THE
Norton
Anthology
OF
American
Literature

Second Edition

Shorter

Early American Literature 1620–1820 • MURPHY
American Literature 1820–1865 • PARKER
American Literature 1865–1914 • GOTTESMAN
American Literature between the Wars 1914–1945
HOLLAND • BAYM
American Prose 1945– • PRITCHARD
American Poetry 1945– • KALSTONE

THE
Norton
Anthology
OF
American
Literature

Second Edition

NINA BAYM
University of Illinois

RONALD GOTTESMAN
University of Southern California

LAURENCE B. HOLLAND
Late of the Johns Hopkins University

FRANCIS MURPHY
Smith College

HERSHEL PARKER
University of Delaware

WILLIAM H. PRITCHARD
Amherst College

DAVID KALSTONE
Rutgers, The State University of New Jersey

Shorter

W • W • NORTON & COMPANY
NEW YORK • LONDON

Library of Congress Cataloging-in-Publication Data
Main entry under title:

The Norton anthology of American literature.

Includes bibliographies and index.
1. American literature. I. Gottesman, Ronald.
PS507.N65   1986   810'.8   85-25861

ISBN 0-393-95386-6 CL
ISBN 0-393-95389-0 PBK

W. W. Norton & Company, Inc., 500 Fifth Avenue, New York, N. Y. 10110

W. W. Norton & Company Ltd., 37 Great Russell Street, London WC1B 3NU
4 5 6 7 8 9 0

Contents

American Literature
1820–1865

American Literature
1865–1914

American Literature between the Wars
1914–1945   1657

American Prose
1945–

American Poetry
1945–   2461

Preface to the Second Edition

LIKE THE FIRST EDITION, this Second Edition—Shorter of *The Norton Anthology of American Literature* has been prepared for the convenience of teachers who wish to have all the materials for a course within a single volume. The book, distilled from the full resources of the Second Edition of the two parent volumes, is designed to serve either a short course in American literature or a longer course in which a "core" anthology is supplemented by individual texts. This edition retains the major innovations which have found favor with a host of teachers and students, but introduces changes in response to the useful suggestions and criticisms of those who have used the book in the classroom. Like other Norton anthologies, then, it is the product of a collaboration between editors and teachers.

One change was born of the realization that the twentieth century is now more than eighty-five years old. To provide a useful ordering of its full and varied literary achievement, the century has been divided into three sections: American Literature between the Wars (1914–1945); American Prose (1945–   ); and American Poetry (1945–   ). In each of these sections, writers who usually get short shrift are introduced judiciously and helpfully by editors who are experts in the periods and are represented by selections that enable students to read them in some depth.

This change was not, however, made at the expense of writers in the earlier periods. For example, in the earliest period (1620–1820), additions to just about every major author enable each of them to be more fully studied. Selections from John Winthrop's *Journal* are coupled with the central excerpt from his famous sermon; a new chapter of Bradford's *Of Plymouth Plantation* looks forward to Hawthorne's story *The May-Pole of Merry Mount*; added poems strengthen the representation of Bradstreet and Taylor; Samuel Sewall, new to the anthology, provides further opportunity for the study of the journal tradition; Cotton Mather's *Life of Winthrop* looks back at our very first author; and the addition of Jonathan Edward's *Divine and Supernatural Light* provides a very different aspect of the writings of this strong author. Among later writers in the period, Benjamin Franklin is more fully represented with humorous short pieces as well as a newly edited text of the selections from his *Autobiography* (including all of Part II), while St. Jean de Crèvecoeur's *Letters from an American Farmer* now include the harrowing account of the slave in the cage.

The section of American literature from 1820 to 1865 has been justly acclaimed for the rich variety of its works. The revisions fall into two categories: those that strengthen even further the representation of the great authors, and those that open up the canon. In the first category, teachers familiar with the first edition will note additions to every major author from Emerson to Dickinson. Paramount among these is the inclusion of Emerson's *Nature* complete. We have also added, for Hawthorne, the popular *Rappaccini's Daughter*; for Poe, a new story, *Ligeia*, and an additional critical work, the *Review of Hawthorne's Twice-Told Tales*; for Thoreau, the central "Ponds" chapter of *Walden*; for Whitman, the 1855 *Preface to Leaves of Grass* and the much-discussed *As I Ebb'd with the Ocean of Life*; for Melville, *Hawthorne and His Mosses* together with a central letter to Hawthorne, Sketch Eighth of *The Encantadas* with its strong portrait of one of Melville's few heroines, and *Billy Budd, Sailor* (which replaces *Benito Cereno*); and for Dickinson, a reconsidered and refined selection of her poems and two revelatory letters to T.W. Higginson. For Emerson and Thoreau there are provided, as well, some useful selections from their journals and letters. In the second category are Augustus Baldwin Longstreet, represented as an early Southern realist; Frederick Douglass, with the three essential chapters of the *Narrative of the Life . . . an American Slave*; and Rebecca Harding Davis, whose searing fictional indictment of pre-Civil War industrialism, *Life in the Iron-Mills*, has been newly recovered for American literature by Tillie Olsen.

It should be noted that some of the changes cited above are in accordance with a commitment on the part of the editors to the presentation of longer works complete—especially essential for the shorter course—as well as a commitment to providing as many opportunities as possible for the teaching of American fiction. These same principles are applied also to later sections. In the next period, for example, which covers American literature from 1865 to 1914, we offer all of Samuel Clemens' *Adventures of Huckleberry Finn* and Henry James' early "international theme" tale, *Daisy Miller*—central masterworks by two great figures of the period. There is, in addition, a story by each of the three finest women authors of the period: Sarah Orne Jewett, Kate Chopin, and Edith Wharton. Newly anthologized are the popular Ambrose Bierce, Joel Chandler Harris, and Jack London, and added writings by Dreiser and by Stephen Crane. Finally, the black polemic tradition is carried on in this period by its two essential exponents, Booker T. Washington and W.E.B. Du Bois.

The twentieth-century sections now include two plays, both of them indubitable masterpieces of modern literature: Eugene O'Neill's culminating tragic work, *Long Day's Journey into Night*, and Tennessee Williams' greatest play, *A Streetcar Named Desire*. We are able to reprint these works by special arrangements with their publishers—arrangements which allow them to be anthologized exclusively in Norton texts.

The important section of literature between the wars has been rethought. To begin with, all the authors have been rearranged in chronological order, so as to make them more easily locatable. In accordance with requests from many teachers, we have reselected and added poems for all the major poets—Robinson, Williams, Pound, Moore, Eliot, Ransom, Cummings, Crane, and especially Frost, Stevens, and H. D.—and have added work by Robinson Jeffers, Edna St. Vincent Millay, and Countee Cullen. Prose fiction has been similarly strengthened. Most notable is that we now offer four stories by Faulkner, a larger selection than is available in any other anthology and which is made possible, again, by an arrangement exclusive to Norton anthologies. New to the edition are Thomas Wolfe, John Steinbeck, and Zora Neale Hurston, an author recovered for American literature by Alice Walker and who has become required reading in the literature of social concern. Fitzgerald is represented now by his complex *May Day*, a novella foreshadowing *The Great Gatsby*, and there are new stories by Anderson and Hemingway.

The changes in the final sections, incorporating literature since 1945, have been made in accordance with a careful reconsideration of the judgments made in the first edition. Prose (1945–   ) is strengthened not only by the inclusion of the play by Williams, but by the fiction of John Cheever, Bernard Malamud, Philip Roth, Thomas Pynchon (the initial chapter of *The Crying of Lot 49* offers a fascinating introduction to his narrative innovations), and the young black "womanist" writer, Alice Walker. Richard Wright and Eudora Welty (originally in the earlier section) now find their proper home in the contemporary section, and new stories have been provided for O'Connor and Updike. The section of Poetry (1945–   ) was from the first praised for establishing a basic canon out of the confusing welter of contemporary writings; that canon is now enlarged by the inclusion of Robert Penn Warren—for the first time anthologized, and justly so, as an important poet. Bishop and Lowell have been reviewed, and significant recent work by Wilbur, Ammons, Ashbery, Merrill, and Rich has been included.

A major responsibility of the anthology is to redress the long neglect of woman writers in America. This new edition offers the work of twenty women (seven more than in the first edition). Another responsibility is to do justice to the contributions of black writers to American literature and culture; we include thirteen black authors who provide the opportunity to trace explicit discussions of what is distinctive in the black experience, as represented both in polemical and in imaginative writings.

The Norton Anthology of American Literature continues to incorporate features that have established a new standard in literary texts for the classroom. The format is not that of the traditional anthology, but of a book to be read for pleasure. There are no forbidding double columns of prose and verse; the text is inviting to the eye; and the special paper reduces the volume to a size and weight that make it easily carried—including to a classroom. Furthermore, the editorial materials—introductions, headnotes, footnotes—are terse but full, and designed to give the student the information needed, without preempting the interpretive function either of the student or of the instructor. The "Selected Bibliographies" at the end of the volume provide guides to further readings and research, and complete the self-sufficiency of the anthology, which permits each of its selections to be read, understood, and placed in historical context without the need for access to a collection of reference books.

The editors have taken scrupulous care to provide the most accurate available version of each work that is represented. And each text is printed in the form which accords, as closely as it is possible to determine, to the intentions of its author. There is one exception: we have modernized the spellings and (very sparingly) the punctuation in the section of early American literature, on the principle that nonfunctional features such as archaic spellings and typography pose unnecessary problems for beginning students. We have, however, since it is a new edition from the manuscript, left Franklin's *Autobiography* unchanged. We have used square brackets to indicate titles that, for the convenience of the student, have been supplied by the editors, and have, whenever a portion of a text has been omitted, indicated that omission by three asterisks.

The editors of this anthology were selected on the basis of their expertness in their individual areas, and also because they combine respect for the best that has been thought and said about literature in the past with an alertness (as participants, as well as observers) to the altering interests, procedures, and evaluations in contemporary scholarship and criticism. Each editor was given ultimate responsibility for his or her own period, but all collaborated in the total enterprise. In the 1820–1865 section, Ronald Gottesman prepared the texts and introductions for Lincoln, Douglass, and Dickinson.

In preparing these volumes, we have incurred obligations to hundreds of teachers throughout the country who have answered our questions; we take this opportunity to thank them warmly for their invaluable assistance. Those teachers who prepared detailed critiques, or who offered special help in selecting or preparing texts, are listed under "Acknowledgments," on a separate page. The editors would like to express appreciation for their assistance to Jill Beerman, Mark Canner, Darius Cooper, Mary Eberle, Deborah Grossman, Mary Hathorn, William Kozlowski, Bea McLean, Patrick Merla, Marilyn Moss, the staff of the Enoch Pratt Library, Heddy Richter (former American Literature Librarian, Doheny Library, University of Southern California), Diane Rosenfeldt, and Tina Stough. The publisher's editor, in turn, would like to express his thanks to his co-workers Sue Crooks, Mike McIver, Diane O'Connor, Hugh O'Neill, Nancy Palmquist, Marian Schwartz, and Carol Stiles. Our greatest debt is to M. H. Abrams (Cornell University), Norton's adviser on English texts, upon whose rich experience in making anthologies we drew often and profitably. All have helped us to achieve the task of representing adequately, in a single convenient volume, a distillation of the extraordinary variety and quality of our American literary heritage.

It remains to record with sadness the untimely death of our coeditor and friend, Laurence B. Holland, who contributed greatly to the initial planning and the first edition of the anthology.

Acknowledgments

THE FOLLOWING TEACHERS were of especial help to the publisher in the arduous task of distilling materials from the parent volumes to make up the Shorter Edition: Pamela Barnes (Pima Community College); Milton Bates (Marquette University); Jerome Bump (University of Texas at Austin); William Dowie (Southeastern Louisiana University); Clayton Eichelberger (University of Texas at Arlington); W. Kenneth Holditch (University of New Orleans); Peter Ohlin (McGill University); Marjorie Pryse (University of Tennessee at Knoxville); Julia Stern (Columbia University); and Richie D. Watson (Randolph-Macon College).

The following provided excellent advice toward the planning of the two-volume second edition, and so we thank them once again: Bruce Abrams (Tuskegee Institute); John Bassett (Wayne State University); Alfred Bendixen (Barnard College); Ronald A. Bosco (State University of New York at Albany); Panthea Reid Broughton (Louisiana State University); Lawrence Buell (Oberlin); William Bedford Clark (Texas A&M University); Hugh J. Dawson (University of San Francisco); Sterling F. Delano (Villanova University); Joanne Feit Diehl (University of California at Davis); Jim Ewing (Mississippi College); Judith Fetterley (State University of New York at Albany); Rosemary F. Franklin (University of Georgia); Albert Gelpi (Stanford University); Donna Gerstenberger (University of Washington); Anthony C. Hilfer (University of Texas at Austin); Paul Lauter (State University of New York/College at Old Westbury); J. A. Leo LeMay (University of Delaware); Wendy Martin (University of North Carolina at Chapel Hill); Adalaide K. Morris (University of Iowa); Frederick Newbury (University of Oregon); Alan Perlis (University of Alabama in Birmingham); William Powers (Michigan Technical University); Marjorie Pryse (University of Tennessee); Jerome H. Rosenberg (Miami University in Ohio); Joan Schulz (State University of New York at Albany); Ann Semel; Daniel B. Shea (Washington University in St. Louis); Merrill Skaggs (Drew University); Catharine R. Stimpson (Rutgers University); J. Maurice Thomas (Wingate College); Linda W. Wagner (Michigan State University); and Lawrence Wharton (University of Alabama in Birmingham).

Early American Literature

1620–1820

Long before Captain John Smith established Jamestown in 1607, the European imagination had been entranced by rumors of the New World's plenty. But it was probably Captain Smith, rather than any other, who convinced English readers that there was an earthly paradise not far from their shores. In his *A Description of New England* (1616) he wrote that "Here nature and liberty afford us that freely which in England we want [lack], or it costs us dearly." What greater satisfaction is there, he asked, than hauling in one's supper by dropping a hook and line into any plentiful river or stream; is it not "pretty sport" to "pull up two pence, six pence, and twelve pence" as fast as you can let out a line? One hundred twenty-five years later another Virginia planter, William Byrd, would add to the fabled accounts of the place in his *History of the Dividing Line*, and it is significant that Thomas Jefferson's one book, *Notes on the State of Virginia* (1785, 1787), was written in response to inquiries made by a French naturalist concerning the geography and resources of his state. William Bartram, of Philadelphia, charmed both Wordsworth and Coleridge with his travels through North and South Carolina in the 1770s. His descriptions of sun-filled pastures and awesome waterfalls convinced them that the landscape of our dreams is grounded on reality. European readers for three centuries were anxious to sort American fable from fact, but as Smith's *Description* convinced them, the facts themselves were fabulous.

THE PURITAN EXPERIMENT: PLYMOUTH PLANTATION

Although those separatists from the Church of England whom we call "Pilgrims" were familiar with Captain Smith's *Description* and followed his map of the Atlantic coast, they were not sympathetic to his proposal that he join their emigration to the New World; for Smith was primarily an adventurer, explorer, and trader, and while this group was not composed entirely of "reborn" Christians (only about twenty-seven of the one hundred persons aboard the *Mayflower* were Puritans), and even those were not indifferent to the material well-being of their venture, their leaders had more in mind than mercantile success. These pilgrims thought of themselves as soldiers in a war against Satan—the Arch-Enemy—who planned to ruin the Kingdom of God on earth by sowing discord among those who professed to be Christians. This small band of believers saw no hope of reforming a national church and its Anglican hierarchy from within. In 1608, five years after the death of Queen Elizabeth and with an enemy of Puritanism, James Stuart, on the throne, they left England and settled in Holland, where, William Bradford tells us, they saw "fair and beautiful cities" and the "grisly face of poverty" confronting them. Isolated by their language, and unable to farm, they turned to mastering trades (Bradford himself became a weaver). Later, fearing that they would eventually lose their identity as a religious community living as strangers in a foreign land, they applied for a charter to settle in the Virginia Plantation—a vast tract of land which included what is now New England. Sponsored by merchants who were anxious to receive repayment in goods from the New World, they sailed from Southampton, England, in September, 1620. Sixty-six days later, taken by strong winds much farther north than they had anticipated, they dropped anchor at Cape Cod and established their colony at Plymouth.

In spite of the fact that their separatism does not make them representative of the large number of emigrants who came to these shores in the seventeenth century (Plymouth was eventually absorbed into the Massachusetts Bay Colony in 1691 when a new charter was negotiated), their story has become an integral part of our literature. Bradford's account of a chosen people, exiles in a "howling wilderness," who struggled against all adversity to bring into being the City of God on earth, is ingrained in our national consciousness. Both in the nineteenth century and in the twentieth, Americans have seen themselves as a "redeemer nation," without, of course, possessing Bradford's Christian ideals. What gives Bradford's book its great strength, in spite of his obvious prejudices, is his ability to keep the ideals of the Pilgrims before us as he describes the harsh reality of their struggle against not only the external forces of nature but the even more damaging corruption of worldliness within the community.

THE PURITAN EXPERIMENT: THE MASSACHUSETTS BAY COLONY

Far more representative in attitude toward the Church of England were the Puritans who joined the Massachusetts Bay Colony under the leadership of John Winthrop. They were dissenting but nonseparating—although it might be argued that geographical distance from London, and a charter which located the seat of their colony in Boston, left them nonseparating in theory rather than practice. Whatever their difference with respect to the Church of England, however, the basic beliefs of both groups were identical: both held with Martin Luther that no Pope or Bishop had a right to impose any law upon a Christian soul without consent and, following John Calvin, that God chose freely those He would save and those He would damn eternally.

Too much can be made of this doctrine of election; those who have not read the actual Puritan sermons often come away from secondary sources with the mistaken notion that Puritans talked about nothing but damnation. Puritans did indeed hold that God had chosen, before their birth, those whom He wished to save; but it does not follow that the Puritans considered most of us to be born damned. While Puritans argued that Adam broke the "Covenant of Works" (the promise God made to Adam that he was immortal and could live in Paradise forever as long as he obeyed God's commandments) when he disobeyed and ate of the tree of knowledge of good and evil, thereby bringing sin and death into the world, their central doctrine was the new "Covenant of Grace," a binding agreement Christ made with all men who believed in Him, and which He sealed with His crucifixion, promising them eternal life. Puritans thus addressed themselves not to the hopelessly unregenerate but to the indifferent, and they addressed the heart more often than the mind, always distinguishing between "historical" or rational understanding and heartfelt "saving faith." There is more joy in Puritan life and thought than we often credit, and this joy is the direct result of meditation on the doctrine of Christ's redeeming power. Edward Taylor is not alone in making his rapturous litany of Christ's attributes: "He is altogether lovely in everything, lovely in His person, lovely in His natures, lovely in His properties, lovely in His offices, lovely in His titles, lovely in His practice, lovely in His purchases and lovely in His relations." All of Taylor's art is a meditation on the miraculous gift of the Incarnation, and, in this respect, his sensibility is typically Puritan. Anne Bradstreet, who is remarkably frank about confessing her religious doubts, told her children that it was "upon this rock Christ Jesus" that she built her faith.

Their lives, however, were hard. Anne Bradstreet's father told people in England to come over and join them if their lives were "endued with grace," but that others were "not fitted for this business"; that there was not a house where one had not died, and that if they survived the terrible winter they had to face the devastating infections that were the result of summer heat. Bradford's account of what he called "the starving time" are among the most moving in his history, and nothing in Captain Smith's *Discovery* had hinted at how oppressive daily life might be. Sarah Kemble Knight of Boston and her Maryland counterpart Ebenezer Cooke provide healthy antidotes to any sentimental notion we might have that life on the frontier was invigorating. Puritan letters, diaries, histories, and poetry all attest to their faith in a larger plan, a "noble design" as Cotton Mather put it, which made daily life bearable.

In this Christocentric world it is not surprising that Puritans held to the strictest requirements regarding communion or, as they preferred to call it, the Lord's Supper. It was the most important of the two sacraments they recognized (baptism being the other), and they guarded it with a zeal which set them apart from all other dissenting churches. In the beginning, communion was taken only by church members—those who had stood before their minister and elders and given an account (or "relation") of their conversion—and was regarded as a sign of election. This insistence on challenging their members made these New England churches more rigorous than any others, and confirmed the feeling that they were a special few. Thus, when John Winthrop addressed the immigrants to the Bay Colony aboard the flagship *Arbella* in 1630, he told them that the eyes of the world were upon them, and that they would be an example for all, a "city upon a hill."

PURITAN HISTORIOGRAPHY

Puritans held the writing of history in high regard; for, as heirs of Renaissance thought, they believed that lasting truths were to be gained by studying the lives of noble men. Cotton Mather urged students of the ministry to read not only early church historians but the classical historians Xenophon, Livy, Tacitus, and Plutarch as well. Puritans saw all of human time as a progression toward the fulfillment of God's design on earth. Therefore, pre-Christian history could be read as a preparation for Christ's

entry into the world. They learned this lesson from medieval Biblical scholars, who interpreted figures in the Old Testament as foreshadowings of
Christ. This method of comparison, called "typology," was an ingrained
habit of Puritan thinking, and it made them compare themselves, as a
chosen people, to the Israelites of old, who had been given the promise of
a new land. Cotton Mather said that John Winthrop was the Puritan Moses
whose education had prepared him to fulfill the "noble design of carrying
a colony of chosen people into an American wilderness."

Puritans believed that God's hand was present in every human event and
that He rewarded good and punished bad. History, therefore, revealed what
God approved of or condemned, and if God looked favorably upon a nation,
His approval could be evidenced in its success. Puritans had enough confidence in God's design to believe that no facts were too small or insignificant
to be included in that design; everything could emblemize something. In
writing about Anne Bradstreet, Adrienne Rich observes that seventeenth-
century Puritan life was perhaps "the most self-conscious ever lived"; that
"faith underwent its hourly testing, the domestic mundanities were episodes in the drama; the piecemeal thoughts of a woman stirring a pot, clues
to her 'justification' in Christ." John Winthrop in his diary records a struggle between a snake and a mouse and is surprised to see the seemingly
weaker emerge the victor. His Boston friend, Mr. Wilson, however, saw
the event as a battle between Satan and a "poor contemptible people, which
God hath brought hither, which should overcome Satan here and dispossess
him of his kingdom." When a young sailor on board the *Mayflower* mocked
those Puritans who were sick, Bradford found it fitting that the sailor
should himself succumb to a "grievous disease." This sense of the universal
significance of all things meant that drama was present in every believer's
life and that individual lives could be as symbolic as the life of a nation.
Mary Rowlandson, who had been captured by the Indians, saw her captivity as a lesson in the life of a representative soul who once wished to
experience affliction and later experienced it only too well. Her Indian cap-
tors were, to her, more than uncivilized savages; they were devils incarnate.

The greatest of all the Puritan historians was Cotton Mather, and in his
Magnalia Christi Americana (1702) the myth of a chosen people took on
its fullest resonance of meaning. By the time Mather undertook his history,
the original Puritan community had vanished, leaving behind heirs to its
lands and fortunes but not to its spirituality. Mather saw himself as one
of the last defenders of the "old New England way," and all the churches
as under attack from new forces of secularism. As a historian, Mather
solved his problem by not focusing on the dissolution of the Puritan community but writing "saints' lives" instead, each of which (like those of
Eliot, Bradford, and Winthrop) would serve as an example of the progress
of the individual Christian soul and an allegory of the potential American
hero. Under Mather's artistry, Winthrop's vision of a community of saints
living in mutual concern and sympathy became an ideal rather than a historical reality. The words "New England" would symbolize the effort to
realize the City of God on earth, and "whether New England may live anywhere else or no," he said, "it must live in our history."

AN EXPANDING UNIVERSE

It should come as no surprise to learn that Cotton Mather was defensively
retrospective in his ecclesiastical history of New England; for the enormous

changes—economic, social, philosophical, and scientific—which occurred between Mather's birth in 1663 and the publication of the *Magnalia* in 1702 inevitably affected the influence and authority of Congregational churches. In 1686 Mather himself joined with Boston merchants in jailing their colonial Governor, Sir Edmund Andros, and was successful in getting him sent back to England. It was a rare occasion when church and trade saw eye to eye; the Puritan clergy disliked Andros's Anglicanism as much as the merchants hated his taxes. It was an act celebrated annually in Boston until it was replaced by celebrations honoring American independence.

The increase in population alone would account for a greater diversity of opinion in the matter of churches. In 1670, for example, the population of the colonies numbered approximately 111,000. Thirty years later the colonies contained more than a quarter of a million persons; by 1760, if one included Georgia, they numbered 1,600,000, and the settled area had tripled. The demand for and price of colonial goods increased in England, and vast fortunes were to be made in New England with any business connected with shipbuilding: especially timber, tar, and pitch. Virginia planters became rich in tobacco, and rice and indigo from the Carolinas were in constant demand.

New England towns were full of acrimonious debate between first settlers and newcomers. Town histories are full of accounts of splinter groups and the establishment of the "Second" church. In the beginning land was apportioned to settlers and allotted free, but by 1713 speculators in land were hard at work, buying as much as possible for as little as possible and selling high. The idea of a "community" of mutually helpful souls was fast disappearing. Life in the colonies was not easy, but the hardships and dangers the first settlers faced were mostly overcome, and compared to crowded cities like London, it was healthier, cheaper, and more hopeful. Those who could arrange their passage came in great numbers. Boston almost doubled in size from 1700 to 1720. It is also important to note that the great emigration to America which occurred in the first half of the eighteenth century was not primarily English. Dutch and Germans came in large numbers and so did French Protestants. Jewish merchants and craftsmen were well known in New York and Philadelphia.

By 1750 Philadelphia had become the unofficial capital of the colonies and was second only to London as a city of commerce. In 1681 the Quaker William Penn exchanged a large claim against the Crown for land in the New World. He was named Proprietor (rather than Governor, since he actually owned the territory) of Pennsylvania and immediately opened the land to settlement by people of all faiths. Penn had the genius to bestow the privilege of self-government on the people of Pennsylvania and in his "Frame of Government" told them that "Liberty without obedience is confusion, and obedience without liberty is slavery." These thousands of emigrants did not think of themselves as displaced Englishmen; they thought of themselves as Americans. In 1702 no one would have dreamed of an independent union of colonies, but by 1762, fifty years later, it was a distinct possibility.

THE ENLIGHTENMENT

Great challenges to seventeenth-century beliefs were posed by scientists and philosophers, and it has sometimes been suggested that the "modern" period dates from 1662 and the founding of the British scientific academy known, because of the patronage of King Charles II, as the Royal Society. The greatest scientists of the age like Sir Isaac Newton (1642–1727) and philosophers like John Locke (1632–1704) saw no conflict between their discoveries and traditionally held Christian truths. They saw nothing heretical in arguing that the universe was an orderly system and that by the application of reason mankind would comprehend its laws. But the inevitable result of their inquiries was to make the universe seem more rational and benevolent than it had been represented by Puritan doctrine. Because the world seemed more comprehensible, people paid less attention to revealed religion, and a number of seventeenth-century modes of thought—Bradford and Winthrop's penchant for the allegorical and emblematic, seeing every natural and human event as a message from God, for instance—seemed almost medieval and decidedly quaint. These new scientists and philosophers were called "Deists"; they deduced the existence of a Supreme Being from the construction of the universe itself rather than from the Bible. "A creation," as one distinguished historian has put it, "presupposes a creator." People were less interested in the metaphysical wit of introspective divines than in the progress of ordinary men as they made their way in the world. They assumed that men were naturally good, and dwelt on neither the Fall nor the Incarnation. A harmonious universe proclaimed the beneficence of God, and Deists argued that man himself should be as generous. They were not interested in theology but in man's own nature. Americans as well as Englishmen knew Alexander Pope's famous couplet:

> Know then thyself, presume not God to scan,
> The proper study of mankind is man.

Locke said that "our business" here on earth "is not to know all things, but those which concern our conduct." In suggesting that we are not born with a set of innate ideas of good or evil and that the mind is rather like a blank wax tablet upon which experiences are inscribed (a *tabula rasa*), Locke qualified traditional belief.

THE GREAT AWAKENING

A conservative reaction against the world view of the new science was bound to follow, and the first half of the eighteenth century witnessed a number of religious revivals in both England and America. They were sometimes desperate efforts to reassert the old values in the face of the new and, oddly enough, were themselves the direct product of the new cult of feeling, a philosophy which argued that man's greatest pleasure was derived from the good he did for others and that his sympathetic emotions (his joy as well as his tears) should not be contained. Phillis Wheatley, whose poem on the death of the Methodist George Whitefield (1714–70) made her famous, said that Whitefield prayed that "grace in every heart might dwell," and longed to see "America excell." Whitefield's revival meetings along the Atlantic seaboard were a great personal triumph; but they were no more famous than the "extraordinary circumstances" which occurred in Northampton, Massachusetts, under the leadership of Jonathan Edwards in the 1730s and which have come to be synonymous with "the Great Awakening."

Edwards also read his Locke, but he wished to liberate human beings from their senses, not define them by those senses. Edwards was fond of pointing out that the five senses are what we share with beasts, and that if our ultimate goal were merely a heightened sensibility, feverish sickness is the condition where the senses are most acute. Edwards was interested in *supernatural* concerns, but he was himself influenced by Locke in arguing that true belief is something which we feel and do not merely comprehend intellectually. Edwards took the one doctrine most difficult for eighteenth-century minds to accept—election—and persuaded his congregation that God's sovereignty was not only the most reasonable doctrine, but that it was the most "delightful," and appeared to him (using adjectives which suggest that the best analogy is to what can be apprehended sensually) "exceeding pleasant, bright, and sweet." In carefully reasoned, calmly argued prose, as harmonious and as ordered as anything the age produced, Edwards brought his great intellect to bear on doctrines that had been current the century before. Most people, when they think about the Puritans, remember Edwards's sermon *Sinners in the Hands of an Angry God*, forgetting that one hundred years had lapsed between that sermon and Winthrop's *Model of Christian Charity*. When Edwards tried to reassert "the old New England way" and demanded accounts of conversion before admission to church membership, he was accused of being a reactionary who thrived on hysteria, was removed from his pulpit, and was effectively silenced. He spent his last years as a missionary to the Indians in Stockbridge, Massachusetts, a town forty miles to the west of Northampton. There he remained until invited to become president of the College of New Jersey. His death in Princeton was the direct result of his willingness to be vaccinated against smallpox and so to set an example for his frightened and superstitious students; it serves as a vivid reminder of how complicated in any one individual the reponse to the "new science" could become.

THE AMERICAN CRISIS

On June 7, 1776, at the second Continental Congress, Richard Henry Lee of Virginia moved that "these united colonies are, and of a right ought to be, free and independent states." A committee was duly appointed to prepare a declaration of independence, and it was approved on July 4. Although these motions and their swiftness took some delegates by surprise—the purpose of the Congress had, after all, not been to declare independence but to protest the usurpation of rights by King and Parliament and to effect a compromise with the mother country—others saw them as the inevitable consequence of the events of the decade preceding. The Stamp Act of 1764, taxing all newspapers, legal documents, and licenses, had infuriated Bostonians and resulted in the burning of the Governor's palace; in Virginia, Patrick Henry had taken the occasion to speak impassionedly against taxation without representation. In 1770 a Boston mob had been fired upon by British soldiers, and three years later the famous "Tea Party" occurred, an act which drew hard lines in the matter of acceptable limits of British rule. The news of the April confrontation with the British in Concord and Lexington, Massachusetts, was still on everyone's tongue in Philadelphia when the second Continental Congress convened in May of 1775.

Although the drama of these events cannot be underestimated, most historians agree that it was Thomas Paine's *Common Sense*, published in January, 1776, that gave the needed push for revolution. In the course of two months it was read by almost every American. In arguing that separation from England was the only reasonable course and that "the Almighty" had planted these feelings in us "for good and wise purposes," Paine was appealing to basic tenets of the Enlightenment. His clarion call to those that "love mankind," those "that dare oppose not only the tyranny but the tyrant, stand forth!" did not go unheeded. Americans needed an apologist for the Revolution, and in December of 1776, when Washington's troops were at their most demoralized, it was, again, Paine's first *Crisis* paper—popularly called *The American Crisis*—which was read to all the regiments and was said to have inspired their future success.

Paine first came to America in 1774 with a note from Benjamin Franklin recommending him to publishers and editors. He was only one of a number of young writers who were able to take advantage of the times. This was, in fact, the great age of the newspaper and the moral essay; Franklin tells us that he modeled his own style on the clarity, good sense, and simplicity of the English essayists Joseph Addison and Richard Steele. The first newspaper in the colonies appeared in 1704, but by the time of the Revolution there were almost fifty papers and forty magazines. The great cry was for a "national literature" (meaning anti-British), and the political events of the 1770s were advantageous for a career. Philip Freneau made his first success as a writer as a satirist of the British, and after the publication of his *Poems Written Chiefly during the Late War* (1786) he turned to newspaper work, editing the New York *Daily Advertiser* and writing anti-Federalist party essays, making himself an enemy of Alexander Hamilton in the process. The most distinguished political writings of the period are, in fact, the essays Hamilton, John Jay, and James Madison wrote for New York newspapers in 1787 and 1788 and collectively known as *The Federalist Papers*. In attempting to get New Yorkers to support the new Constitution they provided an eloquent defense of the framework of the Republic. Joel Barlow also published anti-British satires in the *New Haven Gazette and Connecticut Magazine*, and envisioned an American literature which would extol our government, our educational institutions, and the arts. He spent most of his life revising a long hymn to the Republic called *The Columbiad*. But Barlow never settled down to the life of the artist; he was too much the entrepreneur and world traveler for that. His best poems are not his philosophical epics but poems, like *The Hasty Pudding*, in praise of the simple life. Freneau's career was also marked by restlessness and indecision, although in his case financial necessity came between his life and his art. The first American writer able to live exclusively by his craft was Washington Irving.

The crisis in American life caused by the Revolution made artists self-conscious about American subjects. It would be another fifty years before writers discovered ways of being American without compromising their integrity. One of the ironies of our history is that the Revolution itself has rarely proved to be a usable subject for American literature and art.

THE PURSUIT OF HAPPINESS

When John Winthrop described his "model" for a Christian community, he envisioned a group of men and women working together for the common good, each one of whom knew his place in the social structure and accepted God's disposition of goods. At all times, he said, "some must be rich, some poor, some high and eminent in power and dignity," others low and "in subjection." Ideally, it was to be a community of love, each made equal by their fallen nature and their concern for the salvation of their souls; but it was to be a stable community, and Winthrop would not have imagined very much social change. One hundred forty years later John Adams, our second President, envisioned a model community, decreed by higher laws, when he said that the American colonies were a part of a "grand scheme and design in Providence for the illumination of the ignorant and the emancipation of the slavish part of mankind all over the earth." Adams witnessed social mobility of a kind and number, however, that no European before him would have dreamed possible. As historians have observed, European critics of America in the eighteenth and nineteenth centuries never understood that great social change was possible without social upheaval primarily because there was no feudal hierarchy to overthrow. When Crèvecoeur wanted to distinguish America from Europe, it was the medievalism of the latter that he wished to stress. The visitor to America, he said, "views not the hostile castle, and the haughty mansion, contrasted with the clay-built hut and miserable cabin, where cattle and men help to keep each other warm, and dwell in meanness, smoke and indigence." Of course, not everyone was free. Some of our founding fathers, like Thomas Jefferson, were large slaveowners, and it was still not possible to vote without owning property. Women had hardly any rights at all: they could not vote, and young women were educated at home, excluded by their studies from anything other than domestic employment. Nevertheless, the same forces that were undermining church authority in New England (in New York and Philadelphia no such hierarchy existed) were effecting social change. The two assumptions held to be true by most eighteenth-century Americans were, as Russel Nye once put it, "the perfectability of man, and the prospect of his future progress." Much of the imaginative energy of the second half of the eighteenth century was expanded in correcting institutional injustices: the tyranny of monarchy, the tolerance of slavery, the misuse of prisons. Few doubted that with the application of intelligence the human lot could be improved; and writers like Freneau, Franklin, and Crèvecoeur argued that, if it were not too late, the white man might learn something about brotherhood and manners from noble savages rather than from rude white settlers, slaveowners, and backwoodsmen.

In many ways it is Franklin who best represents the spirit of the Enlightenment in America: self-educated, social, assured, a man of the world, ambitious and public-spirited, speculative about the nature of the universe, but in matters of religion content to observe the actual conduct of men rather than to debate supernatural matters which are unprovable. When Ezra Stiles asked him about his religion, he said he believed in the "creator of the universe" but he doubted the "divinity of Jesus." He would never dogmatize about it, however, because he expected soon "an opportunity of knowing the truth with less trouble." Franklin always presents himself as a man depending on firsthand experience, too worldly-wise to be caught off guard. His posture, however, belies one side of the eighteenth century which can be accounted for neither by the inheritance of Calvin nor by the empiricism of Locke: those idealistic assumptions which underlie the great public documents of the American Revolution, especially the Declaration of Independence. There are truths which, Joel Barlow once said, were "as perceptible when first presented to the mind as age or world of experience could make them." Given the representative nature of Franklin's character, it seems right that of the documents most closely associated with the formation of the American Republic—the Declaration of Independence, the treaty of alliance with France, the Treaty of Paris, and the Constitution—only he should have signed all four.

The fact that Americans in the last quarter of the eighteenth century would hold that "certain truths are self-evident, that all men are created equal, that they are endowed by their Creator with certain unalienable Rights, that among these are Life, Liberty and the pursuit of Happiness," is the result, as both Leon Howard and Gary Wills have argued, of their reading the Scottish philosophers, particularly Francis Hutcheson and Lord Kames (Henry Home), who argued that all men in all places possess a sense common to all—a moral sense—which contradicted the notion of the mind as an empty vessel awaiting experience. This idealism paved the way for writers like Bryant, Emerson, Thoreau, and Whitman, but in the 1770s its presence is found chiefly in politics and ethics. The assurance of a universal sense of right and wrong made possible both the overthrow of tyrants and the restoration of order; and it allowed men to make new earthly covenants, not, as was the case with Bradford and Winthrop, for the glory of God, but, as Thomas Jefferson argued, for man's right to happiness on earth.

JOHN WINTHROP
1588–1649

John Winthrop was born in Groton, England, on an estate which his father purchased from Henry VIII. It was a prosperous farm, and Winthrop had all the advantages which his father's social and economic position would allow. He went to Cambridge University for two years and married at the age of seventeen. It was probably at Cambridge University that Winthrop was exposed to Puritan ideas. Unlike Bradford and the Pilgrims, however, Winthrop was not a separatist; that is, he wished to reform the national church from within, purging it of everything that harked back to Rome, especially the hierarchy of the clergy and all the traditional Catholic rituals. For a time Winthrop thought of becoming a clergyman himself, but instead he turned to the practice of law.

In the 1620s severe economic depression in England made Winthrop realize that he could not depend upon the support of his father's estate. The ascension of Charles I to the throne—who was known to be sympathetic to Roman Catholicism and impatient with Puritan reformers—was also taken as an ominous sign for Puritans, and Winthrop was not alone in predicting that "God will bring some heavy affliction upon the land, and that speedily." Winthrop came to realize that he could not antagonize the King by expressing openly the Puritan cause without losing all that he possessed. The only recourse seemed to be to obtain the King's permission to emigrate. In March of 1629 a group of enterprising merchants, all sympathetic believers, were able to get a charter from the Council for New England for land in the New World. They called themselves "The Company of Massachusetts Bay in New England."

From four candidates, Winthrop was chosen Governor in October, 1629; for the next twenty years most of the responsibility for the Colony rested in his hands. On April 8, 1630, an initial group of some seven hundred emigrants sailed from England. The ship carrying Winthrop was called the *Arbella*. Somewhere in the middle of the Atlantic ocean Winthrop delivered his sermon *A Model of Christian Charity*. It set out clearly and eloquently the ideals of a harmonious Christian community, and reminded all those on board that they would stand as an example to the world either of the triumph or else the failure of this Christian enterprise. When Cotton Mather wrote his history of New England some fifty years after Winthrop's death, he chose Winthrop as his model of the perfect earthly ruler. Although the actual history of the Colony showed that Winthrop's ideal of a perfectly selfless community was impossible to realize in fact, Winthrop emerges from the story as a man of unquestioned integrity and deep humanity.

From A Model of Christian Charity[1]

I
A MODEL HEREOF

God Almighty in His most holy and wise providence, hath so dis-

---

1. The text is from Old South Leaflets, Old South Association, Old South Meet- inghouse, Boston, Massachusetts, No. 207, edited by Samuel Eliot Morison. The

posed of the condition of mankind, as in all times some must be rich, some poor, some high and eminent in power and dignity; others mean and in subjection.

THE REASON HEREOF

First, to hold conformity with the rest of His works, being delighted to show forth the glory of His wisdom in the variety and difference of the creatures; and the glory of His power, in ordering all these differences for the preservation and good of the whole; and the glory of His greatness, that as it is the glory of princes to have many officers, so this great King will have many stewards, counting Himself more honored in dispensing His gifts to man by man than if He did it by His own immediate hands.

Secondly, that He might have the more occasion to manifest the work of His Spirit: first upon the wicked in moderating and restraining them, so that the rich and mighty should not eat up the poor, nor the poor and despised rise up against their superiors and shake off their yoke; secondly in the regenerate, in exercising His graces, in them, as in the great ones, their love, mercy, gentleness, temperance, etc.; in the poor and inferior sort, their faith patience, obedience etc.

Thirdly, that every man might have need of other, and from hence they might be all knit more nearly together in the bonds of brotherly affection. From hence it appears plainly that no man is made more honorable than another or more wealthy, etc., out of any particular and singular respect to himself, but for the glory of his creator and the common good of the creature, man. Therefore God still reserves the property of these gifts to Himself as [in] Ezekiel 16.17. He there calls wealth His gold and His silver.[2] [In] Proverbs 3.9, he claims their service as His due, honor the Lord with thy riches etc.[3] All men being thus (by divine providence) ranked into two sorts, rich and poor; under the first are comprehended all such as are able to live comfortably by their own meanes duly improved; and all others are poor according to the former distribution.

There are two rules whereby we are to walk one towards another: justice and mercy. These are always distinguished in their act and in their object, yet may they both concur in the same subject in each respect; as sometimes there may be an occasion of showing mercy to a rich man in some sudden danger of distress, and also doing of mere justice to a poor man in regard of some particular contract, etc.

---

original manuscript for Winthrop's sermon is lost; but a copy made during Winthrop's lifetime was published by the Massachusetts Historical Society in 1838.
2. "Thou hast also taken thy fair jewels of my gold and of my silver, which I had given thee, and madest to thyself images of men, and didst commit whoredom with them."
3. "Honor the Lord with thy substance, and with the firstfruits of all thine increase: So shall thy barns be filled with plenty, and thy presses burst out with new wine."

There is likewise a double law by which we are regulated in our conversation one towards another in both the former respects: the law of nature and the law of grace, or the moral law or the law of the Gospel, to omit the rule of justice as not properly belonging to this purpose otherwise than it may fall into consideration in some particular cases. By the first of these laws man as he was enabled so withal [is] commanded to love his neighbor as himself.[4] Upon this ground stands all the precepts of the moral law, which concerns our dealings with men. To apply this to the works of mercy, this law requires two things: first, that every man afford his help to another in every want or distress; secondly, that he performed this out of the same affection which makes him careful of his own goods, according to that of our Savior. Matthew: "Whatsoever ye would that men should do to you."[5] This was practiced by Abraham and Lot in entertaining the Angels and the old man of Gibeah.[6]

The law of grace or the Gospel hath some difference from the former, as in these respects: First, the law of nature was given to man in the estate of innocency; this of the Gospel in the estate of regeneracy.[7] Secondly, the former propounds one man to another, as the same flesh and image of God; this as a brother in Christ also, and in the communion of the same spirit and so teacheth us to put a difference between Christians and others. *Do good to all, especially to the household of faith*: Upon this ground the Israelites were to put a difference between the brethren of such as were strangers though not of Canaanites.[8] Third, the law of nature could give no rules for dealing with enemies, for all are to be considered as friends in the state of innocency, but the Gospel commands love to an enemy. Proof. If thine Enemy hunger, feed him; Love your Enemies, do good to them that hate you. Matthew: 5.44.

* * *

II

* * *

Thus stands the cause between God and us. We are entered into covenant[9] with Him for this work. We have taken out a commis-

---

4. Matthew 5.43; 19.19.
5. "All things therefore whatsoever ye would that men should do unto you even so do ye also unto them: for this is the law of the prophets" (Matthew 7.12).
6. Abraham entertains the angels in Genesis 18: "And the Lord appeared unto him in the plains of Mamre: and he sat in the tent door in the heat of the day; And he lifted up his eyes and looked, and, lo, three men stood by him: and when he saw them, he ran to meet them * * *" (Genesis 18.1–2). Lot was Abraham's nephew, and he escaped the destruction of the city of Sodom because he defended two angels who were his guests from a

mob (Genesis 19.1–14). In Judges, 19.16–21, an old citizen of Gibeah offered shelter to a traveling priest or Levite and defended him from enemies from a neighboring city.
7. Men lost their natural innocence when Adam fell; that state is called unregenerate. When Christ came to ransom man for Adam's sin, he offered salvation for those who believed in Him and became regenerate, or saved.
8. One who lived in Canaan, the Land of Promise for the Israelites.
9. A legal contract; the Israelites entered into a covenant with God in which He promised to protect them if they kept His word and were faithful to Him.

sion, the Lord hath given us leave to draw our own articles. We have professed to enterprise these actions, upon these and those ends, we have hereupon besought Him of favour and blessing. Now if the Lord shall please to hear us, and bring us in peace to the place we desire, then hath He ratified this covenant and sealed our commission, [and] will expect a strict performance of the articles contained in it; but if we shall neglect the observation of these articles which are the ends we have propounded, and, dissembling with our God, shall fall to embrace this present world and prosecute our carnal intentions, seeking great things for ourselves and our posterity, the Lord will surely break out in wrath against us; be revenged of such a perjured people and make us know the price of the breach of such a covenant.

Now the only way to avoid this shipwreck, and to provide for our posterity, is to follow the counsel of Micah,[1] to do justly, to love mercy, to walk humbly with our God. For this end, we must be knit together in this work as one man. We must entertain each other in brotherly affection, we must be willing to abridge ourselves of our superfluities, for the supply of other's necessities. We must uphold a familiar commerce together in all meekness, gentleness, patience and liberality. We must delight in each other, make other's conditions our own, rejoice together. mourn together, labour and suffer together, always having before our eyes our commission and community in the work, our community as members of the same body. So shall we keep the unity of the spirit in the bond of peace. The Lord will be our God, and delight to dwell among us as His own people, and will command a blessing upon us in all our ways, so that we shall see much more of His wisdom, power, goodness and truth, than formerly we have been acquainted with. We shall find that the God of Israel is among us, when ten of us shall be able to resist a thousand of our enemies; when He shall make us a praise and glory that men shall say of succeeding plantations, "the lord make it like that of NEW ENGLAND." For we must consider that we shall be as a city upon a hill.[2] The eyes of all people are upon us, so that if we shall deal falsely with our God in this work we have undertaken, and so cause Him to withdraw His present help from us, we shall be made a story and a by-word through the world. We shall open the mouths of enemies to speak evil of the ways of God, and all professors for God's sake. We shall shame the faces of many of God's worthy servants, and cause their prayers to be turned into curses upon us 'til we be consumed out of

1. The Book of Micah preserves the words of this eighth-century-B.C. prophet. Micah speaks continually of the judgment of God on His people and the necessity to hope for salvation: "I will bear the indignation of the Lord, because I have sinned against him, until he plead my cause, and execute judgment for me: he will bring me forth to the light, and I shall behold his righteousness" (Micah 7.9).
2. "Ye are the light of the world. A city that is set on a hill cannot be hid. Neither do men light a candle, and put it under a bushel, but on a candlestick; and it giveth light unto all that are in the house" (Matthew 5.14-15).

the good land whither we are agoing.

And to shut up this discourse with that exhortation of Moses, that faithful servant of the Lord, in his last farewell to Israel, Deuteronomy 30.[3] Beloved, there is now set before us life and good, death and evil, in that we are commanded this day to love the Lord our God, and to love one another, to walk in His ways and to keep His commandments and His ordinance and His laws, and the articles of our covenant with Him, that we may live and be multiplied, and that the Lord our God may bless us in the land whither we go to possess it. But if our hearts shall turn away, so that we will not obey, but shall be seduced, and worship other gods, our pleasures and profits, and serve them; it is propounded unto us this day, we shall surely perish out of the good land whither we pass over this vast sea to possess it.

Therefore let us choose life,
that we and our seed
may live by obeying His
voice and cleaving to Him,
for He is our life and
our prosperity.

1630   1838

From The Journal of John Winthrop[1]

[June 8, 1630] The wind still W. and by S., fair weather, but close and cold. We stood N. N. W. with a stiff gale, and, about three in the afternoon, we had sight of land to the N. W. about ten leagues, which we supposed was the Isles of Monhegan, but it proved Mount Mansell.[2] Then we tacked and stood W. S. W. We had now fair sunshine weather, and so pleasant a sweet air as did much refresh us, and there came a smell off the shore like the smell of a garden.

There came a wild pigeon into our ship, and another small land bird.

[July 5, 1632] At Watertown there was (in the view of divers witnesses) a great combat between a mouse and a snake; and, after a long fight, the mouse prevailed and killed the snake. The pastor of Boston, Mr. Wilson, a very sincere, holy man, hearing of it, gave this interpretation: That the snake was the devil; the mouse was a

3. "And it shall come to pass, when all these things are come upon thee, the blessing and the curse, which I have set before thee, and thou shalt call them to mind among all the nations, whither the Lord thy God hath driven thee, And shalt return unto the Lord thy God, and shalt obey his voice according to all that I command thee this day, thou and thy children, with all thine heart, and with all thy soul; That then the Lord thy God will turn thy captivity, and have compassion upon thee, and will return and gather thee from all the nations, whither the Lord thy God hath scattered thee" (Deuteronomy 30.1–3).

1. The text used here is from *Winthrop's Journal: History of New England 1630–1649*, edited by James Kendall Hosmer (New York: Charles Scribner's Sons, 1908).

2. What Winthrop saw was Mount Desert, Maine, named by the French explorer Champlain in 1604.

poor contemptible people, which God had brought hither, which should overcome Satan here, and dispossess him of his kingdom. Upon the same occasion, he told the governor,[3] that, before he was resolved to come into this country, he dreamed he was here, and that he saw a church arise out of the earth, which grew up and became a marvellous goodly church.

[December 27, 1633] The governor and assistants met at Boston, and took into consideration a treatise, which Mr. Williams[4] (then of Salem) had sent to them, and which he had formerly written to the governor and council of Plymouth, wherein, among other things, he disputes their right to the lands they possessed here, and concluded that, claiming by the king's grant, they could have no title, nor otherwise, except they compounded[5] with the natives. For this, taking advice with some of the most judicious ministers, (who much condemned Mr. Williams's error and presumption,) they gave order, that he should be convented[6] at the next court, to be censured, etc. There were three passages chiefly whereat they were much offended: 1, for that he chargeth King James to have told a solemn public lie, because in his patent he blessed God that he was the first Christian prince that had discovered this land; 2, for that he chargeth him and others with blasphemy for calling Europe Christendom, or the Christian world; 3, for that he did personally apply to our present king, Charles, these three places in the Revelations,[7] viz., [*blank*].

Mr. Endicott being absent, the governor wrote to him to let him know what was done, and withal added divers arguments to confute the said errors, wishing him to deal with Mr. Williams to retract the same, etc. Whereto he returned a very modest and discreet answer. Mr. Williams also wrote to the governor,[8] and also to him and the rest of the council, very submissively, professing his intent to have been only to have written for the private satisfaction of the governor, etc., of Plymouth, without any purpose to have stirred any further in it, if the governor here had not required a copy of him; withal offering his book, or any part of it, to be burnt.

At the next court he appeared penitently, and gave satisfaction of his intention and loyalty. So it was left, and nothing done in it.

[January 20, 1634] Hall and the two others,[9] who went to Connecticut November 3, came now home, having lost themselves and endured much misery. They informed us that the small pox was gone as far as any Indian plantation was known to the west, and much people dead of it, by reason whereof they could have no trade.

---

3. I.e., Winthrop himself.
4. Roger Williams (c. 1603–83), who had emigrated to New England in 1630 and refused a call to the First Church of Boston because he would not preach to "an unseparated people."
5. Arranged to purchase.
6. Summoned to appear.
7. I.e., the biblical Book of Revelations. Winthrop never added the citations.
8. In 1633 Edward Winslow was governor.
9. Not further identified.

At Naragansett, by the Indians' report, there died seven hundred; but, beyond Pascataquack, none to the eastward.

[January 24, 1634] The governor and council met again at Boston, to consider of Mr. Williams's letter, etc., when, with the advice of Mr. Cotton[1] and Mr. Wilson, and weighing his letter, and further considering of the aforesaid offensive passages in his book,[2] (which, being written in very obscure and implicative phrases, might well admit of doubtful interpretation,) they found the matters not to be so evil as at first they seemed. Whereupon they agreed, that, upon his retractation, etc., or taking an oath of allegiance to the king, etc., it should be passed over.

[January 11, 1636] The governor[3] and assistants met at Boston to consider about Mr. Williams, for that they were credibly informed, that, notwithstanding the injunction laid upon him (upon the liberty granted him to stay till the spring) not to go about to draw others to his opinions, he did use to entertain company in his house, and to preach to them, even of such points as he had been censured for; and it was agreed to send him into England by a ship then ready to depart. The reason was, because he had drawn above twenty persons to his opinion, and they were intended to erect a plantation about the Naragansett Bay,[4] from whence the infection would easily spread into these churches, (the people being, many of them, much taken with the apprehension of his godliness). Whereupon a warrant was sent to him to come presently to Boston, to be shipped,[5] etc. He returned answer, (and divers of Salem came with it,) that he could not come without hazard of his life, etc. Whereupon a pinnace[6] was sent with commission to Capt. Underhill, etc., to apprehend him, and carry him aboard the ship, (which then rode at Natascutt;) but, when they came at his house, they found he had been gone three days before; but whither they could not learn.

He had so far prevailed at Salem, as many there (especially of devout women) did embrace his opinions, and separated from the churches, for this cause, that some of their members, going into England, did hear the ministers there, and when they came home the churches here held [to be in] communion with them.

[October 21, 1636] One Mrs. Hutchinson,[7] a member of the church of Boston, a woman of a ready wit and bold spirit, brought

1. John Cotton (1584–1652) emigrated to Boston in 1633 and from that time until his death was a major figure in the hierarchy of the town. He was pastor of the First Church of Boston.
2. Winthrop is referring to a now-lost Williams manuscript or treatise, mentioned in the entry for December 27, 1633, rather than a published book.
3. John Hays (1594–1654). Winthrop was re-elected governor in 1637.
4. Providence Plantation in Rhode Island received its patent in 1644.

5. I.e., returned to Boston by ship.
6. A small, light vessel, usually with two masts.
7. Anne Hutchinson (1591–1643), originally a follower of John Cotton, soon pursued an extreme position in which she argued that the elect were joined in personal union with God and superior to those lacking Inner Light. She also denied that good works were in any way a sign of God's favor, arguing that Justification was by faith alone and had nothing to do with either piety or worldly success.

over with her two dangerous errors: 1. That the person of the Holy Ghost dwells in a justified[8] person. 2. That no sanctification can help to evidence to us our justification.[9]—From these two grew many branches; as, 1. Our union with the Holy Ghost, so as a Christian remains dead to every spritual action, and hath no gifts nor graces, other than such as are in hypocrites, nor any other sanctification but the Holy Ghost himself.

There joined with her in these opinions a brother of hers, one Mr. Wheelwright, a silenced[1] minister sometimes in England.

[October 25, 1636] The other ministers in the bay, hearing of these things, came to Boston at the time of a general court, and entered conference in private with them, to the end they might know the certainty of these things; that if need were, they might write to the church of Boston about them, to prevent (if it were possible) the dangers, which seemed hereby to hang over that and the rest of the churches. At this conference, Mr. Cotton was present, and gave satisfaction to them, so as he agreed with them all in the point of sanctification, and so did Mr. Wheelwright; so as they all did hold, that sanctification did help to evidence justification. The same he had delivered plainly in public, divers times; but, for the indwelling of the person of the Holy Ghost, he held that still, as some other of the ministers did, but not union with the person of the Holy Ghost, (as Mrs. Hutchinson and others did,) so as to amount to a personal union.

[November 1, 1637] There was great hope that the late general assembly would have had some good effect in pacifying the troubles and dissensions about matters of religion; but it fell out otherwise. For though Mr. Wheelwright and those of his party had been clearly confuted and confounded in the assembly, yet they persisted in their opinions, and were as busy in nourishing contentions (the principal of them) as before. * * *

The court also sent for Mrs. Hutchinson, and charged her with divers matters, as her keeping two public lectures every week in her house, whereto sixty or eighty persons did usually resort, and for reproaching most of the ministers (viz., all except Mr. Cotton) for not preaching a covenant of free grace, and that they had not the seal of the spirit, nor were able ministers of the New Testament; which were clearly proved against her, though she sought to shift it off.[2] And, after many speeches to and fro, at last she was so full as she could not contain, but vented her revelations; amongst which this was one, that she had it revealed to her, that she should come into New England, and should here be persecuted, and that God would ruin us and our posterity, and the whole state, for the same.

---

8. I.e., one elected or chosen for salvation by God.
9. In the eyes of most Puritans, worldly success could be looked upon as a sign of God's favor.

1. Mr. Wheelwright had probably refused to take an oath of loyalty to the Church of England.
2. I.e., to qualify her statements.

So the court proceeded and banished her; but, because it was winter, they committed her to a private house, where she was well provided, and her own friends and the elders permitted to go to her, but none else.

The court called also Capt. Underhill, and some five or six more of the principal, whose hands were to the said petition; and because they stood to justify it, they were disfranchised, and such as had public places were put from them.

The court also ordered, that the rest, who had subscribed the petition, (and would not acknowledge their fault, and which near twenty of them did,) and some others, who had been chief stirrers in these contentions, etc., should be disarmed. This troubled some of them very much, especially because they were to bring them in themselves; but at last, when they saw no remedy, they obeyed.[3]

All the proceedings of this court against these persons were set down at large, with the reasons and other observations, and were sent into England to be published there, to the end that all our godly friends might not be discouraged from coming to us, etc.

[March, 1638] While Mrs. Hutchinson continued at Roxbury,[4] divers of the elders and others resorted to her, and finding her to persist in maintaining those gross errors beforementioned, and many others, to the number of thirty or thereabout, some of them wrote to the church at Boston, offering to make proof of the same before the church, etc., 15; whereupon she was called, (the magistrates being desired to give her license to come,) and the lecture was appointed to begin at ten. (The general court being then at Newtown, the governor[5] and the treasurer, being members of Boston, were permitted to come down, but the rest of the court continued at Newtown.) When she appeared, the errors were read to her. The first was, that the souls of men are mortal by generation,[6] but, after, made immortal by Christ's purchase. This she maintained a long time; but at length she was so clearly convinced by reason and scripture, and the whole church agreeing that sufficient had been delivered for her conviction, that she yielded she had been in an error. Then they proceeded to three other errors: 1. That there was no resurrection of these bodies, and that these bodies were not united to Christ, but every person united hath a new body, etc. These were also clearly confuted, but yet she held her own; so as the church (all but two of her sons) agreed she should be admonished, and because her sons would not agree to it, they were admonished also.

Mr. Cotton pronounced the sentence of admonition with great solemnity, and with much zeal and detestation of her errors and pride of spirit. The assembly continued till eight at night, and all

3. They were also forbidden to borrow or buy guns until "the court shall take further order therein . . ."
4. Near Boston.

5. Winthrop himself.
6. I.e., from the beginning. Orthodox believers hold the soul immortal.

did acknowledge the special presence of God's spirit therein; and she was appointed to appear again the next lecture day.

[March 22, 1638] Mrs. Hutchinson appeared again; (she had been licensed by the court, in regard she had given hope of her repentance, to be at Mr. Cotton's house, that both he and Mr. Davenport[7] might have the more opportunity to deal with her;) and the articles being again read to her, and her answer required, she delivered it in writing, wherein she made a retractation of near all, but with such explanations and circumstances as gave no satisfaction to the church; so as she was required to speak further to them. Then she declared, that it was just with God to leave her to herself, as He had done, for her slighting His ordinances, both magistracy and ministry;[8] and confessed that what she had spoken against the magistrates at the court (by way of revelation) was rash and ungrounded; and desired the church to pray for her. This gave the church good hope of her repentance; but when she was examined about some particulars, as that she had denied inherent righteousness, etc., she affirmed that it was never her judgment; and though it was proved by many testimonies, that she had been of that judgment, and so had persisted, and maintained it by argument against divers, yet she impudently persisted in her affirmation, to the astonishment of all the assembly. So that, after much time and many arguments had been spent to bring her to see her sin, but all in vain, the church, with one consent, cast her out. Some moved to have her admonished[9] once more; but, it being for manifest evil in matter of conversation, it was agreed otherwise; and for that reason also the sentence was denounced[1] by the pastor, matter of manners belonging properly to his place.

After she was excommunicated,[2] her spirits, which seemed before to be somewhat dejected, revived again, and she gloried in her sufferings, saying, that it was the greatest happiness, next to Christ, that ever befell her. Indeed, it was a happy day to the churches of Christ here, and to many poor souls, who had been seduced by her, who, by what they heard and saw that day, were (through the grace of God) brought off quite from her errors, and settled again in the truth.

* * *

After two or three days, the governor sent a warrant to Mrs. Hutchinson to depart this jurisdiction before the last of this month, according to the order of court, and for that end set her at liberty from her former constraint, so as she was not to go forth of her own house till her departure; and upon the 28th she went by water to her farm at the Mount, where she was to take water, with Mr.

---

7. John Davenport (1597–1670), a Puritan minister.
8. Because her unorthodox beliefs threatened both civil and ecclesiastical law.
9. Warned.

1. Publicly condemned.
2. Excluded, banished; not to be confused with the rite of excommunication performed by the Roman Catholic church.

Wheelwright's wife and family, to go to Pascataquack; but she changed her mind, and went by land to Providence, and so to the island in the Naragansett Bay, which her husband and the rest of that sect had purchased of the Indians. * * *

[September, 1638] . . . Mrs. Hutchinson, being removed to the Isle of Aquiday, in the Naragansett Bay, after her time was fulfilled, that she expected deliverance of a child, was delivered of a monstrous birth, which, being diversely related in the country, (and, in the open assembly at Boston, upon a lecture day, [was] declared by Mr. Cotton to be twenty-seven several lumps of man's seed, without any alteration or mixture of anything from the woman, and thereupon gathered that it might signify her error in denying inherent righteousness, but that all was Christ in us, and nothing of ours in our faith, love, etc.). Hereupon the governor wrote to Mr. Clarke, a physician and a preacher to those of the island, to know the certainty thereof.

* * *

[July 3 1645] * * * Then was the deputy governor[3] desired by the court to go up and take his place again upon the bench, which he did accordingly, and the court being about to arise, he desired leave for a little speech, which was to this effect.

I suppose something may be expected from me, upon this charge that is befallen me, which moves me to speak now to you; yet I intend not to intermeddle in the proceedings of the court, or with any of the persons concerned therein. Only I bless God, that I see an issue of this troublesome business. I also acknowledge the justice of the court, and, for mine own part, I am well satisfied, I was publicly charged, and I am publicly and legally acquitted, which is all I did expect or desire. And though this be sufficient for my justification before men, yet not so before the God, who hath seen so much amiss in my dispensations (and even in this affair) as calls me to be humble. For to be publicly and criminally charged in this court, is matter of humiliation, (and I desire to make a right use of it,) notwithstanding I be thus acquitted. If her father had spit in her face, (saith the Lord concerning Miriam,) should she not have been ashamed seven days?[4] Shame had lien upon her, whatever the occasion had been. I am unwilling to stay you from your urgent affairs, yet give me leave (upon this special occasion) to speak a little more to this assembly. It may be of some good use, to inform and rectify the judgments of some of the people, and may prevent such distempers as have arisen amongst us. The great questions that have troubled the country, are about the authority of the magistrates and the liberty of

3. Winthrop. The governor in 1645 was Thomas Dudley (1576–1654).
4. The sister of Moses and Aaron. "And the Lord said to Moses, If her father had but spit in her face, should she not be ashamed seven days? Let her be shut out from the camp seven days, and after that let her be received in again" (Numbers 12.14).

the people. It is yourselves who have called us to this office, and being called by you, we have our authority from God, in way of an ordinance, such as hath the image of God eminently stamped upon it, the contempt and violation whereof hath been vindicated with examples of divine vengeance. I entreat you to consider, that when you choose magistrates, you take them from among yourselves, men subject to like passions as you are. Therefore when you see infirmities in us, you should reflect upon your own, and that would make you bear the more with us, and not be severe censurers of the failings of your magistrates, when you have continual experience of the like infirmities in yourselves and others. We account him a good servant, who breaks not his covenant. The covenant between you and us is the oath you have taken of us, which is to this purpose, that we shall govern you and judge your causes by the rules of God's laws and our own, according to our best skill. When you agree with a workman to build you a ship or house, etc., he undertakes as well for his skill as for his faithfulness, for it is his profession, and you pay him for both. But when you call one to be a magistrate, he doth not profess nor undertake to have sufficient skill for that office, nor can you furnish him with gifts, etc., therefore you must run the hazard of his skill and ability. But if he fail in faithfulness, which by his oath he is bound unto, that he must answer for. If it fall out that the case be clear to common apprehension, and the rule clear also, if he transgress here, the error is not in the skill, but in the evil of the will: it must be required of him. But if the case be doubtful, or the rule doubtful, to men of such understanding and parts as your magistrates are, if your magistrates should err here, yourselves must bear it.

For the other point concerning liberty, I observe a great mistake in the country about that. There is a twofold liberty, natural (I mean as our nature is now corrupt[5]) and civil or federal. The first is common to man with beasts and other creatures. By this, man, as he stands in relation to man simply, hath liberty to do what he lists; it is a liberty to evil as well as to good. This liberty is incompatible and inconsistent with authority, and cannot endure the least restraint of the most just authority. The exercise and maintaining of this liberty makes men grow more evil, and in time to be worse than brute beasts: *omnes sumus licentia deteriores.*[6] This is that great enemy of truth and peace, that wild beast, which all the ordinances of God are bent against, to restrain and subdue it. The other kind of liberty I call civil or federal, it may also be termed moral, in reference to the covenant between God and man, in the moral law, and the politic covenants and constitutions, amongst men themselves. This liberty is the proper end and object of authority, and cannot subsist without it; and it is a liberty to that only which is good, just, and honest. This

5. I.e., since we are fallen and subject to death.   6. We are all the worse for license.

liberty you are to stand for, with the hazard (not only of your goods, but) of your lives, if need be. Whatsoever crosseth this, is not authority, but a distemper thereof. This liberty is maintained and exercised in a way of subjection to authority; it is of the same kind of liberty wherewith Christ hath made us free. The woman's own choice makes such a man her husband; yet being so chosen, he is her lord, and she is to be subject to him, yet in a way of liberty, not of bondage; and a true wife accounts her subjection her honor and freedom, and would not think her condition safe and free, but in her subjection to her husband's authority. Such is the liberty of the church under the authority of Christ, her king and husband; his yoke is so easy and sweet to her as a bride's ornaments; and if through forwardness or wantonness, etc., she sake it off, at any time, she is at no rest in her spirit, until she take it up again; and whether her lord smiles upon her, and embraceth her in his arms, or whether he frowns, or rebukes, or smites her, she apprehends the sweetness of his love in all, and is refreshed, supported, and instructed by every such dispensation of his authority over her. On the other side, ye know who they are that complain of this yoke and say, let us break their bands, etc., we will not have this man to rule over us. Even so, brethren, it will be between you and your magistrates. If you stand for your natural corrupt liberties, and will do what is good in your own eyes, you will not endure the least weight of authority, but will murmur, and oppose, and be always striving to shake off that yoke; but if you will be satisfied to enjoy such civil and lawful liberties, such as Christ allows you, then will you quietly and cheerfully submit unto that authority which is set over you, in all the administrations of it, for your good. Wherein, if we fail at any time, we hope we shall be willing (by God's assistance) to hearken to good advice from any of you, or in any other way of God; so shall your liberties be preserved, in upholding the honor and power of authority amongst you.

The deputy governor having ended his speech, the court arose, and the magistrates and deputies retired to attend their other affairs. * * *

1630–49　　　　　　　　　　　　　　　　　　　　　　1826

WILLIAM BRADFORD
1590–1657

William Bradford epitomizes the spirit of determination and self-sacrifice that seems to us characteristic of our first "Pilgrims," a word Bradford himself used to describe the community of believers who sailed from Southampton, England, on the *Mayflower* and settled in Plymouth, Massachusetts, in 1620. For Bradford, as well as for the other members of this community, the decision to settle at Plymouth was the last step in a long march of exile from England, and the hardships they suffered in the new land were tempered with the knowledge that they were in a place they had chosen for themselves, where they were safe from persecution. Shortly after their arrival Bradford was elected Governor. His duties involved more than that title might imply today: he was chief judge and jury, superintended agriculture and trade, and made allotments of land. It would be hard to imagine a historian better prepared to write the history of this colony.

Bradford's own life provides a model of the life of the community as a whole. He was born in Yorkshire, in the town of Austerfield, of parents who were modestly well off. Bradford's father died when he was a child, and he was brought up by his grandparents and uncles. He did not receive a university education; instead, he was taught the arts of farming. When he was only twelve or thirteen, he heard the sermons of the nonconformist minister Richard Clyfton, who preached in a neighboring parish; these sermons changed Bradford's life. For Clyfton was the religious guide of a small community of believers who met at the house of William Brewster in Scrooby, Nottinghamshire, and it was with this group, in 1606, that Bradford wished to be identified. Much against the opposition of uncles and grandparents, he left home and joined them. They were known as "separatists," because unlike the majority of Puritans, they saw no hope of reforming the Church of England from within. They wished to follow Calvin's model and to set up "particular" churches, each one founded on a formal covenant, entered into by those who professed their faith and swore to the covenant. Their model was the Old Testament covenant God made with Adam and which Christ renewed. In their covenanted churches God offered Himself as a contractual partner to each believer; it was a contract freely initiated but perpetually binding. They were not sympathetic to the idea of a national church. Separating was, however, by English law an act of treason, and many believers paid a high price for their dreams of purity. Sick of the hidden life that the Church of England forced upon them, the Scrooby community took up residence in Holland. Bradford joined them in 1609 and there learned to be a weaver. When he came into his inheritance he went into business for himself.

Living in a foreign land was not easy, and eventually the Scrooby community petitioned for a grant of land in the New World. Their original grant was for land in the Virginia territory, but high seas prevented them from reaching those shores and they settled at Plymouth, Massachusetts, instead. In the second book of Bradford's history he describes the signing of the "Mayflower Compact," a civil covenant designed to allow the temporal state to serve the godly citizen. It was the first of a number of "plantation covenants" designed to protect the rights of citizens beyond the reach of established governments.

Bradford was a self-educated man, deeply committed to the Puritan cause. In his ecclesiastical history of New England, Cotton Mather describes him as "a person for study as well as action; and hence notwithstanding the difficulties which he passed in his youth, he attained unto a notable skill in languages * * * but the Hebrew he most of all studied, because, he said, he would see with his own eyes the ancient oracles of God in their native beauty * * * the crown of all his life was his holy, prayerful, watchful and fruitful walk with God, wherein he was exemplary." Bradford served as Governor for all but five of the remaining years of his life.

The manuscript of Bradford's *History*, although known to early historians, disappeared from Boston after the Revolution. The first book (through Chapter IX) had been copied into the Plymouth church records and was thus preserved, but the second book was assumed lost. The manuscript was found in the residence of the Bishop of London and published for the first time in 1856. In 1897 it was returned to this country by ecclesiastical decree and was deposited in the State House in Boston.

From Of Plymouth Plantation[1]

From *Book I, Chapter I*.
[*The Separatist Interpretation of the Reformation in England, 1550–1607*]

* * * When as by the travail and diligence of some godly and zealous preachers, and God's blessing on their labors, as in other places of the land, so in the North parts,[2] many became enlightened by the Word of God and had their ignorance and sins discovered[3] unto them, and began by His grace to reform their lives and make conscience of their ways; the work of God was no sooner manifest in them but presently they were both scoffed and scorned by the profane[4] multitude; and the ministers urged with the yoke of subscription,[5] or else must be silenced. And the poor people were so vexed with apparitors and pursuivants and the commissary courts,[6] as truly their affliction was not small. Which, notwithstanding, they bore sundry years with much patience, till they were occasioned by the continuance and increase of these troubles, and other means which the Lord raised up in those days, to see further into things by the light of the Word of God. How not only these base and beggarly ceremonies were unlawful, but also that the lordly and tyrannous power of the prelates ought not to be submitted unto; which thus, contrary to the freedom of the gospel, would load and burden men's consciences and by their compulsive power make a profane mixture of persons and things in the worship of God. And that their offices and callings, courts and canons, etc. were unlawful and antichristian; being such as have no warrant in the Word of God, but the same that were used in popery and still retained. Of which a famous author thus writeth in his Dutch commentaries, at the coming of King James into England:

> The new king (saith he) found there established the reformed religion according to the reformed religion of King Edward VI, retaining or keeping still the spiritual state of the bishops, etc. after the old manner, much varying and differing

---

1. The text is from *Of Plymouth Plantation*, ed. Samuel Eliot Morison (New York: Knopf, 1953), pp. 8–10, 58–63, 73–79, 204–10, 252–54.
2. I.e., of England and Scotland.
3. Revealed.

4. Unholy.
5. I.e., to subscribe to the tenets of the Church of England; "urged": threatened.
6. I.e., vexed with officers and summoners of the Church of England, and the court of a Bishop's jurisdiction.

from the reformed churches in Scotland, France and the Netherlands, Emden, Geneva, etc., whose reformation is cut, or shapen much nearer the first Christian churches, as it was used in the Apostles' times.[7]

So many, therefore, of these professors as saw the evil of these things in these parts, and whose hearts the Lord had touched with heavenly zeal for His truth, they shook off this yoke of antichristian bondage, and as the Lord's free people joined themselves (by a covenant[8] of the Lord) into a church estate, in the fellowship of the gospel, to walk in all His ways made known, or to be made known unto them, according to their best endeavours, whatsoever it should cost them, the Lord assisting them. And that it cost them something this ensuing history will declare.

These people became two distinct bodies or churches, and in regard of distance of place did congregate severally; for they were of sundry towns and villages, some in Nottinghamshire, some of Lincolnshire, and some of Yorkshire where they border nearest together. In one of these churches (besides others of note) was Mr. John Smith,[9] a man of able gifts and a good preacher, who afterwards was chosen their pastor. But these afterwards falling into some errors in the Low Countries,[10] there (for the most part) buried themselves and their names.

But in this other church (which must be the subject of our discourse) besides other worthy men, was Mr. Richard Clyfton, a grave and reverend preacher, who by his pains and diligence had done much good, and under God had been a means of the conversion of many. And also that famous and worthy man Mr. John Robinson, who afterwards was their pastor for many years, till the Lord took him away by death. Also Mr. William Brewster a reverend man, who afterwards was chosen an elder of the church and lived with them till old age.

But after these things they could not long continue in any peaceable condition, but were hunted and persecuted on every side, so as their former afflictions were but as flea-bitings in comparison of these which now came upon them. For some were taken and clapped up in prison, others had their houses beset and watched night and day, and hardly escaped their hands; and the most were fain to flee and leave their houses and habitations, and the means of their livelihood.

7. From Emanuel van Meteren's *General History of the Netherlands* (1608). King James (1566–1625) ascended the throne in 1603. Most Puritans preferred the model of the Calvinist system in Geneva or the Church of Scotland, which replaced a hierarchy of Archbishops, Bishops, and priests with a national assembly and a parish presbytery consisting of ministers and elders.
8. A solemn agreement between the members of a church to act together in harmony with the precepts of the Gospel.
9. A Cambridge University graduate who seceded from the Church of England in 1605. Richard Clyfton and John Robinson were also Cambridge University graduates who were separatists. William Brewster (1576–1644) was a church leader of the Pilgrims in both Leyden and Plymouth.
10. Holland.

Yet these and many other sharper things which afterward befell them, were no other than they looked for, and therefore were the better prepared to bear them by the assistance of God's grace and Spirit.

Yet seeing themselves thus molested, and that there was no hope of their continuance there, by a joint consent they resolved to go into the Low Countries, where they heard was freedom of religion for all men; as also how sundry from London and other parts of the land had been exiled and persecuted for the same cause, and were gone thither, and lived at Amsterdam and in other places of the land. So after they had continued together about a year, and kept their meetings every Sabbath in one place or other, exercising the worship of God amongst themselves, notwithstanding all the diligence and malice of their adversaries, they seeing they could no longer continue in that condition, they resolved to get over into Holland as they could. Which was in the year 1607 and 1608; of which more at large in the next chapter.

Book I, Chapter IX. Of their Voyage and how they Passed the Sea; and of their Safe Arrival at Cape Cod

September 6. These troubles[1] being blown over, and now all being compact together in one ship, they put to sea again with a prosperous wind, which continued divers days together, which was some encouragement unto them; yet, according to the usual manner, many were afflicted with seasickness. And I may not omit here a special work of God's providence. There was a proud and very profane young man, one of the seamen, of a lusty,[2] able body, which made him the more haughty; he would alway be contemning the poor people in their sickness and cursing them daily with grievous execrations; and did not let[3] to tell them that he hoped to help to cast half of them overboard before they came to their journey's end, and to make merry with what they had; and if he were by any gently reproved, he would curse and swear most bitterly. But it pleased God before they came half seas over, to smite this young man with a grievous disease, of which he died in a desperate manner, and so was himself the first that was thrown overboard. Thus his curses light on his own head, and it was an astonishment to all his fellows for they noted it to be the just hand of God upon him.

After they had enjoyed fair winds and weather for a season, they were encountered many times with cross winds and met with many fierce storms with which the ship was shroudly[4] shaken, and her upper works made very leaky; and one of the main beams in the

---

1. Some of the Scrooby community originally sailed from Delftshaven about August 1, 1620, on board the *Speedwell*, but it proved unseaworthy and it was necessary to transfer everything to the *Mayflower*.
2. Strong, energetic.
3. Hesitate.
4. Shrewdly, in its original sense of wickedly.

midships was bowed and cracked, which put them in some fear that the ship could not be able to perform the voyage. So some of the chief of the company, perceiving the mariners to fear the sufficiency of the ship as appeared by their mutterings, they entered into serious consultation with the master and other officers of the ship, to consider in time of the danger, and rather to return than to cast themselves into a desperate and inevitable peril. And truly there was great distraction and difference of opinion amongst the mariners themselves; fain would they do what could be done for their wages' sake (being now near half the seas over) and on the other hand they were loath to hazard their lives too desperately. But in examining of all opinions, the master and others affirmed they knew the ship to be strong and firm under water; and for the buckling of the main beam, there was a great iron screw the passengers brought out of Holland, which would raise the beam into his place; the which being done, the carpenter and master affirmed that with a post put under it, set firm in the lower deck and otherways bound, he would make it sufficient. And as for the decks and upper works, they would caulk them as well as they could, and though with the working of the ship they would not long keep staunch,[5] yet there would otherwise be no great danger, if they did not overpress her with sails. So they committed themselves to the will of God and resolved to proceed.

In sundry of these storms the winds were so fierce and the seas so high, as they could not bear a knot of sail, but were forced to hull[6] for divers days together. And in one of them, as they thus lay at hull in a mighty storm, a lusty young man called John Howland, coming upon some occasion above the gratings was, with a seele[7] of the ship, thrown into sea; but it pleased God that he caught hold of the topsail halyards which hung overboard and ran out at length. Yet he held his hold (though he was sundry fathoms under water) till he was hauled up by the same rope to the brim of the water, and then with a boat hook and other means got into the ship again and his life saved. And though he was something ill with it, yet he lived many years after and became a profitable member both in church and commonwealth. In all this voyage there died but one of the passengers, which was William Butten, a youth, servant to Samuel Fuller, when they drew near the coast.

But to omit other things (that I may be brief) after long beating at sea they fell with that land which is called Cape Cod; the which being made and certainly known to be it, they were not a little joyful. After some deliberation had amongst themselves and with the master of the ship, they tacked about and resolved to stand for the southward (the wind and weather being fair) to find some place about Hudson's River for their habitation. But after they had sailed that course about half the day, they fell amongst dangerous

5. **Watertight.**
6. **Drift with the wind under short sail.**
7. **Roll.**

shoals and roaring breakers, and they were so far entangled therewith as they conceived themselves in great danger; and the wind shrinking upon them withal, they resolved to bear up again for the Cape and thought themselves happy to get out of those dangers before night overtook them, as by God's good providence they did. And the next day they got into the Cape Harbor[8] where they rid in safety.

A word or two by the way of this cape. It was thus first named by Captain Gosnold and his company, Anno 1602, and after by Captain Smith was called Cape James; but it retains the former name amongst seamen. Also, that point which first showed those dangerous shoals unto them they called Point Care, and Tucker's Terror; but the French and Dutch to this day call it Malabar[9] by reason of those perilous shoals and the losses they have suffered there.

Being thus arrived in a good harbor, and brought safe to land, they fell upon their knees and blessed the God of Heaven who had brought them over the vast and furious ocean, and delivered them from all the perils and miseries thereof, again to set their feet on the firm and stable earth, their proper element. And no marvel if they were thus joyful, seeing wise Seneca was so affected with sailing a few miles on the coast of his own Italy, as he affirmed, that he had rather remain twenty years on his way by land than pass by sea to any place in a short time, so tedious and dreadful was the same unto him.[1]

But here I cannot but stay and make a pause, and stand half amazed at this poor people's present condition; and so I think will the reader, too, when he well considers the same. Being thus passed the vast ocean, and a sea of troubles before in their preparation (as may be remembered by that which went before), they had now no friends to welcome them nor inns to entertain or refresh their weatherbeaten bodies; no houses or much less towns to repair to, to seek for succor. It is recorded in Scripture as a mercy to the Apostle and his shipwrecked company, that the barbarians showed them no small kindness in refreshing them,[2] but these savage barbarians, when they met with them (as after will appear) were readier to fill their sides full of arrows than otherwise. And for the season it was winter, and they that know the winters of that country know them to be sharp and violent, and subject to cruel and fierce storms, dangerous to travel to known places, much more to search an unknown coast. Besides, what could they see but a hideous and

---

8. Cape Harbor is now Provincetown Harbor; they arrived on November 11, 1620, the journey from England having taken 65 days.
9. The prefix "mal" means bad; the reference here is to the dangerous sandbars.
1. Bradford notes that this remark may be found in the *Moral Epistles to Lucilius*, line 5, of the Roman Stoic philosopher (4? B.C.–A.D. 65).
2. "And when they were escaped, then they knew that the island was called Melita. And the barbarous people showed us no little kindness: for they kindled a fire, and received us every one, because of the present rain, and because of the cold" (Acts 28.1–2).

desolate wilderness, full of wild beasts and wild men—and what multitudes there might be of them they knew not. Neither could they, as it were, go up to the top of Pisgah[3] to view from this wilderness a more goodly country to feed their hopes; for which way soever they turned their eyes (saved upward to the heavens) they could have little solace or content in respect of any outward objects. For summer being done, all things stand upon them with a weatherbeaten face, and the whole country, full of woods and thickets, represented a wild and savage hue. If they looked behind them, there was the mighty ocean which they had passed and was now as a main bar and gulf to separate them from all the civil parts of the world. If it be said they had a ship to succor them, it is true; but what heard they daily from the master and company? But that with speed they should look out a place (with their shallop)[4] where they would be, at some near distance; for the season was such as he would not stir from thence till a safe harbor was discovered by them, where they would be, and he might go without danger; and that victuals consumed apace but he must and would keep sufficient for themselves and their return. Yea, it was muttered by some that if they got not a place in time, they would turn them and their goods ashore and leave them. Let it also be considered what weak hopes of supply and succor they left behind them, that might bear up their minds in this sad condition and trials they were under; and they could not but be very small. It is true, indeed, the affections and love of their brethren at Leyden[5] was cordial and entire towards them, but they had little power to help them or themselves; and how the case stood between them and the merchants at their coming away hath already been declared.

What could now sustain them but the Spirit of God and His grace? May not and ought not the children of these fathers rightly say: "Our fathers were Englishmen which came over this great ocean, and were ready to perish in this wilderness; but they cried unto the Lord, and He heard their voice and looked on their adversity,"[6] etc. "Let them therefore praise the Lord, because He is good: and His mercies endure forever." "Yea, let them which have been redeemed of the Lord, show how He hath delivered them from the hand of the oppressor. When they wandered in the desert wilderness out of the way, and found no city to dwell in, both hungry and thirsty, their soul was overwhelmed in them. Let them confess before the Lord His loving kindness and His wonderful works before the sons of men."[7]

3. Mountain from which Moses saw the Promised Land (Deuteronomy 34.1–4).
4. Small boat.
5. In Holland. A substantial number of separatists remained in the Netherlands.
6. "And the Egyptians evil entreated us, and afflicted us, and laid upon us hard bondage: And we cried unto the Lord God of our fathers, the Lord heard our voice, and looked on our affliction, and our labor and our oppression: And the Lord brought us forth out of Egypt with a mighty hand * * *" (Deuteronomy 26.6–8).
7. "O give thanks unto the Lord, for he is good: for his mercy endureth for ever. Let the redeemed of the Lord say so, whom he hath redeemed from the hand

From *Book II, Chapter XI.*[1] *The Remainder of Anno 1620*
[THE MAYFLOWER COMPACT]

I shall a little return back, and begin with a combination[2] made by them before they came ashore; being the first foundation of their government in this place. Occasioned partly by the discontented and mutinous speeches that some of the strangers[3] amongst them had let fall from them in the ship: That when they came ashore they would use their own liberty, for none had power to command them, the patent they had being for Virginia and not for New England, which belonged to another government, with which the Virginia Company had nothing to do. And partly that such an act by them done, this their condition considered, might be as firm as any patent,[4] and in some respects more sure.

The form was as followeth:
IN THE NAME OF GOD, AMEN.

We whose names are underwritten, the loyal subjects of our dread Sovereign Lord King James, by the Grace of God of Great Britain, France, and Ireland King, Defender of the Faith, etc.

Having undertaken, for the glory of God and advancement of the Christian Faith and Honour of our King and Country, a Voyage to plant the First Colony in the Northern Parts of Virginia, do by these presents solemnly and mutually in the presence of God and one of another, Covenant and Combine ourselves together into a Civil Body Politic, for our better ordering and preservation and furtherance of the ends aforesaid; and by virtue hereof to enact, constitute and frame such just and equal Laws, Ordinances, Acts, Constitutions and Offices, from time to time, as shall be thought most meet and covenient for the general good of the Colony, unto which we promise all due submission and obedience. In witness whereof we have hereunder subscribed our names at Cape Cod, the 11th of November, in the year of the reign of our Sovereign Lord King James, of England, France and Ireland the eighteenth, and of Scotland the fifty-fourth. Anno Domini 1620.

After this they chose, or rather confirmed, Mr. John Carver[5] (a man godly and well approved amongst them) their Governor for that year. And after they had provided a place for their goods, or common store (which were long in unlading[6] for want of boats,

---

of the enemy; And gathered them out of the lands, from the east, and from the west, from the north, and from the south" (Psalm 107.1–5).

1. Bradford numbered only the first 10 chapters of his manuscript.
2. A form of union, a joining together.
3. Puritans called themselves "saints" and those outside their churches "strangers." Many of those who came to Plymouth with them were not church members but adventurers looking forward to business success and making new lives in the New World.
4. A document signed by a sovereign granting privileges to those named in it.
5. Carver (c. 1576–1621), like Bradford, was an original member of the group who went to Holland and, like Bradford, a tradesman. Bradford was elected Governor after Carver's death.
6. Unloading.

foulness of the winter weather and sickness of divers) and begun
some small cottages for their habitation; as time would admit, they
met and consulted of laws and orders, both for their civil and military government as the necessity of their condition did require, still
adding thereunto as urgent occasion in several times, and as cases
did require.

In these hard and difficult beginnings they found some discontents and murmurings arise amongst some, and mutinous speeches
and carriages in other; but they were soon quelled and overcome by
the wisdom, patience, and just and equal carriage of things, by the
Governor and better part, which clave[7] faithfully together in the
main.

[THE STARVING TIME]

But that which was most sad and lamentable was, that in two or
three months' time half of their company died, especially in January
and February, being the depth of winter, and wanting houses and
other comforts; being infected with the scurvy and other diseases
which this long voyage and their inaccommodate condition had
brought upon them. So as there died some times two or three of a
day in the foresaid time, that of 100 and odd persons, scarce fifty
remained. And of these, in the time of most distress, there was but
six or seven persons who to their great commendations, be it
spoken, spared no pains night nor day, but with abundance of toil
and hazard of their own health, fetched them wood, made them
fires, dressed them meat, made their beds, washed their loathsome
clothes, clothed and unclothed them. In a word, did all the homely[8]
and necessary offices for them which dainty and queasy stomachs
cannot endure to hear named; and all this willingly and cheerfully,
without any grudging in the least, showing herein their true love
unto their friends and brethren; a rare example and worthy to be
remembered. Two of these seven were Mr. William Brewster, their
reverend Elder, and Myles Standish, their Captain and military
commander, unto whom myself and many others were much beholden in our low and sick condition. And yet the Lord so upheld
these persons as in this general calamity they were not at all
infected either with sickness or lameness. And what I have said of
these I may say of many others who died in this general visitation,
and others yet living; that whilst they had health, yea, or any
strength continuing, they were not wanting[9] to any that had need
of them. And I doubt not but their recompense is with the Lord.

But I may not here pass by another remarkable passage not to be
forgotten. As this calamity fell among the passengers that were to
be left here to plant, and were hasted ashore and made to drink
water that the seamen might have the more beer, and one[1] in his

---

7. Past tense of *cleave*.
8. Intimate.
9. Lacking in attention.

1. "Which was this author himself" [Brad-
ford's note].

sickness desiring but a small can of beer, it was answered that if he were their own father he should have none. The disease began to fall amongst them also, so as almost half of their company died before they went away, and many of their officers and lustiest men, as the boatswain, gunner, three quartermasters, the cook and others. At which the Master was something strucken and sent to the sick ashore and told the Governor he should send for beer for them that had need of it, though he drunk water homeward bound.

But now amongst his company there was far another kind of carriage in this misery than amongst the passengers. For they that before had been boon companions in drinking and jollity in the time of their health and welfare, began now to desert one another in this calamity, saying they would not hazard their lives for them, they should be infected by coming to help them in their cabins; and so, after they came to lie by it, would do little or nothing for them but, "if they died, let them die." But such of the passengers as were yet aboard showed them what mercy they could, which made some of their hearts relent, as the boatswain (and some others) who was a proud young man and would often curse and scoff at the passengers. But when he grew weak, they had compassion on him and helped him; then he confessed he did not deserve it at their hands, he had abused them in word and deed. "Oh!" (saith he) "you, I now see, show your love like Christians indeed one to another, but we let one another lie and die like dogs." Another lay cursing his wife, saying if it had not been for her he had never come this unlucky voyage, and anon cursing his fellows, saying he had done this and that for some of them; he had spent so much and so much amongst them, and they were now weary of him and did not help him, having need. Another gave his companion all he had, if he died, to help him in his weakness; he went and got a little spice and made him a mess of meat once or twice. And because he died not so soon as he expected, he went amongst his fellows and swore the rogue would cozen[2] him, he would see him choked before he made him any more meat; and yet the poor fellow died before morning.

From *Book II, Chapter XIX. Anno Dom: 1628*
[THOMAS MORTON OF MERRYMOUNT][1]

About some three or four years before this time, there came over one Captain Wollaston (a man of pretty[2] parts) and with him three or four more of some eminency, who brought with them a great many servants, with provisions and other implements for to

---

2. Cheat.

1. Almost nothing is known of either Thomas Morton or Captain Wollaston other than what Bradford tells us. By all accounts Morton left England with a bad reputation and a history of unrests behind him. Unlike the Puritans, however, Morton relished the sensuality of the wild and took great pleasure in the American landscape. Bradford tells us that Morton did not think that "in all the world it could be paralleled" for its plenitude and beauty.

2. I.e., of a clever nature.

begin a plantation. And pitched themselves in a place within the Massachusetts which they called after their Captain's name, Mount Wollaston. Amongst whom was one Mr. Morton, who it should seem had some small adventure of his own or other men's amongst them, but had little respect amongst them, and was slighted by the meanest servants. Having continued there some time, and not finding things to answer their expectations nor profit to arise as they looked for, Captain Wollaston takes a great part of the servants[3] and transports them to Virginia, where he puts them off at good rates, selling their time to other men; and writes back to one Mr. Rasdall (one of his chief partners and accounted their merchant) to bring another part of them to Virginia likewise, intending to put them off there as he had done the rest. And he, with the consent of the said Rasdall, appointed one Fitcher to be his Lieutenant and govern the remains of the Plantation till he or Rasdell returned to take further order thereabout. But this Morton abovesaid, having more craft than honesty (who had been a kind of pettifogger[4] of Furnival's Inn) in the others' absence watches an opportunity (commons being but hard amongst them)[5] and got some strong drink and other junkets[6] and made them a feast; and after they were merry, he began to tell them he would give them good counsel. "You see," saith he, "that many of your fellows are carried to Virginia, and if you stay till this Rasdall return, you will also be carried away and sold for slaves with the rest. Therefore I would advise you to thrust out this Lieutenant Fitcher, and I, having a part in the Plantation, will receive you as my partners and consociates; so may you be free from service, and we will converse, plant, trade, and live together as equals and support and protect one another," or to like effect. This counsel was easily received, so they took opportunity and thrust Lieutenant Fitcher out o' doors, and would suffer him to come no more amongst them, but forced him to seek bread to eat and other relief from his neighbors till he could get passage for England.

After this they fell to great licentiousness and led a dissolute life, pouring out themselves into all profaneness. And Morton became Lord of Misrule,[7] and maintained (as it were) a School of Atheism. And after they had got some goods into their hands, and got much by trading with the Indians, they spent it as vainly in quaffing and drinking, both wine and strong waters in great excess (and, as some reported) £10 worth in a morning. They also set up a maypole, drinking and dancing about it many days together, inviting

---

3. A servant was anyone who worked for another in agriculture or domestic economy. An indentured servant was one who agreed to work for another for seven years in order to pay for his transportation to the New World.
4. A shifty lawyer; Furnival's Inn is a ward in the city of London.

5. I.e., there were few responsible citizens among them.
6. Delicacies; food for banqueting.
7. One who presides over games and revels, usually at Christmastime in a great man's house; here one who presides over revelry and licentiousness.

the Indian women for their consorts, dancing and frisking together like so many fairies, or furies, rather; and worse practices. As if they had anew revived and celebrated the feast of the Roman goddess Flora,[8] or the beastly practices of the mad Bacchanalians. Morton likewise, to show his poetry composed sundry rhymes and verses, some tending to lasciviousness, and others to the detraction and scandal of some persons, which he affixed to this idle or idol maypole. They changed also the name of their place, and instead of calling it Mount Wollaston they call it Merry-mount, as if this jollity would have lasted ever. But this continued not long, for after Morton was sent for England (as follows to be declared) shortly after came over that worthy gentleman Mr. John Endicott, who brought over a patent under the broad seal for the government of the Massachusetts. Who, visiting those parts, caused that maypole to be cut down and rebuked them for their profaneness and admonished them to look there should be better walking. So they or others now changed the name of their place again and called it Mount Dagon.[9]

Now to maintain this riotous prodigality and profuse excess, Morton, thinking himself lawless, and hearing what gain the French and fishermen made by trading of pieces,[1] powder and shot to the Indians, he as the head of this consortship began the practice of the same in these parts. And first he taught them how to use them, to charge and discharge, and what proportion of powder to give the piece, according to the size or bigness of the same; and what shot to use for fowl and what for deer. And having thus instructed them, he employed some of them to hunt and fowl for him, so as they became far more active in that employment than any of the English, by reason of their swiftness of foot and nimbleness of body, being also quick-sighted and by continual exercise well knowing the haunts of all sorts of game. So as when they saw the execution that a piece would do, and the benefit that might come by the same, they became mad (as it were) after them and would not stick to give any price they could attain to for them; according their bows and arrows but baubles in comparison of them. * * *

This Morton having thus taught them the use of pieces, he sold them all he could spare, and he and his consorts determined to send for many out of England and had by some of the ships sent for above a score. The which being known, and his neighbours meeting the Indians in the woods armed with guns in this sort, it was a terror unto them who lived stragglingly[2] and were of no strength in

8. Roman goddess of flowers and vegetation; the Maenads or Bacchantes were women drunk with wine who worshiped Bacchus and tore anyone they met to pieces.
9. Named after the god of the Philistines: "Then the lords of the Philistines gathered them together for to offer a great sacrifice unto Dagon their god, and to rejoice; for they said, Our god hath delivered Samson our enemy into our hand" (Judges 16.23).
1. Guns.
2. Spread out in a scattered fashion; far apart.

any place. And other places (though more remote) saw this mischief would quickly spread over all, if not prevented. Besides, they saw they should keep no servants, for Morton would entertain any, how vile soever, and all the scum of the country or any discontents would flock to him from all places, if this nest was not broken. And they should stand in more fear of their lives and goods in short time from this wicked and debased crew than from the savages themselves.

So sundry of the chief of the straggling plantations, meeting together, agreed by mutual consent to solicit those of Plymouth (who were then of more strength than them all) to join with them to prevent the further growth of this mischief, and suppress Morton and his consorts before they grew to further head and strength. Those that joined in this action, and after contributed to the charge of sending him for England, were from Piscataqua, Naumkeag, Winnisimmet, Wessagusset, Nantasket and other places where any English were seated. Those of Plymouth being thus sought to by their messengers and letters, and weighing both their reasons and the common danger, were willing to afford them their help though themselves had least cause of fear or hurt. So, to be short, they first resolved jointly to write to him, and in a friendly and neighborly way to admonish him to forbear those courses, and sent a messenger with their letters to bring his answer.

But he was so high as scorned all advice, and asked who had to do with him, he had and would trade pieces with the Indians, in despite of all, with many other scurrilous terms full of disdain. They sent to him a second time and bade him be better advised and more temperate in his terms, for the country could not bear the injury he did. It was against their common safety and against the King's proclamation. He answered in high terms as before; and that the King's proclamation was no law, demanding what penalty was upon it. It was answered, more than he could bear—His Majesty's displeasure. But insolently he persisted and said the King was dead and his displeasure with him, and many the like things. And threatened withal that if any came to molest him, let them look to themselves for he would prepare for them.

Upon which they saw there was no way but to take him by force; and having so far proceeded, now to give over would make him far more haughty and insolent. So they mutually resolved to proceed, and obtained of the Governor of Plymouth to send Captain Standish and some other aid with him, to take Morton by force. The which accordingly was done. But they found him to stand stiffly in his defense, having made fast his doors, armed his consorts, set divers dishes of powder and bullets ready on the table; and if they had not been over-armed with drink, more hurt might have been done. They summoned him to yield, but he kept his house and they could get nothing but scoffs and scorns from him. But at length, fearing they would do some violence to the house, he and some of his crew came out, but not to yield but to shoot; but they were so steeled[3] with drink as their pieces were too heavy for them. Himself with a carbine, overcharged and almost half filled with powder and shot, as was after found, had thought to have shot Captain Standish; but he stepped to him and put by his piece and took him. Neither was there any hurt done to any of either side, save that one was so drunk that he ran his own nose upon the point of a sword that one held before him, as he entered the house; but he lost but a little of his hot blood.[4]

Morton they brought away to Plymouth, where he was kept till a ship went from the Isle of Shoals for England, with which he was sent to the Council of New England, and letters written to give them information of his course and carriage. And also one was sent at their common charge to inform their Honours more particularly and to prosecute against him. But he fooled of the messenger, after he was gone from hence, and though he went for England yet nothing was done to him, not so much as rebuked, for aught was heard, but returned the next year. Some of the worst of the company were dispersed and some of the more modest kept the house till he should be heard from. But I have been too long about so unworthy a person, and bad a cause.

1856

3. Insensible.
4. Morton refers to Captain Standish in his *New England Canaan* (1637) as Captain Shrimp, and tells us that it would have been easy for him to destroy these nine "worthies" like a "flock of wild geese" but that he loathed violence and asked for his freedom to leave. He suggests that he was treated brutally because the Puritans wished to shame him before the Indians.

ANNE BRADSTREET
c. 1612–1672

Anne Bradstreet's father, Thomas Dudley, was the manager of the country estate of the Puritan Earl of Lincoln, and his daughter was very much the apple of his eye. When she was about seven she had eight tutors in languages, music, and dancing and her father took great care to see that she received an education superior to that of most young women of the time. When she was only sixteen she married a young man, Simon Bradstreet, a recent graduate of Cambridge University, who was associated with her father in conducting the affairs of the Earl of Lincoln's estate. He also shared her father's Puritan beliefs. A year after the marriage her husband was appointed to assist in the preparations of the Company of the Massachusetts Bay, and the following year the Bradstreets and the Dudleys sailed with Winthrop's fleet. Anne Bradstreet tells us that when she first "came into this country" she "found a new world and new manners," at which her "heart rose" in resistance, "But after I was convinced it was the way of God, I submitted to it and joined the church at Boston."

We know very little of Anne Bradstreet's daily life, except that it was a hard existence. The wilderness, Samuel Eliot Morison once observed, "made men stern and silent, children unruly, servants insolent." William Bradford's wife, Dorothy, staring at the barren dunes of Cape Cod, said that she preferred the surety of drowning to the unknown life ashore. Added to the hardship of daily living was the fact that Anne Bradstreet was never very strong. She had rheumatic fever as a child and as a result suffered recurrent periods of severe fatigue; nevertheless, she risked death by childbirth eight times. Her husband was secretary to the Company and later Governor of the Bay Colony; he was always involved in the colony's diplomatic missions; and in 1661 he went to England to renegotiate the Bay Company charter with Charles II. All of Simon's tasks must have added to her responsibilities at home. And like any good Puritan she added to the care of daily life the examination of her conscience. She tells us in one of the "Meditations" written for her children that she was troubled many times about the truth of the Scriptures; that she never saw any convincing miracles, and that she always wondered if those of which she read "were feigned." What proved to her finally that God exists was not her reading but the evidence of her own eyes. She is the first in a long line of American poets who took their consolation not from theology but from the "wonderous works," as she wrote, "that I see, the vast frame of the heaven and the earth, the order of all things, night and day, summer and winter, spring and autumn, the daily providing for this great household upon the earth, the preserving and directing of all to its proper end."

When Anne Bradstreet was a young girl she had written poems to please her father, and he made much of their reading them together. After her marriage she continued writing. Quite unknown to her, her brother-in-law, John Woodbridge, pastor of the Andover church, brought with him to London a manuscript collection of her poetry and had it printed there in 1650. It was the first published volume of poems written by a resident in the New World and was widely read. Reverend Edward Taylor, also a poet, and living in the frontier community of Westfield, Massachusetts, had a copy of the second edition of Bradstreet's poems (1678) in his library. Although she herself probably took greatest pride in her long meditative poems on the ages of man and on the seasons, the poems which have attracted present-day readers are the more intimate ones which reflect her concern for her family and home and the pleasures she took in everyday life rather than in the life to come.

The text used is the *Works of Anne Bradstreet*, ed. Jeannine Hensley (Cambridge: Harvard University Press, 1967).

The Prologue

1

To sing of wars, of captains, and of kings,
Of cities founded, commonwealths begun,
For my mean[1] pen are too superior things:
Or how they all, or each their dates have run
Let poets and historians set these forth,   5
My obscure lines shall not so dim their worth.

---

1. Humble.

2

But when my wond'ring eyes and envious heart
Great Bartas'[2] sugared lines do but read o'er,
Fool[3] I do grudge the Muses[4] did not part
'Twixt him and me that overfluent store;   10
A Bartas can do what a Bartas will
But simple I according to my skill.

3

From schoolboy's tongue no rhet'ric we expect,
Nor yet a sweet consort[5] from broken strings,
Nor perfect beauty where's a main defect: 15
My foolish, broken, blemished Muse so sings,
And this to mend, alas, no art is able,
'Cause nature made it so irreparable.

4

Nor can I, like that fluent sweet tongued Greek,
Who lisped at first, in future times speak plain.[6]   20
By art he gladly found what he did seek,
A full requital of his striving pain.
Art can do much, but this maxim's most sure:
A weak or wounded brain admits no cure.

5

I am obnoxious to each carping tongue   25
Who says my hand a needle better fits,
A poet's pen all scorn I should thus wrong,
For such despite they cast on female wits:
If what I do prove well, it won't advance,
They'll say it's stol'n, or else it was by chance.   30

6

But sure the antique Greeks were far more mild
Else of our sex, why feigned they those nine
And poesy made Calliope's[7] own child;
So 'mongst the rest they placed the arts divine:
But this weak knot they will full soon untie.   35
The Greeks did nought, but play the fools and lie.

7

Let Greeks be Greeks, and women what they are;
Men have precedency and still excel,
It is but vain unjustly to wage war;
Men can do best, and women know it well.   40
Preeminence in all and each is yours;
Yet grant some small acknowledgement of ours.

8

And oh ye high flown quills[8] that soar the skies,
And ever with your prey still catch your praise,
If e'er you deign these lowly lines your eyes,   45

2. Guillaume du Bartas (1544–90) was a French writer much admired by the Puritans. He was most famous as the author of *The Divine Weeks*, an epic poem translated by Joshua Sylvester and intended to recount the great moments in Christian history.
3. I.e., like a fool.
4. In Greek mythology, the nine goddesses of the arts and sciences.
5. Accord, harmony of sound.
6. The Greek orator Demosthenes (c. 383–322 B.C.) conquered a speech defect.
7. The muse of epic poetry.
8. Pens.

Give thyme or parsley wreath, I ask no bays;[9]
This mean and unrefined ore of mine
Will make your glist'ring gold but more to shine.

1650

Contemplations

Some time now past in the autumnal tide,
When Phoebus[1] wanted but one hour to bed,
The trees all richly clad, yet void of pride,
Were gilded o'er by his rich golden head.
Their leaves and fruits seemed painted, but was true,   5
Of green, of red, of yellow, mixed hue;
Rapt were my senses at this delectable view.

2

I wist not what to wish, yet sure thought I,
If so much excellence abide below,
How excellent is He that dwells on high,   10
Whose power and beauty by his works we know?
Sure he is goodness, wisdom, glory, light,
That hath this under world so richly dight;[2]
More heaven than earth was here, no winter and no night.

3

Then on a stately oak I cast mine eye,   15
Whose ruffling top the clouds seemed to aspire;
How long since thou wast in thine infancy?
Thy strength, and stature, more thy years admire,
Hath hundred winters past since thou wast born?
Or thousand since thou brakest thy shell of horn?   20
If so, all these as nought, eternity doth scorn.

4

Then higher on the glistering Sun I gazed,
Whose beams was shaded by the leafy tree;
The more I looked, the more I grew amazed,
And softly said, "What glory's like to thee?"   25
Soul of this world, this universe's eye,
No wonder some made thee a deity;
Had I not better known, alas, the same had I.

5

Thou as a bridegroom from thy chamber rushes,
And as a strong man, joys to run a race;[3]   30
The morn doth usher thee with smiles and blushes;
The Earth reflects her glances in thy face.
Birds, insects, animals with vegative,
Thy heat from death and dullness doth revive,
And in the darksome womb of fruitful nature dive.   35

6

Thy swift annual and diurnal course,
Thy daily straight and yearly oblique path,

9. Garlands of laurel, used to crown the
head of a poet.
1. Apollo, the sun god.
2. Furnished, adorned.

3. The sun "is as a bridegroom coming
out of his chamber, and rejoiceth as a
strong man to run a race" (Psalms
19.4–5).

Thy pleasing fervor and thy scorching force,
All mortals here the feeling knowledge hath.
Thy presence makes it day, thy absence night,   40
Quaternal seasons cabeséd by thy might:
Hail creature, full of sweetness, beauty, and delight.

7

Art thou so full of glory that no eye
Hath strength thy shining rays once to behold?
And is thy splendid throne erect so high,   45
As to approach it, can no earthly mould?
How full of glory then must thy Creator be,
Who gave this bright light luster unto thee?
Admired, adored for ever, be that Majesty.

8

Silent alone, where none or saw, or heard,   50
In pathless paths I lead my wand'ring feet,
My humble eyes to lofty skies I reared
To sing some song, my mazéd[4] Muse thought meet.
My great Creator I would magnify,
That nature had thus decked liberally;   55
But Ah, and Ah, again, my imbecility!

9

I heard the merry grasshopper then sing.
The black-clad cricket bear a second part;
They kept one tune and played on the same string,
Seeming to glory in their little art.   60
Shall creatures abject thus their voices raise
And in their kind resound their Maker's praise,
Whilst I, as mute, can warble forth no higher lays?

10

When present times look back to ages past,
And men in being fancy those are dead,   65
It makes things gone perpetually to last,
And calls back months and years that long since fled.
It makes a man more aged in conceit
Than was Methuselah,[5] or's grandsire great,
While of their persons and their acts his mind doth treat.   70

11

Sometimes in Eden fair he seems to be,
Sees glorious Adam there made lord of all,
Fancies the apple, dangle on the tree,
That turned his sovereign to a naked thrall.[6]
Who like a miscreant's driven from that place,   75
To get his bread with pain and sweat of face,
A penalty imposed on his backsliding race.

12

Here sits our grandame[7] in retired place,
And in her lap her bloody Cain new-born;

---

4. Amazed.
5. Methuselah was thought to have lived 969 years (Genesis 5.18–27); "conceit": apprehension, the processes of thought.

6. Slave.
7. By believing in the "father of lies," Eve lost Paradise; her elder son, Cain, slew his brother, Abel (Genesis 10–16).

The weeping imp oft looks her in the face,   80
Bewails his unknown hap[8] and fate forlorn;
His mother sighs to think of Paradise,
And how she lost her bliss to be more wise,
Believing him that was, and is, father of lies.

13

Here Cain and Abel come to sacrifice,   85
Fruits of the earth and fatlings[9] each do bring,
On Abel's gift the fire descends from skies,
But no such sign on false Cain's offering;
With sullen hateful looks he goes his ways,
Hath thousand thoughts to end his brother's days,   90
Upon whose blood his future good he hopes to raise.

14

There Abel keeps his sheep, no ill he thinks;
His brother comes, then acts his fratricide;
The virgin Earth of blood her first draught drinks,
But since that time she often hath been cloyed.   95
The wretch with ghastly face and dreadful mind
Thinks each he sees will serve him in his kind,
Though none on earth but kindred near then could he find.

15

Who fancies not his looks now at the bar,
His face like death, his heart with horror fraught,   100
Nor malefactor ever felt like war,
When deep despair with wish of life hath fought,
Branded with guilt and crushed with treble woes,
A vagabond to Land of Nod[1] he goes.
A city builds, that walls might him secure from foes.   105

16

Who thinks not oft upon the father's ages,
Their long descent, how nephews' sons they saw,
The starry observations of those sages,
And how their precepts to their sons were law,
How Adam sighed to see his progeny,   110
Clothed all in his black sinful livery,
Who neither guilt nor yet the punishment could fly.

17

Our life compare we with their length of days
Who to the tenth of theirs doth now arrive?
And though thus short, we shorten many ways,   115
Living so little while we are alive;
In eating, drinking, sleeping, vain delight
So unawares comes on perpetual night,
And puts all pleasures vain unto eternal flight.

18

When I behold the heavens as in their prime,   120
And then the earth (though old) still clad in green,
The stones and trees, insensible of time,

---

8. Fortune, circumstances.
9. Animals for slaughter.
1. An unidentified region east of Eden

where Cain dwelled after slaying Abel
(Genesis 4.16).

Nor age nor wrinkle on their front are seen;
If winter come and greenness then do fade,
A spring returns, and they more youthful made;   125
But man grows old, lies down, remains where once he's laid.

19

By birth more noble than those creatures all,
Yet seems by nature and by custom cursed,
No sooner born, but grief and care makes fall
That state obliterate he had at first;   130
Nor youth, nor strength, nor wisdom spring again,
Nor habitations long their names retain,
But in oblivion to the final day remain.

20

Shall I then praise the heavens, the trees, the earth
Because their beauty and their strength last longer?   135
Shall I wish there, or never to had birth,
Because they're bigger, and their bodies stronger?
Nay, they shall darken, perish, fade and die,
And when unmade, so ever shall they lie,
But man was made for endless immortality.   140

21

Under the cooling shadow of a stately elm
Close sat I by a goodly river's side,
Where gliding streams the rocks did overwhelm,
A lonely place, with pleasures dignified.
I once that loved the shady woods so well,   145
Now thought the rivers did the trees excel,
And if the sun would ever shine, there would I dwell.

22

While on the stealing stream I fixt mine eye,
Which to the longed-for ocean held its course,
I marked, nor crooks, nor rubs,[2] that there did lie   150
Could hinder aught,[3] but still augment its force.
"O happy flood," quoth I, "that holds thy race
Till thou arrive at thy beloved place,
Nor is it rocks or shoals that can obstruct thy pace,

23

Nor is't enough, that thou alone mayst slide,   155
But hundred brooks in thy clear waves do meet,
So hand in hand along with thee they glide
To Thetis' house,[4] where all embrace and greet.
Thou emblem true of what I count the best,
O could I lead my rivulets to rest,   160
So may we press to that vast mansion, ever blest."

24

Ye fish, which in this liquid region 'bide,
That for each season have your habitation,
Now salt, now fresh where you think best to glide
To unknown coasts to give a visitation,   165
In lakes and ponds you leave your numerous fry;

---

2. Difficult ties.
3. Anything.

4. I.e., the sea; Thetis was Achilles' mother and a sea nymph.

So nature taught, and yet you know not why,
You wat'ry folk that know not your felicity.

25

Look how the wantons frisk to taste the air,
Then to the colder bottom straight they dive;   170
Eftsoon to Neptune's[5] glassy hall repair
To see what trade they great ones there do drive,
Who forage o'er the spacious sea-green field,
And take the trembling prey before it yield,
Whose armor is their scales, their spreading fins their shield. 175

26

While musing thus with contemplation fed,
And thousand fancies buzzing in my brain,
The sweet-tongued Philomel[6] perched o'er my head
And chanted forth a most melodious strain
Which rapt me so with wonder and delight,   180
I judged my hearing better than my sight,
And wished me wings with her a while to take my flight.

27

"O merry Bird," said I, "that fears no snares,
That neither toils nor hoards up in thy barn,
Feels no sad thoughts nor cruciating[7] cares   185
To gain more good or shun what might thee harm.
Thy clothes ne'er wear, thy meat is everywhere,
Thy bed a bough, thy drink the water clear,
Reminds not what is past, nor what's to come dost fear."

28

"The dawning morn with songs thou dost prevent,[8]   190
Sets hundred notes unto thy feathered crew,
So each one tunes his pretty instrument,
And warbling out the old, begin anew,
And thus they pass their youth in summer season,
Then follow thee into a better region,   195
Where winter's never felt by that sweet airy legion."

29

Man at the best a creature frail and vain,
In knowledge ignorant, in strength but weak,
Subject to sorrows, losses, sickness, pain,
Each storm his state, his mind, his body break,   200
From some of these he never finds cessation,
But day or night, within, without, vexation,
Troubles from foes, from friends, from dearest, near'st relation.

30

And yet this sinful creature, frail and vain,
This lump of wretchedness, of sin and sorrow,   205
This weatherbeaten vessel wracked with pain,
Joys not in hope of an eternal morrow;

---

5. Roman god of the ocean; "eftsoon":
soon afterward.
6. I.e., the nightingale. Philomela, the
daughter of King Attica, was transformed into a nightingale after her

brother-in-law raped her and tore out
her tongue.
7. I.e., excruciating, painful.
8. Anticipate.

Nor all his losses, crosses, and vexation,
In weight, in frequency and long duration
Can make him deeply groan for that divine translation.[9] 210

31
The mariner that on smooth waves doth glide
Sings merrily and steers his bark with ease,
As if he had command of wind and tide,
And now become great master of the seas:
But suddenly a storm spoils all the sport, 215
And makes him long for a more quiet port,
Which 'gainst all adverse winds may serve for fort.

32
So he that saileth in this world of pleasure,
Feeding on sweets, that never bit of th' sour,
That's full of friends, of honor, and of treasure, 220
Fond fool, he takes this earth ev'n for heav'n's bower.
But sad affliction comes and makes him see
Here's neither honour, wealth, nor safety;
Only above is found all with security.

33
O Time the fatal wrack[1] of mortal things, 225
That draws oblivion's curtains over kings;
Their sumptuous monuments, men know them not,
Their names without a record are forgot,
Their parts, their ports, their pomp's[2] all laid in th' dust
Nor wit nor gold, nor buildings scape times rust; 230
But he whose name is graved in the white stone[3]
Shall last and shine when all of these are gone.

1650

The Flesh and the Spirit

In secret place where once I stood
Close by the banks of Lacrim[1] flood,
I heard two sisters reason on
Things that are past and things to come;
One flesh was called, who had her eye 5
On worldly wealth and vanity;
The other Spirit, who did rear
Her thoughts unto a higher sphere:
Sister, quoth Flesh, what liv'st thou on,
Nothing but meditation? 10
Doth contemplation feed thee so
Regardlessly to let earth go?
Can speculaton satisfy
Notion[2] without reality?

---

9. Transformation.
1. Destroyer.
2. Vanity; "parts": features; "ports": places of refuge.
3. "To him that overcometh, will I give to eat of the hidden manna, and will give him a white stone, and in the stone a new name written, which no man knoweth saving him that receiveth it" (Revelation 2.17).
1. In Latin *lacrima* means tear.
2. Thought.

Dost dream of things beyond the moon,   15
And dost thou hope to dwell there soon?
Hast treasures there laid up in store
That all in th' world thou count'st but poor?
Art fancy sick,[3] or turned a sot
To catch at shadows which are not?   20
Come, come, I'll show unto thy sense,
Industry hath its recompense.
What canst desire, but thou may'st see
True substance in variety?
Dost honor like? Acquire the same,   25
As some to their immortal fame,
And trophies[4] to thy name erect
Which wearing time shall ne'er deject.
For riches doth thou long full sore?
Behold enough of precious store.   30
Earth hath more silver, pearls, and gold,
Than eyes can see or hands can hold.
Affect's thou pleasure? Take thy fill,
Earth hath enough of what you will.
Then let not go, what thou may'st find   35
For things unknown, only in mind.

Spirit: Be still thou unregenerate[5] part,
Disturb no more my settled heart,
For I have vowed (and so will do)
Thee as a foe still to pursue.   40
And combat with thee will and must,
Until I see thee laid in th' dust.
Sisters we are, yea, twins we be,
Yet deadly feud 'twixt thee and me;
For from one father are we not,   45
Thou by old Adam wast begot.
But my arise is from above,
Whence my dear Father I do love.
Thou speak'st me fair, but hat'st me sore,
Thy flatt'ring shows[6] I'll trust no more.   50
How oft thy slave, hast thou me made,
When I believed what thou hast said,
And never had more cause of woe
Than when I did what thou bad'st do.
I'll stop mine ears at these thy charms,   55
And count them for my deadly harms.
Thy sinful pleasures I do hate,
Thy riches are to me no bait,
Thine honors do, nor will I love;
For my ambition lies above.   60
My greatest honor it shall be
When I am victor over thee,

3. I.e., do you have hallucinations;   5. Unrepentant.
"sot": fool.   6. Exhibitions, displays.
4. Monuments.

And triumph shall with laurel head,[7]
When thou my captive shalt be led,
How I do live, thou need'st not scoff,   65
For I have meat thou know'st not of;
The hidden manna[8] I do eat,
The word of life it is my meat.
My thoughts do yield me more content
Than can thy hours in pleasure spent.   70
Nor are they shadows which I catch,
Nor fancies vain at which I snatch,
But reach at things that are so high,
Beyond thy dull capacity;
Eternal substance I do see,   75
With which enrichéd I would be.
Mine eye doth pierce the heavens and see
What is invisible to thee.

My garments are not silk nor gold,
Nor such like trash which earth doth hold,   80
But royal robes I shall have on,
More glorious than the glist'ring sun;
My crown not diamonds, pearls, and gold,
But such as angels' heads enfold.
The city[9] where I hope to dwell,   85
There's none on earth can parallel;
The stately walls both high and strong,
Are made of precious jasper stone;
The gates of pearl, both rich and clear,
And angels are for porters there;   90
The streets thereof transparent gold,
Such as no eye did e'er behold;
A crystal river there doth run,
Which doth proceed from the Lamb's throne.
Of life, there are the waters sure,   95
Which shall remain forever pure,
Nor sun, nor moon, they have no need,
For glory doth from God proceed.
No candle there, nor yet torchlight,
For there shall be no darksome night.   100
From sickness and infirmity
For evermore they shall be free;
Nor withering age shall e'er come there,
But beauty shall be bright and clear;
This city pure is not for thee,   105
For things unclean there shall not be.
If I of heaven may have my fill,
Take thou the world and all that will.

                                              1650

---

7. In Roman times a crown of laurel was a sign of victory for poets, heroes, and athletes.
8. The food sent by God to the Israel-ites in the wilderness (Exodus 16.15).
9. Lines 85 to 106 follow the description of the heavenly city of the New Jerusa-lem in Revelation 21 and 22.

The Author to Her Book[1]

Thou ill-formed offspring of my feeble brain,
Who after birth didst by my side remain,
Till snatched from thence by friends, less wise than true,
Who thee abroad, exposed to public view,
Made thee in rags, halting to th' press to trudge,   5
Where errors were not lessened (all may judge).
At thy return my blushing was not small,
My rambling brat (in print) should mother call,
I cast thee by as one unfit for light,
Thy visage was so irksome in my sight;   10
Yet being mine own, at length affection would
Thy blemishes amend, if so I could:
I washed thy face, but more defects I saw,
And rubbing off a spot still made a flaw.
I stretched thy joints to make thee even feet,[2]   15
Yet still thou run'st more hobbling than is meet;
In better dress to trim thee was my mind,
But nought save homespun cloth i' th' house I find.
In this array 'mongst vulgars[3] may'st thou roam.
In critic's hands beware thou dost not come,   20
And take thy way where yet thou art not known;
If for thy father asked, say thou hadst none;
And for thy mother, she alas is poor,
Which caused her thus to send thee out of door.

                      1678

Before the Birth of One of Her Children

All things within this fading world hath end,
Adversity doth still our joys attend;
No ties so strong, no friends so dear and sweet,
But with death's parting blow is sure to meet.
The sentence past is most irrevocable,   5
A common thing, yet oh, inevitable.
How soon, my Dear, death may my steps attend,
How soon't may be thy lot to lose thy friend,
We both are ignorant, yet love bids me
These farewell lines to recommend to thee,   10
That when that knot's untied that made us one,
I may seem thine, who in effect am none.
And if I see not half my days that's due,
What nature would, God grant to yours and you;
The many faults that well you know I have   15
Let be interred in my oblivious grave;
If any worth or virtue were in me,
Let that live freshly in thy memory
And when thou feel'st no grief, as I no harms,

1. *The Tenth Muse* was published in 1650 without Anne Bradstreet's knowledge. She is thought to have written this poem in 1666 when a second edition was contemplated.
2. I.e., metrical feet; to smooth out the lines.
3. The common people.

Yet love thy dead, who long lay in thine arms.   20
And when thy loss shall be repaid with gains
Look to my little babes, my dear remains.
And if thou love thyself, or loved'st me,
These O protect from stepdame's[1] injury.
And if chance to thine eyes shall bring this verse,   25
With some sad sighs honor my absent hearse;
And kiss this paper for thy love's dear sake,
Who with salt tears this last farewell did take.

   1678

To My Dear and Loving Husband

If ever two were one, then surely we.
If ever man were loved by wife, then thee;
If ever wife was happy in a man,
Compare with me, ye women, if you can.
I prize thy love more than whole mines of gold   5
Or all the riches that the East doth hold.
My love is such that rivers cannot quench,
Nor ought but love from thee, give recompense.
Thy love is such I can no way repay,
The heavens reward thee manifold, I pray.   10
Then while we live, in love let's so persevere
That when we live no more, we may live ever.

   1678

In Memory of My Dear Grandchild Elizabeth Bradstreet, Who Deceased August, 1665, Being a Year and Half Old

Farewell dear babe, my heart's too much content,
Farewell sweet babe, the pleasure of mine eye,
Farewell fair flower that for a space was lent,
Then ta'en away unto eternity.
Blest babe, why should I once bewail thy fate,   5
Or sigh thy days so soon were terminate,
Sith[1] thou art settled in an everlasting state.

2

By nature trees do rot when they are grown,
And plums and apples thoroughly ripe do fall,
And corn and grass are in their season mown,   10
And time brings down what is both strong and tall.
But plants new set to be eradicate,
And buds new blown to have so short a date,
Is by His hand alone that guides nature and fate.

   1678

For Deliverance from a Fever

When sorrows had begirt me round,
And pains within and out,

---

1. I.e., stepmother's.   1. Since.

When in my flesh no part was found,[1]
Then didst Thou rid[2] me out.
My burning flesh in sweat did boil,   5
My aching head did break,
From side to side for ease I toil,
So faint I could not speak.
Beclouded was my soul with fear
Of Thy displeasure sore,   10
Nor could I read my evidence
Which oft I read before.
"Hide not Thy face from me!" I cried,
"From burnings keep my soul.
Thou know'st my heart, and hast me tried;   15
I on Thy mercies roll."
"O heal my soul," Thou know'st I said,
"Though flesh consume to nought,
What though in dust it shall be laid,
To glory t' shall be brought."   20
Thou heard'st, Thy rod Thou didst remove
And spared my body frail,
Thou show'st to me Thy tender love,
My heart no more might quail.
O, praises to my mighty God,   25
Praise to my Lord, I say,
Who hath redeemed my soul from pit,[3]
Praises to Him for aye.[4]

1867

Here Follows Some Verses upon the Burning of Our House July 10th, 1666

Copied Out of a Loose Paper

In silent night when rest I took
For sorrow near I did not look
I wakened was with thund'ring noise
And piteous shrieks of dreadful voice.
That fearful sound of "Fire!" and "Fire!"   5
Let no man know is my desire.
I, starting up, the light did spy,
And to my God my heart did cry
To strengthen me in my distress
And not to leave me succorless.   10
Then, coming out, beheld a space
The flame consume my dwelling place.
And when I could no longer look,
I blest His name that gave and took,[1]
That laid my goods now in the dust.   15
Yea, so it was, and so 'twas just.

1. I.e., when nothing was spared.
2. Cleanse. "Thou": God.
3. Hell.
4. Ever.

1. "The Lord gave, and the Lord hath taken away; blessed be the name of the Lord" (Job 1.21).

It was His own, it was not mine,
Far be it that I should repine;
He might of all justly bereft
But yet sufficient for us left.   20
When by the ruins oft I past
My sorrowing eyes aside did cast,
And here and there the places spy
Where oft I sat and long did lie:
Here stood that trunk, and there that chest,   25
There lay that store I counted best.
My pleasant things in ashes lie,
And them behold no more shall I.
Under thy roof no guest shall sit,
Nor at thy table eat a bit.   30
No pleasant tale shall e'er be told,
Nor things recounted done of old.
No candle e'er shall shine in thee,
Nor bridegroom's voice e'er heard shall be.
In silence ever shall thou lie,   35
Adieu, Adieu, all's vanity.
Then straight I 'gin my heart to chide,
And did thy wealth on earth abide?
Didst fix thy hope on mold'ring dust?
The arm of flesh didst make thy trust?   40
Raise up thy thoughts above the sky
That dunghill mists away may fly.
Thou hast an house on high erect,
Framed by that mighty Architect,
With glory richly furnished,   45
Stands permanent though this be fled.
It's puchaséd and paid for too
By Him who hath enough to do.
A price so vast as is unknown
Yet by His gift is made thine own;   50
There's wealth enough, I need no more,
Farewell, my pelf,[2] farewell my store.
The world no longer let me love,
My hope and treasure lies above.

                                                                              1867

2. Possessions, usually in the sense of being falsely gained.

EDWARD TAYLOR

c. 1642–1729

Given the importance of Edward Taylor's role in the town in which he
lived for fifty-eight years, it is curious that we should know so little about
his life. Taylor was probably born in Sketchly, Leicestershire County,
England; his father was a "yeoman farmer"—that is, he was not a "gentleman" with large estates, but an independent landholder with title to his
farm. Although his poetry contains no images which reflect his boyhood in

Leicestershire, the dialect of that farming country is ever-present and gives his verse an air of provincial charm, but also, it must be admitted, makes it difficult and complex for the modern reader. Taylor did not enter Harvard until he was twenty-nine years old, and he stayed only three years. It is assumed, therefore, that he had some university education in England, but it is not known where. We do know that he taught school and that he left his family and sailed to New England in 1668 because he would not sign an oath of loyalty to the Church of England. Rather than compromise his religious principles as a Puritan, he preferred exile in what he once called a "howling wilderness." It was at Harvard that he must have decided to leave teaching and prepare himself for the ministry.

In 1671 a delegation from the frontier town of Westfield, Massachusetts, asked Taylor to join them as their minister, and after a good deal of soul-searching he journeyed with them the hundred miles west to Westfield, where he remained the rest of his life. As by far the most educated member of that community, he served as minister, physician, and public servant. Taylor married twice and had fourteen children, many of whom died in infancy. A rigorous observer of all churchly functions, Taylor did not shy away from the religious controversies of the period. He was a strict observer of the "old" New England way, demanding a public account of conversion before admission to church membership and the right to partake of the sacrament of communion.

Taylor was a learned man as well as a pious one. Like most Harvard ministers, he knew Latin, Hebrew, and Greek. He had a passion for books and copied out in his own hand volumes that he borrowed from his college roommate Samuel Sewall. He was known to Sewall and others as a good preacher, and on occasion he sent poems and letters to Boston friends, some parts of which were published during his lifetime. But Taylor's work as a poet was generally unknown until, in the 1930s, Thomas H. Johnson discovered that most of Taylor's poems had been deposited in the Yale University Library by Taylor's grandson, Ezra Stiles, a former president of Yale. It was one of the major literary discoveries of the twentieth century, and revealed a body of work by a Puritan divine that was remarkable both in its quantity and quality.

Taylor's interest in poetry was lifelong, and he tried his hand at a variety of poetic genres: elegies on the death of public figures; lyrics in the manner of Elizabethan songs; a long poem, *God's Determinations*, in the tradition of the medieval "debate"; and an almost unreadable five-hundred-page *Metrical History of Christianity*, primarily a book of martyrs. But Taylor's best verse is to be found in a series called *Preparatory Meditations*. These poems, written for his own pleasure and never a part of any religious service, followed upon his preparation for a sermon to be delivered at monthly communion. They gave the poet an occasion to summarize the emotional and intellectual content of his sermon and to speak directly and fervently to God. Sometimes these poems are gnarled and difficult to follow, but they also reveal a unique voice, unmistakably Taylor's. They are written in an idiom which harkens back to the verse Taylor must have known as a child in England—the metaphysical lyrics of John Donne and George Herbert—and so delight in puns and paradoxes and a rich profusion of metaphors and images. Nothing previously discovered about Puritan literature had suggested that there was a writer in New England who had sustained such a long-term love affair with poetry.

From PREPARATORY MEDITATIONS[1]
Prologue

Lord, can a crumb of dust the earth outweigh,
    Outmatch all mountains, nay, the crystal sky?
Embosom in't designs that shall display
    And trace into the boundless deity?
    Yea, hand a pen whose moisture doth guide o'er   5
    Eternal glory with a glorious glore.[2]

If it its pen had of an angel's quill,
    And sharpened on a precious stone ground tight,
And dipped in liquid gold, and moved by skill
    In Crystal leaves should golden letters write,   10
    It would but blot and blur, yea, jag, and jar
    Unless thou mak'st the pen, and scrivener.

I am this crumb of dust which is designed
    To make my pen unto Thy praise alone,
And my dull fancy[3] I would gladly grind   15
    Unto an edge on Zion's[4] precious stone.
    And write in liquid gold upon Thy name
    My letters till Thy glory forth doth flame.

Let not th'attempts break down my dust, I pray,
    Nor laugh Thou them to scorn but pardon give.   20
Inspire this crumb of dust 'til it display
    Thy glory through't: and then thy dust shall live.
    Its failings then thou'lt overlook, I trust,
    They being slips slipped from Thy crumb of dust.

Thy crumb of dust breathes two words from its breast,   25
    That Thou wilt guide its pen to write aright
To prove Thou art, and that Thou art the best
    And show Thy properties to shine most bright.
    And then Thy works will shine as flowers on stems
    Or as in jewelry shops, do gems.   30

c. 1682   1939

1. The full title is *Preparatory Meditations before my Approach to the Lord's Supper. Chiefly upon the Doctrine preached upon the Day of Administration [of Communion]*. Taylor administered communion once a month to those members of his congregation who had made a declaration of their faith. He wrote these meditations in private; they are the result of his contemplation of the Biblical texts which served as the basis for the communion sermon. One hundred ninety-five of these poems survive, dating from 1682 to 1725. The text used here is from *Poems of Edward Taylor*, ed. Donald E. Stanford (New Haven, Conn.: Yale University Press, 1960).
2. Scottish form of "glory."
3. I.e., imagination.
4. A hill in Jerusalem where the Jews built their temple; the city of God on earth.

Meditation 8 (First Series)

John 6.51. I am the living bread.[1]

I kenning through astronomy divine
    The world's bright battlement,[2] wherein I spy
A golden path my pencil cannot line,
    From that bright throne unto my threshold lie.
    And while my puzzled thoughts about it pour   5
    I find the bread of life in't at my door.

When that this bird of paradise[3] put in
    This wicker cage (my corpse) to tweedle praise
Had pecked the fruit forbade: and so did fling
    Away its food; and lost its golden days;   10
    It fell into celestial famine sore:
    And never could attain a morsel more.

Alas! alas! poore bird, what wilt thou do?
    The creatures' field no food for souls e'er gave.
And if thou knock at angels' doors they show   15
    An empty barrel: they no soul bread have.
    Alas! poor bird, the world's white loaf is done.
    And cannot yield thee here the smallest crumb.

In this sad state, God's tender bowels[4] run
    Out streams of grace: and He to end all strife   20
The purest wheat in heaven His dear-dear son
    Grinds, and kneads up into this bread of life.
    Which bread of life from Heaven down came and stands
    Dished on thy table up by Angels' hands.

Did God mold up this bread in heaven, and bake,   25
    Which from His table came, and to thine goeth?
Doth He bespeak thee thus, this soul bread take.
    Come eat thy fill of this thy God's white loaf?
    It's food too fine for angels, yet come, take
    And eat thy fill. It's heaven's sugar cake.   30

What grace is this knead in this loaf? This thing
    Souls are but petty things it to admire.
Ye angels, help: This fill would to the brim

---

1. "The Jews then murmured at him, because he said, I am the bread which came down from heaven. And they said, Is not this Jesus, the son of Joseph, whose father and mother we know? how is it then that he saith, I came down from heaven? Jesus therefore answered * * * Verily, verily, I say unto you, He that believeth on me hath everlasting life. I am that bread of life" (John 6.41–51). Christ offers a "New Covenant of Faith" in place of the "Old Covenant of Works" which Adam broke when he disobeyed God's commandment.
2. I.e., discerning, by means of "divine astronomy," the towers of heaven. Taylor goes on to suggest that there is an invisible golden path from this world to the gates of Heaven.
3. I.e., the soul, which is like a bird kept in the body's cage.
4. Here used in the sense of the interior of the body, the "seat of the tender and sympathetic emotions," the heart.

Heav'ns whelmed-down[5] crystal meal bowl, yea and higher
This bread of life dropped in thy mouth, doth cry.   35
    Eat, eat me, Soul, and thou shalt never die.

June 8, 1684   1939

Meditation 16 (First Series)

Luke 7.16. A great prophet is risen up.[1]

Leaf gold, Lord of thy golden wedge[2] o'erlaid
    My Soul at first, Thy Grace in every part
Whose pert,[3] fierce eye thou such a sight hadst made
    Whose brightsome beams could break into Thy heart
    Till Thy cursed foe had with my fist mine eye   5
    Dashed out, and did my soul unglorify.

I cannot see, nor will thy will aright.
    Nor see to wail my woe, my loss and hue
Nor all the shine in all the sun can light
    My candle, nor its heat my heart renew.   10
    See, wail, and will thy will, I must, or must
    From heaven's sweet shine to hell's hot flame be thrust.

Grace then concealed in God Himself, did roll
    Even snow ball like into a sunball shine
And nestles all its beams bunched in Thy soul   15
    My Lord, that sparkle in prophetic lines.
    Oh! wonder more than wonderful! this will
    Lighten the eye which sight divine did spill.

What art Thou, Lord, this ball of glory bright?
    A bundle of celestial beams up bound   20
In grace's band fixed in heaven's topmost height
    Pouring Thy golden beams thence, circling round
    Which show Thy Glory, and Thy glory's way
    And everywhere will make celestial day.

Lord, let Thy golden beams pierce through mine eye   25
    And leave therein an heavenly light to glaze
My soul with glorious grace all o'er, whereby
    I may have sight, and grace in me may blaze.
    Lord ting[4] my candle at Thy burning rays,
    To give a gracious glory to Thy praise.   30

5. Turned over. The *Oxford English Dictionary* quotes a passage from Dryden which is relevant: "That the earth is like a trencher and the Heavens a dish whelmed over it."

1. Taylor refers to the passage in the New Testament in which Jesus raised from the dead the only son of a widow. When the dead man spoke, fear took hold of all the witnesses to this miracle and they said: "That a great prophet is risen up among us; and That God hath visited his people. And this rumor of Him went forth throughout all Judea, and throughout all the region round about" (Luke 7.11–17).

2. In gilding it is customary to apply small squares of gold leaf to a surface; here the shape would seem to be triangular.

3. Sharp, quick to see.

4. Perhaps to "ring" with light.

Thou lightening eye, let some bright beams of Thine
  Stick in my soul, to light and liven it:
Light, life, and glory, things that are divine;
  I shall be graced withall for glory fit.
    My heart then stuffed with grace, light, life, and glee   35
    I'll sacrifice in flames of love to Thee.

March 6, 1686   1960

Meditation 22 (First Series)

Philippians 2.9. God hath highly exalted him.[1]

When thy bright beams, my Lord, do strike mine eye,
  Methinks I then could truly chide outright
My hide-bound soul that stands so niggardly
  That scarce a thought gets glorified by't.
    My quaintest[2] metaphors are ragged stuff,   5
    Making the sun seem like a mullipuff.[3]

It's my desire, Thou shouldst be glorified:
  But when Thy glory shines before mine eye,
I pardon crave, lest my desire be pride.
  Or bed Thy glory in a cloudy sky.   10
    The sun grows wan; and angels palefaced shrink,
    Before Thy shine, which I besmear with ink.

But shall the bird sing forth Thy praise, and shall
  The little bee present her thankful hum?
But I who see Thy shining glory fall   15
  Before mine eyes, stand blockish, dull, and dumb?
    Whether I speak, or speechless stand, I spy,
    I fail Thy glory: therefore pardon cry.

But this I find; my rhymes do better suit
  Mine own dispraise than tune forth praise to Thee.   20
Yet being chid, whether consonant,[4] or mute,
  I force my tongue to tattle, as You see.
    That I Thy glorious praise may trumpet right,
    Be thou my song, and make, Lord, me thy pipe.

This shining sky will fly away apace,   25
  When Thy bright glory splits the same to make
Thy majesty a pass, whose fairest face
  Too foul a path is for Thy feet to take.

1. "Let this mind be in you, which was also in Christ Jesus: Who, being in the form of God, thought it not robbery to be equal with God: But made himself no reputation, and took upon him the form of a servant, and was made in the likeness of men: And being found in fashion as a man, he humbled himself, and became obedient unto death, even the death of the cross. Wherefore God also hath highly exalted him, and given him a name which is above every name: That at the name of Jesus every knee should bow, of things in heaven, and things in earth, and things under the earth; And that every tongue should confess that Jesus Christ is Lord, to the glory of God the Father" (Philippians 2.5–11).
2. Most skilled, wise.
3. Fuzz ball.
4. Talkative, making sounds.

What glory then, shall tend Thee through the sky
    Draining the heaven much of angels dry?   30

What light then flame will in Thy judgment seat,
    'Fore which all men and angels shall appear?
How shall Thy glorious righteousness them treat,
    Rend'ring to each after his works done here?
    Then saints with angels thou wilt glorify: 35
    And burn lewd[5] men, and devils gloriously.

One glimpse, my Lord, of Thy bright judgment day,
    And glory piercing through, like fiery darts,
All devils, doth me make for grace to pray,
    For filling grace had I ten thousand hearts.   40
    I'd through ten hells to see Thy judgment day
    Wouldst Thou but gild my soul with Thy bright ray.

June 12, 1687   1960

Meditation 38 (First Series)

1 John 2.1. An Advocate with the Father.[1]

Oh! what a thing is man? Lord, who am I?
    That Thou shouldst give him law[2] (Oh! golden line)
To regulate his thoughts, words, life thereby.
    And judge him wilt thereby too in Thy time.
    A court of justice Thou in heaven hold'st   5
    To try his case while he's here housed on mold.[3]

How do Thy angels lay before Thine eye
    My deeds both white and black I daily do?
How doth Thy court Thou Panelist[4] there them try?
    But flesh complains. What right for this? let's know.   10
    For right, or wrong I can't appear unto't.
    And shall a sentence pass on such a suite?

Soft; blemish not this golden bench, or place.
    Here is no bribe, nor colorings[5] to hide
Nor pettifogger[6] to befog the case   15
    But justice hath her glory here well tried.
    Her spotless law all spotted cases tends.
    Without respect or disrespect them ends.

God's judge Himself: and Christ attorney is,
    The Holy Ghost registerer[7] is found.   20

1. "And if any man sin, we have an advocate with the Father, Jesus Christ the righteous: And he is the propitiation for our sins; and not for ours only, but also for the sins of the whole world" (1 John 2.1–2).
2. I.e., the Ten Commandments set forth in the Old Testament prescribing our behavior. This inheritance is our "golden line," or lineage.
3. I.e., the body will decay; only the soul is immortal.
4. I.e., impanel, as a jury.
5. Deceitful appearances.
6. Lawyer who handles trivial cases and is given to professional tricks and quibblings.
7. I.e., registrar, court recorder and keeper of records.

Angels the sergeants[8] are, all creatures kiss
    The book, and do as Evidences[9] abound.
All cases pass according to pure law
    And in the sentence is no fret,[1] nor flaw.

What sayst, my soul? Here all thy deeds are tried.   25
    Is Christ thy advocate to plead thy cause?
Art thou His client? Such shall never slide.
    He never lost His case: He pleads such laws
    As carry do the same, nor doth refuse
    The vilest sinner's case that doth Him choose.   30

This is His honor, not dishonor: nay,
    No habeas-corpus[2] against His clients came
For all their fines His purse doth make down pay.
    He non-suits Satan's suit or casts[3] the same.
    He'll plead thy case, and not accept a fee.   35
    He'll plead sub forma pauperis[4] for thee.

My case is bad. Lord, be my advocate.
    My sin is red: I'm under God's arrest.
Thou hast the hint of pleading; plead my state.
    Although it's bad Thy plea will make it best.   40
    If Thou wilt plead my case before the King:
    I'll wagonloads of love and glory bring.

July 6, 1690   1939

Upon Wedlock, and Death of Children[1]

A curious knot[2] God made in paradise,
    And drew it out enameled[3] neatly fresh.
It was the true-love knot, more sweet than spice,
    And set with all the flowers of Grace's dress.
    It's wedden's[4] knot, that ne're can be untied: 5
    No Alexander's sword[5] can it divide.

The slips[6] here planted, gay and glorious grow:
    Unless an hellish breath do singe their plumes.
Here primrose, cowslips, roses, lilies blow[7]
    With violets and pinks that void[8] perfumes: 10

8. Attendants at court who maintain order.
9. Witnesses.
1. Malice, ill will.
2. "Thou shalt have the body"; i.e., no person may be kept in jail without the charge against him being quickly brought before a judge. Christ's clients are brought to trial immediately; He has Himself paid for man's sins with His crucifixion and covered their fines with His own blood.
3. I.e., stops a suit because of insufficient evidence; "casts": dismisses.
4. "According to form of poverty," a procedure in which an impoverished person is able to sue another without threat of costs in the event that he should lose.
1. The text used here is from *The Poems of Edward Taylor*, ed. Donald E. Stanford (New Haven, Conn.: Yale University Press, 1960).
2. Flower bed.
3. Polished, shining.
4. I.e., wedding's.
5. Alexander the Great cut the Gordian knot devised by the king of Phyrgia when he learned that anyone who could undo it would rule Asia.
6. Cuttings.
7. Bloom.
8. Emit.

Whose beautious leaves o'erlaid with honey dew,
And chanting birds chirp out sweet music true.

When in this knot I planted was, my stock[9]
    Soon knotted, and a manly flower out brake.[1]
And after it, my branch again did knot,   15
    Brought out another flower, its sweet-breathed mate.
    One knot gave one tother[2] the tother's place.
    Whence chuckling smiles fought in each other's face.

But oh! a glorious hand from glory came
    Guarded with angels, soon did crop this flower[3]   20
Which almost tore the root up of the same,
    At that unlooked for, dolesome, darksome hour.
    In prayer to Christ perfumed it did ascend,
    And angels bright did it to heaven 'tend.

But pausing on't, this sweet perfumed my thought: 25
    Christ would in glory have a flower, choice, prime,
And having choice, chose this my branch forth brought.
    Lord take't. I thank Thee, thou tak'st ought of mine:
    It is my pledge in glory, part of me
    Is now in it, Lord, glorified with Thee.   30

But praying o're my branch, my branch did sprout,
    And bore another manly flower, and gay,[4]
And after that another, sweet brake[5] out,
    The which the former hand soon got away.
    But oh! the tortures, vomit, screechings, groans,   35
    And six week's fever would pierce hearts like stones.[6]

Grief o're doth flow: and nature fault would find
    Were not Thy will, my spell, charm, joy, and gem:
That as I said, I say, take, Lord, they're Thine.
    I piecemeal pass to glory bright in them.   40
    In joy, may I sweet flowers for glory breed,
    Whether thou get'st them green, or lets them seed.

c. 1682   1939

Upon a Wasp Chilled with Cold[1]

The bear that breathes the northern blast[2]
Did numb, torpedo-like,[3] a wasp

9. Stem.
1. Samuel Taylor was born on August 27, 1675, and lived to maturity.
2. To the other.
3. Elizabeth Taylor was born on December 27, 1676, and died on December 25, 1677.
4. James Taylor was born on October 12, 1678, and lived to maturity.
5. I.e., broke out.
6. Abigail Taylor was born on August 6, 1681, and died on August 22, 1682.

1. The text used here is from *The Poems of Edward Taylor*, ed. Donald E. Stanford (New Haven, Conn.: Yale University Press, 1960).
2. The northern constellation Ursa Major, or the Great Bear.
3. The torpedo is a fish, like a stingray, and discharges a shock to one who touches it, causing numbness. Sir Thomas Browne writes: "Torpedoes deliver their opium at a distance and stupify beyond themselves" (1646).

Whose stiffened limbs encramped, lay bathing
In Sol's[4] warm breath and shine as saving,
Which with her hands she chafes and stands   5
Rubbing her legs, shanks, thighs, and hands.
Her petty toes, and fingers' ends
Nipped with this breath, she out extends
Unto the sun, in great desire
To warm her digits at that fire.   10
Doth hold her temples in this state
Where pulse doth beat, and head doth ache.
Doth turn, and stretch her body small,
Doth comb her velvet capital.[5]
As if her little brain pan were   15
A volume of choice precepts clear.
As if her satin jacket hot
Contained apothecary's shop[6]
Of nature's receipts, that prevails
To remedy all her sad ails,   20
As if her velvet helmet high
Did turret[7] rationality.
She fans her wing up to the wind
As if her pettycoat were lined,
With reason's fleece, and hoists sails   25
And humming flies in thankful gales
Unto her dun curled[8] palace hall
Her warm thanks offering for all.

    Lord, clear my misted sight that I
May hence view Thy divinity,   30
Some sparks whereof thou up dost hasp[9]
Within this little downy wasp
In whose small corporation[1] we
A school and a schoolmaster see,
Where we may learn, and easily find   35
A nimble spirit bravely mind
Her work in every limb: and lace
It up neat with a vital grace,
Acting each part though ne'er so small
Here of this fustian[2] animal.   40
Till I enravished climb into
The Godhead on this ladder do,
Where all my pipes inspired upraise
An heavenly music furred[3] with praise.

1960

---

4. The sun personified.
5. Head.
6. What we would now call a drugstore or pharmacy; "receipts": remedies, prescriptions.
7. Contain, encompass.

8. Dark curved.
9. Enclosed, confined.
1. Body.
2. Coarse-clothed.
3. Trimmed or embellished, as with fur.

Huswifery[1]

Make me, O Lord, Thy spining wheel complete.
    Thy Holy Word my distaff make for me.
Make mine affections Thy swift flyers neat
    And make my soul Thy holy spool to be.
My conversation make to be Thy reel   5
And reel the yarn thereon spun of Thy wheel.[2]

Make me Thy loom then, knit therein this twine:
    And make Thy Holy Spirit, Lord, wind quills:[3]
Then weave the web Thyself. The yarn is fine.
    Thine ordinances make my fulling mills.[4]   10
Then dye the same in heavenly colors choice,
All pinked with varnished[5] flowers of paradise.

Then clothe therewith mine understanding, will,
    Affections, judgment, conscience, memory,
My words, and actions, that their shine may fill   15
    My ways with glory and Thee glorify.
Then mine apparel shall display before Ye
That I am clothed in holy robes for glory.

                                                                    1939

1. Housekeeping: used here to mean weaving. In Taylor's *Treatise Concerning the Lord's Supper* (see the following selection) he considers the significance of the sacrament of communion and takes as his text a passage from the New Testament: "And he saith unto him, Friend, how camest thou in hither not having a wedding garment? And he was speechless" (Matthew 22.12). Taylor argues that the wedding garment is the proper sign of the regenerate Christian. The text used here is from *Poems of Edward Taylor*, ed. Donald E. Stanford

(New Haven, Conn: Yale University Press, 1960).
2. In the lines above Taylor refers to the working parts of a spinning wheel: the "distaff" holds the raw wool or flax; the "flyers" regulate the spinning; the "spool" twists the yarn; and the "reel" takes up the finished thread.
3. I.e., be like a spool or bobbin.
4. Where cloth is beaten and cleansed with fuller's earth, or soap.
5. "Pinked": adorned; "varnished": glossy, sparkling.

SAMUEL SEWALL

1652–1730

Samuel Sewall's pursuit of the hand of the widow Katherine Winthrop has provided most readers of American literature with needed comic relief in the drama of Puritan salvation. There is something very satisfying in looking over the shoulder of the distinguished jurist subjecting his pride and reputation to the whims of courtship and adopting the role of a petitioner which, after a happy marriage of forty-two years, he probably never thought he would have to assume again. But Samuel Sewall is a more complicated figure than this small episode in his career would suggest. He became a part of the public life of Massachusetts in his late twenties and rose to a position of great authority. In the late 1870s, when the Massachusetts Historical Society began to publish his diary, his private life intrigued colonial historians, but before that Samuel Sewall was best known as the hanging judge of the Salem witch trials, a man who presided over one of the saddest episodes in our history and was a symbol of misguided authority and self-satisfied complacency.

Samuel Sewall's self-confidence was derived, in part, from having had every material advantage. Although his father had served briefly as a Puritan minister, his chief interest was business, and when the vast landholdings in New England held by Samuel Sewall's grandfather, Henry Sewall, Sr., passed to him, he determined to stay in Massachusetts rather than try to manage his estates while living abroad. He summoned his wife and children to him and they arrived in Boston on July 6, 1661. Samuel was only nine.

It was said of young Samuel that he was "born to be educated," and upon arrival at the house in Newbury that his father had prepared for them, he was placed under the care of the minister of the town and instructed in those subjects which would make him eligible for admission to Harvard in the class of 1671. He loved books and debated matters of theology with a passion. It seems fitting that Edward Taylor became his "chum and bedfellow" their senior year. Both were a little old before their time, very conservative in matters of church doctrine and apprehensive about the secularization of the age. Sewall stayed on as a resident tutor and teaching fellow and after completing his master's degree (his thesis concerned the nature of original sin) he was given an appointment as Keeper of the College Library. He maintained close ties with Harvard and his classmates, eventually outliving them all.

Seven out of the eleven members of Sewall's class became ministers, and all of Sewall's education was directed toward that end. He remained bookish and familiar with new theological subtleties all his life, and because he traveled extensively in Massachusetts regularly few people were more informed than he about the activities of local churches. But it must have become clear to him in his last years at Harvard that his true bent was in another direction; he refused a call to a pulpit in Woodbridge, New Jersey. One reason must have been that the town of Boston was attractive to him; for in spite of an introspective side, Sewall's temperament was basically outgoing and social. His marriage in 1676 to Hannah Hull, the daughter of the affluent merchant John Hull, determined Sewall's career. He learned how to manage his father-in-law's interests and after John Hull's death in 1684 became a central figure in the great mercantile life of the town. He learned when to borrow and when to lend, filled his ships with goods Londoners were eager to buy (timber, molasses, pitch), and learned to anticipate public demand in New England for English goods (metalwares, fabrics, tiles) which his agent in London purchased for him and loaded in his ships for their return.

Sewall's ability to manage his fortune left him with the time to indulge his passion for civic duties. His diary, which he began in 1673 and continued for fifty-six years, reveals just how much the public and private life for Sewall were one. In 1679 he was elected a "constable" and represented the king in military affairs and from then until 1729 he worked to become identified more as a public servant than as an importer. He represented Edward Taylor's town of Westfield in the General Court (or Legislature) of Massachusetts; he moderated public meetings; he served as magistrate; he performed marriages and executed wills; he became a judge of the Superior Court in 1692 and Chief Justice in 1717. He delighted in the ceremonies of his office and preferred the old forms to the new. His respect for tradition makes him seem at times inflexible and pompous, but for Samuel Sewall appearances mattered. He was not, however, ignorant of his own sins or the sins of the Commonwealth. On January 14, 1697, a fast day, Samuel Sewall placed in the hand of his minister, Samuel Willard, a statement acknowledging his wrong in the trials at Salem. He was the only witchcraft judge to do so. It was read aloud from the pulpit and posted for all to read. Three years later he published the first antislavery tract in America, *The Selling of Joseph*, and tells us that he received "frowns and hard words" for his pains. In matters of church discipline he was as strict as his friend Edward Taylor, but in the matter of slavery he welcomed change. "Perfect servitude," he wrote, "can have no place by right . . . because our liberty in the natural account, is the very next thing to life itself, yea by many is preferred before it."

From The Diary of Samuel Sewall[1]

March 21[, 1677] Mane.[2] * * *

Remember, since I had thoughts of joining to the Church, I have been exceedingly tormented in my mind, sometimes lest the Third church [the South] should not be in God's way in breaking off from the old. (I resolved to speak with Mr. Torrey about that, but he passed home when I was called to business at the Warehouse. Another time I got Mr. Japheth Hobart to promise me a Meeting at our House after Lecture,—but she that is now his wife, being in town, prevented him.) Sometimes with my own unfitness and want of Grace: yet through importunity of friends, and hope that God might communicate himself to me in the ordinance, and because of my child (then hoped for) its being baptised, I offered myself, and was not refused. Besides what I had written, when I was speaking [about admission to the church] I resolved to confess what a great Sinner I had been, but going on in the method of the Paper, it came not to my mind. And now that Scruple of the Church vanished, and I began to be more afraid of myself. And on Saturday Goodman [Robert] Walker[3] came in, who used to be very familiar with me. But he said nothing of my coming into the Church, nor wished God to show me grace therein, at which I was almost overwhelmed, as thinking that he deemed me unfit for it. And I could hardly sit down to the Lord's Table. But I feared that if I went away I might be less fit next time, and thought that it would be strange for me

1. The first entry of Sewall's diary is dated December 3, 1673, and the last entry December 25, 1728. The text used here is from *The Diary of Samuel Sewall*, ed. M. Halsey Thomas (New York: Farrar, Straus and Giroux, 1973). To preserve the special flavor of Sewall's style, the text has not been modernized.
2. "In the morning."
3. Goodman was the appropriate title for the head of a household. Robert Walker was one of the founders of the Old South Church in 1669.

who was just then joined to the Church, to withdraw, wherefore I stayed. But I never experienced more unbelief. I feared at least that I did not believe there was such an one as Jesus Xt.,[4] and yet was afraid that because I came to the ordinance without belief, that for the abuse of Xt. I should be stricken dead; yet I had some earnest desires that Xt. would, before the ordinance were done, though it were when he was just going away, give me some glimpse of himself; but I perceived none. Yet I seemed then to desire the coming of the next Sacrament day, that I might do better, and was stirred up hereby dreadfully to seek God who many times before had touched my heart by Mr. Thatcher's praying and preaching more than now. The Lord pardon my former grieving of his Spirit, and circumcise my heart to love him with all my heart and soul.

March 30, 1677. I, together with Gilbert Cole, was admitted into Mr. Thatcher's Church, making a Solemn covenant to take the L. Jehovah for our God, and to walk in Brotherly Love and watchfulness to Edification. Goodm. Cole first spake, then I, then the Relations of the Women were read: as we spake so were we admitted; then alltogether covenanted.[5] Prayed before, and after.

Satterday, Jany 2^d [1686] Last night had a very unusual Dream; *viz.* That our Saviour in the dayes of his Flesh when upon Earth, came to Boston and abode here sometime, and moreover that He Lodged in that time at Father Hull's; upon which in my Dream had two Reflections, One was how much more Boston had to say than Rome boasting of Peter's being there. The other a sense of great Respect that I ought to have shewed Father Hull since Christ chose when in Town, to take up His Quarters at his House. Admired the goodness and Wisdom of Christ in coming hither and spending some part of His short Life here. The Chronological absurdity never came into my mind, as I remember. Jany 1. 1686 finished reading the Godly Learned ingenious Pareus on the Revelation.[6]

April 11th 1692. Went to Salem, where, in the Meeting-house, the persons accused of Witchcraft were examined; was a very great Assembly; 'twas awfull to see how the afflicted persons were agitated. Mr. Noyes pray'd at the beginning, and Mr. Higginson concluded. [*In the margin*], Væ, Væ, Væ, Witchcraft.[7]

July 30, 1692. Mrs. Cary makes her escape out of Cambridge-Prison, who was Committed for Witchcraft.[8]

Thorsday, Augt. 4. [1692] At Salem, Mr. Waterhouse brings the

4. Christ.
5. Admitted to church membership. Statements of conversion for women were usually read from testimony recorded in conversations with the pastor.
6. David Pareus (1548–1622) was a theologian and biblical commentator and one of Sewall's favorite authors.
7. "Woe, woe, woe, witchcraft." Governor William Phips (1651–95) appointed Sewall one of seven councillors of a court of Oyer and Terminer (that is, to hear and determine) to judge those accused of witchcraft in Salem on May 24, 1692. The court met in Salem on June 2 and Bridget Bishop was hanged on June 10. On June 30 they met again and five more accused were executed on July 19. Unfortunately for us, Sewall kept his entries regarding the trials at Salem to a minimum.
8. Mrs. Cary was given protection in New York.

news of the desolation at Jamaica, June 7th. 1700 persons kill'd, besides the Loss of Houses and Goods by the Earthquake.

Augt. 19th 1692 * * * This day [*in the margin*, Dolefull Witchcraft] George Burrough, John Willard, Jn[o] Procter, Martha Carrier and George Jacobs were executed at Salem, a very great number of Spectators being present. Mr. Cotton Mather was there, Mr. Sims, Hale, Noyes, Chiever, &c. All of them said they were innocent, Carrier and all. Mr. Mather says they all died by a Righteous Sentence. Mr. Burrough by his Speech, Prayer, protestation of his Innocence, did much move unthinking persons, which occasions their speaking hardly[9] concerning his being executed.

Augt. 25. [1692] Fast at the old [First] Church, respecting the Witchcraft, Drought, &c.

Monday, Sept. 19, 1692. About noon, at Salem, Giles Corey was press'd to death[1] for standing Mute; much pains was used with him two days, one after another, by the Court and Capt. Gardner of Nantucket who had been of his acquaintance: but all in vain.

Sept. 20. [1692] Now I hear from Salem that about 18 years agoe, he was suspected to have stamped and press'd a man to death, but was cleared. Twas not remembred till Anne Putnam was told of it by said Corey's Spectre the Sabbath-day night before Execution.[2]

Sept. 20, 1692. The Swan[3] brings in a rich French Prize of about 300 Tuns, laden with Claret, White Wine, Brandy, Salt, Linnen Paper, &c.

Sept. 21. [1692] A petition is sent to Town in behalf of Dorcas Hoar, who now confesses: Accordingly an order is sent to the Sheriff to forbear her Execution, notwithstanding her being in the Warrant to die to morrow. This is the first condemned person who has confess'd.[4]

Nov. 6. [1692] Joseph threw a knop of Brass and hit his Sister Betty on the forhead so as to make it bleed and swell; upon which, and for his playing at Prayer-time, and eating when Return Thanks, I whipd him pretty smartly. When I first went in (call'd by his Grandmother) he sought to shadow and hide himself from me behind the head of the Cradle: which gave me the sorrowfull remembrance of Adam's carriage.

Jany 15. [1697] * * * Copy of the Bill I put up on the Fast day [January 14]; giving it to Mr. Willard as he pass'd by, and standing up at the reading of it, and bowing when finished; in the Afternoon.

Samuel Sewall, sensible of the reiterated strokes of God upon himself and family,[5] and being sensible, that as to the Guilt con-

9. Vigorously.
1. Giles Corey was 80 years old at the time. Heavy stones were placed on him until he died.
2. Anne Putnam was only 12 when she made, along with her mother, accusations against "witches."
3. A ship.
4. Confession of witchcraft automatically set the accused free.
5. On May 22, 1696, Sewall buried an unborn son and on December 23 his daughter Sarah died. When his son Samuel read from Matthew 12.7 ("But if ye had

tracted, upon the opening of the late Commission of Oyer and Terminer at Salem (to which the order for this Day relates) he is, upon many accounts, more concerned than any that he knows of, Desires to take the Blame and Shame of it, Asking pardon of Men, And especially desiring prayers that God, who has an Unlimited Authority, would pardon that Sin and all other his Sins; personal and Relative: And according to his infinite Benignity, and Soveraignty, Not Visit the Sin of him, or of any other, upon himself or any of his, nor upon the Land: But that He would powerfully defend him against all Temptations to Sin, for the future; and vouchsafe him the Efficacious, Saving Conduct of his Word and Spirit.

Fourth-day, June 19, 1700 * * * Having been long and much dissatisfied with the Trade of fetching Negros from Guinea; at last I had a strong Inclination to Write something about it; but it wore off. At last reading Bayne, Ephes.[6] about servants, who mentions Blackamoors; I began to be uneasy that I had so long neglected doing any thing. When I was thus thinking, in came Bro[r] Belknap to shew me a Petition he intended to present to the Gen[l] Court for the freeing a Negro and his wife, who were unjustly held in Bondage. And there is a Motion by a Boston Comittee to get a Law that all Importers of Negros shall pay 40[s] *per* head, to discourage the bringing of them. And Mr. C. Mather resolves to publish a sheet to exhort Masters to labour their Conversion. Which makes me hope that I was call'd of God to Write this Apology[7] for them; Let his Blessing accompany the same.

Febr. 6. [1718] This morning wandering in my mind whether to live a Single or a Married Life;[8] I had a sweet and very affectionat Meditation Concerning the Lord Jesus; Nothing was to be objected against his Person, Parentage, Relations, Estate, House, Home! Why did I not resolutely, presently close with Him! And I cry'd mightily to God that He would help me so to doe! * * *

March, 14. [1718] Deacon Marion comes to me, sits with me a great while in the evening; after a great deal of Discourse about his Courtship—He told [me] the Olivers said they wish'd I would Court their Aunt.[9] I said little, but said twas not five Moneths since I buried my dear Wife. Had said before 'twas hard to know whether best to marry again or no; whom to marry. Gave him a book of the Berlin Jewish Converts.

---

known what *this* meaneth, I will have mercy, and not sacrifice, ye would not have condemned the guiltless.") it did "awfully bring to mind," Sewall noted, "the Salem tragedy."

6. Paul Baynes, *A Commentary upon the First Chapter of the Epistle of Saint Paul, Written to the Ephesians* (London, 1618).

7. *The Selling of Joseph* was published on June 24, 1700.

8. Hannah Hull Sewall had died on October 19, 1717; they had been married almost 42 years. Sewall married Mrs. Abigail Tilley on October 29, 1719, and she died suddenly in May of 1720. Sewall's courtship of Madame Winthrop began seriously in the fall of 1720. On March 29, 1722, Sewall married a widow, Mary Gibbs, and she survived him.

9. Katherine Brattle Winthrop was the widow of Chief Justice Wait Still Winthrop, Sewall's friend. Instead, he married Mrs. Tilley.

Septr 5. [1720] Mary Hirst goes to Board with Madam Oliver and her Mother Loyd, Going to Son Sewall's I there meet with Madam Winthrop, told her I was glad to meet her there, had not seen her a great while; gave her Mr. Homes's Sermon.

Sept. 30. [1720] Mr. Colman's Lecture: Daughter Sewall acquaints Madam Winthrop that if she pleas'd to be within at 3. P.M. I would wait on her. She answer'd she would be at home.

October 1. [1720] *Satterday*, I dine at Mr. Stoddard's: from thence I went to Madam Winthrop's just at 3. Spake to her, saying, my loving wife[1] died so soon and suddenly, 'twas hardly convenient for me to think of Marrying again; however I came to this Resolution, that I would not make my Court to any person without first Consulting with her. * * *

Octob^r 3. 2. [1720] Waited on Madam Winthrop again; 'twas a little while before she came in. Her daughter Noyes[2] being there alone with me, I said, I hoped my Waiting on her Mother would not be disagreeable to her. She answer'd she should not be against that that might be for her Comfort. I Saluted her, and told her I perceiv'd I must shortly wish her a good Time; (her mother had told me, she was with Child, and within a Moneth or two of her Time). By and by in came Mr. Airs, Chaplain of the Castle,[3] and hang'd up his Hat, which I was a little startled at, it seeming as if he was to lodge there. At last Madam Winthrop came in. After a considerable time, I went up to her and said, if it might not be inconvenient I desired to speak with her. She assented, and spake of going into another Room; but Mr. Airs and Mrs. Noyes presently rose up, and went out, leaving us there alone. Then I usher'd in Discourse from the names in the Fore-seat; at last I pray'd that Katharine [Mrs. Winthrop] might be the person assign'd for me. She instantly took it up in way of Denyal, as if she had catch'd at an Opportunity to do it, saying she could not do it before she was asked. Said that was her mind unless she should Change it, which she believed she should not; could not leave her Children. I express'd my Sorrow that she should do it so Speedily, pray'd her Consideration, and ask'd her when I should wait on her agen. She setting no time, I mention'd that day Sennight.[4] Gave her Mr. Willard's Fountain[5] open'd with the little print and verses; saying I hop'd if we did well read that book, we should meet together hereafter, if we did not now. She took the Book, and put it in her Pocket. Took Leave.

[Oct.] 6th[, 1720] A little after 6 P.M. I went to Madam Winthrop's. She was not within. I gave Sarah Chickering the Maid 2^s, Juno, who brought in wood, 1^s Afterward the Nurse came in, I gave her 18^d, having no other small Bill. After awhile Dr. Noyes

---

1. I.e., Abigail.
2. The wife of Dr. Oliver Noyes.
3. I.e., Castle Island in Boston Harbor; "saluted": kissed.
4. A week hence.

5. Samuel Willard, *The Fountain Opened, or the Great Gospel Privilege of Having Christ Exhibited to Sinful Men* (Boston, 1700).

came in with his Mother; and quickly after his wife came in: They sat talking, I think, till eight a-clock. I said I fear'd I might be some Interruption to their Business: Dr. Noyes reply'd pleasantly: He fear'd they might be an Interruption to me, and went away. Madam seem'd to harp upon the same string. Must take care of her Children; could not leave that House and Neighbourhood where she had dwelt so long. I told her she might doe her children as much or more good by bestowing what she laid out in Hous-keeping, upon them. Said her Son would be of Age the 7th of August. I said it might be inconvenient for her to dwell with her Daughter-in-Law, who must be Mistress of the House. I gave her a piece of Mr. Belcher's Cake and Ginger-Bread wrapped up in a clean sheet of Paper; told her of her Father's kindness to me when Treasurer, and I Constable. My Daughter Judith was gon from me and I was more lonesom—might help to forward one another in our Journey to Canaan.6 * * *

[*Oct.*] 12[, 1720] At Madm Winthrop's Steps I took leave of Capt Hill, &c.

Mrs. Anne Cotton came to door (twas before 8.) said Madam Winthrop was within, directed me into the little Room, where she was full of work7 behind a Stand; Mrs. Cotton came in and stood. Madam Winthrop pointed to her to set me a Chair. Madam Winthrop's Countenance was much changed from what 'twas on Monday, look'd dark and lowering. At last, the work, (black stuff or Silk) was taken away, I got my Chair in place, had some Converse, but very Cold and indifferent to what 'twas before. Ask'd her to acquit me of Rudeness if I drew off her Glove. Enquiring the reason, I told her twas great odds between handling a dead Goat, and a living Lady. Got it off. I told her I had one Petition to ask of her, that was, that she would take off the Negative she laid on me the third of October; She readily answer'd she could not, and enlarg'd upon it; She told me of it so soon as she could; could not leave her house, children, neighbours, business. I told her she might do som Good to help and support me. * * * Sarah fill'd a Glass of Wine, she drank to me, I to her, She sent Juno home with me with a good Lantern, I gave her 6d and bid her thank her Mistress. In some of our Discourse, I told her I had rather go to the Stone-House8 adjoining to her, than to come to her against her mind. Told her the reason why I came every other night was lest I should drink too deep draughts of Pleasure. She had talk'd of Canary,9 her Kisses were to me better than the best Canary. * * *

Oct. 13. [1720] I tell my Son and daughter Sewall, that the Weather was not so fair as I apprehended. * * *

[*Oct.*] 17. [1720] *Monday,* * * * In the Evening I visited Madam Winthrop, who Treated me Courteously, but not in Clean Linen

---

6. I.e., to paradise.
7. I.e., her needlework.

8. A prison.
9. A sweet wine from the Canary Isles.

as somtimes. She said, she did not know whether I would come again, or no. I ask'd her how she could so impute inconstancy to me. (I had not visited her since Wednesday night being unable to get over the Indisposition received by the Treatment received that night, and I *must* in it seem'd to sound like a made piece of Formality.) Gave her this day's Gazett. * * *

[*Oct.*] 19. [1720] Midweek, Visited Madam Winthrop; Sarah told me she was at Mr. Walley's, would not come home till late. I gave her Hannah's 3 oranges with her Duty, not knowing whether I should find her or no. Was ready to go home: but said if I knew she was there, I would go thither. Sarah seemd to speak with pretty good Courage, She would be there. I went and found her there, with Mr. Walley and his wife in the little Room below. At 7 a-clock I mentioned going home; at 8. I put on my Coat, and quickly waited on her home. She found occasion to speak loud to the servant, as if she had a mind to be known. Was Courteous to me; but took occasion to speak pretty earnestly about my keeping a Coach: I said twould cost £100. per annum: she said twould cost but £40. * * *

Oct. 20. [1720] Mr. Colman preaches from Luke 15.10. Joy among the Angels: made an Excellent Discourse.

At Council, Col. Townsend spake to me of my Hood: Should get a Wigg.[1] I said twas my chief[2] Ornament: I wore it for sake of the Day. Bro[r] Odlin, and Sam, Mary, and Jane Hirst dine with us. Promis'd to wait on the Govr about 7. Madam Winthrop not being at Lecture, I went thither first; found her very Serene with her dâter Noyes, Mrs. Dering, and the widow Shipreev sitting at a little Table, she in her arm'd Chair. She drank to me, and I to Mrs. Noyes. After awhile pray'd the favour to speak with her. She took one of the Candles, and went into the best Room, clos'd the shutters, sat down upon the Couch. She told me Madam Usher had been there, and said the Coach must be set on Wheels, and not by Rusting. She spake something of my needing a Wigg. Ask'd me what her Sister said to me. I told her, She said, If her Sister were for it, She would not hinder it. But I told her, she did not say she would be glad to have me for her Brother. Said, I shall keep you in the Cold, and ask her if she would be within tomorrow night, for we had had but a running Feast. She said she could not tell whether she should, or no. I took Leave. As were drinking at the Governour's, he said: In England the Ladies minded little more than that they might have Money, and Coaches to ride in. I said, And New-England brooks its Name.[3] At which Mr. Dudley smiled. Gov[r] said they were not quite so bad here.

1. I.e., in addition to Sewall's judicial hood, he should acquire a wig such as English judges wear today, and to be distinguished from the periwig which Madame Winthrop wanted Sewall to wear to disguise his baldness. Sewall chose to wear a velvet cap instead.
2. Principal.
3. I.e., it is the same in New England.

Oct. 21. [1720] *Friday*, My Son, the Minister, came to me p. m.
by appointment and we pray one for another in the Old Chamber;
more especially respecting my Courtship. About 6. a-clock I go to
Madam Winthrop's; Sarah told me her Mistress was gon out, but
did not tell me whither she went. She presently order'd me a Fire;
so I went in, having Dr. Sibb's Bowels[4] with me to read. I read the
two first Sermons, still no body came in: at last about 9. a-clock
Mr. Jn⁰ Eyre came in; I took the opportunity to say to him as I
had done to Mrs. Noyes before, that I hoped my Visiting his
Mother would not be disagreeable to him; He answered me with
much Respect. When twas after 9. a-clock He of himself said he
would go and call her, she was but at one of his Brothers: A while
after I heard Madam Winthrop's voice, enquiring something about
John. After a good while and Clapping the Garden door twice or
thrice, she came in. I mention'd somthing of the lateness; she
banter'd me, and said I was later. She receiv'd me Courteously. I
ask'd when our proceedings should be made publick: She said They
were like to be no more publick than they were already. Offer'd me
no Wine that I remember. I rose up at 11 a-clock to come away,
saying I would put on my Coat, She offer'd not to help me. I pray'd
her that Juno might light me home, she open'd the Shutter, and
said twas pretty light abroad; Juno was weary and gon to bed. So I
came hôme by Star-light as well as I could. At my first coming in, I
gave Sarah five Shillings. I write Mr. Eyre his Name in his book
with the date Octob^r 21. 1720. It cost me 8ˢ. Jehovah jireh![5]
Madam told me she had visited M. Mico, Wendell, and Wᵐ Clark
of the South [Church].

Octob^r 24. [1720] I went in the Hackny Coach through the
Common, stop't at Madam Winthrop's (had told her I would take
my departure from thence). Sarah came to the door with Katee in
her Arms: but I did not think to take notice of the Child. Call'd her
Mistress. I told her, being encourag'd by David Jeffries loving eyes,
and sweet Words, I was come to enquire whether she could find in
her heart to leave that House and Neighbourhood, and go and
dwell with me at the South-end; I think she said softly, Not yet. I
told her It did not ly in my hands to keep a Coach. If I should, I
should be in danger to be brought to keep company with her
Neighbour Brooker, (he was a little before sent to prison for
Debt). Told her I had an Antipathy against those who would
pretend to give themselves; but nothing of their Estate. I would a
proportion of my Estate with my self. And I suppos'd she would do
so. As to a Perriwig, My best and greatest Friend, I could not
possibly have a greater, began to find me with Hair before I was
born, and had continued to do so ever since; and I could not find in

4. **Heart.** Dr. Richard Sibbes was the
author of *Bowels Opened; or a Discovery
of the Neere and Deere Love, Union,*
*and Communion between Christ and the
Church* (London, 1641).
5. The Lord will provide (Genesis 22.14).

my heart to go to another. She commended the book I gave her, Dr. Preston, the Church's Marriage; quoted him saying 'twas inconvenient keeping out of a Fashion commonly used. I said the Time and Tide did circumscribe my Visit. She gave me a Dram of Black-Cherry Brandy, and gave me a lump of the Sugar that was in it. She wish'd me a good Journy. I pray'd God to keep her, and came away. Had a very pleasant Journy to Salem.

Novr 2. [1720] *Midweek,* went again, and found Mrs. Alden there, who quickly went out. Gave her [Madam Winthrop] about ½ pound of Sugar Almonds, cost 3^s per £. Carried them on Monday. She seem'd pleas'd with them, ask'd what they cost. Spake of giving her a Hundred pounds per annum if I dy'd before her. Ask'd her what sum she would give me, if she should dy first? Said I would give her time to Consider of it. She said she heard as if I had given all to my Children by Deeds of Gift. I told her 'twas a mistake, Point-Judith was mine &c. That in England, I own'd, my Father's desire was that it should go to my eldest Son; 'twas 20£ per annum; she thought 'twas forty. I think when I seem'd to excuse pressing this, she seem'd to think twas best to speak of it; a long winter was coming on. Gave me a Glass or two of Canary.

Novr 4th [1720] *Friday,* Went again about 7. a-clock; found there Mr. John Walley and his wife: sat discoursing pleasantly. I shew'd them Isaac Moses's [an Indian] Writing. Madam W. serv'd Comfeits[6] to us. After a-while a Table was spread, and Supper was set. I urg'd Mr. Walley to Crave a Blessing; but he put it upon me. About 9. they went away. I ask'd Madam what fashioned Necklace I should present her with, She said, None at all. I ask'd her Whereabout we left off last time; mention'd what I had offer'd to give her; Ask'd her what she would give me; She said she could not Change her Condition: She had said so from the beginning; could not be so far from her Children, the Lecture. Quoted the Apostle Paul affirming that a single Life was better than a Married. I answer'd That was for the present Distress. Said she had not pleasure in things of that nature as formerly: I said, you are the fitter to make me a Wife. If she held in that mind, I must go home and bewail my Rashness in making more haste than good Speed. However, considering the Supper, I desired her to be within next Monday night, if we liv'd so long. Assented. She charg'd me with saying, that she must put away Juno, if she came to me: I utterly deny'd it, it never came in my heart; yet she insisted upon it; saying it came in upon discourse about the Indian woman that obtained her Freedom this Court. About 10. I said I would not disturb the good orders of her House, and came away. She not seeming pleas'd with my Coming away. Spake to her about David Jeffries, had not seen him.

Monday, Novr 7th [,1720] My Son pray'd in the Old Chamber.

6. Sweetmeats; fruits preserved in sugar.

Our time had been taken up by Son and Daughter Cooper's Visit; so that I only read the 130th and 143. Psalm. Twas on the Account of my Courtship. I went to Mad. Winthrop; found her rocking her little Katee in the Cradle. I excus'd my Coming so late (near Eight). She set me an arm'd Chair and Cusheon; and so the Cradle was between her arm'd Chair and mine. Gave her the remnant of my Almonds; She did not eat of them as before; but laid them away; I said I came to enquire whether she had alter'd her mind since Friday, or remained of the same mind still. She said, There-abouts. I told her I loved her, and was so fond[7] as to think that she loved me: She said had a great respect for me. I told her, I had made her an offer, without asking any advice; she had so many to advise with, that twas a hindrance. The Fire was come to one short Brand besides the Block, which Brand was set up in end; at last it fell to pieces, and no Recruit was made:[8] She gave me a Glass of Wine. I think I repeated again that I would go home and bewail my Rashness in making more haste than good Speed. I would en-deavour to contain myself, and not go on to sollicit her to do that which she could not Consent to. Took leave of her. As came down the steps she bid me have a Care. Treated me Courteously. Told her she had enter'd the 4th year of her Widowhood. I had given her the News-Letter before: I did not bid her draw off her Glove as some-time I had done. Her Dress was not so clean as sometime it had been. Jehovah jireh!

Midweek, [*Nov.*] 9th [1720] Dine at Bror Stoddard's: were so kind as to enquire of me if they should invite Mm Winthrop; I answer'd No. * * *

Novr 11th [1720] Went not to Mm Winthrop's. This is the 2d *Withdraw*.[9]

March, 29th. [1722] Samuel Sewall, and Mrs. Mary Gibbs were joined together in Marriage by the Revd Mr. William Cooper; Mr. Sewall pray'd once. Mr. Jno Cotton was at Sandwich, sent for by Madam Cotton after her Husband's death.

1673–1729   1878–82

7. Foolish.
8. Added logs would indicate that Se-wall was expected to stay longer.

9. I.e., the second time he decided not to visit.

COTTON MATHER
1663–1728

Cotton Mather, as the eldest son of Increase Mather and the grandson of Richard Mather and John Cotton, was the heir apparent to the Congrega-tional hierarchy which had dominated the churches of New England for almost fifty years. Like his father before him, Cotton Mather attended Har-

vard College. He was admitted at the age of twelve, and when he graduated
in 1678, President Urian Oakes told the commencement audience that his
hope was great that "in this youth, Cotton and Mather shall, in fact as well
as name, joint together and once more appear in life." He was expected by his
family to excel and did not disappoint them, but there is no doubt he had
to pay a price for his ambition: he stammered badly when young, so much
so that it was assumed he could never be a preacher, and he was subject all
his life to nervous disorders which drove him alternatively to ecstasy and
despair. His enemies often complained that he was vain and aggressive. But
he was also a genius of sorts, competent in the natural sciences and gifted
in the study of ancient languages. He possessed a strong mind, and by the
time he had stopped writing he could boast that he had published more
than four hundred separate works. A worthy successor to his father's position as pastor of the Second Church of Boston, he remained connected
with that church from 1685, when he was ordained, until his death.

Like Benjamin Franklin, Mather found great satisfaction in doing good
works, and organized societies for building churches, supported schools for
the children of slaves, and worked to establish funds for indigent clergy.
But for all his worldly success, Mather's life was darkened by disappointment and tragedy. He lost two wives and saw his third wife go insane, and
of his fifteen children, only two lived until his death. More than one of his
contemporaries observed that he never overcame his bitterness at being
rejected for the presidency of Harvard. It was the one thing his father had
achieved that he could not succeed in doing.

Although he was a skillful preacher and an eminent theologian, it is his
work as a historian which has earned Mather a significant place in American
literature. No one has described more movingly the hopes of the first generation of Puritans, and what gives Mather's best writing its urgency is the
sense that the Puritan community as he knew it was fading away. By the
time that Mather was writing his history of New England, the issues which
seemed most pressing to his parishioners were political and social rather
than theological. In his diary of 1700 he noted that "there was hardly any
but my father and myself to appear in defense of our invaded churches."
Everything that Mather wrote can be seen as a call to defend the old order
of church authority against the encroachment of an increasingly secular
world. As an apologist for the "old New England way" there is no doubt
that Mather left himself open to attack, and by the end of the seventeenth
century he had become a scapegoat for the worst in Puritan culture. He is
often blamed for the Salem witch trials, for example, but he never actually
attended one of them; his greatest crime was in not speaking out against
those who he knew had exceeded the limits of authority. Mather saw the
devil's presence in Salem as a final effort to undermine and destroy religious
community.

In spite of its rambling and sometimes self-indulgent nature, the *Magnalia Christi Americana* (the title may be translated as "A History of the
Wonderful Works of Christ in America") remains Mather's most impressive work. It is described on the title page as an "ecclesiastical history of
New England," and in the course of its seven books, Mather attempts to
record for future readers not only a history of the New England churches
and the college (Harvard) where its ministers were trained, but representative biographies of "saint's" lives. Although it is true that Mather was so

caught up in his vision of a glorious past that he was sometimes quite blind to the suffocating realities of the world in which he lived, no one has set forth more clearly the history of a people who transformed a wilderness into a garden and the ideal of a harmonious community which has been characterized time and again as the "American dream." It is, however, in Mather's biographical sketches—his lives of Bradford, Winthrop, Eliot, and Phips—that the *Magnalia* is most arresting; for it is in his account of a particular saint's reconciliation with God on earth that New England's story is most eloquently realized.

Much has been said about Mather's style, mostly by those who hate his pedantry. But Mather did not favor any one manner of writing. He is fond of paradoxes and repetition, and he sometimes displays his learning shamelessly, but his prose can be quite straightforward when the occasion demands it. Mather also tolerated a variety of prose styles, but clearly liked the allusive style best. He tells us in his guide to young ministers (*Manuductio ad Ministerium,* 1726) that the prose which he likes best is that in which "there is not only a vigor sensible in every sentence, but the paragraph is embellished with profitable references, even to something beyond what is directly spoken. Formal and painful quotations are not studied; yet all that could be learnt from them is insinuated. The writer pretends not unto reading, yet he could not have written as he does if he had not read very much in his time; and his composures are not only a cloth of gold, but also stuck with as many jewels as the gown of a Russian ambassador."

From The Wonders of the Invisible World[1]
[*A People of God in the Devil's Territories*]

The New Englanders are a people of God settled in those, which were once the devil's territories; and it may easily be supposed that the devil was exceedingly disturbed, when he perceived such a people here accomplishing the promise of old made unto our blessed Jesus, that He should have the utmost parts of the earth for His possession.[2] There was not a greater uproar among the Ephesians,[3] when the Gospel was first brought among them, than there was among the powers of the air (after whom those Ephesians walked) when first the silver trumpets of the Gospel here made the joyful sound. The devil thus irritated, immediately tried

1. In May, 1692, Governor William Phips of Massachusetts appointed a court to "hear and determine" the cases against some 19 persons in Salem, Massachusetts, accused of witchcraft. Mather had long been interested in the subject of witchcraft, and in this work, written at the request of the judges, he describes the case against the accused. Mather, like many others, saw the evidence of witchcraft as the devil's work, a last-ditch effort to undermine the Puritan ideal. Mather was himself skeptical of much of the evidence used against the accused, especially as the trials proceeded in the summer of 1692, but like a number of prominent persons in the community, he made no public protest. First published in 1693, the text used here is taken from the reprint by John Russell Smith (London, 1862).
2. After Jesus was baptized he went into the desert to fast for 40 days; it was there that the devil tempted him and offered him the world. See Luke 4.
3. Ephesus was an ancient city of Ionia in west Asia Minor and famous for its temples to the goddess Diana. When St. Paul preached there he received hostile treatment, and riots followed the sermons of missionaries who attempted to convert the Ephesians.

all sorts of methods to overturn this poor plantation: and so much of the church, as was fled into this wilderness, immediately found the serpent cast out of his mouth a flood for the carrying of it away. I believe that never were more satanical devices used for the unsettling of any people under the sun, than what have been employed for the extirpation of the vine which God has here planted, casting out the heathen, and preparing a room before it, and causing it to take deep root, and fill the land, so that it sent its boughs unto the Atlantic Sea eastward, and its branches unto the Connecticut River westward, and the hills were covered with the shadow thereof. But all those attempts of hell have hitherto been abortive, many an Ebenezer[4] has been erected unto the praise of God, by his poor people here: and having obtained help from God, we continue to this day Wherefore the devil is now making one attempt more upon us; an attempt more difficult, more surprising, more snarled with unintelligible circumstances than any that we have hitherto encountered; an attempt so critical, that if we get well through, we shall soon enjoy halcyon days with all the vultures of hell trodden under our feet. He has wanted his incarnate legions to persecute us, as the people of God have in the other hemisphere been persecuted: he has therefore drawn forth his more spiritual ones to make an attack upon us. We have been advised by some credible Christians yet alive, that a malefactor, accused of witchcraft as well as murder, and executed in this place more than forty years ago, did then give notice of an horrible plot against the country by witchcraft, and a foundation of witchcraft then laid, which if it were not seasonably discovered, would probably blow up, and pull down all the churches in the country. And we have now with horror seen the discovery of such a witchcraft! An army of devils is horribly broke in upon the place which is the center, and after a sort, the first-born of our English settlements: and the houses of the good people there are filled with the doleful shrieks of their children and servants, tormented by invisible hands, with tortures altogether preternatural. After the mischiefs there endeavored, and since in part conquered, the terrible plague of evil angels hath made its progress into some other places, where other persons have been in like manner diabolically handled. These our poor afflicted neighbors, quickly after they become infected and infested with these demons, arrive to a capacity of discerning those which they conceive the shapes of their troublers; and notwithstanding the great and just suspicion that the demons might impose the shapes of innocent persons in their spectral exhibitions upon the sufferers (which may perhaps prove no small part of the witch-plot in the issue), yet many of the persons thus represented, being examined, several of them have been convicted of a very damnable witchcraft: yea, more than one twenty

---

4. Literally a stone of help; a commemorative monument like the one Samuel erected to commemorate victory over the Philistines (1 Samuel 7.12).

have confessed, that they have signed unto a book, which the devil showed them, and engaged in his hellish design of bewitching and ruining our land. We know not, at least I know not, how far the delusions of Satan may be interwoven into some circumstances of the confessions; but one would think all the rules of understanding human affairs are at an end, if after so many most voluntary harmonious confessions, made by intelligent persons of all ages, in sundry towns, at several times, we must not believe the main strokes wherein those confessions all agree: especially when we have a thousand preternatural things every day before our eyes, wherein the confessors do acknowledge their concernment, and give demonstration of their being so concerned. If the devils now can strike the minds of men with any poisons of so fine a composition and operation, that scores of innocent people shall unite, in confessions of a crime, which we see actually committed, it is a thing prodigious, beyond the wonders of the former ages, and it threatens no less than a sort of a dissolution upon the world. Now, by these confessions 'tis agreed that the Devil has made a dreadful knot of witches in the country, and by the help of witches has dreadfully increased that knot: that these witches have driven a trade of commissioning their confederate spirits to do all sorts of mischiefs to the neighbors, whereupon there have ensued such mischievous consequences upon the bodies and estates of the neighborhood, as could not otherwise be accounted for: yea, that at prodigious witch-meetings, the wretches have proceeded so far as to concert and consult the methods of rooting out the Christian religion from this country, and setting up instead of it perhaps a more gross diabolism than ever the world saw before. And yet it will be a thing little short of miracle, if in so spread a business as this, the Devil should not get in some of his juggles,[5] to confound the discovery of all the rest.

* * *

But I shall no longer detain my reader from his expected entertainment, in a brief account of the trials which have passed upon some of the malefactors lately executed at Salem, for the witchcrafts whereof they stood convicted. For my own part, I was not present at any of them; nor ever had I any personal prejudice at the persons thus brought upon the stage; much less at the surviving relations of those persons, with and for whom I would be as hearty a mourner as any man living in the world: The Lord comfort them! But having received a command[6] so to do, I can do no other than shortly relate the chief matters of fact, which occurred in the trials of some that were executed, in an abridgment collected out of the court papers on this occasion put into my hands. You are to take the truth, just as it was; and the truth will hurt no good man.

5. Tricks.
6. I.e., the request by the judges of the Salem trials to explain the sentencing of people accused of witchcraft.

There might have been more of these, if my book would not thereby have swollen too big; and if some other worthy hands did not perhaps intend something further in these collections; for which cause I have only singled out four or five, which may serve to illustrate the way of dealing, wherein witchcrafts use to be concerned; and I report matters not as an advocate, but as an historian.

* * *

The Trial of Martha Carrier
AT THE COURT OF OYER AND TERMINER,[7]
HELD BY ADJOURNMENT AT SALEM, AUGUST 2. 1692

I. Martha Carrier was indicted for the bewitching certain persons, according to the form usual in such cases, pleading not guilty to her indictment; there were first brought in a considerable number of the bewitched persons who not only made the court sensible[8] of an horrid witchcraft committed upon them, but also deposed that it was Martha Carrier, or her shape, that grievously tormented them, by biting, pricking, pinching and choking of them. It was further deposed that while this Carrier was on her examination before the magistrates, the poor people were so tortured that every one expected their death upon the very spot, but that upon the binding of Carrier they were eased. Moreover the look of Carrier then laid the afflicted people for dead; and her touch, if her eye at the same time were off them, raised them again: which things were also now seen upon her trial. And it was testified that upon the mention of some having their necks twisted almost round, by the shape of this Carrier, she replied, "It's no matter though their necks had been twisted quite off."

II. Before the trial of this prisoner, several of her own children had frankly and fully confessed not only that they were witches themselves, but that this their mother had made them so. This confession they made with great shows of repentance, and with much demonstration of truth. They related place, time, occasion; they gave an account of journeys, meetings and mischiefs by them performed, and were very credible in what they said. Nevertheless, this evidence was not produced against the prisoner at the bar,[9] inasmuch as there was other evidence enough to proceed upon.

III. Benjamin Abbot gave his testimony that last March was a twelvemonth, this Carrier was very angry with him, upon laying out some land near her husband's: her expressions in this anger were that she would stick as close to Abbot as the bark stuck to the tree; and that he should repent of it afore seven years came to an end, so as Doctor Prescot should never cure him. These words were heard

7. To hear and determine.
8. Aware.

9. Court.

by others besides Abbot himself; who also heard her say, she would hold his nose as close to the grindstone as ever it was held since his name was Abbot. Presently after this, he was taken with a swelling in his foot, and then with a pain in his side, and exceedingly tormented. It bred into a sore, which was lanced[1] by Doctor Prescot, and several gallons of corruption[2] ran out of it. For six weeks it continued very bad, and then another sore bred in the groin, which was also lanced by Doctor Prescot. Another sore than bred in his groin, which was likewise cut, and put him to very great misery: he was brought unto death's door, and so remained until Carrier was taken, and carried away by the constable, from which very day he began to mend, and so grew better every day, and is well ever since.

Sarah Abbot also, his wife, testified that her husband was not only all this while afflicted in his body, but also that strange, extraordinary and unaccountable calamities befell his cattle; their death being such as they could guess at no natural reason for.

IV. Allin Toothaker testified that Richard, the son of Martha Carrier, having some difference with him, pulled him down by the hair of the head. When he rose again he was going to strike at Richard Carrier but fell down flat on his back to the ground, and had not power to stir hand or foot, until he told Carrier he yielded; and then he saw the shape of Martha Carrier go off his breast.

This Toothaker had received a wound in the wars; and he now testified that Martha Carrier told him he should never be cured. Just afore the apprehending of Carrier, he could thrust a knitting needle into his wound four inches deep; but presently after her being seized, he was thoroughly healed.

He further testified that when Carrier and he some times were at variance, she would clap her hands at him, and say he should get nothing by it; whereupon he several times lost his cattle, by strange deaths, whereof no natural causes could be given.

V. John Rogger also testified that upon the threatening words of this malicious Carrier, his cattle would be strangely bewitched; as was more particularly then described.

VI. Samuel Preston testified that about two years ago, having some difference with Martha Carrier, he lost a cow in a strange, preternatural, unusual manner; and about a month after this, the said Carrier, having again some difference with him, she told him he had lately lost a cow, and it should not be long before he lost another; which accordingly came to pass; for he had a thriving and well-kept cow, which without any known cause quickly fell down and died.

VII. Phebe Chandler testified that about a fortnight before the apprehension of Martha Carrier, on a Lordsday, while the Psalm was singing in the Church, this Carrier then took her by the shoulder and shaking her, asked her, where she lived: she made her no

---

1. Cut open.   2. Pus; infected matter.

answer, although as Carrier, who lived next door to her father's house, could not in reason but know who she was. Quickly after this, as she was at several times crossing the fields, she heard a voice, that she took to be Martha Carrier's, and it seemed as if it was over her head. The voice told her she should within two or three days be poisoned. Accordingly, within such a little time, one half of her right hand became greatly swollen and very painful; as also part of her face: whereof she can give no account how it came. It continued very bad for some days; and several times since she has had a great pain in her breast; and been so seized on her legs that she has hardly been able to go. She added that lately, going well to the house of God, Richard, the son of Martha Carrier, looked very earnestly upon her, and immediately her hand, which had formerly been poisoned, as is abovesaid, began to pain her greatly, and she had a strange burning at her stomach; but was then struck deaf, so that she could not hear any of the prayer, or singing, till the two or three last words of the Psalm.

VIII. One Foster, who confessed her own share in the witchcraft for which the prisoner stood indicted, affirmed that she had seen the prisoner at some of their witch-meetings, and that it was this Carrier, who persuaded her to be a witch. She confessed that the Devil carried them on a pole to a witch-meeting; but the pole broke, and she hanging about Carrier's neck, they both fell down, and she then received an hurt by the fall, whereof she was not at this very time recovered.

IX. One Lacy, who likewise confessed her share in this witch-craft, now testified, that she and the prisoner were once bodily present at a witch-meeting in Salem Village; and that she knew the prisoner to be a witch, and to have been at a diabolical sacrament, and that the prisoner was the undoing of her and her children by enticing them into the snare of the devil.

X. Another Lacy, who also confessed her share in this witchcraft, now testified, that the prisoner was at the witch-meeting, in Salem Village, where they had bread and wine administered unto them.

XI. In the time of this prisoner's trial, one Susanna Sheldon in open court had her hands unaccountably tied together with a wheel-band[3] so fast that without cutting it, it could not be loosed: it was done by a specter; and the sufferer affirmed it was the prisoner's.

Memorandum. This rampant hag, Martha Carrier, was the person of whom the confessions of the witches, and of her own children among the rest, agreed that the devil had promised her she should be Queen of Hebrews.

1692, 1693

---

3. A band or strap that goes around a wheel.

From MAGNALIA CHRISTI AMERICANA[1]

Nehemias Americanus:[2] The Life of John Winthrop, Esq., Governor of the Massachusetts Colony

Quicunque Venti erunt, Ars nostra certe non aberit.
—CICERO.[3]

Let Greece boast of her patient Lycurgus,[4] the lawgiver, by whom diligence, temperance, fortitude, and wit were made the fashions of a therefore long-lasting and renowned commonwealth: let Rome tell of her devout Numa,[5] the lawgiver, by whom the most famous commonwealth saw peace triumphing over extinguished war and cruel plunders; and murders giving place to the more mollifying exercises of his religion. Our New England shall tell and boast of her Winthrop, a lawgiver as patient as Lycurgus, but not admitting any of his criminal disorders; as devout as Numa, but not liable to any of his heathenish madnesses; a governor in whom the excellencies of Christianity made a most improving addition unto the virtues, wherein even without those he would have made a parallel for the great men of Greece, or of Rome, which the pen of a Plutarch[6] has eternized.

A stock of heroes by right should afford nothing but what is heroical; and nothing but an extreme degeneracy would make anything less to be expected from a stock of Winthrops. Mr. Adam Winthrop,[7] the son of a worthy gentleman wearing the same name, was himself a worthy, a discreet, and a learned gentleman, particularly eminent for skill in the law, nor without remark for[8] love to the gospel, under the reign of King Henry VIII, and brother to a memorable favorer of the Reformed religion in the days of Queen

1. "A History of the Wonderful Works of Christ in America." Mather's book is subtitled *The ecclesiastical History of New England from its first planting, in the year 1620, unto the year of our Lord, 1698.* The *Magnalia* contains seven books. The first book is concerned with the discovery of America and the founding and history of the New England settlements. The second book contains lives of Governors of New England, and the life of William Bradford may be found there; the third book contains lives of 60 famous "Divines, by whose ministry the churches of New England have been planted and continued." Other books contain a history of Harvard University, a record of church ordinances passed in synods, and a record of "illustrious" and "wonderous" events which have been witnessed by people in New England. First published in London in 1702, the text used here is taken from that edited by Thomas Robbins (Hartford, Conn.: Silas Andrus & Son, 1855).

2. "The American Nehemiah." As governor of Judea, Nehemiah rebuilt the walls of Jerusalem after they had been destroyed by Nebuzaradan (Nehemiah 1.3).

3. "Whatever winds may blow, this art of ours can never be lost." The quotation is from the Roman orator Cicero's (106–43 B.C.) *Epistulae ad Familiares* 12.25.5.

4. Ninth-century B.C. Spartan reformer who reshaped the nation's constitution and made it an efficient military state.

5. Numa Pompilius (715–673 B.C.), second legendary King of Rome.

6. The Greek biographer (A.D. 46?–120?), best known for his lives of Greeks and Romans.

7. Mather refers here to Winthrop's grandfather (1498–1562), father 1548–1623), and uncle William (1529–82).

8. I.e., not noted for. Henry VIII (1491–1547) founded the Church of England and was despised by Puritans.

Mary,[9] into whose hands the famous martyr Philpot[1] committed his papers, which afterwards made no inconsiderable part of our martyr-books. This Mr. Adam Winthrop had a son of the same name also, and of the same endowments and employments with his father; and this third Adam Winthrop was the father of that renowned John Winthrop, who was the father of New England, and the founder of a colony, which, upon many accounts, like him that founded it, may challenge the first place among the English glories of America. Our John Winthrop, thus born at the mansion-house of his ancestors, at Groton in Suffolk, on June 12, 1587,[2] enjoyed afterwards an agreeable education. But though he would rather have devoted himself unto the study of Mr. John Calvin, than of Sir Edward Cook;[3] nevertheless, the accomplishments of a lawyer were those wherewith heaven made his chief opportunities to be serviceable.

Being made, at the unusually early age of eighteen, a justice of peace, his virtues began to fall under a more general observation; and he not only so bound himself to the behavior of a Christian, as to become exemplary for a conformity to the laws of Christianity in his own conversation, but also discovered a more than ordinary measure of those qualities which adorn an officer of humane society. His justice was impartial, and used the balance to weigh not the cash, but the case of those who were before him: *prosopolatria* he reckoned as bad as *idolatria*.[4] His wisdom did exquisitely temper things according to the art of governing, which is a business of more contrivance than the seven arts of the schools;[5] *oyer* still went before *terminer* in all his administrations.[6] His courage made him dare to do right, and fitted him to stand among the lions that have sometimes been the supporters of the throne.[7] All which virtues he rendered the more illustrious, by emblazoning them with the constant liberality and hospitality of a gentleman. This made him the terror of the wicked, and the delight of the sober, the envy of the many, but the hope of those who had any hopeful design in hand for the common good of the nation and the interests of religion.

Accordingly, when the noble design of carrying a colony of chosen people into an American wilderness was by some eminent

9. Mary Tudor (1516–58) reestablished Roman Catholicism in England in 1555.
1. John Philpot (1516–55) was a Puritan martyr burned at the stake, and is included in John Foxe's *Book of Martyrs* (1563).
2. Should read January 12, 1588.
3. I.e., he would have preferred to study for the ministry and read John Calvin's *Institutes* (1536) rather than prepare for the law by reading Lord-Chief-Justice Edward Coke's *Institutes of English Law* (1628–44).

4. Hero worship (literally "face-worship") he considered no better than the worship of idols or "false gods."
5. The trivium and quadrivium of a classical education consisted of grammar, rhetoric, and logic, as well as arithmetic, music, geometry, and astronomy.
6. I.e., in the parlance of English law, "hearing" all the evidence came before "judging."
7. Daniel was saved from the Roman

persons undertaken, this eminent person was, by the consent of all, chosen for the Moses,[8] who must be the leader of so great an undertaking: and indeed nothing but a Mosaic spirit could have carried him through the temptations, to which either his farewell to his own land, or his travel in a strange land, must needs expose a gentleman of his education. Wherefore, having sold a fair estate of six or seven hundred[9] a year, he transported himself with the effects of it into New England in the year 1630, where he spent it upon the service of a famous plantation, founded and formed for the seat of the most reformed Christianity: and continued there, conflicting with temptations of all sorts, as many years as the nodes of the moon take to dispatch a revolution.[1] Those persons were never concerned in a new plantation, who know not that the unavoidable difficulties of such a thing will call for all the prudence and patience of a mortal man to encounter therewithal; and they must be very insensible of the influence, which the just wrath of heaven has permitted the devils to have upon this world, if they do not think that the difficulties of a new plantation, devoted unto the evangelical worship of our Lord Jesus Christ, must be yet more than ordinary. How prudently, how patiently, and with how much resignation to our Lord Jesus Christ, our brave Winthrop waded through these difficulties, let posterity consider with admiration. And know, that as the picture of this their governor was, after his death, hung up with honor in the State House of his country, so the wisdom, courage, and holy zeal of his life, were an example well worthy to be copied by all that shall succeed him in government.

Were he now to be considered only as a Christian, we might therein propose him as greatly imitable. He was a very religious man; and as he strictly kept his heart, so he kept his house, under the laws of piety;[2] there he was every day constant in holy duties, both morning and evening, and on the Lord's days, and lectures,[3] though he wrote not after the preacher,[4] yet such was his attention, and such his retention in hearing, that he repeated unto his family the sermons which he had heard in the congregation. But it is chiefly as a governor that he is now to be considered. Being the governor over the considerablest part of New England, he maintained the figure and honor of his place with the spirit of a true gentleman; but yet with such obliging condescension to the circumstances of the colony, that when a certain troublesome and malicious calumniator, well known in those times, printed his libelous nick-

lions by his faith (Daniel 6.23). King Solomon's throne had carved lions on both sides (I Kings 10.19–20).
8. Moses led the Jews out of Egypt into Israel.
9. I.e., English pounds.
1. Approximately the same number of years that Winthrop lived in Massachusetts: 18.6 years. In astronomy a node is either of two diametrically opposite points at which the orbit (or revolution) of a planet intersects the ecliptic.
2. "(For if a man know not how to rule his own house, how shall he take care of the church of God?)" (I Timothy 3.5).
3. Days in which less formal sermons were delivered.
4. I.e., although he did not take the sermon down in shorthand.

names upon the chief persons here, the worst nickname he could find for the governor was John Temperwell;[5] and when the calumnies of that ill man caused the Archbishop to summon one Mr. Cleaves[6] before the King, in hopes to get some accusation from him against the country, Mr. Cleaves gave such an account of the governor's laudable carriage in all respects, and the serious devotion wherewith prayers were both publicly and privately made for his Majesty, that the King expressed himself most highly pleased therewithal, only sorry that so worthy a person should be no better accommodated than with the hardships of America. He was, indeed, a governor, who had most exactly studied that book which, pretending to teach politics, did only contain three leaves, and but one word in each of those leaves, which word was, MOD-ERATION. Hence, though he were a zealous enemy to all vice, yet his practice was according to his judgment thus expressed: "In the infancy of plantations, justice should be administered with more lenity than in a settled state; because people are more apt then to transgress; partly out of ignorance of new laws and orders, partly out of oppression of business, and other straits. [LENTO GRADU][7] was the old rule; and if the strings of a new instrument be wound up unto their height, they will quickly crack." But when some leading and learned men took offense at his conduct in this matter, and upon a conference gave it in as their opinion, "That a stricter discipline was to be used in the beginning of a plantation, than after its being with more age established and confirmed," the governor being readier to see his own errors than other men's, professed his purpose to endeavor their satisfaction with less of lenity in his administrations. At that conference there were drawn up several other articles to be observed between the governor and the rest of the magistrates, which were of this import: That the magistrates, as far as might be, should aforehand ripen their consultations, to produce that unanimity in their public votes, which might make them liker to the voice of God; that if differences fell out among them in their public meetings, they should speak only to the case, without any reflection,[8] with all due modesty, and but by way of question; or desire the deferring of the cause to further time; and after sentence to imitate privately no dislike; that they should be more familiar, friendly and open unto each other, and more frequent in their visitations, and not any way expose each other's infirmities, but seek the honor of each other, and all the court; that one magistrate shall not cross the proceedings of another, without first advising with him; and that they should in all their appearances abroad, be so circumstanced as to prevent all contempt of

5. Thomas Morton (d. 1649) in *New English Canaan* (1637), Pt. 4, Chap. 23.
6. George Cleaves settled in Maine in 1630 and returned to England in 1636. Archbishop William Laud (1573–1645)

was an enemy of the Puritans.
7. "By slow degrees."
8. I.e., without imputing any ill will on the part of another.

authority; and that they should support and strengthen all under-officers. All of which articles were observed by no man more than by the governor himself.

But whilst he thus did, as our New English Nehemiah, the part of a ruler in managing the public affairs of our American Jerusalem, when there were Tobijahs and Sanballats enough to vex him,[9] and give him the experiment of Luther's observation, *Omnis qui regit est tanquam signum, in guod omnia jacula, Satan et Mundus dirigunt*;[1] he made himself still an exacter parallel unto that governor of Israel, by doing the part of a neighbor among the distressed people of the new plantation. To teach them the frugality necessary for those times, he abridged himself of a thousand comfortable things, which he had allowed himself elsewhere: his habit was not that soft raiment, which would have been disagreeable to a wilderness;[2] his table was not covered with the superfluities that would have invited unto sensualities: water was commonly his own drink, though he gave wine to others. But at the same time his liberality unto the needy was even beyond measure generous; and therein he was continually causing "the blessing of him that was ready to perish to come upon him, and the heart of the widow and the orphan to sing for joy,"[3] but none more than those of deceased ministers, whom he always treated with a very singular compassion; among the instances whereof we still enjoy with us the worthy and now aged son of that Reverend Higginson, whose death left his family in a wide world soon after his arrival here, publicly acknowledging the charitable Winthrop for his foster-father.[4] It was oftentimes no small trial unto his faith, to think how a table for the people should be furnished when they first came into the wilderness![5] and for very many of the people his own good works were needful, and accordingly employed for the answering of his faith. Indeed, for a while the governor was the Joseph, unto whom the whole body of the people repaired when their corn failed them;[6] and he continued relieving of them with his open-handed bounties, as long as he had any stock to do it with; and a lively faith to see the return of the "bread after many days,"[7] and not starve in the days that were to pass till that return should be seen, carried him cheerfully through those expenses.

9. Both the governor of Samaria, Sanballat, and a Persian officer, Tobijah, opposed the rebuilding of the walls of Jerusalem (Nehemiah 2.10; 4.7).
1. "A man in authority is a target at which Satan and the world launch all their darts," from Martin Luther's (1483–1546) *Loci Communes*.
2. "But what went ye out for to see? a man clothed in soft raiment? behold, they that wear soft clothing are in king's houses" (Matthew 11.8).
3. Job 29.13.
4. Francis Higginson (1587–1630) died after only a year's residence in Salem.

His "aged son" John (1616–1708) wrote an "Attestation" prefixed to the *Magnalia*.
5. "Yea, they spake against God; they said, Can God furnish a table in the wilderness" (Psalm 78.19–20).
6. "And the famine was over all the face of the earth; and Joseph opened all the storehouses and sold unto the Egyptians; and the famine waxed sore in the land of Egypt" (Geneiss 41.50).
7. "Cast thy bread upon the waters: for thou shalt find it after many days" (Ecclesiastes 11.1).

Once it was observable that, on February 5, 1630, when he was distributing the last handful of the meal in the barrel unto a poor man distressed by the "wolf at the door," at that instant they spied a ship arrived at the harbor's mouth, laden with provisions for them all. Yea, the governor sometimes made his own private purse to be the public: not by sucking into it, but by squeezing out of it; for when the public treasure had nothing in it, he did himself defray the charges of the public. And having learned that lesson of our Lord, "that it is better to give than to receive,"[8] he did, at the General Court, when he was a third time chosen governor, make a speech unto this purpose: That he had received gratuities from divers towns, which he accepted with much comfort and content; and he had likewise received civilities from particular persons, which he could not refuse without incivility in himself: nevertheless, he took them with a trembling heart, in regard of God's word, and the conscience of his own infirmities; and therefore he desired them that they would not hereafter take it ill if he refused such presents for the time to come. 'Twas his custom also to send some of his family upon errands unto the houses of the poor, about their mealtime, on purpose to spy whether they wanted;[9] and if it were found that they wanted, he would make that the opportunity of sending supplies unto them. And there was one passage of his charity that was perhaps a little unusual: in an hard and long winter, when wood was very scarce at Boston, a man gave him a private information that a needy person in the neighborhood stole wood sometimes from his pile; whereupon the governor in a seeming anger did reply, "Does he so? I'll take a course with him; go, call that man to me; I'll warrant you I'll cure him of stealing." When the man came, the governor considering that if he had stolen, it was more out of necessity than disposition, said unto him, "Friend, it is a severe winter, and I doubt you are but meanly provided for wood; wherefore I would have you supply yourself at my woodpile till this cold season be over." And he then merrily asked his friends whether he had not effectually cured this man of stealing his wood.

One would have imagined that so good a man could have had no enemies, if we had not had a daily and woeful experience to convince us that goodness itself will make enemies. It is a wonderful speech of Plato (in one of his books, *De Republica*), "For the trial of true virtue, 'tis necessary that a good man μηδὲν ἀδικῶν, δόξαν ἔχει τὴν μεγίστην ἀδικίας: Though he do no unjust thing, should suffer the infamy of the greatest injustice."[1] The governor had by his unspotted integrity procured himself a great reputation among

---

8. "I have showed you all things, how that so laboring ye ought to support the weak, and to remember the words of the Lord Jesus, how he said, It is more blessed to give than to receive" (Acts 20.35).
9. I.e., lacked anything.
1. From *The Republic* of Plato (427?–347 B.C.).

the people; and then the crime of popularity was laid unto his charge by such, who were willing to deliver him from the danger of having all men speak well of him.[2] Yea, there were persons eminent both for figure and for number, unto whom it was almost essential to dislike everything that came from him; and yet he always maintained an amicable correspondence with them; as believing that they acted according to their judgment and conscience, or that their eyes were held by some temptation in the worst of all their oppositions. Indeed, his right works were so many, that they exposed him unto the envy of his neighbors;[3] and of such power was that envy, that sometimes he could not stand before it; but it was by not standing that he most effectually withstood it all.[4] Great attempts were sometimes made among the freemen to get him left out from his place in the government upon little pretenses, lest by the too frequent choice of one man, the government should cease to be by choice; and with a particular aim at him, sermons were preached at the anniversary Court of election, to dissuade the freemen from choosing one man twice together. This was the reward of his extraordinary serviceableness! But when these attempts did succeed, as they sometimes did, his profound humility appeared in that equality of mind, wherewith he applied himself cheerfully to serve the country in whatever station their votes had allotted for him. And one year when the votes came to be numbered, there were found six less for Mr. Winthrop than for another gentleman who then stood in competition: but several other persons regularly tendering their votes before the election was published, were, upon a very frivolous objection, refused by some of the magistrates that were afraid lest the election should at last fall upon Mr. Winthrop: which, though it was well perceived, yet such was the self-denial of this patriot, that he would not permit any notice to be taken of the injury. But these trials were nothing in comparison of those harsher and harder treats which he sometimes had from the forwardness of not a few in the days of their paroxisms; and from the faction of some against him, not much unlike that of the Piazzi in Florence against the family of the Medicis:[5] all of which he at last conquered by conforming to the famous Judge's motto, *Prudens qui Patiens*.[6] The oracles of God have said, "Envy is rottenness to the bones;"[7] and Gulielmus Parisiensis[8] applies it unto rulers, who are

2. "Woe unto you, when all men shall speak well of you! for so did their fathers to the false prophets" (Luke 6.26).
3. "Again, I consider all travail, and every right work, that for this a man is envied of his neighbor. This is also vanity and vexation of spirit" (Ecclesiastes 4.4).
4. "Wrath is cruel, and anger is outrageous, but who is able to stand before envy" (Proverbs 27.4).
5. In 1478 an important member of the

Medici family was assassinated by one of the Piazzis and all Italy became involved in the war which followed.
6. "He is prudent who is patient," a maxim attributed to Sir Edward Coke.
7. "A sound heart is the life of the flesh: but envy the rottenness of the bones" (Proverbs 14.30).
8. William of St. Amour (d. 1272), Bishop of Paris, was also known as a satirist.

as it were the bones of the societies which they belong unto: "Envy," says he, "is often found among them, and it is rottenness unto them." Our Winthrop encountered this envy from others, but conquered it, by being free from it himself.

Were it not for the sake of introducing the exemplary skill of this wise man, at giving soft answers, one would not choose to relate those instances of wrath which he had sometimes to encounter with; but he was for his gentleness, his forbearance, and longanimity,[9] a pattern so worthy to be written *after*, that something must here be written *of* it. He seemed indeed never to speak any other language than that of Theodosius:[1] "If any man speak evil of the governour, if it be through lightness, 'tis to be contemned;[2] if it be through madness, 'tis to be pitied; if it be through injury, 'tis to be remitted." Behold, reader, the "meekness of wisdom" notably exemplified! There was a time when he received a very sharp letter from a gentleman who was a member of the Court,[3] but he delivered back the letter unto the messengers that brought it, with such a Christian speech as this: "I am not willing to keep such a matter of provocation by me!" Afterwards the same gentleman was compelled by the scarcity of provisions to send unto him that he would sell him some of his cattle; whereupon the governor prayed him to accept what he had sent for as a token of his good will; but the gentleman returned him this answer: "Sir, your overcoming of yourself hath overcome me:" and afterwards gave demonstration of it.

The French have a saying that *"Un honesté homme, est un homme mesle!"*—a good man is a mixed man; and there hardly ever was a more sensible mixture of those two things, resolution and condescension, than in this good man. There was a time when the Court of Election being, for fear of tumult, held at Cambridge, May 17, 1637, the sectarian part of the country, who had the year before gotten a governor more unto their mind,[4] had a project now to have confounded the election, by demanding that the court would consider a petition then tendered before their proceeding thereunto. Mr. Winthrop saw that this was only a trick to throw all into confusion, by putting off the choice of the governor and assistants until the day should be over; and therefore he did, with a strenuous resolution, procure a disappointment unto that mischievous and ruinous contrivance. Nevertheless, Mr. Winthrop himself being by the voice of the freemen in this exigency chosen the governor, and all of the other party left out, that ill-affected party discovered the dirt and mire, which remained with them, after

9. Patience.
1. Theodosius Flavius I (A.D. 346–395) was a Christian Roman Emperor.
2. Despised.
3. Thomas Dudley (1574–1653); the messengers were John Haynes and Thomas Hooker.
4. Sir Henry Vane returned to England in 1637; he was sympathetic toward the views expressed by the followers of Anne Hutchinson.

the storm was over; particularly the sergeants, whose office 'twas to attend the governor, laid down their halberd;[5] but such was the condescension of this governor, as to take no present notice of this anger and contempt, but only order some of his own servants to take the halberds; and when the country manifested their deep resentments of the affront thus offered him, he prayed them to overlook it. But it was not long before a compensation was made for these things by the doubled respects which were from all parts paid unto him. Again, there was a time when the suppression of an *Antinomian* and *Familistical* faction,[6] which extremely threatened the ruin of the country, was generally thought much owing unto this renowned man; and therefore when the friends of that faction could not wreak[7] their displeasure on him with any politic vexations, they set themselves to do it by ecclesiastical ones. Accordingly, when a sentence of banishment was passed on the ringleaders of those disturbances, who

> ——*Maria et Terras, Cœlumque profundum,*
> *Quippe ferant Rapidi, secum vertanique per Auras;*[8]

many at the church of Boston, who were then that way too much inclined, most earnestly solicited the elders of that church, whereof the governor was a member, to call him forth as an offender, for passing of that sentence. The elders were unwilling to do any such thing; but the governor understanding the ferment among the people took that occasion to make a speech in the congregation to this effect:

BRETHREN: Understanding that some of you have desired that I should answer for an offense lately taken among you; had I been called upon so to do, I would, first, have advised with the ministers of the country, whether the church had power to call in question the civil court; and I would, secondly, have advised with the rest of the court, whether I might discover their counsels unto the church. But though I know that the reverend Elders of this church, and some others, do very well apprehend that the church cannot inquire into the proceedings of the court; yet, for the satisfaction of the weaker, who do not apprehend it, I will declare my mind concerning it. If the church have any such power, they have it from the Lord Jesus Christ; but the Lord Jesus Christ hath disclaimed it, not only by practice, but also by precept, which we have in his gospel, Matt. xx. 25, 26.[9] It is true, indeed, that magistrates, as they are church-

---

5. A weapons which is a combination spear and battle-ax; "condescension": humility.

6. Both Antinomianism and Familism (a word derived from an English religious sect called The Family of Love) hold the regenerate self above ecclesiastical and civil law.

7. Inflict.

8. "Rack sea and land and sky with mingled wrath,/ In the wild tumult of their stormy path" (Virgil's *Aeneid* I. 59–60).

9. "But Jesus called them *unto him,* and said, Ye know that the princes of the Gentiles exercise dominion over them, and they that are great exercise authority upon them. But it shall not be so among you: but whosoever will be great among you, let him be your minister."

members, are accountable unto the church for their failings; but that is when they are out of their calling. When Uzziah would go offer incense in the temple, the officers of the church called him to an account, and withstood him; but when Asa put the prophet in prison, the officers of the church did not call him to an account for that.[1] If the magistrate shall in a private way wrong any man, the church may call him to an account for it; but if he be in pursuance of a course of justice, though the thing that he does be unjust, yet he is not accountable for it before the church. As for myself, I did nothing in the causes of any of the brethren but by the advice of the Elders of the church. Moreover, in the oath which I have taken there is this clause: "In all cases wherein you are to give your vote, you shall do as in your judgment and conscience you shall see to be just, and for the public good." And I am satisfied, it is most for the glory of God, and the public good, that there has been such a sentence passed; yea, those brethren are so divided from the rest of the country in their opinions and practices, that it cannot stand with the public peace for them to continue with us; Abraham saw that Hagar and Ishmael must be sent away.[2]

By such a speech he marvelously convinced, satisfied and mollified the uneasy brethren of the church; *Sic cunctus Pelagi cecidit Fragor*—.[3] And after a little patient waiting, the differences all so wore away, that the church, merely as a token of respect unto the governor when he had newly met with some losses in his estate, sent him a present of several hundreds of pounds.

Once more there was a time when some active spirits among the deputies of the colony, by their endeavors not only to make themselves a court of Judicature, but also to take away the negative by which the magistrates might check their votes, had like by over-driving to have run the whole government into something too democratical. And if there were a town in Spain undermined by coneys, another town in Thrace destroyed by moles, a third in Greece ranversed[4] by frogs, a fourth in Germany subverted by rats; I must on this occasion add, that there was a country in America like to be confounded by a swine. A certain stray sow being found, was claimed by two several persons with a claim so equally maintained on both sides, that after six or seven years' hunting the business from one court unto another, it was brought at last into the General Court, where the final determination was "that it was impossible to proceed unto any judgment in the case."[5] However,

---

1. Uzziah, King of Judea, was afflicted with leprosy when he tried to burn incense on the altar in spite of the protests of the priests (Ecclesiastes 30.78; Numbers 16.40). Asa was the third king of Judea and put the prophet Hanani in prison when he accused him of not relying on the Lord (2 Chronicles 16.7–10).
2. Ishmael was the son of Abraham and his wife's servant Hagar; Abraham sent them into the wilderness at the insistence of his wife, Sarah (Genesis 16.1–16; 21.9–14).
3. "To silence sunk the thunder of the wave" (*Aeneid* I.154).
4. Overturned; "coneys": rabbits.
5. Mather refers to a case involving the merchant Robert Krayne (1595–1656) and Goody Sherman, a Boston widow, in 1634.

in the debate of this matter, the negative of the upper-house upon the lower in that court was brought upon the stage; and agitated with so hot a zeal, that a little more, and all had been in the fire. In these agitations, the governor was informed that an offense had been taken by some eminnent persons at certain passages in a discourse by him written thereabout; whereupon, with his usual condescendency, when he next came into the General Court, he made a speech of this import:

I understand that some have taken offense at something that I have lately written; which offense I desire to remove now, and begin this year in a reconciled state with you all. As for the matter of my writing, I had the concurrence of my brethren; it is a point of judgment which is not at my own disposing. I have examined it over and over again by such light as God has given me, from the rules of religion, reason and custom; and I see no cause to retract anything of it: wherefore I must enjoy my liberty in that, as you do yourselves. But for the manner, this, and all that was blameworthy in it, was wholly my own; and whatsoever I might allege for my own justification therein before men, I wave it, as now setting myself before another Judgment seat. However, what I wrote was upon great provocation, and to vindicate myself and others from great aspersion; yet that was no sufficient warrant for me to allow any distemper of spirit in myself; and I doubt I have been too prodigal of my brethren's reputation; I might have maintained my cause without casting any blemish upon others, when I made that my conclusion, "And now let religion and sound reason give judgment in the case;" it looked as if I had arrogated too much unto myself, and too little to others. And when I made that profession, "That I would maintain what I wrote before all the world," though such words might modestly be spoken, yet I perceive an unbeseeming pride of my own heart breathing in them. For these failings, I ask pardon of God and man.

Sic ait, et dicto citius Tumida Æquora placut,
Collectasque fugát Nubes, Solemque reducit.[6]

This acknowledging disposition in the governor made them all acknowledge that he was truly "a man of an excellent spirit."[7] In fine, the victories of an Alexander, an Hannibal, or a Cæsar[8] over other men were not so glorious as the victories of this great man over himself, which also at last proved victories over other men.

But the stormiest of all the trials that ever befell this gentleman was in the year 1645, when he was, in title, no more than deputy

---

6. "He speaks—but ere the word is said,/ Each mounting billow droops its head,/ And brightening clouds one moment stay/ To pioneer returning day" (*Aeneid* I.142–143).
7. "He that hath knowledge spareth his words: *and* a man of understanding is of an excellent spirit" (Proverbs 17.27).
8. Alexander the Great (356–323 B.C.), King of Macedonia, Hannibal (247–183 B.C.), the Carthaginian general, and Julius Caesar (100–44 B.C.), Roman general and statesman, were all pre-Christian warriors.

governor of the colony. If the famous Cato were forty-four times called into judgment but as often acquitted; let it not be wondered, and if[9] our famous Winthrop were one time so. There happening certain seditious and mutinous practices in the town of Hingham,[1] the deputy governor, as legally as prudently, interposed his authority for the checking of them: whereupon there followed such an enchantment[2] upon the minds of the deputies in the General Court, that upon a scandalous petition of the delinquents unto them, wherein a pretended invasion made upon the liberties of the people was complained of, the deputy governor was most irregularly called forth unto an ignominious hearing before them in a vast assembly; whereto with a sagacious humilitude he consented, although he showed them how he might have refused it. The rest of that hearing was, that notwithstanding the touchy jealousy of the people about their liberties lay at the bottom of all this prosecution, yet Mr. Winthrop was publicly acquitted, and the offenders were severally fined and censured. But Mr. Winthrop then resuming the place of deputy governor on the bench, saw cause to speak unto the root of the matter after this manner:[3]

I shall not now speak anything about the past proceedings of this court, or the persons therein concerned. Only I bless God that I see an issue[4] of this troublesome affair. I am well satisfied that I was publicly accused, and that I am now publicly acquitted. But though I am justified before men, yet it may be the Lord hath seen so much amiss in my administrations, as calls me to be humbled; and indeed for me to have been thus charged by men, is itself a matter of humiliation, whereof I desire to make a right use before the Lord. If Miriam's father spit in her face, she is to be ashamed.[5] But give me leave, before you go, to say something that may rectify the opinions of many people, from whence the distempers have risen that have lately prevailed upon the body of this people. The questions that have troubled the country have been about the authority of the magistracy, and the liberty of the people. It is you who have called us unto this office; but being thus called, we have our authority from God; it is the ordinance of God, and it hath the image of God stamped upon it; and the contempt of it has been vindicated by God with terrible examples of his vengeance. I entreat you to consider, that when you choose magistrates, you take them from among yourselves, "men subject

9. "And if" is the archaic form of if; Cato: the Roman orator (234–149 B.C.).
1. A town about 25 miles south of Boston. These challenges to authority were made against the captain of the town militia who was appointed by the state authorities.
2. I.e., a delusion in judgment.
3. "But ye should say, why persecute we him, seeing the root of the matter is found in me?" (Job 19.28). Mather's version of Winthrop's speech to the Gen-

eral Court differs somewhat from that quoted in Winthrop's *Journal.*
4. End.
5. "And the Lord said unto Moses, if her father had but spit in her face, should she not be ashamed seven days? let her be shut out from the camp seven days, and after that let her be received in again" (Numbers 12.14). Miriam was Moses' sister, and was punished for challenging his choice in a wife.

unto like passions with yourselves." If you see our infirmities, reflect on your own, and you will not be so severe censurers of ours. We count him a good servant who breaks not his covenant: the covenant between us and you is the oath you have taken of us, which is to this purpose, "that we shall govern you, and judge your causes, according to God's laws, and our own, according to our best skill." As for our skill, you must run the hazard of it; and if there be an error, not in the will, but only in skill, it becomes you to bear it. Nor would I have you to mistake in the point of your own liberty. There is a liberty of corrupt nature, which is affected both by men and beasts, to do what they list; and this liberty is inconsistent with authority, impatient of all restraint; by this liberty, *Sumus Omnes Deteriores*;[6] 'tis the grand enemy of truth and peace, and all the ordinances of God are bent against it. But there is a civil, a moral, a federal liberty, which is the proper end and object of authority; it is a liberty for that only which is just and good; for this liberty you are to stand with the hazard of your very lives; and whatsoever crosses it is not authority, but a distemper thereof. This liberty is maintained in a way of subjection to authority; and the authority set over you will in all administrations for your good be quietly submitted unto, by all but such as have a disposition to shake off the yoke, and lose their true liberty, by their murmuring at the honor and power of authority.

The spell that was upon the eyes of the people being thus dissolved, their distorted and enraged notions of things all vanished; and the people would not afterwards entrust the helm of the weather-beaten bark in any other hands but Mr. Winthrop's until he died.

Indeed, such was the mixture of distant qualities in him, as to make a most admirable temper; and his having a certain greatness of soul, which rendered him grave, generous, courageous, resolved, well-applied, and every way a gentleman in his demeanor, did not hinder him from taking sometimes the old Roman's way to avoid confusions, namely, *Cedendo*;[7] or from discouraging some things which are agreeable enough to most that wear the name of gentlemen. Hereof I will give no instances, but only oppose two passages of his life.

In the year 1632, the governor, with his pastor, Mr. Wilson,[8] and some other gentlemen, to settle a good understanding between the two colonies, traveled as far as Plymouth, more than forty miles, through an howling wilderness, no better accommodated in those early days than the princes that in Solomon's time saw "servants on horseback,"[9] or than genus and species in the old

---

6. "We are all the worse for it," from Terence's *Heaucton Timorumenos* (3.1).
7. "By yielding the point."
8. John Wilson (c. 1591–1667).
9. "I have seen servants upon horses, and princes walking as servants upon the earth" (Ecclesiastes 10.7). The Book of Ecclesiastes was mistakenly attributed to Solomon.

epigram, "going on foot."[1] The difficulty of the walk, was abundantly compensated by the honorable, first reception, and then dismission, which they found from the rulers of Plymouth, and by the good correspondence thus established between the new colonies, who were like the floating bottles wearing this motto: *Si Collidimur Frangimur*.[2] But there were at this time in Plymouth two ministers,[3] leavened so far with the humors of the rigid Separation, that they insisted vehemently upon the unlawfulness of calling any unregenerate man by the name of "Goodman Such-an-One," until by their indiscreet urging of this whimsy, the place began to be disquieted.[4] The wiser people being troubled at these trifles, they took the opportunity of Governor Winthrop's being there, to have the thing publicly propounded in the congregation; who in answer thereunto, distinguished between a theological and a moral goodness; adding, that when juries were first used in England, it was usual for the crier, after the names of persons fit for that service were called over, to bid them all, "Attend, good men and true;" whence it grew to be a civil custom in the English nation, for neighbors living by one another, to call one another "Goodman Such-an-One;" and it was [a] pity now to make a stir about a civil custom, so innocently introduced. And that speech of Mr. Winthrop's put a lasting stop to the little, idle, whimsical conceits, then beginning to grow obstreperous.

Nevertheless, there was one civil custom used in (and in few but) the English nation, which this gentleman did endeavor to abolish in this country; and that was, the usage of drinking to one another. For although by drinking to one another, no more is meant than an act of courtesy, when one going to drink, does invite another to do so too, for the same ends with himself, nevertheless the governor (not altogether unlike to Cleomenes, of whom 'tis reported by Plutarch, ἄκοντι οὐδεὶς ποτήριον προσέφερε, *Nolenti poculum nunquam proebuit*,)[5] considered the impertinency and insignificancy of this usage, as to any of those ends that are usually pretended for it; and that indeed it ordinarily served for no ends at all, but only to provoke persons unto unseasonable and perhaps unreasonable drinking, and at last produce that abominable health-drinking, which the Fathers of old[6] so severely rebuked in the pagans, and which the Papists themselves do condemn, when their casuists pronounce it, *Peccatum mortale, provocare ad Æquales Calices, et Nefas Respondere*.[7] Wherefore in his own most hos-

---

1. "Better on foot go, than a wicked horse to ride."
2. "If we come into collision, we break."
3. Ralph Smith (1590–1661), Plymouth's first minister (1629–36), and Roger Williams (c. 1604–83) were both Separatists.
4. I.e., they used the title "Goodman" to mean only regeneracy and visible sainthood.

5. "Never urge the reluctant to drink." Plutarch (A.D. 46?–120?) writes about the Roman Emperor Cleomenes III (r. 235–222 B.C.) in his *Parallel Lives*.
6. I.e., Church Fathers.
7. "It is a deadly sin to challenge another to a drinking match, and it is impious to accept such challenges."

pitable house he left it off; not out of any silly or stingy fancy, but merely that by his example a greater temperance, with liberty of drinking, might be recommended, and sundry inconveniences in drinking avoided; and his example accordingly began to be much followed by the sober people in this country, as it now also begins among persons of the highest rank in the English nation itself; until an order of court came to be made against that ceremony in drinking, and then, the old wont violently returned, with a *Nitimur in Vetitum*.[8]

Many were the afflictions of this righteous man![9] He lost much of his estate in a ship, and in an house, quickly after his coming to New England, besides the prodigious expense of it in the difficulties of his first coming hither. Afterwards his assiduous application unto the public affairs, (wherein *Ipse se non habuit, postquam Respublica eum Gubernatorem habere cœpit*)[1] made him so much to neglect his own private interests, that an unjust steward[2] ran him £2,500 in debt before he was aware; for the payment whereof he was forced, many years before his decease, to sell the most of what he had left unto him in the country. Albeit, by the observable blessings of God upon the posterity of this liberal man, his children all of them came to fair estates, and lived in good fashion and credit. Moreover, he successively buried three wives; the first of which was the daughter and heiress of Mr. Forth, of Much Stambridge in Essex, by whom he had "wisdom with an inheritance;" and an excellent son. The second was the daughter of Mr. William Clopton, of London, who died with her child, within a very little while. The third was the daughter of the truly worshipful Sir John Tyndal, who made it her whole care to please, first God, and then her husband; and by whom he had four sons, which survived and honored their father.[3] And unto all these, the addition of the distempers, ever now and then raised in the country, procured unto him a very singular share of trouble; yea, so hard was the measure which he found even among pious men, in the temptations of a wilderness, that when the thunder and lightning had smitten a windmill whereof he was owner, some had such things in their heads as publicly to reproach this charitablest of men as if the voice of the Almighty had rebuked, I know not what oppression, which they judged him guilty of; which things I would not have mentioned, but that the instances may fortify the expectations of my best readers for such afflictions.

He that had been for his attainments, as they said of the blessed

8. "A bias towards the forbidden usage," from Ovid's *Amores* (3.4.17).
9. "Many are the afflictions of the righteous: But the Lord delivereth him of them all" (Psalm 34.19).
1. "He no longer belonged to himself, after the Republic had once made him her chief magistrate."

2. One James Luxford.
3. Winthrop married Mary Forth (1583–1615) in 1606. Much Stambridge is also known as Great Stambridge. They had six children but only one, John (b. 1606), survived his father. He married Thomasine Clopton (1583–1616) in 1615 and Margaret Tyndal in 1618.

Macarius,[4] a Παιδαριογερων, (an old man, while a young one,) and that had in his young days met with many of those ill days, whereof he could say, he had "little pleasure in them;" now found old age in its infirmities advancing earlier upon him, than it came upon his much longer-lived progenitors. While he was yet seven years off of that which we call "the grand climacterical,"[5] he felt the approaches of his dissolution; and finding he could say,

> *Non Habitus, non ipse Color, non Gressus Euntis,*
> *Non Species Eadem, quæ fuit ante, manet;*[6]

he then wrote this account of himself: "Age now comes upon me, and infirmities therewithal, which makes me apprehend, that the time of my departure out of this world is not far off.[7] However, our times are all in the Lord's hand, so as we need not trouble our thoughts how long or short they may be, but how we may be found faithful when we are called for." But at last when that year came, he took a cold which turned into a fever, whereof he lay sick about a month, and in that sickness, as it hath been observed, that there was allowed unto the serpent the "bruising of the heel;"[8] and accordingly at the heel or the close of our lives the old serpent will be nibbling more than ever in our lives before; and when the devil sees that we shall shortly be, "where the wicked cease from troubling," that wicked one will trouble us more than ever; so this eminent saint now underwent sharp conflicts with the tempter, whose wrath grew great, as the time to exert it grew short; and he was buffeted with the disconsolate thoughts of black and sore desertions, wherein he could use that sad representation of his own condition:

> *Nuper eram Judex; Jam Judicor; Ante Tribunal*
> *Subsistens paveo; Judicor ipse modo.*[9]

But it was not long before those clouds were dispelled, and he enjoyed in his holy soul the great consolations of God! While he thus lay ripening for heaven, he did out of obedience unto the ordinance of our Lord send for the Elders of the church to pray with him; yea, they and the whole church fasted as well as prayed for him; and in that fast the venerable Cotton[1] preached on Psalm 35.13–14: "When they were sick, I humbled myself with fasting; I

---

4. Macarius, a 4th-century Egyptian, had a reputation for having accomplished much while still young.
5. I.e., when he was 63; the "grand climacterial" would be age 70.
6. "I am not what I was in form or face, / In healthful color or in vigorous pace," from the *Elegies* of Maximianus (I.210–211).
7. "For I am now ready to be offered, and the time of my departure is at hand" (2 Timothy 4.6).

8. In his anger after the Fall, God tells the devil (in the form of a serpent): "And I will put enmity between thee and the woman, and between thy seed and her seed; it shall bruise thy head, and thou shalt bruise his heel" (Genesis 3.15).
9. "I once judged others, but now trembling stand/ Before a dread tribunal, to be judged."
1. John Cotton (1584–1652), Mather's grandfather and namesake.

behaved myself as though he had been my friend or brother; I bowed down heavily, as one that mourned for his mother." From whence I find him raising that observation, "The sickness of one that is to us as a friend, a brother, a mother, is a just occasion of deep humbling our souls with fasting and prayer;" and making this application:

Upon this occasion we are now to attend this duty for a governor, who has been to us as a friend in his counsel for all things, and help for our bodies by physic, for our estates by law, and of whom there was no fear of his becoming an enemy, like the friends of David:[2] a governor who has been unto us as a brother; not usurping authority over the church; often speaking his advice, and often contradicted, even by young men, and some of low degree; yet not replying, but offering satisfaction also when any supposed offenses have arisen; a governor who has been unto us as a mother, parent-like distributing his goods to brethren and neighbors at his first coming; and gently bearing our infirmities without taking notice of them.

Such a governor, after he had been more than ten several times by the people chosen their governor, was New England now to lose; who having, like Jacob, first left his council and blessing with his children gathered about his bedside;[3] and, like David, "served his generation by the will of God,"[4] he "gave up the ghost," and fell asleep on March 26, 1649. Having, like the dying Emperor Valentinian,[5] this above all his other victories for his triumphs, his overcoming of himself.

The words of Josephus[6] about Nehemiah, the governor of Israel, we will now use upon this governor of New England, as his

EPITAPH

Ἀνὴρ ἐγένετο χρηστὸσ τὴν φύσιν, καὶ δίκαιος,
Καὶ περὶ τοὺς ὁμοευνεῖς φιλοτιμότατος:
Μνημεῖον ἰώνιον ἀυτῳ καταλιπὼν τὰ τῶν
Ἱεροσολύμων Τείχη:

VIR FUIT INDOLE BONUS, AC JUSTUS:
ET POPULARIUM GLORIÆ AMANTISSIMUS:
QUIBUS ETERNUM RELIQUIT MONUMENTUM,
Novanglorum MŒNIA.[7]

1702

2. King David's friends and counselors joined Absalom in his revolt against his father (2 Samuel).
3. The aged patriarch Jacob was the second son of Isaac and Rebekah. In Genesis 49 he called his sons about him and told them what would befall them "in the last days" of the world.
4. "For David, after he had served his own generation by the will of God, fell on sleep, and was laid unto his fathers . . ." (Acts 13.36).

5. Christian Emperor of Rome (d. 375).
6. Josephus (37–100?) was a Jewish historian and author of *Antiquities of the Jews* where the following quotation appears (Book 11, Chap. 5).
7. "He was by nature a man at once benevolent and just: most zealous for the honor of his countrymen and to them he left an imperishable monument—the walls of New England." The Latin paraphrase of the Greek substitutes "New England" for "Jerusalem."

JONATHAN EDWARDS
1703–1758

Although it is certainly true that, as Perry Miller once put it, the true life of Jonathan Edwards is the life of a mind, the circumstances surrounding Edwards's career are not without their drama, and his rise to eminence and fall from power remain one of the most moving stories in American literature.

Edwards was born in East Windsor, Connecticut, a town not far from Hartford, the son of the Reverend Timothy Edwards and Esther Stoddard Edwards. There was little doubt from the beginning as to his career. Edwards's mother was the daughter of the Reverend Solomon Stoddard of Northampton, Massachusetts, one of the most influential and independent figures in the religious life of New England. Western Massachusetts clergymen were so anxious for his approval, that he was sometimes called the "Pope of the Connecticut Valley," and his gifted grandson, the only male child in a family of eleven children, was groomed to be his heir.

Edwards was a studious and dutiful child, and from an early age showed remarkable gifts of observation and exposition. When he was eleven he wrote an essay on the flying spider which is still very readable. Most of Edwards's early education he received at home. In 1716, when he was thirteen, Edwards was admitted to Yale College; he stayed on to read theology in New Haven for two years after his graduation in 1720. Like Benjamin Franklin, Edwards determined to perfect himself, and in one of his early notebooks he resolved "never to lose one moment of time, but to improve it in the most profitable way" he could. As a student he always rose at four in the morning, studied thirteen hours a day, and reserved part of each day for walking. It was a routine that Edwards varied little, even when, after spending two years in New York, he came to Northampton to assist his grandfather in his church. He married in 1727. In 1729 Solomon Stoddard died, and Edwards was named to succeed him. In the twenty-four years that Edwards lived in Northampton he managed to tend his duties as pastor of a growing congregation and deliver brilliant sermons, to write some of his most important books—concerned primarily with defining the nature of true religious experience—and watch his five children grow up. Until the mid-1740s his relations with the town seemed enviable.

In spite of the awesome—even imposing—quality of Jonathan Edwards's mind, all of his work is of a piece and, in essence, readily graspable. What Edwards was trying to do was to restore to his congregation and to his readers that original sense of religious commitment which he felt had been lost since the first days of the Puritan exodus, and he wanted to do this by transforming his congregation from mere believers who understood the logic of Christian doctrine to converted Christians who were genuinely moved by the principles of their belief. Edwards says that he read the work of the English philosopher John Locke (1632–1704) with more pleasure "than the greedy miser finds when gathering up handfuls of silver and gold, from some newly discovered treasure." For Locke confirmed Edwards's conviction that we must do more than comprehend religious ideas; we must be *moved* by them, we must know them experientially: the difference, as he says, is like that between reading the word "fire" and actually being burned. Basic to this newly felt belief is the recognition that nothing that man can do warrants his salvation—that man is totally dependent on God, and that he is saved solely by God's grace. In his progress as a Christian, Edwards says that he experienced several steps toward conversion, but that his true conversion came only when he had achieved a "full and constant sense of the absolute sovereignty of God, and a delight in that sovereignty." The word "delight" reminds us that Edwards is trying to inculcate and describe a religious feeling that approximates a physical sensation, recognizing always that supernatural feelings and natural ones are actually very different. In his patient and lucid prose Edwards became a master at the art of persuading his congregation that they could—and *must*—possess this intense awareness of their precarious condition. The exaltation which his parishioners felt when they experienced delight in God's sovereignty was the characteristic fervid emotion of religious revivalism.

For fifteen years, beginning in 1734, this spirit of revivalism transformed complacent believers all along the eastern seaboard. This period of new religious fervor has been called "The Great Awakening," and in the early years Edwards could do no wrong. His meetinghouse was filled with newly converted believers, and the details of the spiritual life of Edwards and his congregation were the subject of inquiry by Christian believers everywhere. But in his attempt to restore the church to the position of authority it held in the years of his grandfather's reign, Edwards went too far. When he named backsliders from his pulpit—including the children and parents of the best families in town—and tried to return to the old order of communion, permitting the sacrament to be taken only by those who had publicly declared themselves to be saved, the people of the town turned against him. Residents of the Connecticut Valley everywhere were tired of religious controversy, and the hysterical behavior of a few fanatics turned many against the spirit of revivalism. On June 22, 1750, by a vote of two hundred to twenty, Edwards was dismissed from his church and effectively silenced. Although the congregation had difficulty naming a successor to Edwards, they preferred to have no sermons rather than let Edwards preach. For the next seven years he served as missionary to the Indians in Stockbridge, Massachusetts, a town thirty-five miles to the west of Northampton. There he wrote his monumental treatises debating the doctrine of the freedom of the will and defining the nature of true virtue: "that consent, propensity and union of heart to Being in general, that is immediately exercised in a general good will." It was in Stockbridge that Edwards received, very reluctantly, a call to become president of the College of New Jersey (later called Princeton). Three months after his arrival in Princeton, Edwards died of smallpox, the result of the inoculation taken to prevent infection.

Personal Narrative[1]

I had a variety of concerns and exercises[2] about my soul from my childhood, but had two more remarkable seasons of awakening[3] before I met with that change by which I was brought to those new dispositions and that new sense of things that I have since had. The first time was when I was a boy, some years before I went to college, at a time of remarkable awakening in my father's congregation. I was then very much affected[4] for many months and concerned about the things of religion and my soul's salvation and was abundant in duties. I used to pray five times a day in secret, and to spend much time in religious talk with other boys and used to meet with them to pray together. I experienced I know not what kind of delight in religion. My mind was much engaged in it, and had much self-righteous pleasure; and it was my delight to abound in religious duties. I, with some of my schoolmates, joined together and built a booth in a swamp, in a very secret and retired place, for a place of prayer. And besides, I had particular secret places of my own in the woods, where I used to retire by myself, and used to be from time to time much affected. My affections seemed to be lively and easily moved, and I seemed to be in my element, when engaged in religious duties. And I am ready to think, many are deceived with such affections and such a kind of delight, as I then had in religion, and mistake it for grace.

But in process of time, my convictions and affections wore off; and I entirely lost all those affections and delights, and left off secret prayer, at least as to any constant performance of it, and returned like a dog to his vomit, and went on in ways of sin.[5]

Indeed, I was at some times very uneasy, especially towards the latter part of the time of my being at college.[6] 'Til it pleased God, in my last year at college, at a time when I was in the midst of many uneasy thoughts about the state of my soul, to seize me with a pleurisy;[7] in which he brought me nigh to the grave, and shook me over the pit of hell.

But yet, it was not long after my recovery before I fell again into my old ways of sin. But God would not suffer me to go on with any quietness; but I had great and violent inward struggles: 'til after

1. Because of Edwards's reference to an evening in January, 1739, this essay must have been written after that date. Edwards's reasons for writing it are not known, and it was not published in his lifetime. After his death his friend Samuel Hopkins had access to his manuscripts and prepared *The Life and Character of the Late Rev. Mr. Jonathan Edwards*, which was published in 1765. In that volume the *Personal Narrative* appeared in Section IV as a chapter entitled "An account of his conversion, experiences, and religious exercises, given

by himself."
2. Agitations.
3. I.e., spiritual awakenings, renewals.
4. Emotionally aroused, as opposed to merely understanding rationally the arguments for Christian faith.
5. "As a dog returneth to his vomit, so a fool returneth to his folly" (Proverbs 26.11).
6. Edwards was an undergraduate at Yale from 1716 to 1720 and a divinity student from 1720 to 1722.
7. A respiratory disorder.

many conflicts with wicked inclinations and repeated resolutions and bonds that I laid myself under by a kind of vows to God, I was brought wholly to break off all former wicked ways and all ways of known outward sin, and to apply myself to seek my salvation and practice the duties of religion, but without that kind of affection and delight that I had formerly experienced. My concern now wrought more by inward struggles and conflicts and self-reflections. I made seeking my salvation the main business of my life. But yet it seems to me I sought after a miserable manner, which has made me sometimes since to question whether ever it issued in that which was saving,[8] being ready to doubt, whether such miserable seeking was ever succeeded. But yet I was brought to seek salvation in a manner that I never was before. I felt a spirit to part with all things in the world for an interest in Christ. My concern continued and prevailed, with many exercising thoughts and inward struggles; but yet it never seemed to be proper to express my concern that I had, by the name of terror.

From my childhood up, my mind had been wont to be full of objections against the doctrine of God's sovereignty, in choosing whom He would to eternal life and rejecting whom He pleased, leaving them eternally to perish and be everlastingly tormented in hell. It used to appear like a horrible doctrine to me. But I remember the time very well when I seemed to be convinced, and fully satisfied, as to this sovereignty of God and His justice in thus eternally disposing of men according to His soverign pleasure. But never could give an account how or by what means I was thus convinced; not in the least imagining, in the time of it nor a long time after, that there was any extraordinary influence of God's spirit in it; but only that now I saw further, and my reason apprehended the justice and reasonableness of it. However, my mind rested in it; and it put an end to all those cavils and objections, that had 'til then abode with me, all the preceding part of my life. And there has been a wonderful alteration in my mind, with respect to the doctrine of God's sovereignty, from that day to this; so that I scarce ever have found so much as the rising of an objection against God's sovereignty, in the most absolute sense, in showing mercy to whom He will show mercy and hardening and eternally damning whom He will.[9] God's absolute sovereignty and justice, with respect to salvation and damnation, is what my mind seems to rest assured of, as much as of anything that I see with my eyes; at least it is so at times. But I have oftentimes since that first conviction had quite another kind of sense of God's sovereignty than I had then. I have often since not only had a conviction, but a delightful conviction. The doctrine of God's sovereignty has very often appeared an

---

8. I.e., truly redeeming, capable of making the penitent a "saint."
9. "Therefore hath he mercy on whom he will have mercy, and whom he will be hardeneth" (Romans 9.18).

exceeding pleasant, bright and sweet doctrine to me; and absolute sovereignty is what I love to ascribe to God. But my first conviction was not with this.

The first that I remember that ever I found anything of that sort of inward, sweet delight in God and divine things, that I have lived much in since, was on reading those words, 1 Timothy 1.17, "Now unto the king eternal, immortal, invisible, the only wise God, be honor and glory for ever and ever, Amen." As I read the words, there came into my soul, and was as it were diffused through it, a sense of the glory of the Divine Being, a new sense, quite different from anything I ever experienced before. Never any words of scripture seemed to me as these words did. I thought with myself, how excellent a being that was, and how happy I should be if I might enjoy that God and be rapt[1] up to God in Heaven, and be as it were swallowed up in Him. I kept saying, and as it were singing over these words of scripture to myself; and went to prayer to pray to God that I might enjoy Him; and prayed in a manner quite different from what I used to do, with a new sort of affection. But it never came into my thought that there was anything spiritual or of a saving nature in this.

From about that time I began to have a new kind of apprehensions and ideas of Christ, and the work of redemption, and the glorious way of salvation by Him. I had an inward, sweet sense of these things, that at times came into my heart; and my soul was led away in pleasant views and contemplations of them. And my mind was greatly engaged to spend my time in reading and meditating on Christ, and the beauty and excellency of His person, and the lovely way of salvation, by free grace in Him. I found no books so delightful to me as those that treated of these subjects. Those words Canticles 2.1, used to be abundantly with me: "I am the Rose of Sharon, the lily of the valleys." The words seemed to me, sweetly to represent the loveliness and beauty of Jesus Christ. And the whole book of Canticles[2] used to be pleasant to me; and I used to be much in reading it, about that time. And found, from time to time, an inward sweetness that used, as it were, to carry me away in my contemplations, in what I know not how to express otherwise, than by a calm, sweet abstraction of soul from all the concerns of this world, and a kind of vision, or fixed ideas and imaginations, of being alone in the mountains or some solitary wilderness, far from all mankind, sweetly conversing with Christ, and rapt and swallowed up in God. The sense I had of divine things would often of a sudden as it were, kindle up a sweet burning in my heart, an ardor of my soul, that I know not how to express.

Not long after I first began to experience these things, I gave an account to my father of some things that had passed in my mind. I was pretty much affected by the discourse we had together. And

1. Lifted.   2. I.e., Song of Solomon.

when the discourse was ended, I walked abroad alone, in a solitary place in my father's pasture, for contemplation. And as I was walking there, and looked up on the sky and clouds; there came into my mind a sweet sense of the glorious majesty and grace of God that I know not how to express. I seemed to see them both in a sweet conjunction, majesty and meekness joined together. It was a sweet and gentle, and holy majesty; and also a majestic meekness; an awful sweetness; a high, and great, and holy gentleness.

After this my sense of divine things gradually increased, and became more and more lively, and had more of that inward sweetness. The appearance of everything was altered: there seemed to be, as it were, a calm, sweet cast, or appearance of divine glory, in almost everything. God's excellency, His wisdom, His purity and love, seemed to appear in everything: in the sun, moon and stars; in the clouds, and blue sky; in the grass, flowers, trees; in the water, and all nature; which used greatly to fix my mind. I often used to sit and view the moon for a long time, and so in the daytime spent much time in viewing the clouds and sky to behold the sweet glory of God in these things, in the meantime, singing forth with a low voice my contemplations of the Creator and Redeemer. And scarce anything, among all the works of nature, was so sweet to me as thunder and lightning. Formerly, nothing had been so terrible to me. I used to be a person uncommonly terrified with thunder, and it used to strike me with terror when I saw a thunderstorm rising. But now, on the contrary, it rejoiced me. I felt God at the first appearance of a thunderstorm. And used to take the opportunity at such times to fix myself to view the clouds, and see the lightnings play, and hear the majestic and awful voice of God's thunder, which often times was exceeding entertaining, leading me to sweet contemplations of my great and glorious God. And while I viewed, used to spend my time, as it always seemed natural to me, to sing or chant forth my meditations, to speak my thoughts in soliloquies, and speak with a singing voice.

I felt then a great satisfaction as to my good estate.[3] But that did not content me. I had vehement longings of soul after God and Christ, and after more holiness, wherewith my heart seemed to be full and ready to break: which often brought to my mind the words of the psalmist, Psalm 119.28: "My soul breaketh for the longing it hath." I often felt a mourning and lamenting in my heart that I had not turned to God sooner, that I might have had more time to grow in grace. My mind was greatly fixed on divine things; I was almost perpetually in the contemplation of them. Spent most of my time in thinking of divine things, year after year. And used to spend abundance of my time in walking alone in the woods and solitary places for meditation, soliloquy and prayer, and converse with

3. Conditions of being.

God. And it was always my manner, at such times, to sing forth my contemplations. And was almost constantly in ejaculatory prayer, wherever I was. Prayer seemed to be natural to me, as the breath by which the inward burnings of my heart had vent.

The delights which I now felt in things of religion were of an exceeding different kind from those forementioned, that I had when I was a boy. They were totally of another kind; and what I then had no more notion or idea of, than one born blind has of pleasant and beautiful colors. They were of a more inward, pure, soul-animating and refreshing nature. Those former delights never reached the heart, and did not arise from any sight of the divine excellency of the things of God or any taste of the soul-satisfying and life-giving good there is in them.

My sense of divine things seemed gradually to increase, 'til I went to preach at New York, which was about a year and a half after they began. While I was there, I felt them, very sensibly,[4] in a much higher degree, than I had done before. My longings after God and holiness, were much increased. Pure and humble, holy and heavenly Christianity appeared exceeding amiable to me. I felt in me a burning desire to be in everything a complete Christian, and conformed to the blessed image of Christ, and that I might live in all things, according to the pure, sweet and blessed rules of the gospel. I had an eager thirsting after progress in these things. My longings after it put me upon pursuing and pressing after them. It was my continual strife day and night, and constant inquiry, how I should be more holy, and live more holily, and more becoming a child of God, and disciple of Christ. I sought an increase of grace and holiness, and that I might live an holy life with vastly more earnestness than ever I sought grace, before I had it. I used to be continually examining myself, and studying and contriving for likely ways and means how I should live holily with far greater diligence and earnestness than ever I pursued anything in my life; but with too great a dependence on my own strength, which afterwards proved a great damage to me. My experience had not then taught me, as it has done since, my extreme feebleness and impotence, every manner of way, and the innumerable and bottomless depths of secret corruption and deceit that there was in my heart. However, I went on with my eager pursuit after more holiness, and sweet conformity to Christ.

The Heaven I desired was a heaven of holiness, to be with God, and to spend my eternity in divine love, and holy communion with Christ. My mind was very much taken up with contemplations on heaven, and the enjoyments of those there, and living there in perfect holiness, humility and love. And it used at that time to appear a great part of the happiness of heaven that there the saints could

4. Edwards was in New York from August, 1722, to April, 1723, assisting at a Presbyterian church; "sensibly": feelingly.

express their love to Christ. It appeared to me a great clog and hindrance and burden to me that what I felt within I could not express to God and give vent to as I desired. The inward ardor of my soul seemed to be hindered and pent up, and could not freely flame out as it would. I used often to think how in heaven this sweet principle should freely and fully vent and express itself. Heaven appeared to me exceeding delightful as a world of love. It appeared to me that all happiness consisted in living in pure, humble, heavenly, divine love.

I remember the thoughts I used then to have of holiness. I remember I then said sometimes to myself, "I do certainly know that I love holiness such as the gospel prescribes." It appeared to me there was nothing in it but what was ravishingly lovely. It appeared to me to be the highest beauty and amiableness, above all other beauties, that it was a divine beauty, far purer than anything here upon earth; and that everything else, was like mire, filth and defilement in comparison of it.

Holiness, as I then wrote down some of my contemplations on it, appeared to me to be of a sweet, pleasant, charming, serene, calm nature. It seemed to me it brought an inexpressible purity, brightness, peacefulness and ravishment to the soul, and that it made the soul like a field or garden of God, with all manner of pleasant flowers; that is, all pleasant, delightful and undisturbed, enjoying a sweet calm, and the gently vivifying beams of the sun. The soul of a true Christian, as I then wrote my meditations, appeared like such a little white flower as we see in the spring of the year, low and humble on the ground, opening its bosom, to receive the pleasant beams of the sun's glory, rejoicing, as it were, in a calm rapture, diffusing around a sweet fragrancy, standing peacefully and lovingly in the midst of other flowers round about, all in like manner opening their bosoms, to drink in the light of the sun.

There was no part of creature holiness that I then, and at other times, had so great a sense of the loveliness of, as humility, brokenness of heart and poverty of spirit, and there was nothing that I had such a spirit to long for. My heart, as it were, panted after this to lie low before God, and in the dust; that I might be nothing, and that God might be all; that I might become as a little child.[5]

While I was there at New York, I sometimes was much affected with reflections on my past life, considering how late it was, before I began to be truly religious and how wickedly I had lived 'til then; and once so as to weep abundantly, and for a considerable time together.

On January 12, 1722–3 I made a solemn dedication of myself to God, and wrote it down; giving up myself, and all that I had to God; to be for the future in no respect my own; to act as one that

5. "Verily I say unto you, Whosoever shall not receive the kingdom of God as a little child, he shall not enter therein" (Mark 10.15).

had no right to himself, in any respect. And solemnly vowed to take God for my whole portion and felicity, looking on nothing else as any part of my happiness, nor acting as if it were: and His law for the constant rule of my obedience, engaging to fight with all my might against the world, the flesh and the devil, to the end of my life. But have reason to be infinitely humbled, when I consider, how much I have failed of answering my obligation.

I had then abundance of sweet religious conversation in the family where I lived, with Mr. John Smith, and his pious mother. My heart was knit in affection to those in whom were appearances of true piety, and I could bear the thoughts of no other companions but such as were holy, and the disciples of the blessed Jesus.

I had great longings for the advancement of Christ's kingdom in the world. My secret prayer used to be in great part taken up in praying for it. If I heard the least hint of anything that happened in any part of the world that appeared to me in some respect or other, to have a favorable aspect on the interest of Christ's kingdom, my soul eagerly catched at it; and it would much animate and refresh me. I used to be earnest to read public newsletters, mainly for that end, to see if I could not find some news favorable to the interest of religion in the world.

I very frequently used to retire into a solitary place, on the banks of Hudson's river, at some distance from the city, for contemplation on divine things and secret converse with God, and had many sweet hours there. Sometimes Mr. Smith and I walked there together to converse of the things of God, and our conversation used much to turn on the advancement of Christ's kingdom in the world, and the glorious things that God would accomplish for His church in the latter days.

I had then, and at other times, the greatest delight in the holy Scriptures, of any book whatsoever. Oftentimes in reading it, every word seemed to touch my heart. I felt an harmony between something in my heart, and those sweet and powerful words. I seemed often to see so much light exhibited by every sentence, and such a refreshing ravishing food communicated, that I could not get along in reading. Used oftentimes to dwell long on one sentence, to see the wonders contained in it; and yet almost every sentence seemed to be full of wonders.

I came away from New York in the month of April, 1723, and had a most bitter parting with Madam Smith and her son. My heart seemed to sink within me, at leaving the family and city, where I had enjoyed so many sweet and pleasant days. I went from New York to Weathersfield[6] by water. As I sailed away, I kept sight of the city as long as I could; and when I was out of sight of it, it would affect me much to look that way, with a kind of melancholy mixed with sweetness. However, that night after this sorrowful part-

---

6. Wethersfield, Connecticut, is very near his father's home in Windsor.

ing, I was greatly comforted in God at Westchester, where we went ashore to lodge, and had a pleasant time of it all the voyage to Saybrook.[7] It was sweet to me to think of meeting dear Christians in heaven, where we should never part more. At Saybrook we went ashore to lodge on Saturday, and there kept sabbath where I had a sweet and refreshing season, walking alone in the fields.

After I came home to Windsor, remained much in a like frame of my mind as I had been in at New York, but only sometimes felt my heart ready to sink with the thoughts of my friends at New York. And my refuge and support was in contemplations on the heavenly state, as I find in my diary of May 1, 1723. It was my comfort to think of that state where there is fulness of joy; where reigns heavenly, sweet, calm and delightful love, without alloy; where there are continually the dearest expressions of this love; where is the enjoyment of the persons loved without ever parting; where these persons that appear so lovely in this world will really be inexpressibly more lovely, and full of love to us. And how sweetly will the mutual lovers join together to sing the praises of God and the Lamb![8] How full will it fill us with joy to think that this enjoyment, these sweet exercises will never cease or come to an end, but will last to all eternity!

Continued much in the same frame in the general that I had been in at New York, 'til I went to New Haven to live there as tutor of the college, having some special seasons of uncommon sweetness; particularly once at Boston in a journey from Boston, walking out alone in the fields. After I went to New Haven, I sunk in religion, my mind being diverted from my eager and violent pursuits after holiness by some affairs that greatly perplexed and distracted my mind.

In September, 1725, was taken ill at New Haven, and, endeavoring to go home to Windsor, was so ill at the North Village that I could go no further, where I lay sick for about a quarter of a year. And in this sickness, God was pleased to visit me again with the sweet influences of His spirit. My mind was greatly engaged there on divine, pleasant contemplations and longings of soul. I observed that those who watched with me would often be looking out for the morning, and seemed to wish for it. Which brought to my mind those words of the psalmist, which my soul with sweetness made its own language: "My soul waitest for the Lord, more than they that watch for the morning, I say, more than they that watch for the morning."[9] And when the light of the morning came, and the beams of the sun came in at the windows, it refreshed my soul from one morning to another. It seemed to me to be some image of the sweet light of God's glory.

I remember, about that time, I used greatly to long for the con-

---

7. Westchester and Saybrook are in New York and Connecticut, respectively.

8. In Revelation the symbol of Christ.
9. Psalm 130.6.

version of some that I was concerned with. It seemed to me I could gladly honor them, and with delight be a servant to them, and lie at their feet, if they were but truly holy.

But sometime after this, I was again greatly diverted in my mind with some temporal concerns that exceedingly took up my thoughts, greatly to the wounding of my soul, and went on through various exercises, that it would be tedious to relate, that gave me much more experience of my own heart than ever I had before.

Since I came to this town,[1] I have often had sweet complacency in God, in views of His glorious perfections and the excellency of Jesus Christ. God has appeared to me a glorious and lovely Being, chiefly on the account of His holiness. The holiness of God has always appeared to me the most lovely of all His attributes. The doctrines of God's absolute sovereignty and free grace in showing mercy to whom He would show mercy, and man's absolute dependence on the operations of God's Holy Spirit, have very often appeared to me as sweet and glorious doctrines. These doctrines have been much my delight. God's sovereignty has ever appeared to me as great part of His glory. It has often been sweet to me to go to God and adore Him as a sovereign God, and ask sovereign mercy of Him.

I have loved the doctrines of the gospel; they have been to my soul like green pastures. The gospel has seemed to me to be the richest treasure, the treasure that I have most desired and longed that it might dwell richly in me. The way of salvation by Christ has appeared in a general way glorious and excellent, and most pleasant and beautiful. It has often seemed to me that it would in a great measure spoil heaven to receive it in any other way. That text has often been affecting and delightful to me, Isaiah 32.2: "A man shall be an hiding place from the wind, and a covert from the tempest, etc."

It has often appeared sweet to me to be united to Christ; to have Him for my head, and to be a member of His body; and also to have Christ for my teacher and prophet. I very often think with sweetness and longings and pantings of soul, of being a little child, taking hold of Christ, to be led by Him through the wilderness of this world. That text, Matthew 18.3 at the beginning, has often been sweet to me, "Except ye be converted, and become as little children, etc." I love to think of coming to Christ, to receive salvation of Him, poor in spirit, and quite empty of self; humbly exalting Him alone; cut entirely off from my own root, and to grow into and out of Christ; to have God in Christ to be all in all; and to live by faith on the Son of God, a life of humble, unfeigned confidence in Him. That Scripture has often been sweet to me, Psalm 115.1: "Not unto us, O Lord, not unto us, but unto Thy name give

1. Northampton, Massachusetts, where, in 1726, Edwards came to help his grandfather in conducting the affairs of his parish; "complacency": contentment.

glory, for Thy mercy, and for Thy truth's sake." And those words of Christ, Luke 10.21: "In that hour Jesus rejoiced in spirit, and said, I thank thee, O Father, Lord of heaven and earth, that Thou hast hid these things from the wise and prudent, and hast revealed them unto babes: Even so Father, for so it seemed good in Thy sight." That sovereignty of God that Christ rejoiced in seemed to me to be worthy to be rejoiced in, and that rejoicing of Christ seemed to me to show the excellency of Christ, and the spirit that He was of.

Sometimes only mentioning a single word causes my heart to burn within me, or only seeing the name of Christ or the name of some attribute of God. And God has appeared glorious to me on account of the Trinity. It has made me have exalting thoughts of God, that He subsists in three persons: Father, Son, and Holy Ghost.

The sweetest joys and delights I have experienced have not been those that have arisen from a hope of my own good estate,[2] but in a direct view of the glorious things of the gospel. When I enjoy this sweetness it seems to carry me above the thoughts of my own safe estate. It seems at such times a loss that I cannot bear, to take off my eye from the glorious, pleasant object I behold without me, to turn my eye in upon myself, and my own good estate.

My heart has been much on the advancement of Christ's kingdom in the world. The histories of the past advancement of Christ's kingdom have been sweet to me. When I have read histories of past ages, the pleasantest thing in all my reading has been to read of the kingdom of Christ being promoted. And when I have expected in my reading to come to any such thing, I have lotted[3] upon it all the way as I read. And my mind has been much entertained and delighted with the Scripture promises and prophecies of the future glorious advancement of Christ's kingdom on earth.

I have sometimes had a sense of the excellent fullness of Christ, and His meetness and suitableness as a Savior; whereby He has appeared to me, far above all, the chief of ten thousands.[4] And His blood and atonement has appeared sweet, and His righteousness sweet; which is always accompanied with an ardency of spirit, and inward strugglings and breathings and groanings, that cannot be uttered, to be emptied of myself, and swallowed up in Christ.

Once, as I rid out into the woods for my health, Anno[5] 1737, and having lit from my horse in a retired place, as my manner commonly has been, to walk for divine contemplation and prayer, I had a view, that for me was extraordinary, of the glory of the Son of God, as mediator between God and man, and His wonderful, great, full, pure and sweet grace and love, and meek and gentle condescen-

---

2. Condition of being.
3. Rejoiced.
4. "My beloved is white and ruddy, the chiefest among ten thousand" (Song of Solomon 5.10).
5. In the year.

sion. This grace, that appeared to me so calm and sweet, appeared great above the heavens. The person of Christ appeared ineffably excellent, with an excellency great enough to swallow up all thought and conception, which continued, as near as I can judge, about an hour, which kept me, the bigger part of the time, in a flood of tears, and weeping aloud. I felt withal an ardency of soul to be, what I know not otherwise how to express, than to be emptied and annihilated; to lie in the dust, and to be full of Christ alone; to love Him with a holy and pure love; to trust in Him; to live upon Him; to serve and follow Him, and to be totally wrapt up in the fullness of Christ; and to be perfectly sanctified and made pure with a divine and heavenly purity. I have several other times had views very much of the same nature and that have had the same effects.

I have many times had a sense of the glory of the third person in the Trinity in His office of sanctifier; in His holy operations communicating divine light and life to the soul. God in the communications of His Holy Spirit has appeared as an infinite fountain of divine glory and sweetness, being full and sufficient to fill and satisfy the soul, pouring forth itself in sweet communications, like the sun in its glory, sweetly and pleasantly diffusing light and life.

I have sometimes had an affecting sense of the excellency of the word of God, as a word of life; as the light of life; a sweet, excellent, life-giving word, accompanied with a thirsting after that word, that it might dwell richly in my heart.

I have often, since I lived in this town, had very affecting views of my own sinfulness and vileness; very frequently so as to hold me in a kind of loud weeping, sometimes for a considerable time together, so that I have often been forced to shut myself up.[6] I have had a vastly greater sense of my wickedness, and the badness of my heart, since my conversion, than ever I had before. It has often appeared to me, that if God should mark iniquity against me, I should appear the very worst of all mankind, of all that have been since the beginning of the world of this time, and that I should have by far the lowest place in hell. When others that have come to talk with me about their soul concerns have expressed the sense they have had of their own wickedness by saying that it seemed to them that they were as bad as the devil himself, I thought their expressions seemed exceeding faint and feeble to represent my wickedness. I thought I should wonder that they should content themselves with such expressions as these, if I had any reason to imagine that their sin bore any proportion to mine. It seemed to me I should wonder at myself if I should express my wickedness in such feeble terms as they did.

My wickedness, as I am in myself, has long appeared to me perfectly ineffable and infinitely swallowing up all thought and imagination, like an infinite deluge or infinite mountains over my head. I

6. I.e., retire to his study.

know not how to express better what my sins appear to me to be
than by heaping infinite upon infinite, and multiplying infinite by
infinite. I go about very often, for this many years, with these
expressions in my mind and in my mouth, "Infinite upon infinite.
Infinite upon infinite!" When I look into my heart and take a view
of my wickedness, it looks like an abyss infinitely deeper than hell.
And it appears to me that were it not for free grace, exalted and
raised up to the infinite height of all the fullness and glory of the
great Jehovah,[7] and the arm of His power and grace stretched forth,
in all the majesty of His power and in all the glory of His sovereignty, I should appear sunk down in my sins infinitely below hell
itself, far beyond sight of everything but the piercing eye of God's
grace, that can pierce even down to such a depth and to the bottom
of such an abyss.

And yet I be not in the least inclined to think that I have a
greater conviction of sin than ordinary. It seems to me my conviction of sin is exceeding small and faint. It appears to me enough
to amaze me that I have no more sense of my sin. I know certainly
that I have very little sense of my sinfulness. That my sins appear
to me so great don't seem to me to be because I have so much more
conviction of sin than other Christians, but because I am so much
worse and have so much more wickedness to be convinced of.
When I have had these turns of weeping and crying for my sins, I
thought I knew in the time of it that my repentance was nothing to
my sin.

I have greatly longed of late for a broken heart and to lie low
before God. And when I ask for humility of God, I can't bear the
thoughts of being no more humble than other Christians. It seems
to me that though their degrees of humility may be suitable
for them, yet it would be a vile self-exaltation in me not to be the
lowest in humility of all mankind. Others speak of their longing to
be humbled to the dust. Though that may be a proper expression
for them I always think for myself that I ought to be humbled
down below hell. 'Tis an expression that it has long been natural for
me to use in prayer to God. I ought to lie infinitely low before God.

It is affecting to me to think how ignorant I was, when I was a
young Christian, of the bottomless, infinite depths of wickedness,
pride, hypocrisy and deceit left in my heart.

I have vastly a greater sense of my universal, exceeding dependence
on God's grace and strength and mere good pleasure, of late, than I
used formerly to have, and have experienced more of an abhorrence
of my own righteousness. The thought of any comfort or joy, arising in me, on any consideration or reflection on my own amiableness, or any of my performances or experiences, or any goodness of
heart or life is nauseous and detestable to me. And yet I am greatly
afflicted with a proud and self-righteous spirit, much more sensibly

7. The God of the Old Testament.

than I used to be formerly. I see that serpent rising and putting forth its head, continually, everywhere, all around me.

Though it seems to me that in some respects I was a far better Christian for two or three years after my first conversion than I am now, and lived in a more constant delight and pleasure, yet of late years I have had a more full and constant sense of the absolute sovereignty of God and a delight in that sovereignty, and have had more of a sense of the glory of Christ as a mediator as revealed in the gospel. On one Saturday night in particular, had a particular discovery of the excellency of the gospel of Christ, above all other doctrines, so that I could not but say to myself, "This is my chosen light, my chosen doctrine," and of Christ, "This is my chosen prophet." It appeared to me to be sweet beyond all expression to follow Christ and to be taught and enlightened and instructed by Him, to learn of Him, and live to Him.

Another Saturday night, January, 1738–9, had such a sense how sweet and blessed a thing it was to walk in the way of duty, to do that which was right and meet to be done and agreeable to the holy mind of God, that it caused me to break forth into a kind of a loud weeping, which held me some time, so that I was forced to shut myself up, and fasten the doors. I could not but as it were cry out, "How happy are they which do that which is right in the sight of God! They are blessed indeed, they are the happy ones!" I had at the same time, a very affecting sense how meet and suitable it was that God should govern the world, and order all things according to His own pleasure, and I rejoiced in it, and God reigned, and that His will was done.

c. 1740   1765

A Divine and Supernatural Light[1]

IMMEDIATELY IMPARTED TO THE SOUL BY THE SPIRIT OF GOD, SHOWN TO BE BOTH A SCRIPTURAL AND RATIONAL DOCTRINE

Matthew 16.17

And Jesus answered and said unto him, Blessed art thou, Simon Bar-jona;[2] for flesh and blood hath not revealed it unto thee, but my Father which is in heaven.

Christ addresses these words to Peter upon occasion of his professing his faith in Him as the Son of God. Our Lord was inquiring of His disciples, whom men said that He was; not that He needed to be informed, but only to introduce and give occasion to what follows. They answer that some said He was John the Baptist, and some Elias, and others Jeremias, or one of the prophets.[3] When

1. Edwards delivered this sermon in Northampton, Massachusetts, in 1733; it was published the following year at the request of his congregation. The text used is from Sereno E. Dwight, ed., *The Works of Jonathan Edwards*, Vol. VI (New York, 1829–30).
2. The apostle Peter (Simon, son of Jona).
3. Matthew 16.14. Elias is the name used in the New Testament for the prophet Elijah.

they had thus given an account whom others said that He was, Christ asks them, whom they said that He was? Simon Peter, whom we find always zealous and forward, was the first to answer: he readily replied to the question, Thou art Christ the Son of the living God.

Upon this occasion, Christ says as He does to him and of him in the text: in which we may observe.

1. That Peter is pronounced blessed on this account.—Blessed art thou—"Thou art an happy man, that thou art not ignorant of this, that I am Christ, the Son of the living God. Thou art distinguishingly happy. Others are blinded, and have dark and deluded apprehensions, as you have now given an account, some thinking that I am Elias, and some that I am Jeremias, and some one thing, and some another: but none of them thinking right, all of them are misled. Happy art thou, that art so distinguished as to know the truth in this matter."

2. The evidence of this his happiness declared, viz., That God, and He only, had revealed it to him. This is an evidence of his being blessed.

First. As it shows how peculiarly favored he was of God above others; q.d.,[4] "How highly favored art thou, that others, wise and great men, the scribes, Pharisees,[5] and rulers, and the nation in general, are left in darkness, to follow their own misguided apprehensions; and that thou shouldst be singled out, as it were, by name, that my heavenly Father should thus set His love on thee, Simon Bar-jona.—This argues thee blessed, that thou shouldst thus be the object of God's distinguishing love."

Secondly. It evidences his blessedness also, as it intimates that this knowledge is above any that flesh and blood can reveal. "This is such knowledge as only my Father which is in heaven can give. It is too high and excellent to be communicated by such means as other knowledge is. Thou art blessed, that thou knowest what God alone can teach thee."

The original of this knowledge is here declared, both negatively and positively. Positively, as God is here delcared the author of it. Negatively, as it is declared, that flesh and blood had not revealed it. God is the author of all knowledge and understanding whatsoever. He is the author of all moral prudence, and of the skill that men have in their secular business. Thus it is said of all in Israel that were wise-hearted and skilled in embroidering, that God had filled them with the spirit of wisdom. Exodus 28.3.[6]

God is the author of such knowledge; yet so that flesh and blood reveals it. Mortal men are capable of imparting the knowledge of hu-

---

4. *Quasi dicat,* "as if he should say."
5. The Pharisees were a sect hostile to Jesus and known for their arrogance and pride (Matthew 9.9–13); "scribes": interpreters of the Jewish law.

6. This passage from Exodus refers to God's command to the people of Israel to make proper garments for Aaron's priesthood.

man arts and sciences, and skill in temporal affairs. God is the author of such knowledge by those means: flesh and blood is employed as the mediate or second cause of it; He conveys it by the power and influence of natural means. But this spiritual knowledge, spoken of in the text, is what God is the author of, and none else: He reveals it, and flesh and blood reveals it not. He imparts this knowledge immediately, not making use of any intermediate natural causes, as He does in other knowledge.

What had passed in the preceding discourse naturally occasioned Christ to observe this; because the disciples had been telling how others did not know Him, but were generally mistaken about him, divided and confounded in their opinions of Him: but Peter had declared his assured faith, that He was the Son of God. Now it was natural to observe how it was not flesh and blood that had revealed it to him, but God; for if this knowledge were dependent on natural causes or means, how came it to pass that they, a company of poor fishermen, illiterate men, and persons of low education, attained to the knowledge of the truth, while the Scribes and Pharisees, men of vastly higher advantages, and greater knowledge and sagacity, in other matters, remained in ignorance? This could be owing only to the gracious distinguishing influence and revelation of the Spirit of God. Hence, what I would make the subject of my present discourse from these words, is this

Doctrine

That there is such a thing as a spiritual and divine light, immediately imparted to the soul by God, of a different nature from any that is obtained by natural means. And on this subject I would,

I. Show what this divine light is.

II. How it is given immediately by God, and not obtained by natural means.

III. Show the truth of the doctrine.

And then conclude with a brief improvement.[7]

I. I would show what this spiritual and divine light is. And in order to it would show,

First, In a few things, what it is not. And here,

1. Those convictions that natural men may have of their sin and misery, is not this spiritual and divine light. Men, in a natural condition, may have convictions of the guilt that lies upon them, and of the anger of God, and their danger of divine vengeance. Such convictions are from the light of truth. That some sinners have a greater conviction of their guilt and misery than others is because some have more light, or more of an apprehension of truth than

---

7. Literally, turning something to profit; here used in the sense of the lesson to be learned.

others. And this light and conviction may be from the Spirit of God; the Spirit convinces men of sin; but yet nature is much more concerned in it than in the communication of that spiritual and divine light that is spoken of in the doctrine; it is from the Spirit of God only as assisting natural principles, and not as infusing any new principles. Common grace differs from special in that it influences only by assisting of nature, and not by imparting grace, or bestowing anything above nature. The light that is obtained is wholly natural, or of no superior kind to what mere nature attains to, though more of that kind be obtained than would be obtained if men were left wholly to themselves; or, in other words, common grace only assists the faculties of the soul to do that more fully which they do by nature, as natural conscience or reason will by mere nature make a man sensible of guilt, and will accuse and condemn him when he has done amiss. Conscience is a principle natural to men; and the work that it doth naturally, or of itself, is to give an apprehension of right and wrong, and to suggest to the mind the relation that there is between right and wrong and a retribution. The Spirit of God, in those convictions which unregenerate men sometimes have, assists conscience to do this work in a further degree than it would do if they were left to themselves. He helps it against those things that tend to stupify it, and obstruct its exercise. But in the renewing and sanctifying work of the Holy Ghost, those things are wrought in the soul that are above nature, and of which there is nothing of the like kind in the soul by nature; and they are caused to exist in the soul habitually, and according to such a stated constitution or law, that lays such a foundation for exercises in a continued course, as is called a principle of nature. Not only are remaining principles assisted to do their work more freely and fully, but those principles are restored that were utterly destroyed by the fall; and the mind thenceforward habitually exerts those acts that the dominion of sin had made it as wholly destitute of as a dead body is of vital acts.

The Spirit of God acts in a very different manner in the one case, from what He doth in the other. He may, indeed, act upon the mind of a natural man, but He acts in the mind of a saint[8] as an indwelling vital principle. He acts upon the mind of an unregenerate[9] person as an extrinsic occasional agent; for, in acting upon them. He doth not unite himself to them: for, notwithstanding all His influences that they may possess, they are still sensual, having not the Spirit. Jude 19.[1] But He unites himself with the mind of a saint, takes him for His temple, actuates and influences him as a new supernatural principle of life and action. There is this

8. Here, a living Christian who has passed from mere understanding of Christ's doctrine to heartfelt commitment; such people were often called "visible saints."
9. One who is not yet saved.
1. "These be they who separate themselves, sensual, having not the Spirit."

difference, that the Spirit of God, in acting in the soul of a godly man, exerts and communicates Himself there in His own proper nature. Holiness is the proper nature of the Spirit of God. The Holy Spirit operates in the minds of the godly, by uniting Himself to them, and living in them, and exerting His own nature in the exercise of their faculties. The Spirit of God may act upon a creature, and yet not in acting communicate Himself. The Spirit of God may act upon inanimate creatures, as, the Spirit moved upon the face of the waters,[2] in the beginning of the creation; so the Spirit of God may act upon the minds of men many ways, and communicate Himself no more than when He acts upon an inanimate creature. For instance, He may excite thoughts in them, may assist their natural reason and understanding, or may assist other natural principles, and this without any union with the soul, but may act, as it were, upon an external object. But as He acts in His holy influences and spiritual operations, He acts in a way of peculiar communication of Himself; so that the subject is thence denominated spiritual.

2. This spiritual and divine light does not consist in any impression made upon the imagination. It is no impression upon the mind, as though one saw anything with the bodily eyes. It is no imagination or idea of an outward light or glory, or any beauty of form or countenance, or a visible luster or brightness of any object. The imagination may be strongly impressed with such things; but this is not spiritual light. Indeed when the mind has a lively discovery of spiritual things, and is greatly affected with the power of divine light, it may, and probably very commonly doth, much affect the imagination; so that impressions of an outward beauty or brightness may accompany those spiritual discoveries. But spiritual light is not that impression upon the imagination, but an exceedingly different thing. Natural men may have lively impressions on their imaginations; and we cannot determine but that the devil, who transforms himself into an angel of light, may cause imaginations of an outward beauty, or visible glory, and of sounds and speeches, and other such things; but these are things of a vastly inferior nature to spiritual light.

3. This spiritual light is not the suggesting of any new truths or propositions not contained in the word of God. This suggesting of new truths or doctrines to the mind, independent of any antecedent revelations of those propositions, either in word or writing, is inspiration; such as the prophets and apostles had, and such as some enthusiasts[3] pretend to. But this spiritual light that I am speaking of, is quite a different thing from inspiration. It reveals no new doctrine, it suggests no new proposition to the mind, it teaches no new thing of God, or Christ, or another world, not taught in the Bible,

2. Genesis 1.2.
3. People who erroneously claim to be inspired by the spirit of God.

but only gives a due apprehension of those things that are taught in the word of God.

4. It is not every affecting view that men have of religious things that is this spiritual and divine light. Men by mere principles of nature are capable of being affected with things that have a special relation to religion as well as other things. A person by mere nature, for instance, may be liable to be affected with the story of Jesus Christ, and the sufferings he underwent, as well as by any other tragical story. He may be the more affected with it from the interest he conceives mankind to have in it. Yea, he may be affected with it without believing it; as well as a man may be affected with what he reads in a romance, or sees acted in a stage play. He may be affected with a lively and eloquent description of many pleasant things that attend the state of the blessed in heaven, as well as his imagination be entertained by a romantic[4] description of the pleasantness of fairyland, or the like. And a common belief of the truth of such things, from education or otherwise, may help forward their affection. We read in Scripture of many that were greatly affected with things of a religious nature, who yet are there represented as wholly graceless, and many of them very ill[5] men. A person therefore may have affecting views of the things of religion, and yet be very destitute of spiritual light. Flesh and blood may be the author of this; one man may give another an affecting view of divine things with but common assistance; but God alone can give a spiritual discovery of them.—But I proceed to show,

Secondly, Positively what this spiritual and divine light is.

And it may be thus described: A true sense of the divine excellency of the things revealed in the word of God, and a conviction of the truth and reality of them thence arising. This spiritual light primarily consists in the former of these, viz., A real sense and apprehension of the divine excellency of things revealed in the word of God. A spiritual and saving conviction of the truth and reality of these things, arises from such a sight of their divine excellency and glory; so that this conviction of their truth is an effect and natural consequence of this sight of their divine glory. There is therefore in this spiritual light,

1. A true sense of the divine and superlative excellency of the things of religion; a real sense of the excellency of God and Jesus Christ, and of the work of redemption, and the ways and works of God revealed in the gospel. There is a divine and superlative glory in these things; an excellency that is of a vastly higher kind, and more sublime nature than in other things; a glory greatly distinguishing them from all that is earthly and temporal. He that is spiritually enlightened truly apprehends and sees it, or has a sense of it. He does not merely rationally believe that God is glorious, but he has a sense of the gloriousness of God in his heart. There is not only a

4. Fanciful, imaginary.   5. I.e., evil.

rational belief that God is holy, and that holiness is a good thing, but there is a sense of the loveliness of God's holiness. There is not only a speculatively judging that God is gracious, but a sense how amiable God is on account of the beauty of this divine attribute.

There is a twofold knowledge of good of which God has made the mind of man capable. The first, that which is merely notional; as when a person only speculatively judges that anything is, which by the agreement of mankind, is called good or excellent, viz., that which is most to general advantage, and between which and a reward there is a suitableness, and the like. And the other is, that which consists in the sense of the heart; as when the heart is sensible[6] of pleasure and delight in the presence of the idea of it. In the former is exercised merely the speculative faculty, or the understanding, in distinction from the will or disposition of the soul. In the latter, the will, or inclination, or heart, are mainly concerned.

Thus there is a difference between having an opinion, that God is holy and gracious, and having a sense of the loveliness and beauty of that holiness and grace. There is a difference between having a rational judgment that honey is sweet, and having a sense of its sweetness. A man may have the former, that knows not how honey tastes; but a man cannot have the latter unless he has an idea of the taste of honey in his mind. So there is a difference between believing that a person is beautiful, and having a sense of his beauty. The former may be obtained by hearsay, but the latter only by seeing the countenance. When the heart is sensible of the beauty and amiableness of a thing, it necessarily feels pleasure in the apprehension. It is implied in a person's being heartily sensible of the loveliness of a thing, that the idea of it is pleasant to his soul; which is a far different thing from having a rational opinion that is is excellent.

2. There arises from this sense of the divine excellency of things contained in the word of God, a conviction of the truth and reality of them; and that, either indirectly or directly.

First, Indirectly, and that two ways:

1. As the prejudices of the heart, against the truth of divine things, are hereby removed; so that the mind becomes susceptive of the due force of rational arguments for their truth. The mind of man is naturally full of prejudices against divine truth. It is full of enmity against the doctrines of the gospel; which is a disadvantage to those arguments that prove their truth, and causes them to lose their force upon the mind. But when a person has discovered to him the divine excellency of Christian doctrines, this destroys the enmity, removes those prejudices, sanctifies the reason, and causes it to lie open to the force of arguments for their truth.

Hence was the different effect that Christ's miracles had to convince the disciples, from what they had to convince the Scribes and

6. Aware.

Pharisees. Not that they had a stronger reason, or had their reason more improved; but their reason was sanctified, and those blinding prejudices, that the Scribes and Pharisees were under, were removed by the sense they had of the excellency of Christ, and his doctrine.

It not only removes the hinderances of reason, but positively helps reason. It makes even the speculative notions more lively. It engages the attention of the mind, with more fixedness and intenseness to that kind of objects; which causes it to have a clearer view of them, and enables it more clearly to see their mutual relations, and occasions it to take more notice of them. The ideas themselves that otherwise are dim and obscure are by this means impressed with the greater strength, and have a light cast upon them, so that the mind can better judge of them. As he that beholds objects on the face of the earth, when the light of the sun is cast upon them, is under greater advantage to discern them in their true forms and natural relations, than he that sees them in a dim twilight.

The mind, being sensible of the excellency of divine objects, dwells upon them with delight; and the powers of the soul are more awakened and enlivened to employ themselves in the contemplation of them, and exert themselves more fully and much more to the purpose. The beauty of the objects draws on the faculties, and draws forth their exercises; so that reason itself is under far greater advantages for its proper and free exercises, and to attain its proper end, free of darkness and delusion. But,

Secondly, A true sense of the divine excellency of the things of God's word doth more directly and immediately convince us of their truth; and that because the excellency of these things is so superlative. There is a beauty in them so divine and godlike, that it greatly and evidently distinguishes them from things merely human, or that of which men are the inventors and authors; a glory so high and great, that when clearly seen, commands assent to their divine reality. When there is an actual and lively discovery of this beauty and excellency, it will not allow of any such thought as that it is the fruit of men's invention. This is a kind of intuitive and immediate evidence. They believe the doctrines of God's word to be divine, because they see a divine, and transcendent, and most evidently distinguishing glory in them; such a glory as, if clearly seen, does not leave room to doubt of their being of God, and not of men.

Such a conviction of the truths of religion as this, arising from a sense of their divine excellency, is included in saving faith. And this original of it is that by which it is most essentially distinguished from that common assent, of which unregenerate men are capable.

II. I proceed now to the second thing proposed, viz., to show how this light is immediately given by God, and not obtained by natural means. And here,

1. It is not intended that the natural faculties are not used in it. They are the subject of this light: and in such a manner, that they are not merely passive, but active in it. God, in letting in this light into the soul, deals with man according to his nature, and makes use of his rational faculties. But yet this light is not the less immediately from God for that; the faculties are made use of as the subject, and not as the cause. As the use we make of our eyes in beholding various objects, when the sun arises, is not the cause of the light that discovers those objects to us.

2. It is not intended that outward means have no concern in this affair. It is not in this affair, as in inspiration, where new truths are suggested; for, by this light is given only a due apprehension of the same truths that are revealed in the word of God, and therefore it is not given without the word. The gospel is employed in this affair. This light is the "light of the glorious gospel of Christ" (2 Corinthians 4.3–4).[7] The gospel is as a glass, by which this light is conveyed to us (1 Corinthians 13.12): "Now we see through a glass."[8] But,

3. When it is said that this light is given immediately by God, and not obtained by natural means, hereby is intended that it is given by God without making use of any means that operate by their own power or natural force. God makes use of means; but it is not as mediate causes to produce this effect. There are not truly any second causes of it; but it is produced by God immediately. The word of God is no proper cause of this effect, but is made use of only to convey to the mind the subject matter of this saving instruction: And this indeed it doth convey to us by natural force or influence. It conveys to our minds these doctrines; it is the cause of a notion of them in our heads, but not of the sense of their divine excellency in our hearts. Indeed a person cannot have spiritual light without the word. But that does not argue, that the word properly causes that light. The mind cannot see the excellency of any doctrine, unless that doctrine be first in the mind; but seeing the excellency of the doctrine may be immediately from the Spirit of God; though the conveying of the doctrine, or proposition, itself, may be by the word. So that the notions which are the subject matter of this light are conveyed to the mind by the word of God; but that due sense of the heart, wherein this light formally consists, is immediately by the Spirit of God. As, for instance, the notion that there is a Christ, and that Christ is holy and gracious, is conveyed to the mind by the word of God. But the sense of the excellency of Christ, by reason of that holiness and grace, is, nevertheless, immediately the work of the Holy Spirit. I come now,

---

7. "But if our gospel be hid, it is hid to them that are lost: In whom the god of this world hath blinded the minds of them which believe not, lest the light of the glorious gospel of Christ, who is the image of God, should shine unto them."

8. "For now we see through a glass, darkly; but then face to face."

III. To show the truth of the doctrine; that is, to show that there is such a thing as that spiritual light that has been described, thus immediately let into the mind by God. And here I would show, briefly, that this doctrine is both scriptural and rational.

First, It is scriptural. My text is not only full to the purpose, but it is a doctrine with which the Scripture abounds. We are there abundantly taught, that the saints differ from the ungodly in this; that they have the knowledge of God, and a sight of God, and of Jesus Christ. I shall mention but few texts out of many: 1 John 3.6: "Whosoever sinneth, hath not seen him, nor known him." 3 John 11: "He that doeth good, is of God: but he that doeth evil, hath not seen God." John 14.19: "The world seeth me no more; but ye see me." John 17.3: "And this is eternal life, that they might know thee, the only true God, and Jesus Christ whom thou hast sent." This knowledge, or sight, of God and Christ cannot be a mere speculative knowledge, because it is spoken of as that wherein they differ from the ungodly. And by these scriptures, it must not only be a different knowledge in degree and circumstances, and different in its effects, but it must be entirely different in nature and kind.

And this light and knowledge is always spoken of as immediately given of God; Matthew 11.25–27: "At that time, Jesus answered and said, I thank thee, O Father, Lord of heaven and earth, because thou hast hid these things from the wise and prudent, and hast revealed them unto babes. Even so, Father, for so it seemed good in thy sight. All things are delivered unto me of my Father: and no man knoweth the Father, save the Son, and he to whomsoever the Son will reveal him." Here this effect is ascribed exclusively to the arbitrary operation and gift of God bestowing this knowledge on whom He will, and distinguishing those with it who have the least natural advantage or means for knowledge, even babes, when it is denied to the wise and prudent. And imparting this knowledge is here appropriated to the Son of God, as His sole prerogative. And again, 2 Corinthians 4.6: "For God, who commanded the light to shine out of darkness, hath shined in our hearts, to give the light of the knowledge of the glory of God, in the face of Jesus Christ." This plainly shows, that there is a discovery of the divine superlative glory and excellency of God and Christ, peculiar to the saints: and, also, that it is as immediately from God, as light from the sun, and that it is the immediate effect of His power and will. For it is compared to God's creating the light by his powerful word in the beginning of the creation; and is said to be by the Spirit of the Lord, in the 18th verse of the preceding chapter. God is spoken of as giving the knowledge of Christ in conversion, as of what before was hidden and unseen; Galatians 1.15–16: "But when it pleased God, who separated me from my mother's womb, and called me by his grace, to reveal his son in me." The scripture also speaks plainly of such a knowledge of the word of God, as has been described as the immediate gift of God; Psalm 119.18: "Open thou mine eyes, that I may behold wondrous things out of thy law." What could the psalmist mean, when he begged of God to open his eyes? Was he ever blind? Might he not have resort to the law, and see every word and sentence in it when he pleased? And what could he mean by those wondrous things? Were they the wonderful stories of the creation, and deluge, and Israel's passing through the Red Sea,[9] and the like? Were not his eyes open to read these strange things when he would? Doubtless, by wondrous things in God's law, he had respect to those distinguishing and wonderful excellencies, and marvelous manifestations of the divine perfections and glory contained in the commands and doctrines of the word, and those works and counsels of God that were there revealed. So the scripture speaks of a knowledge of God's dispensation, and covenant of mercy,[1] and way of grace towards His people, as peculiar to the saints, and given only by God; Psalm 25.14: "The secret of the Lord is with them that fear him; and he will show them his covenant."

And that a true and saving belief of the truth of religion is that which arises from such a discovery is, also, what the scripture teaches. As John 6.40: "And this is the will of him that sent me, that every one who seeth the Son, and believeth on him, may have everlasting life"; where it is plain that a true faith is what arises from a spiritual sight of Christ. And John 17.6–8: "I have manifested thy name unto the men which thou gavest me out of the world. Now, they have known, that all things whatsoever thou hast given me, are of thee. For I have given unto them the words which thou gavest me, and they have received them, and have known surely, that I came out from thee, and they have believed that thou didst send me"; where Christ's manifesting God's name to the disciples, or giving them the knowledge of God, was that whereby they knew that Christ's doctrine was of God, and that Christ Himself proceeded from Him, and was sent by Him. Again, John 12.44–46: "Jesus cried, and said, He that believeth on me, believeth not on me but on him that sent me. And he that seeth me, seeth him that sent me. I am come a light into the world, that whosoever believeth on me, should not abide in darkness." Their believing in Christ, and spiritually seeing Him, are parallel.

Christ condemns the Jews, that they did not know that He was the Messiah, and that His doctrine was true, from an inward distinguishing taste and relish of what was divine, in Luke 12.56–57. He having there blamed the Jews, that, though they could discern the face of the sky and of the earth, and signs of the weather, that yet they could not discern those times—or, as it is expressed in Mat-

9. The waters of the Red Sea divided for the Israelites in their exodus from Egypt (Exodus 14.2).
1. The agreement between Christ and those who believe in Him that they would be saved; also known as the Covenant of Faith, as distinct from the Covenant of Works which Adam broke.

thew, the signs of those times—adds, "yea, and why even of your ownselves, judge ye not what is right?" i.e., without extrinsic signs. Why have ye not that sense of true excellency, whereby ye may distinguish that which is holy and divine? Why have ye not that savor of the things of God, by which you may see the distinguishing glory, and evident divinity of me and my doctrine?

The apostle Peter mentions it as what gave him and his companions good and well-grounded assurance of the truth of the gospel, that they had seen the divine glory of Christ. 2 Peter 1.16: "For we have not followed cunningly-devised fables, when we made known unto you the power and coming of our Lord Jesus Christ, but were eye-witnesses of his majesty." The apostle has respect to that visible glory of Christ which they saw in His transfiguration. That glory was so divine, having such an ineffable appearance and semblance of divine holiness, majesty, and grace, that it evidently denoted Him to be a divine person. But if a sight of Christ's outward glory might give a rational assurance of His divinity,why may not an apprehension of His spiritual glory do so too? Doubtless Christ's spiritual glory is in itself as distinguishing, and as plainly shows His divinity, as His outward glory—nay, a great deal more, for His spiritual glory is that wherein His divinity consists; and the outward glory of His transfiguration showed Him to be divine, only as it was a remarkable image or representation of that spiritual glory. Doubtless, therefore, he that has had a clear sight of the spiritual glory of Christ may say, "I have not followed cunningly-devised fables, but have been an eye-witness of His majesty, upon as good grounds as the apostle, when he had respect to the outward glory of Christ that he had seen." But this brings me to what was proposed next, viz., to show that,

Secondly, This doctrine is rational.[2]

1. It is rational to suppose, that there is really such an excellency in divine things—so transcendent and exceedingly different from what is in other things—that if it were seen, would most evidently distinguish them. We cannot rationally doubt but that things divine, which appertain to the supreme Being, are vastly different from things that are human; that there is a high, glorious, and godlike excellency in them that does most remarkably difference them from the things that are of men insomuch that if the difference were but seen, it would have a convincing, satisfying influence upon anyone that they are divine. What reason can be offered against it unless we would argue that God is not remarkably distinguished in glory from men.

If Christ should now appear to any one as He did on the mount at His transfiguration,[3] or if He should appear to the world in His

2. Capable of being grasped by the mind, understandable.
3. In Matthew 17.1–8, Christ appeared to Peter, James, and John shining "as the sun" and his garments "white as the light."

heavenly glory, as He will do at the day of judgment;[4] without doubt, His glory and majesty would be such as would satisfy everyone that He was a divine person, and that His religion was true; and it would be a most reasonable, and well grounded conviction too. And why may there not be that stamp of divinity or divine glory on the word of God, on the scheme and doctrine of the gospel, that may be in like manner distinguishing and as rationally convincing, provided it be but seen? It is rational to suppose, that when God speaks to the world, there should be something in His word vastly different from men's word. Supposing that God never had spoken to the world, but we had notice that He was about to reveal Himself from heaven and speak to us immediately Himself, or that He should give us a book of His own inditing;[5] after what manner should we expect that He would speak? Would it not be rational to suppose, that His speech would be exceeding different from men's speech, that there should be such an excellency and sublimity in His word, such a stamp of wisdom, holiness, majesty, and other divine perfections, that the word of men, yea of the wisest of men, should appear mean and base in comparison of it? Doubtless it would be thought rational to expect this, and unreasonable to think otherwise. When a wise man speaks in the exercise of His wisdom, there is something in every thing He says, that is very distinguishable from the talk of a little child. So, without doubt, and much more is the speech of God, to be distinguished from that of the wisest of men; agreeable to Jeremiah 23.28–29. God, having there been reproving the false prophets that prophesied in his name, and pretended that what they spake was His word, when indeed it was their own word, says, "The prophet that hath a dream, let him tell a dream; and he that hath my word let him speak my word faithfully: what is the chaff to the wheat? saith the Lord. Is not my word like as a fire? saith the Lord: and like a hammer that breaketh the rock in pieces?"

2. If there be such a distinguishing excellency in divine things, it is rational to suppose that there may be such a thing as seeing it. What should hinder but that it may be seen? It is no argument that there is no such distinguishing excellency, or that it cannot be seen, because some do not see it, though they may be discerning men in temporal matters. It is not rational to suppose, if there be any such excellency in divine things, that wicked men should see it. It is rational to suppose that those whose minds are full of spiritual pollution, and under the power of filthy lusts, should have any relish or sense of divine beauty or excellency; or that their minds should be susceptive of that light that is in its own nature so pure and heavenly? It need not seem at all strange that sin should so blind the mind, seeing that men's particular natural tempers and dispositions will so much blind them in secular matters; as when

4. See Revelation 4.   5. Composition.

men's natural temper is melancholy, jealous, fearful, proud, or the like.

3. It is rational to suppose that this knowledge should be given immediately by God, and not be obtained by natural means. Upon what account should it seem unreasonable that there should be any immediate communication between God and the creature? It is strange, that men should make any matter of difficulty of it. Why should not He that made all things still have something immediately to do with the things that He has made? Where lies the great difficulty, if we own the being of a God, and that He created all things out of nothing, of allowing some immediate influence of God on the creation still? And if it be reasonable to suppose it with respect to any part of the creation, it is especially so with respect to reasonable, intelligent creatures; who are next to God in the gradation of the different orders of beings, and whose business is most immediately with God; and reason teaches, that man was made to serve and glorify his Creator. And if it be rational to suppose that God immediately communicates Himself to man in any affair, it is in this. It is rational to suppose that God would reserve that knowledge and wisdom, which is of such a divine and excellent nature, to be bestowed immediately by Himself, and that it should not be left in the power of second causes. Spiritual wisdom and grace is the highest and most excellent gift that ever God bestows on any creature; in this, the highest excellency and perfection of a rational creature consists. It is also immensely the most important of all divine gifts: it is that wherein man's happiness consists, and on which his everlasting welfare depends. How rational is it to suppose that God, however He has left lower gifts to second causes, and in some sort in their power, yet should reserve this most excellent, divine, and important of all divine communications in His own hands to be bestowed immediately by Himself, as a thing too great for second causes to be concerned in. It is rational to suppose that this blessing should be immediately from God, for there is no gift or benefit that is in itself so nearly related to the divine nature. Nothing which the creature receives is so much a participation of the Deity; it is a kind of emanation of God's beauty, and is related to God as the light is to the sun. It is, therefore, congruous and fit, that when it is given of God, it should be immediately from Himself, and by Himself, according to His own sovereign will.

It is rational to suppose, that it should be beyond man's power to obtain this light by the mere strength of natural reason; for it is not a thing that belongs to reason to see the beauty and loveliness of spiritual things; it is not a speculative thing, but depends on the sense of the heart. Reason, indeed, is necessary, in order to it, as it is by reason only that we are become the subjects of the means of it; which means, I have already shown to be necessary in order to it, though they have no proper causal influence in the affair. It is by reason that we become possessed of a notion of those doctrines that are the subject matter of this divine light or knowledge; and reason may many ways be indirectly and remotely an advantage to it. Reason has also to do in the acts that are immediately consequent on this discovery: for, seeing the truth of religion from hence, is by reason, though it be but by one step, and the inference be immediate. So reason has to do in that accepting of and trusting in Christ that is consequent on it. But if we take reason strictly—not for the faculty of mental perception in general, but for ratiocination, or a power of inferring by arguments—the perceiving of spiritual beauty and excellency no more belongs to reason than it belongs to the sense of feeling to perceive colors, or to the power of seeing to perceive the sweetness of food. It is out of reason's province to perceive the beauty or loveliness of any thing; such a perception does not belong to that faculty. Reason's work is to perceive truth and not excellency. It is not ratiocination that gives men the perception of the beauty and amiableness of a countenance, though it may be many ways indirectly an advantage to it; yet it is no more reason that immediately perceives it than it is reason that perceives the sweetness of honey; it depends on the sense of the heart. Reason may determine that a countenance is beautiful to others, it may determine that honey is sweet to others, but it will never give me a perception of its sweetness.

I will conclude with a very brief improvement of what has been said.

First, this doctrine may lead us to reflect on the goodness of God, that has so ordered it, that a saving evidence of the truth of the gospel is such as is attainable by persons of mean capacities and advantages, as well as those that are of the greatest parts and learning. If the evidence of the gospel depended only on history and such reasonings as learned men only are capable of, it would be above the reach of far the greatest part of mankind. But persons with an ordinary degree of knowledge are capable, without a long and subtle train of reasoning, to see the divine excellency of the things of religion; they are capable of being taught by the Spirit of God, as well as learned men. The evidence that is this way obtained is vastly better and more satisfying than all that can be obtained by the arguings of those that are most learned and greatest masters of reason. And babes are as capable of knowing these things as the wise and prudent; and they are often hid from these when they are revealed to those. 1 Corinthians 1.26–27: "For ye see your calling, brethren, how that not many wise men, after the flesh, not many mighty, not many noble, are called. But God hath chosen the foolish things of the world."

Secondly, This doctrine may well put us upon examining ourselves, whether we have ever had this divine light let into our souls. If there be such a thing, doubtless it is of great importance whether we have thus been taught by the Spirit of God; whether the light of the glorious gospel of Christ, who is the image of God, hath shined unto us, giving us the light of the knowledge of the glory of God in the face of Jesus Christ; whether we have seen the Son, and believed on Him, or have that faith of gospel doctrines which arises from a spiritual sight of Christ.

Thirdly, All may hence be exhorted earnestly to seek this spiritual light. To influence and move to it, the following things may be considered.

1. This is the most excellent and divine wisdom that any creature is capable of. It is more excellent than any human learning; it is far more excellent than all the knowledge of the greatest philosophers or statesmen. Yea, the least glimpse of the glory of God in the face of Christ doth more exalt and ennoble the soul than all the knowledge of those that have the greatest speculative understanding in divinity without grace. This knowledge has the most noble object that can be, viz., the divine glory and excellency of God and Christ. The knowledge of these objects is that wherein consists the most excellent knowledge of the angels, yea, of God Himself.

2. This knowledge is that which is above all others sweet and joyful. Men have a great deal of pleasure in human knowledge, in studies of natural things; but this is nothing to that joy which arises from this divine light shining into the soul. This light gives a view of those things that are immensely the most exquisitely beautiful and capable of delighting the eye of the understanding. The spiritual light is the dawning of the light of glory in the heart. There is nothing so powerful as this to support persons in affliction, and to give the mind peace and brightness in this stormy and dark world.

3. This light is such as effectually influences the inclination and changes the nature of the soul. It assimilates our nature to the divine nature, and changes the soul into an image of the same glory that is beheld. 2 Corinthians 3.18: "But we all with open face, beholding as in a glass the glory of the Lord, are changed into the same image, from glory to glory, even as by the Spirit of the Lord." This knowledge will wean[6] from the world, and raise the inclination to heavenly things. It will turn the heart to God as the fountain of good, and to choose Him for the only portion. This light, and this only, will bring the soul to a saving close with Christ. It conforms the heart to the gospel, mortifies its enmity and opposition against the scheme of salvation therein revealed; it causes the heart to embrace the joyful tidings, and entirely to adhere to, and acquiesce in, the revelation of Christ as our Savior; it causes the whole soul to accord and symphonize with it, admitting it with entire credit and respect, cleaving to it with full inclination and affection; and it effectually disposes the soul to give up itself entirely to Christ.

4. This light, and this only, has its fruit in an universal holiness of life. No merely notional or speculative understanding of the doc-

6. Draw us away from.

trines of religion will ever bring to this. But this light, as it reaches the bottom of the heart, and changes the nature, so it will effectually dispose to an universal obedience. It shows God as worthy to be obeyed and served. It draws forth the heart in a sincere love to God, which is the only principle of a true, gracious, and universal obedience, and it convinces of the reality of those glorious rewards that God has promised to them that obey Him.

1733   1734

Sinners in the Hands of an Angry God[1]

Deuteronomy 32.35

Their foot shall slide in due time.[2]

In this verse is threatened the vengeance of God on the wicked unbelieving Israelites, who were God's visible people, and who lived under the means of grace,[3] but who, notwithstanding all God's wonderful works towards them, remained (as in verse 28.)[4] void of counsel, having no understanding in them. Under all the cultivations of heaven, they brought forth bitter and poisonous fruit, as in the two verses next preceding the text.[5] The expression I have chosen for my text, "Their foot shall slide in due time," seems to imply the following things, relating to the punishment and destruction to which these wicked Israelites were exposed.

1. That they were always exposed to destruction; as one that stands or walks in slippery places is always exposed to fall. This is implied in the manner of their destruction coming upon them, being represented by their foot sliding. The same is expressed, Psalm 73.18: "Surely thou didst set them in slippery places; thou castedst them down into destruction."

2. It implies that they were always exposed to sudden unexpected destruction. As he that walks in slippery places is every moment liable to fall, he cannot foresee one moment whether he shall stand or fall the next; and when he does fall, he falls at once without warning. Which is also expressed in Psalm 73. 18–19: "Surely thou didst set them in slippery places; thou castedst them down into

1. Edwards delivered this sermon in Enfield, Connecticut, a town about 30 miles south of Northampton, on Sunday, July 8, 1741. In Benjamin Trumbull's *A Complete History of Connecticut* (1797, 1818) we are told that Edwards read his sermon in a level voice with his sermon book in his left hand, and in spite of his calm "there was such a breathing of distress, and weeping, that the preacher was obliged to speak to the people and desire silence, that he might be heard." The text is from Sereno E. Dwight, ed., *The Works of Jonathan Edwards*, Vol. VII (New York, 1829–30).
2. "To me belongeth vengeance, and recompense; their foot shall slide in due time: for the day of their calamity is at hand, and the things that shall come

upon them make haste."
3. I.e., the Ten Commandments. For Protestants following the Westminster Confession (1646), the "means of grace" consist of "preaching of the word and the administration of the sacraments of baptism and the Lord's Supper."
4. "They are a nation void of counsel, neither is there any understanding in them" (Deuteronomy 32.28).
5. "For their vine is of the vine of Sodom, and the fields of Gomorrah: their grapes are grapes of gall, their clusters are bitter: their wine is the poison of dragons, and the cruel venom of asps" (Deuteronomy 32.32–33). Sodom and Gomorrah were wicked cities destroyed by a rain of fire and sulphur from heaven (Genesis 19.28).

destruction: How are they brought into desolation as in a moment!"

3. Another thing implied is, that they are liable to fall of themselves, without being thrown down by the hand of another; as he that stands or walks on slippery ground needs nothing but his own weight to throw him down.

4. That the reason why they are not fallen already, and do not fall now, is only that God's appointed time is not come. For it is said, that when that due time or appointed times comes, their foot shall slide. Then they shall be left to fall, as they are inclined by their own weight. God will not hold them up in these slippery places any longer, but will let them go; and then, at that very instant, they shall fall into destruction; as he that stands on such slippery declining ground, on the edge of a pit, he cannot stand alone, when he is let go he immediately falls and is lost.

The observation from the words that I would now insist upon is this. "There is nothing that keeps wicked men at any one moment out of hell, but the mere pleasure of God." By the mere pleasure of God, I mean His sovereign pleasure, His arbitrary will, restrained by no obligation, hindered by no manner of difficulty, any more than if nothing else but God's mere will had in the least degree, or in any respect whatsoever, any hand in the preservation of wicked men one moment. The truth of this observation may appear by the following considerations.

1. There is no want of power in God to cast wicked men into hell at any moment. Men's hands cannot be strong when God rises up. The strongest have no power to resist Him, nor can any deliver[6] out of His hands. He is not only able to cast wicked men into hell, but He can most easily do it. Sometimes an earthly prince meets with a great deal of difficulty to subdue a rebel, who has found means to fortify himself, and has made himself strong by the numbers of his followers. But it is not so with God. There is no fortress that is any defense from the power of God. Though hand join in hand, and vast multitudes of God's enemies combine and associate themselves, they are easily broken in pieces. They are as great heaps of light chaff before the whirlwind; or large quantities of dry stubble before devouring flames. We find it easy to tread on and crush a worm that we see crawling on the earth; so it is easy for us to cut or singe a slender thread that any thing hangs by: thus easy is it for God, when he pleases, to cast His enemies down to hell. What are we, that we should think to stand before him, at whose rebuke the earth trembles, and before whom the rocks are thrown down?

2. They deserve to be cast into hell; so that divine justice never stands in the way, it makes no objection against God's using His power at any moment to destroy them. Yea, on the contrary, justice calls aloud for an infinite punishment of their sins. Divine justice

6. I.e., rescue others.

says of the tree that brings forth such grapes of Sodom, "Cut it down, why cumbereth it the ground? Luke 13.7. The sword of divine justice is every moment brandished over their heads, and it is nothing but the hand of arbitrary mercy, and God's will, that holds it back.

3. They are already under a sentence of condemnation to hell. They do not only justly deserve to be cast down thither, but the sentence of the law of God, that eternal and immutable rule of righteousness that God has fixed between Him and mankind, is gone out against them, and stands against them; so that they are bound over already to hell. John 3.18: "He that believeth not is condemned already." So that every unconverted man properly belongs to hell; that is his place; from thence he is, John 8.23: "Ye are from beneath." And thither he is bound; it is the place that justice, and God's word, and the sentence of his unchangeable law assign to him.

4. They are now the objects of that very same anger and wrath of God that is expressed in the torments of hell. And the reason why they do not go down to hell at each moment is not because God, in whose power they are, is not then very angry with them as He is with many miserable creatures now tormented in hell, who there feel and bear the fierceness of His wrath. Yea, God is a great deal more angry with great numbers that are now on earth: yea, doubtless, with many that are now in this congregation, who it may be are at ease, than He is with many of those who are now in the flames of hell.

So that it is not because God is unmindful of their wickedness, and does not resent it, that He does not let loose His hand and cut them off. God is not altogether such an one as themselves, though they may imagine Him to be so. The wrath of God burns against them, their damnation does not slumber; the pit is prepared, the fire is made ready, the furnace is now hot, ready to receive them; the flames do now rage and glow. The glittering sword is whet,[7] and held over them, and the pit hath opened its mouth under them.

5. The devil stands ready to fall upon them, and seize them as his own, at what moment God shall permit him. They belong to him; he has their souls in his possession, and under his dominion. The scripture represents them as his goods, Luke 11.12.[8] The devils watch them; they are ever by them at their right hand; they stand waiting for them, like greedy hungry lions that see their prey, and expect to have it, but are for the present kept back. If God should withdraw His hand, by which they are restrained, they would in one moment fly upon their poor souls. The old serpent is gaping for them; hell opens it mouth wide to receive them; and if God should permit it, they would be hastily swallowed up and lost.

7. Sharpened.
8. "Or if he shall ask an egg, will he offer him a scorpion?"

6. There are in the souls of wicked men those hellish principles reigning that would presently kindle and flame out into hell fire, if it were not for God's restraints. There is laid in the very nature of carnal men a foundation for the torments of hell. There are those corrupt principles, in reigning power in them, and in full possession of them, that are seeds of hell fire. These principles are active and powerful, exceeding violent in their nature, and if it were not for the restraining hand of God upon them, they would soon break out, they would flame out after the same manner as the same corruptions, the same enmity does in the hearts of damned souls, and would beget the same torments as they do in them. The souls of the wicked are in scripture compared to the troubled sea, Isaiah 57.20[9] For the present, God restrains their wickedness by His mighty power, as He does the raging waves of the troubled sea, saying, "Hitherto shalt thou come, but no further;"[1] but if God should withdraw that restraining power, it would soon carry all before it. Sin is the ruin and misery of the soul; it is destructive in its nature; and if God should leave it without restraint, there would need nothing else to make the soul perfectly miserable. The corruption of the heart of man is immoderate and boundless in its fury; and while wicked men live here, it is like fire pent up by God's restraints, whereas if it were let loose, it would set on fire the course of nature; and as the heart is now a sink of sin, so if sin was not restrained, it would immediately turn the soul into a fiery oven, or a furnace of fire and brimstone.

7. It is no security to wicked men for one moment that there are no visible means of death at hand. It is no security to a natural man that he is now in health and that he does not see which way he should now immediately go out of the world by any accident, and that there is no visible danger in any respect in his circumstances. The manifold and continual experience of the world in all ages, shows this is no evidence that a man is not on the very brink of eternity, and that the next step will not be into another world. The unseen, unthought-of ways and means of persons going suddenly out of the world are innumerable and inconceivable. Unconverted men walk over the pit of hell on a rotten covering, and there are innumerable places in this covering so weak that they will not bear their weight, and these places are not seen. The arrows of death fly unseen at noonday;[2] the sharpest sight cannot discern them. God has so many different unsearchable ways of taking wicked men out of the world and sending them to hell, that there is nothing to make it appear that God had need to be at the expense of a miracle, or go out of the ordinary course of His providence, to destroy any wicked man at any moment. All the means that there

9. "But the wicked are like the troubled sea, when it cannot rest, whose waters cast up mire and dirt."
1. Job 38.11.

2. "Thou shalt not be afraid for the terror by night; nor for the arrow that flieth by day" (Psalm 91.5).

are of sinners going out of the world are so in God's hands, and so universally and absolutely subject to His power and determination, that it does not depend at all the less on the mere will of God whether sinners shall at any moment go to hell than if means were never made use of or at all concerned in the case.

8. Natural men's prudence and care to preserve their own lives, or the care of others to preserve them, do not secure them a moment. To this, divine providence and universal experience do also bear testimony. There is this clear evidence that men's own wisdom is no security to them from death; that if it were otherwise we should see some difference between the wise and politic men of the world, and others, with regard to their liableness to early and unexpected death: but how is it in fact? Ecclesiastes 2.16: "How dieth the wise man? even as the fool."

9. All wicked men's pains and contrivance which they use to escape hell, while they continue to reject Christ, and so remain wicked men, do not secure them from hell one moment. Almost every natural[3] man that hears of hell, flatters himself that he shall escape it; he depends upon himself for his own security; he flatters himself in what he has done, in what he is now doing, or what he intends to do. Every one lays out matters in his own mind how he shall avoid damnation, and flatters himself that he contrives well for himself, and that his schemes will not fail. They hear indeed that there are but few saved, and that the greater part of men that have died heretofore are gone to hell; but each one imagines that he lays out matters better for his own escape than others have done. He does not intend to come to that place of torment; he says within himself that he intends to take effectual care, and to order matters so for himself as not to fail.

But the foolish children of men miserably delude themselves in their own schemes, and in confidence in their own strength and wisdom; they trust to nothing but a shadow. The greater part of those who heretofore have lived under the same means of grace, and are now dead, are undoubtedly gone to hell; and it was not because they were not as wise as those who are now alive: it was not because they did not lay out matters as well for themselves to secure their own escape. If we could speak with them, and inquire of them, one by one, whether they expected, when alive, and when they used to hear about hell, ever to be the subjects of that misery, we doubtless, should hear one and another reply, "No, I never intended to come here: I had laid out matters otherwise in my mind; I thought I should contrive well for myself: I thought my scheme good. I intended to take effectual care; but it came upon me unexpected; I did not look for it at that time, and in that manner; it came as a thief: Death outwitted me: God's wrath was too quick for me. Oh, my cursed foolishness! I was flattering myself, and pleasing myself with

3. I.e., unregenerate, unsaved.

vain dreams of what I would do hereafter; and when I was saying, peace and safety, then suddenly destruction came upon me."

10. God has laid Himself under no obligation by any promise to keep any natural man out of hell one moment. God certainly has made no promises either of eternal life or of any deliverance or preservation from eternal death but what are contained in the covenant of grace,[4] the promises that are given in Christ, in whom all the promises are yea and amen. But surely they have no interest in the promises of the covenant of grace who are not the children of the covenant, who do not believe in any of the promises, and have no interest in the Mediator of the covenant.[5]

So that, whatever some have imagined and pretended[6] about promises made to natural men's earnest seeking and knocking, it is plain and manifest that whatever pains a natural man takes in religion, whatever prayers he makes, till he believes in Christ, God is under no manner of obligation to keep him a moment from eternal destruction.

So that, thus it is that natural men are held in the hand of God, over the pit of hell; they have deserved the fiery pit, and are already sentenced to it; and God is dreadfully provoked, His anger is as great towards them as to those that are actually suffering the executions of the fierceness of His wrath in hell, and they have done nothing in the least to appease or abate that anger, neither is God in the least bound by any promise to hold them up one moment; the devil is waiting for them, hell is gaping for them, the flames gather and flash about them, and would fain lay hold on them, and swallow them up; the fire pent up in their own hearts is struggling to break out: and they have no interest in any Mediator, there are no means within reach that can be any security to them. In short, they have no refuge, nothing to take hold of; all that preserves them every moment is the mere arbitrary will, and uncovenanted, unobliged forbearance of an incensed God.

Application

The use of this awful[7] subject may be for awakening unconverted persons in this congregation. This that you have heard is the case of every one of you that are out of Christ. That world of misery, that lake of burning brimstone is extended abroad under you. There is the dreadful pit of the glowing flames of the wrath of God; there is hell's wide gaping mouth open; and you have nothing to stand upon, nor any thing to take hold of; there is nothing between you and hell but the air; it is only the power and mere pleasure of God that holds you up.

---

4. The original covenant God made with Adam is called the Covenant of Works; the second covenant Christ made with fallen man—declaring that if he believed in Him he would be saved—is called the Covenant of Grace.
5. I.e., Christ, who took upon Himself man's sins and suffered for them.
6. Claimed.
7. Awesome.

You probably are not sensible[8] of this; you find you are kept out of hell, but do not see the hand of God in it; but look at other things, as the good state of your bodily constitution, your care of your own life, and the means you use for your own preservation. But indeed these things are nothing; if God should withdraw His hand, they would avail no more to keep you from falling, than the thin air to hold up a person that is suspended in it.

Your wickedness makes you as it were heavy as lead, and to tend downwards with great weight and pressure towards hell; and if God should let you go, you would immediately sink and swiftly descend and plunge into the bottomless gulf, and your healthy constitution, and your own care and prudence, and best contrivance, and all your righteousness, would have no more influence to uphold you and keep you out of hell, than a spider's web would have to stop a fallen rock. Were it not for the sovereign pleasure of God, the earth would not bear you one moment; for you are a burden to it; the creation groans with you; the creature is made subject to the bondage of your corruption, not willingly; the sun does not willingly shine upon you to give you light to serve sin and Satan; the earth does not willingly yield her increase to satisfy your lusts; nor is it willingly a stage for your wickedness to be acted upon; the air does not willingly serve you for breath to maintain the flame of life in your vitals, while you spend your life in the service of God's enemies. God's creatures are good, and were made for men to serve God with, and do not willingly subserve to any other purpose, and groan when they are abused to purposes so directly contrary to their nature and end. And the world would spew you out, were it not for the sovereign hand of Him who hath subjected it in hope. There are black clouds of God's wrath now hanging directly over your heads, full of the dreadful storm, and big with thunder; and were it not for the restraining hand of God, it would immediately burst forth upon you. The sovereign pleasure of God, for the present, stays His rough wind; otherwise it would come with fury, and your destruction would come like a whirlwind, and you would be like the chaff of the summer threshing floor.

The wrath of God is like great waters that are dammed for the present; they increase more and more, and rise higher and higher, till an outlet is given; and the longer the stream is stopped, the more rapid and mighty is its course when once it is let loose. It is true that judgment against your evil works has not been executed hitherto; the floods of God's vengeance have been withheld; but your guilt in the meantime is constantly increasing, and you are every day treasuring up more wrath; the waters are constantly rising, and waxing more and more mighty; and there is nothing but the mere pleasure of God that holds the waters back, that are unwilling to be stopped, and press hard to go forward. If God should only

8. **Aware.**

withdraw His hand from the floodgate, it would immediately fly open, and the fiery floods of the fierceness and wrath of God, would rush forth with inconceivable fury, and would come upon you with omnipotent power; and if your strength were ten thousand times greater than it is, yea, ten thousand times greater than the strength of the stoutest, sturdiest devil in hell, it would be nothing to withstand or endure it.

The bow of God's wrath is bent, and the arrow made ready on the string, and justice bends the arrow at your heart, and strains the bow, and it is nothing but the mere pleasure of God, and that of an angry God, without any promise or obligation at all, that keeps the arrow one moment from being made drunk with your blood. Thus all you that never passed under a great change of heart, by the mighty power of the Spirit of God upon your souls, all you that were never born again, and made new creatures, and raised from being dead in sin, to a state of new, and before altogether unexperienced light and life, are in the hands of an angry God. However you may have reformed your life in many things, and may have had religious affections,[9] and may keep up a form of religion in your families and closets,[1] and in the house of God, it is nothing but His mere pleasure that keeps you from being this moment swallowed up in everlasting destruction. However unconvinced you may now be of the truth of what you hear, by and by you will be fully convinced of it. Those that are gone from being in the like circumstances with you see that it was so with them; for destruction came suddenly upon most of them; when they expected nothing of it and while they were saying, peace and safety: now they see that those things on which they depended for peace and safety, were nothing but thin air and empty shadows.

The God that holds you over the pit of hell, much as one holds a spider or some loathsome insect over the fire, abhors you, and is dreadfully provoked: His wrath towards you burns like fire; He looks upon you as worthy of nothing else but to be cast into the fire; He is of purer eyes than to bear to have you in His sight; you are ten thousand times more abominable in His eyes than the most hateful venomous serpent is in ours. You have offended Him infinitely more than ever a stubborn rebel did his prince; and yet it is nothing but His hand that holds you from falling into the fire every moment. It is to be ascribed to nothing else, that you did not go to hell the last night; that you was suffered to awake again in this world, after you closed your eyes to sleep. And there is no other reason to be given, why you have not dropped into hell since you arose in the morning, but that God's hand has held you up. There is no other reason to be given why you have not gone to hell, since you have sat here in the house of God, provoking His pure eyes by your sinful wicked manner of attending His solemn worship. Yea,

9. Feelings.   1. Studies; rooms for meditation.

there is nothing else that is to be given as a reason why you do not this very moment drop down into hell.

O sinner! Consider the fearful danger you are in: it is a great furnace of wrath, a wide and bottomless pit, full of the fire of wrath, that you are held over in the hand of that God, whose wrath is provoked and incensed as much against you, as against many of the damned in hell. You hang by a slender thread, with the flames of divine wrath flashing about it, and ready every moment to singe it, and burn it asunder; and you have no interest in any Mediator, and nothing to lay hold of to save yourself, nothing to keep off the flames of wrath, nothing of your own, nothing that you ever have done, nothing that you can do, to induce God to spare you one moment. And consider here more particularly,

1. Whose wrath it is? It is the wrath of the infinite God. If it were only the wrath of man, though it were of the most potent prince, it would be comparatively little to be regarded. The wrath of kings is very much dreaded, especially of absolute monarchs, who have the possessions and lives of their subjects wholly in their power, to be disposed of at their mere will. Proverbs 20.2: "The fear of a king is as the roaring of a lion: Whoso provoketh him to anger, sinneth against his own soul." The subject that very much enrages an arbitrary prince, is liable to suffer the most extreme torments that human art can invent, or human power can inflict. But the greatest earthly potentates in their greatest majesty and strength, and when clothed in their greatest terrors, are but feeble, despicable worms of the dust, in comparison of the great and almighty Creator and King of heaven and earth. It is but little that they can do, when most enraged, and when they have exerted the utmost of their fury. All the kings of the earth, before God, are as grasshoppers; they are nothing, and less than nothing: both their love and their hatred is to be despised. The wrath of the great King of kings, is as much more terrible than theirs, as His majesty is greater. Luke 12.4–5: "And I say unto you, my friends, Be not afraid of them that kill the body, and after that, have no more that they can do. But I will forewarn you whom you shall fear: fear him, which after he hath killed, hath power to cast into hell: yea, I say unto you, Fear him."

2. It is the fierceness of His wrath that you are exposed to. We often read of the fury of God; as in Isaiah 59.18: "According to their deeds, accordingly he will repay fury to his adversaries." So Isaiah 66.15: "For behold, the Lord will come with fire, and with his chariots like a whirlwind, to render his anger with fury, and his rebuke with flames of fire." And in many other places. So, Revelation 19.15: we read of "the wine press of the fierceness and wrath of Almighty God."[2] The words are exceeding terrible. If it had only been said, "the wrath of God," the words would have

2. "He treadeth the winepress of the fierceness and wrath of Almighty God."

implied that which is infinitely dreadful: but it is "the fierceness and wrath of God." The fury of God! the fierceness of Jehovah![3] Oh, how dreadful must that be! Who can utter or conceive what such expressions carry in them! But it is also "the fierceness and wrath of Almighty God." As though there would be a very great manifestation of His almighty power in what the fierceness of His wrath should inflict, as though omnipotence should be as it were enraged, and exerted, as men are wont to exert their strength in the fierceness of their wrath. Oh! then, what will be the consequence! What will become of the poor worms that shall suffer it! Whose hands can be strong? And whose heart can endure? To what a dreadful, inexpressible, inconceivable depth of misery must the poor creature be sunk who shall be the subject of this!

Consider this, you that are here present that yet remain in an unregenerate state. That God will execute the fierceness of His anger implies that He will inflict wrath without any pity. When God beholds the ineffable extremity of your case, and sees your torment to be so vastly disproportioned to your strength, and sees how your poor soul is crushed, and sinks down, as it were, into an infinite gloom; He will have no compassion upon you, He will not forbear the executions of His wrath, or in the least lighten His hand; there shall be no moderation or mercy, nor will God then at all stay His rough wind; He will have no regard to your welfare, nor be at all careful lest you should suffer too much in any other sense, than only that you shall not suffer beyond what strict justice requires. Nothing shall be withheld because it is so hard for you to bear. Ezekiel 8.18: "Therefore will I also deal in fury: mine eye shall not spare, neither will I have pity; and though they cry in mine ears with a loud voice, yet I will not hear them." Now God stands ready to pity you; this is a day of mercy; you may cry now with some encouragement of obtaining mercy. But when once the day of mercy is past, your most lamentable and dolorous cries and shrieks will be in vain; you will be wholly lost and thrown away of God as to any regard to your welfare. God will have no other use to put you to, but to suffer misery; you shall be continued in being to no other end; for you will be a vessel of wrath fitted to destruction; and there will be no other use of this vessel, but to be filled full of wrath. God will be so far from pitying you when you cry to Him, that it is said He will only "laugh and mock." Proverbs 1.25–26, etc.[4]

How awful are those words, Isaiah 63.3, which are the words of the great God: "I will tread them in mine anger, and will trample them in my fury, and their blood shall be sprinkled upon my garments, and I will stain all my raiment." It is perhaps impossible to conceive of words that carry in them greater manifestations of these three things, viz., contempt, and hatred, and fierceness of indigna-

3. The God of the Old Testament, the Hebrew God.
4. "But ye have set at nought all my counsel, and would none of my reproof: I also will laugh at your calamity; I will mock you when your fear cometh."

tion. If you cry to God to pity you, He will be so far from pitying you in your doleful case, or showing you the least regard or favor, that instead of that, He will only tread you under foot. And though He will know that you cannot bear the weight of omnipotence treading upon you, yet He will not regard that, but He will crush you under His feet without mercy; He will crush out your blood, and make it fly and it shall be sprinkled on His garments, so as to stain all His raiment. He will not only hate you, but He will have you in the utmost contempt: no place shall be thought fit for you, but under His feet to be trodden down as the mire of the streets.

3. The misery you are exposed to is that which God will inflict to that end, that He might show what that wrath of Jehovah is. God hath had it on His heart to show to angels and men both how excellent His love is, and also how terrible His wrath is. Sometimes earthly kings have a mind to show how terrible their wrath is, by the extreme punishments they would execute on those that would provoke them. Nebuchadnezzar, that mighty and haughty monarch of the Chaldean empire, was willing to show his wrath when enraged with Shadrach, Meshech, and Abednego; and accordingly gave orders that the burning fiery furnace should be heated seven times hotter than it was before; doubtless, it was raised to the utmost degree of fierceness that human art could raise it.[5] But the great God is also willing to show His wrath, and magnify His awful majesty and mighty power in the extreme sufferings of His enemies. Romans 9.22: "What if God, willing to show his wrath, and to make his power known, endure with much long-suffering the vessels of wrath fitted to destruction?" And seeing this in His design, and what He has determined, even to show how terrible the restrained wrath, the fury and fierceness of Jehovah is, He will do it to effect. There will be something accomplished and brought to pass that will be dreadful with a witness. When the great and angry God hath risen up and executed His awful vengeance on the poor sinner, and the wretch is actually suffering the infinite weight and power of His indignation, then will God call upon the whole universe to behold that awful majesty and mighty power that is to be seen in it. Isaiah 33.12–14: "And the people shall be as the burnings of lime, as thorns cut up shall they be burnt in the fire. Hear ye that are far off, what I have done; ye that are near, acknowledge my might. The sinners in Zion are afraid; fearfulness hath surprised the hypocrites," etc.

Thus it will be with you that are in an unconverted state, if you continue in it; the infinite might, and majesty, and terribleness of the omnipotent God shall be magnified upon you, in the ineffable strength of your torments. You shall be tormented in the presence of the holy angels, and in the presence of the Lamb; and when you shall be in this state of suffering, the glorious inhabitants of heaven

5. See Daniel 3.1–30.

shall go forth and look on the awful spectacle, that they may see what the wrath and fierceness of the Almighty is; and when they have seen it, they will fall down and adore that great power and majesty. Isaiah 66.23–24: "And it shall come to pass, that from one new moon to another, and from one sabbath to another, shall flesh come to worship before me, saith the Lord. And they shall go forth and look upon the carcasses of the men that have transgressed against me; for their worm shall not die, neither shall their fire be quenched, and they shall be an abhorring unto all flesh."

4. It is everlasting wrath. It would be dreadful to suffer this fierceness and wrath of Almighty God one moment; but you must suffer it to all eternity. There will be no end to this exquisite horrible misery. When you look forward, you shall see a long forever, a boundless duration before you, which will swallow up your thoughts, and amaze your soul; and you will absolutely despair of ever having any deliverance, any end, any mitigation, any rest at all. You will know certainly that you must wear out long ages, millions of millions of ages, in wrestling and conflicting with this almighty merciless vengeance; and then when you have so done, when so many ages have actually been spent by you in this manner, you will know that all is but a point to what remains. So that your punishment will indeed be infinite. Oh, who can express what the state of a soul in such circumstances is! All that we can possibly say about it gives but a very feeble, faint representation of it; it is inexpressible and inconceivable: For "who knows the power of God's anger?"[6]

How dreadful is the state of those that are daily and hourly in the danger of this great wrath and infinite misery! But this is the dismal case of every soul in this congregation that has not been born again, however moral and strict, sober and religious, they may otherwise be. Oh that you would consider it, whether you be young or old! There is reason to think that there are many in this congregaton now hearing this discourse that will actually be the subjects of this very misery to all eternity. We know not who they are, or in what seats they sit, or what thoughts they now have. It may be they are now at ease, and hear all these things without much disturbance, and are now flattering themselves that they are not the persons, promising themselves that they shall escape. If they knew that there was one person, and but one, in the whole congregation, that was to be the subject of this misery, what an awful thing would it be to think of! If we knew who it was, what an awful sight would it be to see such a person! How might all the rest of the congregation lift up a lamentable and bitter cry over him! But, alas! instead of one, how many is it likely will remember this discourse in hell? And it would be a wonder, if some that are now present should not be in hell in a very short time, even before this year is

6. "Who knoweth the power of thine anger? even according to thy fear, so is thy wrath" (Psalm 90.11).

out. And it would be no wonder if some persons, that now sit here, in some seats of this meetinghouse, in health, quiet and secure, should be there before tomorrow morning. Those of you that finally continue in a natural condition, that shall keep out of hell longest will be there in a little time! your damnation does not slumber; it will come swiftly, and, in all probability, very suddenly upon many of you. You have reason to wonder that you are not already in hell. It is doubtless the case of some whom you have seen and known, that never deserved hell more than you, and that heretofore appeared as likely to have been now alive as you. Their case is past all hope; they are crying in extreme misery and perfect despair; but here you are in the land of the living and in the house of God, and have an opportunity to obtain salvation. What would not those poor damned hopeless souls give for one day's opportunity such as you now enjoy!

And now you have an extraordinary opportunity, a day wherein Christ has thrown the door of mercy wide open, and stands in calling and crying with a loud voice to poor sinners; a day wherein many are flocking to Him, and pressing into the kingdom of God. Many are daily coming from the east, west, north and south; many that were very lately in the same miserable condition that you are in are now in a happy state, with their hearts filled with love to Him who has loved them, and washed them from their sins in His own blood, and rejoicing in hope of the glory of God. How awful is it to be left behind at such a day! To see so many others feasting, while you are pining and perishing! To see so many rejoicing and singing for joy of heart, while you have cause to mourn for sorrow of heart, and howl for vexation of spirit! How can you rest one moment in such a condition? Are not your souls as precious as the souls of the people at Suffield,[7] where they are flocking from day to day to Christ?

Are there not many here who have lived long in the world, and are not to this day born again? and so are aliens from the commonwealth of Israel,[8] and have done nothing ever since they have lived, but treasure up wrath against the day of wrath? Oh, sirs, your case, in an especial manner, is extremely dangerous. Your guilt and hardness of heart is extremely great. Do you not see how generally persons of your years are passed over and left, in the present remarkable and wonderful dispensation of God's mercy? You had need to consider yourselves, and awake thoroughly out of sleep. You cannot bear the fierceness and wrath of the infinite God. And you, young men, and young women, will you neglect this precious season which you now enjoy, when so many others of your age are renouncing all youthful vanities, and flocking to Christ? You especially have now an extraordinary opportunity; but if you neglect it, it will soon be

7. "A town in the neighborhood" [Edwards's note].

8. I.e., not among the chosen people and, therefore, saved.

with you as with those persons who spent all the precious days in youth in sin, and are now come to such a dreadful pass in blindness and hardness. And you, children, who are unconverted, do not you know that you are going down to hell, to bear the dreadful wrath of that God, who is now angry with you every day and every night? Will you be content to be the children of the devil, when so many other children in the land are converted, and are become the holy and happy children of the King of kings?

And let every one that is yet of Christ, and hanging over the pit of hell, whether they be old men and women, or middle-aged, or young people, or little children, now hearken to the loud calls of God's word and providence. This acceptable year of the Lord, a day of such great favors to some, will doubtless be a day of as remarkable vengeance to others. Men's hearts harden, and their guilt increases apace at such a day as this, if they neglect their souls; and never was there so great danger of such person being given up to hardness of heart and blindness of mind. God seems now to be hastily gathering in His elect in all parts of the land; and probably the greater part of adult persons that ever shall be saved, will be brought in now in a little time, and that it will be as it was on the great outpouring of the Spirit upon the Jews in the apostles' days;[9] the election will obtain, and the rest will be blinded. If this should be the case with you, you will eternally curse this day, and will curse the day that ever you was born, to see such a season of the pouring out of God's Spirit, and will wish that you had died and gone to hell before you had seen it. Now undoubtedly it is, as it was in the days of John the Baptist, the axe is in an extraordinary manner laid at the root of the trees,[1] that every tree which brings not forth good fruit, may be hewn down and cast into the fire.

Therefore, let everyone that is out of Christ, now awake and fly from the wrath to come. The wrath of Almighty God is now undoubtedly hanging over a great part of this congregation: Let everyone fly out of Sodom: "Haste and escape for your lives, look not behind you, escape to the mountain, lest you be consumed."[2]

1741

[The Beauty of the World][1]

The beauty of the world consists wholly of sweet mutual consents,[2] either within itself or with the Supreme Being. As to the

9. In Acts 2 the apostle Peter admonishes a crowd to repent and be converted, saying, "Save yourselves from this untoward generation. Then they that gladly received his word were baptized: and the same day there were added unto them about three thousand souls" (Acts 2.40–41).

1. "And now also the axe is laid unto the root of the trees: therefore every tree which brings not forth good fruit is hewn down, and cast into the fire" (Matthew 3.10).

2. Genesis 19.17.

1. This fragment was found among Edwards's papers and first published, with this title, by Perry Miller in *Images or Shadows of Divine Things* (New Haven, Conn.: Yale University Press, 1948). The editorial emendations are by Perry Miller.

2. Agreements.

corporeal world, though there are many other sorts of consents, yet the sweetest and most charming beauty of it is its resemblance of spiritual beauties. The reason is that spiritual beauties are infinitely the greatest, and bodies being but the shadows of beings, they must be so much the more charming as they shadow forth spiritual beauties. This beauty is peculiar to natural things, it surpassing the art of man.

Thus there is the resemblance of a decent trust, dependence and acknowledgment in the planets continually moving around the sun, receiving his influences by which they are made happy, bright and beautiful: a decent attendance in the secondary planets, an image of majesty, power, glory, and beneficence in the sun in the midst of all, and so in terrestrial things, as I have shown in another place.

It is very probable that that wonderful suitableness of green for the grass and plants, the blues of the skie, the white of the clouds, the colors of flowers, consists in a complicated proportion that these colors make one with another, either in their magnitude of the rays, the number of vibrations that are caused in the atmosphere, or some other way. So there is a great suitableness between the objects of different sense, as between sounds, colors, and smells; as between colors of the woods and flowers and the smells and the singing of birds, which it is probable consist in a certain proportion of the vibrations that are made in the different organs. So there are innumerable other agreeablenesses of motions, figures, etc. The gentle motions of waves, of [the] lily, etc., as it is agreeable to other things that represent calmness, gentleness, and benevolence, etc. the fields and woods seem to rejoice, and how joyful do the birds seem to be in it. How much a resemblance is there of every grace in the field covered with plants and flowers when the sun shines serenely and undisturbedly upon them, how a resemblance, I say, of every grace and beautiful disposition of mind, of an inferior towards a superior cause, preserver, benevolent benefactor, and a fountain of happiness.

How great a resemblance of a holy and virtuous soul is a calm, serene day. What an infinite number of such like beauties is there in that one thing, the light, and how complicated an harmony and proportion is it probable belongs to it.

There are beauties that are more palpable and explicable, and there are hidden and secret beauties. The former pleases, and we can tell why; we can explain the particular point for the agreement that renders the thing pleasing. Such are all artificial regularities; we can tell wherein the regularity lies that affects us. [The] latter sort are those beauties that delight us and we cannot tell why. Thus, we find ourselves pleased in beholding the color of the violets, but we know not what secret regularity or harmony it is that creates that pleasure in our minds. These hidden beauties are commonly by far the greatest, because the more complex a beauty is, the more hidden is it. In this latter fact consists principally the beauty of the world, and very much in light and colors. Thus mere light is pleasing to the mind. If it be to the degree of effulgence, it is very sensible, and mankind have agreed in it: they all represent glory and extraordinary beauty by brightness. The reason of it is either that light or our organ of seeing is so contrived that an harmonious motion is excited in the animal spirits and propogated to the brain. That mixture we call white is a proportionate mixture that is harmonious, as Sir Isaac Newton[3] has shown, to each particular simple color, and contains in it some harmony or other that is delightful. And each sort of rays play a distinct tune to the soul, besides those lovely mixtures that are found in nature. Those beauties, how lovely is the green of the face of the earth in all manner of colors, in flowers the color of the skies, and lovely tinctures of the morning and evening.

Corollary:[4] Hence the reason why almost all men, and those that seem to be very miserable, love life, because they cannot bear to lose sight of such a beautiful and lovely world. The ideas, that every moment whilst we live have a beauty that we take not distinct notice of, brings a pleasure that, when we come to the trial, we had rather live in much pain and misery than lose.

1948

3. Sir Isaac Newton (1642–1727), in his *Opticks* (1704), explained the phenomena of color, proving that differences in color are caused by differing degrees of refrangibility.

4. Something which naturally follows from a proved proposition.

BENJAMIN FRANKLIN
1706–1790

Benjamin Franklin was born on Milk Street in Boston, the tenth son in a family of fifteen children. His father, Josiah, was a tallow chandler and soap boiler who came to Boston in 1682 from Ecton in Northamptonshire, England, and was proud of his Protestant ancestors. He married Abiah Folger, whose father was a teacher to the Indians. Josiah talked of offering his son Benjamin as his "tithe" to the church and enrolled him in Boston Grammar School as a preparation for the study of the ministry, but his plans were too ambitious and Benjamin was forced to leave school and work for his father. He hated his father's occupation and threatened to run away to sea. A compromise was made, and when Benjamin was twelve he was apprenticed to his brother, a printer. He must have been a natural student of the printing trade; he loved books and reading, he learned quickly, and he liked to write. His brother unwittingly published Benjamin's first essay when he printed an editorial left on his desk signed "Silence Dogood." When his brother was imprisoned in 1722 for offending Massachusetts officials, Franklin carried on publication of the paper by himself.

In 1723 Franklin broke with his brother and ran away to Philadelphia.

It was a serious act for an apprentice, and his brother was justly indignant and angry. But the break was inevitable; for Franklin was proud and independent by nature, and too clever for his brother by far. At seventeen, with little money in his pocket but already an expert printer, he proceeded to make his way in the world, subject to the usual "errata," as he liked to call his mistakes, but confident that he could profit from lessons learned and not repeat them. His most serious error was in trusting a foolish man who wanted to be important to everyone. As a result of Governor Keith's "favors," Benjamin found himself alone and without employment in London in 1724. He returned to the colonies two years later.

Franklin had an uncanny instinct for success. He taught himself French, Spanish, Italian, and Latin, yet was shrewd enough to know that people did not like to do business with merchants who were smarter than they. He dressed plainly and sometimes carried his own paper in a wheelbarrow through Philadelphia streets to assure future customers that he was hard-working and not above doing things for himself. By the time he was twenty-four he was the sole owner of a successful printing shop and editor and publisher of the *Pennsylvania Gazette*. He offered his *Poor Richard's Almanac* for sale in 1733 and made it an American institution, filling it with maxims for achieving wealth and preaching hard work and thrift. In 1730 he married Deborah Read, the daughter of his first landlady, and they had two children. Franklin had two illegitimate children, and Deborah took Franklin's son William into the household. He was later to become Governor of New Jersey and a Loyalist during the Revolution; Franklin addressed the first part of his *Autobiography* to him. Before he retired from business at the age of forty-two, Franklin had founded a library, invented a stove, established a fire company, subscribed to an academy which was to become the University of Pennsylvania, and served as secretary to the American Philosophical Society. It was his intention when he retired to devote himself to public affairs and his lifelong passion for the natural sciences, especially the phenomena of sound, vapors, earthquakes, and electricity.

Franklin's observations on electricity were published in London in 1751 and, despite his disclaimers in the *Autobiography*, brought him the applause of British scientists. Science was Franklin's great passion, the only thing, the American historian Charles Beard once said, about which Franklin was not ironic. His inquiring mind was challenged most by the mechanics of the ordinary phenomena of the world, and he was convinced that man's rational powers would enable him to solve riddles that had puzzled mankind for centuries. Franklin believed that man was naturally innocent, that all the mysteries which charmed the religious mind could be explained to our advantage, and that education, properly undertaken, would transform our lives and set us free from the tyrannies of church and monarchy. Franklin had no illusions about the "errata" of mankind, but his metaphor suggests that we can change and alter our past in a way that the word *sins* does not.

Franklin's remaining years, however, were not spent in a laboratory, but at the diplomatic table in London, Paris, and Philadelphia, where his gift for irony served him well. For he was a born diplomat, detached, adaptable, witty, urbane, charming, and clever, and of the slightly more than forty years left to him after his retirement, more than half were spent abroad. In 1757 he went to England to represent the colonies and stayed for five years, returning in 1763. It was in England in 1768 that Franklin first noted his growing sense of alienation from England and the impossibility of compromise with the mother country. Parliament can make *all* laws for the colonies or *none*, he said, and "I think the arguments for the latter more numerous and weighty, than those for the former." When he returned to Philadelphia in May, 1775, he was chosen as a representative to the second Continental Congress, and he served on the committee to draft the Declaration of Independence. In October, 1776, he was appointed Minister to France, where he successfully negotiated a treaty of allegiance and became something of a cult hero. In 1781 he was a member of the American delegation to the Paris peace conference, and he signed the Treaty of Paris which brought the Revolutionary War to an end. Franklin protested his too long stay in Europe and returned to Philadelphia in 1785, serving as a delegate to the Constitutional Convention. When he died in 1790, he was one of the most beloved Americans. Twenty thousand people attended his funeral.

This hero of the eighteenth century, however, has not universally charmed our own. For a number of readers Franklin has been identified as a garrulous but insensitive man of the world, too adaptable for a man of integrity and too willing to please. D. H. Lawrence is only one of a number of Franklin's critics who have charged him with insensitivity and indifference to the darker recesses of the soul. There is no question but that Franklin, like Emerson, has been reduced by his admirers—the hero of those who seek only the way to wealth. But such critics often ignore Franklin's own comments on the follies of humankind.

The Way to Wealth[1]
Preface to Poor Richard Improved

Courteous Reader,

I have heard that nothing gives an author so great pleasure, as to find his works respectfully quoted by other learned authors. This pleasure I have seldom enjoyed; for though I have been, if I may say it without vanity, an eminent author of almanacs annually now a full quarter of a century, my brother authors in the same way, for what reason I know not, have ever been very sparing in their applauses, and no other author has taken the least notice of me, so that did not my writings produce me some solid pudding, the great deficiency of praise would have quite discouraged me.

I concluded at length, that the people were the best judges of my merit; for they buy my works; and besides, in my rambles, where I am not personally known, I have frequently heard one or other of my adages repeated, with "as Poor Richard says" at the end on 't; this gave me some satisfaction, as it showed not only that my instructions were regarded, but discovered likewise some respect for

1. Franklin composed this essay for the 25th anniversary issue of his *Almanac*, the first issue of which, under the fictitious editorship of "Richard Saunders," appeared in 1733. For this essay Franklin brought together the best of his maxims in the guise of a speech by Father Abraham. It is frequently reprinted as *The Way to Wealth*, but is also known by earlier titles: *Poor Richard Improved* and *Father Abraham's Speech*. The text used here is from *The Writings of Benjamin Franklin*, Vol. III, ed. Albert Henry Smyth (New York: Macmillan, 1907).

my authority; and I own, that to encourage the practice of remembering and repeating those wise sentences, I have sometimes quoted myself with great gravity.

Judge, then, how much I must have been gratified by an incident I am going to relate to you. I stopped my horse lately where a great number of people were collected at a vendue[2] of merchant goods. The hour of sale not being come, they were conversing on the badness of the times and one of the company called to a plain clean old man, with white locks, "Pray, Father Abraham, what think you of the times? Won't these heavy taxes quite ruin the country? How shall we be ever able to pay them? What would you advise us to?" Father Abraham stood up, and replied, "If you'd have my advice, I'll give it you in short, for a *word to the wise is enough, and many words won't fill a bushel,* as Poor Richard says." They joined in desiring him to speak his mind, and gathering round him, he proceeded as follows:

"Friends," says he, "and neighbors, the taxes are indeed very heavy, and if those laid on by the government were the only ones we had to pay, we might more easily discharge them; but we have many others, and much more grievous to some of us. We are taxed twice as much by our idleness, three times as much by our pride, and four times as much by our folly; and from these taxes the commissioners cannot ease or deliver us by allowing an abatement. However, let us hearken to good advice, and something may be done for us; *God helps them that help themselves,* as Poor Richard says, in his Almanack of 1733.

"It would be thought a hard government that should tax its people one-tenth part of their time, to be employed in its service. But idleness taxes many of us much more, if we reckon all that is spent in absolute sloth, or doing of nothing, with that which is spent in idle employments or amusements, that amount to nothing. Sloth, by bringing on diseases, absolutely shortens life. *Sloth, like rust, consumes faster than labor wears; while the used key is always bright,* as Poor Richard says. *But dost thou love life, then do not squander time, for that's the stuff life is made of,* as Poor Richard says. How much more than is necessary do we spend in sleep, forgetting that *the sleeping fox catches no poultry* and that *there will be sleeping enough in the grave,* as Poor Richard says.

"*If time be of all things the most precious, wasting time must be,* as Poor Richard says, *the greatest prodigality;* since, as he elsewhere tells us, *lost time is never found again; and what we call time enough, always proves little enough:* let us then up and be doing, and doing to the purpose; so by diligence shall we do more with less perplexity. *Sloth makes all things difficult, but industry all easy,* as Poor Richard says; *and he that riseth late must trot all day, and shall scarce overtake his business at night;* while *laziness travels so*

2. Auction or sale.

slowly, that poverty soon overtakes him, as we read in Poor Richard, who adds, *drive thy business, let not that drive thee,* and *early to bed, and early to rise, makes a man healthy, wealthy, and wise.*

"So what signifies wishing and hoping for better times. We may make these times better, if we bestir ourselves. *Industry need not wish,* as Poor Richard says, *and he that lives upon hope will die fasting. There are no gains without pains; then help hands, for I have no lands,* or if I have, they are smartly taxed. And, as Poor Richard likewise observes, *he that hath a trade hath an estate; and he that hath a calling, hath an office of profit and honor;* but then the trade must be worked at, and the calling well followed, or neither the estate nor the office will enable us to pay our taxes. If we are industrious, we shall never starve; for, as Poor Richard says, *at the workingman's house hunger looks in, but dares not enter.* Nor will the bailiff or the constable enter, for *industry pays debts, while despair increaseth them,* says Poor Richard. What though you have found no treasure, nor has any rich relation left you a legacy, *diligence is the mother of goodluck,* as Poor Richard says, and *God gives all things to industry. Then plow deep, while sluggards sleep, and you shall have corn to sell and to keep,* says Poor Dick. Work while it is called today, for you know not how much you may be hindered tomorrow, which makes Poor Richard say, *one today is worth two tomorrows,* and farther, *have you somewhat to do tomorrow, do it today.* If you were a servant, would you not be ashamed that a good master should catch you idle? Are you then your own master, *be ashamed to catch yourself idle,* as Poor Dick says. When there is so much to be done for yourself, your family, your country, and your gracious king, be up by peep of day; *let not the sun look down and say, inglorious here he lies.* Handle your tools without mittens; remember that *the cat in gloves catches no mice,* as Poor Richard says. 'Tis true there is much to be done, and perhaps you are weak-handed, but stick to it steadily; and you will see great effects, for *constant dropping wears away stones,* and *by diligence and patience the mouse ate in two the cable;* and *little strokes fell great oaks,* as Poor Richard says in his Almanack, the year I cannot just now remember.

"Methinks I hear some of you say, "must a man afford himself no leisure?" I will tell thee, my friend, what Poor Richard says, *employ thy time well, if thou meanest to gain leisure; and, since thou art not sure of a minute, throw not away an hour.* Leisure is time for doing something useful; this leisure the diligent man will obtain, but the lazy man never; so that, as Poor Richard says *a life of leisure and a life of laziness are two things.* Do you imagine that sloth will afford you more comfort than labour? No, for as Poor Richard says, *trouble springs from idleness, and grievous toil from needless ease. Many without labor, would live by their wits only, but they break for want of stock.* Whereas industry gives comfort, and plenty, and respect: *fly pleasures, and they'll follow you. The diligent spinner has a large shift;*[3] *and now I have a sheep and a cow, everybody bids me good morrow;* all which is well said by Poor Richard.

"But with our industry, we must likewise be steady, settled, and careful, and oversee our own affairs with our own eyes, and not trust too much to others; for, as Poor Richard says

> *I never saw an oft-removed tree,*
> *Nor yet an oft-removed family,*
> *That throve so well as those that settled be.*

And again, *three removes*[4] *is as bad as a fire;* and again, *keep thy shop, and thy shop will keep thee;* and again, *if you would have your business done, go; if not, send.* And again,

> *He that by the plough would thrive,*
> *Himself must either hold or drive.*

And again, *the eye of a master will do more work than both his hands;* and again, *want of care does us more damage than want of knowledge;* and again, *not to oversee workmen is to leave them your purse open.* Trusting too much to others' care is the ruin of many; for, as the Almanack says, *in the affairs of this world, men are saved, not by faith, but by the want of it;* but a man's own care is profitable; for, saith Poor Dick, *learning is to the studious,* and *riches to the careful,* as well as *power to the bold,* and *heaven to the virtuous,* and farther, *if you would have a faithful servant, and one that you like, serve yourself.* And again, he adviseth to circumspection and care, even in the smallest matters, because sometimes *a little neglect may breed great mischief;* adding, *for want of a nail the shoe was lost; for want of a shoe the horse was lost; and for want of a horse the rider was lost, being overtaken and slain by the enemy; all for want of care about a horseshoe nail.*

"So much for industry, my friends, and attention to one's own business; but to these we must add frugality, if we would make our industry more certainly successful. A man may, if he knows not how to save as he gets, keep his nose all his life to the grindstone, and die not worth a groat[5] at last. A *fat kitchen makes a lean will,* as Poor Richard says; and

> *Many estates are spent in the getting,*
> *Since women for tea forsook spinning and knitting,*
> *And men for punch forsook hewing and splitting.*

If you would be wealthy, says he, in another Almanack, *think of saving as well as of getting: the Indies have not made Spain rich, because her outgoes are greater than her incomes.*

"Away then with your expensive follies, and you will not then

3. Wardrobe.
4. Moves.
5. A silver coin worth about four pence.

have so much cause to complain of hard times, heavy taxes, and chargeable families; for, as Poor Dick says,

> *Women and wine, game and deceit,*
> *Make the wealth small and the wants great.*

And farther, *what maintains one vice would bring up two children.* You may think perhaps, that a little tea, or a little punch now and then, diet a little more costly, clothes a little finer, and a little entertainment now and then, can be no great matter; but remember what Poor Richard says, *many a little makes a mickle*;[6] and farther, *Beware of little expenses; a small leak will sink a great ship*; and again, *who dainties love shall beggars prove*; and moreover, *fools make feasts, and wise men eat them.*

"Here you are all got together at this vendue of fineries and knick-nacks. You call them goods; but if you do not take care, they will prove evils to some of you. You expect they will be sold cheap, and perhaps they may for less than they cost; but if you have no occasion for them, they must be dear to you. Remember what Poor Richard says; *buy what thou hast no need of, and ere long thou shalt sell thy necessaries.* And again, *at a great pennyworth pause a while*: he means, that perhaps the cheapness is apparent only, and not real; or the bargain, by straightening thee in thy business, may do thee more harm than good. For in another place he says, *many have been ruined by buying good pennyworths.* Again, Poor Richard says, *'tis foolish to lay out money in a purchase of repentance*; and yet this folly is practiced every day at vendues, for want of minding the Almanack. *Wise men*, as Poor Dick says, *learn by others' harms, fools scarcely by their own*; but *felix quem faciunt aliena pericula cautum.*[7] Many a one, for the sake of finery on the back, have gone with a hungry belly, and half-starved their families. *Silks and satins, scarlet and velvets*, as Poor Richard says, *put out the kitchen fire.*

"These are not the necessaries of life; they can scarcely be called the conveniences; and yet only because they look pretty, how many want to have them! The artificial wants of mankind thus become more numerous than the natural; and, as Poor Dick says, *for one poor person, there are an hundred indigent.* By these, and other extravagancies, the genteel are reduced to poverty, and forced to borrow of those whom they formerly despised, but who through industry and frugality have maintained their standing; in which case it appears plainly, that *a plowman on his legs is higher than a gentleman on his knees*, as Poor Richard says. Perhaps they have had a small estate left them, which they knew not the getting of; they think, " 'Tis day, and will never be night"; that a little to be spent out of so much is not worth minding; *a child and a fool*, as Poor Richard says, *imagine twenty shillings and twenty years can*

---

6. Lot.
7. A Latin version of the proverb just quoted.

never be spent but, *always taking out of the meal-tub, and never putting in, soon comes to the bottom;* as Poor Dick says, *when the well's dry, they know the worth of water.* But this they might have known before, if they had taken his advice; *if you would know the value of money, go and try to borrow some; for, he that goes a-borrowing goes a-sorrowing;* and indeed so does he that lends to such people, when he goes to get it in again. Poor Dick farther advises, and says,

> *Fond pride of dress is sure a very curse;*
> *E'er fancy you consult, consult your purse.*

And again, *pride is as loud a beggar as want, and a great deal more saucy.* When you have bought one fine thing, you must buy ten more, that your appearance may be all of a piece; but Poor Dick says, *'tis easier to suppress the first desire, than to satisfy all that follow it.* And 'tis as truly folly for the poor to ape the rich, as for the frog to swell, in order to equal the ox.

> *Great estates may venture more,*
> *But little boats should keep near shore.*

'Tis, however, a folly soon punished; for *pride that dines on vanity sups on contempt,* as Poor Richard says. And in another place, *pride breakfasted with plenty, dined with poverty, and supped with infamy.* And after all, of what use is this pride of appearance, for which so much is risked so much is suffered? It cannot promote health, or ease pain; it makes no increase of merit in the person, it creates envy, it hastens misfortune.

> *What is a butterfly? At best*
> *He's but a caterpillar dressed*
> *The gaudy fop's his picture just,*

as Poor Richard says.

"But what madness must it be to run in debt for these superfluities! We are offered, by the terms of this vendue, *six months' credit;* and that perhaps has induced some of us to attend it, because we cannot spare the ready money, and hope now to be fine without it. But, ah, think what you do when you run in debt; you give to another power over your liberty. If you cannot pay at the time, you will be ashamed to see your creditor; you will be in fear when you speak to him; you will make poor pitiful sneaking excuses, and by degrees come to lose your veracity, and sink into base downright lying; for, as Poor Richard says, *the second vice is lying, the first is running in debt.* And again, to the same purpose, *lying rides upon debt's back.* Whereas a free-born Englishman ought not to be ashamed or afraid to see or speak to any man living. But poverty often deprives a man of all spirit and virtue: *'tis hard for an empty bag to stand upright,* as Poor Richard truly says.

"What would you think of that prince, or that government, who should issue an edict forbidding you to dress like a gentleman or a gentlewoman, on pain of imprisonment or servitude? Would you not say, that you were free, have a right to dress as you please, and that such an edict would be a breach of your privileges, and such a government tyrannical? And yet you are about to put yourself under that tyranny, when you run in debt for such dress! Your creditor has authority, at his pleasure to deprive you of your liberty, by confining you in gaol[8] for life, or to sell you for a servant, if you should not be able to pay him! When you have got your bargain, you may, perhaps, think little of payment; but *creditors*, Poor Richard tells us, *have better memories than debtors*; and in another place says, *creditors are a superstitious sect, great observers of set days and times*. The day comes round before you are aware, and the demand is made before you are prepared to satisfy it, or if you bear your debt in mind, the term which at first seemed so long will, as it lessens, appear extremely short. Time will seem to have added wings to his heels as well as shoulders. *Those have a short Lent*, saith Poor Richard, *who owe money to be paid at Easter*. Then since, as he says, *The borrower is a slave to the lender, and the debtor to the creditor*, disdain the chain, preserve your freedom; and maintain your independency: be industrious and free; be frugal and free. At present, perhaps, you may think yourself in thriving circumstances, and that you can bear a little extravagance without injury; but,

> *For age and want, save while you may;*
> *No morning sun lasts a whole day,*

as Poor Richard says. Gain may be temporary and uncertain, but ever while you live, expense is constant and certain; and *'tis easier to build two chimneys than to keep one in fuel*, as Poor Richard says. So, *rather go to bed supperless than rise in debt*.

> *Get what you can, and what you get hold;*
> *'Tis the stone that will turn all your lead into gold,*

as Poor Richard says. And when you have got the philosopher's stone,[9] sure you will no longer complain of bad times, or the difficulty of paying taxes.

"This doctrine, my friends, is reason and wisdom; but after all, do not depend too much upon your own industry, and frugality, and prudence, though excellent things, for they may all be blasted without the blessing of heaven; and therefore, ask that blessing humbly, and be not uncharitable to those that at present seem to want it, but comfort and help them. Remember, Job[1] suffered, and was afterwards prosperous.

---

8. Jail.
9. A substance thought to transform base metals into gold, much sought after by alchemists.
1. The Old Testament patriarch who suffered with faith.

"And now to conclude, *experience keeps a dear[2] school, but fools will learn in no other, and scarce in that*; for it is true, *we may give advice, but we cannot give conduct*, as Poor Richard says: however, remember this, *they that won't be counseled, can't be helped*, as Poor Richard says: and farther, that, *if you will not hear reason, she'll surely rap your knuckles.*"

Thus the old gentleman ended his harangue. The people heard it, and approved the doctrine, and immediately practiced the contrary, just as if it had been a common sermon; for the vendue opened, and they began to buy extravangantly, notwithstanding, his cautions and their own fear of taxes. I found the good man had thoroughly studied my almanacs, and digested all I had dropped on these topics during the course of five and twenty years. The frequent mention he made of me must have tired any one else, but my vanity was wonderfully delighted with it, though I was conscious that not a tenth part of the wisdom was my own, which he ascribed to me, but rather the gleanings I had made of the sense of all ages and nations. However, I resolved to be the better for the echo of it; and though I had at first determined to buy stuff for a new coat, I went away resolved to wear my old one a little longer. Reader, if thou wilt do the same, thy profit will be as great as mine. I am, as ever, thine to serve thee,

Richard Saunders
July 7, 1757

1757

1758

The Sale of the Hessians[1]

From *the Count de Schaumbergh to the Baron Hohendorf, Commanding the Hessian Troops in America*

Rome, February 18, 1777.

MONSIEUR LE BARON:——On my return from Naples, I received at Rome your letter of the 27th December of last year. I have learned with unspeakable pleasure the courage our troops exhibited at Trenton, and you cannot imagine my joy on being told that of the 1,950 Hessians engaged in the fight, but 345 escaped.[2] There were just 1,605 men killed, and I cannot sufficiently commend your prudence in sending an exact list of the dead to my minister in London. This precaution was the more necessary, as the report sent to the English ministry does not give but 1,455 dead. This would

---

2. Expensive.

1. The text used here is from *The Writings of Benjamin Franklin*, ed. Albert Henry Smyth (New York: Macmillan, 1907). The American colonists were angry to find themselves defending their soil against German mercenaries purchased by Britain, and so Franklin's satire is based on rumors that Frederick

II (1744–97), head of the central West German state of Hesse-Cassel, was paid 30 pounds each for 15,700 Hessians killed on American soil.

2. The Battle of Trenton (New Jersey) was fought on Christmas Eve, 1776. Washington took 950 Hessian prisoners and between 20 and 30 were killed.

make 483,450 florins instead of 643,500 which I am entitled to demand under our convention. You will comprehend the prejudice which such an error would work in my finances, and I do not doubt you will take the necessary pains to prove that Lord North's[3] list is false and yours correct.

The court of London objects that there were a hundred wounded who ought not to be included in the list, nor paid for as dead; but I trust you will not overlook my instructions to you on quitting Cassel, and that you will not have tried by human succor to recall the life of the unfortunates whose days could not be lengthened but by the loss of a leg or an arm. That would be making them a pernicious present, and I am sure they would rather die than live in a condition no longer fit for my service. I do not mean by this that you should assassinate them; we should be humane, my dear Baron, but you may insinuate to the surgeons with entire propriety that a crippled man is a reproach to their profession, and that there is no wiser course than to let every one of them die when he ceases to be fit to fight.

I am about to send to you some new recruits. Don't economize them. Remember glory before all things. Glory is true wealth. There is nothing degrades the soldier like the love of money. He must care only for honor and reputation, but this reputation must be acquired in the midst of dangers. A battle gained without costing the conqueror any blood is an inglorious success, while the conquered cover themselves with glory by perishing with their arms in their hands. Do you remember that of the 300 Lacedæmonians who defended the defile[4] of Thermopylæ, not one returned? How happy should I be could I say the same of my brave Hessians!

It is true that their king, Leonidas, perished with them: but things have changed, and it is no longer the custom for princes of the empire to go and fight in America for a cause with which they have no concern. And besides, to whom should they pay the thirty guineas per man if I did not stay in Europe to receive them? Then, it is necessary also that I be ready to send recruits to replace the men you lose. For this purpose I must return to Hesse. It is true, grown men are becoming scarce there, but I will send you boys. Besides, the scarcer the commodity the higher the price. I am assured that the women and little girls have begun to till our lands, and they get on not badly. You did right to send back to Europe that Dr. Crumerus who was so successful in curing dysentery. Don't bother with a man who is subject to looseness of the bowels. That disease makes bad soldiers. One coward will do more mischief in an engagement than ten brave men will do good. Better that they

3. Frederick North, Earl of Guilford and British prime minister from 1770 to 1782.
4. A narrow mountain gorge or pass which necessitates troops marching through only by files. The Spartans unsuccessfully defended their lands against the Persians in 480 B.C.

burst in their barracks than fly in a battle, and tarnish the glory of our arms. Besides, you know that they pay me as killed for all who die from disease, and I don't get a farthing for runaways. My trip to Italy, which has cost me enormously, makes it desirable that there should be a great mortality among them. You will therefore promise promotion to all who expose themselves; you will exhort them to seek glory in the midst of dangers; you will say to Major Maundorff that I am not at all content with his saving the 345 men who escaped the massacre of Trenton. Through the whole campaign he has not had ten men killed in consequence of his orders. Finally, let it be your principal object to prolong the war and avoid a decisive engagement on either side, for I have made arrangements for a grand Italian opera, and I do not wish to be obliged to give it up. Meantime I pray God, my dear Baron de Hohendorf, to have you in His holy and gracious keeping.

1778

The Ephemera[1]

An Emblem of Human Life

You may remember, my dear friend,[2] that when we lately spent that happy day in the delightful garden and sweet society of the Moulin Joly,[3] I stopped a little in one of our walks, and stayed some time behind the company. We had been shown numberless skeletons of a kind of little fly, called an ephemera, whose successive generations, we were told, were bred and expired within the day. I happened to see a living company of them on a leaf, who appeared to be engaged in conversation. You know I understand all the inferior animal tongues: my too great application to the study of them is the best excuse I can give for the little progress I have made in your charming language. I listened through curiosity to the discourse of these little creatures; but as they, in their national vivacity, spoke three or four together, I could make but little of their conversation. I found, however, by some broken expressions that I heard now and then, they were disputing warmly on the merit of two foreign musicians, one a *cousin,* the other a *moscheto;*[4] in which dispute they spent their time, seemingly as regardless of the shortness of life as if they had been sure of living a month.

1. The text used here is from *The Writings of Benjamin Franklin*, ed. Albert Henry Smyth (New York: Macmillan, 1907). Franklin printed his "Bagatelles," of which this is the first, on his own press while he was in residence in France from 1776 to 1785. This essay was printed in both English and French but the date of first publication is unknown. It was included in W. T. Franklin's edition of the *Writings* in 1818.

2. Mme. d'Hardancourt Brillon de Jouy was about 35 years younger than Franklin and together with the widow Catherine Helvétius was the subject of much attention on Franklin's part. Her husband seems to have shown little concern over Franklin's presence in her company every Wednesday and Saturday. She was a musician and occasionally set Franklin's verses to music.

3. An estate on an island in the river Seine.

4. A gnat and a mosquito.

Happy people! thought I, you live certainly under a wise, just, and mild government, since you have no public grievances to complain of, nor any subject of contention but the perfections and imperfections of foreign music. I turned my head from them to an old gray-headed one, who was single on another leaf, and talking to himself. Being amused with his soliloquy, I put it down in writing, in hopes it will likewise amuse her to whom I am so much indebted for the most pleasing of all amusements, her delicious company and heavenly harmony.

"It was," said he, "the opinion of learned philosophers of our race, who lived and flourished long before my time, that this vast world, the Moulin Joly, could not itself subsist more than eighteen hours; and I think there was some foundation for that opinion, since, by the apparent motion of the great luminary that gives life to all nature, and which in my time has evidently declined considerably towards the ocean at the end of our earth, it must then finish its course, be extinguished in the waters that surround us, and leave the world in cold and darkness, necessarily producing universal death and destruction. I have lived seven of those hours, a great age, being no less than four hundred and twenty minutes of time. How very few of us continue so long! I have seen generations born, flourish, and expire. My present friends are the children and grandchildren of the friends of my youth, who are now, alas, no more! And I must soon follow them; for, by the course of nature, though still in health, I cannot expect to live above seven or eight minutes longer. What now avails all my toil and labor, in amassing honey-dew on this leaf, which I cannot live to enjoy! What the political struggles I have been engaged in, for the good of my compatriot inhabitants of this bush, or my philosophical studies for the benefit of our race in general! for, in politics, what can laws do without morals? Our present race of ephemeræ will in a course of minutes become corrupt, like those of other and older bushes, and consequently as wretched. And in philosophy how small our progress! Alas! art is long, and life is short! My friends would comfort me with the idea of a name, they say, I shall leave behind me; and they tell me I have lived long enough to nature and to glory. But what will fame be to an ephemera who no longer exists? And what will become of all history in the eighteenth hour, when the world itself, even the whole Moulin Joly, shall come to its end, and be buried in universal ruin?"

To me, after all my eager pursuits, no solid pleasures now remain, but the reflection of a long life spent in meaning well, the sensible conversation of a few good lady ephemeræ, and now and then a kind smile and a tune from the ever amiable *Brillante*.[5]

B. FRANKLIN

5. A pun on Madame Brillon's name.

Remarks Concerning the Savages of
North America[1]

Savages we call them, because their manners differ from ours, which we think the perfection of civility; they think the same of theirs.

Perhaps, if we could examine the manners of different nations with impartiality, we should find no people so rude, as to be without any rules of politeness; nor any so polite, as not to have some remains of rudeness.

The Indian men, when young, are hunters and warriors; when old, counselors; for all their government is by counsel of the sages; there is no force, there are no prisons, no officers to compel obedience, or inflict punishment. Hence they generally study oratory, the best speaker having the most influence. The Indian women till the ground, dress the food, nurse and bring up the children, and preserve and hand down to posterity the memory of public transactions. These employments of men and women are accounted natural and honorable. Having few artificial wants, they have abundance of leisure for improvement by conversation. Our laborious manner of life, compared with theirs, they esteem slavish and base; and the learning, on which we value ourselves, they regard as frivolous and useless. An instance of this occurred at the Treaty of Lancaster, in Pennsylvania, *anno* 1744, between the government of Virginia and the Six Nations.[2] After the principal business was settled, the commissioners from Virginia acquainted the Indians by a speech, that there was at Williamsburg a college, with a fund for educating Indian youth; and that, if the Six Nations would send down half a dozen of their young lads to that college, the government would take care that they should be well provided for, and instructed in all the learning of the white people. It is one of the Indian rules of politeness not to answer a public proposition the same day that it is made; they think it would be treating it as a light matter, and that they show it respect by taking time to consider it, as of a matter important. They therefore deferred their answer till the day following; when their speaker began, by expressing their deep sense of the kindness of the Virginia government, in making them that offer; "for we know," says he, "that you highly esteem the kind of learning taught in those Colleges, and that the maintenance of our young men, while with you, would be very expensive to you. We are convinced, therefore, that you mean to do us good by your proposal; and we thank you heartily. But you, who are wise, must know that different nations have different conceptions of things; and you will therefore not take it amiss, if our ideas of this kind of educa-

1. The text used here is from *The Writings of Benjamin Franklin*, Vol. X, ed. Albert Henry Smyth (New York: Macmillan, 1907).

2. A confederation of Iroquois tribes: Seneca, Cayuga, Oneida, Onondaga, Mohawk, and Tuscarora.

tion happen not to be the same with yours. We have had some experience of it; several of our young people were formerly brought up at the colleges of the northern provinces; they were instructed in all your sciences; but, when they came back to us, they were bad runners, ignorant of every means of living in the woods, unable to bear either cold or hunger, knew neither how to build a cabin, take a deer, or kill an enemy, spoke our language imperfectly, were therefore neither fit for hunters, warriors, nor counselors; they were totally good for nothing. We are however not the less obliged by your kind offer, though we decline accepting it; and, to show our grateful sense of it, if the gentlemen of Virginia will send us a dozen of their sons, we will take great care of their education, instruct them in all we know, and make *men* of them."

Having frequent occasions to hold public councils, they have acquired great order and decency in conducting them. The old men sit in the foremost ranks, the warriors in the next, and the women and children in the hindmost. The business of the women is to take exact notice of what passes, imprint it in their memories (for they have no writing), and communicate it to their children. They are the records of the council, and they preserve traditions of the stipulations in treaties 100 years back; which, when we compare with our writings, we always find exact. He that would speak, rises. The rest observe a profound silence. When he has finished and sits down, they leave him 5 or 6 minutes to recollect, that, if he has omitted anything he intended to say, or has anything to add, he may rise again and deliver it. To interrupt another, even in common conversation, is reckoned highly indecent. How different this from the conduct of a polite British House of Commons, where scarce a day passes without some confusion, that makes the speaker hoarse in calling *to order*; and how different from the mode of conversation in many polite companies of Europe, where, if you do not deliver your sentence with great rapidity, you are cut off in the middle of it by the impatient loquacity of those you converse with, and never suffered to finish it!

The politeness of these savages in conversation is indeed carried to excess, since it does not permit them to contradict or deny the truth of what is asserted in their presence. By this means they indeed avoid disputes; but then it becomes difficult to know their minds, or what impression you make upon them. The missionaries who have attempted to convert them to Christianity, all complain of this as one of the great difficulties of their mission. The Indians hear with patience the truths of the Gospel explained to them, and give their usual tokens of assent and approbation; you would think they were convinced. No such matter. It is mere civility.

A Swedish minister, having assembled the chiefs of the Susquehanah Indians, made a sermon to them, acquainting them with the principal historical facts on which our religion is founded; such as the fall of our first parents by eating an apple, the coming of Christ to repair the mischief, His miracles and suffering, &c. When he had finished, an Indian orator stood up to thank him. "What you have told us," says he, "is all very good. It is indeed bad to eat apples. It is better to make them all into cider. We are much obliged by your kindness in coming so far, to tell us these things which you have heard from your mothers. In return, I will tell you some of those we have heard from ours. In the beginning, our fathers had only the flesh of animals to subsist on; and if their hunting was unsuccessful, they were starving. Two of our young hunters, having killed a deer, made a fire in the woods to broil some part of it. When they were about to satisfy their hunger, they beheld a beautiful young woman descend from the clouds, and seat herself on that hill, which you see yonder among the blue mountains. They said to each other, it is a spirit that has smelled our broiling vension, and wishes to eat of it; let us offer some to her. They presented her with the tongue; she was pleased with the taste of it, and said, 'Your kindness shall be rewarded; come to this place after thirteen moons, and you shall find something that will be of great benefit in nourishing you and your children to the latest generations.' They did so, and, to their surprise, found plants they had never seen before; but which, from that ancient time, have been constantly cultivated among us, to our great advantage. Where her right hand had touched the ground, they found maize; where her left hand had touch it, they found kidney-beans; and where her backside had sat on it, they found tobacco." The good missionary, disgusted with this idle tale, said, "What I delivered to you were sacred truths; but what you tell me is mere fable, fiction, and falsehood." The Indian, offended, replied, "My brother, it seems your friends have not done you justice in your education; they have not well instructed you in the rules of common civility. You saw that we, who understand and practice those rules, believed all your stories; why do you refuse to believe ours?"

When any of them come into our towns, our people are apt to crowd round them, gaze upon them, and incommode them, where they desire to be private; this they esteem great rudeness, and the effect of the want of instruction in the rules of civility and good manners. "We have," say they, "as much curiosity as you, and when you come into our towns, we wish for opportunities of look-ing at you; but for this purpose we hide ourselves behind bushes, where you are to pass, and never intrude ourselves into your com-pany."

Their manner of entering one another's village has likewise its rules. It is reckoned uncivil in traveling strangers to enter a village abruptly, without giving notice of their approach. Therefore, as soon as they arrive within hearing, they stop and hollow,[3] remain-

3. Cry out; announce themselves.

ing there till invited to enter. Two old men usually come out to them, and lead them in. There is in every village a vacant dwelling, called *the strangers' house*. Here they are placed, while the old men go round from hut to hut, acquainting the inhabitants, that strangers are arrived, who are probably hungry and weary; and every one sends them what he can spare of victuals, and skins to repose on. When the strangers are refreshed, pipes and tobacco are brought; and then, but not before, conversation begins, with inquiries who they are, whither bound, what news, &c.; and it usually ends with offers of service, if the strangers have occasion of guides, or any necessaries for continuing their journey; and nothing is exacted for the entertainment.

The same hospitality, esteemed among them as a principal virtue, is practiced by private persons; of which Conrad Weiser, our interpreter, gave me the following instances. He had been naturalized among the Six Nations, and spoke well the Mohawk language. In going through the Indian country, to carry a message from our Governor to the Council at Onondaga, he called at the habitation of Canassatego, an old acquaintance, who embraced him, spread furs for him to sit on, placed before him some boiled beans and venison, and mixed some rum and water for his drink. When he was well refreshed, and had lit his pipe, Canassatego began to converse with him; asked how he had fared the many years since they had seen each other; whence he then came; what occasioned the journey, &c. Conrad answered all his questions; and when the discourse began to flag, the Indian, to continue it, said, "Conrad, you have lived long among the white people, and know something of their customs; I have been sometimes at Albany, and have observed, that once in seven days they shut up their shops, and assemble all in the great house; tell me what it is for? What do they do there?" "They meet there," says Conrad, "to hear and learn *good things*." "I do not doubt," says the Indian, "that they tell you so; they have told me the same; but I doubt the truth of what they say, and I will tell you my reasons. I went lately to Albany to sell my skins and buy blankets, knives, powder, rum, &c. You know I used generally to deal with Hans Hanson; but I was a little inclined this time to try some other merchant. However, I called first upon Hans, and asked him what he would give for beaver. He said he could not give any more than four shillings a pound; 'but,' says he, 'I cannot talk on business now; this is the day when we meet together to learn *good things*, and I am going to the meeting.' So I thought to myself, 'Since we cannot do any business today, I may as well go to the meeting too,' and I went with him. There stood up a man in black, and began to talk to the people very angrily. I did not understand what he said; but, perceiving that he looked much at me and at Hanson, I imagined he was angry at seeing me there; so I went out, sat down near the house, struck fire, and lit my pipe, waiting till the meeting should break up. I thought too, that the man had mentioned something of beaver, and I suspected it might be the subject of their meeting. So, when they came out, I accosted my merchant. 'Well, Hans,' says I, 'I hope you have agreed to give more than four shillings a pound.' 'No,' says he, 'I cannot give so much; I cannot give more than three shillings and sixpence.' I then spoke to several other dealers, but they all sung the same song,—three and sixpence, —three and sixpence. This made it clear to me, that my suspicion was right; and, that whatever they pretended of meeting to learn *good things*, the real purpose was to consult how to cheat Indians in the price of beaver. Consider but a little, Conrad, and you must be of my opinion. If they met so often to learn *good things*, they would certainly have learned some before this time. But they are still ignorant. You know our practice. If a white man, in traveling through our country, enters one of our cabins, we all treat him as I treat you; we dry him if he is wet, we warm him if he is cold, we give him meat and drink, that he may allay his thirst and hunger; and we spread soft furs for him to rest and sleep on; we demand nothing in return. But, if I go into a white man's house at Albany, and ask for victuals and drink, they say, 'Where is your money?' and if I have none, they say, 'Get out, you Indian dog.' You see they have not yet learned those little *good things*, that we need no meetings to be instructed in, because our mothers taught them to us when we were children; and therefore it is impossible their meetings should be, as they say, for any such purpose, or have any such effect; they are only to contrive *the cheating of Indians in the price of beaver*."[4]

1784

The Autobiography Franklin turned to the manuscript of *The Autobiography* on four different occasions over a period of nineteen years. The first part, addressed to his son William Franklin (c. 1731–1813), who was Governor of New Jersey when Franklin was writing this section, was composed while Franklin was visiting the country home of Bishop Jonathan Shipley at Twyford, a village about fifty miles from London. It was begun on July 30 and concluded on or about August 13, 1771. Franklin did not work on the manuscript again until he was living in France and was Minister of the newly formed United States, about thirteen years later. The last two sections were written in August, 1788, and the winter of 1789–90, when Franklin stopped because of illness. Before he died he carried his life up to the year 1758. The account ends, therefore, before Franklin's great triumphs as a diplomat and public servant.

4. "It is remarkable that in all ages and countries hospitality has been allowed as the virtue of those whom the civilized were pleased to call barbarians. The Greeks celebrated the Scythians for it. The Saracens possessed it eminently, and it is to this day the reigning virtue of the wild Arabs. St. Paul, too, in the relation of his voyage and shipwreck on the island of Melité says the barbarous people showed us no little kindness; for they kindled a fire, and received us every one, because of the present rain, and because of the cold" [Franklin's note]. Saint Paul's account of his visit to Melita may be found in Acts 28. The Scythians were nomadic tribes of southeastern Europe known for their plundering.

The first part of *The Autobiography* was published in 1791 by Jacques Buisson in a French translation; William Temple Franklin, Franklin's grandson, published an edition of *The Autobiography* in 1818, but he did not possess the last section which his grandfather wrote because he unwittingly exchanged it for the French translator's Part One. It was not until 1868 that John Bigelow published *The Autobiography* as we know it, with all four sections complete.

The text for *The Autobiography* here reprinted is entirely new; it is the first to have been taken directly from the manuscript itself (all other editors have merely corrected earlier printed texts). The text was established by J. A. Leo Lemay and Paul Zall for their Norton Critical Edition of *The Autobiography*, and is here reprinted with their kind permission. The text has been only slightly modernized. All manuscript abbreviations and symbols have been expanded. The editors note that they have omitted short dashes which Franklin often wrote after sentences, and punctuation marks which "have been clearly superseded by revisions or additions." Careless slips have been corrected silently but may be found in their section on emendations in their complete text. Professors Lemay and Zall have been very generous in letting us see their footnotes and biographical sketches. Every student of Franklin's *Autobiography* must also acknowledge the extremely helpful edition of Leonard W. Labaree *et al.* (New Haven, Conn.: Yale University Press, 1964).

From The Autobiography

From [*Part One*]

Twyford, at the Bishop of St. Asaph's 1771.

Dear Son,

I have ever had a Pleasure in obtaining any little Anecdotes of my Ancestors. You may remember the Enquiries I made among the Remains[1] of my Relations when you were with me in England; and the Journey I took for that purpose. Now imaging it may be equally agreeable to you to know the Circumstances of *my* Life, many of which you are yet unacquainted with; and expecting a Week's uninterrupted Leisure in my present Country Retirement, I sit down to write them for you. To which I have besides some other Inducements. Having emerg'd from the Poverty and Obscurity in which I was born and bred, to a State of Affluence and some Degree of Reputation in the World, and having gone so far thro' Life with a considerable Share of Felicity, the conducting Means I made use of, which, with the Blessing of God, so well succeeded, my Posterity may like to know, as they may find some of them suitable to their own Situations, and therefore fit to be imitated. That Felicity, when I reflected on it, has induc'd me sometimes to

THE AUTOBIOGRAPHY OF BENJA-MIN FRANKLIN: A Norton Critical Edition, edited by J. A. Leo Lemay and Paul M. Zall. Copyright © 1984 by W. W. Norton & Company, Inc. Reprinted by permission of the editors and

W. W. Norton & Company, Inc.
1. I.e., the remaining representatives of a family. Franklin and his son toured England in 1758 and visited ancestral homes at Ecton and Banbury, Northamptonshire, England.

say, that were it offer'd to my Choice, I should have no Objection to a Repetition of the same Life from its Beginning, only asking the Advantage Authors have in a second Edition to correct some Faults of the first. So would I if I might, besides correcting the Faults, change some sinister Accidents and Events of it for others more favorable, but tho' this were denied, I should still accept the Offer. However, since such a Repetition is not to be expected, the Thing most like living one's Life over again, seems to be a *Recollection* of that Life; and to make that Recollection as durable as possible, the putting it down in Writing. Hereby, too, I shall indulge the Inclination so natural in old Men, to be talking of themselves and their own past Actions, and I shall indulge it, without being troublesome to others who thro' respect to Age might think themselves oblig'd to give me a Hearing, since this may be read or not as any one pleases. And lastly, (I may as well confess it, since my Denial of it will be believ'd by no body) perhaps I shall a good deal gratify my own *Vanity*. Indeed I scarce ever heard or saw the introductory Words, *Without Vanity I may say*, etc. but some vain thing immediately follow'd. Most People dislike Vanity in others whatever Share they have of it themselves, but I give it fair Quarter wherever I meet with it, being persuaded that it is often productive of Good to the Possessor and to others that are within his Sphere of Action: And therefore in many Cases it would not be quite absurd if a Man were to thank God for his Vanity among the other Comforts of Life.

And now I speak of thanking God, I desire with all Humility to acknowledge, that I owe the mention'd Happiness of my past Life to his kind Provdience, which led me to the Means I us'd and gave them Success. My Belief of This, induces me to *hope*, tho' I must not *presume*, that the same Goodness will still be exercis'd towards me in continuing that Happiness, or in enabling me to bear a fatal Reverso,[2] which I may experience as others have done, the Complexion of my future Fortune being known to him only: and in whose Power it is to bless to us even our Afflictions.

* * *

At Ten Years old, I was taken home to assist my Father in his Business, which was that of a Tallow Chandler and Soap-Boiler.[3] A Business he was not bred to, but had assumed on his Arrival in New England on finding his Dying Trade would not maintain his Family, being in little Request. Accordingly I was employed in cutting Wick for the Candles, filling the Dipping Mold, and the Molds for cast Candles, attending the Shop, going of Errands, etc. I dislik'd the Trade and had a strong Inclination for the Sea; but my Father declar'd against it; however, living near the Water, I was much in and about it, learned early to swim well, and to manage Boats, and when in a Boat or Canoe with other Boys I was com-

---

2. I.e., a backhanded stroke, a word used in dueling with rapiers.　　3. Maker of candles and soap.

monly allow'd to govern,[4] especially in any case of Difficulty; and upon other Occasions I was generally a Leader among the Boys, and sometimes led them into Scrapes, of which I will mention one Instance, as it shows an early projecting public Spirit, tho' not then justly conducted. There was a Salt Marsh that bounded part of the Mill Pond, on the Edge of which at Highwater, we us'd to stand to fish for Minnows. By much Trampling, we had made it a mere Quagmire. My Proposal was to build a Wharf there fit for us to stand upon, and I show'd my Comrades a large Heap of Stones which were intended for a new House near the Marsh, and which would very well suit our Purpose. Accordingly in the Evening when the Workmen were gone, I assembled a Number of my Playfellows, and working with them diligently like so many Emmets,[5] sometimes two or three to a Stone, we brought them all away and built our little Wharf. The next Morning the Workmen were surpris'd at Missing the Stones; which were found in our Wharf; Enquiry was made after the Removers; we were discovered and complain'd of; several of us were corrected by our Fathers; and tho' I pleaded the Usefulness of the Work, mine convinc'd me that nothing was useful which was not honest.

* * *

* * * I continu'd thus employ'd in my Father's Business four two Years, that is till I was 12 Years old; and my Brother John[2] who was bred to that Business having left my Father, married and set up for himself at Rhode Island, there was all Appearance that I was destin'd to supply his Place and be a Tallow Chandler. But my Dislike to the Trade continuing, my Father was under Apprehensions that if he did not find one for me more agreeable, I should break away and get to Sea, as his Son Josiah had done to his great Vexation. He therefore sometimes took me to walk with him, and see Joiners, Bricklayers, Turners, Braziers,[7] etc. at their Work, that he might observe my Inclination, and endeavour to fix it on some Trade or other on Land. It has ever since been a Pleasure to me to see good Workmen handle their Tools; and it has been useful to me, having learned so much by it, as to be able to do little Jobs myself in my House, when a Workman could not readily be got; and to construct little Machines for my Experiments while the Intention of making the Experiment was fresh and warm in my Mind. My Father at last fix'd upon the Cutler's Trade, and my Uncle Benjamin's Son Samuel who was bred to that Business in London being about that time establish'd in Boston, I was sent to be with him some time on liking. But his Expectations of a Fee with me displeasing my Father, I was taken home again.

4. Steer.
5. Ants.
6. John Franklin (1690–1756), Franklin's favorite brother; he was to become Post-

master of Boston.
7. Woodworkers, bricklayers, latheworkers, brassworkers.

From a Child I was fond of Reading, and all the little Money that came into my Hands was ever laid out in Books. Pleas'd with the Pilgrim's Progress, my first Collection was of John Bunyan's[8] Works, in separate little Volumes. I afterwards sold them to enable me to buy R. Burton's[9] Historical Collections; they were small Chapmen's Books[1] and cheap, 40 or 50 in all. My Father's little Library consisted chiefly of Books in polemic Divinity, most of which I read, and have since often regretted, that at a time when I had such a Thirst for Knowledge, more proper Books had not fallen in my Way, since it was now resolv'd I should not be a Clergyman. Plutarch's Lives[2] there was, in which I read abundantly, and I still think that time spent to great Advantage. There was also a Book of Defoe's[3] called an Essay on Projects and another of Dr. Mather's[4] call'd Essays to do Good, which perhaps gave me a Turn of Thinking that had an Influence on some of the principal future Events of my Life.

This Bookish Inclination at length determin'd my Father to make me a Printer, tho' he had already one Son, (James) of that Profession. In 1717 my Brother James return'd from England with a Press and Letters[5] to set up his Business in Boston. I lik'd it much better than that of my Father, but still had a Hankering for the Sea. To prevent the apprehended Effect of such an Inclination, my Father was impatient to have me bound[6] to my Brother. I stood out some time, but at last was persuaded and signed the Indentures,[7] when I was yet but 12 Years old. I was to serve as an Apprentice till I was 21 Years of Age, only I was to be allow'd Journeyman's Wages[8] during the last Year. In a little time I made great Proficiency in the Business, and became a useful Hand to my Brother. I now had Access to better Books. An Acquaintance with the Apprentices of Booksellers enable me sometimes to borrow a small one, which I was careful to return soon and clean. Often I sat up in my Room reading the greatest Part of the Night, when the Book was borrow'd in the Evening and to be return'd early in the Morning lest it should be miss'd or wanted. And after some time an ingenious Tradesman[9] who had a pretty Collection of Books, and who frequented our Printing-House, took Notice me, invited me to his Library, and very kindly lent me such Books as I chose to read. I now took a Fancy to Poetry, and made some little Pieces. My

---

8. John Bunyan (1628–88) published *Pilgrim's Progess* in 1678; his works were enormously popular and available in cheap one-shilling editions.
9. Burton was a pseudonym for Nathaniel Crouch (1632?–1725?), a popularizer of British history.
1. Peddlers' books, hence inexpensive.
2. Plutarch (A.D. 46?–120?), Greek biographer who wrote *Parallel Lives* of noted Greek and Roman figures.
3. Daniel Defoe's *Essay on Projects* (1697) proposed remedies for economic improvement.
4. Cotton Mather published *Bonifacius: An Essay upon the Good* in 1710.
5. Type.
6. Apprenticed.
7. A contract binding him to work for his brother for nine years. James Franklin (1697–1735) had learned the printer's trade in England.
8. I.e., be paid for each day's work, having served his apprenticeship.
9. "Mr. Matthew Adams" [Franklin's note]. "Pretty": exceptionally fine.

Brother, thinking it might turn to account encourag'd me, and put me on composing two occasional Ballads. One was called the *Light House Tragedy*, and contain'd an Account of the drowning of Capt. Worthilake with his Two Daughters; the other was a Sailor Song on the Taking of *Teach* or Blackbeard the Pirate.[1] They were wretched Stuff, in the Grubstreet Ballad Style,[2] and when they were printed he sent me about the Town to sell them. The first sold wonderfully, the Event being recent, having made a great Noise. This flatter'd my Vanity. But my Father discourag'd me, by ridiculing my Performances, and telling me Verse-makers were generally Beggars; so I escap'd being a Poet, most probably a very bad one. But as Prose Writing has been of great Use to me in the Course of my Life, and was a principal Means of my Advancement, I shall tell you how in such a Situation I acquir'd what little Ability I have in that Way.

There was another Bookish Lad in the Town, John Collins by Name, with whom I was intimately acquainted. We sometimes disputed, and very fond we were of Argument, and very desirous of confuting one another. Which disputatious Turn, by the way, is apt to become a very bad Habit, making People often extremely disagreeable in Company, by the Contradiction that is necessary to bring it into Practice, and thence, besides souring and spoiling the Conversation, is productive of Disgusts and perhaps Enmities where you may have occasion for Friendship. I had caught it by reading my Father's Books of Dispute about Religion. Persons of good Sense, I have since observ'd, seldom fall into it, except Lawyers, University Men, and Men of all Sorts that have been bred at Edinburgh.[3] A Question was once some how or other started between Collins and me, of the Propriety of educating the Female Sex in Learning, and their Abilities for Study. He was of Opinion that it was improper; and that they were naturally unequal to it. I took the contrary Side, perhaps a little for Dispute sake. He was naturally more eloquent, had a ready Plenty of Words, and sometimes as I thought bore me down more by his Fluency than by the Strength of his Reasons. As we parted without settling the Point, and were not to see one another again for some time, I sat down to put my Arguments in Writing, which I copied fair and sent to him. He answer'd and I replied. Three or four Letters of a Side had pass'd, when my Father happen'd to find my Papers, and read them. Without entering into the Discussion, he took occasion to talk to me about the Manner of my Writing, observ'd that tho' I had the Advantage of my Antagonist in correct Spelling and pointing[4]

1. The full texts of these ballads cannot be found; George Worthylake, lighthouse keeper on Beacon Island, Boston Harbor, and his wife and daughter were drowned on November 3, 1718; the pirate Blackbeard, Edward Teach, was killed off the Carolina coast on November 22, 1718.

2. Grub Street in London was inhabited by poor literary hacks who capitalized on poems of topical interest.

3. Scottish Presbyterians were noted for their argumentative nature.

4. Punctuation. Spelling and punctuation were not standardized in this period.

(which I ow'd to the Printing House) I fell far short in elegance of Expression, in Method and in Perspicuity, of which he convinc'd me by several Instances. I saw the Justice of his Remarks, and thence grew more attentive to the *Manner* in Writing, and determin'd to endeavour at Improvement.

About this time I met with an odd Volume of the Spectator.[5] I had never before seen any of them. I bought it, read it over and over, and was much delighted with it. I thought the Writing excellent, and wish'd if possible to imitate it. With that View, I took some of the Papers, and making short Hints of the Sentiment in each Sentence, laid them by a few Days, and then without looking at the Book, tried to complete the Papers again, by expressing each hinted Sentiment at length and as fully as it had been express'd before, in any suitable Words that should come to hand.

Then I compar'd my Spectator with the Original, discover'd some of my Faults and corrected them. But I found I wanted a Stock of Words or a Readiness in recollecting and using them, which I thought I should have acquir'd before that time, if I had gone on making Verses, since the continual Occasion for Words of the same Import but of different Length, to suit the Measure,[6] or of different Sound for the Rhyme, would have laid me under a constant Necessity of searching for Variety, and also have tended to fix that Variety in my Mind, and make me Master of it. Therefore I took some of the Tales and turn'd them into Verse: And after a time, when I had pretty well forgotten the Prose, turn'd them back again. I also sometimes jumbled my Collections of Hints into Confusion, and after some Weeks, endeavour'd to reduce them into the best Order, before I began to form the full Sentences, and complete the Paper. This was to teach me Method in the Arrangement of Thoughts. By comparing my Work afterwards with the original, I discover'd many faults and amended them; but I sometimes had the Pleasure of Fancying that in certain Particulars of small Import, I had been lucky enough to improve the Method or the Language and this encourag'd me to think I might possibly in time come to be a tolerable English Writer, of which I was extremely ambitious.

* * *

My Brother had in 1720 or 21, begun to print a Newspaper. It was the second[7] that appear'd in America, and was called *The New England Courant*. The only one before it, was *the Boston News Letter*. I remember his being dissuaded by some of his Friends from the Undertaking, as not likely to succeed, one Newspaper being in their judgment enough for America. At this time 1771 there are not less than five and twenty. He went on however with the Undertaking, and after having work'd in composing the Types and printing

5. An English periodical published daily from March 1, 1711, to December 6, 1712, and revived in 1714. It contained essays by Joseph Addison (1672–1719) and Richard Steele (1672–1729). It addressed itself primarily to matters of literature and morality.

6. Meter.

7. Actually the fifth; James Franklin's paper appeared on August 7, 1721.

off the Sheets I was employ'd to carry the Papers thro' the Streets to the Customers. He had some ingenious Men among his Friends who amus'd themselves by writing little Pieces for this Paper, which gain'd it Credit, and made it more in Demand; and these Gentlemen often visited us. Hearing their Conversations, and their Accounts of the Approbation their Papers were receiv'd with, I was excited to try my Hand among them. But being still a Boy, and suspecting that my Brother would object to printing any Thing of mine in his Paper if he knew it to be mine, I contriv'd to disguise my Hand, and writing an anonymous Paper I put it in at Night under the Door of the Printing-House.

It was found in the Morning and communicated to his Writing Friends when they call'd in as Usual. They read it, commented on it in my Hearing, and I had the exquisite Pleasure, of finding it met with their Approbation, and that in their different Guesses at the Author none were named but Men of some Character among us for Learning and Ingenuity. I suppose now that I was rather lucky in my Judges: And that perhaps they were not really so very good ones as I then esteem'd them. Encourag'd however by this, I wrote and convey'd in the same Way to the Press several more Papers,[8] which were equally approv'd, and I kept my Secret till my small Fund of Sense for such Performances was pretty well exhausted, and then I discovered[9] it; when I began to be considered a little more by my Brothers' Acquaintance, and in a manner that did not quite please him, as he thought, probably with reason, that it tended to make me too vain. And perhaps this might be one Occasion of the Differences that we began to have about this Time. Tho' a Brother, he considered himself as my Master, and me as his Apprentice; and accordingly expected the same Services from me as he would from another; while I thought he demean'd me too much in some he requir'd of me, who from a Brother expected more Indulgence. Our Disputes were often brought before our Father, and I fancy I was either generally in the right, or else a better Pleader, because the Judgment was generally in my favor. But my Brother was passionate and had often beaten me, which I took extremely amiss; and thinking my Apprenticeship very tedious, I was continually wishing for some Opportunity of shortening it, which at length offered in a manner unexpected.[1]

One of the Pieces in our Newspaper, on some political Point which I have now forgotten, gave Offence to the Assembly.[2] He was taken up, censur'd and imprison'd for a Month by the Speak-

---

8. *The Silence Dogood Letters* (April 12–October 8, 1722) were the earliest essay series in America.
9. Revealed.
1. "I fancy his harsh and tyrannical Treatment of me, might be a means of impressing me with that Aversion to arbitrary Power that has stuck to me thro' my whole Life" [Franklin's note].

2. On June 11, 1722, the *Courant* hinted that there was collusion between local authorities and pirates raiding off Boston Harbor. James Franklin was jailed from June 12 to July 7. "Assembly": Massachusetts legislative body; the lower house, with representatives elected by towns of the Massachusetts General Court.

er's Warrant, I suppose because he would not discover his Author. I too was taken up and examin'd before the Council; but tho' I did not give them any Satisfaction, they contented themselves with admonishing me, and dismiss'd me; considering me perhaps as an Apprentice who was bound to keep his Master's Secrets. During my Brother's Confinement, which I resented a good deal, notwithstanding our private Differences, I had the Management of the Paper, and I made bold to give our Rulers some Rubs[3] in it, which my Brother took very kindly, while others began to consider me in an unfavorable Light, as a young Genius that had a Turn for Libelling and Satire.[4] My Brother's Discharge was accompanied with an Order of the House, (a very odd one) that *James Franklin should no longer print the Paper called the New England Courant.* There was a Consultation held in our Printing-House among his Friends what he should do in this Case. Some propos'd to evade the Order by changing the Name of the Paper; but my Brother seeing Inconveniences in that, it was finally concluded on as a better Way, to let it be printed for the future under the Name of *Benjamin Franklin.* And to avoid the Censure of the Assembly that might fall on him, as still printing it by his Apprentice, the Contrivance was, that my old Indenture should be return'd to me with a full Discharge on the Back of it, to be shown on Occasion; but to secure to him the Benefit of my Service I was to sign new Indentures for the Remainder of the Term, which were to be kept private. A very flimsy Scheme it was, but however it was immediately executed, and the Paper went on accordingly under my Name for several Months.[5] At length a fresh Difference arising between my Brother and me, I took upon me to assert my Freedom, presuming that he would not venture to produce the new Indentures. It was not fair in me to take this Advantage, and this I therefore reckon one of the first Errata[6] of my Life: But the Unfairness of it weigh'd little with me, when under the Impressions of Resentment, for the Blows his Passion too often urg'd him to bestow upon me. Tho' he was otherwise not an ill-natur'd Man: Perhaps I was too saucy and provoking.

When he found I would leave him, he took care to prevent my getting Employment in any other Printing-House of the Town, by going round and speaking to every Master, who accordingly refus'd to give me Work. I then thought of going to New York as the nearest Place where there was a Printer: and I was the rather inclin'd to leave Boston, when I reflected that I had already made myself a little obnoxious to the governing Party; and from the arbitrary Proceedings of the Assembly in my Brother's Case it was likely I might if I stay'd soon bring myself into Scrapes; and farther that my indiscreet Disputations about Religion began to make me

---

3. Insults, annoyances.
4. Satirizing.
5. The paper continued under Franklin's

name until 1726, nearly three years after he left Boston.
6. Printer's term for errors.

pointed at with Horror by good People, as an Infidel or Atheist; I
determin'd on the Point: but my Father now siding with my
Brother, I was sensible that if I attempted to go openly, Means
would be used to prevent me. My Friend Collins therefore undertook to manage a little for me. He agreed with the Captain of a
New York Sloop for my Passage, under the Notion of my being a
young Acquaintance of his that had got a naughty Girl with Child,
whose Friends would compel me to marry her, and therefore I
could not appear or come away publicly. So I sold some of my
Books to raise a little Money, was taken on board privately, and as
we had a fair Wind, in three Days I found myself in New York
near 300 Miles from home, a Boy of but 17, without the least
Recommendation to or Knowledge of any Person in the Place, and
with very little Money in my Pocket.

My Inclinations for the Sea, were by this time worn out, or I
might now have gratified them. But having a Trade, and supposing
myself a pretty good Workman, I offer'd my Service to the Printer
of the Place, old Mr. William Bradford.[7] He could give me no
Employment, having little to do, and Help enough already: But,
says he, my Son at Philadelphia has lately lost his principal Hand,
Aquila Rose, by Death. If you go thither I believe he may employ
you. Philadelphia was 100 Miles farther. I set out, however, in a
Boat for Amboy;[8] leaving my Chest and Things to follow me
round by Sea. * * *

* * *

I have been the more particular in this Description of my Journey, and shall be so of my first Entry into that City, that you may
in your Mind compare such unlikely Beginning with the Figure I
have since made there. I was in my working Dress, my best Clothes
being to come round by Sea. I was dirty from my Journey; my
Pockets were stuff'd out with Shirts and Stockings; I knew no Soul,
nor where to look for Lodging. I was fatigu'd with Travelling,
Rowing and Want of Rest. I was very hungry, and my whole Stock
of Cash consisted of a Dutch Dollar and about a Shilling in Cop-
per. The latter I gave the People of the Boat for my Passage, who
at first refus'd it on Account of my Rowing; but I insisted on their
taking it, a Man being sometimes more generous when he has but a
little Money than when he has plenty, perhaps thro' Fear of being
through to have but little. Then I walk'd up the Street, gazing
about, till near the Market House I met a Boy with Bread. I had
made many a Meal on Bread, and inquiring where he got it, I went
immediately to the Baker's he directed me to in Second Street; and
ask'd for Biscuit, intending such as we had in Boston, but they it
seems were not made in Philadelphia, then I ask'd for a three-penny

---

7. William Bradford (1663–1752), one of
the first American printers and father of
Andrew Bradford (1686–1742), Franklin's future competitor in Philadelphia.
8. Perth Amboy, New Jersey.

Loaf, and was told they had none such: so not considering or knowing the Difference of Money and the greater Cheapness nor the Names of his Bread, I bad him give me three pennyworth of any sort. He gave me accordingly three great Puffy Rolls. I was surpris'd at the Quantity, but took it, and having no Room in my Pockets, walk'd off, with a Roll under each Arm, and eating the other. Thus I went up Market Street as far as Fourth Street, passing by the Door of Mr. Read, my future Wife's Father, when she standing at the Door saw me, and thought I made as I certainly did a most awkward ridiculous Appearance. Then I turn'd and went down Chestnut Street and part of Walnut Street, eating my Roll all the Way, and coming round found myself again at Market Street Wharf, near the Boat I came in, to which I went for a Draught of the River Water, and being fill'd with one of my Rolls, gave the other two to a Woman and her Child that came down the River in the Boat with us and were waiting to go farther. Thus refresh'd I walk'd again up the Street, which by this time had many clean dress'd People in it who were all walking the same Way; I join'd them, and thereby was led into the great Meeting House of the Quakers near the Market. I sat down among them, and after looking round a while and hearing nothing said, being very drowsy thro' Labour and want of Rest the preceding Night, I fell fast asleep, and continu'd so till the Meeting broke up, when one was kind enough to rouse me. This was therefore the first House I was in or slept in, in Philadelphia.

Walking again down towards the River, and looking in the Faces of People, I met a young Quaker Man whose Countenance I lik'd, and accosting him requested he would tell me where a Stranger could get Lodging. We were then near the Sign of the Three Mariners. Here, says he, is one Place that entertains Strangers, but it is not a reputable House; if thee wilt walk with me, I'll show thee a better. He brought me to the Crooked Billet in Water Street. Here I got a Dinner. And while I was eating it, several sly Questions were ask'd me, as it seem'd to be suspected from my youth and Appearance, that I might be some Runaway. After Dinner my Sleepiness return'd: and being shown to a Bed, I lay down without undressing, and slept till Six in the Evening; was call'd to Supper; went to Bed again very early and slept soundly till the next Morning. Then I made myself as tidy as I could, and went to Andrew Bradford the Printer's. I found in the Shop the old Man his Father, whom I had seen at New York, and who travelling on horse back had got to Philadelphia before me. He introduc'd me to his Son, who receiv'd me civilly, gave me a Breakfast, but told me he did not at present want a Hand, being lately supplied with one. But there was another Printer in town lately set up, one Keimer,[9] who

9. Samuel Keimer (c. 1688–1742) was a printer in London before coming to Philadelphia.

perhaps might employ me; if not, I should be welcome to lodge at his House, and he would give me a little Work to do now and then till fuller Business should offer.

The old Gentleman said, he would go with me to the new Printer: And when we found him, Neighbor, says Bradford, I have brought to see you a young Man of your Business, perhaps you may want such a One. He ask'd me a few Questions, put a Composing Stick[1] in my Hand to see how I work'd, and then said he would employ me soon, tho' he had just then nothing for me to do. And taking old Bradford whom he had never seen before, to be one of the Townspeople that had a Goodwill for him, enter'd into a Conversation on his present Undertaking and Prospects; while Bradford not discovering that he was the other Printer's Father; on Keimer's Saying he expected soon to get the greatest Part of the Business into his own Hands, drew him on by artful Questions and starting little Doubts, to explain all his Views, what Interest he relied on, and in what manner he intended to proceed. I who stood by and heard all, saw immediately that one of them was a crafty old Sophister,[2] and the other a mere Novice. Bradford left me with Keimer, who was greatly surpris'd when I told him who the old Man was.

Keimer's Printing-House I found, consisted of an old shatter'd Press and one small worn-out Fount of English,[3] which he was then using himself, composing in it an Elegy on Aquila Rose[4] before-mentioned, an ingenious young Man of excellent Character much respected in the Town, Clerk of the Assembly,[5] and a pretty Poet. Keimer made Verses, too, but very indifferently. He could not be said to write them, for his Manner was to compose them in the Types directly out of his Head; so there being no Copy, but one Pair of Cases,[6] and the Elegy likely to require all the Letter, no one could help him. I endeavour'd to put his Press (which he had not yet us'd, and of which he understood nothing) into Order fit to be work'd with; and promising to come and print off his Elegy as soon as he should have got it ready, I return'd to Bradford's who gave me a little Job to do for the present, and there I lodged and dieted.[7] A few Days after Keimer sent for me to print off the Elegy. And now he had got another Pair of Cases, and a Pamphlet to reprint, on which he set me to work.

These two Printers I found poorly qualified for their Business. Bradford had not been bred to it, and was very illiterate; and Keimer tho' something of a Scholar, was a mere Compositor,

1. An instrument of adjustable width in which type is set before being put on a galley.
2. Trickster, rationalizer.
3. An oversized type, not practicable for books and newspapers.
4. Aquila Rose (c. 1695–1723), journeyman printer for Andrew Bradford; his son Joseph apprenticed with Franklin.
5. One who has charge of the records, documents, and correspondence of any organized body; here, the Pennsylvania legislative council.
6. Two shallow trays which contain uppercase and lowercase type.
7. Boarded.

knowing nothing of Presswork. He had been one of the French Prophets[8] and could act their enthusiastic Agitations. At this time he did not profess any particular Religion, but something of all on occasion; was very ignorant of the World, and had, as I afterwards found, a good deal of the Knave in his Composition. He did not like my Lodging at Bradford's while I work'd with him. He had a House indeed, but without Furniture, so he could not lodge me: But he got me a Lodging at Mr. Read's before-mentioned, who was the Owner of his House. And my Chest and Clothes being come by this time, I made rather a more respectable Appearance in the Eyes of Miss Read, than I had done when she first happen'd to see me eating my Roll in the Street.

I began now to have some Acquaintance among the young People of the Town, that were Lovers of Reading with whom I spent my Evenings very pleasantly and gaining Money by my Industry and Frugality, I lived very agreeably, forgetting Boston as much as I could, and not desiring that any there should know where I resided except my Friend Collins who was in my Secret, and kept it when I wrote to him. At length an Incident happened that sent me back again much sooner than I had intended.

I had a Brother-in-law, Robert Homes,[9] Master of a Sloop that traded between Boston and Delaware. He being at New Castle 40 Miles below Philadelphia, heard there of me, and wrote me a Letter, mentioning the Concern of my Friends in Boston at my abrupt Departure, assuring me of their Goodwill to me, and that everything would be accommodated to my Mind if I would return, to which he exhorted me very earnestly. I wrote an Answer to his Letter, thank'd him for his Advice, but stated my Reasons for quitting Boston fully, and in such a Light as to convince him I was not so wrong as he had apprehended. Sir William Keith[1] Governor of the Province, was then at New Castle, and Captain Homes happening to be in Company with him when my Letter came to hand, spoke to him of me, and show'd him the Letter. The Governor read it, and seem'd surpris'd when he was told my Age. He said I appear'd a young Man of promising Parts, and therefore should be encouraged: The Printers at Philadelphia were wretched ones, and if I would set up there, he made no doubt I should succeed; for his Part, he would procure me the public Business, and do me every other Service in his Power. This my Brother-in-Law afterwards told me in Boston. But I knew as yet nothing of it; when one Day Keimer and I being at Work together near the Window, we saw the Governor and another Gentleman (which prov'd to be Colonel French, of New Castle) finely dress'd, come directly across

---

8. An English sect which preached doomsday and cultivated emotional fits.
9. Robert Homes (d. before 1743), husband of Franklin's sister Mary, and a ship's captain.

1. Sir William Keith (1680–1749), governor of Pennsylvania, 1717–26; he fled to England in 1728 to escape debtor's prison.

the Street to our House, and heard them at the Door.

Keimer ran down immediately, thinking it a Visit to him. But the Governor enquir'd for me, came up, and with a Condescension and Politeness I had been quite unus'd to, made me many Compliments, desired to be acquainted with me, blam'd me kindly for not having made myself known to him when I first came to the Place, and would have me away with him to the Tavern where he was going with Colonel French to taste as he said some excellent Madeira. I was not a little surpris'd, and Keimer star'd like a Pig poison'd. I went however with the Governor and Colonel French, to a Tavern the Corner of Third Street, and over the Madeira he propos'd my Setting up my Business, laid before me the Probabilities of Success, and both he and Colonel French assur'd me I should have their Interest and Influence in procuring the Public-Business of both Governments. On my doubting whether my Father would assist me in it, Sir William said he would give me a Letter to him, in which he would state the Advantages, and he did not doubt of prevailing with him. So it was concluded I should return to Boston in the first Vessel with the Governor's Letter recommending me to my Father.

In the meantime the Intention was to be kept secret, and I went on working with Keimer as usual, the Governor sending for me now and then to dine with him, a very great Honor I thought it, and conversing with me in the most affable, familiar, and friendly manner imaginable. About the End of April 1724, a little Vessel offer'd for Boston. I took Leave of Keimer as going to see my Friends. The Governor gave me an ample Letter, saying many flattering things of me to my Father, and strongly recommending the Project of my setting up at Philadelphia, as a Thing that must make my Fortune. We struck on a Shoal in going down the Bay and sprung a Leak, we had a blustring time at Sea, and were oblig'd to pump almost continually, at which I took my Turn. We arriv'd safe however at Boston in about a Fortnight. I had been absent Seven Months and my Friends had heard nothing of me, for my Brother Homes was not yet return'd; and had not written about me. My unexpected Appearance surpris'd the Family; all were however very glad to see me and made me Welcome, except my Brother.

I went to see him at his Printing-House: I was better dress'd than ever while in his Service, having a genteel new Suit from Head to foot, a Watch, and my Pockets lin'd with near Five Pounds Sterling in Silver. He receiv'd me not very frankly, look'd me all over, and turn'd to his Work again. The Journeymen were inquisitive where I had been, what sort of a Country it was, and how I lik'd it? I prais'd it much, and the happy Life I led in it; expressing strongly my Intention of returning to it; and one of them asking what kind of Money we had there, I produc'd a handful of Silver and spread it before them, which was a kind of Raree-Show[2] they had not been

2. A sidewalk peep show; silver coins were rare in the colonies.

us'd to, Paper being the Money of Boston. Then I took an Opportunity of letting them see my Watch: and lastly, (my Brother still grum and sullen) I gave them a Piece of Eight to drink[3] and took my Leave. This Visit of mine offended him extremely. For when my Mother some time after spoke to him of a Reconciliation, and of her Wishes to see us on good Terms together, and that we might live for the future as Brothers, he said, I had insulted him in such a Manner before his People that he could never forget or forgive it. In this however he was mistaken.

My Father receiv'd the Governor's Letter with some apparent Surprise; but said little of it to me for some Days; when Captain Homes returning, he show'd it to him, ask'd if he knew Keith, and what kind of a Man he was: Adding his Opinion that he must be of small Discretion, to think of setting a Boy up in Business who wanted yet 3 Years of being at Man's Estate. Homes said what he could in favor of the Project; but my Father was clear in the Impropriety of it; and at last gave a flat Denial to it. Then he wrote a civil Letter to Sir William thanking him for the Patronage he had so kindly offered me, but declining to assist me as yet in Setting up, I being in his Opinion too young to be trusted with the Management of a Business so important; and for which the Preparation must be so expensive.

* * *

Keimer and I liv'd on a pretty good familiar Footing and agreed tolerably well: for he suspected nothing of my Setting up. He retain'd a great deal of his old Enthusiasms, and lov'd an Argumentation. We therefore had many Disputations. I us'd to work him so with my Socratic Method, and had trapann'd[4] him so often by Questions apparently so distant from any Point we had in hand, and yet by degrees led to the Point, and brought him into Difficulties and Contradictions, that at last he grew ridiculously cautious, and would hardly answer me the most common Question, without asking first, *What do you intend to infer from that?* However it gave him so high an Opinion of my Abilities in the Confuting Way, that he seriously propos'd my being his Colleague in a Project he had of setting up a new Sect. He was to preach the Doctrines, and I was to confound all Opponents. When he came to explain with me upon the Doctrines, I found several Conundrums[5] which I objected to, unless I might have my Way a little too, and introduce some of mine. Keimer wore his Beard at full Length, because somewhere in the Mosaic Law it is said, *thou shalt not mar the Corners of thy Beard*.[6] He likewise kept the seventh-day Sabbath; and these two Points were Essentials with him. I dislik'd both, but agreed to admit

---

3. A Spanish dollar for them to buy drinks with.
4. Trapped.
5. Puzzles, difficult questions.

6. "Ye shall not round the corners of your heads, neither shalt thou mar the corners of thy beard" (Leviticus 19.27). Keimer probably also wore his hair long.

them upon Condition of his adopting the Doctrine of using no animal Food. I doubt, says he, my Constitution will not bear that. I assur'd him it would, and that he would be the better for it. He was usually a great Glutton, and I promis'd myself some Diversion in half-starving him. He agreed to try the Practice if I would keep him Company. I did so and we held it for three Months. We had our Victuals dress'd and brought to us regularly by a Woman in the Neighborhood, who had from me a List of 40 Dishes to be prepar'd for us at different times, in all which there was neither Fish Flesh nor Fowl, and the Whim suited me the better at this time from the Cheapness of it, not costing us above 18 Pence Sterling each, per Week. I have since kept several Lents most strictly, leaving the common Diet for that, and that for the common, abruptly, without the least Inconvenience: So that I think there is little in the Advice of making those Changes by easy Gradations. I went on pleasantly, but Poor Keimer suffer'd grievously, tir'd of the Project, long'd for the Flesh Pots of Egypt,[7] and order'd a roast Pig. He invited me and two Women Friends to dine with him, but it being brought too soon upon table, he could not resist the Temptation, and ate it all up before we came.

I had made some Courtship during this time to Miss Read. I had a great Respect and Affection for her, and had some Reason to believe she had the same for me: but as I was about to take a long Voyage, and we were both very young, only a little above 18, it was thought most prudent by her Mother to prevent our going too far at present, as a Marriage if it was to take place would be more convenient after my Return, when I should be as I expected set up in my Business. Perhaps too she thought my Expectations not so well founded as I imagined them to be.

My chief Acquaintances at this time were, Charles Osborne, Joseph Watson, and James Ralph,[8] All Lovers of Reading. The two first were Clerks to an eminent Scrivener or Conveyancer[9] in the Town, Charles Brockden; the other was Clerk to a Merchant. Watson was a pious sensible young Man, of great integrity. The others rather more lax in their Principles of Religion, particularly Ralph, who as well as Collins had been unsettled by me, for which they both made me suffer. Osborne was sensible, candid, frank, sincere, and affectionate to his Friends; but in literary Matters too fond of Criticizing. Ralph, was ingenious, genteel in his Manners, and extremely eloquent; I think I never knew a prettier Talker. Both of them great Admirers of Poetry, and began to try their Hands in

7. "And the whole congregation of the children of Israel murmured against Moses and Aaron in the wilderness: And the children of Israel said unto them, Would to God we had died by the hand of the Lord in the land of Egypt, when we sat by the flesh pots, and when we did eat bread to the full" (Exodus 16.2–3).

8. Charles Osborne's dates are unknown; Joseph Watson died about 1728; James Ralph (c. 1695–1762) became well known as a political journalist.

9. One who draws up leases and deeds; Charles Brockden (1683–1769) came to Philadelphia in 1706.

little Pieces. Many pleasant Walks we four had together, on Sundays into the Woods near Skuylkill,[1] where we read to one another and conferr'd on what we read. Ralph was inclin'd to pursue the Study of Poetry, not doubting but he might become eminent in it and make his Fortune by it, alledging that the best Poets must when they first began to write, make as many Faults as he did. Osborne dissuaded him, assur'd him he had no Genius for Poetry, and advis'd him to think of nothing beyond the Business he was bred to; that in the mercantile way tho' he had no Stock, he might by his Diligence and Punctuality recommend himself to Employment as a Factor,[2] and in time acquire wherewith to trade on his own Account. I approv'd the amusing oneself with Poetry now and then, so far as to improve one's Language, but no farther. On this it was propos'd that we should each of us at our next Meeting produce a Piece of our own Composing, in order to improve by our mutual Observations, Criticisms and Corrections. As Language and Expression was what we had in View, we excluded all Considerations of Invention[3] by agreeing that the Task should be a Version of the 18th Psalm, which describes the Descent of a Deity.[4] When the Time of our Meeting drew nigh, Ralph call'd on me first, and let me know his Piece was ready. I told him I had been busy, and having little Inclination had done nothing. He then show'd me his Piece for my Opinion; and I much approv'd it, as it appear'd to me to have great Merit. Now, says he, Osborne never will allow the least Merit in any thing of mine, but makes 1000 Criticisms out of mere Envy. He is not so jealous of you. I wish therefore you would take this Piece, and produce it as yours. I will pretend not to have had time, and so produce nothing. We shall then see what he will say to it. It was agreed, and I immediately transcrib'd it that it might appear in my own hand. We met.

Watson's Performance was read: there were some Beauties in it: but many Defects. Osborne's was read: It was much better. Ralph did it Justice, remark'd some Faults, but applauded the Beauties. He himself had nothing to produce. I was backward, seem'd desirous of being excus'd, had not had sufficient Time to correct; etc. but no Excuse could be admitted, produce I must. It was read and repeated; Watson and Osborne gave up the Contest; and join'd in applauding it immoderately. Ralph only made some Criticisms and propos'd some Amendments, but I defended my Text. Osborne was against Ralph, and told him he was no better a Critic than Poet; so he dropped the Argument. As they two went home together, Osborne express'd himself still more strongly in favor of what he thought my Production, having restrain'd himself before as he said, lest I should think it Flattery. But who would have imagin'd, says

1. Schuylkill River, at Philadelphia.
2. Business agent.
3. I.e., originality.

4. "He bowed the heavens also, and came down: and darkness was under his feet" (Psalm 18.9).

he, that Franklin had been capable of such a Performance; such Painting, such Force! such Fire! He has even improv'd the Original! In his common Conversation, he seems to have no Choice of Words; he hesitates and blunders; and yet, good God, how he writes!

When we next met, Ralph discover'd the Trick we had played him, and Osborne was a little laughed at. This Transaction fix'd Ralph in his Resolution of becoming a Poet. I did all I could to dissuade him from it, but he continu'd scribbling Verses, till *Pope*[5] cur'd him. He became however a pretty good Prose Writer. More of him hereafter. But as I may not have occasion again to mention the other two, I shall just remark here, that Watson died in my Arms a few Years after, much lamented, being the best of our Set. Osborne went to the West Indies, where he became an eminent Lawyer and made Money, but died young. He and I had made a serious Agreement, that the one who happen'd first to die, should if possible make a friendly Visit to the other, and acquaint him how he found things in that separate State. But he never fulfill'd his Promise.

The Governor, seeming to like my Company, had me frequently to his House; and his Setting me up was always mention'd as a fix'd thing. I was to take with me Letters recommendatory to a Number of his Friends, besides the Letter of Credit to furnish me with the necessary Money for purchasing the Press and Types, Paper, etc. For these Letters I was appointed to call at different times, when they were to be ready, but a future time was still[6] named. Thus we went on till the ship whose Departure too had been several times postponed was on the Point of sailing. Then when I call'd to take my Leave and receive the Letters, his Secretary, Dr. Bard,[7] came out to me and said the Governor was extremely busy, in writing, but would be down at New Castle[8] before the Ship, and there the Letters would be delivered to me.

Ralph, tho' married and having one Child, had determined to accompany me in this Voyage. It was thought he intended to establish a Correspondence, and obtain Goods to sell on Commission. But I found afterwards, that thro' some Discontent with his Wife's Relations, he purposed to leave her on their Hands, and never return again. Having taken leave of my Friends, and interchang'd some Promises with Miss Read, I left Philadelphia in the Ship, which anchor'd at New Castle. The Governor was there. But when I went to his Lodging, the Secretary came to me from him with the civillest Message in the World, that he could not then see me being

---

5. In the second edition of the *Dunciad* (1728), a poem which attacks ignorance of all kinds, Alexander Pope responded to Ralph's slur against him in *Sawney*: "Silence, ye Wolves: while Ralph to Cynthia howls, / And makes Night hideous—Answer him ye Owls" (Book 3, lines 159–60). In the 1742 edition Pope included another dig at Ralph: "And see: The very Gazeteers give o'er, / Ev'n Ralph repents" (Book 1, lines 215–16).
6. Always.
7. Patrick Bard or Baird resided in Philadelphia as Port Physician after 1720.
8. Delaware.

engag'd in Business of the utmost Importance, but should send the Letters to me on board, wish'd me heartily a good Voyage and a speedy Return, etc. I return'd on board, a little puzzled, but still not doubting.

Mr. Andrew Hamilton,[9] a famous Lawyer of Philadelphia, had taken Passage in the same Ship for himself and Son: and with Mr. Denham[1] a Quaker Merchant, and Messrs. Onion and Russel Masters of an Iron Work in Maryland, had engag'd the Great Cabin; so that Ralph and I were forc'd to take up with a Berth in the Steerage: And none of board knowing us, were considered as ordinary Persons. But Mr. Hamilton and his Son (it was James, since Governor) return'd from New Castle to Philadelphia the Father being recall'd by a great Fee to plead for a seized Ship. And just before we sail'd Colonel French coming on board, and showing me great Respect, I was more taken Notice of, and with my Friend Ralph invited by the other Gentlemen to come into the Cabin, there being now Room. Accordingly we remov'd thither.

Understanding that Colonel French had brought on board the Governor's Dispatches, I ask'd the Captain for those Letters that were to be under my Care. He said all were put into the Bag together; and he could not then come at them; but before we landed in England, I should have an Opportunity of picking them out. So I was satisfied for the present, and we proceeded on our Voyage. We had a sociable Company in the Cabin, and lived uncommonly well, having the Addition of all Mr. Hamilton's Stores, who had laid in plentifully. In this Passage Mr. Denham contracted a Friendship for me that continued during his Life. The Voyage was otherwise not a pleasant one, as we had a great deal of bad Weather.

When we came into the Channel, the Captain kept his Word with me, and gave me an Opportunity of examining the Bag for the Governor's Letters. I found none upon which my Name was put, as under my Care; I pick'd out 6 or 7 that by the Handwriting I thought might be the promis'd Letters, especially as one of them was directed to Basket[2] the King's Printer, and another to some Stationer. We arriv'd in London the 24th of December, 1724. I waited upon the Stationer who came first in my Way, delivering the Letter as from Governor Keith. I don't know such a Person, says he: but opening the Letter, O, this is from Riddlesden;[3] I have lately found him to be a complete Rascal, and I will have nothing to do with him, nor receive any Letters from him. So putting the Letter into my Hand, he turn'd on his Heel and left me to serve some Customer. I was surprised to find these were not the Gov-

9. Andrew Hamilton (c. 1678–1741); his son James Hamilton (c. 1710–83) was governor of Pennsylvania four times between 1748 and 1773.
1. Thomas Denham (d. 1728), merchant and benefactor, left Bristol, England, in 1715.
2. John Baskett (d. 1742).
3. William Riddlesden (d. before 1733), well known in Maryland as a man of "infamy."

ernor's Letters. And after recollecting and comparing Circumstances, I began to doubt his Sincerity. I found my Friend Denham, and opened the whole Affair to him. He let me into Keith's Character, told me there was not the least Probability that he had written any Letters for me, that no one who knew him had the smallest Dependence on him, and he laughed at the Notion of the Governor's giving me a Letter of Credit, having as he said no Credit to give. On my expressing some Concern about what I should do: He advis'd me to endeavour getting some Employment in the Way of my Business. Among the Printers here, says he, you will improve yourself; and when you return to America, you will set up to greater Advantage.

* * *

Thus I spent about 18 Months in London. Most Part of the Time, I work'd hard at my Business, and spent but little upon myself except in seeing Plays, and in Books. My Friend Ralph had kept me poor. He owed me about 27 Pounds; which I was now never likely to receive; a great Sum out of my small Earnings. I lov'd him notwithstanding, for he had many amiable Qualities. Tho' I had by no means improv'd my Fortune, I had pick'd up some very ingenious Acquaintance whose Conversation was of great Advantage to me, and I had read considerably.

We sail'd from Gravesend on the 23d of July 1726. For The Incidents of the Voyage, I refer you to my Journal, where you will find them all minutely related. Perhaps the most important Part of that Journal is the *Plan*[4] to be found in it which I formed at Sea for regulating my future Conduct in Life. It is the more remarkable, as being form'd when I was so young, and yet being pretty faithfully adhered to quite thro' to old Age. We landed in Philadelphia the 11th of October, where I found sundry Alterations. Keith was no longer Governor, being superseded by Major Gordon.[5] I met him walking the Streets as a common Citizen. He seem'd a little asham'd at seeing me, but pass'd without saying anything. I should have been as much asham'd at seeing Miss Read, had not her Friends despairing with Reason of my Return, after the Receipt of my Letter, persuaded her to marry another, one Rogers, a Potter, which was done in my Absence. With him however she was never happy, and soon parted from him, refusing to cohabit with him, or bear his Name. It being now said that he had another Wife. He was a worthless Fellow tho' an excellent Workman which was the Temptation to her Friends. He got into Debt, and ran away in 1727 or 28, went to the West Indies, and died there. Keimer had got a better House, a Shop well supplied with Stationery, plenty of new Types, a number of Hands tho' none good, and seem'd to have a great deal of Business.

4. Only the "Outline" and "Preamble" of Franklin's *Plan* survive.

5. Patrick Gordon (1644–1736), governor of Pennsylvania from 1726 to 1736.

Mr. Denham took a Store in Water Street, where we open'd our Goods. I attended the Business diligently, studied Accounts, and grew in a little Time expert at selling. We lodg'd and boarded together, he counsell'd me as a Father, having a sincere Regard for me: I respected and lov'd him: and we might have gone on together very happily: But in the Beginning of February 1726/7 when I had just pass'd my 21st Year, we both were taken ill. My Distemper was a Pleurisy,[6] which very nearly carried me off: I suffered a good deal, gave up the Point[7] in my own mind, and was rather disappointed when I found myself recovering; regretting in some degree that I must now sometime or other have all that disagreeable Work to do over again. I forget what his Distemper was. It held him a long time, and at length carried him off. He left me a small Legacy in a nuncupative Will,[8] as a Token of his Kindness for me, and he left me once more to the wide World. For the Store was taken into the Care of his Executors, and my Employment under him ended: My Brother-in-law Homes, being now at Philadelphia, advis'd my Return to my Business. And Keimer tempted me with an Offer of large Wages by the Year to come and take the Management of his Printing-House that he might better attend his Stationer's Shop. I had heard a bad Character of him in London, from his Wife and her Friends, and was not fond of having any more to do with him. I tried for farther Employment as a Merchant's Clerk; but not readily meeting with any, I clos'd again with Keimer.

* * *

Before I enter upon my public Appearance in Business, it may be well to let you know the then State of my Mind, with regard to my Principles and Morals, that you may see how far those influenc'd the future Events of my Life. My Parents had early given me religious Impressions, and brought me through my Childhood piously in the Dissenting Way.[9] But I was scarce 15 when, after doubting by turns of several Points as I found them disputed in the different Books I read, I began to doubt of Revelation itself. Some Books against Deism fell into my Hands; they were said to be the Substance of Sermons preached at Boyle's Lectures.[1] It happened that they wrought an Effect on me quite contrary to what was intended by them: For the Arguments of the Deists which were quoted to be refuted, appeared to me much Stronger than the Refutations. In short I soon became a thorough Deist. My Arguments perverted some others, particularly Collins and Ralph: but

---

6. A disease of the lungs.
7. End; i.e., resigned himself to death.
8. An oral will.
9. I.e., in the Congregational or Presbyterian way, as opposed to the Church of England.
1. Robert Boyle (1627–91), English physicist and chemist, endowed annual lectures for preaching eight sermons a year against "infidels." Deism accepts a Supreme Being as the author of finite existence, but denies Christian doctrines of revelation and supernaturalism.

each of them having afterwards wrong'd me greatly without the least Compunction, and recollecting Keith's Conduct towards me, (who was another Freethinker) and my own towards Vernon and Miss Read which at Times gave me great Trouble, I began to suspect that this Doctrine tho' it might be true, was not very useful. My London Pamphlet, which had for its Motto those Lines of Dryden

> ———*Whatever is, is right*
> *Tho' purblind Man Sees but a Part of*
> *The Chain, the nearest Link,*
> *His Eyes not carrying to the equal Beam,*
> *That poizes all, above.*[2]

And from the Attributes of God, his infinite Wisdom, Goodness and Power concluded that nothing could possibly be wrong in the World, and that Vice and Virtue were empty Distinctions, no such Things existing: appear'd now not so clever a Performance as I once thought it; and I doubted whether some Error had not insinuated itself unperceiv'd into my Argument, so as to infect all that follow'd, as is common in metaphysical Reasonings. I grew convinc'd that *Truth, Sincerity* and *Integrity* in Dealings between Man and Man, were of the utmost Importance to the Felicity of Life, and I form'd written Resolutions, (which still remain in my Journal Book) to practice them ever while I lived. Revelation had indeed no weight with me as such; but I entertain'd an Opinion, that tho' certain Actions might not be bad *because* they were forbidden by it, or good *because* it commanded them; yet probably those Actions might be forbidden *because* they were bad for us, or commanded *because* they were beneficial to us, in their own Natures, all the Circumstances of things considered. And this Persuasion, with the kind hand of Providence, or some guardian Angel, or accidental favorable Circumstances and Situations, or all together, preserved me (thro' this dangerous Time of Youth and the hazardous Situations I was sometimes in among Strangers, remote from the Eye and Advice of my Father) without any *willful* gross Immorality or Injustice that might have been expected from my Want of Religion. I say *willful,* because the Instances I have mentioned, had something of *Necessity* in them, from my Youth, Inexperience, and the Knavery of others. I had therefore a tolerable Character to begin the World with, I valued it properly, and determin'd to preserve it.

* * *

2. The first line is not from John Dryden (1631–1700) but from Alexander Pope's *Essay on Man* (1733), Epistle I, line 294; however, Dryden's line is close: "Whatever is, is in its Causes just." The rest of the poem is recalled accurately from Dryden's *Oedipus* (III.i. 244–48).

From [Part Two][1]

* * *

CONTINUATION OF THE ACCOUNT OF MY LIFE.
BEGUN AT PASSY, 1784.

It is some time since I receiv'd the above Letters,[2] but I have been too busy till now to think of complying with the Request they contain. It might too be much better done if I were at home among my Papers, which would aid my Memory, and help to ascertain Dates. But my Return being uncertain, and having just now a little Leisure, I will endeavour to recollect and write what I can; if I live to get home, it may there be corrected and improv'd.

Not having any Copy here of what is already written, I know not whether an Account is given of the means I used to establish the Philadelphia public Library, which from a small Beginning is now become so considerable, though I remember to have come down to near the Time of that Transaction, 1730. I will therefore begin here, with an Account of it, which may be struck out if found to have been already given.

At the time I establish'd myself in Pennsylvania, there was not a good Bookseller's Shop in any of the Colonies to the Southward of Boston. In New York and Philadelphia the Printers were indeed Stationers, they sold only Paper, etc., Almanacs, Ballads, and a few common School Books. Those who lov'd Reading were oblig'd to send for their Books from England. The Members of the Junto had each a few. We had left the Alehouse where we first met, and hired a Room to hold our Club in. I propos'd that we should all of us bring our Books to that Room, where they would not only be ready to consult in our Conferences, but become a common Benefit, each of us being at Liberty to borrow such as he wish'd to read at home. This was accordingly done, and for some time contented us. Finding the Advantage of this little Collection, I propos'd to render the Benefit from Books more common by commencing a Public Sub-scripion Library. I drew a Sketch of the Plan and Rules that would be necessary, and got a skillful Conveyancer Mr. Charles Brock-den[3] to put the whole in Form of Articles of Agreement to be subscribed, by which each Subscriber engag'd to pay a certain Sum

---

1. Franklin wrote the second part of his autobiography at the Hôtel de Valentenois in Passy, a Paris suburb. He had been sent to Paris as American representative to the peace treaty, ending the war with Britain, September 3, 1783. Franklin remained in Paris until July 1785, when Thomas Jefferson replaced him as minister.

2. I.e., letters from James Abel and Benjamin Vaughan, two friends, urging Franklin to continue his memoirs.

3. Charles Brockden (1683–1769) was Philadelphia's leading drafter of legal documents, "Conveyance": an attorney who specializes in the transfer of real estate and property.

down for the first Purchase of Books and an annual Contribution for increasing them. So few were the Readers at that time in Philadelphia, and the Majority of us so poor, that I was not able with great Industry to find more than Fifty Persons, mostly young Tradesmen, willing to pay down for this purpose Forty shillings each, and Ten Shillings per Annum. On this little Fund we began. The Books were imported. The Library was open one Day in the Week for lending them to the Subscribers, on their Promissory Notes to pay Double the Value if not duly returned. The Institution soon manifested its Utility, was imitated by other Towns and in other Provinces, the Libraries were augmented by Donations, Reading became fashionable, and our People having no public Amusements to divert their Attention from Study became better acquainted with Books, and in a few Years were observ'd by Strangers to be better instructed and more intelligent than People of the same Rank generally are in other Countries.

When we were about to sign the above-mentioned Articles, which were to be binding on us, our Heirs, etc. for fifty Years, Mr. Brockden, the Scrivener, said to us, "You are young Men, but it is scarce probable that any of you will live to see the Expiration of the Term fix'd in this Instrument." A Number of us, however, are yet living: But the Instrument was after a few Years rendered null by a Charter that incorporated and gave Perpetuity to the Company.

The Objections, and Reluctances I met with in Soliciting the Subscriptions, made me soon feel the Impropriety of presenting oneself as the Proposer of any useful Project that might be suppos'd to raise one's Reputation in the smallest degree above that of one's Neighbors, when one has need of their Assistance to accomplish that Project. I therefore put myself as much as I could out of sight, and stated it as a Scheme of *a Number of Friends*, who had requested me to go about and propose it to such as they thought Lovers of Reading. In this way my Affair went on more smoothly, and I ever after practic'd it on such Occasions; and from my frequent Successes, can heartily recommend it. The present little Sacrifice of your Vanity will afterwards be amply repaid. If it remains a while uncertain to whom the Merit belongs, someone more vain than yourself will be encourag'd to claim it, and then even Envy will be dispos'd to do you Justice, by plucking those assum'd Feathers, and restoring them to their right Owner.

This Library afforded me the Means of Improvement by constant Study, for which I set apart an Hour or two each Day; and thus repair'd in some Degree the Loss of the Learned Education my Father once intended for me. Reading was the only Amusement I allow'd myself. I spent no time in Taverns, Games, or Frolics of any kind. And my Industry in my Business continu'd as indefatigable as it was necessary. I was in debt for my Printing-House, I had a young Family coming on to be educated,[4] and I had to contend with for Business two Printers who were establish'd in the Place before me. My Circumstances however grew daily easier: my original Habits of Frugality continuing. And My Father having among his Instructions to me when a Boy, frequently repeated a Proverb of Solomon, *"Seest thou a Man diligent in his Calling, he shall stand before Kings, he shall not stand before mean Men."*[5] I from thence consider'd Industry as a Means of obtaining Wealth and Distinction, which encourag'd me: tho' I did not think that I should ever literally stand before Kings, which however has since happened; for I have stood before five,[6] and even had the honor of sitting down with one, the King of Denmark, to Dinner.

We have an English Proverb that says,

> He that would thrive
> Must ask his Wife,[7]

it was lucky for me that I had one as much dispos'd to Industry and Frugality as myself. She assisted me cheerfully in my Business, folding and stitching Pamphlets, tending Shop, purchasing old Linen Rags for the Paper-makers, etc., etc. We kept no idle Servants, our Table was plain and simple, our Furniture of the cheapest. For instance my Breakfast was a long time Bread and Milk, (no Tea,) and I ate it out of a twopenny earthen Porringer[8] with a Pewter Spoon. But mark how Luxury will enter Families, and make a Progress, in Spite of Principle. Being Call'd one Morning to Breakfast, I found it in a China[9] Bowl with a Spoon of Silver. They had been bought for me without my Knowledge by my Wife, and had cost her the enormous Sum of three and twenty Shillings, for which she had no other Excuse or Apology to make, but that she thought *her* Husband deserv'd a Silver Spoon and China Bowl as well as any of his Neighbors. This was the first Appearance of Plate[1] and China in our House, which afterwards in a Course of Years as our Wealth increas'd, augmented gradually to several Hundred Pounds in Value.

I had been religiously educated as a Presbyterian, and tho' some of the Dogmas of that Persuasion, such as the Eternal Decrees of God, Election, Reprobation,[2] etc. appear'd to me unintelligible, others doubtful, and I early absented myself from the Public Assemblies of the Sect, Sunday being my Studying-Day, I never was without some religious Principles; I never doubted, for instance, the Existence of the Deity, that he made the World, and govern'd it by

4. Franklin had three children: William, born c. 1731; Francis, born in 1732; Sarah, born in 1743.
5. Proverbs 22.29.
6. Louis XV and Louis XVI of France, George II and George III of England, and Christian VI of Denmark.
7. More commonly: "He that will thrive must ask leave of his wife."
8. Bowl.
9. I.e., porcelain.
1. Silver.
2. Punishment. "Election": God's choosing who is to be saved and who is to be damned.

his Providence; that the most acceptable Service of God was the doing Good to Man; that our Souls are immortal; and that all Crime will be punished and Virtue reward either here or hereafter; these I esteem'd the Essentials of every Religion, and being to be found in all the Religions we had in our Country I respected them all, tho' with different degrees of Respect as I found them more or less mix'd with other Articles which without any Tendency to inspire, promote or confirm Morality, serv'd principally to divide us and make us unfriendly to one another. This Respect to all, with an Opinion that the worst had some good Effects, induc'd me to avoid all Discourse that might tend to lessen the good Opinion another might have of his own Religion; and as our Province increas'd in People and new Places of worship were continually wanted, and generally erected by voluntary Contribution, my Mite[3] for such purpose, whatever might be the Sect, was never refused.

Tho' I seldom attend any Public Worship, I had still an Opinion of its Propriety, and of its Utility when rightly conducted, and I regularly paid my annual Subscription for the Support of the only Presbyterian Minister or Meeting we had in Philadelphia. He us'd to visit me sometimes as a Friend, and admonish me to attend his Administrations, and I was now and then prevail'd on to do so, once for five Sundays successively. Had he been, *in my Opinion*, a good Preacher perhaps I might have continued, notwithstanding the occasion I had for the Sunday's Leisure in my Course of Study: But his Discourses were chiefly either polemic Arguments, or Explications of the peculiar Doctrines of our Sect, and were all to me very dry, uninteresting and unedifying, since not a single moral Principle was inculcated or enforc'd, their Aim seeming to be rather to make us Presbyterians than good Citizens. At length he took for his Text that Verse of the 4th Chapter of Philippians, *Finally, Brethren, Whatsoever Things are true, honest, just, pure, lovely, or of good report, if there be any virtue, or any praise, think on these Things;*[4] and I imagin'd in a Sermon on such a Text, we could not miss of having some Morality; But he confin'd himself to five Points only as meant by the Apostle, viz. 1. Keeping holy the Sabbath Day. 2. Being diligent in Reading the Holy Scriptures. 3. Attending duly the Public Worship. 4. Partaking of the Sacrament. 5. Paying a due Respect to God's Ministers.—These might be all good Things, but as they were not the kind of good Things that I expected from that Text, I despaired of ever meeting with them from any other, was disgusted, and attended his Preaching no more. I had some Years before compos'd a little Liturgy or Form of Prayer for my own private Use, viz. in 1728, entitled, *Articles of Belief and Acts of Religion.*[5] I return'd to the Use of this, and went

3. Small contribution.
4. A paraphrase of Philippians 4.8.
5. Only the first part of Franklin's *Articles of Belief and Acts of Religion* sur-

vives. It can be found in *The Papers of Benjamin Franklin*, Vol. I, ed. Leonard W. Labaree *et al.* (New Haven, Conn.: Yale University Press, 1964).

no more to the public Assemblies. My Conduct might be blame-able, but I leave it without attempting farther to excuse it, my present purpose being to relate Facts, and not to make Apologies for them.

It was about this time that I conceiv'd the bold and arduous Project of arriving at moral Perfection. I wish'd to live without committing any Fault at anytime; I would conquer all that either Natural Inclination, Custom, or Company might lead me into. As I knew, or thought I knew, what was right and wrong, I did not see why I might not *always* do the one and avoid the other. But I soon found I had undertaken a Task of more Difficulty than I had imagined: While my Care was employ'd in guarding against one Fault, I was often surpris'd by another. Habit took the Advantage of Inattention. Inclination was somethines too strong for Reason. I concluded at length, that the mere speculative Conviction that it was our Interest to be completely virtuous, was not sufficient to prevent our Slipping, and that the contrary Habits must be broken and good Ones acquired and established, before we can have any Dependence on a steady uniform Rectitude of Conduct. For this purpose I therefore contriv'd the following Method.

In the various Enumerations of the moral Virtues I had met with in my Reading, I found the Catalogue more or less numerous, as different Writers included more or fewer Ideas under the same Name. Temperance, for Example, was by some confin'd to Eating and Drinking, while by others it was extended to mean the mod-erating every other Pleasure, Appetite, Inclination or Passion, bod-ily or mental, even to our Avarice and Ambition. I propos'd to myself, for the sake of Clearness, to use rather more Names with fewer Ideas annex'd to each, than a few Names with more Ideas; and I included after Thirteen Names of Virtues all that at that time occurr'd to me as necessary or desirable, and annex'd to each a short Precept, which fully express'd the Extent I gave to its Meaning.

These Names of Virtues with their Precepts were

1. TEMPERANCE.
Eat not to Dulness. Drink not to Elevation.

2. SILENCE.
Speak not but what may benefit others or yourself. Avoiding trifling Conversation.

3. ORDER
Let all your Things have their Places. Let each Part of your Business have its Time.

4. RESOLUTION.
Resolve to perform what you ought. Perform without fail what you resolve.

5. FRUGALITY.
Make no Expense but to do good to others or yourself: i.e. Waste nothing.

6. INDUSTRY.
Lose no Time. Be always employ'd in something useful. Cut off all unnecessary Actions.

7. SINCERITY.
Use no hurtful Deceit. Think innocently and justly; and, if you speak; speak accordingly.

8. JUSTICE.
Wrong none, by doing Injuries or omitting the Benefits that are your Duty.

9. MODERATION.
Avoid Extremes. Forbear resenting Injuries so much as you think they deserve.

10. CLEANLINESS.
Tolerate no Uncleanness in Body, Clothes or Habitation.

11. TRANQUILITY.
Be not disturbed at Trifles, or Accidents common or unavoidable.

12. CHASTITY.
Rarely use Venery but for Health or offspring; Never to Dulness, Weakness, or the Injury of your own or another's Peace or Reputation.

13. HUMILITY.
Imitate Jesus and Socrates.

My intention being to acquire the *Habitude*[6] of all these Virtues, I judg'd it would be well not to distract my Attention by attempting the whole at once, but to fix it on one of them at a time, and when I should be Master of that, then to proceed to another, and so on till I should have gone thro' the thirteen. And as the previous Acquisition of some might facilitate the Acquisition of certain others, I arrang'd them with that View as they stand above. *Temperance* first, as it tends to procure that Coolness and Clearness of Head, which is so necessary where Constant Vigilance was to be kept up, and Guard maintained, against the unremitting Attraction of Ancient Habits, and the Force of perpetual Temptations. This being acquir'd and establish'd, *Silence* would be more easy, and my Desire being to gain Knowledge at the same time that I improv'd in Virtue, and considering that in Conversation it was obtain'd rather by the Use of the Ears than of the Tongue, and therefore wishing to break a Habit I was getting into of Prattling, Punning and Joking, which only made me acceptable to trifling Company, I gave *Silence* the second Place. This, and the next, *Order*, I expected

---

6. I.e., making these virtues an integral part of his nature.

would allow me more Time for attending to my Project and my studies; RESOLUTION once become habitual, would keep me firm in my Endeavours to obtain all the subsequent Virtues; *Frugality* and *Industry*, by freeing me from my remaining Debt, and producing Affluence and Independence would make more easy the Practice of *Sincerity* and *Justice*, etc. etc. Conceiving then that agreeable to the Advice of Pythagoras[7] in his Golden Verses, daily Examination would be necessary, I contriv'd the following Method for conducting that Examination.

I made a little Book in which I allotted a Page for each of the Virtues. I rul'd each Page with red Ink so as to have seven Columns, one for each Day of the Week, marking each Column with a Letter for the Day. I cross'd these Columns with thirteen red Lines, marking the Beginning of each Line with the first Letter of one of the Virtues, on which Line and in its proper Column I might mark by a little black Spot every Fault I found upon Examination, to have been committed respecting that Virtue upon that Day.

I determined to give a Week's strict Attention to each of the Virtues successively. Thus in the first Week my great Guard was to avoid every the least Offence against Temperance, leaving the other Virtues to their ordinary Chance, only marking every Evening the Faults of the Day. Thus if in the first Week I could keep my first Line marked T clear of Spots, I suppos'd the Habit of that Virtue so much strengthen'd and its opposite weaken'd, that I might venture extending my Attention to include the next, and for the following Week keep both Lines clear of Spots. Proceeding thus to the last, I could go thro' a Course complete in Thirteen Weeks, and four Courses in a Year. And like him who having a Garden to weed, does not attempt to eradicate all the bad Herbs at once, which would exceed his Reach and his Strength, but works on one of the Beds at a time, and having accomplish'd the first proceeds to a second; so I should have, (I hoped) the encouraging Pleasure of seeing on my Pages the Progress I made in Virtue, by clearing successively my Lines of their Spots, till in the End by a Number of Courses, I should be happy in viewing a clean Book after a thirteen Weeks' daily Examination.

This my little Book had for its Motto these Lines from *Addison's Cato*,[8]

> *Here will I hold: If there is a Pow'r above us,*
> *(And that there is, all Nature cries aloud*
> *Thro' all her Works) he must delight in Virtue,*
> *And that which he delights in must be happy.*

7. Pythagoras (sixth century B.C.) was a Greek philosopher and mathematician. Franklin added a note here: "Insert those Lines that direct it in a Note," and wished to include verses translated: "Let sleep not close your eyes till you have thrice examined the transactions of the day: where have I strayed, what have I done, what good have I omitted?"
8. Joseph Addison, *Cato, a Tragedy* (1713; V.i.15–18). Franklin also used these lines as an epigraph for his *Articles of Belief and Acts of Religion.*

Form of the Pages

TEMPERANCE.

Eat not to Dulness.
Drink not to Elevation.

	S	M	T	W	T	F	S
T							
S	•	•	•		•	•	
O	•	•	•		•	•	•
R			•			•	
F			•		•		
I			•				
S							
J							
M							
Cl.							
T							
Ch							
H							

Another from *Cicero*.[9]

*O Vitæ Philosophia Dux! O Virtutum indagatrix, expultrixque
vitiorum! Unus dies bene, et ex preceptis tuis actus, peccanti
immortalitati est anteponendus.*

Another from the Proverbs of Solomon speaking of Wisdom or
Virtue;

Length of Days is in her right hand, and in her Left Hand
Riches and Honors; Her Ways are Ways of Pleasantness, and
all her Paths are Peace.

III, 16, 17

And conceiving God to be the Fountain of Wisdom, I thought it
right and necessary to solicit his Assistance for obtaining it; to this
End I form'd the following little Prayer, which was prefix'd to my
Tables of Examination, for daily Use.

*O Powerful Goodness! bountiful Father! merciful Guide! In-
crease in me that Wisdom which discovers my truest Interests;
Strengthen my Resolutions to perform what that Wisdom dictates.
"Accept my kind Offices to thy other Children, as the only Return
in my Power for thy continual Favors to me.*

I us'd also sometimes a little Prayer which I took from *Thomson's*[1] Poems, viz.

*Father of Light and Life, thou Good supreme,
O teach me what is good, teach me thy self!
Save me from Folly, Vanity and Vice,
From every low Pursuit, and fill my Soul
With Knowledge, conscious Peace, and Virtue pure,
Sacred, substantial, neverfading Bliss!*

The Precept of Order requiring that *every Part of my Business
should have its allotted Time,* one Page in my little Book contain'd
the following Scheme of Employment for the Twenty-four Hours
of a natural Day.

I enter'd upon the Execution of this Plan for Self-examination,
and continu'd it with occasional Intermissions for some time. I was
surpris'd to find myself so much fuller of Faults than I had imagined, but I had the Satisfaction of seeing them diminish. To avoid
the Trouble of renewing now and then my little Book, which by
scraping out the Marks on the Paper of old Faults to make room
for new Ones in a new Course, became full of Holes: I transferr'd
my Tables and Precepts to the Ivory Leaves of a Memorandum

9. Marcus Tullius Cicero (106–43 B.C.),
Roman philosopher and orator. The
quotation is from *Tusculan Disputations*
(V.ii.5), but several lines are omitted
after *vitiorum*: "Oh, philosophy, guide
of life: Oh, searcher out of virtues and
expeller of vices! * * * One day lived
well and according to thy precepts is to
be preferred to an eternity of sin."
1. James Thomson (1700–48), *The Seasons*, "Winter" (1726), lines 218–23.

The Morning Question, What Good shall I do this Day?	5 6 7	Rise, wash, and address *Powerful Goodness;* contrive Day's Business and take the Resolution of the Day; prosecute the present Study: and breakfast.—
	8 9 10 11	Work.
	12 1	Read, or overlook my Accounts, and dine.
	2 3 4 5	Work.
	6 7 8 9	Put Things in their Places, Supper, Musick, or Diversion, or Conversation, Examination of the Day.
Evening Question, What Good have I done to day?	10 11 12 1 2 3 4	Sleep.—

Book, on which the Lines were drawn with red Ink that made a durable Stain, and on those Lines I mark'd my Faults with a black Lead Pencil, which Marks I could easily wipe out with a wet Sponge. After a while I went thro' one Course only in a Year, and afterwards only one in several Years; till at length I omitted them entirely, being employ'd in Voyages and Business abroad with a Multiplicity of Affairs, that interfered. But I always carried my little Book with me.

My Scheme of ORDER, gave me the most Trouble, and I found, that tho' it might be practicable where a Man's Business was such as to leave him the Disposition of his Time, that of a Journeyman Printer for instance, it was not possible to be exactly observ'd by a Master, who must mix with the World, and often receive People of Business at their own Hours. *Order* too, with regard to Places for Things, Papers, etc. I found extremely difficult to acquire. I had not been early accustomed to it, and having an exceeding good Memory, I was not so sensible of the Inconvenience attending Want of Method. This Article therefore cost me so much painful Attention and my Faults in it vex'd me so much, and I made so little Progress in Amendment, and had such frequent Relapses, that I was almost ready to give up the Attempt, and content myself with a faulty Character in that respect. Like the Man who in buying an Axe of a Smith my Neighbor, desired to have the whole of its Surface as bright as the Edge; the Smith consented to grind it bright for him if he would turn the Wheel. He turn'd while the Smith press'd the broad Face of the Axe hard and heavily on the Stone, which made the Turning of it very fatiguing. The Man came every now and then from the Wheel to see how the Work went on; and at length would take his Axe as it was without farther Grinding. No, says the Smith, Turn on, turn on; we shall have it bright by and by; as yet 'tis only speckled. Yes, says the Man; but—*I think I like a speckled Axe best.*—And I believe this may have been the Case with many who having for want of some such Means as I employ'd found the Difficulty of obtaining good, and breaking bad Habits, in other Points of Vice and Virtue, have given up the Struggle, and concluded that *a speckled Axe was best.* For something that pretended to be Reason was every now and then suggesting to me, that such extreme Nicety as I exacted of myself might be a kind of Foppery in Morals, which if it were known would make me ridiculous; that a perfect Character might be attended with the Inconvenience of being envied and hated; and that a benevolent Man should allow a few Faults in himself, to keep his Friends in Countenance.

In Truth I found myself incorrigible with respect to *Order*; and now I am grown old, and my Memory bad, I feel very sensibly the want of it. But on the whole, tho' I never arrived at the Perfection I had been so ambitious of obtaining, but fell far short of it, yet I was by the Endeavour made a better and a happier Man than I otherwise should have been, if I had not attempted it; As those who aim at perfect Writing by imitating the engraved Copies,[2] tho' they never reach the wish'd for Excellence of those Copies, their Hand is mended by the Endeavour, and is tolerable while it continues fair and legible.

And it may be well my Posterity should be informed, that to this little Artifice, with the Blessing of God, their Ancestor ow'd the constant Felicity of his Life down to his 79th Year in which this is written. What Reverses may attend the Remainder is in the Hand of Providence: But if they arrive, the Reflection on past Happiness enjoy'd ought to help his Bearing them with more Resignation. To *Temperance* he ascribes his long-continu'd Health, and what is still left to him of a good Constitution. To *Industry* and *Frugality* the early Easiness of his Circumstances, and Acquisition of his Fortune, with all that Knowledge which enabled him to be an useful Citizen, and obtain'd for him some Degree of Reputation among the Learned. To *Sincerity* and *Justice* the Confidence of his Country, and the honorable Employs it conferr'd upon him. And to the joint Influence of the whole Mass of the Virtues, even in their imperfect State he was able to acquire them, all that Evenness of Temper, and that Cheerfulness in Conversation which makes his Company still sought for, and agreeable even to his younger Acquaintance. I hope therefore that some of my Descendants may follow the Example and reap the Benefit.

It will be remark'd[3] that, tho' my Scheme was not wholly without Religion there was in it no Mark of any of the distinguishing Tenets of any particular Sect. I had purposely avoided them; for being fully persuaded of the Utility and Excellency of my Method, and that it might be serviceable to People in all Religions, and intending some time or other to publish it, I would not have anything in it that should prejudice anyone of any Sect against it. I purposed writing a little Comment on each Virtue, in which I would have shown the Advantages of possessing it, and the Mischiefs attending its opposite Vice; and I should have called my Book the ART *of Virtue*, because it would have shown the *Means and Manner* of obtaining Virtue; which would have distinguish'd it from the mere Exhortation to be good, that does not instruct and indicate the Means; but is like the Apostle's Man of verbal Charity, who only, without showing to the Naked and the Hungry *how* or where they might get Clothes or Victuals, exhorted them to be fed and clothed. *James* II, 15, 16.[4]

But it so happened that my Intention of writing and publishing this Comment was never fulfilled. I did indeed, from time to time

---

2. I.e., the models in the printed book.
3. Observed.
4. "If a brother or sister be naked, and destitute of daily food, And one of you say unto them, Depart in peace, be ye warmed and filled; notwithstanding ye give them not those things which are needful to the body; what doth it profit?"

put down short Hints of the Sentiments, Reasonings, etc. to be made use of in it; some of which I have still by me: But the necessary close Attention to private Business in the earlier part of Life, and public Business since, have occasioned my postponing it. For it being connected in my Mind with a *great and extensive Project* that required the whole Man to execute, and which an unforeseen Succession of Employs prevented my attending to, it has hitherto remain'd unfinish'd.

In this Piece it was my Design to explain and enforce this Doctrine, that vicious Actions are not hurtful because they are forbidden, but forbidden because they are hurtful, the Nature of Man alone consider'd: That it was therefore every one's Interest to be virtuous, who wish'd to be happy even in this World. And I should from this Circumstance (there being always in the World a Number of rich Merchants, Nobility, States and Princes, who have need of honest Instruments for the Management of their Affairs, and such being so rare) have endeavoured to convince young Persons, that no Qualities were so likely to make a poor Man's Fortune as those of Probity and Integrity.

My List of Virtues contain'd at first but twelve: But a Quaker Friend having kindly inform'd me that I was generally thought proud; that my Pride show'd itself frequently in Conversation; that I was not content with being in the right when discussing any Point, but was overbearing and rather insolent; of which he convinc'd me by mentioning several Instances; I determined endeavouring to cure myself if I could of this Vice or Folly among the rest, and I added *Humility* to my List, giving an extensive Meaning to the Word. I cannot boast of much Success in acquiring the *Reality* of this Virtue; but I had a good deal with regard to the *Appearance* of it. I made it a Rule to forbear all direct Contradiction to the Sentiments of others, and all positive Assertion of my own. I even forbid myself, agreeable to the old Laws of our Junto, the Use of every Word or Expression in the Language that imported[5] a fix'd Opinion; such as *certainly, undoubtedly*, etc. and I adopted instead of them, I *conceive*, I *apprehend*, or I *imagine* a thing to be so or so, or it so appears to me at present. When another asserted something that I thought an Error, I denied myself the Pleasure of contradicting him abruptly, and of showing immediately some Absurdity in his Proposition; and in answering I began by observing that in certain Cases or Circumstances his Opinion would be right, but that in the present case there *appear'd* or *seem'd* to me some Difference, etc. I soon found the Advantage of this Change in my Manners. The Conversations I engag'd in went on more pleasantly. The modest way in which I propos'd my Opinions, procur'd them a readier Reception and less Contradiction; I had less Mortifi-

5. Suggested.

cation when I was found to be in the wrong, and I more easily prevail'd wtih others to give up their Mistakes and join with me when I happen'd to be in the right. And this Mode, which I at first put on, with some violence to natural Inclination, became at length so easy and so habitual to me, that perhaps for these Fifty Years past no one has ever heard a dogmatical Expression escape me. And to this Habit (after my Character of Integrity) I think it principally owing, that I had early so much Weight with my Fellow Citizens, when I proposed new Institutions, or Alterations in the old; and so much Influence in public Councils when I became a Member. For I was but a bad Speaker, never eloquent, subject to much Hesitation in my choice of Words, hardly correct in Language, and yet I generally carried my Points.

In reality there is perhaps no one of our natural Passions so hard to subdue as *Pride*. Disguise it, struggle with it, beat it down, stifle it, mortify it as much as one pleases, it is still alive, and will every now and then peep out and show itself. You will see it perhaps often in this History. For even if I could conceive that I had completely overcome it, I should probably be proud of my Humility.

Thus far written at Passy, 1784.

* * *

1771–90   1868

ST. JEAN DE CRÈVECOEUR
1735–1813

Crèvecoeur was a man with a mysterious past, and a number of details of his life have puzzled his biographers. He was born Michel-Guillaume-Jean de Crèvecoeur in Caen, Normandy, in 1735. When he was nineteen, he left home and sailed to England, where he took up residence with distant relatives. He planned to marry, but his fiancée died before the ceremony took place, and in 1755 he went to Canada; he enlisted in the Canadian militia, served the government as a surveyor and cartographer, and was wounded in the defense of Quebec. His military career came to an end in 1759, and for the next ten years Crèvecoeur traveled extensively in the colonies as a surveyor and Indian trader. In 1769 he bought land in Orange County, New York, and, newly married, settled into the life of an American farmer.

Given the history of Crèvecoeur's restlessness, it is hard to know whether or not he would have been happy forever at Pine Hill, but the advent of the American Revolution and his Tory sympathies were enough to determine his return to France. He claimed that he wished to re-establish ownership of family lands, and it is ironic, given his political sympathies, that he was arrested and imprisoned as a rebel spy when he tried to sail from the port of New York. Not until 1780 did Crèvecoeur succeed in reaching

London. He remained in France until 1783, when he returned as French consul to New York, Connecticut, and New Jersey, only to learn that his farm had been burned in an Indian attack, his wife was dead, and his children were housed with strangers.

Crèvecoeur was a great success as a diplomat—he was made an honorary citizen of a number of American cities, and the town of St. Johnsbury, Vermont, was named in his honor—but he did not remain long in America. He returned to France in 1785 and after 1790 remained there permanently, first living in Paris and retiring, after 1793, to Normandy.

The first year that Crèvecoeur spent at Pine Hill he began to write a series of essays about America based on his travels and experience as a farmer. He brought them to London in 1780 and, suppressing those essays most unsympathetic to the American cause, sold them to the bookseller Thomas Davies. *Letters from an American Farmer* appeared in 1782 and was an immediate success. Crèvecoeur found himself a popular hero when the expanded French edition appeared in 1783. Its publication followed close enough upon the American Revolution to satisfy an almost insatiable demand for things American and confirmed, for most readers, a vision of a new land, rich and promising, where industry prevailed over class and fashion. George Washington said the book was "too flattering" to be true, but more careful readers of these twelve letters will take note of a more ambiguous attitude throughout: Crèvecoeur's hymn to the land does not make him blind to the ignorant frontiersman or the calculating slaveholder. His final letter, "Distresses of a Frontiersman," affirms the possibility of a harmonious relationship with Nature, but he writes from an Indian village and with no successful historical models in mind.

From Letters from an American Farmer[1]
From *Letter III. What Is an American*

I wish I could be acquainted with the feelings and thoughts which must agitate the heart and present themselves to the mind of an enlightened Englishman, when he first lands on this continent. He must greatly rejoice that he lived at a time to see this fair country discovered and settled; he must necessarily feel a share of national pride, when he views the chain of settlements which embellishes these extended shores. When he says to himself, this is the work of my countrymen, who, when convulsed by factions,[2] afflicted by a variety of miseries and wants, restless and impatient, took refuge here. They brought along with them their national genius,[3] to which they principally owe what liberty they enjoy, and what substance they possess. Here he sees the industry of his native country displayed in a new manner, and traces in their works the embryos of all the arts, sciences, and ingenuity which flourish in Europe. Here he beholds fair cities, substantial villages, extensive fields, an immense country filled with decent houses, good roads, orchards, meadows, and bridges,

---

1. From *Letters from an American Farmer*, ed. Albert Boni and Charles Boni (New York, 1925).
2. Disputes.
3. Spirit; distinctive national character.

where an hundred years ago all was wild, woody, and uncultivated! What a train of pleasing ideas this fair spectacle must suggest; it is a prospect which must inspire a good citizen with the most heartfelt pleasure. The difficulty consists in the manner of viewing so extensive a scene. He is arrived on a new continent; a modern society offers itself to his contemplation, different from what he had hitherto seen. It is not composed, as in Europe, of great lords who possess everything, and of a herd of people who have nothing. Here are no aristocratical families, no courts, no kings, no bishops, no ecclesiastical dominion, no invisible power giving to a few a very visible one; no great manufacturers employing thousands, no great refinements of luxury. The rich and the poor are not so far removed from each other as they are in Europe. Some few towns excepted, we are all tillers of the earth, from Nova Scotia to West Florida. We are a people of cultivators, scattered over an immense territory, communicating with each other by means of good roads and navigable rivers, united by the silken bands of mild government, all respecting the laws, without dreading their power, because they are equitable. We are all animated with the spirit of an industry which is unfettered and unrestrained, because each person works for himself. If he travels through our rural districts he views not the hostile castle, and the haughty mansion, contrasted with the clay-built hut and miserable cabin, where cattle and men help to keep each other warm, and dwell in meanness, smoke, and indigence. A pleasing uniformity of decent competence appears throughout our habitations. The meanest of our log-houses is a dry and comfortable habitation. Lawyer or merchant are the fairest titles our towns afford; that of a farmer is the only appellation of the rural inhabitants of our country. It must take some time ere he can reconcile himself to our dictionary, which is but short in words of dignity, and names of honor. There, on a Sunday, he sees a congregation of respectable farmers and their wives, all clad in neat homespun, well mounted, or riding in their own humble wagons. There is not among them an esquire, saving the unlettered magistrate. There he sees a parson as simple as his flock, a farmer who does not riot[4] on the labor of others. We have no princes, for whom we toil, starve, and bleed: we are the most perfect society now existing in the world. Here man is free as he ought to be; nor is this pleasing equality so transitory as many others are. Many ages will not see the shores of our great lakes replenished with inland nations, nor the unknown bounds of North America entirely peopled. Who can tell how far it extends? Who can tell the millions of men whom it will feed and contain? for no European foot has as yet traveled half the extent of this mighty continent!

The next wish of this traveler will be to know whence came all

---

4. I.e., indulge himself.

these people? They are a mixture of English, Scotch, Irish, French, Dutch, Germans, and Swedes. From this promiscuous breed, that race now called Americans have arisen. The eastern provinces[5] must indeed be excepted, as being the unmixed descendants of Englishmen. I have heard many wish that they had been more intermixed also: for my part, I am no wisher, and think it much better as it has happened. They exhibit a most conspicuous figure in this great and variegated picture; they too enter for a great share in the pleasing perspective displayed in these thirteen provinces. I know it is fashionable to reflect on them, but respect them for what they have done; for the accuracy and wisdom with which they have settled their territory; for the decency of their manners; for their early love of letters; their ancient college,[6] the first in this hemisphere; for their industry, which to me who am but a farmer is the criterion of everything. There never was a people, situated as they are, who with so ungrateful a soil have done more in so short a time. Do you think that the monarchical ingredients which are more prevalent in other governments have purged them from all foul stains? Their histories assert the contrary.

In this great American asylum, the poor of Europe have by some means met together, and in consequence of various causes; to what purpose should they ask one another what countrymen they are? Alas, two thirds of them had no country. Can a wretch who wanders about, who works and starves, whose life is a continual scene of sore affliction or pinching penury, can that man call England or any other kingdom his country? A country that had no bread for him, whose fields procured him no harvest, who met with nothing but the frowns of the rich, the severity of the laws, with jails and punishments; who owned not a single foot of the extensive surface of this planet? No! Urged by a variety of motives, here they came. Everything has tended to regenerate them; new laws, a new mode of living, a new social system; here they are become men: in Europe they were as so many useless plants, wanting vegetative mold and refreshing showers; they withered, and were mowed down by want, hunger, and war; but now by the power of transplantation, like all other plants they have taken root and flourished! Formerly they were not numbered in any civil lists[7] of their country, except in those of the poor; here they rank as citizens. By what invisible power has this surprising metamorphosis been performed? By that of the laws and that of their industry. The laws, the indulgent laws, protect them as they arrive, stamping on them the symbol of adoption; they receive ample rewards for their labors; these accumulated rewards procure them lands; those lands confer on them the title of freemen, and to that title every benefit is affixed which men

5. New England.
6. Harvard College was founded in 1636.
7. Recognized employees of the civil government: ambassadors, judges, secretaries, etc.

can possibly require. This is the great operation daily performed by our laws. From whence proceed these laws? From our government. Whence the government? It is derived from the original genius and strong desire of the people ratified and confirmed by the crown. This is the great chain which links us all, this is the picture which every province exhibits, Nova Scotia excepted. There the crown has done all;[8] either there were no people who had genius, or it was not much attended to: the consequence is that the province is very thinly inhabited indeed; the power of the crown in conjunction with the mosquitoes has prevented men from settling there. Yet some parts of it flourished once, and it contained a mild, harmless set of people. But for the fault of a few leaders, the whole were banished. The greatest political error the crown ever committed in America was to cut off men from a country which wanted nothing but men!

What attachment can a poor European emigrant have for a country where he had nothing? The knowledge of the language, the love of a few kindred as poor as himself, were the only cords that tied him: his country is now that which gives him land, bread, protection, and consequence: *Ubi panis ibi patria*[9] is the motto of all emigrants. What then is the American, this new man? He is either a European, or the descendant of a European, hence that strange mixture of blood, which you will find in no other country. I could point out to you a family whose grandfather was an Englishman, whose wife was Dutch, whose son married a French woman, and whose present four sons have now four wives of different nations. He is an American, who, leaving behind him all his ancient prejudices and manners, receives new ones from the new mode of life he has embraced, the new government he obeys, and the new rank he holds. He becomes an American by being received in the broad lap of our great *Alma Mater*.[1] Here individuals of all nations are melted into a new race of men, whose labors and posterity will one day cause great changes in the world. Americans are the western pilgrims, who are carrying along with them that great mass of arts, sciences, vigor, and industry which began long since in the east; they will finish the great circle. The Americans were once scattered all over Europe; here they are incorporated into one of the finest systems of population which has ever appeared, and which will hereafter become distinct by the power of the different climates they inhabit. The American ought therefore to love this country much better than that wherein either he or his forefathers were born. Here the rewards of his industry follow with equal steps the progress of his labor; his labor is founded on the basis of nature, *self-interest*; can it want a stronger allurement? Wives and children, who

8. In 1755 the French Acadians were banished from Nova Scotia by the British, who took it in 1710.

9. "Where there is bread, there is one's fatherland."

1. Literally, dear mother.

before in vain demanded of him a morsel of bread, now, fat and frolicsome, gladly help their father to clear those fields whence exuberant crops are to arise to feed and to clothe them all; without any part being claimed, either by a despotic prince, a rich abbot, or a mighty lord. Here religion demands but little of him; a small voluntary salary to the minister, and gratitude to God; can he refuse these? The American is a new man, who acts upon new principles; he must therefore entertain new ideas, and form new opinions. From involuntary idleness, servile dependence, penury, and useless labor, he has passed to toils of a very different nature, rewarded by ample subsistence.—This is an American.

British America is divided into many provinces, forming a large association, scattered along a coast 1,500 miles extent and about 200 wide. This society I would fain examine, at least such as it appears in the middle provinces; if it does not afford that variety of tinges and gradations which may be observed in Europe, we have colors peculiar to ourselves. For instance, it is natural to conceive that those who live near the sea must be very different from those who live in the woods; the intermediate space will afford a separate and distinct class.

Men are like plants; the goodness and flavor of the fruit proceeds from the peculiar soil and exposition in which they grow. We are nothing but what we derive from the air we breathe, the climate we inhabit, the government we obey, the system of religion we profess, and the nature of our employment. Here you will find but few crimes; these have acquired as yet no root among us. I wish I was able to trace all my ideas; if my ignorance prevents me from describing them properly, I hope I shall be able to delineate a few of the outlines, which are all I propose.

Those who live near the sea feed more on fish than on flesh, and often encounter that boisterous element. This renders them more bold and enterprising; this leads them to neglect the confined occupations of the land. They see and converse with a variety of people, their intercourse with mankind becomes extensive. The sea inspires them with a love of traffic, a desire of transporting produce from one place to another; and leads them to a variety of resources which supply the place of labor. Those who inhabit the middle settlements, by far the most numerous, must be very different; the simple cultivation of the earth purifies them, but the indulgences of the government, the soft remonstrances of religion, the rank of independent freeholders, must necessarily inspire them with sentiments, very little known in Europe among people of the same class. What do I say? Europe has no such class of men; the early knowledge they acquire, the early bargains they make, give them a great degree of sagacity. As freemen they will be litigious; pride and obstinacy are often the cause of lawsuits; the nature of our laws and governments may be another. As citizens it is easy to imagine that they will carefully read the newspapers, enter into every political disquisition, freely blame or censure governors and others. As farmers they will be careful and anxious to get as much as they can, because what they get is their own. As northern men they will love the cheerful cup. As Christians, religion curbs them not in their opinions; the general indulgence leaves everyone to think for themselves in spiritual matters; the laws inspect our actions, our thoughts are left to God. Industry, good living, selfishness, litigiousness, country politics, the pride of freemen, religious indifference are their characteristics. If you recede still farther from the sea, you will come into more modern settlements; they exhibit the same strong lineaments, in a ruder appearance. Religion seems to have still less influence, and their manners are less improved.

Now we arrive near the great woods, near the last inhabited districts;[2] there men seem to be placed still farther beyond the reach of government, which in some measure leaves them to themselves. How can it pervade every corner; as they were driven there by misfortunes, necessity of beginnings, desire of acquiring large tracts of land, idleness, frequent want of economy,[3] ancient debts; the reunion of such people does not afford a very pleasing spectacle. When discord, want of unity and friendship; when either drunkenness or idleness prevail in such remote districts; contention, inactivity, and wretchedness must ensue. There are not the same remedies to these evils as in a long-established community. The few magistrates they have are in general little better than the rest; they are often in a perfect state of war; that of man against man, sometimes decided by blows, sometimes by means of the law; that of man against every wild inhabitant of these venerable woods, of which they are come to dispossess them. There men appear to be no better than carnivorous animals of a superior rank, living on the flesh of wild animals when they can catch them, and when they are not able, they subsist on grain. He who would wish to see America in its proper light, and have a true idea of its feeble beginnings and barbarous rudiments, must visit our extended line of frontiers where the last settlers dwell, and where he may see the first labors of settlement, the mode of clearing the earth, in all their different appearances; where men are wholly left dependent on their native tempers and on the spur of uncertain industry, which often fails when not sanctified by the efficacy of a few moral rules. There, remote from the power of example and check of shame, many families exhibit the most hideous parts of our society. They are a kind of forlorn hope, preceding by ten or twelve years the most respectable army of veterans which come after them. In that space, prosperity will polish some, vice and the law will drive off the rest, who unit-

2. I.e., the frontier; the land west of the original colonies and east of the Mississippi.

3. I.e., they were improvident and spent beyond their means.

ing again with others like themselves will recede still farther; making room for more industrious people, who will finish their improvements, convert the loghouse into a convenient habitation, and rejoicing that the first heavy labors are finished, will change in a few years that hitherto barbarous country into a fine fertile, well-regulated district. Such is our progress, such is the march of the Europeans toward the interior parts of this continent. In all societies there are offcasts; this impure part serves as our precursors or pioneers; my father himself was one of that class,[4] but he came upon honest principles, and was therefore one of the few who held fast; by good conduct and temperance, he transmitted to me his fair inheritance, when not above one in fourteen of his contemporaries had the same good fortune.

Forty years ago this smiling country was thus inhabited; it is now purged, a general decency of manners prevails throughout, and such has been the fate of our best countries.

Exclusive of those general characteristics, each province has its own, founded on the government, climate, mode of husbandry, customs, and peculiarity of circumstances. Europeans submit insensibly to these great powers, and become, in the course of a few generations, not only Americans in general, but either Pennsylvanians, Virginians, or provincials under some other name. Whoever traverses the continent must easily observe those strong differences, which will grow more evident in time. The inhabitants of Canada, Massachusetts, the middle provinces, the southern ones will be as different as their climates; their only points of unity will be those of religion and language.

As I have endeavored to show you how Europeans become Americans, it may not be disagreeable to show you likewise how the various Christian sects introduced wear out, and how religious indifference becomes prevalent. When any considerable number of a particular sect happen to dwell contiguous to each other, they immediately erect a temple, and there worship the Divinity agreeably to their own peculiar ideas. Nobody disturbs them. If any new sect springs up in Europe it may happen that many of its professors[5] will come and settle in America. As they bring their zeal with them, they are at liberty to make proselytes if they can, and to build a meeting and to follow the dictates of their consciences; for neither the government nor any other power interferes. If they are peaceable subjects, and are industrious, what is it to their neighbors how and in what manner they think fit to address their prayers to the Supreme Being? But if the sectaries are not settled close together, if they are mixed with other denominations, their zeal will cool for want of fuel, and will be extinguished in a little time. Then the Americans become as to religion what they are as to country, allied

---

4. His father never came to America.   5. Believers.

to all. In them the name of Englishman, Frenchman, and European is lost, and in like manner, the strict modes of Christianity as practiced in Europe are lost also. This effect will extend itself still farther hereafter, and though this may appear to you as a strange idea, yet it is a very true one. I shall be able perhaps hereafter to explain myself better; in the meanwhile, let the following example serve as my first justification.

Let us suppose you and I to be traveling; we observe that in this house, to the right, lives a Catholic, who prays to God as he has been taught, and believes in transubstantiation;[6] he works and raises wheat, he has a large family of children, all hale and robust; his belief, his prayers offend nobody. About one mile farther on the same road, his next neighbor may be a good honest plodding German Lutheran, who addresses himself to the same God, the God of all, agreeably to the modes he has been educated in, and believes in consubstantiation;[7] by so doing he scandalizes nobody; he also works in his fields, embellishes the earth, clears swamps, etc. What has the world to do with his Lutheran principles? He persecutes nobody, and nobody persecutes him, he visits his neighbors, and his neighbors visit him. Next to him lives a seceder,[8] the most enthusiastic of all sectaries;[9] his zeal is hot and fiery, but separated as he is from others of the same complexion, he has no congregation of his own to resort to, where he might cabal and mingle religious pride with worldly obstinacy. He likewise raises good crops, his house is handsomely painted, his orchard is one of the fairest in the neighborhood. How does it concern the welfare of the country, or of the province at large, what this man's religious sentiments are, or really whether he has any at all? He is a good farmer, he is a sober, peaceable, good citizen: William Penn[1] himself would not wish for more. This is the visible character, the invisible one is only guessed at, and is nobody's business. Next again lives a Low Dutchman, who implicitly believes the rules laid down by the synod of Dort.[2] He conceives no other idea of a clergyman than that of a hired man; if he does his work well he will pay him the stipulated sum; if not he will dismiss him, and do without his sermons, and let his church be shut up for years. But notwithstanding this coarse idea, you will find his house and farm to be the neatest in all the country; and you will judge by his wagon and fat horses that he thinks more of the affairs of this world than of those of the next.

---

6. The doctrine followed by Roman Catholics that the bread and wine used in the sacrament of communion have been changed into the real presence of Christ's body and blood.
7. As distinguished from transubstantiation; the doctrine which affirms that Christ's body is not present in or under the elements of bread and wine, but that the bread and wine are signs of Christ's presence through faith.

8. One who has withdrawn from any religious body.
9. One who dissents from the established church.
1. William Penn (1644–1718), English Quaker and founder of Philadelphia.
2. The Synod of Dort met in Holland in 1618 and attempted to settle disputes between Protestant Reformed Churches; "Low Dutchman": someone from Holland, not Belgium.

He is sober and laborious, therefore he is all he ought to be as to the affairs of this life; as for those of the next, he must trust to the great Creator. Each of these people instruct their children as well as they can, but these instructions are feeble compared to those which are given to the youth of the poorest class in Europe. Their children will therefore grow up less zealous and more indifferent in matters of religion than their parents. The foolish vanity, or rather the fury of making proselytes, is unknown here; they have no time, the seasons call for all their attention, and thus in a few years, this mixed neighborhood will exhibit a strange religious medley, that will be neither pure Catholicism nor pure Calvinism. A very perceptible indifference, even in the first generation, will become apparent; and it may happen that the daughter of the Catholic will marry the son of the seceder, and settle by themselves at a distance from their parents. What religious education will they give their children? A very imperfect one. If there happens to be in the neighborhood any place of worship, we will suppose a Quaker's meeting; rather than not show their fine clothes, they will go to it, and some of them may perhaps attach themselves to that society. Others will remain in a perfect state of indifference; the children of these zealous parents will not be able to tell what their religious principles are, and their grandchildren still less. The neighborhood of a place of worship generally leads them to it, and the action of going thither is the strongest evidence they can give of their attachment to any sect. The Quakers are the only people who retain a fondness for their own mode of worship; for be they ever so far separated from each other, they hold a sort of communion with the society, and seldom depart from its rules, at least in this country. Thus all sects are mixed as well as all nations; thus religious indifference is imperceptibly disseminated from one end of the continent to the other; which is at present one of the strongest characteristics of the Americans. Where this will reach no one can tell, perhaps it may leave a vacuum fit to receive other systems. Persecution, religious pride, the love of contradiction are the food of what the world commonly calls religion. These motives have ceased here; zeal in Europe is confined; here it evaporates in the great distance it has to travel; there it is a grain of powder inclosed, here it burns away in the open air, and consumes without effect.

But to return to our back settlers. I must tell you that there is something in the proximity of the woods which is very singular. It is with men as it is with the plants and animals that grow and live in the forests; they are entirely different from those that live in the plains. I will candidly tell you all my thoughts but you are not to expect that I shall advance any reasons. By living in or near the woods, their actions are regulated by the wildness of the neighborhood. The deer often come to eat their grain, the wolves to destroy their sheep, the bears to kill their hogs, the foxes to catch their

poultry. This surrounding hostility immediately puts the gun into
their hands; they watch these animals, they kill some; and thus by
defending their property, they soon become professed hunters; this
is the progress; once hunters, farewell to the plow. The chase renders them ferocious, gloomy, and unsociable; a hunter wants no
neighbor, he rather hates them, because he dreads the competition.
In a little time their success in the woods makes them neglect their
tillage. They trust to the natural fecundity of the earth, and therefore do little; carelessness in fencing often exposes what little they
sow to destruction; they are not at home to watch; in order therefore to make up the deficiency, they go oftener to the woods. That
new mode of life brings along with it a new set of manners, which I
cannot easily describe. These new manners, being grafted on the old
stock, produce a strange sort of lawless profligacy, the impressions
of which are indelible. The manners of the Indian natives are
respectable, compared with this European medley. Their wives and
children live in sloth and inactivity; and having no proper pursuits,
you may judge what education the latter receive. Their tender
minds have nothing else to contemplate but the example of their
parents; like them they grow up a mongrel breed, half civilized, half
savage, except nature stamps on them some constitutional propensities. That rich, that voluptuous sentiment is gone that struck them
so forcibly; the possession of their freeholds[3] no longer conveys to
their minds the same pleasure and pride. To all these reasons you
must add their lonely situation, and you cannot imagine what an
effect on manners the great distances they live from each other
has! Consider one of the last settlements in its first view: of what is
it composed? Europeans who have not that sufficient share of
knowledge they ought to have, in order to prosper; people who have
suddenly passed from oppression, dread of government, and fear of
laws into the unlimited freedom of the woods. This sudden change
must have a very great effect on most men, and on that class particularly. Eating of wild meat, whatever you may think, tends to alter
their temper: though all the proof I can adduce is that I have seen
it: and having no place of worship to resort to, what little society
this might afford is denied them. The Sunday meetings, exclusive of
religious benefits, were the only social bonds that might have inspired them with some degree of emulation in neatness. Is it then
surprising to see men thus situated, immersed in great and heavy
labors, degenerate a little? It is rather a wonder the effect is not
more diffusive. The Moravians[4] and the Quakers are the only instances in exception to what I have advanced. The first never settle

3. Land held outright for a specified period of time.
4. The Moravians were followers of
Jacob Hutter, who was executed in 1536;
they were Christian family communities
who gave up private property and were
noted for their industry and thrift. They
suffered a number of persecutions in the
17th century and emigrated to other
lands.

singly, it is a colony of the society which emigrates; they carry with them their forms, worship, rules, and decency: the others never begin so hard, they are always able to buy improvements, in which there is a great advantage, for by that time the country is recovered from its first barbarity. Thus our bad people are those who are half cultivators and half hunters; and the worst of them are those who have degenerated altogether into the hunting state. As old plowmen and new men of the woods, as Europeans and new-made Indians, they contract the vices of both; they adopt the moroseness and ferocity of a native, without his mildness, or even his industry at home. If manners are not refined, at least they are rendered simple and inoffensive by tilling the earth; all our wants are supplied by it, our time is divided between labor and rest, and leaves none for the commission of great misdeeds. As hunters it is divided between the toil of the chase, the idleness of repose, or the indulgence of inebriation. Hunting is but a licentious idle life, and if it does not always pervert good dispositions; yet, when it is united with bad luck, it leads to want: want stimulates that propensity to rapacity and injustice, too natural to needy men, which is the fatal gradation. After this explanation of the effects which follow by living in the woods, shall we yet vainly flatter ourselves with the hope of converting the Indians? We should rather begin with converting our back-settlers; and now if I dare mention the name of religion, its sweet accents would be lost in the immensity of these woods. Men thus placed are not fit either to receive or remember its mild instructions; they want[5] temples and ministers, but as soon as men cease to remain at home, and begin to lead an erratic life, let them be either tawny or white, they cease to be its disciples.

* * *

Europe contains hardly any other distinctions but lords and tenants; this fair country alone is settled by freeholders, the possessors of the soil they cultivate, members of the government they obey, and the framers of their own laws, by means of their representatives. This is a thought which you have taught me to cherish; our difference from Europe, far from diminishing, rather adds to our usefulness and consequence as men and subjects. Had our forefathers remained there, they would only have crowded it, and perhaps prolonged those convulsions which had shook it so long. Every industrious European who transports himself here may be compared to a sprout growing at the foot of a great tree; it enjoys and draws but a little portion of sap; wrench it from the parent roots, transplant it, and it will become a tree bearing fruit also. Colonists are therefore entitled to the consideration due to the most useful subjects; a hundred families barely existing in some parts of

5. Lack.

Scotland will here in six years cause an annual exportation of 10,000 bushels of wheat; 100 bushels being but a common quantity for an industrious family to sell, if they cultivate good land. It is here then that the idle may be employed, the useless become useful, and the poor become rich; but by riches I do not mean gold and silver, we have but little of those metals; I mean a better sort of wealth, cleared lands, cattle, good houses, good clothes, and an increase of people to enjoy them.

There is no wonder that this country has so many charms, and presents to Europeans so many temptations to remain in it. A traveler in Europe becomes a stranger as soon as he quits his own kingdom; but it is otherwise here. We know, properly speaking, no strangers; this is every person's country; the variety of our soils, situations, climates, governments, and produce hath something which must please everybody. No sooner does a European arrive, no matter of what condition, than his eyes are opened upon the fair prospect; he hears his language spoken, he retraces many of his own country manners, he perpetually hears the names of families and towns with which he is acquainted; he sees happiness and prosperity in all places disseminated; he meets with hospitality, kindness, and plenty everywhere; he beholds hardly any poor; he seldom hears of punishments and executions; and he wonders at the elegance of our towns, those miracles of industry and freedom. He cannot admire enough our rural districts, our convenient roads, good taverns, and our many accommodations; he involuntarily loves a country where everything is so lovely.

* * *

After a foreigner from any part of Europe is arrived, and become a citizen, let him devoutly listen to the voice of our great parent, which says to him, "Welcome to my shores, distressed European; bless the hour in which thou didst see my verdant fields, my fair navigable rivers, and my green mountains!—If thou wilt work, I have bread for thee; if thou wilt be honest, sober, and industrious, I have greater rewards to confer on thee—ease and independence. I will give thee fields to feed and clothe thee; a comfortable fireside to sit by, and tell thy children by what means thou hast prospered; and a decent bed to repose on. I shall endow thee beside with the immunities of a freeman. If thou wilt carefully educate thy children, teach them gratitude to God, and reverence to that government, that philanthropic government, which has collected here so many men and made them happy. I will also provide for thy progeny; and to every good man this ought to be the most holy, the most powerful, the most earnest wish he can possibly form, as well as the most consolatory prospect when he dies. Go thou and work and till; thou shalt prosper, provided thou be just, grateful, and industrious."

From *Letter IX. Description of Charles-Town; Thoughts on Slavery; on Physical Evil; A Melancholy Scene*

Charles-Town is, in the north, what Lima is in the south; both are capitals of the richest provinces of their respective hemispheres: you may therefore conjecture, that both cities must exhibit the appearances necessarily resulting from riches. Peru abounding in gold, Lima is filled with inhabitants who enjoy all those gradations of pleasure, refinement, and luxury, which proceed from wealth. Carolina produces commodities, more valuable perhaps than gold, because they are gained by greater industry; it exhibits also on our northern stage, a display of riches and luxury, inferior indeed to the former, but far superior to what are to be seen in our northern towns. Its situation is admirable, being built at the confluence of two large rivers, which receive in their course a great number of inferior streams; all navigable in the spring, for flat-boats. Here the produce of this extensive territory concenters; here therefore is the seat of the most valuable exportation; their wharfs, their docks, their magazines,[1] are extremely convenient to facilitate this great commercial business. The inhabitants are the gayest in America; it is called the center of our beau monde, and it [is] always filled with the richest planters of the province, who resort hither in quest of health and pleasure. Here are always to be seen a great number of valetudinarians from the West Indies, seeking for the renovation of health, exhausted by the debilitating nature of their sun, air, and modes of living. Many of these West Indians have I seen, at thirty, loaded with the infirmities of old age; for nothing is more common in those countries of wealth, than for persons to lose the abilities of enjoying the comforts of life, at a time when we northern men just begin to taste the fruits of our labor and prudence. The round of pleasure, and the expenses of those citizens' tables, are much superior to what you would imagine: indeed the growth of this town and province has been astonishingly rapid. It is [a] pity that the narrowness of the neck on which it stands prevents it from increasing; and which is the reason why houses are so dear. The heat of the climate, which is sometimes very great in the interior parts of the country, is always temperate in Charles-Town; though sometimes when they have no sea breezes the sun is too powerful. The climate renders excesses of all kinds very dangerous, particularly those of the table; and yet, insensible or fearless of danger, they live on, and enjoy a short and a merry life: the rays of their sun seem to urge them irresistably to dissipation and pleasure: on the contrary, the women, from being abstemious, reach to a longer period of life, and seldom die without having had several husbands. An European at his first arrival must be greatly surprised when he sees

1. Warehouses.

the elegance of their houses, their sumptuous furniture, as well as the magnificence of their tables. Can he imagine himself in a country, the establishment of which is so recent?

The three principal classes of inhabitants are, lawyers, planters, and merchants; this is the province which has afforded to the first the richest spoils, for nothing can exceed their wealth, their power, and their influence. They have reached the *ne plus ultra*[2] of worldly felicity; no plantation is secured, no title is good, no will is valid, but what they dictate, regulate, and approve. The whole mass of provincial property is become tributary to this society; which, far above priests and bishops, disdain to be satisfied with the poor Mosaical portion of the tenth.[3] I appeal to the many inhabitants, who, while contending perhaps for their right to a few hundred acres, have lost by the mazes of the law their whole patrimony. These men are more properly law givers than interpreters of the law; and have united here, as well as in most other provinces, the skill and dexterity of the scribe with the power and ambition of the prince: who can tell where this may lead in a future day? The nature of our laws, and the spirit of freedom, which often tends to make us litigious, must necessarily throw the greatest part of the property of the colonies into the hands of these gentlemen. In another century, the law will possess in the north, what now the church possesses in Peru and Mexico.

While all is joy, festivity, and happiness in Charles-Town, would you imagine that scenes of misery overspread in the country? Their ears by habit are become deaf, their hearts are hardened; they neither see, hear, nor feel for the woes of their poor slaves, from whose painful labors all their wealth proceeds. Here the horrors of slavery, the hardship of incessant toils, are unseen; and no one thinks with compassion of those showers of sweat and of tears which from the bodies of Africans, daily drop, and moisten the ground they till. The cracks of the whip urging these miserable beings to excessive labor, are far too distant from the gay capital to be heard. The chosen race eat, drink, and live happy, while the unfortunate one grubs up the ground, raises indigo, or husks the rice; exposed to a sun full as scorching as their native one; without the support of good food, without the cordials of any cheering liquor. This great contrast has often afforded me subjects of the most afflicting meditation. On the one side, behold a people enjoying all that life affords most bewitching and pleasurable, without labor, without fatigue, hardly subjected to the trouble of wishing. With gold, dug from Peruvian mountains, they order vessels to the coasts of Guinea; by virtue of that gold, wars, murders, and devastations are committed in some harmless, peaceable African

2. Latin: literally, *no more beyond*; the point of highest achievement.
3. The law set forth in the first six books of the Old Testament that one tenth of one's worldly goods should be offered to God.

neighborhood, where dwelt innocent people, who even knew not but that all men were black. The daughter torn from her weeping mother, the child from the wretched parents, the wife from the loving husband; whole families swept away and brought through storms and tempests to this rich metropolis! There, arranged like horses at a fair, they are branded like cattle, and then driven to toil, to starve, and to languish for a few years on the different plantations of these citizens. And for whom must they work? For persons they know not, and who have no other power over them than that of violence; no other right than what this accursed metal has given them! Strange order of things! Oh, Nature, where art thou?—Are not these blacks thy children as well as we? On the other side, nothing is to be seen but the most diffusive misery and wretchedness, unrelieved even in thought or wish! Day after day they drudge on without any prospect of ever reaping for themselves; they are obliged to devote their lives, their limbs, their will, and every vital exertion to swell the wealth of masters; who look not upon them with half the kindness and affection with which they consider their dogs and horses. Kindness and affection are not the portion of those who till the earth, who carry the burdens, who convert the logs into useful boards. This reward, simple and natural as one would conceive it, would border on humanity; and planters must have none of it!

* * *

A clergyman settled a few years ago at George-Town, and feeling as I do now, warmly recommended to the planters, from the pulpit, a relaxation of severity; he introduced the benignity of Christianity, and pathetically made use of the admirable precepts of that system to melt the hearts of his congregation into a greater degree of compassion toward their slaves than had been hitherto customary; "Sir (said one of his hearers) we pay you a genteel salary to read to us the prayers of the liturgy, and to explain to us such parts of the Gospel as the rule of the church directs; but we do not want you to teach us what we are to do with our blacks." The clergyman found it prudent to withhold any farther admonition. Whence this astonishing right, or rather this barbarous custom, for most certainly we have no kind of right beyond that of force? We are told, it is true, that slavery cannot be so repugnant to human nature as we at first imagine, because it has been practiced in all ages, and in all nations: the Lacedemonians[4] themselves, those great assertors of liberty, conquered the Helotes with the design of making them their slaves; the Romans, whom we consider as our masters in civil and military policy, lived in the exercise of the most horrid oppression; they conquered to plunder and to enslave. What a hideous aspect the face of the earth must then have exhibited! Provinces, towns, districts, often depopulated; their inhabitants driven to Rome, the

4. Another name for Spartans, who enslaved the people of Helos, a town in Laconia.

greatest market in the world, and there sold by thousands! The Roman dominions were tilled by the hands of unfortunate people, who had once been, like their victors free, rich, and possessed of every benefit society can confer; until they became subject to the cruel right of war, and to lawless force. Is there then no superintending power who conducts the moral operations of the world, as well as the physical? The same sublime hand which guides the planets round the sun with so much exactness, which preserves the arrangement of the whole with such exalted wisdom and paternal care, and prevents the vast system from falling into confusion; doth it abandon mankind to all the errors, the follies, and the miseries, which their most frantic rage, and their most dangerous vices and passions can produce?

* * *

Everywhere one part of the human species are taught the art of shedding the blood of the other; of setting fire to their dwellings; of leveling the works of their industry: half of the existence of nations regularly employed in destroying other nations. What little political felicity is to be met with here and there, has cost oceans of blood to purchase; as if good was never to be the portion of unhappy man. Republics, kingdoms, monarchies, founded either on fraud or successful violence, increase by pursuing the steps of the same policy, until they are destroyed in their turn, either by the influence of their own crimes, or by more successful but equally criminal enemies.

If from this general review of human nature, we descend to the examination of what is called civilized society; there the combination of every natural and artificial want, makes us pay very dear for what little share of political felicity we enjoy. It is a strange heterogeneous assemblage of vices and virtues, and of a variety of other principles, forever at war, forever jarring, forever producing some dangerous, some distressing extreme. Where do you conceive then that nature intended we should be happy? Would you prefer the state of men in the woods, to that of men in a more improved situation? Evil preponderates in both; in the first they often eat each other for want of food, and in the other they often starve each other for want of room. For my part, I think the vices and miseries to be found in the latter, exceed those of the former; in which real evil is more scarce, more supportable, and less enormous. Yet we wish to see the earth peopled; to accomplish the happiness of kingdoms, which is said to consist in numbers. Gracious God! to what end is the introduction of so many beings into a mode of existence in which they must grope amidst as many errors, commit as many crimes, and meet with as many diseases, wants, and sufferings!

The following scene will I hope account for these melancholy reflections, and apologize for the gloomy thoughts with which I have filled this letter: my mind is, and always has been, oppressed since I became a witness to it. I was not long since invited to dine with a planter who lived three miles from ——, where he then resided. In order to avoid the heat of the sun, I resolved to go on foot, sheltered in a small path, leading through a pleasant wood. I was leisurely traveling along, attentively examining some peculiar plants which I had collected, when all at once I felt the air strongly agitated; though the day was perfectly calm and sultry. I immediately cast my eyes toward the cleared ground, from which I was but at a small distance, in order to see whether it was not occasioned by a sudden shower; when at that instant a sound resembling a deep rough voice, uttered, as I thought, a few inarticulate monosyllables. Alarmed and surprised, I precipitately looked all round, when I perceived at about six rods distance something resembling a cage, suspended to the limbs of a tree; all the branches of which appeared covered with large birds of prey, fluttering about, and anxiously endeavoring to perch on the cage. Actuated by an involuntary motion of my hands, more than by any design of my mind, I fired at them; they all flew to a short distance, with a most hideous noise: when, horrid to think and painful to repeat, I perceived a negro, suspended in the cage, and left there to expire! I shudder when I recollect that the birds had already picked out his eyes, his cheek bones were bare; his arms had been attacked in several places, and his body seemed covered with a multitude of wounds. From the edges of the hollow sockets and from the lacerations with which he was disfigured, the blood slowly dropped, and tinged the ground beneath. No sooner were the birds flown, than swarms of insects covered the whole body of this unfortunate wretch, eager to feed on his mangled flesh and to drink his blood. I found myself suddenly arrested by the power of affright and terror; my nerves were convulsed; I trembled, I stood motionless, involuntarily contemplating the fate of this negro, in all its dismal latitude. The living specter, though deprived of his eyes, could still distinctly hear, and in his uncouth dialect begged me to give him some water to allay his thirst. Humanity herself would have recoiled back with horror; she would have balanced whether to lessen such reliefless distress, or mercifully with one blow to end this dreadful scene of agonizing torture! Had I had a ball in my gun, I certainly should have dispatched him; but finding myself unable to perform so kind an office, I sought, though trembling, to relieve him as well as I could. A shell ready fixed to a pole, which had been used by some negroes, presented itself to me; filled it with water, and with trembling hands I guided it to the quivering lips of the wretched sufferer. Urged by the irresistible power of thirst, he endeavored to meet it, as he instinctively guessed its approach by the noise it made in passing through the bars of the cage. "Tankè, you whitè man, tankè you, putè somè poison and givè me." "How long have you been hanging there?" I asked him. "Two days, and me no die; the birds, the birds; aaah me!" Oppressed with the reflections which this shocking spectacle afforded me, I mustered strength enough to walk away, and soon reached the house at which I intended to dine. There I heard that the reason for this slave being thus punished, was on account of his having killed the overseer of the plantation. They told me that the laws of self-preservation rendered such executions necessary; and supported the doctrine of slavery with the arguments generally made use of to justify the practice; with the repetition of which I shall not trouble you at present.

Adieu.

c. 1769–80   1782

THOMAS PAINE
1737–1809

The author of two of the most popular books in eighteenth-century America, and the most persuasive rhetorician of the cause for independence that our country has ever known, Thomas Paine· was born in England in 1737, the son of a Quaker father and an Anglican mother, and did not come to America until he was thirty-seven years old. Paine's early years prepared him to be a supporter of the Revolution. The discrepancy between his high intelligence and the limitations imposed upon him by poverty and caste made him long for a new social order. He once said that a sermon he heard at the age of eight impressed him with the cruelty inherent in Christianity and made him a rebel forever. When he arrived in Philadelphia with letters of introduction from Benjamin Franklin, recommending him as an "ingenious, worthy young man," he had already had a remarkably full life. Until he was thirteen he went to grammar school, and then was apprenticed in his father's corset shop; at nineteen he ran away from home to go to sea. From 1757 to 1774 he was a corsetmaker, a tobacconist and grocer, a schoolteacher, and an exciseman (a government employee who taxed goods). His efforts to organize the excisemen and make Parliament raise their salary was unprecedented. He lost his job when he admitted he had stamped as examined goods which had not been opened. His first wife died less than a year after his marriage, and he was separated from his second wife after three years. Scandals about his private life and questions about his integrity while employed as an exciseman provided his critics with ammunition for the rest of his life. Franklin was right, however, in recognizing Paine's genius; for, like Franklin himself, he was a remarkable man, self-taught and curious about everything, from the philosophy of law to natural science.

In Philadelphia he seemed to find himself as a journalist, and he made his way quickly in that city, first as a spokesman against slavery and then as the anonymous author of *Common Sense*, the first pamphlet published in this country to urge immediate independence from Britain. Paine was obviously the right man in the right place at the right time. Relations with England were at their lowest ebb: Boston was under siege, and the Second Continental Congress had convened in Philadelphia. *Common Sense* sold almost half a million copies, and its authorship (followed by the charge of traitor) could not be kept a secret for long. Paine enlisted in the Revolutionary Army and served as an aide-de-camp in battles in New York, New Jersey, and Pennsylvania. He followed his triumph of *Common Sense* with the first of sixteen pamphlets entitled *Crisis*. The first *Crisis* paper ("These are the times that try men's souls") was read to Washington's troops at Trenton and did much to shore up the spirits of the Revolutionary soldiers.

Paine received a number of political appointments as rewards for his services as a writer for the American cause, but he misused his privileges and lost the most lucrative offices. He was too indiscreet and hot-tempered for public employment. In 1787 he returned to England, determined to get financial assistance to construct an iron bridge for which he had devised plans. It came to nothing. But in England he wrote his second most successful work, his *Rights of Man* (1791–92), an impassioned plea against hereditary monarchy, the traditional institution Paine never tired of arguing against. Paine was charged with treason and fled to France, where he was made a citizen and lionized as a spokesman for revolution. The horrors of the French Revolution, however, brought home to Paine the fact that the mere overthrow of monarchy did not usher in light and order. When he protested the execution of Louis XVI, he was accused of sympathy with the crown and imprisoned. He was saved from trial by the American ambassador, James Monroe, who offered him an American citizenship and safe passage back to New York.

Paine spent the last years of his life in New York City and in New Rochelle, New York. They were unhappy, impoverished years, and his reputation suffered enormously as a result of *The Age of Reason* (1794). Paine's attempt to define his beliefs was viewed as an attack on Christianity and, by extension, on conventional society. He was ridiculed and despised. Even George Washington, who had supported Paine's early writing, thought English criticism of him was "not a bad thing." Paine had clearly outlived his time. He was buried on his farm at New Rochelle after his request for a Quaker grave site was refused. Ten years later an enthusiastic admirer exhumed his bones with the intention of having him reburied in England. The admirer's plans came to nothing, and the whereabouts of Paine's grave is, at present, unknown.

Paine's great gift as a stylist was "plainness." He said he needed no "ceremonious expressions." "It is my design," he wrote, "to make those who can scarcely read understand," to put his arguments in a language "as plain as the alphabet," and to shape everything "to fit the powers of thinking and the turn of language to the subject, so as to bring out a clear conclusion that shall hit the point in question and nothing else."

From Common Sense[1]
Introduction

Perhaps the sentiments contained in the following pages are not yet sufficiently fashionable to procure them general favor; a long habit of not thinking a thing wrong, gives it a superficial appearance of being right, and raises at first a formidable outcry in defence of

---

1. The full title is *Common Sense: Addressed to the Inhabitants of America, on the following Interesting Subjects: viz.: I. Of the Origin and Design of Government in General; with Concise Remarks on the English Constitution. II. Of Monarchy and Hereditary Succession. III.* *Thoughts on the Present State of American Affairs. IV. Of the Present Ability of America; with some Miscellaneous Reflections.* The text used here is from *The Writings of Thomas Paine*, Vol. 1, ed. M. D. Conway (New York, 1894–96).

custom. But the tumult soon subsides. Time makes more converts than reason.

As a long and violent abuse of power is generally the means of calling the right of it in question (and in matters too which might never have been thought of, had not the sufferers been aggravated into the inquiry), and as the King of England hath undertaken in his own right, to support the Parliament in what he calls theirs, and as the good people of this country are grievously oppressed by the combination, they have an undoubted privilege to inquire into the pretensions of both, and equally to reject the usurpation of either.

In the following sheets, the author hath studiously avoided everything which is personal among ourselves. Compliments as well as censure to individuals make no part thereof. The wise and the worthy need not the triumph of a pamphlet; and those whose sentiments are injudicious or unfriendly will cease of themselves, unless too much pains is bestowed upon their conversions.

The cause of America is in a great measure the cause of all mankind. Many circumstances have, and will, arise which are not local, but universal, and through which the principles of all lovers of mankind are affected, and in the event of which their affections are interested. The laying a country desolate with fire and sword, declaring war against the natural rights of all mankind, and extirpating the defenders thereof from the face of the earth, is the concern of every man to whom nature hath given the power of feeling; of which class, regardless of party censure, is

The Author

From *III. Thoughts on the Present State of American Affairs*

In the following pages I offer nothing more than simple facts, plain arguments, and common sense: and have no other preliminaries to settle with the reader, than that he will divest himself of prejudice and prepossession, and suffer his reason and his feelings to determine for themselves: that he will put on, or rather that he will not put off, the true character of a man, and generously enlarge his views beyond the present day.

Volumes have been written on the subject of the struggle between England and America. Men of all ranks have embarked in the controversy, from different motives, and with various designs; but all have been ineffectual, and the period of debate is closed. Arms as the last resource decide the contest; the appeal was the choice of the King, and the continent has accepted the challenge.

It hath been reported of the late Mr. Pelham[2] (who though an able minister was not without his faults) that on his being attacked in the House of Commons on the score that his measures were only of a temporary kind, replied, "they will last my time." Should a thought so fatal and unmanly possess the colonies in the present

2. Prime Minister of Britain (1743–54).

contest, the name of ancestors will be remembered by future generations with detestation.

The sun never shined on a cause of greater worth. 'Tis not the affair of a city, a county, a province, or a kingdom; but of a continent—of at least one eighth part of the habitable globe. 'Tis not the concern of a day, a year, or an age; posterity are virtually involved in the contest, and will be more or less affected even to the end of time, by the proceedings now. Now is the seed time of continental union, faith and honor. The least fracture now will be like a name engraved with the point of a pin on the tender rind of a young oak; the wound would enlarge with the tree, and posterity read it in full grown characters.

By referring the matter from argument to arms, a new era for politics is struck—a new method of thinking hath arisen. All plans, proposals, etc. prior to the nineteenth of April, i.e., to the commencement of hostilities,[3] are like the almanacs of the last year; which though proper then, are superceded and useless now. Whatever was advanced by the advocates on either side of the question then, terminated in one and the same point, viz., a union with Great Britain; the only difference between the parties was the method of effecting it; the one proposing force, the other friendship; but it hath so far happened that the first hath failed, and the second hath withdrawn her influence.

As much hath been said of the advantages of reconciliation, which, like an agreeable dream, hath passed away and left us as we were, it is but right that we should examine the contrary side of the argument, and inquire into some of the many material injuries which these colonies sustain, and always will sustain, by being connected with and dependent on Great Britain. To examine that connection and dependence, on the principles of nature and common sense, to see what we have to trust to, if separated, and what we are to expect, if dependent.

I have heard it asserted by some, that as America has flourished under her former connection with Great Britain, the same connection is necessary towards her future happiness, and will always have the same effect. Nothing can be more fallacious than this kind of argument. We may as well assert that because a child has thrived upon milk, that it is never to have meat, or that the first twenty years of our lives is to become a precedent for the next twenty. But even this is admitting more than is true; for I answer roundly, that America would have flourished as much, and probably much more, had no European power taken any notice of her. The commerce by which she hath enriched herself are the necessaries of life, and will always have a market while eating is the custom of Europe.

But she has protected us, say some. That she hath engrossed[4] us

3. The "Minutemen" of Lexington, Massachusetts, defended their ammunition stores against the British on April 19. 1775, and engaged in the first armed conflict of the American Revolution. 4. Dominated.

is true, and defended the continent at our expense as well as her own, is admitted; and she would have defended Turkey from the same motive, viz., for the sake of trade and dominion.

Alas! we have been long led away by ancient prejudices and made large sacrifices to superstition. We have boasted the protection of Great Britain without considering that her motive was interest not attachment; and that she did not protect us from our enemies on our account; but from her enemies on her own account, from those who had no quarrel with us on any other account, and who will always be our enemies on the same account. Let Britain waive her pretensions to the continent, or the continent throw off the dependence, and we should be at peace with France and Spain, were they at war with Britain. The miseries of Hanover's last war[5] ought to warn us against connections.

It hath lately been asserted in Parliament, that the colonies have no relation to each other but through the parent country, i.e., that Pennsylvania and the Jerseys,[6] and so on for the rest, are sister colonies by the way of England; this is certainly a very roundabout way of proving relationship, but it is the nearest and only true way of proving enmity (or enemyship, if I may so call it). France and Spain never were, nor perhaps ever will be, our enemies as Americans, but as our being the subjects of Great Britain.

But Britain is the parent country, say some. Then the more shame upon her conduct. Even brutes do not devour their young, nor savages make war upon their families; Wherefore, the assertion, if true, turns to her reproach; but it happens not to be true, or only partly so, and the phrase parent or mother country hath been jesuitically[7] adopted by the King and his parasites, with a low papistical design of gaining an unfair bias on the credulous weakness of our minds. Europe, and not England, is the parent country of America. This new world hath been the asylum for the persecuted lovers of civil and religious liberty from every part of Europe. Hither have they fled, not from the tender embraces of the mother, but from the cruelty of the monster; and it is so far true of England, that the same tyranny which drove the first emigrants from home, pursues their descendants still.

In this extensive quarter of the globe, we forget the narrow limits of three hundred and sixty miles (the extent of England) and carry our friendship on a larger scale; we claim brotherhood with every European Christian, and triumph in the generosity of the sentiment.

It is pleasant to observe by what regular gradations we surmount

5. King George III of Great Britain was a descendant of the Prussian House of Hanover; Paine is referring to the Seven Years' War (1756–63), which originally involved Prussia and Austria and grew to involve all the major European powers. American losses in the French and Indian campaigns were heavy, even though the war was settled in Britain's favor.
6. The colony was divided into East and West Jersey.
7. I.e., cunningly.

the force of local prejudices, as we enlarge our acquaintance with the world. A man born in any town in England divided into parishes, will naturally associate most with his fellow parishioners (because their interests in many cases will be common) and distinguish him by the name of neighbor; if he meet him but a few miles from home, he drops the narrow idea of a street, and salutes him by the name of townsman; if he travel out of the county and meet him in any other, he forgets the minor divisions of street and town, and calls him countryman, i.e., countyman: but if in their foreign excursions they should associate in France, or any other part of Europe, their local remembrance would be enlarged into that of Englishmen. And by a just parity of reasoning, all Europeans meeting in America, or any other quarter of the globe, are countrymen; for England, Holland, Germany, or Sweden, when compared with the whole, stand in the same places on the larger scale, which the divisions of street, town, and county do on the smaller ones; distinctions too limited for continental minds. Not one third of the inhabitants, even of this province,[8] are of English descent. Wherefore, I reprobate the phrase of parent or mother country applied to England only, as being false, selfish, narrow and ungenerous.

But, admitting that we were all of English descent, what does it amount to? Nothing. Britain, being now an open enemy, extinguishes every other name and title: and to say that reconciliation is our duty is truly farcical. The first King of England of the present line (William the Conqueror) was a Frenchman, and half the peers of England are descendants from the same country; wherefore, by the same method of reasoning, England ought to be governed by France.

Much hath been said of the united strength of Britain and the colonies, that in conjunction they might bid defiance to the world: but this is mere presumption; the fate of war is uncertain, neither do the expressions mean anything; for this continent would never suffer itself to be drained of inhabitants to support the British arms in either Asia, Africa, or Europe.

Besides, what have we to do with setting the world at defiance? Our plan is commerce, and that, well attended to, will secure us the peace and friendship of all Europe; because it is the interest of all Europe to have America a free port. Her trade will always be a protection, and her barrenness of gold and silver secure her from invaders.

I challenge the warmest advocate for reconciliation to show a single advantage that this continent can reap by being connected with Great Britain. I repeat the challenge; not a single advantage is derived. Our corn will fetch its price in any market in Europe, and our imported goods must be paid for buy them where we will.

But the injuries and disadvantages which we sustain by that

8. I.e., Pennsylvania.

connection, are without number; and our duty to mankind at large, as well as to ourselves, instruct us to renounce the alliance: because, any submission to, or dependence on, Great Britain tends directly to involve this continent in European wars and quarrels, and set us at variance with nations who would otherwise seek our friendship, and against whom we have neither anger nor complaint. As Europe is our market for trade, we ought to form no partial connection with any part of it. It is the true interest of America to steer clear of European contentions, which she never can do, while, by her dependence on Britain, she is made the makeweight in the scale of British politics.

Europe is too thickly planted with kingdoms to be long at peace, and whenever a war breaks out between England and any foreign power, the trade of America goes to ruin, because of her connection with Britain. The next war may not turn out like the last,[9] and should it not, the advocates for reconciliation now will be wishing for separation then, because neutrality in that case would be a safer convoy than a man of war. Everything that is right or reasonable pleads for separation. The blood of the slain, the weeping voice of nature cries, " 'Tis time to part." Even the distance at which the Almighty hath placed England and America is a strong and natural proof that the authority of the one over the other was never the design of Heaven. The time likewise at which the continent was discovered adds weight to the argument, and the manner in which it was peopled increases the force of it. The Reformation was preceded by the discovery of America: as if the Almighty graciously meant to open a sanctuary to the persecuted in future years, when home should afford neither friendship nor safety.

The authority of Great Britain over this continent is a form of government which sooner or later must have an end: and a serious mind can draw no true pleasure by looking forward, under the painful and positive conviction that what he calls "the present constitution" is merely temporary. As parents, we can have no joy, knowing that this government is not sufficiently lasting to insure anything which we may bequeath to posterity: and by a plain method of argument, as we are running the next generation into debt, we ought to do the work of it, otherwise we use them meanly and pitifully. In order to discover the line of our duty rightly, we should take our children in our hand, and fix our station a few years farther into life; that eminence will present a prospect which a few present fears and prejudices conceal from our sight.

Though I would carefully avoid giving unnecessary offense, yet I am inclined to believe, that all those who espouse the doctrine of reconciliation, may be included within the following descriptions. Interested men who are not to be trusted, weak men who cannot

9. The Seven Years' War concluded with the Treaty of Paris (1763), and Britain gained all the French territory in North America.

see, prejudiced men who will not see, and a certain set of moderate men who think better of the European world than it deserves; and this last class, by an ill-judged deliberation, will be the cause of more calamities to this continent than all the other three.

It is the good fortune of many to live distant from the scene of present sorrow; the evil is not sufficiently brought to their doors to make them feel the precariousness with which all American property is possessed. But let our imaginations transport us a few moments to Boston; that seat of wretchedness will teach us wisdom, and instruct us forever to renounce a power in whom we can have no trust.[1] The inhabitants of that unfortunate city, who but a few months ago were in ease and affluence, have now no other alternative than to stay and starve, or turn out to beg. Endangered by the fire of their friends if they continue within the city, and plundered by the soldiery if they leave it, in their present situation they are prisoners without the hope of redemption, and in a general attack for their relief they would be exposed to the fury of both armies.

Men of passive tempers look somewhat lightly over the offenses of Great Britain, and, still hoping for the best, are apt to call out, "Come, come, we shall be friends again for all this." But examine the passions and feelings of mankind: bring the doctrine of reconciliation to the touchstone of nature, and then tell me whether you can hereafter love, honor, and faithfully serve the power that hath carried fire and sword into your land? If you cannot do all these, then are you only deceiving yourselves, and by your delay bringing ruin upon posterity. Your future connection with Britain, whom you can neither love nor honor, will be forced and unnatural, and, being formed only on the plan of present convenience, will in a little time fall into a relapse more wretched than the first. But if you say, you can still pass the violations over, then I ask, hath your house been burnt? Hath your property been destroyed before your face? Are your wife and children destitute of a bed to lie on, or bread to live on? Have you lost a parent or a child by their hands, and yourself the ruined and wretched survivor? If you have not, then are you not a judge of those who have. But if you have, and can still shake hands with the murderers, then are you unworthy the name of husband, father, friend, or lover, and whatever may be your rank or title in life, you have the heart of a coward, and the spirit of a sycophant.

This is not inflaming or exaggerating matters, but trying them by those feelings and affections which nature justifies, and without which we should be incapable of discharging the social duties of life, or enjoying the felicities of it. I mean not to exhibit horror for the purpose of provoking revenge, but to awaken us from fatal and unmanly slumbers, that we may pursue determinately some fixed object. 'Tis not in the power of Britain or of Europe to conquer

---

1. Boston was under British military occupation and blockaded for six months.

America, if she doth not conquer herself by delay and timidity. The present winter is worth an age if rightly employed, but if lost or neglected the whole continent will partake of the misfortune; and there is no punishment which that man doth not deserve, be he who, or what, or where he will, that may be the means of sacrificing a season so precious and useful.

'Tis repugnant to reason, to the universal order of things, to all examples from former ages, to suppose that this continent can long remain subject to any external power. The most sanguine in Britain doth not think so. The utmost stretch of human wisdom cannot, at this time, compass a plan, short of separation, which can promise the continent even a year's security. Reconciliation is now a fallacious dream. Nature hath deserted the connection, and art cannot supply her place. For, as Milton wisely expresses, "never can true reconcilement grow where wounds of deadly hate have pierced so deep."[2]

* * *

A government of our own is our natural right: and when a man seriously reflects on the precariousness of human affairs, he will become convinced that it is infinitely wiser and safer to form a constitution of our own in a cool deliberate manner, while we have it in our power, than to trust such an interesting event to time and chance. If we omit it now, some Massanello[3] may hereafter arise, who, laying hold of popular disquietudes, may collect together the desperate and the discontented, and by assuming to themselves the powers of government, finally sweep away the liberties of the continent like a deluge. Should the government of America return again into the hands of Britain, the tottering situation of things will be a temptation for some desperate adventurer to try his fortune; and in such a case, what relief can Britain give? Ere she could hear the news, the fatal business might be done; and ourselves suffering like the wretched Britons under the oppression of the conqueror. Ye that oppose independence now, ye know not what ye do: ye are opening a door to eternal tyranny by keeping vacant the seat of government. There are thousands and tens of thousands, who would think it glorious to expel from the continent that barbarous and hellish power, which hath stirred up the Indians and the Negroes to destroy us; the cruelty hath a double guilt: it is dealing brutally by us, and treacherously by them.

To talk of friendship with those in whom our reason forbids us to have faith, and our affections wounded through a thousand pores instruct us to detest, is madness and folly. Every day wears out the little remains of kindred between us and them; and can there be

---

2. *Paradise Lost*, IV.98–99.
3. "Thomas Anello, otherwise Massanello, a fisherman of Naples, who after spiriting up his countrymen in the public market place, against the oppression of the Spaniards, to whom the place was then subject, prompted them to revolt, and in the space of a day became King" [Paine's note].

any reason to hope, that as the relationship expires, the affection will increase, or that we shall agree better when we have ten times more and greater concerns to quarrel over than ever?

Ye that tell us of harmony and reconciliation, can ye restore to us the time that is past? Can ye give to prostitution its former innocence? Neither can ye reconcile Britian and America. The last cord now is broken, the people of England are presenting addresses against us. There are injuries which nature cannot forgive; she would cease to be nature if she did. As well can the lover forgive the ravisher of his mistress, as the continent forgive the murders of Britain. The Almighty hath implanted in us these unextinguishable feelings for good and wise purposes. They are the guardians of His image in our hearts. They distinguish us from the herd of common animals. The social compact would dissolve, and justice be extirpated from the earth, or have only a casual existence were we callous to the touches of affection. The robber and the murderer would often escape unpunished, did not the injuries which our tempers sustain provoke us into justice.

O! ye that love mankind! Ye that dare oppose not only the tyranny but the tyrant, stand forth! Every spot of the old world is overrun with oppression. Freedom hath been hunted round the globe. Asia and Africa have long expelled her. Europe regards her like a stranger, and England hath given her warning to depart. O! receive the fugitive, and prepare in time an asylum for mankind.

1776

The Crisis,[1] No. 1

These are the times that try men's souls. The summer soldier and the sunshine patriot will, in this crisis, shrink from the service of their country; but he that stands it now, deserves the love and thanks of man and woman. Tyranny, like hell, is not easily conquered; yet we have this consolation with us, that the harder the conflict, the more glorious the triumph. What we obtain too cheap, we esteem too lightly: it is dearness only that gives everything its value. Heaven knows how to put a proper price upon its goods; and it would be strange indeed if so celestial an article as freedom should not be highly rated. Britain, with an army to enforce her tyr-

1. The first of 16 pamphlets which appeared under this title. Paine sometimes referred to this particular essay as *The American Crisis.* There were three pamphlet editions in one week: one undated, one dated December 19, and the one reprinted here, dated December 23. The text used here is from *The Writings of Thomas Paine,* Vol. 1, ed. M. D. Conway (New York, 1894–96).
2. "The present winter is worth an age, if rightly employed; but, if lost or neglected, the whole continent will partake of the evil; and there is no punishment that man does not deserve, be he who, or what, or where he will, that may be the means of sacrificing a season so precious and useful" [Paine's note, taken from *Common Sense*]. Paine wanted an immediate declaration of independence, uniting the colonies and enlisting the aid of France and Spain.
3. Lord William Howe (1729–1814) was Commander of the British army in America from 1775 to 1778.
4. The colony was divided into East and West Jersey.
5. I.e., like one who is chilled.

anny, has declared that she has a right (not only to tax) but "to bind us in all cases whatsoever," and if being bound in that manner is not slavery, then is there not such a thing as slavery upon earth. Even the expression is impious; for so unlimited a power can belong only to God.

Whether the independence of the continent was declared too soon, or delayed too long, I will not now enter into as an argument; my own simple opinion is, that had it been eight months earlier, it would have been much better. We did not make a proper use of last winter, neither could we, while we were in a dependent state. However, the fault, if it were one, was all our own;[2] we have none to blame but ourselves. But no great deal is lost yet. All that Howe[3] has been doing for this month past is rather a ravage than a conquest, which the spirit of the Jerseys,[4] a year ago, would have quickly repulsed, and which time and a little resolution will soon recover.

I have as little superstition in me as any man living, but my secret opinion has ever been, and still is, that God Almighty will not give up a people to military destruction, or leave them unsupportedly to perish, who have so earnestly and so repeatedly sought to avoid the calamities of war, by every decent method which wisdom could invent. Neither have I so much of the infidel in me as to suppose that He has relinquished the government of the world, and given us up to the care of devils; and as I do not, I cannot see on what grounds the King of Britain can look up to heaven for help against us: a common murderer, a highwayman, or a housebreaker has as good a pretense as he.

'Tis surprising to see how rapidly a panic will sometimes run through a country. All nations and ages have been subject to them: Britain has trembled like an ague[5] at the report of a French fleet of flat-bottomed boats; and in the fourteenth[6] century the whole English army, after ravaging the kingdom of France, was driven back like men petrified with fear; and this brave exploit was performed by a few broken forces collected and headed by a woman, Joan of Arc. Would that heaven might inspire some Jersey maid to spirit up her countrymen, and save her fair fellow sufferers from ravage and ravishment! Yet panics, in some cases, have their uses; they produce as much good as hurt. Their duration is always short; the mind soon grows through them, and acquires a firmer habit than before. But their peculiar advantage is that they are the touchstones of sincerity and hypocrisy, and bring things and men to light, which might otherwise have lain forever undiscovered. In fact, they have the same effect on secret traitors, which an imaginary apparition would have upon a private murderer. They sift out the hidden thoughts of man, and hold them up in public to the world. Many a disguised tory[7]

6. Properly, the 15th century. Joan of Arc led the French to victory over the English in 1429.

7. I.e., supporter of the King.

has lately shown his head, that shall penitentially solemnize with curses the day on which Howe arrived upon the Delaware.

As I was with the troops at Fort Lee, and marched with them to the edge of Pennsylvania, I am well acquainted with many circumstances, which those who live at a distance know but little or nothing of. Our situation there was exceedingly cramped, the place being a narrow neck of land between the North River[8] and the Hackensack. Our force was inconsiderable, being not one fourth so great as Howe could bring against us. We had no army at hand to have relieved the garrison, had we shut ourselves up and stood on our defense. Our ammunition, light artillery, and the best part of our stores had been removed on the apprehension that Howe would endeavor to penetrate the Jerseys, in which case Fort Lee could be of no use to us; for it must occur to every thinking man, whether in the army or not, that these kind of field forts are only for temporary purposes, and last in use no longer than the enemy directs his force against the particular object, which such forts are raised to defend. Such was our situation and condition at Fort Lee on the morning of the 20th of November, when an officer arrived with information that the enemy with 200 boats had landed about seven miles above: Major General Green,[9] who commanded the garrison, immediately ordered them under arms, and sent express to General Washington at the town of Hackensack, distant, by the way of the ferry, six miles. Our first object was to secure the bridge over the Hackensack, which laid up the river between the enemy and us, about six miles from us, and three from them. General Washington arrived in about three quarters of an hour, and marched at the head of the troops towards the bridge, which place I expected we should have a brush for; however, they did not choose to dispute it with us, and the greatest part of our troops went over the bridge, the rest over the ferry, except some which passed at a mill on a small creek, between the bridge and the ferry, and made their way through some marshy grounds up to the town of Hackensack, and there passed the river. We brought off as much baggage as the wagons could contain, the rest was lost. The simple object was to bring off the garrison, and march them on till they could be strengthened by the Jersey or Pennsylvania militia, so as to be enabled to make a stand. We staid four days at Newark, collected our outposts with some of the Jersey militia, and marched out twice to meet the enemy, on being informed that they were advancing, though our numbers were greatly inferior to theirs. Howe, in my little opinion, committed a great error in generalship in not throwing a body of forces off from Staten Island through Amboy, by which means he might have seized all our stores at Brunswick, and intercepted our march into Pennsylvania; but if we believe the

8. I.e., the Hudson River.
9. Paine was aide-de-camp to Major General Nathanael Greene (1742–86).

power of hell to be limited, we must likewise believe that their agents are under some providential control.[1]

I shall not now attempt to give all the particulars of our retreat to the Delaware; suffice it for the present to say, that both officers and men, though greatly harassed and fatigued, frequently without rest, covering, or provision, the inevitable consequences of a long retreat, bore it with a manly and martial spirit. All their wishes centered in one, which was that the country would turn out and help them to drive the enemy back. Voltaire has remarked that King William never appeared to full advantage but in difficulties and in action;[2] the same remark may be made on General Washington, for the character fits him. There is a natural firmness in some minds which cannot be unlocked by trifles, but which, when unlocked, discovers a cabinet[3] of fortitude; and I reckon it among those kind of public blessings, which we do not immediately see, that God hath blessed him with uninterrupted health, and given him a mind that can even flourish upon care.

I shall conclude this paper with some miscellaneous remarks on the state of our affairs; and shall begin with asking the following question: Why is it that the enemy have left the New England provinces, and made these middle ones the seat of war? The answer is easy: New England is not infested with tories, and we are. I have been tender in raising the cry against these men, and used numberless arguments to show them their danger, but it will not do to sacrifice a world either to their folly or their baseness. The period is now arrived, in which either they or we must change our sentiments, or one or both must fall. And what is a tory? Good God! what is he? I should not be afraid to go with a hundred whigs[4] against a thousand tories, were they to attempt to get into arms. Every tory is a coward; for servile, slavish, self-interested fear is the foundation of toryism; and a man under such influence, though he may be cruel, never can be brave.

But, before the line of irrecoverable separation be drawn between us, let us reason the matter together: Your conduct is an invitation to the enemy, yet not one in a thousand of you has heart enough to join him. Howe is as much deceived by you as the American cause is injured by you. He expects you will all take up arms, and flock to his standard, with muskets on your shoulders. Your opinions are of no use to him, unless you support him personally, for 'tis soldiers, and not tories, that he wants.

I once felt all that kind of anger, which a man ought to feel, against the mean principles that are held by the tories: a noted one,

---

1. The American losses were larger than Paine implies. General Howe took 3,000 prisoners and a large store of military supplies when he captured Fort Lee. Paine wrote *The Crisis, No. 1* while serving with Washington's army as it retreated through New Jersey.

2. Voltaire (1694–1778) made this remark about King William III of England (1650–1702) in his *History of Louis the Fourteenth* (1751).
3. Storehouse.
4. Supporters of the Revolution.

who kept a tavern at Amboy,[5] was standing at his door, with as pretty a child in his hand, about eight or nine years old, as I ever saw, and after speaking his mind as freely as he thought was prudent, finished with this unfatherly expression, "Well! give me peace in my day." Not a man lives on the continent but fully believes that a separation must some time or other finally take place, and a generous parent should have said, "If there must be trouble, let it be in my day, that my child may have peace"; and this single reflection, well applied, is sufficient to awaken every man to duty. Not a place upon earth might be so happy as America. Her situation is remote from all the wrangling world, and she has nothing to do but to trade with them. A man can distinguish himself between temper and principle, and I am as confident, as I am that God governs the world, that America will never be happy till she gets clear of foreign dominion. Wars, without ceasing, will break out till that period arrives, and the continent must in the end be conqueror; for though the flame of liberty may sometimes cease to shine, the coal can never expire.

America did not, nor does not, want force; but she wanted a proper application of that force. Wisdom is not the purchase of a day, and it is no wonder that we should err at the first setting off. From an excess of tenderness, we were unwilling to raise an army, and trusted our cause to the temporary defense of a well-meaning militia. A summer's experience has now taught us better; yet with those troops, while they were collected, we were able to set bounds to the progress of the enemy, and thank God! they are again assembling. I always considered militia as the best troops in the world for a sudden exertion, but they will not do for a long campaign. Howe, it is probable, will make an attempt on this city;[6] should he fail on this side the Delaware, he is ruined: if he succeeds, our cause is not ruined. He stakes all on his side against a part on ours; admitting he succeeds, the consequences will be that armies from both ends of the continent will march to assist their suffering friends in the middle states; for he cannot go everywhere, it is impossible. I consider Howe as the greatest enemy the tories have; he is bringing a war into their country, which, had it not been for him and partly for themselves, they had been clear of. Should he now be expelled, I wish with all the devotion of a Christian, that the names of whig and tory may never more be mentioned; but should the tories give him encouragement to come, or assistance if he come, I as sincerely wish that our next year's arms may expel them from the continent, and the congress appropriate their possessions to the relief of those who have suffered in well-doing. A single successful battle next year will settle the whole. America could carry on a two years' war by the confiscation of the property of disaffected persons, and be made happy by

5. Paine was stationed at Perth Amboy, New Jersey, while in the Continental Army.

6. Philadelphia.

their expulsion. Say not that this is revenge; call it rather the soft resentment of a suffering people, who, having no object in view but the good of all, have staked their own all upon a seemingly doubtful event. Yet it is folly to argue against determined hardness; eloquence may strike the ear, and the language of sorrow draw forth the tear of compassion, but nothing can reach the heart that is steeled with prejudice.

Quitting this class of men, I turn with the warm ardor of a friend to those who have nobly stood, and are yet determined to stand the matter out: I call not upon a few, but upon all: not on this state or that state, but on every state: up and help us; lay your shoulders to the wheel; better have too much force than too little, when so great an object is at stake. Let it be told to the future world that in the depth of winter, when nothing but hope and virtue could survive, that the city and the country, alarmed at one common danger, came forth to meet and to repulse it. Say not that thousands are gone, turn out your tens of thousands;[7] throw not the burden of the day upon Providence, but "show your faith by your works"[8] that God may bless you. It matters not where you live, or what rank of life you hold, the evil or the blessing will reach you all. The far and the near, the home counties and the back,[9] the rich and poor will suffer or rejoice alike. The heart that feels not now is dead: the blood of his children will curse his cowardice who shrinks back at a time when a little might have saved the whole, and made them happy. I love the man that can smile in trouble, that can gather strength from distress, and grow brave by reflection. 'Tis the business of little minds to shrink; but he whose heart is firm, and whose conscience approves his conduct, will pursue his principles unto death. My own line of reasoning is to myself as straight and clear as a ray of light. Not all the treasures of the world, so far as I believe, could have induced me to support an offensive war, for I think it murder; but if a thief breaks into my house, burns and destroys my property, and kills or threatens to kill me, or those that are in it, and to "bind me in all cases whatsoever"[1] to his absolute will, am I to suffer it? What signifies it to me, whether he who does it is a king or a common man; my countryman or not my countryman; whether it be done by an individual villain, or an army of them? If we reason to the root of things we shall find no difference; neither can any just cause be assigned why we should punish in the one case and pardon in the other. Let them call me rebel, and welcome, I feel no concern from it; but I should suffer the misery of devils were I to make a whore of my soul by swearing allegiance to one whose character is that of

7. "Saul hath slain his thousands, and David his ten thousands" (1 Samuel 18.7).
8. "Show me thy faith without thy works, and I will show thee my faith by my works" (James 2.18).

9. I.e., the backwoods.
1. From the Declaratory Act of Parliament, February 24, 1766, establishing British authority over the American colonies.

a sottish, stupid, stubborn, worthless, brutish man. I conceive likewise a horrid idea in receiving mercy from a being, who at the last day shall be shrieking to the rocks and mountains to cover him, and fleeing with terror from the orphan, the widow, and the slain of America.

There are cases which cannot be overdone by language, and this is one. There are persons, too, who see not the full extent of the evil which threatens them; they solace themselves with hopes that the enemy, if he succeed, will be merciful. It is the madness of folly to expect mercy from those who have refused to do justice; and even mercy, where conquest is the object, is only a trick of war; the cunning of the fox is as murderous as the violence of the wolf, and we ought to guard equally against both. Howe's first object is, partly by threats and partly by promises, to terrify or seduce the people to deliver up their arms and receive mercy. The ministry recommended the same plan to Gage,[2] and this is what the tories call making their peace, "a peace which passeth all understanding" indeed![3] A peace which would be the immediate forerunner of a worse ruin than any we have yet thought of. Ye men of Pennsylvania, do reason upon these things! Were the back counties to give up their arms, they would fall an easy prey to the Indians, who are all armed: this perhaps is what some tories would not be sorry for. Were the home counties to deliver up their arms, they would be exposed to the resentment of the back counties, who would then have it in their power to chastise their defection at pleasure. And were any one state to give up its arms, that state must be garrisoned by all Howe's army of Britons and Hessians[4] to preserve it from the anger of the rest. Mutual fear is the principal link in the chain of mutual love, and woe be to that state that breaks the compact. Howe is mercifully inviting you to barbarous destruction, and men must be either rogues or fools that will not see it. I dwell not upon the vapors of imagination: I bring reason to your ears, and, in language as plain as A, B, C, hold up truth to your eyes.

I thank God that I fear not. I see no real cause for fear. I know our situation well, and can see the way out of it. While our army was collected, Howe dared not risk a battle; and it is no credit to him that he decamped from the White Plains,[5] and waited a mean opportunity to ravage the defenceless Jerseys; but it is great credit to us, that, with a handful of men, we sustained an orderly retreat for near an hundred miles, brought off our ammunition, all our field pieces, the greatest part of our stores, and had four rivers to pass. None can say that our retreat was precipitate, for we were near

---

2. General Thomas Gage, who commanded the British armies in America from 1763 to 1775, prior to Howe.
3. "And the peace of God, which passeth all understanding, shall keep your hearts and minds through Christ Jesus" (Philippians 4.7).
4. German mercenaries.
5. At White Plains, New York, on October 28, 1776, General Howe successfully overcame Washington's troops, but failed to take full advantage of his victory.

three weeks in performing it, that the country[6] might have time to come in. Twice we marched back to meet the enemy, and remained out till dark. The sign of fear was not seen in our camp, and had not some of the cowardly and disaffected inhabitants spread false alarms through the country, the Jerseys had never been ravaged. Once more we are again collected and collecting; our new army at both ends of the continent is recruiting fast, and we shall be able to open the next campaign with sixty thousand men, well armed and clothed. This is our situation, and who will may know it. By perseverance and fortitude we have the prospect of a glorious issue; by cowardice and submission, the sad choice of a variety of evils—a ravaged country—a depopulated city—habitations without safety, and slavery without hope—our homes turned into barracks and bawdyhouses for Hessians, and a future race to provide for, whose fathers we shall doubt of. Look on this picture and weep over it! and if there yet remains one thoughtless wretch who believes it not, let him suffer it unlamented.

Common Sense
1776

6. I.e., the local volunteers.

THOMAS JEFFERSON
1743–1826

President of the United States, first Secretary of State, and Minister to France, Governor of Virginia, and Congressman, Thomas Jefferson once said that he wished to be remembered for only three things: drafting the Declaration of Independence, writing and supporting the Virginia Statute for Religious Freedom (1786), and founding the University of Virginia. Jefferson might well have included a number of other accomplishments in this list: he was a remarkable architect and designed the Virginia state capital, his residence Monticello, and the original buildings for the University of Virginia; he farmed thousands of acres and built one of the most beautiful plantations in America; he had a library of some 10,000 volumes, which served as the basis for the Library of Congress, and a collection of paintings and sculpture that made him America's greatest patron of the arts; and was known the world over for his spirit of scientific inquiry and as the creator of a number of remarkable inventions. The three acts for which he wished to be remembered, however, have this in common: they all testify to Jefferson's lifelong passion to liberate the human mind from tyranny, whether imposed by the state, the church, or our own ignorance.

Jefferson was born at Shadwell, in what is now Albemarle County, Virginia. Peter Jefferson, his father, was a county official and surveyor. He made the first accurate map of Virginia, something of which Jefferson was always proud. When his father died Thomas was only fourteen. Peter Jefferson left his son 2,750 acres of land, and Jefferson added to this acreage until he died; at one time he owned almost 10,000 acres. Jefferson tells us in his *Autobiography* that his father's education had been "quite neglected" but that he was always "eager after information" and determined to improve himself. In 1760, when Jefferson entered William and Mary College in Williamsburg, Virginia, he had mastered Latin and Greek, played the violin respectably, and was a skilled horseman. He was tall and a bit awkward looking, but a good companion. Williamsburg was the capital of Virginia as well as a college town, and Jefferson was fortunate enough to make the acquaintance of three men who strongly influenced his life: Governor Francis Fauquier, a Fellow of the Royal Society; George Wythe, one of the best teachers of law in the country; and Dr. William Small, an emigrant from Scotland who taught mathematics and philosophy and who introduced Jefferson, as Garry Wills has put it, "to the invigorating realm of the Scottish Enlightenment," especially the work of Francis Hutcheson, author of *An Inquiry into the Original of Our Ideas of Beauty and Virtue* (1725), and Lord Kames (Henry Home), author of *Essays on the Principles of Morality and Natural Religion* (1751). Jefferson flourished in Williamsburg, and it is hard to imagine a city in America where his natural interests and talents could have been more sympathetically encouraged.

Jefferson stayed on in Williamsburg to read law after graduation, and was admitted to the bar. In 1769 he was elected to the Virginia House of Burgesses and began a distinguished career in the legislature. In 1774 he wrote an influential and daring pamphlet on *A Summary View of the Rights of British America*, denying all parliamentary authority over America and arguing that ties to the British monarchy were voluntary and not irrevocable. Jefferson's reputation as a writer preceded him to Philadelphia, where he was a delegate to the second Continental Congress, and on June 11, 1776, he was elected to join Benjamin Franklin, John Adams, Roger Sherman, and Robert Livingston in drafting a declaration of independence. Although committee members made suggestions, the draft was very much Jefferson's own. As Garry Wills has recently shown, Jefferson was unhappy with the changes made by Congress to his draft, and rightly so; for congressional changes went contrary to some of his basic arguments. Jefferson wished to place the British *people* on record as the ultimate cause of the Revolution, because they tolerated a corrupt Parliament and King; and he wished to include a strong statement against slavery. Congress tolerated neither passage. Jefferson was justified, however, in asking that he be remembered as the author of the Declaration. It was, as Dumas Malone, Jefferson's biographer, once put it, a "dangerous but glorious opportunity." Whether as the result of these frustrations, or merely Jefferson's wish to be nearer his family, he left the Congress in September, 1776, and entered the Virginia House of Delegates. In 1779 he was elected Governor, and although re-elected the following year, Jefferson's term of office came to an ignominious end when he resigned. After the British captured Richmond in 1781, Jefferson and the legislature moved to Charlottesville, and he and the legislators barely escaped imprisonment when the pursuing British army descended on them at Monticello. Jefferson's resignation and the lack of preparations for the defense of the city were held against him, and it was some time before he regained the confidence of Virginians.

From 1781 to 1784 Jefferson withdrew from public life and remained at Monticello, completing his only book, *Notes on the State of Virginia*. In 1784 he was appointed Minister to France and served with Benjamin Franklin on the commission which signed the Treaty of Paris, ending the

Revolutionary War. He returned to Monticello in 1789, and in 1790 Washington appointed him the first Secretary of State under the newly adopted Constitution. After three years he announced his plans for retirement once again and withdrew to Monticello, where he rotated his crops and built a grist mill. But Jefferson's political blood was too thick for retirement, and in 1796 he ran for the office of President, losing to John Adams and taking the office of Vice-President instead. In 1800 he was elected President, the first to be inaugurated in Washington. He named Benjamin Latrobe surveyor of public buildings, and he worked with Latrobe in planning a great city.

When Jefferson returned to Monticello in 1809, he knew that this time his public life was over. For the final seventeen years of his life he kept a watchful eye on everything that grew in Monticello. But Jefferson was never far from the world. He rose every morning to attack his voluminous correspondence. The Library of Congress holds more than 55,000 Jefferson manuscripts and letters, and the most recent edition of his writings will run to sixty volumes. Jefferson left no treatise on political philosophy and, in a sense, was no political thinker. He was always more interested in the practical consequences of ideas. He remained an agrarian aristocrat all his life, and it is to the liberty of mind and the values of the land that he always returned. As Dumas Malone puts it: he was a "homely aristocrat in manner of life and personal tastes; he distrusted all rulers and feared the rise of an industrial proletariat, but more than any of his eminent contemporaries, he trusted the common man, if measurably enlightened and kept in rural virtue." Jefferson died a few hours before John Adams on the Fourth of July, 1826.

From The Autobiography of Thomas Jefferson[1]
From *The Declaration of Independence*

* * *

It appearing in the course of these debates, that the colonies of New York, New Jersey, Pennsylvania, Delaware, Maryland, and South Carolina were not yet matured for falling from the parent stem, but that they were fast advancing to that state, it was thought most prudent to wait a while for them, and to postpone the final decision to July 1st; but, that this might occasion as little delay as possible, a committee was appointed to prepare a Declaration of Independence. The committee were John Adams, Dr. Franklin, Roger Sherman, Robert R. Livingston, and myself. Committees were also appointed, at the same time, to prepare a plan of con-

1. On June 7, 1776, Richard Henry Lee of Virginia proposed to the second Continental Congress, meeting in Philadelphia, that "these united Colonies are, and of a right ought to be, free and independent states." On June 11, a committee of five—John Adams of Massachusetts, Benjamin Franklin of Pennsylvania, Roger Sherman of Connecticut, Robert Livingston of New York, and Thomas Jefferson of Virginia—was instructed to draft a declaration of independence. The draft presented to Congress on June 28 was primarily the work of Jefferson. Lee's resolution was passed on July 2, and the Declaration was adopted on July 4 with the changes noted by Jefferson in this text, taken from his *Autobiography*. On August 2 a copy in parchment was signed by all the delegates but three, and they signed later. The text used here is from *The Writings of Thomas Jefferson*, ed. A. A. Lipscomb and A. E. Bergh (1903).

federation for the colonies, and to state the terms proper to be proposed for foreign alliance. The committee for drawing the Declaration of Independence, desired me to do it. It was accordingly done, and being approved by them, I reported it to the House on Friday, the 28th of June, when it was read, and ordered to lie on the table. On Monday, the 1st of July, the House resolved itself into a committee of the whole, and resumed the consideration of the original motion made by the delegates of Virginia, which, being again debated through the day, was carried in the affirmative by the votes of New Hampshire, Connecticut, Massachusetts, Rhode Island, New Jersey, Maryland, Virginia, North Carolina and Georgia. South Carolina and Pennsylvania voted against it. Delaware had but two members present, and they were divided. The delegates from New York declared they were for it themselves, and were assured their constituents were for it; but that their instructions having been drawn near a twelve-month before, when reconciliation was still the general object, they were enjoined by them to do nothing which should impede that object. They, therefore, thought themselves not justifiable in voting on either side, and asked leave to withdraw from the question; which was given them. The committee rose and reported their resolution to the House. Mr. Edward Rutledge, of South Carolina, then requested the determination might be put off to the next day, as he believed his colleagues, though they disapproved of the resolution, would then join in it for the sake of unanimity. The ultimate question, whether the House would agree to the resolution of the committee, was accordingly postponed to the next day, when it was again moved, and South Carolina concurred in voting for it. In the meantime, a third member had come post[2] from the Delaware counties, and turned the vote of that colony in favor of the resolution. Members of a different sentiment attending that morning from Pennsylvania also, her vote was changed, so that the whole twelve colonies who were authorized to vote at all, gave their voices for it; and, within a few days, the convention of New York approved of it, and thus supplied the void occasioned by the withdrawing of her delegates from the vote.

Congress proceeded the same day to consider the Declaration of Independence, which had been reported and lain on the table the Friday preceding, and on Monday referred to a committee of the whole. The pusillanimous idea that we had friends in England worth keeping terms with, still haunted the minds of many. For this reason, those passages which conveyed censures on the people of England were struck out, lest they should give them offense. The clause too, reprobating the enslaving the inhabitants of Africa, was struck out in complaisance to South Carolina and Georgia, who had never attempted to restrain the importation of slaves, and who, on the contrary, still wished to continue it. Our northern brethren also,

2. I.e., by stagecoach.

I believe, felt a little tender under those censures; for though their people had very few slaves themselves, yet they had been pretty considerable carriers of them to others. The debates, having taken up the greater parts of the 2d, 3d, and 4th days of July, were, on the evening of the last, closed; the Declaration was reported by the committee, agreed to by the House, and signed by every member present, except Mr. Dickinson.[3] As the sentiments of men are known not only by what they receive, but what they reject also, I will state the form of the Declaration as originally reported. The parts struck out by Congress shall be distinguished by a black line drawn under them, and those inserted by them shall be placed in the margin, or in a concurrent column.

A DECLARATION BY THE REPRESENTATIVES OF THE UNITED STATES OF AMERICA, IN GENERAL CONGRESS ASSEMBLED.

When, in the course of human events, it becomes necessary for one people to dissolve the political bands which have connected them with another, and to assume among the powers of the earth the separate and equal station to which the laws of nature and of nature's God entitle them, a decent respect to the opinions of mankind requires that they should declare the causes which impel them to the separation.

We hold these truths to be self evident: that all men are created equal;[4] that they are endowed by their Creator with inherent and inalienable rights; that certain among these are life, liberty, and the pursuit of happiness;[5] that to secure these rights, governments are instituted among men, deriving their just powers from the consent of the governed; that whenever any form of government becomes destructive of these ends, it is the right of the people to alter or to abolish it, and to institute new government, laying its foundation on such principles, and organizing its powers in such form, as to them shall seem most likely to effect their safety and happiness. Prudence, indeed, will dictate that govern-

3. John Dickinson of Pennsylvania, who opposed it.
4. Garry Wills, in his study of the Declaration (*Inventing America*, 1978), tells us that Jefferson means "equal" in possessing a moral sense: "The moral sense is not only man's *highest* faculty, but the one that is *equal* to all men."
5. In his *Second Treatise on Government* (1689) John Locke defined man's natural rights to "life, liberty, and property." Jefferson's substitution of "pursuit of happiness" has puzzled a number of critics. Wills suggests that Jefferson was less influenced by Locke than the Scottish philosophers, particularly Francis Hutcheson and his *Inquiry into the Original of Our Ideas of Beauty and Virtue* (1725). Wills tells us that "the pursuit of happiness is a phenomenon both obvious and paradoxical. It supplies us with the ground of human right and the goal of human virtue. It is the basic drive of the self, and the only means given for transcending the self. * * * Men in the eighteenth century felt they could become conscious of their freedom only by discovering how they were bound: When they found what they *must* pursue, they knew they had a *right* to pursue it."

ments long established should not be changed for light and transient causes; and accordingly all experience hath shown that mankind are more disposed to suffer while evils are sufferable, than to right themselves by abolishing the forms to which they are accustomed. But when a long train of abuses and usurpations, begun at a distinguished[6] period and pursuing invariably the same object, evinces a design to reduce them under absolute despotism, it is their right, it is their duty to throw off such government, and to provide new guards for their future security. Such has been the patient sufferance of these colonies; and such is now the necessity which constrains them to expunge their former systems alter of government. The history of the present king of Great Britain[7] is a history of unremitting injuries and usurpa- repeated tions, among which appears no solitary fact to contra- all having dict the uniform tenor of the rest, but all have in direct object the establishment of an absolute tyranny over these states. To prove this, let facts be submitted to a candid world for the truth of which we pledge a faith yet unsullied by falsehood.

He has refused his assent to laws the most wholesome and necessary for the public good.

He has forbidden his governors to pass laws of immediate and pressing importance, unless suspended in their operation till his assent should be obtained; and, when so suspended, he has utterly neglected to attend to them.

He has refused to pass other laws for the accommodation of large districts of people, unless those people would relinquish the right of representation in the legislature, a right inestimable to them, and formidable to tyrants only.

He has called together legislative bodies at places unusual, uncomfortable, and distant from the depository of their public records, for the sole purpose of fatiguing them into compliance with his measures.

He has dissolved representative houses repeatedly and continually for opposing with manly firmness his invasions on the rights of the people.

He has refused for a long time after such dissolutions to cause others to be elected, whereby the legislative powers, incapable of annihilation, have returned to the people at large for their exercise, the state remaining, in the meantime, exposed to all the dangers of invasion from without and convulsions within.

---

6. I.e., discernible.   7. King George III (1738–1820).

He has endeavored to prevent the population of these states; for that purpose obstructing the laws for naturalization of foreigners, refusing to pass others to encourage their migrations hither, and raising the conditions of new appropriations of lands.

He has <u>suffered</u> the administration of justice <u>totally</u> ^{obstructed} <u>to cease in some of these states</u> refusing his assent to ^{by} laws for establishing judiciary powers.

He has made <u>our</u> judges dependent on his will alone for the tenure of their offices, and the amount and payment of their salaries.

He has erected a multitude of new offices, <u>by a self-assumed power</u> and sent hither swarms of new officers to harass our people and eat out their substance.

He has kept among us in times of peace standing armies <u>and ships of war</u> without the consent of our legislatures.

He has affected to render the military independent of, and superior to, the civil power.

He has combined with others[8] to subject us to a jurisdiction foreign to our constitutions and unacknowledged by our laws, giving his assent to their acts of pretended legislation for quartering large bodies of armed troops among us; for protecting them by a mock trial from punishment for any murders which they should commit on the inhabitants of these states; for cutting off our trade with all parts of the world; for imposing taxes on us without our consent; for depriving us [ ] of the benefits of trial by jury; for transporting ^{in many cases} us beyond seas to be tried for pretended offenses; for abolishing the free system of English laws in a neighboring province,[9] establishing therein an arbitrary government, and enlarging its boundaries, so as to render it at once an example and fit instrument for introducing the same absolute rule into these <u>states;</u> for taking away ^{colonies} our charters, abolishing our most valuable laws, and altering fundamentally the forms of our governments; for suspending our own legislatures, and declaring themselves invested with power to legislate for us in all cases whatsoever.

He has abdicated government here <u>withdrawing his</u> ^{by declaring} <u>governors, and declaring us out of his allegiance and</u> ^{us out of his protection,} <u>protection.</u> ^{and waging war against}

He has plundered our seas, ravaged our coasts, burnt ^{us.}

8. I.e., the British Parliament.
9. The Quebec Act of 1774 recognized the Roman Catholic religion in Quebec and extended the borders of the province to the Ohio River; it restored French civil law and thus angered the New England colonies. It was often referred to as one of the "intolerable acts."

our towns, and destroyed the lives of our people.

He is at this time transporting large armies of foreign mercenaries to complete the works of death, desolation and tyranny already begun with circumstances of cruelty and perfidy [ ] unworthy the head of a civilized nation.[1] *scarcely paralleled in the most barbarous ages, and totally*

He has constrained our fellow citizens taken captive on the high seas, to bear arms against their country, to become the executioners of their friends and brethren, or to fall themselves by their hands.

He has [ ] endeavored to bring on the inhabitants of our frontiers, the merciless Indian savages, whose known rule of warfare is an undistinguished destruction of all ages, sexes and conditions of existence. *excited domestic insurrection among us, and has*

He has incited treasonable insurrections of our fellow citizens, with the allurements of forfeiture and confiscation of our property.

He has waged cruel war against human nature itself, violating its most sacred rights of life and liberty in the persons of a distant people who never offended him, captivating and carrying them into slavery in another hemisphere, or to incur miserable death in their transportation thither. This piratical warfare, the opprobrium of INFIDEL powers, is the warfare of the CHRISTIAN king of Great Britain. Determined to keep open a market where MEN should be bought and sold, he has prostituted his negative for suppressing every legislative attempt to prohibit or to restrain this execrable commerce. And that this assemblage of horrors might want no fact of distinguished die, he is now exciting those very people to rise in arms among us, and to purchase that liberty of which he has deprived them, by murdering the people on whom he also obtruded them: thus paying off former crimes committed against the LIBERTIES of one people, with crimes which he urges them to commit against the LIVES of another.

In every stage of these oppressions we have petitioned for redress in the most humble terms: our repeated petitions have been answered only by repeated injuries.

A prince whose character is thus marked by every act which may define a tyrant is unfit to be the ruler of a [ ] people who mean to be free. Future ages will scarcely believe that the hardiness of one man adventured, within the short compass of twelve years only, to lay a foundation so broad and so undisguised for *free*

1. German soldiers hired by the King for colonial service.

tyranny over a people fostered and fixed in principles of freedom.

Nor have we been wanting in attentions to our British brethren. We have warned them from time to time of attempts by their legislature to extend a jurisdiction over these our states. We have reminded them of the circumstances of our emigration and settlement here, no one of which could warrant so strange a pretension: that these were effected at the expense of our own blood and treasure, unassisted by the wealth or the strength of Great Britain: that in constituting indeed our several forms of government, we had adopted one common king, thereby laying a foundation for perpetual league and amity with them: but that submission to their parliament was no part of our constitution, nor ever in idea, if history may be credited: and, we [ ] appealed to their native justice and magnanimity as well as to the ties of our common kindred to disavow these usurpations which were likely to interrupt our connection and correspondence. They too have been deaf to the voice of justice and of consanguinity, and when occasions have been given them, by the regular course of their laws, of removing from their councils the disturbers of our harmony, they have, by their free election, reestablished them in power. At this very time too, they are permitting their chief magistrate to send over not only soldiers of our common blood, but Scotch and foreign mercenaries to invade and destroy us. These facts have given the last stab to agonizing affection, and manly spirit bids us to renounce forever these unfeeling brethren. We must endeavor to forget our former love for them, and hold them as we hold the rest of mankind, enemies in war, in peace friends. We might have been a free and a great people together; but a communication of grandeur and of freedom, it seems, is below their dignity. Be it so, since they will have it. The road to happiness and to glory is open to us, too. We will tread it apart from them, and acquiesce in the necessity which denounces[2] our eternal separation [ ]!

Marginal notes:
an unwarrantable us

have

and we have conjured them by would inevitably

We must therefore

and hold them as we hold the rest of mankind, enemies in war, in peace friends.

We therefore the representatives of the United States of America in General Congress assembled, do in the name, and

We, therefore, the representatives of the United States of America in General Congress assembled, appealing to the su-

2. Proclaims.

by the authority of the good people of these states reject and renounce all allegiance and subjection to the kings of Great Britain and all others who may hereafter claim by, through or under them; we utterly dissolve all political connection which may heretofore have subsisted between us and the people or parliament of Great Britain: and finally we do assert and declare these colonies to be free and independent states, and that as free and independent states, they have full power to levy war, conclude peace, contract alliances, establish commerce, and to do all other acts and things which independent states may of right do.

And for the support of this declaration, we mutually pledge to each other our lives, our fortunes, and our sacred honor.

1821

preme judge of the world for the rectitude of our intentions, do in the name, and by the authority of the good people of these colonies, solemnly publish and declare, that these united colonies are, and of right ought to be free and independent states; that they are absolved from all allegiance to the British crown, and that all political connection between them and the state of Great Britain is, and ought to be, totally dissolved; and that as free and independent states, they have full power to levy war, conclude peace, contract alliances, establish commerce, and to do all other acts and things which independent states may of right do.

And for the support of this declaration, with a firm reliance on the protection of divine providence, we mutually pledge to each other our lives, our fortunes, and our sacred honor.

1829

The Declaration thus signed on the 4th, on paper, was engrossed on parchment, and signed again on the 2d of August.

From Notes on the State of Virginia[1]
Query XIX. Manufactures

We never had an interior trade of any importance. Our exterior commerce has suffered very much from the beginning of the present contest. During this time we have manufactured within our families the most necessary articles of clothing. Those of cotton will bear

---

1. In 1781, the year Jefferson retired as Governor of Virginia, he received a request from the Marquis de Barbé-Marbois, secretary of the French legation at Philadelphia, to answer 23 questions concerning the geographical boundaries, the ecology, and the social history of Virginia. Jefferson took the occasion to make some observations on slavery, manufacturing, and government. He wanted especially to counter the notion, prevalent among European naturalists, that species in North America had degenerated and were inferior to Old World types. Jefferson's replies were published privately in 1784–85. The threat of an unauthorized French translation prompted Jefferson to publish an authorized edition in London in 1787. The text used here is from the Norton edition, edited by William Peden (1954).

some comparison with the same kinds of manufacture in Europe; but those of wool, flax and hemp are very coarse, unsightly, and unpleasant: and such is our attachment to agriculture, and such our preference for foreign manufactures, that be it wise or unwise, our people will certainly return as soon as they can, to the raising raw materials, and exchanging them for finer manufactures than they are able to execute themselves.

The political economists of Europe have established it as a principle that every state should endeavor to manufacture for itself: and this principle, like many others, we transfer to America, without calculating the difference of circumstance which should often produce a difference of result. In Europe the lands are either cultivated, or locked up against the cultivator. Manufacture must therefore be resorted to of necessity not of choice, to support the surplus of their people. But we have an immensity of land courting the industry of the husbandman.[2] Is it best then that all our citizens should be employed in its improvement, or that one half should be called off from that to exercise manufactures and handicraft arts for the other? Those who labor in the earth are the chosen people of God, if ever He had a chosen people, whose breasts He has made his peculiar deposit for substantial and genuine virtue. It is the focus in which He keeps alive that sacred fire, which otherwise might escape from the face of the earth. Corruption of morals in the mass of cultivators is a phenomenon of which no age nor nation has furnished an example. It is the mark set on those, who not looking up to heaven, to their own soil and industry, as does the husbandman, for their subsistence, depend for it on the casualties and caprice of customers. Dependence begets subservience and venality, suffocates the germ of virtue, and prepares fit tools for the designs of ambition. This, the natural progress and consequence of the arts, has sometimes perhaps been retarded by accidental circumstances: but, generally speaking, the proportion which the aggregate of the other classes of citizens bears in any state to that of its husbandmen is the proportion of its unsound to its healthy parts, and is a good enough barometer whereby to measure its degree of corruption. While we have land to labor then, let us never wish to see our citizens occupied at a workbench, or twirling a distaff.[3] Carpenters, masons, smiths are wanting in husbandry: but, for the general operations of manufacture, let our workshops remain in Europe. It is better to carry provisions and materials to workmen there, than bring them to the provisions and materials, and with them their manners and principles. The loss by the transportation of commodities across the Atlantic will be made up in happiness and permanence of government. The mobs of great cities add just so much to the support of pure government as sores do to the strength of the human body. It

2. Farmer.
3. A short stick on which wool or flax is wound.

is the manners and spirit of a people which preserve a republic in vigor. A degeneracy in these is a canker which soon eats to the heart of its laws and constitution.

1780–81   1787

Letter to John Adams[1]
[The Natural Aristocrat]

Monticello, October 28, 1813

Dear Sir,—According to the reservation between us, of taking up one of the subjects of our correspondence at a time, I turn to your letters of August the 16th and September the 2d. * * * I agree with you that there is a natural aristocracy among men. The grounds of this are virtue and talents. Formerly bodily powers gave place among the aristoi.[2] But since the invention of gunpowder has armed the weak as well as the strong with missile death, bodily strength, like beauty, good humor, politeness and other accomplishments, has become but an auxiliary ground of distinction. There is also an artificial aristocracy, founded on wealth and birth, without either virtue or talents; for with these it would belong to the first class. The natural aristocracy I consider as the most precious gift of nature for the instruction, the trusts, and government of society. And indeed, it would have been inconsistent in creation to have formed man for the social state, and not to have provided virtue and wisdom enough to manage the concerns of the society. May we not even say that that form of government is the best which provides the most effectually for a pure selection of these natural aristoi into the offices of government? The artificial aristocracy is a mischievous ingredient in government, and provision should be made to prevent its ascendency. On the question, what is the best provision, you and I differ; but we differ as rational friends, using the free exercise of our own reason, and mutually indulging its errors. You think it best to put the pseudo-aristoi into a separate chamber of legislation, where they may be hindered from doing mischief by their co-ordinate branches, and where, also, they may be a protection to wealth against the agrarian and plundering enterprises of the majority of the people. I think that to give them power in order to prevent them from doing mischief is arming them for it, and increasing instead of remedying the evil. For if the co-ordinate branches

---

1. Thomas Jefferson and John Adams (1735–1826) became estranged when Adams was elected second President in 1796. Adams's Federalist positions were opposed by Jefferson, who succeeded him as President in 1801. In 1812 they began to correspond and were able to debate their differences. The text used here is from *The Writings of Thomas Jefferson*, Vol. 13, ed. A. A. Lipscomb and A. E. Bergh (1903).
2. The best. On July 9, 1813, Adams wrote to Jefferson that he recalled a maxim from the work of Theognis which said that " 'nobility in men is worth as much as it is in horses, asses, or rams; but the meanest [i.e., poorest] blooded puppy in the world, if he gets a little money is as good a man as the best of them.' Yet birth and wealth together have prevailed over virtue and talents in all ages. The many will acknowledge no other *aristoi*."

can arrest their action, so may they that of the co-ordinates. Mischief may be done negatively as well as positively. Of this, a cabal in the Senate of the United States has furnished many proofs. Nor do I believe them necessary to protect the wealthy; because enough of these will find their way into every branch of the legislation, to protect themselves. From fifteen to twenty legislatures of our own, in action for thirty years past, have proved that no fears of an equalization of property are to be apprehended from them. I think the best remedy is exactly that provided by all our constitutions, to leave to the citizens the free election and separation of the aristoi from the pseudo-aristoi, of the wheat from the chaff. In general they will elect the really good and wise. In some instances, wealth may corrupt, and birth blind them; but not in sufficient degree to endanger the society.

It is probable that our difference of opinion may, in some measure, be produced by a difference of character in those among whom we live. From what I have seen of Massachusetts and Connecticut myself, and still more from what I have heard, and the character given of the former by yourself,[3] who know them so much better, there seems to be in those two states a traditionary reverence for certain families, which has rendered the offices of the government nearly hereditary in those families. I presume that from an early period of your history, members of those families happening to possess virtue and talents, have honestly exercised them for the good of the people, and by their services have endeared their names to them. In coupling Connecticut with you, I mean it politically only, not morally. For having made the Bible the common law of their land, they seem to have modeled their morality on the story of Jacob and Laban.[4] But although this hereditary succession to office with you, may, in some degree, be founded in real family merit, yet in a much higher degree, it has proceeded from your strict alliance of Church and State. These families are canonized in the eyes of the people on common principles, "you tickle me, and I will tickle you." In Virginia we have nothing of this. Our clergy, before the Revolution, having been secured against rivalship by fixed salaries, did not give themselves the trouble of acquiring influence over the people. Of wealth, there were great accumulations in particular families, handed down from generation to generation, under the English law of entails.[5] But the only object of ambition for the wealthy was a seat in the King's Council.[6] All their court then was paid to the crown and its creatures; and they philippized[7] in all collisions

3. "Vol. 1, page 111" [Jefferson's note]. A reference to Adams's *Defense of the Constitutions of Government of the United States of America*, 3 vols. (Philadelphia, 1797). This work was first published in 1787.
4. I.e., a dynastic family, founded on the marital relations between the daughters of Jacob and Laban (Genesis 24–31).

5. An estate which cannot be willed but must pass from a proscribed list of successors.
6. The Privy Council, a select group of advisors, appointed by the King.
7. Argued against liberty for the people; spoke corrupted by their desire to please the King.

between the King and the people. Hence they were unpopular; and that unpopularity continues attached to their names. A Randolph, a Carter, or a Burwell[8] must have great personal superiority over a common competitor to be elected by the people even at this day. At the first session of our legislature after the Declaration of Independence, we passed a law abolishing entails. And this was followed by one abolishing the privilege of primogeniture, and dividing the lands of intestates[9] equally among all their children, or other representatives. These laws, drawn by myself, laid the axe to the foot of pseudo-aristocracy. And had another which I prepared been adopted by the legislature, our work would have been complete. It was a bill for the more general diffusion of learning. This proposed to divide every county into wards of five or six miles square, like your townships; to establish in each ward a free school for reading, writing and common arithmetic; to provide for the annual selection of the best subjects from these schools, who might receive, at the public expense, a higher degree of education at a district school; and from these district schools to select a certain number of the most promising subjects, to be completed at an university, where all the useful sciences should be taught. Worth and genius would thus have been sought out from every condition of life, and completely prepared by education for defeating the competition of wealth and birth for public trusts. My proposition had, for a further object, to impart to these wards those portions of self-government for which they are best qualified, by confiding to them the care of their poor, their roads, police, elections, the nomination of jurors, administration of justice in small cases, elementary exercises of militia; in short, to have made them little republics, with a warden at the head of each, for all those concerns which, being under their eye, they would better manage than the larger republics of the county or state. A general call of ward meetings by their wardens on the same day through the state, would at any time produce the genuine sense of the people on any required point, and would enable the state to act in mass, as your people have so often done, and with so much effect by their town meetings. The law for religious freedom,[1] which made a part of this system, having put down the aristocracy of the clergy, and restored to the citizen the freedom of the mind, and those of entails and descents nurturing an equality of condition among them, this on education would have raised the mass of the people to the high ground of moral respectability necessary to their own safety, and to orderly government; and would have completed the great object of qualifying them to select the veritable aristoi, for the trusts of government, to the exclusion of the pseudalists; and the same Theognis who has furnished the epigraphs of your two

8. John Randolph, Landon Carter, and Lewis Burwell were all Virginia aristocrats.
9. Those who died without wills; "primogeniture": a law which gave estates to the eldest son.
1. Passed in 1786.

letters, assures us that "Ουδεμιαν πω, Κυρν', αγαθοι πολιν ωλεσαν ανδρες."[2] Although this law has not yet been acted on but in a small and inefficient degree, it is still considered as before the legislature, with other bills of the revised code, not yet taken up, and I have great hope that some patriotic spirit will, at a favorable moment, call it up, and make it the keystone of the arch of our government.

With respect to aristocracy, we should further consider, that before the establishment of the American states, nothing was known to history but the man of the old world, crowded within limits either small or overcharged, and steeped in the vices which that situation generates. A government adapted to such men would be one thing; but a very different one, that for the man of these states. Here every one may have land to labor for himself, if he chooses; or, preferring the exercise of any other industry, may exact for it such compensation as not only to afford a comfortable subsistence, but wherewith to provide for a cessation from labor in old age. Every one, by his property, or by his satisfactory situation, is interested in the support of law and order. And such men may safely and advantageously reserve to themselves a wholesome control over their public affairs, and a degree of freedom, which, in the hands of the canaille[3] of the cities of Europe, would be instantly perverted to the demolition and destruction of everything public and private. The history of the last twenty-five years of France,[4] and of the last forty years in America, nay of its last two hundred years, proves the truth of both parts of this observation.

But even in Europe a change has sensibly taken place in the mind of man. Science had liberated the ideas of those who read and reflect, and the American example had kindled feelings of right in the people. An insurrection has consequently begun, of science, talents, and courage, against rank and birth, which have fallen into contempt. It has failed in its first effort, because the mobs of the cities, the instrument used for its accomplishment, debased by ignorance, poverty, and vice, could not be restrained to rational action. But the world will recover from the panic of this first catastrophe. Science is progressive, and talents and enterprise on the alert. Resort may be had to the people of the country, a more governable power from their principles and subordination; and rank, and birth, and tinsel-aristocracy will finally shrink into insignificance, even there. This, however, we have no right to meddle with. It suffices for us, if the moral and physical condition of our own citizens qualifies them to select the able and good for the direction of their government, with a recurrence of elections at such short periods as will

2. "Curnis, good men have never harmed any city." Theognis was a Greek elegiac poet of the sixth century B.C.

3. Mob.

4. I.e., since the French Revolution (1789).

enable them to displace an unfaithful servant, before the mischief he meditates may be irremediable.

I have thus stated my opinion on a point on which we differ, not with a view to controversy, for we are both too old to change opinions which are the result of a long life of inquiry and reflection; but on the suggestions of a former letter of yours, that we ought not to die before we have explained ourselves to each other. We acted in perfect harmony, through a long and perilous contest for our liberty and independence. A constitution has been acquired, which, though neither of us thinks perfect, yet both consider as competent to render our fellow citizens the happiest and the securest on whom the sun has ever shone. If we do not think exactly alike as to its imperfections, it matters little to our country, which, after devoting to it long lives of disinterested labor, we have delivered over to our successors in life, who will be able to take care of it and of themselves.

Of the pamphlet on aristocracy which has been sent to you, or who may be its author, I have heard nothing but through your letter. If the person you suspect, it may be known from the quaint, mystical, and hyperbolical ideas, involved in affected, newfangled and pedantic terms which stamp his writings. Whatever it be, I hope your quiet is not to be affected at this day by the rudeness or intemperance of scribblers; but that you may continue in tranquility to live and to rejoice in the prosperity of our country, until it shall be your own wish to take your seat among the aristoi who have gone before you. Ever and affectionately yours.

PHILIP FRENEAU
1752–1832

Philip Freneau had all the advantages that wealth and social position could bestow, and the Freneau household in Manhattan was frequently visited by well-known writers and painters. Philip received a good education at the hands of tutors and at fifteen entered the sophomore class at the College of New Jersey (now Princeton University). There he became fast friends with his roommate, James Madison, a future President, and a classmate, Hugh Henry Brackenridge, who was to become a successful novelist. In their senior year Freneau and Brackenridge composed an ode on *The Rising Glory of America*, and Brackenridge read the poem at commencement. It establishes early in Freneau's career his recurrent vision of a glorious future in which America would fulfill the collective hope of humankind:

> Paradise anew
> Shall flourish, by no second Adam lost,

No dangerous tree with deadly fruit shall grow,
No tempting serpent to allure the soul
From native innocence. . . . The lion and the lamb
In mutual friendship linked, shall browse the shrub,
And timorous deer with softened tigers stray
O'er mead, or lofty hill, or grassy plain * * *

For a short time Freneau taught school and hoped to make a career as a writer, but it was an impractical wish. When he was offered a position as secretary on a plantation in the West Indies in 1776, he sailed to Santa Cruz and remained there almost three years. It was in that country, where "Sweet orange groves in lonely valleys rise," that Freneau wrote some of his most sensuous lyrics; but as he tells us in *To Sir Toby*, he could not talk of "blossoms" and an "endless spring" forever in a land which abounded in poverty and misery and where the owners grew wealthy on a slave economy. In 1778 he returned home and enlisted as a seaman on a blockade runner; two years later he was captured at sea and imprisoned on the British ship *Scorpion*, anchored in New York Harbor. He was treated brutally, and when he was exchanged from the hospital ship *Hunter* his family feared for his life.

Freneau was to spend ten more years of his life at sea, first as a master of a merchant ship in 1784, and again in 1803, but immediately after he regained his health he moved to Philadelphia to work in the post office, and it was in that city that he gained his reputation as a satirist, journalist, and poet. As editor of the *Freeman's Journal*, Freneau wrote impassioned verse in support of the American Revolution and turned all his rhetorical gifts against anyone who was thought to be in sympathy with the British monarchy. It was during this period in his life that he became identified as the "Poet of the American Revolution." In 1791, after he returned from duties at sea, Jefferson, as Secretary of State, offered him a position as translator in his department, understanding that Freneau would have plenty of free time to devote to his newspaper, *The National Gazette*. Like Thomas Paine, Freneau was a strong supporter of the French Revolution, and he had a sharp eye for anyone not sympathetic to the democratic cause. He had a special grudge against Alexander Hamilton, Secretary of the Treasury, as chief spokesman for the Federalists. President Washington thought it was ironic that "that rascal Freneau" should be employed by his administration when he attacked it so outspokenly.

The National Gazette ceased publication in 1793, and after Jefferson resigned his office, Freneau left Philadelphia for good, alternating between ship's captain and newspaper editor in New York and New Jersey. He spent his last years on his New Jersey farm, unable to make it supporting and with no hope of further employment. Year after year he sold all the land he inherited from his father and was finally reduced to applying for a pension as a veteran of the American Revolution. He died impoverished and unknown, lost in a blizzard.

Freneau's biographer, Lewis Leary, subtitled his book *A Study in Literary Failure* and began that work by observing that "Philip Freneau failed in almost everything he attempted." Freneau's most sympathetic readers have always felt that he was born in a time not ripe for poetry, and that his genuine lyric gifts were always in conflict with his political pamphleteering. Had he been born fifty years later, perhaps he could have joined Cooper and Irving in a life devoted exclusively to letters. There is no doubt that he did much to pave the way for these later writers. Freneau is not "the Father of American Poetry" (as his readers, anxious for a spokesman for a national literary consciousness, liked to call him), but his obsession with the beautiful, transient things of nature, and the conflict in his art between the sensuous and the didactic, are central to the concerns of American poetry.

Texts used are *The Poems of Philip Freneau*, ed. F. L. Pattee (Princeton: The University Library, 1902) and *The Poems of Freneau*, ed. H. H. Clark (New York: Harcourt, Brace, 1929).

The Wild Honey Suckle

Fair flower, that dost so comely grow,
Hid in this silent, dull retreat,
Untouched thy honeyed blossoms blow,[1]
Unseen thy little branches greet:
  No roving foot shall crush thee here,   5
  No busy hand provoke a tear.

By Nature's self in white arrayed,
She bade thee shun the vulgar[2] eye,
And planted here the guardian shade,
And sent soft waters murmuring by;   10
  Thus quietly thy summer goes,
  Thy days declining to repose.

Smit with those charms, that must decay,
I grieve to see your future doom;
They died—nor were those flowers more gay,   15
The flowers that did in Eden bloom;
  Unpitying frosts, and Autumn's power
  Shall leave no vestige of this flower.

From morning suns and evening dews
At first thy little being came: 20
If nothing once, you nothing lose,
For when you die you are the same;
  The space between, is but an hour,
  The frail duration of a flower.

1786

The Indian Burying Ground

In spite of all the learned have said,
I still my old opinion keep;
The posture, that we give the dead,
Points out the soul's eternal sleep.

---

1. **Bloom.**   2. **Common; unfeeling.**

Not so the ancients of these lands— 5
The Indian, when from life released,
Again is seated with his friends,
And shares again the joyous feast.[1]

His imaged birds, and painted bowl,
And vension, for a journey dressed, 10
Bespeak the nature of the soul,
Activity, that knows no rest.

His bow, for action ready bent,
And arrows, with a head of stone,
Can only mean that life is spent, 15
And not the old ideas gone.

Thou, stranger, that shalt come this way,
No fraud upon the dead commit—
Observe the swelling turf, and say
They do not lie, but here they sit. 20

Here still a lofty rock remains,
On which the curious eye may trace
(Now wasted, half, by wearing rains)
The fancies of a ruder race.

Here still an agéd elm aspires, 25
Beneath whose far-projecting shade
(And which the shepherd still admires)
The children of the forest played!

There oft a restless Indian queen
(Pale Sheba,[2] with her braided hair) 30
And many a barbarous form is seen
To chide the man that lingers there.

By midnight moons, o'er moistening dews,
In habit for the chase arrayed,
The hunter still the deer pursues, 35
The hunter and the deer, a shade!

And long shall timorous fancy see
The painted chief, and pointed spear,
And Reason's self shall bow the knee
To shadows and delusions here. 40

1788

---

1. "The North American Indians bury
their dead in a sitting posture; decorat-
ing the corpse with wampum, the images
of birds, quadrupeds, &: And (if that of
a warrior) with bows, arrows, tomhawks

and other military weapons" [Freneau's
note].
2. Sheba is the Queen who visited Solomon to test his wisdom. 1 Kings 10.1–13

To Sir Toby[1]

A Sugar Planter in the Interior Parts of Jamaica, Near the City of San Jago de la Vega, (Spanish Town) 1784

"The motions of his spirit are black as night,
And his affections dark as Erebus."[2]
—SHAKESPEARE[3]

If there exists a hell—the case is clear—
Sir Toby's slaves enjoy that portion here:
Here are no blazing brimstone lakes—'tis true;
But kindled rum too often burns as blue;
In which some fiend, whom nature must detest,   5
Steeps Toby's brand, and marks poor Cudjoe's breast.[4]
Here whips on whips excite perpetual fears,
And mingled howlings vibrate on my ears:
Here nature's plagues abound, to fret and tease,
Snakes, scorpions, despots, lizards, centipedes—   10
No art, no care escapes the busy lash;
All have their dues—and all are paid in cash—
The eternal driver keeps a steady eye
On a black herd, who would his vengeance fly,
But chained, imprisoned, on a burning soil,   15
For the mean avarice of a tyrant toil![5]
The lengthy cart-whip guards this monster's reign—
And cracks, like pistols, from the fields of cane.
Ye powers! who formed these wretched tribes, relate,
What had they done, to merit such a fate!   20
Why were they brought from Eboe's[6] sultry waste,
To see that plenty which they must not taste—
Food, which they cannot buy, and dare not steal;
Yams and potatoes—many a scanty meal!—
One, with a gibbet[7] wakes his negro's fears,   25
One to the windmill nails him by the ears;
One keeps his slave in darkened dens, unfed,
One puts the wretch in pickle ere he's dead:
This, from a tree suspends him by the thumbs,
That, from his table grudges even the crumbs!   30
O'er yond' rough hills a tribe of females go,
Each with her gourd,[8] her infant, and her hoe;
Scorched by a sun that has no mercy here,
Driven by a devil, whom men call overseer—

1. First published in the *National Gazette*, July 21, 1792, entitled *The Island Field Hand*.
2. Night.
3. *The Merchant of Venice* 5.1.79. Freneau has substituted the word "black" for "dull."
4. Cudge or Cudjoe was a common name for a slave. "This passage has a reference to the West Indian custom (sanctioned by law) of branding a newly imported slave on the breast, with a red hot iron, as evidence of the purchaser's property" [Freneau's note].
5. Lines 13–16 were added in 1809.
6. "A small Negro kingdom near the river Senegal" [Freneau's note].
7. Gallows.
8. Water cup.

In chains, twelve wretches to their labours haste;   35
Twice twelve I saw, with iron collars graced!—
    Are such the fruits that spring from vast domains?
Is wealth, thus got, Sir Toby, worth your pains!—
Who would your wealth on terms, like these, possess,
Where all we see is pregnant with distress—   40
Angola's[9] natives scourged by ruffian hands,
And toil's hard product shipped to foreign lands.

    Talk not of blossoms, and your endless spring;
What joy, what smile, can scenes of misery bring?—
Though Nature, here, has every blessing spread,   45
Poor is the laborer—and how meanly fed!—

    Here Stygian[1] paintings light and shade renew,
Pictures of hell, that Virgil's[2] pencil drew:
Here, surly Charons[3] make their annual trip,
And ghosts arrive in every Guinea ship,[4]   50
To find what beasts these western isles afford,
Plutonian[5] scourges, and despotic lords:—

    Here, they, of stuff determined to be free,
Must climb the rude cliffs of the Liguanee;[6]
Beyond the clouds, in sculking haste repair,   55
And hardly safe from brother traitors[7] there.—

1784   1792

On the Religion of Nature

    The power, that gives with liberal hand
      The blessings man enjoys, while here,
    And scatters through a smiling land
      Abundant products of the year;
        That power of nature, ever blessed,   5
        Bestowed religion with the rest.

    Born with ourselves, her early sway
      Inclines the tender mind to take
    The path of right, fair virtue's way
      Its own felicity to make.   10
        This universally extends
        And leads to no mysterious ends.

9. West African Portuguese colony.
1. Hellish; taken from the river Styx which, in Greek mythology, souls must cross.
2. "See *Aeneid*, Book 6th.—and Fenelon's Telemachus, Book 18" [Freneau's note]. Aeneas descends to the underworld in the sixth book of the Latin poet Virgil's (70–19 B.C.) epic; François de Salignac de la Mothe-Fénelon (1651–1715) was a theologian as well as the author of *Télémaque* (1699), a didactic romance concerning the son of Ulysses as he searches for his father.

3. In Greek mythology, the ferryman who carried souls of the dead over the river Styx to Hades.
4. Slave ships from West Africa.
5. Hellish; in Greek mythology Pluto was the god of the underworld.
6. "The mountains northward of the kingdom" [Freneau's note].
7. "Alluding to the *Independent* negroes in the blue mountains, who, for a stipulated reward, deliver up every fugitive that falls into their hands, to the English Government" [Freneau's note].

Religion, such as nature taught,
   With all divine perfection suits;
Had all mankind this sytem sought   15
   Sophists[1] would cease their vain disputes,
   And from this source would nations know
   All that can make their heaven below.

This deals not curses on mankind,
   Or dooms them to perpetual grief,   20
If from its aid no joys they find,
   It damns them not for unbelief;
   Upon a more exalted plan
   Creatress nature dealt with man—

Joy to the day, when all agree   25
   On such grand systems to proceed,
From fraud, design, and error free,
   And which to truth and goodness lead:
   Then persecution will retreat
   And man's religion be complete.   30

                                                    1815

1. Teachers of philosophy.

PHILLIS WHEATLEY

c. 1753–1784

Phillis Wheatley was only nineteen years old when her *Poems on Various Subjects, Religious and Moral* was published in London in 1773. At the time of their publication she was the object of considerable public attention because, in addition to being a child prodigy, Phillis Wheatley was a black slave. She had been born in Africa, probably somewhere in present-day Senegal or Gambia, and was brought to Boston in 1761 when she was about seven years of age. She was purchased by a wealthy tailor, John Wheatley, for his wife, Susannah, probably as a companion. Phillis Wheatley was fortunate in her surroundings for Mrs. Wheatley had a sympathetic heart. Phillis was both very frail and remarkably intelligent, and the Wheatley household seems to have been alert to her gifts. In an age when few white women were given an education, she was taught to read and write, and in a very short time began also to read Latin writers. She came to know the Bible well; and three English poets—Milton, Pope, and Gray—touched her deeply and exerted a strong influence on her verse. It is clear that the Wheatleys were deeply committed Christians and thought of her as, first of all, a soul in need of salvation. Her poem in 1770 on the death of the Reverend George Whitefield, the great English evangelical preacher who frequently toured New England, made her famous. She had been taken to London partly for reasons of health, but also to meet a number of distinguished persons (the Countess of Huntington and the Lord Mayor of London) who knew her poetry and wanted to assist her in its publication.

Her literary gifts, intelligence, and piety were a striking example to her English and American audience of the triumph of native human capacities over the circumstances of birth. Phillis returned to Boston sooner than had been planned, when she received news of Mrs. Wheatley's fatal illness.

After the death of the Wheatleys, Phillis was freed and in 1778 married John Peters, a freedman. Almost nothing is known about Peters other than the fact that the Wheatley family disliked him, that he may have been a spokesman for Negro rights, that he moved from job to job and was imprisoned for debt in 1784, and was probably in prison when Phillis died. She spent her last years alone and in great poverty in a wreck of a house in Boston. She had lost two children; and when she was on her deathbed her third child lay ill beside her and died soon after she did. Both mother and child were buried together in an unmarked grave.

Until the 1830s, when Massachusetts abolitionists reprinted her poetry, Phillis Wheatley's verse remained forgotten. Hers was a thoroughly conventional poetic talent, tied too strongly to Miltonic cadences and the balanced couplets of Alexander Pope; but given the stringencies of the time and of her situation, it would be unrealistic to expect anything more. The only hint of injustice found in her poetry is in the line "Some view our sable race with scornful eye." It would be almost a hundred years before a black American writer could drop the mask of convention and write about the formation of his own unique sensibility. Nevertheless, Phillis Wheatley expresses the popular sentiments of the age in matters of poetic taste, religious feeling, and national identity. She is the first black writer of consequence in America; and her life constitutes a deeply moving account of unfulfilled promise.

The text used here is from *The Poems of Phillis Wheatley*, ed. Julian D. Mason, Jr. (Chapel Hill: University of North Carolina Press, 1966).

On Being Brought from Africa to America

'Twas mercy brought me from my pagan land,
Taught my benighted soul to understand
That there's a God, that there's a Savior too:
Once I redemption neither sought nor knew.
Some view our sable[1] race with scornful eye,   5
"Their color is a diabolic dye."
Remember, Christians, Negroes, black as Cain,[2]
May be refined, and join the angelic train.

1773

To S. M.,[1] a Young African Painter, on Seeing His Works

To show the laboring bosom's deep intent,
And thought in living characters to paint,
When first thy pencil did those beauties give,

---

1. Black.
2. Cain slew his brother Abel and was "marked" by God for doing so. This mark has sometimes been taken to be the origin of the Negro (Genesis 4.1–15).
1. Scipio Moorhead, a servant to the Reverend John Moorhead of Boston.

And breathing figures learnt from thee to live,
How did those prospects give my soul delight,   5
A new creation rushing on my sight?
Still, wondrous youth! each noble path pursue,
On deathless glories fix thine ardent view:
Still may the painter's and the poet's fire
To aid thy pencil, and thy verse conspire!   10
And may the charms of each seraphic² theme
Conduct thy footsteps to immortal fame!
High to the blissful wonders of the skies
Elate thy soul, and raise thy wishful eyes.
Thrice happy, when exalted to survey   15
That splendid city, crowned with endless day,
Whose twice six gates³ on radiant hinges ring:
Celestial Salem⁴ blooms in endless spring.

Calm and serene thy moments glide along,
And may the muse inspire each future song!   20
Still, with the sweets of contemplation blest,
May peace with balmy wings your soul invest!
But when these shades of time are chased away,
And darkness ends in everlasting day,
On what seraphic pinions shall we move,   25
And view the landscapes in the realms above?
There shall thy tongue in heavenly murmurs flow,
And there my muse with heavenly transport glow:
No more to tell of Damon's⁵ tender sighs,
Or rising radiance of Aurora's⁶ eyes,   30
For nobler themes demand a nobler strain,
And purer language on the ethereal plain.
Cease, gentle muse! the solemn gloom of night
Now seals the fair creation from my sight.

                                                              1773

To His Excellency General Washington¹

Sir. I have taken the freedom to address your Excellency in the
enclosed poem, and entreat your acceptance, though I am not
insensible of its inaccuracies. Your being appointed by the Grand
Continental Congress to be Generalissimo of the armies of North
America, together with the fame of your virtues, excite sensations
not easy to suppress. Your generosity, therefore, I presume, will
pardon the attempt. Wishing your Excellency all possible success in
the great cause you are so generously engaged in. I am,

Your Excellency's most obedient humble servant,
Phillis Wheatley

2. Angelic.
3. Heaven, like the city of Jerusalem, is thought to have had 12 gates (as many gates as tribes of Israel).
4. Heavenly Jerusalem.
5. In classical mythology Damon pledged his life for his friend Pythias.

6. The Roman goddess of the dawn.
1. This poem was first published in *The Pennsylvania Magazine* when Thomas Paine was editor. Washington invited Wheatley to meet him in Cambridge, Massachusetts, in February, 1776, after reading it.

Providence, Oct. 26, 1775.
His Excellency Gen. Washington.

> Celestial choir! enthroned in realms of light,
>   Columbia's[2] scenes of glorious toils I write.
> While freedom's cause her anxious breast alarms,
> She flashes dreadful in refulgent arms.
> See mother earth her offspring's fate bemoan,   5
> And nations gaze at scenes before unknown!
> See the bright beams of heaven's revolving light
> Involved in sorrows and the veil of night!
>   The goddess comes, she moves divinely fair,
> Olive and laurel[3] binds her golden hair: 10
> Wherever shines this native of the skies,
> Unnumbered charms and recent graces rise.
>   Muse! bow propitious while my pen relates
> How pour her armies through a thousand gates,
> As when Eolus[4] heaven's fair face deforms,   15
> Enwrapped in tempest and a night of storms;
> Astonished ocean feels the wild uproar,
> The refluent surges beat the sounding shore;
> Or thick as leaves in Autumn's golden reign,
> Such, and so many, moves the warrior's train.   20
> In bright array they seek the work of war,
> Where high unfurled the ensign[5] waves in air.
> Shall I to Washington their praise recite?
> Enough thou know'st them in the fields of fight.
> Thee, first in peace and honors—we demand   25
> The grace and glory of thy martial band.
> Famed for thy valor, for thy virtues more,
> Hear every tongue thy guardian aid implore!
>   One century scarce performed its destined round,
> When Gallic[6] powers Columbia's fury found;   30
> And so may you, whoever dares disgrace
> The land of freedom's heaven-defended race!
> Fixed are the eyes of nations on the scales,
> For in their hopes Columbia's arm prevails.
> Anon Britannia droops the pensive head,   35
> While round increase the rising hills of dead.
> Ah! cruel blindness to Columbia's state!
> Lament thy thirst of boundless power too late.
>   Proceed, great chief, with virtue on thy side,
> Thy every action let the goddess guide.   40
> A crown, a mansion, and a throne that shine,
> With gold unfading, WASHINGTON! be thine.

1775–76   1776, 1834

2. This reference to America as the land Columbus found is believed to be the first in print.
3. Emblems of victory.
4. Keeper of the winds.
5. Flag or banner.

6. The French and Indian War, which lasted half a century, may be thought to have begun with King William's War in 1689–97 and Queen Anne's War in 1702–3.

American Literature
1820–1865

IN A PAINTING popular during the late nineteenth century, Christian Schussele reverentially depicted *Washington Irving and His Literary Friends at Sunnyside*. Working in 1863, four years after Irving's death, Schussele portrayed an astonishing number of elegantly clad notables in Irving's snug study in his Gothic cottage-castle on the Hudson River, north of New York City. Among them were several writers in this anthology: Irving himself, Oliver Wendell Holmes, Nathaniel Hawthorne, Henry Wadsworth Longfellow, Ralph Waldo Emerson, William Cullen Bryant, and James Fenimore Cooper. Intermingled with these men were poets and novelists now seldom read: William Gilmore Simms, Fitz-Greene Halleck, Nathaniel Parker Willis, James Kirke Paulding, John Pendleton Kennedy, and Henry T. Tuckerman, along with the historians William H. Prescott and George Bancroft. The Schussele painting was a pious hoax, for these guests never assembled together at one time, at Sunnyside or anywhere else, and while a few of those depicted were indeed among Irving's friends, he barely knew some of them and never met others at all. But in several ways the scene is profoundly true to American literary history.

As Schussele's painting suggests, Irving, beloved by ordinary readers and by most of his fellow writers, was the central figure in the American literary world between 1809 (the year of his parody *History of New York*) and the Civil War, especially after he demonstrated in *The Sketch Book* (1819–20) that memorable fiction—*Rip Van Winkle* and *The Legend of Sleepy Hollow*—could be set in the United States; he also proved, by the book's international success, that an American writer could win a British and Continental audience. Irving's legion of imitators included several of the persons in the painting, and among his fellow writers Irving's reputation was enhanced by his generosity, as in his gallantly relinquishing the subject of the conquest of Mexico to Prescott or in urging the publisher George P. Putnam to bring out an American edition of the first book by the unknown Herman Melville. Although James Fenimore Cooper's fame as a fiction writer rivaled Irving's in the 1820s and 1830s, his influence never approached the breadth of Irving's. Nor did the influence of Ralph Waldo Emerson, despite his profoundly provocative effects on such writers as Margaret Fuller, Henry David Thoreau, Walt Whitman, Herman Melville, and Emily Dickinson—effects that make modern literary historians see him as the seminal writer of the century.

Mentioning the names of Fuller, Thoreau, Melville, and Dickinson suggests still another way the Schussele painting is exemplary. Since the painter set out to depict representative literary men (not literary women) as much as to depict genuine intimates of Irving, it is striking that he omitted writers who now seem among the most important of the century: Edgar Allan Poe, Thoreau, Whitman, Melville, John Greenleaf Whittier (who was frowned upon as a militant abolitionist until 1866, when *Snow-Bound* made him seem a safe poet to admire), and Dickinson (in the 1860s an all but unpublished recluse). The painter would probably have considered Augustus Baldwin Longstreet, George Washington Harris, and other Southern or backwoods humorists in this volume to be subliterary, despite the fact that Irving had influenced such writing and had delighted in reading it.

THE SMALL WORLD OF AMERICAN WRITERS

Perhaps most important, paintings like the one by Schussele (and the similar wishful fad of depicting famous literary people in cozy association through the then-new technique of composite photography) capture the fact that in the nineteenth century the American literary world was very small indeed, so small that most of the writers in this period knew each other, often intimately, or else knew much about each other. They lived, if not in each other's pockets, at least in each other's houses, or boardinghouses: Lemuel Shaw, from 1830 to 1860 Chief Justice of the Massachusetts Supreme Court, and Herman Melville's father-in-law after 1847, for a time stayed in a Boston boardinghouse run by Ralph Waldo Emerson's widowed mother; the Longfellows summered in the 1840s at the Pittsfield boardinghouse run by Melville's cousin, a house where Melville had stayed in his early teens; in Pittsfield and Lenox, Hawthorne and Melville paid each other overnight visits, in Concord the Hawthornes rented the Old Manse, the Emerson ancestral home, and later bought a house there from the educator Bronson Alcott and made it famous as the Wayside; in Concord the Emersons welcomed many guests, including Margaret Fuller, and when the master was away Thoreau sometimes stayed in the house to help Mrs. Emerson with the children and the property. The popular Manhattan hostess Anne Lynch assigned the young travel-writer Bayard Taylor to write a valentine for a slightly older travel-writer, Herman Melville, in 1848, and three years later, apparently with matchmaking in mind, brought together Taylor's intimate friend R. H. Stoddard and Elizabeth Barstow, a distant relative of Hawthorne. In 1853 Hawthorne received at Wayside young Mr. Stoddard, by then husband of Elizabeth Barstow, and pulled wires to get him a job in the New York Custom House, Hawthorne having the year before written the campaign biography for his old friend, the candidate for president, Franklin Pierce. (When Melville finally got his own appointment to the Custom House in 1866, Stoddard was on desk duty to welcome him; Stoddard kept Melville from being fired once, but Melville outlasted him many years in that nest of corruption.) On a visit to Washington after the Civil War had broken out, the still reclusive, and ailing, Hawthorne seriously considered making the hazardous trip to Wheeling to meet the extraordinary new contributor to *The Atlantic Monthly*, Rebecca Harding; later he welcomed her at Wayside. At Litchfield, Connecticut, the young Georgian Longstreet greatly admired one of the minister Lyman Beecher's daughters (not Harriet, then a small child).

Many of the writers of this period came together casually for dining and drinking, the hospitality at the editor Evert A. Duyckinck's house in New York being famous, open to southerners like Simms as well as New Yorkers like Melville and Bostanians like the elder Richard Henry Dana. In the late 1850s a Bohemian group of newspaper and theater people and writers drank together at Pfaff's saloon on Broadway above Bleecker Street; for a time Whitman was a fixture there. Of the clubs formed by writers, artists, and other notables (usually male), the three most memorable are the Bread and Cheese Club, which Cooper organized in 1824 in the back room of his publisher's Manhattan bookstore; the Transcendental Club, started in Boston in 1836 and lasting four years; the Saturday Club, a more convivial Boston group formed in 1856; and the Authors Club, founded in New York in 1882. Members of the Bread and Cheese Club included the poet William Cullen Bryant, Samuel F. B. Morse (the painter who later invented the telegraph), the poet Fitz-Greene Halleck, and Thomas Cole, the English-born painter of the American landscape. Emerson was the leading spirit of the Transcendental Club, but other members included Bronson Alcott, later Margaret Fuller, and George Ripley, the organizer of the Transcendental commune at Brook Farm, near Roxbury. Among the members of the Saturday Club were Emerson, James Russell Lowell, Henry Wadsworth Longfellow, Oliver Wendell Holmes, and the historians John Lothrop Motley and William H. Prescott; Nathaniel Hawthorne attended some meetings. Brander Matthews cofounded the Authors Club, from the first a beloved resource for the literary establishment, which included dominant magazine editors of the time such as Richard Watson Gilder, and critics and poets such as R. H. Stoddard and Edmund Clarence Stedman (an intimate of Samuel L. Clemens and William Dean Howells who also befriended Melville in his last years and whose son Arthur became Melville's literary executor); Matthews recalled that once or twice "the shy and elusive Herman Melville dropped in for an hour or two."

THE SMALL COUNTRY

Such intimacy was inevitable in a country which had only a few literary and publishing centers, all of them along the Atlantic seaboard. Despite the acquisition of the Louisiana Territory from France in 1803 and the vast Southwest from Mexico in 1848, most of the writers we still read lived all their lives in the original thirteen states, except for trips abroad, and their practical experience was of a compact country: in 1840 the "northwestern" states were those covered by the Northwest Ordinance of 1787 (Ohio, Indiana, Illinois, and Michigan; Wisconsin was still a territory), while the "southwestern" humor writers such as George Washington Harris, Thomas Bangs Thorpe, and Johnson Jones Hooper wrote in the region bounded by Georgia, Louisiana, and Tennessee.

Improvements in transportation were shrinking the country even while territorial gains were enlarging it. When Irving went from Manhattan to Albany in 1800, steamboats had not yet been invented, although William

Longstreet, the father of the writer, had been planning one for a decade; the Hudson voyage was slow and dangerous, and in 1803 the wagons of Irving's Canada-bound party barely made it through the bogs beyond Utica. The Erie Canal, completed in 1825, changed things: in the 1830s and 1840s Hawthorne, Melville, and Fuller took the canal boats in safety, suffering only from crowded and stuffy sleeping conditions. When Irving went buffalo hunting in Indian territory (now Oklahoma) in 1832 he left the steamboat at St. Louis and went on horseback, camping out at night except when his party reached one of the line of missions built to accommodate whites who were Christianizing the Indians. By the 1840s railroads had replaced stagecoaches between many eastern towns, although to get to New Orleans in 1848 Whitman had to change from railroad to stagecoach to steamboat. Despite frequent train wrecks, steamboat explosions, and Atlantic shipwrecks, by the 1850s travel had ceased to be the hazardous adventure it had been. But the few American writers who saw much of the country were still provincials in their practical attitude toward their literary careers, for their publishers and purchasers were concentrated mainly in or near New York, Philadelphia, and Boston.

And the New York, Philadelphia, and Boston of this period were themselves tiny in comparison to their modern size. The site of Brook Farm, now long since a victim of urban sprawl, was chosen because it was nine miles remote from Boston and two miles away from the nearest farm. The population of New York City at the start of the 1840s was only a third of a million and was concentrated in Lower Manhattan: Union Square was the edge of town. Horace Greeley, the editor of the New York *Tribune*, escaped the bustle of the city by living on a ten-acre farm up the East River on Turtle Bay, where the East Fifties are now; there he and his wife provided a bucolic retreat for Margaret Fuller when she was his literary critic and metropolitan reporter. In 1853 the Crystal Palace, an exposition of arts, crafts, and sciences, created in imitation of the great Crystal Palace at the London World's Fair of 1851, failed—largely because it was too far out of town, up west of the new Croton Water Reservoir that had recently brought running water to the city. The reservoir was on the spot where the New York Public Library now stands, at Forty-second Street and Fifth Avenue, and the Crystal Palace was on the site of the modern Bryant Park, named for the nature poet but now long inured to sadder urban visitors than those who made their way to the Fair in the 1850s.

THE ECONOMICS OF AMERICAN LETTERS

Geography and modes of transportation bore directly upon publishing procedures in the United States of this period. For a long time writers who wanted to publish a book carried the manuscript to a local printer and paid job rates to have it printed and bound. Longfellow worked in this fashion with a firm in Brunswick, Maine, when he printed his translation of *Elements of French Grammar* and other textbooks during his first years as a teacher. Fiction was also sometimes sent to a local printer, as when Longstreet had his own firm in Augusta print *Georgia Scenes* or when Johnson Jones Hooper paid a firm in Tuscaloosa, Alabama, to print *A Ride with Old Kit Kuncker* before having it brought out the next year by a regular Philadelphia publisher. However, the true publishing centers were major seaports which could receive the latest British books by the fastest ships and, hastily reprinting them, distribute them inland by river traffic as well as in coastal cities. After 1820 the leading publishing towns were New York and Philadelphia, with the Erie Canal soon giving New York an advantage in the Ohio trade. Boston remained only a provincial publishing center until after 1850, when publishers realized the value of the new railroad connections to the West. Despite the aggressive merchandizing techniques of a few firms, the creation of a national book-buying market for literature, especially American literature, was long delayed.

The problem was that the economic interests of American publisher-booksellers were antithetical to the interests of American writers. A national copyright law became effective in the United States in 1790, but it was 1891 before American writers had international protection and foreign writers received protection in the United States. Until the end of the century, American printers routinely pirated English writers, paying nothing to Sir Walter Scott or Charles Dickens for their novels, which were rushed into print and sold very cheaply in New York, Philadelphia, and other cities. American readers benefited from the situation, for they could buy the best British—and Continental—writings cheaply, but American writers suffered, since if they were to receive royalties, their books had to be priced above the prices charged for works of the most famous British writers. American publishers were willing to carry a few native novelists and poets as prestige items for a while, but they were businessmen, not philanthropists.

To compound the problem, Irving's apparent conquest of the British publishing system, by which he received large sums for *The Sketch Book* and succeeding volumes, proved delusory. Cooper and others followed in Irving's track and were paid by magnanimous British publishers under a system whereby works first printed in Great Britain were presumed to hold a British copyright. But this practice was ruled illegal by a British judge in 1849, and the British market dried up for American writers.

Throughout this period, making a serious American contribution to the literature of the world was no guarantee at all of monetary rewards. Except possibly for a few authors of sentimental best sellers, including what Hawthorne jealously called "that damned mob of scribbling women," the United States was not a country in which one could make a living by writing. It was not even a place where the best authors could always publish what they wrote. The only writers who could consistently find a publisher were Irving and Cooper, who kept their appeal on the basis of early success (though more copies had to be sold in order to make the same profit) and the magazine or newspaper editors who could fill some of their own columns when they wanted. These editors included (for various periods of time) Poe, Longstreet, Harris, Thorpe, Hooper, Lowell, and four other notable examples: Fuller, who for several years reported for the New York *Tribune* at home and from Europe; Whitman, who for much of the 1840s and 1850s was free to editorialize in one Brooklyn or Manhattan newspaper or another; Whittier, who for more than two decades before the Civil War was corresponding editor of the Washington *National Era*; and, most conspicuously, Bryant, long-time owner of the New York *Evening Post*. Whitman was his own publisher for most editions of *Leaves of Grass*, and filled mail orders himself, as Thoreau also did when an occasional request came for one of the 700 copies of his first book which the publisher had turned back to him. At crucial moments in his career Melville was balked from writing what he wanted to write, as when he sacrificed his literary aspirations after the failure of *Mardi* and wrote *Redburn* and *White-Jacket*, which he regarded as mere drudgery; and at other times he was "prevented from publishing" works he had written, including at least one which was subsequently destroyed. Ironically, the writer freest to pursue literary greatness in this period was probably Emily Dickinson, whose "letter to the world" remained unmailed during her lifetime.

THE QUEST FOR AN AMERICAN LITERARY DESTINY

In the first half of the nineteenth century, lobbying for the existence of an American literature in magazines seemed to take up more space than the literature itself. Especially after the War of 1812 confirmed American independence, theorists called for a great literature which would match the emerging political greatness of the nation. Huckstering critics soon developed specific notions as to the subjects which would-be writers should choose: preferably the distant colonial past (the nearest we could hope to come to the medieval settings which were serving Sir Walter Scott so well), or possibly Indian legends, or still less desirable (because too near the mundane present), subjects from the recent Revolutionary past. Such exhortations were the stock-in-trade of commencement speakers and literary critics in the 1820s and 1830s. But in *The Poet* (1842) Emerson boldly called for a poet who would write of the United States as it was, not as it might have been:

> We have yet had no genius in America, with tyrannous eye, which knew the value of our incomparable materials, and saw, in the barbarism and materialism of the times, another carnival of the same gods whose picture he so much admires in Homer; then in the middle age; then in Calvinism. Banks and tariffs, the newspaper and caucus, methodism and unitarianism, are flat and dull to dull people, but rest on the same foundations of wonder as the town of Troy, and the temple of Delphos, and are as swiftly passing away. Our logrolling, our stumps and their politics, our fisheries, our Negroes, and Indians, our boasts, and our repudiations, the wrath of rogues, and the pusillanimity of honest men, the northern trade, the southern planting, the western clearing, Oregon, and Texas, are yet unsung. Yet America is a poem in our eyes; its ample geography dazzles the imagination, and it will not wait long for metres.

Later Whitman was to say that he had remained simmering, simmering, until Emerson brought him to a boil.

During the 1840s Evert A. Duyckinck and other New York literary men and women (primarily through the columns of the *Democratic Review* and the *Literary World*) mustered a squad of promoters of the great literature that was to come. The propagandists perfected the rhetorical strategy of linking literary destiny to geography and political destiny: the "great nation of futurity" must have a literature to match Niagara Falls and the Rocky Mountains. Herman Melville for several years was associated with Duyckinck's magazines, and he half-champions and half-spoofs the chauvinistic rhetoric in the essay on Hawthorne which he wrote for the *Literary World* in 1850. An American, he proclaimed, was "bound to carry republican progressiveness into Literature, as well as into Life," even to the point of believing that sooner or later American writers would rival Shakespeare, whom a generation of Bardolators regarded as unapproachable. This was literary manifest destiny with a vengeance, warranted only because as he wrote the essay Melville had already written his way well into what he later titled *Moby-Dick*.

None of the American writers of the period was chauvinistic enough to think that a great American literature could be written without reference to past English and European literature. As Cooper protested in *Notions of the Americans* (1828), writers in the United States possessed the same literary heritage that writers in Great Britain did. Shakespeare, Spenser, Milton, Bunyan, Addison, Pope, Fielding, Johnson, and Burns, along with many others (especially some now neglected writers of the eighteenth century) were the possession of all educated Americans born in the late eighteenth century or early in the nineteenth. Americans were not long behind the British in responding to the Romantics Wordsworth and Coleridge, then to Byron, Moore, and Scott. By the 1830s Carlyle was a force in the lives of several American writers through his translations of recent German philosophical works and his own jeremiads against contemporary British values. Americans had access to the latest British and Continental discussions of art, religion, politics, and science, for British magazines, especially the quarterly reviews, were imported promptly and widely reprinted. Nineteenth-century American writing reveals its full meanings only in the light of European influences and parallel developments.

THE NEW AMERICANNESS OF AMERICAN LITERATURE

Despite the cultural cross-connections with Europe, the best literature that emerged in the United States was distinctively new, and a few perceptive critics very early began trying to define its special quality. This analysis from the review of *The Whale* (the English title of *Moby-Dick*) in the London *Leader* had currency in America as well, for the popular *Harper's New Monthly Magazine* quoted it approvingly:

> Want [lack] of originality has long been the just and standing reproach to American literature; the best of its writers were but second-hand Englishmen. Of late some have given evidence of originality, not *absolute* originality, but such genuine outcomings of the American intellect as can be safely called national. Edgar Poe, Nathaniel Hawthorne, Herman Melville are assuredly no British offshoots; nor is Emerson—the *German* American that he is! The observer of this commencement of an American literature, properly so called, will notice as significant that these writers have a wild and mystic love of the supersensual, peculiarly their own. To move a horror skilfully, with something of the earnest faith in the Unseen, and with weird imagery to shape these Phantasms so vividly that the most incredulous mind is hushed, absorbed—to do this no European pen has apparently any longer the power—to do this American literature is without a rival. What *romance* writer can be named with Hawthorne? Who knows the terrors of the seas like Herman Melville?"

Plainly, this was meant as praise, but to employ "weird imagery" in order to "move a horror skilfully" was hardly the ambition of any American writer of the period besides Poe; for their part, Hawthorne and Melville were not concerned with the supernatural except as stage devices for heightening their psychological analyses.

But literary historians have not improved much on the reviewer in the *Leader* in deciding what was American about American literature. American writers were not achieving originality in form: Irving's sentences were accepted as models of English prose style precisely because they were themselves modeled upon the sentences of Addison and Goldsmith, long the prime exemplars of decorous English prose. Melville's sentences often looked like those of whatever powerful master of the English language he had most recently been reading—Shakespeare, Milton, Burton, Taylor, Sterne, De Quincey, Carlyle. Nor was the content of the best American writing of this period original in anything like an "absolute" sense. Modern scholars have shown that in his most "American" stories, *Rip Van Winkle* and *The Legend of Sleepy Hollow*, Irving drew upon, and even closely translated, parts of German tales. In *Moby-Dick* Melville's metaphysics are recognizably of the generation of Goethe, Byron, and Carlyle. Thoreau's recurrent ideas came mainly from Emerson (at least Emerson himself insisted they did), but Emerson had picked them up from dozens of ancient and modern philosophers.

Yet, as everyone in the country sensed by the 1850s, there was some elusive quality about its new literature that was *American*. Irving's German-influenced stories were profoundly moving to Americans, who knew more than most Britons what it was to feel the trauma of rapid change, especially to experience repeated physical uprootings, and Americans found in the ne'er-do-well Rip a model for making a success of failure. In Cooper's novels was a sense of the immensity of physical nature and the power of human beings to destroy nature that most European writers could experience only vicariously. In Melville's *Moby-Dick* was a sense of the grandeur of the physical universe and man's role in it long suppressed in European consciousness. In *Leaves of Grass* Whitman undertook another elemental task—to become the national poet of a new people on a new continent. What proved most enduringly "American" about Emerson was his wide streak of Yankee individualism best displayed in *Self-Reliance*, which became an inspiration to thousands of Americans who were determined to hitch their wagons, as Emerson said, to a star. Even Thoreau's *Walden*, which many contemporaries took merely as an American counterpart of the English naturalist Gilbert White's *Natural History and Antiquities of Selbourne*, was in fact consciously an American counterscripture, a Franklinesque retort to Poor Richard, a how-to book on getting a living by working at what you love. At a time when grandiloquence in political rhetoric was often taken for eloquence, Abraham Lincoln mastered both the majestic cadences of the King James Version of the Bible and the extravagant toughness of backwoods tall talk. Dickinson's poems in their minute intensity were as ambitious as Whitman's, magnificent attempts to define her experience at whatever cost in wrenched syntax and rhyme. At best, beyond question, American writers were accomplishing things yet unattempted in the English language.

THE AESTHETICS OF A NATIONAL LITERATURE

The great writers of the period for the most part defined their aesthetic problems by themselves, though Emerson's *The Poet* aided some of the others. The primary difficulty of how to keep from being secondhand English writers had not been squarely faced by the theorists of nationality in literature, who most often seemed to think that adoption of an American setting or, more vaguely, the infusion of an American "spirit" guaranteed Americanness. Insofar as the issues had been addressed by Americans before the 1840s, it was primarily by painters and sculptors, the most prominent of whom had received their training abroad, then had found it impossible to reconcile their European notions of noble subject and style with Americanness. The Hudson River school of painters, led by Thomas Cole (one of whose notable followers was Asher B. Durand, the painter of *Kindred Spirits*, a detail of which is reproduced on the cover of this volume), found a pantheistic majesty in American landscapes not anticipated by the history-filled landscapes of European painting. Some of Cole's own work was marred by a tendency to allegorize as inveterate as Hawthorne's own, but others of the Hudson River school, including Frederic Edwin Church, faced in North—and South—America a New World, a landscape with primeval power both to awe and destroy. Artistic tributes could be as clichéd as Whitman's catalogues (everyone from Church to T. B. Thorpe painted inevitable Niagaras), but Church's recently rediscovered *Icebergs* (1861) is only a decade away from *Moby-Dick*, a work by a spirit that was in truth kindred. Other Americans, notably Martin Johnson Heade, born the same year as Melville, found compelling mystery not only in the exotica of South America but also in the salt hay marshes and low coasts of New England. The genre painters who formed so conspicuous a part of the artistic establishment—Melville's and Whitman's acquaintance William Sidney Mount, for instance—were pleasantly but unchallengingly continuing the familiar Dutch tradition—familiar from paintings brought across the Atlantic by Dutch settlers as well as those more recently brought over. Of the major writers of the period Whitman, from his friendships with the members of the Brooklyn Art Union in the early 1850s, was exposed to controversies in art in time to have them affect his poetry—his own aesthetic statements reflect Horatio Greenough's championship of the nude and his disparagement of mere embellishment. Most of the writers, despite the theorizing about painting and sculpting and the actual painting and sculpting available for them to see, were pretty much on their own when they were solving their crucial aesthetic problems—such as Hawthorne's attempts to strike a balance between the allegorical and the realistic, Emerson's difficulty in achieving unity from the mutually repellent particles of his thought, Thoreau's attempts to unite the Transcendentalist and the naturalist in himself, Whitman's struggle to domesticate the epic catalogue without falling into self-parody, Melville's attempt to create a tragedy in a democracy, and Dickinson's attempts to walk the hairline between mere coyness and psychological precision.

THE WRITERS AND THEIR AMERICA

When the great American writers of the mid-nineteenth century took stock of their country, they sometimes caught the contagion of an ebullient, expansionist mood that struck many observers as the dominant one of the time, and even Thoreau, the most relentless critic of the values of his society, insisted that to some extent he counted himself among "those who find their encouragement and inspiration in precisely the present condition of things, and cherish it with the fondness and enthusiasm of lovers." But often they felt a profound alienation. Emerson was a preacher who had renounced his pulpit, and the other great writers—also preachers without pulpits—devoted much of their artistic effort to analyzing conditions of life in America and to exhorting their fellow citizens to live more wisely.

CONFORMITY, MATERIALISM, AND THE ECONOMY

The eccentricity of Americans, especially in rural areas and smaller towns, was notorious among visitors from abroad and was recorded in some of its aspects by writers as diverse as Longstreet, Harris, Melville, and Stowe. In Stowe's novels of the late 1850s and early 1860s there is a gallery of portraits of such mentally angular or gnarled characters. In Amherst, Emily Dickinson out-Thoreaued Thoreau in her resolute privacy, idiosyncracies, and individuality. But she could be understood in relation to real and fictional characters. The night her correspondent Thomas Wentworth Higginson met her in 1870 he strove to convey her character in a letter to his wife without staying up too late; "if you had read Mrs. Stoddard's novels you could understand a house where each member runs his or her own selves." Despite such powerful individualists, it seemed to some of the writers that Americans, even while deluding themselves that they were the most self-reliant populace in the world, were systematically selling out their individuality. Emerson sounded the alarm: "Society everywhere is in conspiracy against the manhood of every one of its members. Society is a joint-stock company in which the members agree for the better securing of his bread to each shareholder, to surrender the liberty and culture of the eater. The virtue in most request is conformity." In *The Celestial Railroad* Hawthorne satirically described the condition at the Vanity Fair of modern America, where there was a "species of machine for the wholesale manufacture of individual morality." He went on: "This excellent result is effected by societies for all manner of virtuous purposes; with which a man has merely to connect himself, throwing, as it were, his quota of virtue into the common stock; and the president and directors will take care that the aggregate amount be well applied." Thoreau repeatedly satirized America as a nation of joiners which tried to force every newcomer "to belong to their desperate odd-fellow society": to Thoreau, members of the Odd Fellows and other social organizations were simply not odd *enough*, not individual enough.

But none of the writers found anything comical in the wholesale loss of Yankee individualism as both men and women deserted worn-out farms for factories, where many began to feel what Emerson called "the disproportion between their faculties and the work offered them." Far too often, the search for a better life had degenerated into a desire to possess factory-made objects. "Things are in the saddle," Emerson said sweepingly, "and ride mankind." In elaboration of that accusation, Thoreau wrote *Walden* as a treatise on expanding the spiritual life by simplifying material wants. Informing Thoreau's outrage at the materialism of his time was the bitter knowledge that even the most impoverished were being led to waste their money (and, therefore, their lives) on trumpery. In a vocabulary echoing Benjamin Franklin, he condemned the emerging consumer economy which was devoted, even in the infancy of advertising, to the creation of "artificial wants" for things which were unneeded or outright pernicious. And to counter the loss of an archetypal Yankee virtue, he made himself into a Jack-of-all-trades and strong master of one, the art of writing. In strangely different ways the four to speak out most profoundly about the emerging American economic system were Melville, Stowe, Whitman, and Harding.

SEX AND SEXUAL ROLES

At a time when sex was banished from the magazines and from almost all books except medical treatises, Whitman alone called for a healthy sense of the relation between body and soul and created a forum for discussing sexual joy and anguish. The other male writers made no challenge to conventional sexual roles; when Emerson, for instance, said that society "is in conspiracy against the manhood of every one of its members," he meant "*man*hood," not "manhood and womanhood." Only Whitman among the male authors regularly employed what we would call nonsexist language, and only Whitman rejected the opinion that woman's proper "sphere" was a limited, subservient, supportive one. While the attitudes of most male—and female—writers of the time reflected and embodied the prevailing sexism, Whitman rejected the "empty dish, gallantry" as a degraded attitude: "This tepid wash, this diluted deferential love, as in songs, fictions, and so forth, is enough to make a man vomit." Instead, he insisted on equality: "Women in These States approach the day of that organic equality with me, without which, I see, men cannot have organic equality among themselves." Of the other writers only Margaret Fuller thought so deeply about sexual roles. Ironically, as the mother of a tardily acknowledged child (and perhaps not the wife of its Italian father), Fuller was an incalculable threat to the little Boston literary society in the months before her death by shipwreck prevented her arrival home. Of the women writers of the time, Dickinson, who never married, was the most bitterly ironic observer of the sacrifices marriage often required of a woman, as in her depiction of the bride who "rose to His Requirement—dropt / The Playthings of Her Life / To take the honorable Work / Of Woman, and of Wife," and Elizabeth Stoddard, overshadowed by her husband, wrote controlled, ironic analyses of the restricted roles women were allowed to assume. But women had no monopoly on sexual anguish. Melville, who as a young man had known the pagan Eden of the South Seas, found that the claims of his intellect and imagination, his pursuit of a literary career, could not be met while also meeting the claims of his wife and children. And Whitman, the only writer of the period to advance a "Programme" for honest depiction of sex in literature, privately recorded the torments he endured from his homoerotic longings.

NATURE

In "a new country," Thoreau said, "fuel is an encumbrance," and his generation acted as if trees existed to be burned (and mountains to be graded and wild animals to be slaughtered). But while Thoreau faced the possibility that like villains we might grub our forests all up, "poaching on our own national domains," he had no deep anxiety that primeval nature like the Maine woods would be destroyed. Melville was likewise sure that the whale would not perish: "hunted from the savannas and glades of the middle seas, the whale-bone whales can at last resort to their Polar citadels, and diving under the ultimate glassy barriers and walls there, come up among icy fields and floes; and in a charmed circle of everlasting December, bid defiance to all pursuit from man." Of the major writers of the period, Emerson, Thoreau, and Whitman felt an intensity of communion with nature that warrants their being called nature-mystics, and Dickinson, bounded by town lots and fields near her house in Amherst, found a profoundly un-Christian, "Druidic difference" which enhanced nature for her with a sense of harmony between it and human beings. The writers diverged in their wider views of the universe, Melville describing in *Moby Dick* the maddening of a cabin-boy abandoned in the immensity of ocean, and Thoreau, by contrast, insisting that he was not lonely at Walden. "Why should I feel lonely? is not our planet in the Milky Way?" But whatever their sense of man's place in the cosmos, they all found nature a force in their lives in ways out of keeping with the times, when the Romantic sense of nature as restorer and healer of mankind seemed to persist, as Thoreau pointed out, in the absurd form of uneasy rest-day strollers anxious to pass their allotted time in the woods and return to town.

ORTHODOX RELIGION AND TRANSCENDENTALISM

All the major writers found themselves at odds with the dominant religion of their time, a nominal Protestant Christianity which exerted practical control over what could be printed in books and magazines. This church, Emerson said, acted "as if God were dead." Whitman was more bitter still: "The churches are one vast lie; the people do not believe them, and they do not believe themselves." The writers all came of Protestant backgrounds where Calvinism was more or less watered down (less in the cases of Melville and Dickinson), but they tended to apply absolute standards toward what passed for Christianity. In *The Celestial Railroad* Hawthorne memorably satirized the American urge to be progressive and liberal in theology as well as in politics, and Melville extended the satire throughout an entire book, *The Confidence-Man*.

Awareness of the fact of religious ecstasy was not at issue. Emerson, for instance, showed in *The Over-Soul* a clinical sense of the varieties of religious experience, the "carying forms of that shudder of awe and delight with which the individual soul always mingles with the universal soul." Similarly, Thoreau acknowledged the validity of the "second birth and peculiar religious experience" available to the "solitary hired man on a farm in the outskirts of Concord," but felt that any religious denomination in America would pervert that mystical experience into something available only under its auspices and something to be brought into line with its particular doctrines. Like Thoreau, Whitman saw all religious ecstasy as equally valid, and came forth in *Song of Myself* outbidding "the old cautious hucksters" like Jehovah, Kronos, Zeus, and Hercules, gods who held too low an estimate of the value of men and women. Among these writers Melville was alone in his anguish at the realization that Christianity was impracticable. Melville also felt the brutal power of the Calvinistic Jehovah with special keenness: mankind was "god-bullied" even as the hull of the *Pequod* was in *Moby-Dick*, and the best way man had of demonstrating his own divinity lay in defying the omnipotent tyrant. To Dickinson also God was a bully—a "Mastiff," whom subservience might, or might not, appease. In a series of novels Harriet Beecher Stowe best described the way rigid Calvinism could cripple young minds.

Transcendentalism in the late 1830s and early 1840s was treated in newspapers and magazines as something between a national laughingstock and a clear menace to organized religion. The running journalistic joke, which Hawthorne echoed in *The Celestial Railroad*, was that no one could define the term, other than that it was highfalutin, foreign, and obscurely dangerous. The conservative Christian view is well represented by a passage which appeared in Stowe's newspaper serialization of *Uncle Tom's Cabin* (1851) but was omitted from the book version, a sarcastic indictment of the reader who might find it hard to believe that Tom could be stirred by a passage in the Bible: "I mention this, of course, philosophic friend, as a psychological phenomenon. Very likely it would do no such a thing for you, because you are an enlightened man, and have out-grown the old myths of past centuries. But then you have Emerson's Essays and Carlyle's Miscellanies, and other productions of the latter day, suited to your advanced development." Such early observers understood well enough that Transcendentalism was more pantheistic than Christian. The "defiant Pantheism" infusing Thoreau's shorter pieces helped keep them out of the magazines, and James Russell Lowell for the *Atlantic Monthly* publication of a section of *The Maine Woods* censored a sentence in which Thoreau declared that a pine tree was as immortal as he was, and perchance would "go to as high a heaven."

Melville was also at least once kept from publication by the religious scruples of the magazines, and often he was harshly condemned for what he had managed to publish. For years he bore the wrath of reviewers such as the one who denounced him for writing *Moby-Dick* and the Harpers for publishing it: "The Judgment day will hold him liable for not turning his talents to better account, when, too, both authors and publishers of injurious books will be conjointly answerable for the influence of those books upon the wide circle of immortal minds on which they have written their mark. The book-maker and the book-publisher had better do their work with a view to the trial it must undergo at the bar of God." The ultimate result was that Melville was silenced. This was extreme, but Emerson, Thoreau, and Whitman all suffered in comparable ways for transgressing the code of the Doctors of Divinity (Thoreau said he wished it were not the D.D.'s but the chickadee-dees who acted as censors). Lowell himself indiscriminately censored Thoreau, Whitman, and Stoddard.

IMMIGRATION AND XENOPHOBIA

However threatened conservative Protestants felt by Transcendentalism and by religious speculations like Melville's, they felt far more threatened by Catholicism when refugees from the Napoleonic wars were followed by refugees from oppressed and famine-struck Ireland. In Boston, Lyman Beecher, father of Harriet Beecher Stowe, thundered out antipapist sermons, then professed dismay when in 1834 a mob in Charlestown, across the Charles River from Boston, burned the Ursuline Convent School where daughters of many wealthy families were educated. Through the 1830s and 1840s and long afterward, the country was saturated with lurid books and pamphlets purporting to reveal the truth about sexual practices in nunneries and monasteries (accounts of how priests and nuns disposed of their babies were specially prized) and about the Pope's schemes to take over the Mississippi Valley (Samuel F. B. Morse and others warned that Jesuits were prowling the Ohio Valley, in disguise). An extreme of xenophobia was reached in the summer of 1844, when rioters in Philadelphia (the city, everyone pointed out, of brotherly love) burned Catholic churches and a seminary. Melville was replying to the current hostility when he followed a description of the pestilent conditions of steerage-passengers in emigrant ships with this plea: "Let us waive that agitated national topic, as to whether such multitudes of foreign poor should be landed on our American shores; let us waive it, with the one only thought, that if they can get here, they have God's right to come; though they bring all Ireland and her miseries with them. For the whole world is the patrimony of the whole world; there is no telling who does not own a stone in the Great Wall of China."

For all his humanitarian eloquence, Melville, like the other writers, realized that the new immigrants were changing the country from the cozy, homogeneous land it had been, or had seemed to be. By the end of the Civil War many native Americans shared Stowe's profound nostalgia for the days before the railroads, before the influx of Catholics, before the even more alien influx of immigrants from southern and eastern Europe, few of whom spoke English and many of whom were not Christian at all. The view of many in the literary establishment was reflected by Thomas Bailey Aldrich in *The Stillwater Tragedy* (1880): what you do with the widow and children of the unionizing Italian (once he has conveniently and agonizingly died) is ship them back to Italy.

POLITICS AND WARS

The major writers of the period lived with the anguishing paradox that the most idealistic nation in the world was implicated in continuing national sins: the near-genocide of the American Indians (whole tribes in colonial times had already become, in Melville's phrase for the Massachusetts Pequods, as extinct as the ancient Medes), the enslavement of blacks, and (partly a by-product of slavery) the staged "Executive's War" against Mexico, started by President Polk before being declared by Congress. Emerson was an exception, but most writers were silent about the successive removal of Indian tribes to less desirable lands: American destiny plainly required a little practical callousness, most whites felt, in a secular version of the colonial notion that God had willed the extirpation of the red men. The imperialistic Mexican War was so gaudily exotic—and so distant— that only a small minority of American writers voiced more than perfunctory opposition; an exception was Thoreau, who spent a night in the Concord jail in symbolic protest against being taxed to support the war.

It was Negro slavery, what Melville called "man's foulest crime," which most stirred the consciences of the white writers; and in describing his own enslavement the fugitive Frederick Douglass developed a notable capacity to stir readers as well as audiences in the lecture halls. When the Fugitive Slave Law was enforced in Boston in 1851 (by Melville's father-in-law, Chief Justice Shaw), Thoreau worked his outrage into his journals; then after another famous case in 1854 he combined the experiences into his most scathing speech, *Slavery in Massachusetts*, for delivery at a Fourth of July countercelebration at which a copy of the Constitution was burned because slavery was written into it. In that speech Thoreau summed up the disillusionment that many of his generation shared. He had felt a vast but indefinite loss after the 1854 case, he said: "I did not know at first what ailed me. At last it occurred to me that what I had lost was a country." (Successive generations of American writers would experience the same trauma: Howells, Twain, and others when the United States turned from savior to conqueror in the Philippines after the Spanish-American War; Robert Lowell and many others after it became clear that the involvement of the United States in Vietnam was not purely a gesture of compassion toward a grateful, beleaguered nation.) More obliquely than Thoreau, Melville explored black slavery in *Benito Cereno* as an index to the emerging national character. At his bitterest, he felt in the mid-1850s that "free Ameriky" was "intrepid, unprincipled, reckless, predatory, with boundless ambition, civilized in externals but a savage at heart."

John Brown's raid on Harpers Ferry in 1859, immediately repudiated by the new Republican party, drew from the now tubercular Thoreau a passionate defense. During the Civil War itself, Lincoln found the genius to suit diverse occasions with right language and length of utterance, but the major writers fell silent. When the war began on April 12, 1861, with the firing of Confederate guns on Fort Sumter, in Charleston harbor, Irving, Cooper, Poe, and Fuller were dead (the younger two earlier than the older two), and before Robert E. Lee's surrender to Ulysses S. Grant at Appomattox, Virginia, on April 9, 1865. Thoreau had been dead three years and Hawthorne one. Some writers in this anthology had in their ways, directly and indirectly, helped to bring the war on: Lincoln was not wholly jesting if in fact he called Stowe the little woman who had started the big war; Whittier had by 1861 devoted decades of his life to the struggle against slavery, arousing furious resistance to him both in the North and in the South; and Douglass's oratory had revealed to many white Northerners a sense of the evils of slavery and the humanness of those of another race (or of mixed races). Firebrand Yankees such as Thoreau and firebrand Southerners such as G. W. Harris had roused the passions of at least some members of their own communities and regions. When the war came most Northern writers were slow to have a sense of its reality. As Rebecca Harding saw during her visit to Concord in 1862, fresh from a portion of a slave state that had chosen to stay with the Union, Emerson had no notion what suffering was involved. Hawthorne, who received her with enthusiasm, had faced the start of the war as a Southern sympathizer in a village that had welcomed John Brown, then had seen Washington in wartime, and retained, as he always did, a practical politician's sense of things. It was for many Northerners an oddly informal war. A man did not have to go when he was drafted: Dickinson's brother Austin was drafted in 1864 but paid $500 for a substitute to be hired. Dickinson, who at first felt the war as "an oblique place," worried about the wounding of the "preceptor" she had not yet seen, Thomas Wentworth Higginson, earlier a co-conspirator with John Brown, then in 1862 the commander of the first black regiment, the First South Carolina Volunteers. When his son Charley ran away to join the Union army, Longfellow had Senator Charles Sumner forward boxes to the boy and was baffled if they did not arrive promptly; he fussed about Charley's not having his rubber overcoat, and sent him a servant and two horses. Melville went down to camp to see a soldier-cousin and, borrowing a flannel shirt, went along on a scouting party. Henry James's brother Wilkinson, injured at Charleston when Colonel Robert Gould Shaw's black regiment was half slaughtered in July 1863, was saved by the civilian father of his closest friend, who did not find the son he was hunting for among the wounded, but found Wilky and delivered him on a stretcher to the James home in Newport. Whitman went to seek his wounded brother, passing piles of amputated limbs on his way to the field hospital, and stayed, nursing the wounded in Washington hospitals, in the single most courageous sacrifice any of these writers made to the war. All the Northern writers felt the reality before the war was over. James Russell Lowell was not a greatly exceptional case in losing three nephews.

Simply because the South was almost exclusively the battlefield, Southerners lived more immediately with the horrors of wounding and death than did most Northerners, and because the South became effectively blockaded from medical supplies and other necessities, Southern civilians suffered directly in deprivation of food, disruption of livelihoods, forced evacuations, and destroyed property, as well as deaths of friends and family members. Harris and Longstreet were made refugees; Simms's magnificent library at Woodlands was burned by stragglers from Sherman's army, with the loss (among other riches) of many letters from Poe and many letters from Evert Duyckinck (which must have contained mentions of Poe, Melville, and other writers, especially New Yorkers and Southerners).

None of the writers in this anthology fought in the war, though Thorpe held Federal office in occupied New Orleans. A younger Connecticut writer, John William DeForest, recruited a company of volunteers at New Haven and served through the war as their captain. His *The First Time under Fire*, published in the September 1864 *Harper's*, deserves to be better known and may find a place in some future edition of this anthology; surely in the opening of the nineteenth-century canon his *Miss Ravenel's Conversion from Secession to Loyalty* will be taught in survey courses as a supplemental text. Samuel L. Clemens after a brief fling at patrolling in Missouri (an episode he later winsomely if speciously recorded in *The Private History of a Campaign that Failed*) saw the war out safely in the West; William Dean Howells sat it out in Venice; and Henry James, seeing both younger brothers off to the war, the opening of which coincided with his suffering what he called an "obscure" injury, spent the war years in Newport and Cambridge. No writer really escaped it, and for most of them, as for most citizens, it was a chasm in personal and national history. In *Clarel* (1876) Melville called the winter of 1860–1861 a "sad arch between contrasted eras"; his modern critics have forgivably misapplied the words to the years 1861–1865.

DeForest's masterpiece aside, the war did not soon evoke great fiction, but Melville's uneven *Battle-Pieces* (1866) included some remarkable meditative poems as well as the technically interesting *Donelson*, in which he conveyed vividly the anxiety of civilians awaiting news during a prolonged and dubious battle and eagerly reading aloud the latest bulletins posted outside the telegraph office. (His contemporaries such as Richard Henry Stoddard liked best the brisk derivative poems such as *Sheridan's Ride*.) Whitman's *Drum-Taps* (1865) is also uneven but contains several great poems. After a few copies had been dispersed, Whitman held back the edition for a "Sequel" mainly consisting of newly written poems on Lincoln, among them *When Lilacs Last in the Dooryard Bloom'd*, the greatest literary work to come out of the war and one of the world's great elegies. Both volumes summed up the national experience. Both writers looked ahead as well as backward, Whitman calling "reconciliation" the "word over all," and Melville urging in a prose "Supplement" that the victorious North "be Christians toward our fellow-whites, as well as philanthropists toward the blacks, our fellow-men." Later in *Specimen Days* Whitman made a memorable attempt to do the impossible—to put the real war realistically into a book.

Both Whitman and Melville, especially in their later years, saw American politics cease to be concerned with great national struggles over momentous issues; rather, politics meant corruption, on a petty or a grand scale. Melville lived out the Gilded Age as an employee at the notoriously corrupt Custom House in New York City. In *Clarel*, foreseeing a descent from the present "civic barbarism" to "the Dark Ages of Democracy," he portrayed his American pilgrims to the Holy Land as recognizing sadly that the time might come to honor the God of Limitations in what had been the Land of Opportunity, a time when Americans might cry: "To Terminus build fanes! / Columbus ended earth's romance: / No New World to mankind remains!"

THE HEROISM OF AMERICAN WRITERS

Against a society which often lost sight of principles, whether aesthetic, social, or political, Emerson offered the challenge which the other great writers took up: "Let us affront and reprimand the smooth mediocrity and squalid contentment of the times, and hurl in the face of custom, and trade, and office, the fact which is the upshot of all history, that there is a great responsible Thinker and Actor moving wherever moves a man: that a true man belongs to no other time or place, but is the centre of things." In the same spirit Melville looked bravely at the risks which lay beyond the imitation of Irving:

> But the graceful writer, who perhaps of all Americans has received the most plaudits from his own country for his productions,—that very popular and amiable writer, however good, and self-reliant in many things, perhaps owes his chief reputation to the self-acknowledged imitation of a foreign model, and to the studied avoidance of all topics but smooth ones. But it is better to fail in originality, than to succeed in imitation. He who has never failed somewhere, that man can not be great. Failure is the true test of greatness.

In the same spirit Whitman commanded his readers: "re-examine all you have been told at school or church or in any book, dismiss whatever insults your own soul, and your very flesh shall be a great poem and have the richest fluency not only in its words but in the silent lines of its lips and face and between the lashes of your eyes and in every motion and joint of your body." As Emerson had warned them they must, the great writers of this time relinquished "display and immediate fame" in order to wrestle, in Melville's phrase, "with the angel—Art," making their writ-

ings into classics from which later generations, and sometimes even their
own, would date eras in their lives. As the selections in this volume dem-
onstrate, all of Emerson's great fellow writers fervently shared his conviction
that "nothing is of any value in books, excepting the transcendental and
extraordinary."

WASHINGTON IRVING

1783–1859

Washington Irving, the first American to achieve an international literary reputation, was born in New York City on April 3, 1783, the last of eleven children of a Scottish-born father and English-born mother. Well into his thirties his brothers routinely tried to make plans for him, and his own devotion to his family was a dominant emotion throughout his life. He read widely in English literature at home, modeling his early prose upon the graceful *Spectator* papers by Joseph Addison, but delighted by many other writers, including Shakespeare, Oliver Goldsmith, and Laurence Sterne. His brothers enjoyed writing poems and essays as pleasant, companionable recreation, and at nineteen Irving wrote a series of satirical essays on the theater and New York society for his brother Peter's newspaper, the *Morning Courier*.

When Irving showed signs of tuberculosis in 1804, his brothers sent him abroad for a two-year tour of Europe, where in his notebooks he steadily became an acute observer and felicitous recorder of what he witnessed. On his return, he began studying law with Judge Josiah Hoffman, but, more important for his career, he and his brother William (along with William's brother-in-law, James Kirke Paulding) started an anonymous satirical magazine, *Salmagundi* (the name of a spicy hash), which ran through 1807 with sketches and poems on politics and drama as well as familiar essays on a great range of topics. Then in 1808 Irving began work on *A History of New York*, at first conceiving it as a parody of Samuel Latham Mitchill's pompously titled *The Picture of New-York; or The Traveller's Guide through the Commercial Metropolis of the United States*, then taking on a variety of satiric targets, including President Jefferson, whom he portrayed as an early Dutch Governor of New Amsterdam, William the Testy. Exuberant, broadly comic, the *History* spoofed historians' pedantries but was itself the result of many months of antiquarian reading in local libraries, where his researches gave Irving refuge from grief over the sudden death of Judge Hoffman's daughter Mitilda, to whom he had become engaged. Then the *History* was launched by a charming publicity campaign. First a newspaper noted the disappearance of a "small elderly gentleman, dressed in an old black coat and cocked hat, by the name of KNICKERBOCKER," adding that there were "some reasons for believing he is not entirely in his right mind." After further "news" items the old man's fictitious landlord announced that he had found in Knickerbocker's room a *"very curious kind of a written book"* which he intended to dispose of to pay the bill that was owed him, and the book at last appeared, ascribed to Diedrich Knickerbocker. With its publication Irving became an American celebrity. Reprinted in England, the *History* reached Sir Walter Scott, who declared that it made his sides hurt from laughter. Like all but the rarest of topical satires, however, it has become increasingly inaccessible to later generations of readers, who can hardly comprehend Irving's strategies and targets without precisely the sort of antiquarian footnotes he found delight in mocking.

During the War of 1812 Irving was editor of the *Analectic Magazine*, which he filled mainly with essays from British periodicals but where he printed his own timely series of patriotic biographical sketches of American naval heroes. Toward the end of the war he was made a colonel in the New York State Militia. Then in May, 1815, a major break occurred in his life: he left for Europe and stayed away for seventeen years. At first he worked in Liverpool with his brother Peter, an importer of English hardware. In 1818 Peter went bankrupt, shortly after their mother died in New York; profoundly grieved and shamed, Irving once again took refuge in writing. During his work on *The Sketch Book* he met Scott, who buoyed him by admiration for the *History* and helpfully directed Irving's attention to the wealth of unused literary material in German folk tales; there, as scholars have shown, Irving found the source for *Rip Van Winkle*, some passages of which are close paraphrases of the original. In 1819 Irving began sending *The Sketch Book* to the United States for publication in installments. When the full version was printed in England the next year, it made Irving famous and brought him the friendship of many of the leading British writers of the time. His new pseudonym, Geoffrey Crayon, became universally recognized, and over the next years selections from *The Sketch Book* entered the classroom as models of English prose just as selections from Addison had long been used. As Irving knew, part of his British success derived from general astonishment that a man born in the United States could write in such an English way about English scenes: Addison lay behind the sketches of English country life, just as Oliver Goldsmith's essays on the Boar's-head Tavern in Eastcheap and on Westminster Abbey lay behind Irving's on the same topics. But in among the graceful, tame tributes to English scenes and characters were two vigorous tales set in rural New York, *Rip Van Winkle* and *The Legend of Sleepy Hollow*. Everyone who read them knew instantly that they were among the literary treasures of the language, and it very soon became hard to remember that they had not always been among the English classics.

Irving's next book, *Bracebridge Hall* (1822), a worshipful tribute to old-fashioned English country life, was, as the author realized, a feeble follow-up, and *Tales of a Traveller* (1824) was widely taken as a sign that he had written himself out. At a loss to sustain his career, Irving gambled on accepting an invitation from an acquaintance, the American Minister to Spain: he was to come to Spain as an attaché of the legation (a device for giving him entree into manuscript collections) and translate Martín Fernández de Navarrete's new compilation of accounts of the voyages of Columbus, including Columbus's own lost journals as copied by an earlier historian. Helped by the American consul in Madrid, Obadiah Rich, who owned a magnificent collection of books and manuscripts on Spanish and Latin American history, Irving worked intensely and in 1828 published *The Life and Voyages of Christopher Columbus*, not a translation of Navarrete (though the Spaniard's volume supplied most of the facts) but a biography of Irving's own, shaped by his skill at evocative re-creation of history. Out of these Spanish years came also *The Conquest of Granada* (1829), *Voyages and Discoveries of the Companions of Columbus* (1831), and *The Alhambra* (1832), which became known as "the Spanish *Sketch Book*."

In 1829 Irving was appointed Secretary to the American legation in

London, where he became a competent, hard-working diplomat, aided by his access to the highest levels of British society. No longer the latest rage, Irving by now was a solidly established author. On his return to the United States in 1832 his reputation was in need of redemption from a different charge—that of becoming too Europeanized. As if in an effort to make amends, Irving turned to three studies of the American West: A *Tour on the Prairies* (1835), based on his horseback journey into what is now Oklahoma; *Astoria* (1836), an account of John Jacob Astor's fur-trading colony in Oregon, written in Astor's own library and based on published accounts as well as research in Astor's archives (in which task Irving was assisted by his nephew Peter); and *The Adventures of Captain Bonneville, U.S.A.* (1837), an account of a Frenchman's explorations in the Rockies and the Far West.

In the late 1830s Irving bought and began refurbishing a house near Tarrytown, along the Hudson north of New York City, just where he had dreamed of settling down in *The Legend of Sleepy Hollow*. At Sunnyside he made a home for several members of his family, including as many as five nieces at a time, but he wrote little. From this somewhat purposeless stage of his life he was rescued by appointment as Minister to Spain in 1842; he served four years in Madrid with great success. After his return he arranged with G. P. Putnam to publish a collected edition of his writings and took the occasion to revise some of them. Using essays he had written years before, he also prepared for the edition a derivative biography of Oliver Goldsmith (1849), after which critics more than ever compared him to the Irish prince of hack writers. Irving's main work after 1851 was his long-contemplated life of George Washington. He worked in libraries, read old newspapers, studied government records, and visited battlefields, but once again he drew very heavily on published biographies, especially the recent one by Jared Sparks. He forced himself, in the most heroic effort of his career, to complete the successive five volumes, the first of which was published in 1855. Just after finishing the last he collapsed, and died a few months later, on November 28, 1859.

Decades before his death, Irving had achieved the status of a classic writer; in his own country he had no rival as a stylist. As schoolboys, Hawthorne and Longfellow were inspired by the success of *The Sketch Book*, and their prose, as well as that of a horde of now-unread writers, owed much to Irving. Although Melville, in his essay on Hawthorne's *Mosses from an Old Manse*, declared his preference for creative geniuses over adept imitators like Irving, he could not escape Irving's influence, which emerges both in his short stories and in a late poem, *Rip Van Winkle's Lilacs*, which showed he saw Rip as an archetypal artist figure. (Melville's debt was even more tangible, for early in 1846 Irving had passed the word to Putnam that *Typee* was worth reprinting in New York; but then Irving had been generous to younger writers all his life, as in his supervision of the London publication of Bryant's poems in 1832.) The southwestern humorists of the 1840s, whom Irving read and enjoyed, were much more robust than Irving in his mature years, yet they learned from him that realistic details of rural life in America could be worked memorably into fiction. From the beginning, Americans identified with Rip as a counter-hero, an anti-Franklinian who made a success of failure, and successive generations have responded profoundly to Irving's pervasive theme of mutability, especially as localized in his portrayal of the bewildering and destructive rapidity of change in American life.

Rip Van Winkle[1]

[The following Tale was found among the papers of the late Diedrich Knickerbocker, an old gentleman of New-York, who was very curious in the Dutch history of the province, and the manners of the descendants from its primitive settlers. His historical researches, however, did not lay so much among books, as among men; for the former are lamentably scanty on his favourite topics; whereas he found the old burghers, and still more, their wives, rich in that legendary lore, so invaluable to true history. Whenever, therefore, he happened upon a genuine Dutch family, snugly shut up in its low-roofed farm house, under a spreading sycamore, he looked upon it as a little clasped volume of black-letter,[2] and studied it with the zeal of a bookworm.

The result of all these researches was a history of the province, during the reign of the Dutch governors, which he published some years since. There have been various opinions as to the literary character of his work, and, to tell the truth, it is not a whit better than it should be. Its chief merit is its scrupulous accuracy, which, indeed, was a little questioned, on its first appearance, but has since been completely established;[3] and it is now admitted into all historical collections, as a book of unquestionable authority.

The old gentleman died shortly after the publication of his work, and now, that he is dead and gone, it cannot do much harm to his memory, to say, that his time might have been much better employed in weightier labours. He, however, was apt to ride his hobby his own way; and though it did now and then kick up the dust a little in the eyes of his neighbours, and grieve the spirit of some friends, for whom he felt the truest deference and affection; yet his errors and follies are remembered "more in sorrow than in anger,"[4] and it begins to be suspected, that he never intended to injure or offend. But however his memory may be appreciated by critics, it is still held dear among many folk, whose good opinion is well worth

1. *Rip Van Winkle* was the last of the sketches printed in the May, 1819, first installment of *The Sketch Book* (New York: C. S. Van Winkle), the source of the present text.
2. Type face in early printed books, resembling medieval script; such books, because of their value, were often equipped with clasps so they could be shut tightly and even locked.
3. Irving knew that most of his first readers would remember with delight the wildly inaccurate Knickerbocker *History*. He is also echoing Cervantes's humorous assurance of accuracy at the outset of *Don Quixote*.
4. Shakespeare's *Hamlet*, 1.1.231–32. To this quotation Irving appended the following footnote: "Vide [see] the excellent discourse of G. C. Verplanck, Esq. before the New-York Historical Society." If Irving's friend Gulian C. Verplanck ever made such an address, it was in fun.

having; particularly certain biscuit bakers, who have gone so far as to imprint his likeness on their new year cakes, and have thus given him a chance for immortality, almost equal to being stamped on a Waterloo medal, or a Queen Anne's farthing.[5]]

Rip Van Winkle
A Posthumous Writing of Diedrich Knickerbocker

> *By Woden, God of Saxons,*
> *From whence comes Wensday, that is Wodensday,*
> *Truth is a thing that ever I will keep*
> *Unto thylke day in which I creep into*
> *My sepulchre——*
>
> —CARTWRIGHT[6]

Whoever has made a voyage up the Hudson, must remember the Kaatskill mountains. They are a dismembered branch of the great Appalachian family, and are seen away to the west of the river, swelling up to a noble height, and lording it over the surrounding country. Every change of season, every change of weather, indeed, every hour of the day, produces some change in the magical hues and shapes of these mountains, and they are regarded by all the good wives, far and near, as perfect barometers. When the weather is fair and settled, they are clothed in blue and purple, and print their bold outlines on the clear evening sky; but some times, when the rest of the landscape is cloudless, they will gather a hood of gray vapours about their summits, which, in the last rays of the setting sun, will glow and light up like a crown of glory.

At the foot of these fairy mountains, the voyager may have descried the light smoke curling up from a village, whose shingle roofs gleam among the trees, just where the blue tints of the upland melt away into the fresh green of the nearer landscape. It is a little village of great antiquity, having been founded by some of the Dutch colonists, in the early times of the province, just about the beginning of the government of the good Peter Stuyvesant,[7] (may he rest in peace!) and there were some of the houses of the original settlers standing within a few years, with lattice windows, gable fronts surmounted with weathercocks, and built of small yellow bricks brought from Holland.

In that same village, and in one of these very houses, (which, to tell the precise truth, was sadly time worn and weather beaten,) there lived many years since, while the country was yet a province

5. Irving's irony cuts in different directions: Waterloo medals were minted liberally after the defeat of Napoleon in 1815, while farthings (tiny coins) from the reign of Queen Anne of England (1702–14) were commonly, though wrongly, considered rare, one story saying only three were minted.
6. In this quotation from *The Ordinary*, 3.1.1050–54, a play by the English writer William Cartwright (1611–43), the speaker is a pedant named Moth. "Woden": Norse god of war.
7. Peter Stuyvesant (1592–1672), last Governor of the Dutch province of New Netherlands, in 1655 (as mentioned below) defeated Swedish colonists at Fort Christina, near what is now Wilmington, Delaware.

of Great Britain, a simple good natured fellow, of the name of Rip Van Winkle. He was a descendant of the Van Winkles who figured so gallantly in the chivalrous days of Peter Stuyvesant, and accompanied him to the siege of Fort Christina. He inherited, however, but little of the martial character of his ancestors. I have observed that he was a simple good natured man; he was moreover a kind neighbour, and an obedient, henpecked husband. Indeed, to the latter circumstance might be owing that meekness of spirit which gained him such universal popularity; for those men are most apt to be obsequious and conciliating abroad, who are under the discipline of shrews at home. Their tempers, doubtless, are rendered pliant and malleable in the fiery furnace of domestic tribulation, and a curtain lecture[8] is worth all the sermons in the world for teaching the virtues of patience and long suffering. A termagant wife may, therefore, in some respects, be considered a tolerable blessing; and if so, Rip Van Winkle was thrice blessed.

Certain it is, that he was a great favourite among all the good wives of the village, who, as usual with the amiable sex, took his part in all family squabbles, and never failed, whenever they talked those matters over in their evening gossippings, to lay all the blame on Dame Van Winkle. The children of the village, too, would shout with joy whenever he approached. He assisted at their sports, made their playthings, taught them to fly kites and shoot marbles, and told them long stories of ghosts, witches, and Indians. Whenever he went dodging about the village, he was surrounded by a troop of them, hanging on his skirts, clambering on his back, and playing a thousand tricks on him with impunity; and not a dog would bark at him throughout the neighbourhood.

The great error in Rip's composition was an insuperable aversion to all kinds of profitable labour. It could not be for the want of assiduity or perseverance; for he would sit on a wet rock, with a rod as long and heavy as a Tartar's lance, and fish all day without a murmur, even though he should not be encouraged by a single nibble. He would carry a fowling piece on his shoulder, for hours together, trudging through woods and swamps, and up hill and down dale, to shoot a few squirrels or wild pigeons. He would never even refuse to assist a neighbour in the roughest toil, and was a foremost man at all country frolicks for husking Indian corn, or building stone fences; the women of the village, too, used to employ him to run their errands, and to do such little odd jobs as their less obliging husbands would not do for them;—in a word, Rip was ready to attend to any body's business but his own; but as to doing family duty, and keeping his farm in order, it was impossible.

In fact, he declared it was no use to work on his farm; it was the

---

8. Tirade delivered by a wife after the curtains around the four-poster bed have been drawn for the night.

most pestilent little piece of ground in the whole country; every thing about it went wrong, and would go wrong, in spite of him. His fences were continually falling to pieces; his cow would either go astray, or get among the cabbages; weeds were sure to grow quicker in his fields than any where else; the rain always made a point of setting in just as he had some out-door work to do. So that though his patrimonial estate had dwindled away under his management, acre by acre, until there was little more left than a mere patch of Indian corn and potatoes, yet it was the worst conditioned farm in the neighbourhood.

His children, too, were as ragged and wild as if they belonged to nobody. His son Rip, an urchin begotten in his own likeness, promised to inherit the habits, with the old clothes of his father. He was generally seen trooping like a colt at his mother's heels, equipped in a pair of his father's cast-off galligaskins,[9] which he had much ado to hold up with one hand, as a fine lady does her train in bad weather.

Rip Van Winkle, however, was one of those happy mortals, of foolish, well-oiled dispositions, who take the world easy, eat white bread or brown, which ever can be got with least thought or trouble, and would rather starve on a penny than work for a pound. If left to himself, he would have whistled life away, in perfect contentment; but his wife kept continually dinning in his ears about his idleness, his carelessness, and the ruin he was bringing on his family. Morning, noon, and night, her tongue was incessantly going, and every thing he said or did was sure to produce a torrent of household eloquence. Rip had but one way of replying to all lectures of the kind, and that, by frequent use, had grown into a habit. He shrugged his shoulders, shook his head, cast up his eyes, but said nothing. This, however, always provoked a fresh volley from his wife, so that he was fain to draw off his forces, and take to the outside of the house—the only side which, in truth, belongs to a henpecked husband.

Rip's sole domestic adherent was his dog Wolf, who was as much henpecked as his master; for Dame Van Winkle regarded them as companions in idleness, and even looked upon Wolf with an evil eye, as the cause of his master's so often going astray. True it is, in all points of spirit befitting an honourable dog, he was as courageous an animal as ever scoured the woods—but what courage can withstand the ever-during and all-besetting terrors of a woman's tongue? The moment Wolf entered the house, his crest fell, his tail drooped to the ground, or curled between his legs, he sneaked about with a gallows air, casting many a sidelong glance at Dame Van Winkle, and at the least flourish of a broomstick or ladle, would fly to the door with yelping precipitation.

9. Loose, wide breeches.

Times grew worse and worse with Rip Van Winkle as years of matrimony rolled on; a tart temper never mellows with age, and a sharp tongue is the only edge tool that grows keener by constant use. For a long while he used to console himself, when driven from home, by frequenting a kind of perpetual club of the sages, philosophers, and other idle personages of the village, that held its sessions on a bench before a small inn, designated by a rubicund portrait of his majesty George the Third. Here they used to sit in the shade, of a long lazy summer's day, talk listlessly over village gossip, or tell endless sleepy stories about nothing. But it would have been worth any statesman's money to have heard the profound discussions that sometimes took place, when by chance an old newspaper fell into their hands, from some passing traveller. How solemnly they would listen to the contents, as drawled out by Derrick Van Bummel, the schoolmaster, a dapper learned little man, who was not to be daunted by the most gigantic word in the dictionary; and how sagely they would deliberate upon public events some months after they had taken place.

The opinions of this junto[1] were completely controlled by Nicholas Vedder, a patriarch of the village, and landlord of the inn, at the door of which he took his seat from morning till night, just moving sufficiently to avoid the sun, and keep in the shade of a large tree; so that the neighbours could tell the hour by his movements as accurately as by a sun dial. It is true, he was rarely heard to speak, but smoked his pipe incessantly. His adherents, however, (for every great man has his adherents,) perfectly understood him, and knew how to gather his opinions. When any thing that was read or related displeased him, he was observed to smoke his pipe vehemently, and send forth short, frequent, and angry puffs; but when pleased, he would inhale the smoke slowly and tranquilly, and emit it in light and placid clouds, and sometimes taking the pipe from his mouth, and letting the fragrant vapour curl about his nose, would gravely nod his head in token of perfect approbation.

From even this strong hold the unlucky Rip was at length routed by his termagant wife, who would suddenly break in upon the tranquillity of the assemblage, call the members all to nought, nor was that august personage, Nicholas Vedder himself, sacred from the daring tongue of this terrible virago, who charged him outright with encouraging her husband in habits of idleness.

Poor Rip was at last reduced almost to despair; and his only alternative to escape from the labour of the farm and the clamour of his wife, was to take gun in hand, and stroll away into the woods. Here he would sometimes seat himself at the foot of a tree, and share the contents of his wallet[2] with Wolf, with whom he sympathised as a fellow sufferer in persecution. "Poor Wolf," he would

1. Ruling committee.   2. Knapsack.

say, "thy mistress leads thee a dogs' life of it; but never mind, my lad, while I live thou shalt never want a friend to stand by thee!" Wolf would wag his tail, look wistfully in his master's face, and if dogs can feel pity, I verily believe he reciprocated the sentiment with all his heart.

In a long ramble of the kind on a fine autumnal day, Rip had unconsciously scrambled to one of the highest parts of the Kaatskill mountains. He was after his favourite sport of squirrel shooting, and the still solitudes had echoed and re-echoed with the reports of his gun. Panting and fatigued, he threw himself, late in the afternoon, on a green knoll, covered with mountain herbage, that crowned the brow of a precipice. From an opening between the trees, he could overlook all the lower country for many a mile of rich woodland. He saw at a distance the lordly Hudson, far, far below him, moving on its silent but majestic course, the reflection of a purple cloud, or the sail of a lagging bark, here and there sleeping on its glassy bosom, and at last losing itself in the blue highlands.

On the other side he looked down into a deep mountain glen, wild, lonely, and shagged, the bottom filled with fragments from the impending cliffs, and scarcely lighted by the reflected rays of the setting sun. For some time Rip lay musing on this scene, evening was gradually advancing, the mountains began to throw their long blue shadows over the valleys, he saw that it would be dark long before he could reach the village, and he heaved a heavy sigh when he thought of encountering the terrors of Dame Van Winkle.

As he was about to descend, he heard a voice from a distance, hallooing, "Rip Van Winkle! Rip Van Winkle!" He looked around, but could see nothing but a crow winging its solitary flight across the mountain. He thought his fancy must have deceived him, and turned again to descend, when he heard the same cry ring through the still evening air; "Rip Van Winkle! Rip Van Winkle!"—at the same time Wolf bristled up his back, and giving a low growl, skulked to his master's side, looking fearfully down into the glen. Rip now felt a vague apprehension stealing over him; he looked anxiously in the same direction, and perceived a strange figure slowly toiling up the rocks, and bending under the weight of something he carried on his back. He was surprised to see any human being in this lonely and unfrequented place, but supposing it to be some one of the neighbourhood in need of his assistance, he hastened down to yield it.

On nearer approach, he was still more surprised at the singularity of the stranger's appearance. He was a short square built old fellow, with thick bushy hair, and a grizzled beard. His dress was of the antique Dutch fashion—a cloth jerkin[3] strapped round the waist— several pair of breeches, the outer one of ample volume, decorated

3. Jacket fitted tightly at the waist.

with rows of buttons down the sides, and bunches at the knees. He bore on his shoulder a stout keg, that seemed full of liquor, and made signs for Rip to approach and assist him with the load. Though rather shy and distrustful of this new acquaintance, Rip complied with his usual alacrity, and mutually relieving each other, they clambered up a narrow gully, apparently the dry bed of a mountain torrent. As they ascended, Rip every now and then heard long rolling peals, like distant thunder, that seemed to issue out of a deep ravine, or rather cleft between lofty rocks, toward which their rugged path conducted. He paused for an instant, but supposing it to be the muttering of one of those transient thunder showers which often take place in mountain heights, he proceeded. Passing through the ravine, they came to a hollow, like a small amphitheatre, surrounded by perpendicular precipices, over the brinks of which impending trees shot their branches, so that you only caught glimpses of the azure sky, and the bright evening cloud. During the whole time, Rip and his companion had laboured on in silence; for though the former marvelled greatly what could be the object of carrying a keg of liquor up this wild mountain, yet there was something strange and incomprehensible about the unknown, that inspired awe, and checked familiarity.

On entering the amphitheatre, new objects of wonder presented themselves. On a level spot in the centre was a company of odd-looking personages playing at nine-pins. They were dressed in a quaint, outlandish fashion: some wore short doublets,[4] others jerkins, with long knives in their belts, and most had enormous breeches, of similar style with that of the guide's. Their visages, too, were peculiar: one had a large head, broad face, and small piggish eyes; the face of another seemed to consist entirely of nose, and was surmounted by a white sugarloaf hat, set off with a little red cockstail. They all had beards, of various shapes and colours. There was one who seemed to be the commander. He was a stout old gentleman, with a weather-beaten countenance; he wore a laced doublet, broad belt and hanger,[5] high crowned hat and feather, red stockings, and high heeled shoes, with roses in them. The whole group reminded Rip of the figures in an old Flemish painting, in the parlour of Dominie[6] Van Schaick, the village parson, and which had been brought over from Holland at the time of the settlement.

What seemed particularly odd to Rip, was, that though these folks were evidently amusing themselves, yet they maintained the gravest faces, the most mysterious silence, and were, withal, the most melancholy party of pleasure he had ever witnessed. Nothing interrupted the stillness of the scene, but the noise of the balls, which, whenever they were rolled, echoed along the mountains like rumbling peals of thunder.

4. Male garment covering from neck to upper thighs, where it hooked to hose.
5. Short, curved sword.
6. Minister.

As Rip and his companion approached them, they suddenly desisted from their play, and stared at him with such fixed statue-like gaze, and such strange, uncouth, lack lustre countenances, that his heart turned within him, and his knees smote together. His companion now emptied the contents of the keg into large flagons, and made signs to him to wait upon the company. He obeyed with fear and trembling; they quaffed the liquor in profound silence, and then returned to their game.

By degrees, Rip's awe and apprehension subsided. He even ventured, when no eye was fixed upon him, to taste the beverage, which he found had much of the flavour of excellent Hollands.[7] He was naturally a thirsty soul, and was soon tempted to repeat the draught. One taste provoked another, and he reiterated his visits to the flagon so often, that at length his senses were overpowered, his eyes swam in his head, his head gradually declined, and he fell into a deep sleep.

On awaking, he found himself on the green knoll from whence he had first seen the old man of the glen. He rubbed his eyes—it was a bright sunny morning. The birds were hopping and twittering among the bushes, and the eagle was wheeling aloft, and breasting the pure mountain breeze. "Surely," thought Rip, "I have not slept here all night." He recalled the occurrences before he fell asleep. The strange man with the keg of liquor—the mountain ravine—the wild retreat among the rocks—the wo-begone party at nine-pins— the flagon—"Oh! that flagon! that wicked flagon!" thought Rip— "what excuse shall I make to Dame Van Winkle?"

He looked round for his gun, but in place of the clean well-oiled fowling-piece, he found an old firelock lying by him, the barrel encrusted with rust, the lock falling off, and the stock worm-eaten. He now suspected that the grave roysters of the mountain had put a trick upon him, and having dosed him with liquor, had robbed him of his gun. Wolf, too, had disappeared, but he might have strayed away after a squirrel or partridge. He whistled after him, shouted his name, but all in vain; the echoes repeated his whistle and shout, but no dog was to be seen.

He determined to revisit the scene of the last evening's gambol, and if he met with any of the party, to demand his dog and gun. As he arose to walk he found himself stiff in the joints, and wanting in his usual activity. "These mountain beds do not agree with me," thought Rip, "and if this frolick should lay me up with a fit of the rheumatism, I shall have a blessed time with Dame Van Winkle." With some difficulty he got down into the glen: he found the gully up which he and his companion had ascended the preceding evening, but to his astonishment a mountain stream was now foaming down it, leaping from rock to rock, and filling the glen with babbling murmurs. He, however, made shift to scramble up its sides,

7. Kind of gin.

working his toilsome way through thickets of birch, sassafras, and witch hazle, and sometimes tripped up or entangled by the wild grape vines that twisted their coils and tendrils from tree to tree, and spread a kind of network in his path.

At length he reached to where the ravine had opened through the cliffs, to the amphitheatre; but no traces of such opening remained. The rocks presented a high impenetrable wall, over which the torrent came tumbling in a sheet of feathery foam, and fell into a broad deep basin, black from the shadows of the surrounding forest. Here, then, poor Rip was brought to a stand. He again called and whistled after his dog; he was only answered by the cawing of a flock of idle crows, sporting high in air about a dry tree that overhung a sunny precipice; and who, secure in their elevation, seemed to look down and scoff at the poor man's perplexities. What was to be done? the morning was passing away, and Rip felt famished for his breakfast. He grieved to give up his dog and gun; he dreaded to meet his wife; but it would not do to starve among the mountains. He shook his head, shouldered the rusty firelock, and, with a heart full of trouble and anxiety, turned his steps homeward.

As he approached the village, he met a number of people, but none that he knew, which somewhat surprised him, for he had thought himself acquainted with every one in the country round. Their dress, too, was of a different fashion from that to which he was accustomed. They all stared at him with equal marks of surprise, and whenever they cast eyes upon him, invariably stroked their chins. The constant recurrence of this gesture, induced Rip, involuntarily, to do the same, when, to his astonishment, he found his beard had grown a foot long!

He had now entered the skirts of the village. A troop of strange children ran at his heels, hooting after him, and pointing at his gray beard. The dogs, too, not one of which he recognized for his old acquaintances, barked at him as he passed. The very village seemed altered: it was larger and more populous. There were rows of houses which he had never seen before, and those which had been his familiar haunts had disappeared. Strange names were over the doors—strange faces at the windows—every thing was strange. His mind now began to misgive him, that both he and the world around him were bewitched. Surely this was his native village, which he had left but the day before. There stood the Kaatskill mountains—there ran the silver Hudson at a distance—there was every hill and dale precisely as it had always been—Rip was sorely perplexed—"That flagon last night," thought he, "has addled my poor head sadly!"

It was with some difficulty he found the way to his own house, which he approached with silent awe, expecting every moment to hear the shrill voice of Dame Van Winkle. He found the house gone to decay—the roof fallen in, the windows shattered, and the doors off the hinges. A half starved dog, that looked like Wolf, was skulking about it. Rip called him by name, but the cur snarled, showed his teeth, and passed on. This was an unkind cut indeed— "My very dog," sighed poor Rip, "has forgotten me!"

He entered the house, which, to tell the truth, Dame Van Winkle had always kept in neat order. It was empty, forlorn, and apparently abandoned. This desolateness overcame all his connubial fears—he called loudly for his wife and children—the lonely chambers rung for a moment with his voice, and then all again was silence.

He now hurried forth, and hastened to his old resort, the little village inn—but it too was gone. A large ricketty wooden building stood in its place, with great gaping windows, some of them broken, and mended with old hats and petticoats, and over the door was painted, "The Union Hotel, by Jonathan Doolittle." Instead of the great tree that used to shelter the quiet little Dutch inn of yore, there now was reared a tall naked pole, with something on top that looked like a red night cap,[8] and from it was fluttering a flag, on which was a singular assemblage of stars and stripes—all this was strange and incomprehensible. He recognised on the sign, however, the ruby face of King George, under which he had smoked so many a peaceful pipe, but even this was singularly metamorphosed. The red coat was changed for one of blue and buff,[9] a sword was stuck in the hand instead of a sceptre, the head was decorated with a cocked hat, and underneath was painted in large characters, GENERAL WASHINGTON.

There was, as usual, a crowd of folk about the door, but none that Rip recollected. The very character of the people seemed changed. There was a busy, bustling, disputatious tone about it, instead of the accustomed phlegm and drowsy tranquillity. He looked in vain for the sage Nicholas Vedder, with his broad face, double chin, and fair long pipe, uttering clouds of tobacco smoke instead of idle speeches; or Van Bummel, the schoolmaster, doling forth the contents of an ancient newspaper. In place of these, a lean bilious looking fellow, with his pockets full of handbills, was haranguing vehemently about rights of citizens—election—members of congress—liberty—Bunker's hill—heroes of seventy-six—and other words, that were a perfect Babylonish jargon[1] to the bewildered Van Winkle.

The appearance of Rip, with his long grizzled beard, his rusty fowling piece, his uncouth dress, and the army of women and children that had gathered at his heels, soon attracted the attention of the tavern politicians. They crowded around him, eyeing him

---

8. Limp, close-fitting cap adopted during the French Revolution as a symbol of liberty; the pole is a "liberty pole"— i.e., a tall flagstaff topped by a liberty cap.
9. Colors of the Revolutionary uniform. Irving's joke is that the new proprietor, being a Yankee, is so parsimonious that he will only touch up the sign, not replace it with a true portrait of Washington.
1. Cf. Genesis 11.1–9, Babel being confused with Babylon.

from head to foot, with great curiosity. The orator bustled up to him, and drawing him partly aside, inquired "which side he voted?" Rip stared in vacant stupidity. Another short but busy little fellow pulled him by the arm, and raising on tiptoe, inquired in his ear, "whether he was Federal or Democrat."[2] Rip was equally at a loss to comprehend the question; when a knowing, self-important old gentleman, in a sharp cocked hat, made his way through the crowd, putting them to the right and left with his elbows as he passed, and planting himself before Van Winkle, with one arm akimbo, the other resting on his cane, his keen eyes and sharp hat penetrating, as it were, into his very soul, demanded, in an austere tone, "what brought him to the election with a gun on his shoulder, and a mob at his heels, and whether he meant to breed a riot in the village?" "Alas! gentlemen," cried Rip, somewhat dismayed, "I am a poor quiet man, a native of the place, and a loyal subject of the King, God bless him!"

Here a general shout burst from the bystanders—"A tory! a tory! a spy! a refugee! hustle him! away with him!" It was with great difficulty that the self-important man in the cocked hat restored order; and having assumed a tenfold austerity of brow, demanded again of the unknown culprit, what he came there for, and whom he was seeking. The poor man humbly assured them that he meant no harm; but merely came there in search of some of his neighbours, who used to keep about the tavern.

"Well—who are they?—name them."

Rip bethought himself a moment, and inquired, "where's Nicholas Vedder?"

There was a silence for a little while, when an old man replied, in a thin piping voice, "Nicholas Vedder? why he is dead and gone these eighteen years! There was a wooden tombstone in the church yard that used to tell all about him, but that's rotted and gone too."

"Where's Brom Dutcher?"

"Oh he went off to the army in the beginning of the war; some say he was killed at the battle of Stoney-Point—others say he was drowned in a squall, at the foot of Antony's Nose.[3] I don't know—he never came back again."

"Where's Van Bummel, the schoolmaster?"

"He went off to the wars too, was a great militia general, and is now in Congress."

Rip's heart died away, at hearing of these sad changes in his home and friends, and finding himself thus alone in the world. Every answer puzzled him, too, by treating of such enormous lapses

2. Political parties which developed in George Washington's administrations, Alexander Hamilton leading the Federalists and Thomas Jefferson the Democrats.

3. "Stoney Point": on the west bank of the Hudson south of West Point, captured by General Anthony Wayne (1745–96) during the Revolution; "Antony's Nose": mountain near West Point.

of time, and of matters which he could not understand: war—congress—Stoney-Point;—he had no courage to ask after any more friends, but cried out in despair, "does nobody here know Rip Van Winkle?"

"Oh, Rip Van Winkle!" exclaimed two or three, "Oh, to be sure! that's Rip Van Winkle yonder, leaning against the tree."

Rip looked, and beheld a precise counterpart of himself, as he went up the mountain: apparently as lazy, and certainly as ragged. The poor fellow was now completely confounded. He doubted his own identity, and whether he was himself or another man. In the midst of his bewilderment, the man in the cocked hat demanded who he was, and what was his name?

"God knows," exclaimed he, at his wit's end; "I'm not myself—I'm somebody else—that's me yonder—no—that's somebody else, got into my shoes—I was myself last night, but I fell asleep on the mountain, and they've changed my gun, and every thing's changed, and I'm changed, and I can't tell what's my name, or who I am!"

The bystanders began now to look at each other, nod, wink significantly, and tap their fingers against their foreheads. There was a whisper, also, about securing the gun, and keeping the old fellow from doing mischief. At the very suggestion of which, the self-important man in the cocked hat retired with some precipitation. At this critical moment a fresh likely woman pressed through the throng to get a peep at the graybearded man. She had a chubby child in her arms, which, frightened at his looks, began to cry. "Hush, Rip," cried she, "hush, you little fool, the old man wont hurt you." The name of the child, the air of the mother, the tone of her voice, all awakened a train of recollections in his mind.

"What is your name, my good woman?" asked he.

"Judith Gardenier."

"And your father's name?"

"Ah, poor man, his name was Rip Van Winkle; it's twenty years since he went away from home with his gun, and never has been heard of since—his dog came home without him; but whether he shot himself, or was carried away by the Indians, nobody can tell. I was then but a little girl."

Rip had but one question more to ask; but he put it with a faltering voice:

"Where's your mother?"

Oh, she too had died but a short time since; she broke a blood vessel in a fit of passion at a New-England pedlar.

There was a drop of comfort, at least, in this intelligence. The honest man could contain himself no longer.—He caught his daughter and her child in his arms.—"I am your father!" cried he—"Young Rip Van Winkle once—old Rip Van Winkle now!—Does nobody know poor Rip Van Winkle!"

All stood amazed, until an old woman, tottering out from among the crowd, put her hand to her brow, and peering under it in his face for a moment, exclaimed, "Sure enough! it is Rip Van Winkle —it is himself. Welcome home again, old neighbour—Why, where have you been these twenty long years?"

Rip's story was soon told, for the whole twenty years had been to him but as one night. The neighbours stared when they heard it; some were seen to wink at each other, and put their tongues in their cheeks; and the self-important man in the cocked hat, who, when the alarm was over, had returned to the field, screwed down the corners of his mouth, and shook his head—upon which there was a general shaking of the head throughout the assemblage.

It was determined, however, to take the opinion of old Peter Vanderdonk, who was seen slowly advancing up the road. He was a descendant of the historian of that name,[4] who wrote one of the earliest accounts of the province. Peter was the most ancient inhabitant of the village, and well versed in all the wonderful events and traditions of the neighbourhood. He recollected Rip at once, and corroborated his story in the most satisfactory manner. He assured the company that it was a fact, handed down from his ancestor the historian, that the Kaatskill mountains had always been haunted by strange beings. That it was affirmed that the great Hendrick Hudson,[5] the first discoverer of the river and country, kept a kind of vigil there every twenty years, with his crew of the Half-moon, being permitted in this way to revisit the scenes of his enterprize, and keep a guardian eye upon the river, and the great city called by his name. That his father had once seen them in their old Dutch dresses playing at nine pins in a hollow of the mountain; and that he himself had heard, one summer afternoon, the sound of their balls, like long peals of thunder.

To make a long story short, the company broke up, and returned to the more important concerns of the election. Rip's daughter took him home to live with her; she had a snug, well-furnished house, and a stout cheery farmer for a husband, whom Rip recollected for one of the urchins that used to climb upon his back. As to Rip's son and heir, who was the ditto of himself, seen leaning against the tree, he was employed to work on the farm; but evinced an hereditary disposition to attend to any thing else but his business.

Rip now resumed his old walks and habits; he soon found many of his former cronies, though all rather the worse for the wear and tear of time; and preferred making friends among the rising generation, with whom he soon grew into great favour.

Having nothing to do at home, and being arrived at that happy

4. Adriaen Van der Donck (1620–55?) wrote a history of New Netherlands (Amsterdam, 1655).
5. Henry Hudson (d. 1611), English navigator in the service of the Dutch;

"great city" is ironic, for the town named for him on the east bank of the Hudson River was flourishing but not a metropolis.

age when a man can do nothing with impunity, he took his place once more on the bench, at the inn door, and was reverenced as one of the patriarchs of the village, and a chronicle of the old times "before the war." It was some time before he could get into the regular track of gossip, or could be made to comprehend the strange events that had taken place during his torpor. How that there had been a revolutionary war—that the country had thrown off the yoke of old England—and that, instead of being a subject of his Majesty George the Third, he was now a free citizen of the United States. Rip, in fact, was no politician; the changes of states and empires made but little impression on him. But there was one species of despotism under which he had long groaned, and that was—petticoat government. Happily, that was at an end; he had got his neck out of the yoke of matrimony, and could go in and out whenever he pleased, without dreading the tyranny of Dame Van Winkle. Whenever her name was mentioned, however, he shook his head, shrugged his shoulders, and cast up his eyes; which might pass either for an expression of resignation to his fate, or joy at his deliverance.

He used to tell his story to every stranger that arrived at Mr. Doolittle's hotel. He was observed, at first, to vary on some points every time he told it, which was, doubtless, owing to his having so recently awaked. It at last settled down precisely to the tale I have related, and not a man, woman, or child in the neighbourhood, but knew it by heart. Some always pretended to doubt the reality of it, and insisted that Rip had been out of his head, and that this was one point on which he always remained flighty. The old Dutch inhabitants, however, almost universally gave it full credit. Even to this day they never hear a thunder storm of a summer afternoon, about the Kaatskill, but they say Hendrick Hudson and his crew are at their game of nine pins; and it is a common wish of all henpecked husbands in the neighbourhood, when life hangs heavy on their hands, that they might have a quieting draught out of Rip Van Winkle's flagon.

NOTE

The foregoing tale, one would suspect, had been suggested to Mr. Knickerbocker by a little German superstition about Charles V. and the Kypphauser mountain;[6] the subjoined note, however, which he had appended to the tale, shows that it is an absolute fact, narrated with his usual fidelity:

6. Later Irving changed "Charles V." (Holy Roman Emperor 1519–56) to "The Emperor Frederick *der Rothbart*" (i.e., Frederick Barbarossa, Holy Roman Emperor 1152–90). ("Rothbart" and "Barbarossa" both mean "redbeard.") In either form, the allusion is a red herring, a disarming way of suggesting indebtedness to a German source while concealing the most specific source, the story of "Peter Klaus" in the folk tales of J. C. C. N. Otmar.

"The story of Rip Van Winkle may seem incredible to many, but nevertheless I give it my full belief, for I know the vicinity of our old Dutch settlements to have been very subject to marvellous events and appearances. Indeed, I have heard many stranger stories than this, in the villages along the Hudson; all of which were too well authenticated to admit of a doubt. I have even talked with Rip Van Winkle myself, who, when last I saw him, was a very venerable old man, and so perfectly rational and consistent on every other point, that I think no conscientious person could refuse to take this into the bargain; nay, I have seen a certificate on the subject taken before a country justice, and signed with a cross, in the justice's own hand writing. The story, therefore, is beyond the possibility of doubt.

D.K."

1819

JAMES FENIMORE COOPER
1789–1851

James Fenimore Cooper, the first successful American novelist, was born on September 15, 1789, in Burlington, New Jersey, but taken in infancy to Cooperstown, on Otsego Lake in central New York, where his wealthy father owned great tracts of land. A few years before, the region had been wilderness, but during Cooper's boyhood there were few backwoodsmen left, and fewer Indians; in his novels the information about Indians came from older people and from books. In 1801 his father sent him to study in Albany in preparation for Yale, where he spent two years in his mid-teens before being expelled for pranks, thereby acquiring a lifelong distaste for New Englanders. He became a sailor in 1806 then two years later a midshipman in the navy. At twenty he inherited a fortune from his father and married Susan De Lancey, whose family had lost possessions by siding with the British in the Revolution but still owned lands in Westchester County. For several years Cooper and his wife wavered between Scarsdale and Otsego as a permanent home. Wherever they settled, Cooper seemed certain to live as a landed gentleman. His first book, *Precaution* (1820), a novel dealing with English high society, was the result of his casual bet with his wife that he could write a better book than the one he had been reading to her. Following that insignificant start, he wrote *The Spy* (1821), the first important historical romance of the Revolution, and on its success he moved to New York City to take up his new career. From the first his faults (such as syntactical awkwardness, arbitrary plotting, and heavy-handed attempts at humor) were obvious enough, but so were his genuine achievements in opening up new American scenes and themes for fiction. Founding the Bread and Cheese Club, he became the center of a circle which included notable painters of the Hudson River school as well as writers (William Cullen Bryant among them) and professional men. In

1823 he published *The Pioneers*, the first of what eventually consisted of five books about Natty Bumppo, known collectively as the *Leather-Stocking Tales*; the second, *The Last of the Mohicans*, followed in 1826. Cooper has other claims to fame—the virtual creation of the sea novel (starting with *The Pilot*, 1824), authorship of the first serious American novels of manners and the first American sociopolitical novels—but with Natty Bumppo, the aged hunter, he had created one of the most popular characters in world literature.

In 1826, at the height of his fame, Cooper sailed for Europe. In Paris, where he became intimate with the aged Lafayette, he wrote *The Prairie* (1827) and *Notions of the Americans* (1828), a defense of the United States against the attacks of European travelers. Smarting under the half-complimentary, half-patronizing epithet of "The American Scott," he wrote three historical novels set in medieval Europe as a realistic corrective to Sir Walter Scott's glorifications of the past. On his return to the United States in 1833 Cooper was so stung by a review of one of these novels that he renounced novel writing in an angry *Letter to His Countrymen* (1834). Then at Cooperstown he gave notice that a point of land on Otsego Lake where the townspeople had been picnicking was private property and not to be used without permission. Newspapers began attacking him as a would-be aristocrat poisoned by his residence abroad, and for years Cooper embroiled himself in lawsuits designed not to gain damages for the journalistic libels but to tame the irresponsible press. Legally in the right, Cooper sacrificed his peace of mind to establish the principle that reviewers must work within the bounds of truth when they deal with the author rather than the book. Even as he was becoming the great national scold of his time, Cooper managed to write book after book—social and political satires growing out of his experiences with the press, a reactionary primer on *The American Democrat* (1838), and, despite his avowal in 1834, a series of sociopolitical novels and two more *Leather-Stocking Tales*, *The Pathfinder* (1840) and *The Deerslayer* (1841). His monumental *History of the Navy of the United States of America* (1839) became the focus of new quarrels and a new lawsuit.

When Cooper died on September 14, 1851, a day before his sixty-second birthday, he was a byword for litigiousness and social pretentiousness. A lifelong defender of American democracy as he knew it in his youth against European aristocracy and then against what American democracy had become, he was out of step with his countrypeople. Yet throughout the century and into the next his *Leather-Stocking Tales* had an incalculable vogue in the United States and abroad. In his own time and shortly afterward, major European writers as diverse as Honoré de Balzac and Leo Tolstoy were profoundly moved by *The Pioneers* and the subsequent Natty Bumppo novels, but gradually the *Leather-Stocking Tales* became something only schoolchildren read. Not until the 1920s did scholars begin to see Cooper's value as the country's first great social critic. It now seems clear that no revolution in taste will lead to widespread admiration of Cooper as a literary artist, but he will always be a major source for the student of ideas in America. Some of his opinions now seem hopelessly reactionary, as when he defends American slavery as legal and, after all, mild ("physical suffering cannot properly be enumerated among its evils") or when he deplores the dangers of universal manhood suffrage and argues for restricting voting on certain issues to property-owners, who have the greater stake in society. What most appeals to modern readers are his profoundly ambivalent dramatizations of such enduring American conflicts as natural right versus legal right, order versus change, primeval wilderness versus civilization. And new readers will always encounter the *Leather-Stocking Tales* with a sense of something long known and loved, for if Cooper is no longer read even by children, everyone has read books—and seen films—which are directly and indirectly influenced by his grand conception of Natty Bumppo.

From The Pioneers
[*The Slaughter of the Pigeons*][1]

"Men, boys, and girls.
Desert th' unpeopled village; and wild crowds
Spread o'er the plain, by the sweet frenzy driven."[2]
—SOMERVILLE

From this time to the close of April, the weather continued to be a succession of great and rapid changes. One day, the soft airs of spring would seem to be stealing along the valley, and, in unison with an invigorating sun, attempting, covertly, to rouse the dormant powers of the vegetable world; while on the next, the surly blasts from the north would sweep across the lake, and erase every impression left by their gentle adversaries. The snow, however, finally disappeared, and the green wheat fields were seen in every direction, spotted with the dark and charred stumps that had, the preceding season, supported some of the proudest trees of the forest.[3] Ploughs were in motion, wherever those useful implements could be used, and the smokes of the sugar-camps[4] were no longer seen issuing from the summits of the woods of maple. The lake had lost all the characteristic beauty of a field of ice, but still a dark and gloomy

1. *The Pioneers, or The Sources of the Susquehanna; A Descriptive Tale* (New York: Charles Wiley, 1823) is the first of five Cooper novels in which Natty Bumppo is the major character. The text is that of the first edition, Vol. II, Chapter 3 (Chapter 22 in later one-volume editions). *The Pioneers* begins in December, 1793, at the settlement of Templeton (modeled on Cooperstown) at Otsego Lake in central New York, some 50 miles west of Albany. The episode reprinted here occurs in the spring of 1794. Natty Bumppo is in his early 70s, six feet tall (then a great height), gray-eyed, with lank, sandy hair, sunburned, robust, but thin almost to emaciation. One yellow tooth survives in his enormous mouth, and he gives forth a remarkable kind of inward laugh. He wears a foxskin hat and is clad in deerskin—coat, moccasins, and even the leggings which

fasten over the keees of his buckskin breeches and give him the nickname of "Leather-Stocking." For his old and unusually long rifle he carries gunpowder in an enormous ox horn slung over his shoulder by a strap of deerskin. This was the unprepossessing figure who captured the imagination of the United States and Europe.
2. From *The Chace*, II, 197–99, by the English poet William Somerville (1675–1742). The last word should be "seized," not "driven."
3. The practice was to chop timber down in the spring, let it dry through the summer, then burn the cleared area so that only blackened logs and stumps remained. Nothing was salvaged except some ashes used as the basis for potash.
4. Where sugar was made from maple sap.

covering concealed its waters, for the absence of currents left them yet hid under a porous crust, which, saturated with the fluid, barely retained enough of its strength to preserve the contiguity of its parts. Large flocks of wild geese were seen passing over the country, which would hover, for a time, around the hidden sheet of water, apparently searching for an opening, where they might obtain a resting-place; and then, on finding themselves excluded by the chill covering, would soar away to the north, filling the air with their discordant screams, as if venting their complaints at the tardy operations of nature.

For a week, the dark covering of the Otsego was left to the undisturbed possession of two eagles, who alighted on the centre of its field, and sat proudly eyeing the extent of their undisputed territory. During the presence of these monarchs of the air, the flocks of migrating birds avoided crossing the plain of ice, by turning into the hills, and apparently seeking the protection of the forests, while the white and bald heads of the tenants of the lake were turned upward, with a look of majestic contempt, as if penetrating to the very heavens, with the acuteness of their vision. But the time had come, when even these kings of birds were to be dispossessed. An opening had been gradually increasing, at the lower extremity of the lake, and around the dark spot where the current of the river had prevented the formation of ice, during even the coldest weather; and the fresh southerly winds, that now breathed freely up the valley, obtained an impression on the waters. Mimic waves begun to curl over the margin of the frozen field, which exhibited an outline of crystallizations, that slowly receded towards the north. At each step the power of the winds and the waves increased, until, after a struggle of a few hours, the turbulent little billows succeeded in setting the whole field in an undulating motion, when it was driven beyond the reach of the eye, with a rapidity, that was as magical as the change produced in the scene by this expulsion of the lingering remnant of winter. Just as the last sheet of agitated ice was disappearing in the distance, the eagles rose over the border of crystals, and soared with a wide sweep far above the clouds, while the waves tossed their little caps of snow into the air, as if rioting in their release from a thraldom of five months duration.

The following morning Elizabeth[5] was awakened by the exhilarating sounds of the martins, who were quarrelling and chattering around the little boxes which were suspended above her windows, and the cries of Richard,[6] who was calling, in tones as animating as the signs of the season itself—

---

5. Elizabeth Temple, daughter of Judge Marmaduke Temple, the founder of Templeton and its chief landowner; at the outset of the story she returns from four years at school.

6. Richard (Dickon) Jones, the sheriff, a cousin of Judge Temple; he superintends "all the minor concerns of Temple's business."

"Awake! awake! my lady fair! the gulls are hovering over the lake already, and the heavens are alive with the pigeons. You may look an hour before you can find a hole, through which, to get a peep at the sun. Awake! awake! lazy ones! Benjamin[7] is overhauling the ammunition, and we only wait for our breakfasts, and away for the mountains and pigeon-shooting."

There was no resisting this animated appeal, and in a few minutes Miss Temple and her friend[8] descended to the parlour. The doors of the hall were thrown open, and the mild, balmy air of a clear spring morning was ventilating the apartment, where the vigilance of the ex-steward had been so long maintaining an artificial heat, with such unremitted diligence. All of the gentlemen, we do not include Monsieur Le Quoi,[9] were impatiently waiting their morning's repast, each being equipt in the garb of a sportsman. Mr. Jones made many visits to the southern door, and would cry—

"See, cousin Bess! see, 'duke![1] the pigeon-roosts of the south have broken up! They are growing more thick every instant. Here is a flock that the eye cannot see the end of. There is food enough in it to keep the army of Xerxes[2] for a month, and feathers enough to make beds for the whole county. Xerxes, Mr. Edwards,[3] was a Grecian king, who—no, he was a Turk, or a Persian, who wanted to conquer Greece, just the same as these rascals will overrun our wheat-fields, when they come back in the fall.—Away! away! Bess; I long to pepper them from the mountain."

In this wish both Marmaduke and young Edwards seemed equally to participate, for really the sight was most exhilarating to a sportsman; and the ladies soon dismissed the party, after a hasty breakfast.

If the heavens were alive with pigeons, the whole village seemed equally in motion, with men, women, and children. Every species of fire-arms, from the French ducking-gun, with its barrel of near six feet in length, to the common horseman's pistol, was to be seen in the hands of the men and boys; while bows and arrows, some made of the simple stick of a walnut sapling, and others in a rude imitation of the ancient cross-bows, were carried by many of the latter.

The houses, and the signs of life apparent in the village, drove the alarmed birds from the direct line of their flight, towards the mountains, along the sides and near the bases of which they were

---

7. Benjamin Penguillan (called Ben Pump), a Cornishman and former sailor, "major-domo" or steward under Jones. In the next paragraph Pump is called "the ex-steward" because he had been a steward to the captain in his seagoing years. One of his charges at the Templeton house is to keep the stove in the parlor hot in winter.

8. Louisa Grant, daughter of the Episco-pal minister.

9. Once a West Indian planter, now a refugee because of the French Revolution.

1. Short for "Marmaduke," the judge.

2. Xerxes the Great (519?–465 B.C.) was King of Persia (486–465 B.C.).

3. Oliver Edwards, a mysterious young stranger.

glancing in dense masses, that were equally wonderful by the rapidity of their motion, as by their incredible numbers.

We have already said, that across the inclined plane which fell from the steep ascent of the mountain to the banks of the Susquehanna, ran the highway, on either side of which a clearing of many acres had been made, at a very early day. Over those clearings, and up the eastern mountain, and along the dangerous path that was cut into its side, the different individuals posted themselves, as suited their inclinations; and in a few moments the attack commenced.

Amongst the sportsmen was to be seen the tall, gaunt form of Leather-stocking,[4] who was walking over the field, with his rifle hanging on his arm, his dogs following close at his heels, now scenting the dead or wounded birds, that were beginning to tumble from the flocks, and then crouching under the legs of their master, as if they participated in his feelings, at this wasteful and unsportsmanlike execution.

The reports of the fire-arms became rapid, whole volleys rising from the plain, as flocks of more than ordinary numbers darted over the opening, covering the field with darkness, like an interposing cloud; and then the light smoke of a single piece would issue from among the leafless bushes on the mountain, as death was hurled on the retreat of the affrighted birds, who would rise from a volley, for many feet into the air, in a vain effort to escape the attacks of man. Arrows, and missiles of every kind, were seen in the midst of the flocks; and so numerous were the birds, and so low did they take their flight, that even long poles, in the hands of those on the sides of the mountain, were used to strike them to the earth.

During all this time, Mr. Jones, who disdained the humble and ordinary means of destruction used by his companions, was busily occupied, aided by Benjamin, in making arrangements for an assault of a more than ordinarily fatal character. Among the relics of the old military excursions, that occasionally are discovered throughout the different districts of the western part of New-York, there had been found in Templeton, at its settlement, a small swivel,[5] which would carry a ball of a pound weight. It was thought to have been deserted by a war-party of the whites, in one of their inroads into the Indian settlements, when, perhaps, their convenience or their necessities induced them to leave such an encumbrance to the rapidity of their march, behind them in the woods. This miniature cannon had been released from the rust, and mounted on little wheels, in a state for actual service. For several years, it was the sole organ for extraordinary rejoicings that was used in those mountains. On the mornings of the Fourth of July, it

4. I.e., Natty Bumppo.
5. Small cannon capable of being swung higher or lower.

would be heard, with its echoes ringing among the hills, and telling forth its sounds, for thirteen times, with all the dignity of a two-and-thirty pounder; and even Captain Hollister,[6] who was the highest authority in that part of the country on all such occasions, affirmed that, considering its dimensions, it was no despicable gun for a salute. It was somewhat the worse for the service it had performed, it is true, there being but a trifling difference in size between the touch-hole and the muzzle.[7] Still, the grand conceptions of Richard had suggested the importance of such an instrument, in hurling death at his nimble enemies. The swivel was dragged by a horse into a part of the open space, that the sheriff thought most eligible for planting a battery of the kind, and Mr. Pump proceeded to load it. Several handfuls of duck-shot were placed on top of the powder, and the Major-domo soon announced that his piece was ready for service.

The sight of such an implement collected all the idle spectators to the spot, who, being mostly boys, filled the air with their cries of exultation and delight. The gun was pointed on high, and Richard, holding a coal of fire in a pair of tongs, patiently took his seat on a stump, awaiting the appearance of a flock that was worthy of his notice.

So prodigious was the number of the birds, that the scattering fire of the guns, with the hurling of missiles, and the cries of the boys, had no other effect than to break off small flocks from the immense masses that continued to dart along the valley, as if the whole creation of the feathered tribe were pouring through that one pass. None pretended to collect the game, which lay scattered over the fields in such profusion, as to cover the very ground with the fluttering victims.

Leather-stocking was a silent, but uneasy spectator of all these proceedings, but was able to keep his sentiments to himself until he saw the introduction of the swivel into the sports.

"This comes of settling a country!" he said—"here have I known the pigeons to fly for forty long years, and, till you made your clearings, there was nobody to scare or to hurt them. I loved to see them come into the woods, for they were company to a body; hurting nothing; being, as it was, as harmless as a garter-snake. But now it gives me sore thoughts when I hear the frighty things whizzing through the air, for I know it's only a motion to bring out all the brats in the village at them. Well! the Lord won't see the waste of his creaters for nothing, and right will be done to the pigeons, as well as others, by-and-by.—There's Mr. Oliver, as bad as the rest of

---

6. The landlord of the major village inn, The Bold Dragoon; his rank comes from his having been an early commander of local militia.

7. Ordinarily the muzzle (or mouth) would be considerably larger than the touch-hole, the vent by which fire is communicated to the powder.

them, firing into the flocks as if he was shooting down nothing but the Mingo[8] warriors."

Among the sportsmen was Billy Kirby,[9] who, armed with an old musket, was loading, and, without even looking into the air, was firing, and shouting as his victims fell even on his own person. He heard the speech of Natty, and took upon himself to reply—

"What's that, old Leather-stocking!" he cried; "grumbling at the loss of a few pigeons! If you had to sow your wheat twice, and three times, as I have done, you wouldn't be so massyfully[1] feeling'd to'ards the divils.—Hurrah, boys! scatter the feathers. This is better than shooting at a turkey's head and neck, old fellow."[2]

"It's better for you, maybe, Billy Kirby," returned the indignant old hunter, "and all them as don't know how to put a ball down a rifle-barrel, or how to bring it up ag'in with a true aim; but it's wicked to be shooting into flocks in this wastey manner; and none do it, who know how to knock over a single bird. If a body has a craving for pigeon's flesh, why! it's made the same as all other creaters, for man's eating, but not to kill twenty and eat one. When I want such a thing, I go into the woods till I find one to my liking, and then I shoot him off the branches without touching a feather of another, though there might be a hundred on the same tree. But you couldn't do such a thing, Billy Kirby—you couldn't do it if you tried."

"What's that you say, you old, dried cornstalk! you sapless stub!" cried the wood-chopper. "You've grown mighty boasting, sin[3] you killed the turkey; but if you're for a single shot, here goes at that bird which comes on by himself."

The fire from the distant part of the field had driven a single pigeon below the flock to which it had belonged, and, frightened with the constant reports of the muskets, it was approaching the spot where the disputants stood, darting first from one side, and then to the other, cutting the air with the swiftness of lightning, and making a noise with its wings, not unlike the rushing of a bullet. Unfortunately for the wood-chopper, notwithstanding his vaunt, he did not see his bird until it was too late for him to fire as it approached, and he pulled his trigger at the unlucky moment when it was darting immediately over his head. The bird continued its course with incredible velocity.

Natty had dropped his piece from his arm, when the challenge was made, and, waiting a moment, until the terrified victim had got in a line with his eyes, and had dropped near the bank of the lake, he raised his rifle with uncommon rapidity, and fired. It might have

<hr>

8. In the *Leather-Stocking* novels set in New York, the Mingos (Iroquois) are made out to be the "bad Indians" while the Delawares are the "good Indians."
9. A woodchopper.

1. Mercifully.
2. In an earlier chapter Natty Bumppo had beaten Kirby in a turkey-shooting contest.
3. Since.

been chance, or it might have been skill, that produced the result; it was probably a union of both; but the pigeon whirled over in the air, and fell into the lake, with a broken wing. At the sound of his rifle, both his dogs started from his feet, and in a few minutes the "slut"[4] brought out the bird, still alive.

The wonderful exploit of Leather-stocking was noised through the field with great rapidity, and the sportsmen gathered in to learn the truth of the report.

"What," said young Edwards, "have you really killed a pigeon on the wing, Natty, with a single ball?"

"Haven't I killed loons before now, lad, that dive at the flash?" returned the hunter. "It's much better to kill only such as you want, without wasting your powder and lead, than to be firing into God's creaters in such a wicked manner. But I come out for a bird, and you know the reason why I like small game, Mr. Oliver, and now I have got one I will go home, for I don't like to see these wasty ways that you are all practysing, as if the least thing was not made for use, and not to destroy."

"Thou sayest well, Leather-stocking," cried Marmaduke, "and I begin to think it time to put an end to this work of destruction."

"Put an ind, Judge, to your clearings. An't the woods his work as well as the pigeons? Use, but don't waste. Wasn't the woods made for the beasts and birds to harbour in? and when man wanted their flesh, their skins, or their feathers, there's the place to seek them. But I'll go to the hut with my own game, for I wouldn't touch one of the harmless things that kiver the ground here, looking up with their eyes at me, as if they only wanted tongues to say their thoughts."

With this sentiment in his mouth, Leather-stocking threw his rifle over his arm, and, followed by his dogs, stepped across the clearing with great caution, taking care not to tread on one, of the hundreds of the wounded birds that lay in his path. He soon entered the bushes on the margin of the lake, and was hid from view.

Whatever might be the impression the morality of Natty made on the Judge, it was utterly lost on Richard. He availed himself of the gathering of the sportsmen, to lay a plan for one "fell swoop"[5] of destruction. The musket-men were drawn up in battle array, in a line extending on each side of his artillery, with orders to await the signal of firing from himself.

"Stand by, my lads," said Benjamin, who acted as an aid-de-camp on this momentous occasion, "stand by, my hearties, and when Squire Dickens heaves out the signal for to begin the firing, d'ye see, you may open upon them in a broadside. Take care and fire low, boys, and you'll be sure to hull the flock."

---

4. Bitch, female dog.
5. Shakespeare's *Macbeth*, 4.3.219, in   Macduff's lament for his dead wife and children.

"Fire low!" shouted Kirby—"hear the old fool! If we fire low, we may hit the stumps, but not ruffle a pigeon."

"How should you know, you lubber?"[6] cried Benjamin, with a very unbecoming heat, for an officer on the eve of battle—"how should you know, you grampus? Havn't I sailed aboard of the Boadishy[7] for five years? and wasn't it a standing order to fire low, and to hull your enemy? Keep silence at your guns, boys, and mind the order that is passed."

The loud laughs of the musketmen were silenced by the authoritative voice of Richard, who called to them for attention and obedience to his signals.

Some millions of pigeons were supposed to have already passed, that morning, over the valley of Templeton; but nothing like the flock that was now approaching had been seen before. It extended from mountain to mountain in one solid blue mass, and the eye looked in vain over the southern hills to find its termination. The front of this living column was distinctly marked by a line, but very slightly indented, so regular and even was the flight. Even Marmaduke forgot the morality of Leather-stocking as it approached, and, in common with the rest, brought his musket to his shoulder.

"Fire!" cried the Sheriff, clapping his coal to the priming of the cannon. As half of Benjamin's charge escaped through the touchhole, the whole volley of the musketry preceded the report of the swivel. On receiving this united discharge of small-arms, the front of the flock darted upward, while, at the same instant, myriads of those in their rear rushed with amazing rapidity into their places, so that when the column of white smoke gushed from the mouth of the little cannon, an accumulated mass of objects was gliding over its point of direction. The roar of the gun echoed along the mountains, and died away to the north, like distant thunder, while the whole flock of alarmed birds seemed, for a moment, thrown into one disorderly and agitated mass. The air was filled with their irregular flights, layer rising over layer, far above the tops of the highest pines, none daring to advance beyond the dangerous pass; when, suddenly, some of the leaders of the feathered tribe shot across the valley, taking their flight directly over the village, and the hundreds of thousands in their rear followed their example, deserting the eastern side of the plain to their persecutors and the fallen.

"Victory!" shouted Richard, "victory! we have driven the enemy from the field."

"Not so, Dickon," said Marmaduke; "the field is covered with them; and, like the Leather-stocking, I see nothing but eyes, in every direction, as the innocent sufferers turn their heads in terror, to examine my movements. Full one half of those that have fallen

---

6. Landlubber, clumsy fellow.
7. "Grampus": variety of small whale, used here as a term of contempt;

"Boadishy": the *Boadicea*, a ship named for the British Queen who led a rebellion against the Roman rulers in A.D. 62.

are yet alive: and I think it is time to end the sport; if sport it be."

"Sport!" cried the Sheriff; "it is princely sport. There are some thousands of the blue-coated boys on the ground, so that every old woman in the village may have a pot-pie for the asking."

"Well, we have happily frightened the birds from this pass," said Marmaduke, "and our carnage must of necessity end, for the present.—Boys, I will give thee sixpence a hundred for the pigeons' heads only; so go to work, and bring them into the village, when I will pay thee."

This expedient produced the desired effect, for every urchin on the ground went industriously to work to wring the necks of the wounded birds. Judge Temple retired towards his dwelling with that kind of feeling, that many a man has experienced before him, who discovers, after the excitement of the moment has passed, that he has purchased pleasure at the price of misery to others. Horses were loaded with the dead; and, after this first burst of sporting, the shooting of pigeons became a business, for the remainder of the season, more in proportion to the wants of the people.[8] Richard, however, boasted for many a year, of his shot with the "cricket;"[9] and Benjamin gravely asserted, that he thought that they killed nearly as many pigeons on that day, as there were Frenchmen destroyed on the memorable occasion of Rodney's victory.[1]

1823

8. The pigeons described in this chapter —the passenger pigeons—are extinct, the last known specimen dying in 1914 at the Cincinnati Zoological Garden.
9. I.e., the little cannon.
1. The British admiral George Brydges, Baron Rodney (1719–92), defeated the French off Dominica, in the West Indies, in April, 1782. Penguillan's nickname comes from his tall tale about manning the pumps to keep the ship from sinking after Rodney's victory.

AUGUSTUS BALDWIN LONGSTREET
1790–1870

Augustus Baldwin Longstreet was born on September 22, 1790, in Augusta, Georgia, of parents from New Jersey; his ancestry was primarily English, French, and Dutch ("Langstraet"); in this time, as later, Georgia had a high percentage of emigrants from Northern states. After attending a notable school in Willington, South Carolina, he consciously followed John C. Calhoun's path, graduating from Yale in 1813 (his teachers included some of the "Connecticut Wits"), then studying law in Litchfield, Connecticut, and passing the Georgia bar examination in 1815. Two years later he married and shared an exceptionally happy family life despite suffering the loss of young children and much later the trauma of the Civil War, until his wife's death in 1868. Longstreet was elected to the state's General Assembly in 1821 and was elected judge of the Superior Court in 1822; in 1824 he abandoned the race for Congress when his first son died. He became a Methodist minister (licensed to preach in 1829), owned and edited the Augusta *State Rights' Sentinel* from 1834 to 1836, then in 1839 became president of Emory College, still in Oxford, Georgia, and only two years old. In 1849 he became president of Centenary College in Jackson, Louisiana, then of the University of Mississippi (his second time at a town named Oxford), and in 1858 president of South Carolina College in Columbia (now the University of South Carolina). In the war he was a refugee, never without funds but piteous because of his age; during the occupation of Oxford, Mississippi, Grant's soldiers burned his house down, destroying his library and private papers.

In the early 1830s, recalling his experiences in traveling through the seven counties of his judicial district (and still other counties, when filling in for a fellow judge), and drawing on his already well-known skill at tale telling, Longstreet began writing realistic, occasionally humorous, sketches for newspaper publication under two pseudonyms: Hall, the name put to stories mainly about men, was taken from a Georgian who signed the Declaration of Independence, and Baldwin, the name put to stories about women, was his own middle name and the name of a Georgian who signed the Constitution. When Longstreet bought his own newspaper he republished some earlier stories as well as new ones, and in 1835, at his own newspaper press but without sufficient supervision, he printed, anonymously, *Georgia Scenes, Characters, Incidents, &c. in the First Half Century of the Republic: By a Native Georgian.* It had, throughout the country, remarkable success; Poe praised it in a long review in the *Southern Literary Messenger.* In the late 1830s and early 1840s Longstreet wrote more stories, some of which he published in his friend William Tappan Thompson's *Augusta Mirror* and *Southern Miscellany,* others in Simms's *The Magnolia,* always keeping in mind an enlarged edition he never found time to complete. By 1840, when his authorship was an open secret, the popular demand for the book in the North led the Harpers to reprint it prefaced by a rueful complaint that they had not been able to prevail upon the author to revise the work.

Neglected but never forgotten, Longstreet has been, as James B. Meriwether explains, mislabeled as "a Southwestern humorist," when he was not a Southwesterner and not primarily a humorist but rather a social historian, an early literary realist as keenly aware as Irving of the mutability of American lives and American landscapes. Longstreet had insisted in his preface: "The following sketches were written, rather in the hope that chance would bring them to light, when time would give them an interest, than in the belief that they would afford any interest to the readers of the present day." A letter he wrote to T. W. White, the publisher of the *Southern Literary Messenger,* whom Longstreet assumed had written the review in that magazine, makes clear that that original purpose applies also to the augmented volume he hoped to publish: "The leading object of the Georgia Scenes, is to enable those who came after us, to see us *precisely as we are.* If my life be spared; they will [be] carried through all ranks of society. I have often desired to see the Greeks and Romans, as they saw each other. . . . The time will come perhaps, when the same desire will be felt to know all about us; and to gratify that desire, I am now writing."

Among those who knew Georgia, the authenticity of the sketches was never doubted, but Longstreet remained, as Meriwether says, "a rather lonely pioneer of literary realism." Yet his influence was enormous. In his own time, he made possible, as much as Irving, the writing of George Washington Harris, and his influence on the young Samuel L. Clemens was strong, as, much later, was his influence on William Faulkner. (The young Faulkner read his way around the library in the home of his friend Phil Stone, the house where Longstreet's son-in-law L. C. Q. Lamar had lived; some of Longstreet's books were still in the house, and Phil Stone had as a boy outraged General James Longstreet, the nephew of the writer, by asking about the General's much disputed delay in obeying Lee's orders at Gettysburg—graphic evidence of how the Civil War impinged on Southern lives into the middle of this century. A. B. Longstreet and William Faulkner are buried not far from each other in St. Peter's Cemetery, in Oxford, Mississippi, fitting proximity for two men who wrote the best horse-swapping stories in our literature.)

Literary scholars are at last giving Longstreet the attention he deserves. Meriwether and Leo Lemay have refined the author's own distinctions between the two personas used in the sketches, and James M. Cox has called *Georgia Scenes* "as 'good' a book as Hawthorne's *Twice-Told Tales*, published two years later. It has as much art, imagination, perception, and insight as Hawthorne's early work possesses." In our search for an aesthetically, historically, and socially honest canon of American literature (especially for the nineteenth century) we are only beginning to challenge the hegemony of the Bearded Poets and New England prose masters; regional prejudice is as real as sexual and racial prejudice, and sometimes as subtle.

A Sage Conversation[1]

I love the aged matrons of our land. As a class, they are the most pious, the most benevolent, the most useful, and the most harmless of the human family. Their life, is a life of good offices. At home, they are patterns of industry, care, economy, and hospitality; abroad, they are ministers of comfort, peace, and consolation. Where affliction is, there are they, to mitigate its pangs; where sorrow is, there are they to assuage its pains. Nor night, nor day,

---

1. *A Sage Conversation* was first printed in the Augusta *State Rights Sentinel* of March 17, 1835, and included in *Georgia Scenes* (1835), the source of the present text; some small changes have been adopted from the Harper text (1840) or made independently.

The short sketch belongs in the tradition of humorous accounts of the accommodations travelers had to content themselves with (contemporaries would have known that the Spouter Inn section of *Moby-Dick* was in the same genre). It also belongs to, and to some extent sets, the tradition of recording the conversation of women—a tradition to which Eudora Welty and Flannery O'Connor have made triumphant contributions. Recently the feminists Julia Penelope Stanley and

Susan J. Wolfe in "Toward a Feminist Aesthetic," *Chrysalis* 6 (1978), have tried to define a connection between women's conversation and women's writing styles, women being more "expressive" than men, using "run-on, infinite syntax" and a "discursive, conjunctive style." Such theory risks treating women reductively. Longstreet does not patronize women, and his follower Samuel L. Clemens delighted in recording male command of such talk as occurs in this story. James B. Meriwether has done his best to gain the story new readers: "Homosexuality, transvestitism, seduction and betrayal are the dark underlying themes of this sketch, skillfully and delicately handled."

nor summer's heat, nor winter's cold, nor angry elements, can deter them from scenes of suffering and distress. They are the first at the fevered couch, and the last to leave it. They hold the first and last cup to the parched lip. They bind the aching head, close the dying eye, and linger in the death-stricken habitation, to pour the last drop of consolation into the afflicted bosoms of the bereaved. I cannot, therefore, ridicule them myself, nor bear to hear them ridiculed in my presence. And yet, I am often amused at their conversations; and have amused *them* with a rehearsal[2] of their own conversations, taken down by me when they little dreamed that I was listening to them. Perhaps my reverence for their character, conspiring with a native propensity to extract amusement from all that passes under my observation, has accustomed me to pay a uniformly strict attention to all they say in my presence.

This much in extraordinary courtesy to those who cannot distinguish between a simple narrative of an amusing interview, and ridicule of the parties to it. Indeed I do not know that the conversation which I am about to record, will be considered amusing by any of my readers. Certainly the amusement of the readers of my own times, is not the leading object of it, or of any of the "Georgia Scenes;" forlorn as may be the hope that their main object will ever be answered.

When I seated myself to the sheet now before me, my intention was merely to detail a conversation between three ladies, which I heard many years since; confining myself to only so much of it as sprung from the ladies' own thoughts, unawakened by the suggestions of others; but, as the manner of its introduction will perhaps interest some of my readers, I will give it.

I was travelling with my old friend, Ned Brace,[3] when we stopped at the dusk of the evening at a house on the road side, for the night. Here we found three nice, tidy, aged matrons, the youngest of whom could not have been under sixty; one of them of course was the lady of the house, whose husband, old as he was, had gone from home upon a land exploring expedition. She received us hospitably, had our horses well attended to, and soon prepared for us a comfortable supper. While these things were doing, Ned and I engaged the other two in conversation; in the course of which, Ned deported himself with becoming seriousness. The kind lady of the house occasionally joined us, and became permanently one of the party, from the time the first dish was placed on the table. At the usual hour, we were summoned to supper; and as soon as we were seated, Ned, unsolicited, and most

---

2. Repetition.
3. Brace is first introduced in *The Character of a Native Georgian* as a satirist of the "beau in the presence of his mistress, the fop, the pedant, the purse-proud, the over-fastidious and sensitive," but also as what we would identify as a consummate put-on artist who plays his roles for the pleasure of his own performance and the observation of his audiences.

unexpectedly to me, said grace.—I knew full well that this was a prelude to some trick, I could not conjecture what. His explanation (except so much as I discovered myself) was, that he knew that one of us would be asked to say grace, and he thought he might as well save the good ladies the trouble of asking. The matter was, however, more fully explained just before the moment of our retiring to bed arrived. To this moment the conversation went round between the good ladies and ourselves, with mutual interest to all.— It was much enlivened by Ned, who was capable, as the reader has been heretofore informed, of making himself extremely agreeable in all company; and who, upon this occasion, was upon his very best behaviour. It was immediately after I had looked at my watch in token of my disposition to retire for the night, that the conversation turned upon marriages, happy and unhappy, strange, unequal, runaways, &c. Ned rose in the midst of it, and asked the landlady where we should sleep. She pointed to an open shed-room adjoining the room in which we were sitting, and separated from it by a log partition, between the spaces of which might be seen all that passed in the dining room; and so close to the fire-place of this apartment, that a loud whisper might be easily heard from one to the other.

"The strangest match," said Ned, resuming the conversation with a parson's gravity, "that ever I heard of, was that of George Scott and David Snow: two most excellent men, who became so much attached to each other that they actually got married——"

"The lackaday!" exclaimed one of the ladies.

"And was it really a fact?" enquired another.

"Oh, yes, ma'am," continued Ned; "I knew them very well, and often went to their house; and no people could have lived happier or managed better than they did. And they raised a lovely parcel of children—as fine a set as I ever saw, except their youngest son, Billy: he was a little wild, but, upon the whole, a right clever boy himself.—Come, friend Baldwin, we're setting up too late for travellers." So saying, Ned moved to the shed-room, and I followed him.

The ladies were left in silent amazement; and Ned, suspecting, doubtless, that they were listening for a laugh from our chamber as we entered it, continued the subject with unabated gravity, thus: "You knew those two men, didn't you?"

"Where did they live!" enquired I, not a little disposed to humor him.

"Why, they lived down there, on Cedar Creek, close by Jacob Denman's—Oh, I'll tell you who their daughter Nancy married— she married John Clarke—you knew *him* very well."

"Oh, yes," said I, "I knew John Clarke very well.—*His* wife *was* a most excellent woman."

"Well, the boys were just as clever, for boys, as she was for a girl, except Bill; and I never heard any thing *very* bad of him, unless it was his laughing in church; that put me more out of conceit of him than any thing I ever knew of him————Now, Baldwin, when I go to bed, I go to bed *to sleep*, and not to talk; and, therefore, from the time my head touches the pillow, there must be no more talking. Besides, we must take an early start to-morrow, and I'm tired." So saying, he hopped into his bed, and I obeyed his injunctions.

Before I followed his example, I could not resist the temptation of casting an eye through the cracks of the partition, to see the effect of Ned's wonderful story upon the kind ladies. Mrs. Barney (it is time to give their names) was setting in a thoughtful posture; her left hand supporting her chin, and her knee supporting her left elbow. Her countenance was that of one who suffers from a slight tooth-ache. Mrs. Shad leaned forward, resting her fore-arm on her knees, and looking into the fire as if she saw *groups of children* playing in it. Mrs. Reed, the landlady, who was the fattest of the three, was thinking and laughing alternately at short intervals. From my bed, it required but a slight change of position to see any one of the group at pleasure.

I was no sooner composed on my pillow, than the old ladies drew their chairs close together, and began the following colloquy in a low undertone, which rose as it progressed:

Mrs. Barney. Didn't that man say them was two *men* that got married to one another?

Mrs. Shad. It seemed to me so.

Mrs. Reed. Why to be sure he did.—I know he said so; for he said what their names was.

Mrs. B. Well, in the name o' sense, what did the man mean by saying they raised a fine pa'cel of children?

Mrs. R. Why, bless your heart and soul, honey! that's what I've been thinkin' about. It seems mighty curious to me some how or other. I can't study it out, no how.

Mrs. S. The man must be jokin', certainly.

Mrs. R. No, he wasn't jokin'; for I looked at him, and he was just as much in yearnest as any body I ever *seed*; and besides, no *Christian* man would tell such a story in that solemn way. And didn't you hear that other man say he knew their da'ter Nancy?

Mrs. S. But, la messy! Mis' Reed, it can't be so. It doesn't stand to reason; don't you know it don't?

Mrs. R. Well, I wouldn't think so; but it's hard for me some how to dispute a *Christian* man's word.

Mrs. B. I've been thinking the thing all over in my mind, and I reckon—now I don't say it is so, for I don't know nothing at all about it—but I reckon that one o' them men was a woman dress'd in men's clothes; for I've often hearn o' women doin' them things, and following their true-love to the wars, and bein' a waitin'-boy to 'em, and all sich.

Mrs. S. Well, may be it's some how in that way—but, la' me! 'twould o' been obliged to been found out; don't you know it would? Only think how many children she had. Now it stands to reason, that at some time or other it must have been found out.

Mrs. R. Well, I'm an old woman any how, and I reckon the good man won't mind what an old woman says to him; so bless the Lord, if I live to see the morning, I'll ask him about it.

I knew that Ned was surpassed by no man living in extricating himself from difficulties; but how he was to escape from this, with even tolerable credit to himself, I could not devise.

The ladies here took leave of Ned's marvellous story, drew themselves closely round the fire, lighted their pipes, and proceeded as follows:

Mrs. B. Jist before me and my old man was married, there was a gal name Nancy Mountcastle (puff——puff,) and she was a mighty likely gal——(puff) I know'd her mighty well—she dressed herself up in men's clothes—(puff, puff,) and followed Jemmy Darden from P'ankatank, in KING AND QUEEN—(puff) clean up to LOUDON.[4]

Mrs. S. (puff, puff, puff, puff, puff.) And did he marry her?

Mrs. B. (sighing deeply). No: Jemmy didn't marry her—pity he hadn't, poor thing.

Mrs. R. Well, I know'd a gal on Tar river,[5] done the same thing— (puff, puff, puff.) She followed Moses Rusher 'way down somewhere in the South State—(puff, puff.)

Mrs. S. (puff, puff, puff, puff.) And what did he do?

Mrs. R. Ah—(puff, puff,) Lord bless your soul, honey, I can't tell you what he did. Bad enough.

Mrs. B. Well, now it seems to me—I don't know much about it—but it seems to me men don't like to marry gals that take on that way. It looks like it puts 'em out o' concait[6] of 'em.

Mrs. S. I know'd one man that married a woman that followed him from Car'lina to this State; but she didn't dress herself in men's clothes. You both know 'em.—You know Simpson Trotty's sister and Rachæl's son Reuben. 'Twas him and his wife.

Mrs. R. and Mrs. B. Oh yes, I know 'em mighty well.

Mrs. S. Well, it was his wife—she followed him out to this State.

Mrs. B. I know'd 'em all mighty well. Her da'ter Lucy was the littlest teeny bit of a thing when it was born I ever did see. But they tell me that when I was born—now I don't know any thing about it myself—but the old folks used to tell me, that when I was born, they put me in a quart-mug, and mought o' covered me up in it.

4. Village on the Piankatank River, in King and Queen County, eastern Virginia; Loudon county is in northern Virginia. (The emphasis on county as a historical-geographical unit persists from English terminology.)
5. River in northeast North Carolina which flows southeast into the Pemlico.
6. Conceit, favorable opinion.

Mrs. S. The lackaday!

Mrs. R. What ailment did Lucy die of, Mis Barney?

Mrs. B. Why, first she took the ager[7] and fever, and took a 'bun-dance o' doctor's means for that. And then she got a powerful bad cough, and it kept gittin' worse and worse, till at last it turned into a consumption, and she jist nat'ly wasted away, till she was nothing but skin and bone, and she died; but, poor creater, she died mighty happy; and I think in my heart, she made the prettiest corpse, considerin', of anybody I most ever seed.

Mrs. R. and Mrs. S. Emph! (solemnly.)

Mrs. R. What did the doctors give her for the fever and ager?

Mrs. B. Oh, they gin' her a 'bundance o' truck[8]—I don't know what all; and none of 'em holp her at all. But at last she got over it, some how or other. If they'd have just gin' her a sweat o' bitter yerbs,[9] jist as the spell was comin' on, it would have cured her right away.

Mrs. R. Well, I reckon sheep-saffron[1] the onliest thing in nater for the ager.

Mrs. B. I've always hearn it was wonderful in hives, and measly ailments.

Mrs. R. Well, it's jist as good for an ager—it's a powerful sweat. Mrs. Clarkson told me, that her cousin Betsey's aunt Sally's Nancy was cured sound and well by it, of a hard shakin' ager.

Mrs. S. Why, you don't tell me so!

Mrs. R. Oh bless your heart, honey, it's every word true; for she told me so with her own mouth.

Mrs. S. "A hard, hard shakin' ager!!"

Mrs. R. Oh yes, honey, it's the truth.

Mrs. S. Well, I'm told that if you'll wrap the inside skin of an egg round your little finger, and go three days reg'lar to a young per-simmon,[2] and tie a string round it, and every day tie three knots in it, and then not go agin for three days, that the ager will leave you.

Mrs. B. I've often hearn o' that, but I don't know about it. Some people don't believe in it.

Mrs. S. Well, Davy Cooper's wife told me, she didn't believe in it; but she tried it, and it cured her sound and well.

Mrs. R. I've hearn of many folks bein' cured in that way. And what did they do for Lucy's cough, Mis' Barney.

Mrs. B. Oh, dear me, they gin' her a powerful chance o' truck. I reckon, first and last, she took at least a pint o' lodimy.[3]

Mrs. S. and Mrs. R. The law!

Mrs. S. Why that ought to have killed her, if nothing else. If

---

7. Ague.
8. Stuff.
9. Herbs.
1. Probably bastard saffron or safflower, used in medicine as a substitute for saffron.
2. I.e., a persimmon tree.
3. Laudanum, a tincture of opium.

they'd jist gin' her a little cumfry and alecampane,[4] stewed in honey, or sugar, or molasses, with a little lump o' mutton suet or butter in it: it would have cured her in two days sound and well.

Mrs. B. I've always counted cumfry and alecampane the lead of all yerbs for colds.

Mrs. S. Horehound and sugar's mazin good.

Mrs. B. Mighty good—mighty good.

Mrs. R. Powerful good. I take mightly to a sweat of sage-tea, in desperate bad colds.

Mrs. S. And so do I, Mis' Reed. Indeed I have a great leanin' to sweats of yerbs, in all ailments sich as colds, and rheumaty pains, and pleurisies, and sich—they're wonderful good. Old brother Smith came to my house from Bethany meeting, in a mighty bad way, with a cold, and cough, and his throat and nose all stopt up; seemed like it would 'most take his breath away, and it was dead o' winter, and I had nothin' but dried yerbs, sich as camomile, sage, penny-ryal, catmint, horehound, and sich;[5] so I put a hot rock to his feet, and made him a large bowl o' catmint tea, and I reckon he drank most two quarts of it through the night, and it put him in a mighty fine sweat, and loosened all the *phleem*, and opened all his head; and the next morning, says he to me, says he, sister Shad—you know he's a mighty kind spoken man, and always was so 'fore he joined society;[6] and the old man likes a joke yet right well, the old man does; but he's a mighty good man, and I think he prays with greater libity,[7] than most any one of his age I most ever seed—don't you think he does, Mis' Reed?

Mrs. R. Powerful.

Mrs. B. Who did he marry?

Mrs. S. Why, he married—stop, I'll tell you directly————— Why, what does make my old head forget so?

Mrs. B. Well, it seems to me I don't remember like I used to. Didn't he marry a Ramsbottom?

Mrs. R. No. Stay, I'll tell you who he married presently—Oh, stay! why I'll tell you who he married!—He married old daddy Johnny Hooer's da'ter, Mournin'.

Mrs. S. Why, la! messy on me, so he did!

Mrs. B. Why, did he marry a Hooer?

Mrs. S. Why, to be sure he did.—You knew Mournin'.

4. Comfrey: plant thought to cause co-agulation of the blood; its root is used in cough mixtures; elecampane, herb the root of which was used as a remedy in pulmonary diseases.
5. Camomile: plant the foliage and flower heads of which are strongly scented and are used as antispasmodics and as diaphoretics (drugs which increase perspiration); pennyryal, or pennyroyal: a mint used as a culicifuge (mosquito killer); catmint: catnip; horehound: a European mint whose hoary (whitish) leaves are used to make cough remedies and stomach tonics and also used as an anthelmintic (a drug used to kill or ex-pell intestinal worms).
6. Technical term from Congregational-ism; here, the communicants enrolled in a particular church.
7. Liberty, facility.

Mrs. B. Oh, mighty well; but I'd forgot that brother Smith married her: I really thought he married a Ramsbottom.

Mrs. R. Oh no, bless your soul, honey, he married Mournin'.

Mrs. B. Well, the law me, I'm clear beat!

Mrs. S. Oh, it's so, you may be sure it is.

Mrs. B. Emp, emph, emph, emph! And brother Smith married Mournin' Hooer! Well, I'm clear put out! Seems to me I'm gittin' mighty forgetful, some how.

Mrs. S. Oh yes, he married Mournin', and I saw her when she joined society.

Mrs. B. Why, you don't tell me so!

Mrs. S. Oh, it's the truth. She didn't join till after he was married, and the church took on mightily about his marrying one out of society. But after she joined they all got satisfied.

Mrs. R. Why, la! me, the seven stars[8] is 'way over here!

Mrs. B. Well, let's light our pipes, and take a short smoke, and go to bed. How did you come on raisin' chickens, this year, Mis' Shad?

Mrs. S. La messy, honey! I have had mighty bad luck. I had the prettiest pa'sel you most ever seed till the varment took to killin' 'em.

Mrs. R. and Mrs. B. The varment!!

Mrs. S. Oh dear, yes. The hawk catched a powerful sight of them; and ahen the varment took to 'em and nat'ly took 'em fore and aft, bodily, till they left most none at all hardly. Sucky counted 'em up t'other day, and there warn't but thirty-nine, she said, countin' in the old speckle hen's chickens that jist come off of her nest.

Mrs. R. and Mrs. B. Humph-h-h-h!

Mrs. R. Well, I've had bad luck too. Billy's hound-dogs broke up most all my nests.

Mrs. B. Well, so they did me, Mis' Reed. I always did despise a hound-dog upon the face of yea'th.[9]

Mrs. R. Oh, they're the bawllinest, squallinest, thievishest things ever was about one; but Billy will have 'em, and I think in my soul his old Troup's the beat of all creaters I ever seed in all my born days a suckin' o' hen's eggs—He's clean most broke me up entirely.

Mrs. S. The lackaday!

Mrs. R. And them that was hatched out, some took to takin' the gaps, and some the pip,[1] and one ailment or other, till they most all died.

Mrs. S. Well I reckon there must be somethin' in the season this

---

8. The Big Dipper.
9. Earth.
1. Gaps: disease of fowls characterized by gaping (yawning), caused by the gapeworm, a parasitic nematode infesting the trachea and bronchi; pip: roup, disease of fowls in which scales form on the dry tip of the tongue.

year that an't good for fowls: for Larkin Goodman's brother Jimmie's wife aunt Penny, told me, she lost most all her fowls with different sorts of ailments, the like of which she never seed before— They'd jist go 'long lookin' right well, and tilt right over backwards, (Mrs. B. The law!) and die right away, (Mrs. R. Did you ever!) with a sort o' somethin' like the blind staggers.

Mrs. B. *and* Mrs. R. Messy on me!

Mrs. B. I reckon they must have eat[2] somethin' didn't agree with them.

Mrs. S. No, they didn't, for she fed 'em every mornin' with her own hand.

Mrs. B. Well, it's mighty curious!

A short pause ensued, which was broken by Mrs. Barney, with— "And brother Smith married Mournin' Hooer!" It came like an opiate upon my senses, and I dropt asleep.

The next morning, when we rose from our beds, we found the good ladies sitting round the fire just as I left them, for they rose long before us.

Mrs. Braney was just in the act of ejaculating, "And brother Smith married Mournin' "—when she was interrupted by our entry into the dining room. We were hardly seated, before Mrs. Reed began to verify her promise. "Mr. ———," said she to Ned, "didn't you say last night, that them was two *men* that got married to one another?"

"Yes, madam," said Ned.

"And didn't you say they raised a fine pa'cel of children?"

"Yes, madam, except Billy.—I said, you know, that he was a little wild."

"Well, yes; I know you said Billy wasn't as clever as the rest of them. But we old women were talking about it last night after you went out, and none of us could make it out, how they could have children; and I said, I reckoned you wouldn't mind an old woman's chat; and, therefore, that I would ask you how it could be? I suppose you won't mind telling an old woman how it was."

"Certainly not, madam. They were both widowers before they fell in love with each other and got married."

"The lack-a-day! I wonder none of us thought o' that. And they had children before they got married?"

"Yes, madam; they had none afterwards that I heard of."

We were here informed that our horses were in waiting, and we bade the good ladies farewell.

BALDWIN.
1835

---

2. Past tense, pronounced to rhyme with "yet."

WILLIAM CULLEN BRYANT
1794–1878

William Cullen Bryant was born in the backwoods of Massachusetts, at Cummington, but his father was a physician who loved the classics, and Cullen, as the boy was called, was trained early in Greek and Latin. For religion he was taught a harsh Calvinism which held that the Fall of Man had brought about the Fall of Nature as well. But Bryant's first published poem was political, not about nature and religion: when he wrote an anti-Jefferson lampoon, *The Embargo*, his Federalist father printed it as a pamphlet (1808). Bryant entered Williams College in 1810 but dropped out after a few months with the expectation of entering Yale. Dr. Bryant could not afford that expense, and instead Cullen read for the law, being admitted to practice in 1815. Meanwhile, in 1813 or 1814, Bryant wrote the first, shorter version of *Thanatopsis*, the poem by which he is best remembered. Since his early teens Bryant had been reading the melancholy and sometimes scarifying meditations of the British "graveyard poets" of the previous decades, especially Robert Blair (*The Grave*), Thomas Gray (*Elegy Written in a Country Churchyard*), Bishop Beilby Porteus (*Death*), and various poems by Henry Kirke White. Such poems by their luxurious sonorousness tempered the Calvinism instilled in the boy, but they often poeticized religious doctrine, as in Blair's account of the resurrection at the Judgment Day: "the time draws on / When not a single spot of burial-earth, / Whether on land, or on the spacious sea, / But must give back its long-committed dust / Inviolate" (*The Grave*). In 1810 or soon afterward Bryant read *Lyrical Ballads* and responded strongly to Wordsworth's near-pantheistic view of Nature. *Thanatopsis* as published in the *North American Review* in 1817 is nondoctrinally meditative. The fuller version of 1821 concludes with a fervent injunction to trust in something or someone who remains unspecified: Bryant's Calvinistic earnestness was outliving his commitment to particular doctrines. (Symptomatically, a reference to the Fall of Nature in the first version of *The Prairies*, 1834, was later removed.) *Thanatopsis* won Bryant immediate acknowledgment in 1817, but a full-time career as a poet was economically impossible. In 1820, the year his father died, Bryant was appointed as justice of the peace in Berkshire County. Early in 1821 he married Frances Fairchild in Great Barrington, Massachusetts, and later that year published a very slim volume of *Poems*.

Stirred by the conflict between his literary ambition and his need to support his family, Bryant in 1825 chanced a move to New York City as an editor of the *New-York Review and Atheneum Magazine*. He was welcomed as a literary celebrity and quickly fitted into metropolitan life, becoming an early member of James Fenimore Cooper's Bread and Cheese Club. His magazine failed, as almost all periodicals did at that time, but Bryant stayed on in New York as editorial assistant on the *Evening Post* (1826), then soon became part owner and editor-in-chief. Bryant was not immune to the pettier temptations of the then brawling occupation of journalism, but over the decades he made the *Evening Post* one of the most respected newspapers in the country, mainly through editorials in which he argued out his

position on many momentous issues. A deeply committed Jacksonian Democrat, despite his youthful Federalism, Bryant rarely let party loyalty inter-
fere with principle. He led the antislavery Free-Soil movement within the
Democratic party as long as this seemed a feasible way of achieving his
ends, then helped to form the Republican party. In 1860 he was an influential advocate of Abraham Lincoln.

As he prospered with his newspaper, Bryant became a great traveler, at
home and abroad, and through his letters to the *Evening Post* he helped
to shape a sense of the world for his countrypeople. *Letters of a Traveller*
appeared in 1850; *Letters of a Traveller, Second Series*, in 1859; and *Letters
from the East* (that is, the Mid-East) in 1869. His community service took
many forms, most tangibly in his campaign for the creation of Central Park.
His private life was happy. In 1844 he moved his family to a fine old farm-
house on the Sound in then rural Long Island, and for many years relieved
his strenuous urban activity with peaceful respites at his estate, Cedarmere.
Left a widower in 1866, Bryant continued to work at the *Evening Post*.
Blessed with patriarchal fame and great wealth, as well as astonishing
health, which owed much to a daily set of vigorous exercises, Bryant in
his seventies undertook the remarkably ambitious task of translating Homer.
His version of the *Iliad* was published in 1870, and that of the *Odyssey*
two years later. Together with the 1876 printing of his *Poems* (a new
accumulation of many old and a few new verses), these translations
crowned his career.

Bryant died of the consequences of a fall suffered after he gave a speech
at the unveiling of a statue of the Italian patriot Joseph Mazzini in Central
Park. In New York City flags were lowered to half mast, and he was
mourned throughout the country as a great poet and editor.

Bryant had, in fact, written very little poetry; his translations from Homer
are many times as long as his own verses. And his poems, early and late, are
for the most part limited to a few subjects treated in ways that soon become predictable. His collected poetry consists of accurately rhymed or
sonorously unrhymed blank verse on landscapes, flora, meteorological phenomena, historical personages and events, friends, Indian legends, and a
few other topics. Yet the country's response showed plainly that he was
providing what it needed at a time of national self-consciousness about the
scarcity of talented poets—a loftiness of diction that at best seemed securely Miltonic, a way of making American landscapes and subjects as
worthy of celebration as Old World scenes and topics, and a moral stance
which blended ecumenical vagueness with didactic earnestness. Bryant's
fame as a poet was accurately analyzed by his early biographer, W. A.
Bradley: "He appeared much more remarkable to his early contemporaries
than he ever can to us, because of the contrast which he presented with
what had gone before. And later, after a period in which he suffered somewhat of an eclipse through the rise of new schools and new poets to contest with him the palm of supremacy, his great age, the traditions of an
earlier day which he represented, his personality which so perfectly embodied the prophetic and seer-like aspect of the poetic ideal, and finally
local pride in the possession of a poet whom New York could produce to
oppose the claims of its rival, Boston, to literary supremacy,—all these
tended to create a regard for Bryant that was rather personal than literary."

On the strength of a few—mainly very early—poems and a notable public life, Bryant passed into what seemed, to his own time, literary immortality. Only as historians describe his part in the great political issues of his time is he passing into a perhaps truer immortality as a man who may not have been a great American poet but who led a great American life.

Thanatopsis[1]

To him who in the love of Nature holds
Communion with her visible forms, she speaks
A various language; for his gayer hours
She has a voice of gladness, and a smile
And eloquence of beauty, and she glides   5
Into his darker musings, with a mild
And gentle sympathy, that steals away
Their sharpness, ere he is aware. When thoughts
Of the last bitter hour come like a blight
Over thy spirit, and sad images   10
Of the stern agony, and shroud, and pall,
And breathless darkness, and the narrow house,
Make thee to shudder, and grow sick at heart;—
Go forth under the open sky, and list
To Nature's teachings, while from all around—   15
Earth and her waters, and the depths of air,—
Comes a still voice—Yet a few days, and thee
The all-beholding sun shall see no more
In all his course; nor yet in the cold ground,
Where thy pale form was laid, with many tears,   20
Nor in the embrace of ocean shall exist
Thy image. Earth, that nourished thee, shall claim
Thy growth, to be resolv'd to earth again;
And, lost each human trace, surrend'ring up
Thine individual being, shalt thou go   25
To mix forever with the elements,
To be a brother to th' insensible rock
And to the sluggish clod, which the rude swain[2]
Turns with his share, and treads upon. The oak
Shall send his roots abroad, and pierce thy mould.   30
Yet not to thy eternal resting place
Shalt thou retire alone—nor couldst thou wish
Couch more magnificent. Thou shalt lie down
With patriarchs of the infant world—with kings
The powerful of the earth—the wise, the good,   35
Fair forms, and hoary seers of ages past,
All in one mighty sepulchre.—The hills

1. The text is that of the first full printing, in Bryant's *Poems* (Cambridge: Hilliard and Metcalf, 1821). The title ("meditation on death") was supplied by an editor for the central section of the poem (lines 17–73) when that section was printed in the *North American Review* (September, 1817).
2. Farmer; "share": plowshare.

Rock-ribb'd and ancient as the sun,—the vales
Stretching in pensive quietness between;
The venerable woods—rivers that move   40
In majesty, and the complaining brooks
That make the meadows green; and pour'd round all,
Old ocean's grey and melancholy waste,—
Are but the solemn decorations all
Of the great tomb of man. The golden sun,   45
The planets, all the infinite host of heaven,
Are shining on the sad abodes of death,
Through the still lapse of ages. All that tread
The globe are but a handful to the tribes
That slumber in its bosom.—Take the wings   50
Of morning—and the Barcan desert[3] pierce,
Or lose thyself in the continuous woods
Where rolls the Oregan, and hears no sound,
Save his own dashings—yet—the dead are there,
And millions in those solitudes, since first   55
The flight of years began, have laid them down
In their last sleep—the dead reign there alone.—
So shalt thou rest—and what if thou shalt fall
Unnoticed by the living—and no friend
Take note of thy departure? All that breathe   60
Will share thy destiny. The gay will laugh
When thou art gone, the solemn brood of care
Plod on, and each one as before will chase
His favourite phantom; yet all these shall leave
Their mirth and their employments, and shall come,   65
And make their bed with thee. As the long train
Of ages glide away, the sons of men,
The youth in life's green spring, and he who goes
In the full strength of years, matron, and maid,
The bow'd with age, the infant in the smiles   70
And beauty of its innocent age cut off,—
Shall one by one be gathered to thy side,
By those, who in their turn shall follow them.
So live, that when thy summons comes to join
The innumerable caravan, that moves   75
To the pale realms of shade, where each shall take
His chamber in the silent halls of death,
Thou go not, like the quarry-slave at night,
Scourged to his dungeon, but sustain'd and sooth'd
By an unfaltering trust, approach thy grave,   80
Like one who wraps the drapery of his couch
About him, and lies down to pleasant dreams.

c. 1814   1821

3. In Barca (northeast Libya); "Oregan" (early variant spelling of Oregon): now the Columbia River. (For his distant ex- amples Bryant ranges across the Atlantic and then westward across the North American continent.)

To a Waterfowl[1]

Whither, 'midst falling dew,
While glow the heavens with the last steps of day,
Far, through their rosy depths, dost thou pursue
Thy solitary way?

Vainly the fowler's eye   5
Might mark thy distant flight to do thee wrong,
As, darkly painted on the crimson sky,
Thy figure floats along.

Seek'st thou the plashy[2] brink
Of weedy lake, or marge of river wide,   10
Or where the rocking billows rise and sink
On the chafed ocean side?

There is a Power whose care
Teaches thy way along that pathless coast,—
The desert and illimitable air,—   15
Lone wandering, but not lost.

All day thy wings have fann'd
At that far height, the cold thin atmosphere;
Yet stoop not, weary, to the welcome land,
Though the dark night is near.   20

And soon that toil shall end,
Soon shalt thou find a summer home, and rest,
And scream among thy fellows; reeds shall bend
Soon o'er thy sheltered nest.

Thou'rt gone, the abyss of heaven   25
Hath swallowed up thy form; yet, on my heart
Deeply hath sunk the lesson thou hast given,
And shall not soon depart.

He, who, from zone to zone,
Guides through the boundless sky thy certain flight,   30
In the long way that I must tread alone,
Will lead my steps aright.

1815   1821

1. The text is that of the printing in   water, Mass., during July, 1815.
Poems (Cambridge: Hilliard and Metcalf,   2. Marshy (plash: pool).
1821); the poem was drafted in Bridge-

The Prairies[1]

These are the Gardens of the Desert, these
The unshorn fields, boundless and beautiful,
And fresh as the young earth, ere man had sinned—
The prairies. I behold them for the first,
And my heart swells, while the dilated sight   5
Takes in the encircling vastness. Lo! they stretch
In airy undulations, far away,
As if the ocean, in his gentlest swell,
Stood still, with all his rounded billows fixed,
And motionless for ever.—Motionless?—   10
No—they are all unchained again. The clouds
Sweep over with their shadows, and beneath
The surface rolls and fluctuates to the eye;
Dark hollows seem to glide along and chase
The sunny ridges. Breezes of the South!   15
Who toss the golden and the flame-like flowers,
And pass the prairie-hawk that, poised on high,
Flaps his broad wings, yet moves not—ye have played
Among the palms of Mexico and vines
Of Texas, and have crisped the limpid brooks   20
That from the fountains of Sonora[2] glide
Into the calm Pacific—have ye fanned
A nobler or a lovelier scene than this?
Man hath no part in all this glorious work:
The hand that built the firmament hath heaved   25
And smoothed these verdant swells, and sown their slopes
With herbage, planted them with island groves,
And hedged them round with forests. Fitting floor
For this magnificent temple of the sky—
With flowers whose glory and whose multitude   30
Rival the constellations! The great heavens
Seem to stoop down upon the scene in love,—
A nearer vault, and of a tenderer blue,
Than that which bends above the eastern hills.
   As o'er the verdant waste I guide my steed,   35
Among the high rank grass that sweeps his sides,
The hollow beating of his footstep seems
A sacrilegious sound. I think of those
Upon whose rest he tramples. Are they here—
The dead of other days!—and did the dust   40
Of these fair solitudes once stir with life
And burn with passion? Let the mighty mounds[3]

1. From the first printing in *Poems* (Boston: Russell, Odiorne, and Metcalf, 1834). Bryant wrote the poem over a year after visiting his brothers in Illinois during 1832. Later he removed the reference to the Fall of Man by substituting this as the third line: "For which the speech of England has no name—" (alluding to the fact that "prairies" was adopted from the French explorers and trappers).
2. River in northwest Mexico.
3. The burial mounds common in Illinois; Bryant follows a contemporary theory that they were built by a race earlier than the American Indians.

That overlook the rivers, or that rise
In the dim forest crowded with old oaks,
Answer. A race, that long has passed away, 45
Built them;—a disciplined and populous race
Heaped, with long toil, the earth, while yet the Greek
Was hewing the Pentelicus[4] to forms
Of symmetry, and rearing on its rock
The glittering Parthenon. These ample fields 50
Nourished their harvests, here their herds were fed,
When haply by their stalls the bison lowed,
And bowed his maned shoulder to the yoke.
All day this desert murmured with their toils,
Till twilight blushed and lovers walked, and wooed 55
In a forgotten language, and old tunes,
From instruments of unremembered form,
Gave the soft winds a voice. The red man came—
The roaming hunter tribes, warlike and fierce,
And the mound-builders vanished from the earth. 60
The solitude of centuries untold
Has settled where they dwelt. The prairie wolf
Hunts in their meadows, and his fresh dug den
Yawns by my path. The gopher mines the ground
Where stood their swarming cities. All is gone— 65
All—save the piles of earth that hold their bones—
The platforms where they worshipped unknown gods—
The barriers which they builded from the soil
To keep the foe at bay—till o'er the walls
The wild beleaguerers broke, and, one by one, 70
The strong holds of the plain were forced, and heaped
With corpses. The brown vultures of the wood
Flocked to those vast uncovered sepulchres,
And sat, unscared and silent, at their feast.
Haply some solitary fugitive, 75
Lurking in marsh and forest, till the sense
Of desolation and of fear became
Bitterer than death, yielded himself to die.
Man's better nature triumphed. Kindly words
Welcomed and soothed him; the rude conquerors 80
Seated the captive with their chiefs. He chose
A bride among their maidens. And at length
Seemed to forget,—yet ne'er forgot,—the wife
Of his first love, and her sweet little ones
Butchered, amid their shrieks, with all his race. 85
    Thus change the forms of being. Thus arise
Races of living things, glorious in strength,
And perish, as the quickening breath of God
Fills them, or is withdrawn. The red man too—
Has left the blooming wilds he ranged so long, 90

4. Greek mountain from which a fine white marble was quarried, including that used in building the Parthenon, the temple of Athena on the Acropolis in Athens.

And, nearer to the Rocky Mountains, sought
A wider hunting ground. The beaver builds
No longer by these streams, but far away,
On waters whose blue surface ne'er gave back
The white man's face—among Missouri's springs,   95
And pools whose issues swell the Oregan,[5]
He rears his little Venice.[6] In these plains
The bison feeds no more. Twice twenty leagues
Beyond remotest smoke of hunter's camp,
Roams the majestic brute, in herds that shake   100
The earth with thundering steps—yet here I meet
His ancient footprints stamped beside the pool.
     Still this great solitude is quick with life.
Myriads of insects, gaudy as the flowers
They flutter over, gentle quadrupeds,   105
And birds, that scarce have learned the fear of man
Are here, and sliding reptiles of the ground,
Startlingly beautiful. The graceful deer
Bounds to the wood at my approach. The bee,
A more adventurous colonist than man,   110
With whom he came across the eastern deep,
Fills the savannas with his murmurings,
And hides his sweets, as in the golden age,
Within the hollow oak. I listen long
To his domestic hum, and think I hear   115
The sound of that advancing multitude
Which soon shall fill these deserts. From the ground
Comes up the laugh of children, the soft voice
Of maidens, and the sweet and solemn hymn
Of Sabbath worshippers. The low of herds   120
Blends with the rustling of the heavy grain
Over the dark-brown furrows. All at once
A fresher wind sweeps by, and breaks my dream,
And I am in the wilderness alone.

1833   1834

5. The Columbia River.   6. I.e., builds a city in the water.

RALPH WALDO EMERSON
1803–1882

Emerson was a man who had no personal excesses such as doomed Poe, no
mysterious decade such as lent glamor to Hawthorne, no exotic adventures
such as Melville founded his career upon, no dramatic struggles for artistic
recognition such as Whitman waged, no local notoriety as a crank and
extremist such as Thoreau acquired. He led a respectable, conventional life
as a family man and decent, solid citizen. Yet in both literature and philosophy this man of conventional life became the American writer with
whom every other significant writer of his time had to come to terms. At

one extreme, Melville reacted so hostilely to the optimistic side of Emerson's thought that he satirized him in *The Confidence-Man* as a great American philosophical con man. At the other extreme, without Emerson's inspiration the writings of Thoreau are all but unthinkable and Whitman's great poetry might never have been written. Emerson's persisting influence upon twentieth-century American writers is evident in astonishing permutations, on writers as diverse as Theodore Dreiser, Robert Frost, Wallace Stevens, his namesake Ralph Waldo Ellison, and A. R. Ammons.

Emerson was born in Boston, Massachusetts, on May 25, 1803, son of a Unitarian minister and the second of five surviving boys. He was eight years old when the death of his father left the family to the meager charity of the church. Determined to send four sons to Harvard (another son, mentally retarded, was cared for by rural relatives), Emerson's mother kept a succession of boardinghouses. Emerson grew up in the city, protected from the lower-class "rough boys" in his early years and sent at nine to the Boston Public Latin School. So poorly clothed that two brothers had to make do at times with one coat, the boys were encouraged by a brilliant eccentric aunt, Mary Moody Emerson, to regard deprivation as ecstatic self-denial. Emerson showed no remarkable literary promise either in his early prose exercises or in his adolescent satires in imitation of Alexander Pope. His Harvard years, 1817–21, were frugal, industrious, and undistinguished. After graduation he served, he said, as "a hopeless Schoolmaster," unable to impose his authority upon his pupils. Escaping into the study of theology in 1825, he began preaching in October, 1826, and early in 1829 was ordained as junior pastor of Boston's Second Church where Increase Mather and Cotton Mather had preached a century and more before.

Biographers have pointed out that Emerson's dedication to the ministry at the age of twenty-one was to a life of public service through eloquence, not to a life of preserving and disseminating religious dogma. In any case, Boston was no longer a Puritan stronghold. Boston Unitarianism, led in the 1820s by William Ellery Channing, still accepted the Bible as the revelation of God's intentions for humankind, but no longer held that human beings were innately depraved or that Jesus was more than the highest type of mankind. Emerson's skepticism toward Christianity was strengthened by his exposure to the German "higher criticism," which heretically interpreted Biblical miracles in the light of comparable stories in other cultures. Emerson was gradually developing a faith greater in individual moral sentiment than in revealed religion. Around 1830–31 his reading of Samuel Taylor Coleridge's *Aids to Reflection* provided him with a basic terminology in his postulation of an intuitive "Reason," which is superior to the mere "Understanding," or ordinary rationality operating on the materials of sense experience. Undogmatic about Christianity as he became, Emerson nevertheless seems to have undergone an intense religious experience around these same years, 1830 or 1831, something comparable to the sweet inward burning which the Calvinist Jonathan Edwards had delighted in describing. Emerson's knowledge of this emotion is clear from his later essay *The Over-Soul*, but he felt no impulse to account for it according to the tenets of a particular church.

In the year of his ordination, Emerson married a young woman from New Hampshire, Ellen Tucker. She died sixteen months later of tuberculosis, the disease which had already infected Emerson and others in his

family. Early in 1832 Emerson notified his church that he had become
so skeptical of the validity of the Lord's Supper that he could no longer
administer it. A few months later he resigned, keeping the sober good will
of many in his flock, and embarked on a leisurely European tour which
constituted a postgraduate education in art and natural science. In the
custom of that time, he called upon literary men, meeting Walter Savage
Landor in Italy, listening to Coleridge converse with such cogent volubility
that he seemed to be reading aloud, and hearing William Wordsworth
recite his poetry. Most important for his intellectual growth and for his
reputation was his visit to Thomas Carlyle at Craigenputtock in Scotland,
beginning a lifelong alliance in which each helped to publish and create an
audience for the other.

In 1834 Emerson drifted into a quiet retreat at Concord, Massachusetts,
where generations of his ancestors had been ministers. That year he received the first installment of his wife's legacy. Soon he was assured of
more than a thousand dollars annually, enough so that he did not need to
hold a steady job again. He continued to preach occasionally, and began
lecturing at New England lyceums, the public halls which brought a variety
of speakers and performers both to the cities and to smaller towns. In 1835,
after a prudent courtship, he married Lydia Jackson of Plymouth, having
explained to her his work and the conditions under which he must pursue
it. One condition was that he must live in rural Concord rather than move
into the bustle of Plymouth. His assessment of his accomplishments was
focused on his being a "poet," even when writing prose: "I am a poet, of a
low class without doubt yet a poet. That is my nature & vocation. My singing be sure is very 'husky,' & is for the most part in prose. Still am I a poet
in the sense of a perceiver & dear lover of the harmonies that are in the
soul & in matter, & specially of the correspondences between these & those.
A sunset, a forest, a snow storm, a certain river-view, are more to me than
many friends & do ordinarily divide my day with books. Wherever I go
therefore I guard & study my rambling propensities with a care that is
ridiculous to people, but to me is the care of my high calling."

At this time, before *Nature* was published and before his essays were
written, Emerson may well have hoped to gain his literary fame by his
verse, and in fact the poems he had written thus far were not so husky or
unmelodious as he implied. His main problem as a poet was not the huski-
ness he complained of but the more serious failure first to arrive at, then
to apply, his great insight: that in true poetry the thought creates its own
meter, the content creates its own form. Emerson's first little book, *Nature*
(1836), did not establish him as an important American writer (for one
thing, it was anonymous, and not every reviewer was in on what became an
open secret around Boston), but it did confirm his future as a prose writer,
however poetic that prose might be. One reviewer noticed the influence of
Wordsworth and Coleridge in the tendency to "look on Nature with the
spiritual eye," so that one creates Nature in perceiving it. Another found
that the author had adopted "the Berkeleyan system" of philosophy which
denies "the outward and real existence" of Nature, and noticed also that
the new school of philosophy called Transcendentalism was "a revival of
the Old Platonic school" in rejecting a scientific attitude toward Nature.
Yet another reviewer stressed the influence of Wordsworth's *Immortality*
ode and of Coleridge's *Dejection: An Ode* in the author's concept of Nature. Another hailed the book as revealing a mind cognate with Thomas

Carlyle's, "however inferior in energies and influences," and defined the philosophy of the book as "an Idealistic Pantheism" like that of Carlyle's *Sartor Resartus* (1834). A Swedenborgian writer in London took *Nature* as self-evidently the work of an American Swedenborgian, especially in "the beautiful and heart-cheering doctrine of correspondences" between Nature's moods and man's. As all these reviewers understood, *Nature* was not a Christian book but one influenced by a range of idealistic philosophies, ancient and very modern, Transcendentalism being merely the latest name for an old way of thinking. Although the favorable reception of the book in England encouraged some American journalists, hitherto skeptical, to take Emerson more seriously as a force in modern thought, Emerson's immediate reward was having the book become the unofficial manifesto for "the Symposium" or the Transcendental Club, which held its first meeting only a few days after *Nature* was published.

The Transcendental Club had influences, on Emerson and on the intellectual life of the country, out of proportion to its small membership and its short life of four years. It was composed mainly of ministers who were repelled by John Locke's views that the mind is a passive receiver of sense impressions and enthusiastic about Coleridge's alternative view of the mind as creative in perception. Among the members were the educator Bronson Alcott, the abolitionist and Unitarian minister Theodore Parker, and the Unitarian minister Orestes A. Brownson (later a major force in American Catholicism). Such friends were welcome, for during the early 1830s deaths broke up the close-knit band of Emerson brothers. Emerson himself had gone South to recover from tuberculosis in 1826–27; weakened by the same disease, Edward Emerson became mentally deranged in 1827 and died in 1834; and the youngest brother, Charles, died in 1836. There was compensation for Emerson in the circle of admirers who began forming about him at the time of his second marriage and the publication of *Nature*. Alcott, Margaret Fuller, and others sought him out, some paying him frequent and prolonged visits or even settling in Concord to be near him.

Nature reached a smaller audience than did many of his lectures, which were often reported by newspapers in substantial part; his formal Harvard addresses to the Phi Beta Kappa Society in 1837 on the American scholar and to the Divinity School graduates in 1838 on the state of Christianity were both printed as pamphlets, according to the custom of the time. The second of these speeches occasioned a brief, virulent series of attacks in the press for its heresies, giving Emerson a notoriety that barred him from speaking at Harvard for three decades. His unsigned contributions to the Transcendentalists' magazine *The Dial* did not enhance his reputation; indeed, he sometimes was attacked in newspapers as the author of Alcott's *Orphic Sayings*, which jocular contemporaries took as the ultimate of transcendental gibberish. Only with the publication of *Essays* (1841) did Emerson's lasting reputation begin. Far more than *Nature*, this book was directed to a popular audience. The essays had been tried out, in whole or large part, in his lectures, so that their final form was shaped by the responses of many audiences.

By the early 1840s, Emerson's life had settled into its enduring routine. He gave intermittent lectures in Boston and made lecture tours in the Northeast and, later, in the Middle Atlantic states to supplement the income from his legacy. Early in 1842 his first son, Waldo, died at the age of five, the last of the untimely deaths in Emerson's immediate family; after that Emerson devoted himself more and more to the personal problems of his circle of family and friends. His editing of *The Dial* from 1842 till 1844, for instance, was undertaken mainly to support his friends, especially Margaret Fuller. He worked steadily at a succession of essays, usually derived from his extensive journals by way of one or more intervening lectures. *Essays* (1841) was followed by *Essays: Second Series* (1844). The second collection demonstrated even more thoroughly than the first that Emerson's intellect had sharpened in the years since *Nature*. In *The Poet* especially his grappling with aesthetic problems was more incisive; he spoke from practical experience as well as theoretical speculation in defining the present state of literature in America, and he brilliantly foretold the nature of the great national poets to come. In *Experience* and other essays he resolutely and realistically faced the conflict between idealism and ordinary life. The deferential minister and the once-tentative lecturer had become a confident American prophet. Emerson slowly gained recognition for his poems, which he collected at the end of 1846. A second trip to Europe (1847–48) capped his secure middle age. He became something of a country squire, buying up many pieces of property in and around Concord. Always aware that there was a certain coldness in his disposition, he deliberately set out to make himself into a more sociable man, taking part in Boston club life (and smoking cigars to mask his diffidence). As his reputation expanded, he widened his lecture tours into the Midwest. His newer books, among them *Representative Men* (1849) and *Conduct of Life* (1860), were less forceful than his earlier ones, though they sold better because of the enlarged market and his established fame. After long resisting attempts by reformers to gain his support for various social issues, Emerson became a fervent advocate in the 1850s for abolitionism, though his efforts were too late and too local to make him a national leader. The rest of Emerson's writing, like the rest of his life, was a slow anticlimax to the intellectual ferment of the years between the mid-1830s and the mid-1840s, though it was only during these later decades that his earlier work first won general recognition. Emerson's memory began to fail more than ten years before his death, and he declined into a benign senility during which the English-speaking world, and even many who read him in translation, continued to honor the intellectual liberator that he had been in his middle life.

Although Emerson's contemporary reputation rested on his essays, he had all along been writing another masterpiece, his journals, which were not published in full until the 1960s and 1970s under the title *Journals and Miscellaneous Notebooks*. It will take time before readers fully grasp the importance of these writings as the historical record of a response to people and events, the most thorough documentation we possess of the growth of a nineteenth-century American writer, and the remarkable account of a spiritual life. A large number of important journal entries is reprinted here, interspersed with some of Emerson's more memorable letters so as to present a picture of his day-to-day life.

A critic said that Emerson wanted to get his whole philosophy into each essay; more than that, he got as much of it as he could into everything he wrote. Emerson's point of view may shift from one pole of a subject to the other even within a single work, for his mind moved like that of a dramatist who embodies felt or imagined moods in various characters, but the subject remains Emersonian. In this there is challenge for the new reader to find pattern in diversity. And for those who have already cherished Emerson through the various stages of life there is the warmth of familiarity, however unsettling this mild-mannered man always remains to any receptive reader.

Nature Since its anonymous publication (Boston: James Munroe and Company, 1836), a little book paid for by the author himself, *Nature* has been recognized as a major document in American Romanticism and Transcendentalism. Merton M. Sealts, Jr., and Alfred R. Ferguson in their *Emerson's "Nature"—Origin, Growth, Meaning* point out "how wide the divergence has been over how to read such a work—whether as doctrine or mysticism, philosophy or poetry." In an earlier Norton anthology, *Eight American Writers* (1963), one of the most conscientious Emersonians, the late Stephen E. Whicher, took the book as "an audacious attempt to rescue nature from the natural scientists and to sketch instead a human or poetical science"; he took Emerson's question "To what end is nature?" as asking how nature can help "to restore our confidence and release our powers, as the fact of historical religion once did." Underlying many passages in *Nature* is the defensiveness of a man who has chosen to be a thinker rather than taking what his contemporaries would have seen as an active role in affairs, a defensiveness, in the sexist terminology which he regularly employed, against the charge of effeminacy. For modern readers there is inescapable pain at Emerson's confidence that wild nature is inexhaustible and invulnerable and at the undreamed-of consequences of the belief that nature is created for man's benefit.

I have drawn on the Sealts-Ferguson list of emendations for the correction of a few obvious typographical errors, and have followed Sealts and Ferguson in two corrections Emerson made in presentation copies at the beginning of Chapter 4, but I have left several oddities of punctuation, spelling, and rough-and-ready subject-verb agreements. The text is thus the one Emerson offered to his circle of American and British friends in the fall of 1836 as his first bid for a national and international reputation.

The Sealts-Ferguson volume is indispensable to serious study of *Nature* for, among other virtues, its printing of source passages in the Harvard University Press edition of *The Journals and Miscellaneous Notebooks of Ralph Waldo Emerson* (abbreviated here *JMN*). I have given the journal and lecture citations only when they reveal Emerson's literary borrowings (which are as often as not second hand, a quotation from a Greek philosopher in a work by Samuel Taylor Coleridge, for example).

Nature

> "Nature is but an image or imitation of wisdom, the last thing of the soul; nature being a thing which doth only do, but not know."
>
> *Plotinus*[1]

Introduction

Our age is retrospective. It builds the sepulchres of the fathers. It writes biographies, histories, and criticism. The foregoing genera-

---

1. Emerson found the motto from the Roman philosopher Plotinus (205?–270?) in his copy of Ralph Cudworth's *The* *True Intellectual System of the Universe* (1820).

tions beheld God and nature face to face; we, through their eyes. Why should not we also enjoy an original relation to the universe? Why should not we have a poetry and philosophy of insight and not of tradition, and a religion by revelation to us, and not the history of theirs? Embosomed for a season in nature, whose floods of life stream around and through us, and invite us by the powers they supply, to action proportioned to nature, why should we grope among the dry bones of the past,[2] or put the living generation into masquerade out of its faded wardrobe? The sun shines to-day also. There is more wool and flax in the fields. There are new lands, new men, new thoughts. Let us demand our own works and laws and worship.

Undoubtedly we have no questions to ask which are unanswerable. We must trust the perfection of the creation so far, as to believe that whatever curiosity the order of things has awakened in our minds, the order of things can satisfy. Every man's condition is a solution in hieroglyphic to those inquiries he would put. He acts it as life, before he apprehends it as truth. In like manner, nature is already, in its forms and tendencies, describing its own design. Let us interrogate the great apparition, that shines so peacefully around us. Let us inquire, to what end is nature?

All science has one aim, namely, to find a theory of nature. We have theories of races and of functions, but scarcely yet a remote approximation to an idea of creation. We are now so far from the road to truth, that religious teachers dispute and hate each other, and speculative men are esteemed unsound and frivolous. But to a sound judgment, the most abstract truth is the most practical. Whenever a true theory appears, it will be its own evidence. Its test is, that it will explain all phenomena. Now many are thought not only unexplained but inexplicable; as language, sleep, dreams, beasts, sex.

Philosophically considered, the universe is composed of Nature and the Soul. Strictly speaking, therefore, all that is separate from us, all which Philosophy distinguishes as the NOT ME,[3] that is, both nature and art, all other men and my own body, must be ranked under this name, NATURE. In enumerating the values of nature and casting up their sum, I shall use the word in both senses;—in its common and in its philosophical import. In inquiries so general as our present one, the inaccuracy is not material; no confusion of thought will occur. *Nature*, in the common sense, refers to essences unchanged by man; space, the air, the river, the leaf. *Art* is applied to the mixture of his will with the same things, as in a house, a

---

2. An echo of Ezekiel 37.1–14, esp. 37.4, where God tells Ezekiel to "Prophesy upon these bones, and say unto them, O ye dry bones, hear the word of the Lord." Emerson had left the ministry but was still writing as a prophet.

3. Emerson takes "NOT ME" from Thomas Carlyle's *Sartor Resartus* (1833–34), where it appears as a translation of the recent German philosophical term for everything but the self.

canal, a statue, a picture. But his operations taken together are so insignificant, a little chipping, baking, patching, and washing, that in an impression so grand as that of the world on the human mind, they do not vary the result.

Chapter I. Nature

To go into solitude, a man needs to retire as much from his chamber as from society. I am not solitary whilst I read and write, though nobody is with me. But if a man would be alone, let him look at the stars. The rays that come from those heavenly worlds, will separate between him and vulgar things. One might think the atmosphere was made transparent with this design, to give man, in the heavenly bodies, the perpetual presence of the sublime. Seen in the streets of cities, how great they are! If the stars should appear one night in a thousand years, how would men believe and adore; and preserve for many generations the remembrance of the city of God which had been shown! But every night come out these preachers of beauty, and light the universe with their admonishing smile.

The stars awaken a certain reverence, because though always present, they are always inaccessible; but all natural objects make a kindred impression, when the mind is open to their influence. Nature never wears a mean appearance. Neither does the wisest man extort all her secret, and lose his curiosity by finding out all her perfection. Nature never became a toy to a wise spirit. The flowers the animals, the mountains, reflected all the wisdom of his best hour, as much as they had delighted the simplicity of his childhood.

When we speak of nature in this manner, we have a distinct but most poetical sense in the mind. We mean the integrity of impression made by manifold natural objects. It is this which distinguishes the stick of timber of the wood-cutter, from the tree of the poet. The charming landscape which I saw this morning, is indubitably made up of some twenty or thirty farms. Miller owns this field, Locke that, and Manning the woodland beyond. But none of them owns the landscape. There is a property in the horizon which no man has but he whose eye can integrate all the parts, that is, the poet. This is the best part of these men's farms, yet to this their land-deeds give them no title.[4]

To speak truly, few adult persons can see nature. Most persons do not see the sun. At least they have a very superficial seeing. The sun illuminates only the eye of the man, but shines into the eye and the heart of the child. The lover of nature is he whose inward and outward senes are still truly adjusted to each other; who has retained the spirit of infancy even into the era of manhood.[5] His

---

4. Compare the opening paragraphs of Thoreau's *Walden*, Chap. 2.
5. An echo of Samuel Taylor Coleridge's *Biographia Literaria*, Chap. 4, in which Coleridge defines the character and privilege of genius as the ability to carry the feelings of childhood into the powers of manhood.

intercourse with heaven and earth, becomes part of his daily food. In the presence of nature, a wild delight runs through the man, in spite of real sorrows. Nature says,—he is my creature, and maugre[6] all his impertinent griefs, he shall be glad with me. Not the sun or the summer alone, but every hour and season yields its tribute of delight; for every hour and change corresponds to and authorizes a different state of the mind, from breathless noon to grimmest midnight. Nature is a setting that fits equally well a comic or a mourning peice. In good health, the air is a cordial of incredible virtue. Crossing a bare common, in snow puddles, at twilight, under a clouded sky, without having in my thoughts any occurrence of special good fortune, I have enjoyed a perfect exhilaration. Almost I fear to think how glad I am. In the woods too, a man casts off his years, as the snake his slough, and at what period soever of life, is always a child. In the woods, is perpetual youth. Within these plantations of God, a decorum and sanctity reign, a perennial festival is dressed, and the guest sees not how he should tire of them in a thousand years. In the woods, we return to reason and faith. There I feel that nothing can befal me in life,—no disgrace, no calamity, (leaving me my eyes,) which nature cannot repair. Standing on the bare ground,—my head bathed by the blithe air, and uplifted into infinite space,—all mean egotism vanishes. I become a transparent eye-ball.[7] I am nothing. I see all. The currents of the Universal Being circulate through me; I am part or particle of God. The name of the nearest friend sounds then foreign and accidental. To be brothers, to be acquaintances,—master or servant, is then a trifle and a disturbance. I am the lover of uncontained and immortal beauty. In the wilderness, I find something more dear and connate[8] than in streets or villages. In the tranquil landscape, and especially in the distant line of the horizon, man beholds somewhat as beautiful as his own nature.

The greatest delight which the fields and woods minister, is the suggestion of an occult relation between man and the vegetable. I am not alone and unacknowledged. They nod to me and I to them. The waving of the boughs in the storm, is new to me and old. It takes me by surprise, and yet is not unknown. Its effect is like that of a higher thought or a better emotion coming over me, when I deemed I was thinking justly or doing right.

Yet it is certain that the power to produce this delight, does not reside in nature, but in man, or in a harmony of both. It is necessary to use these pleasures with great temperance. For, nature is

6. Despite.
7. The most famous phrase in the essay, endlessly ridiculed and explicated. As Sealts says in *The Composition of Nature*," Emerson is not "merely repeating what he had already said about the implications of the preceding sentence on the bare common." When the speaker leaves the village for the woods, "the level of discourse is significantly shifted along with the setting, and the ensuing episode takes place on what Emerson would later call another 'platform' of experience."
8. Related.

not always tricked in holiday attire, but the same scene which yesterday breathed perfume and glittered as for the frolic of the nymphs, is overspread with melancholy today. Nature always wears the colors of the spirit.[9] To a man laboring under calamity, the heat of his own fire hath sadness in it. Then, there is a kind of contempt of the landscape felt by him who has just lost by death a dear friend. The sky is less grand as it shuts down over less worth in the population.

Chapter II. Commodity[1]

Whoever considers the final cause[2] of the world, will discern a multitude of uses that enter as parts into that result. They all admit of being thrown into one of the following classes; Commodity; Beauty; Language; and Discipline.

Under the general name of Commodity, I rank all those advantages which our senses owe to nature. This, of course, is a benefit which is temporary and mediate, not ultimate, like its service to the soul. Yet although low, it is perfect in its kind, and is the only use of nature which all men apprehend. The misery of man appears like childish petulance, when we explore the steady and prodigal provision that has been made for his support and delight on this green ball which floats him through the heavens. What angels invented these splendid ornaments, these rich conveniences, this ocean of air above, this ocean of water beneath, this firmament of earth between? this zodiac of lights, this tent of dropping clouds, this striped coat of climates, this fourfold year? Beasts, fire, water, stones, and corn serve him. The field is at once his floor, his work-yard, his play-ground, his garden, and his bed.

> "More servants wait on man
> Than he'll take notice of."——[3]

Nature, in its ministry to man, is not only the material, but is also the process and the result. All the parts incessantly work into each other's hands for the profit of man. The wind sows the seed; the sun evaporates the sea; the wind blows the vapor to the field; the ice, on the other side of the planet, condenses rain on this; the rain feeds the plant; the plant feeds the animal; and thus the endless circulations of the divine charity nourish man.

The useful arts are but reproductions or new combinations by the wit of man, of the same natural benefactors. He no longer waits for favoring gales, but by means of steam, he realizes[4] the fable of Æolus's bag, and carries the two and thirty winds in the boiler of

9. See Emerson's maturer broodings on subjectivity in *Experience*.
1. Usefulness.
2. In the sense of "purpose."
3. From *Man*, by the English poet George Herbert (1593–1633), quoted at length in Chap. 8, "Prospects."
4. Brings into real existence. In the

Odyssey, X Aeolus, the god of winds, gives Odysseus a bag containing favorable winds, but they create a storm when his unwary sailors let them all out at once; here, Emerson refers only to the harnessing of the powers of nature by human beings.

his boat. To diminish friction, he paves the road with iron bars, and, mounting a coach with a ship-load of men, animals, and merchandise behind him, he darts through the country, from town to town, like an eagle or a swallow through the air. By the aggregate of these aids, how is the face of the world changed, from the era of Noah to that of Napoleon! The private poor man hath cities, ships, canals, bridges, built for him. He goes to the post-office, and the human race run on his errands; to the book-shop, and the human race read and write of all that happens, for him; to the court-house, and nations repair his wrongs. He sets his house upon the road, and the human race go forth every morning, and shovel out the snow, and cut a path for him.

But there is no need of specifying particulars in this class of uses. The catalogue is endless, and the examples so obvious, that I shall leave them to the reader's reflection, with the general remark, that this mercenary benefit is one which has respect to a farther good. A man is fed, not that he may be fed, but that he may work.

Chapter III. Beauty

A nobler want of man is served by nature, namely, the love of Beauty.

The ancient Greeks called the world κοσμος,[5] beauty. Such is the constitution of all things, or such the plastic[6] power of the human eye, that the primary forms, as the sky, the mountain, the tree, the animal, give us a delight *in and for themselves*; a pleasure arising from outline, color, motion, and grouping. This seems partly owing to the eye itself. The eye is the best of artists. By the mututal action of its structure and of the laws of light, perspective is produced, which integrates every mass of objects, of what character soever, into a well colored and shaded globe, so that where the particular objects are mean and unaffecting, the landscape which they compose, is round and symmetrical. And as the eye is the best composer so light is the first of painters. There is no object so foul that intense light will not make beautiful. And the stimulus it affords to the sense, and a sort of infinitude which it hath, like space and time, make all matter gay. Even the corpse hath its own beauty. But beside this general grace diffused over nature, almost all the individual forms are agreeable to the eye, as is proved by our endless imitations[7] of some of them, as the acorn, the grape, the pine-cone, the wheat-ear, the egg, the wings and forms of most birds, the lion's claw, the serpent, the butterfly, sea-shells, flames, clouds, buds, leaves, and the forms of many trees, as the palm.

For better consideration, we may distribute the aspects of Beauty in a threefold manner.

1. First, the simple perception of natural forms is a delight. The

5. Cosmos (order).
6. Creative.

7. As in architectural and furniture design and decoration.

influence of the forms and actions in nature, is so needful to man, that, in its lowest functions, it seems to lie on the confines of commodity and beauty. To the body and mind which have been cramped by noxious work or company, nature is medicinal and restores their tone. The tradesman, the attorney comes out of the din and craft[8] of the street, and sees the sky and the woods, and is a man again. In their eternal calm, he finds himself. The health of the eye seems to demand a horizon. We are never tired, so long as we can see far enough.

But in other hours, Nature satisfies the soul purely by its loveliness, and without any mixture of corporeal benefit. I have seen the spectacle of morning from the hill-top over against my house, from day-break to sun-rise, with emotions which an angel might share. The long slender bars of cloud float like fishes in the sea of crimson light. From the earth, as a shore, I look out into that silent sea. I seem to partake its rapid transformations: the active enchantment reaches my dust, and I dilate and conspire with[9] the morning wind. How does Nature deify us with a few and cheap elements! Give me health and a day, and I will make the pomp of emperors ridiculous. The dawn is my Assyria; the sun-set and moon-rise my Paphos, and unimaginable realms of faerie; broad noon shall be my England of the senses and the understanding; the night shall be my Germany of mystic philosophy and dreams.[1]

Not less excellent, except for our less susceptibility in the afternoon, was the charm, last evening, of a January sunset. The western clouds divided and subdivided themselves into pink flakes modulated with tints of unspeakable softness; and the air had so much life and sweetness, that it was a pain to come within doors. What was it that nature would say? Was there no meaning in the live repose of the valley behind the mill, and which Homer or Shakespeare could not re-form for me in words? The leafless trees become spires of flame in the sunset, with the blue east for their background, and the stars of the dead calices[2] of flowers, and every withered stem and stubble rimed with frost, contribute something to the mute music.

The inhabitants of cities suppose that the country landscape is pleasant only half the year. I please myself with observing the graces of the winter scenery, and believe that we are as much touched by it as by the genial[3] influences of summer. To the attentive eye, each moment of the year has its own beauty, and in the same field, it beholds, every hour, a picture which was never seen before, and which shall never be seen again. The heavens

---

8. Craftiness, materialism.
9. Breathe with.
1. The ancient Near Eastern Empire and the ancient city in Cyprus (site of worship of Aphrodite). In the next part of the passage Emerson is contrasting the

Scottish Common Sense philosophy with German post-Kantian idealism.
2. Calyx, the outer whorl of leaves or sepals at the base of a flower; just below, rimed: coated.
3. Generative, creative.

change every moment, and reflect their glory or gloom on the plains beneath. The state of the crop in the surrounding farms alters the expression of the earth from week to week. The succession of native plants in the pastures and roadsides, which make the silent clock by which time tells the summer hours, will make even the divisions of the day sensible to a keen observer. The tribes of birds and insects, like the plants punctual to their time, follow each other, and the year has room for all. By water-courses, the variety is greater. In July, the blue pontederia or pickerel-weed blooms in large beds in the shallow parts of our pleasant river,[4] and swarms with yellow butterflies in continual motion. Art cannot rival this pomp of purple and gold. Indeed the river is a perpetual gala, and boasts each month a new ornament.

But this beauty of Nature which is seen and felt as beauty, is the least part. The shows of day, the dewy morning, the rainbow, mountains, orchards in blossom, stars, moonlight, shadows in still water, and the like, if too eagerly hunted, become shows merely, and mock us with their unreality. Go out of the house to see the moon, and 't is mere tinsel; it will not please as when its light shines upon your necessary journey. The beauty that shimmers in the yellow afternoons of October, who ever could clutch it? Go forth to find it, and it is gone: 't is only a mirage as you look from the windows of diligence.

2. The presence of a higher, namely, of the spiritual element is essential to its perfection. The high and divine beauty which can be loved without effeminacy, is that which is found in combination with the human will, and never separate. Beauty is the mark God sets upon virtue. Every natural action is graceful. Every heroic act is also decent,[5] and causes the place and the bystanders to shine. We are taught by great actions that the universe is the property of every individual in it. Every rational creature has all nature for his dowry and estate. It is his, if he will. He may divest himself of it; he may creep into a corner, and abdicate his kingdom, as most men do, but he is entitled to the world by his constitution. In proportion to the energy of his thought and will, he takes up the world into himself. "All those things for which men plough, build, or sail, obey virtue;" said an ancient historian.[6] "The winds and waves," said Gibbon, "are always on the side of the ablest navigators."[7] So are the sun and moon and all the stars of heaven. When a noble act is done,—perchance in a scene of great natural beauty; when Leonidas[8] and his three hundred martyrs consume one day in

4. The Concord River.
5. Beautiful.
6. Sallust, Roman historian of the 1st century B.C., in *The Conspiracy of Cataline*, Chap. 2.
7. Edward Gibbon (1737–94), English historian, from *The Decline and Fall of the Roman Empire*, Chap. 68 (*JMN*

V.108.
8. Leonidas, king of Sparta, was killed defending the pass at Thermopylae against the Persian army led by Xerxes, 480 B.C.; below, Arnold Winkelried was a Swiss hero in a battle against the Austrians at Sempach in 1386.

dying, and the sun and moon come each and look at them once in the steep defile of Thermopylæ; when Arnold Winkelried, in the high Alps, under the shadow of the avalanche, gathers in his side a sheaf of Austrian spears to break the line for his comrades; are not these heroes entitled to add the beauty of the scene to the beauty of the deed? When the bark of Columbus nears the shore of America; —before it, the beach lined with savages, fleeing out of all their huts of cane; the sea behind; and the purple mountains of the Indian Archipelago around, can we separate the man from the living picture? Does not the New World clothes his form with her palm-groves and savannahs as fit drapery? Ever does natural beauty steal in like air, and envelope great actions. When Sir Harry Vane was dragged up the Tower-hill, sitting on a sled, to suffer death, as the champion of the English laws, one of the multitude cried out to him, "You never sate on so glorious a seat."[9] Charles II., to intimidate the citizens of London, caused the patriot Lord Russel to be drawn in an open coach, through the principal streets of the city, on his way to the scaffold.[1] "But," to use the simple narrative of his biographer, "the multitude imagined they saw liberty and virtue sitting by his side." In private places, among sordid objects, an act of truth or heroism seems at once to draw to itself the sky as its temple, the sun as its candle. Nature stretcheth out her arms to embrace man, only let his thoughts be of equal greatness. Willingly does she follow his steps with the rose and the violet, and bend her lines of grandeur and grace to the decoration of her darling child. Only let his thoughts be of equal scope, and the frame will suit the picture. A virtuous man, is in unison with her works, and makes the central figure of the visible sphere. Homer, Pindar, Socrates, Phocion, associate themselves fitly in our memory with the whole geography and climate of Greece.[2] The visible heavens and earth sympathize with Jesus. And in common life, whosoever has seen a person of powerful character and happy genius, will have remarked how easily he took all things along with him,—the persons, the opinions, and the day, and nature became ancillary to a man.

3. There is still another aspect under which the beauty of the world may be viewed, namely, as it becomes an object of the intellect. Beside the relation of things to virtue, they have a relation to thought. The intellect searches out the absolute order of things as they stand in the mind of God, and without the colors of affection.[3] The intellectual and the active powers seem to succeed each

9. Sir Harry Vane, a Puritan, once colonial governor of Massachustts, was executed for treason in 1662.
1. William, Lord Russell, b. 1639, executed for treason in 1683 after perjurous testimony. *JMN* (V.76) cites Emerson's source as Alexander Chalmer's *General Biographical Dictionary*.
2. Homer, legendary Greek author of *The Iliad* and *The Odyssey*; Pindar, Greek lyric poet of the 5th and 6th centuries B.C.; Socrates, Greek philosopher of the 5th century B.C.; Phocion, Athenian statesman and general of the 4th century B.C., of whom Emerson knew from Plutarch's *Lives*.
3. Modifying emotions.

other in man, and the exclusive activity of the one, generates the exclusive activity of the other. There is something unfriendly in each to the other, but they are like the alternate periods of feeding and working in animals; each prepares and certainly will be followed by the other. Therefore does beauty, which, in relation to actions, as we have seen comes unsought, and comes because it is unsought, remain for the apprehension and pursuit of the intellect; and then again, in its turn, of the active power. Nothing divine dies. All good is eternally reproductive. The beauty of nature reforms itself in the mind, and not for barren contemplation, but for new creation.

All men are in some degree impressed by the face of the world. Some men even to delight. This love of beauty is Taste. Others have the same love in such excess, that, not content with admiring, they seek to embody it in new forms. The creation of beauty is Art.

The production of a work of art throws a light upon the mystery of humanity. A work of art is an abstract or opitome of the world. It is the result or expression of nature, in miniature. For although the works of nature are innumerable and all different, the result or the expression of them all is similar and single. Nature is a sea of forms radically alike and even unique.[4] A leaf, a sun-beam, a landscape, the ocean, make an analogous impression on the mind. What is common to them all,—that perfectness and harmony, is beauty. Therefore the standard of beauty, is the entire circuit of natural forms,—the totality of nature; which the Italians expressed by defining beauty "il piu nell' uno."[5] Nothing is quite beautiful alone: nothing but is beautiful in the whole. A single object is only so far beautiful as it suggests this universal grace. The poet, the painter, the sculptor, the musician, the architect seek each to concentrate this radiance of the world on one point, and each in his several work to satisfy the love of beauty which stimulates him to produce. Thus is Art, a nature passed through the alembic[6] of man. Thus in art, does nature work through the will of a man filled with the beauty of her first works.

The world thus exists to the soul to satisfy the desire of beauty. Extend this element to the uttermost, and I call it an ultimate end. No reason can be asked or given why the soul seeks beauty. Beauty, in its largest and profoundest sense, is one expression for the universe. God is the all-fair. Truth, and goodness, and beauty, are but different faces of the same All. But beauty in nature is not ultimate. It is the herald of inward and eternal beauty, and is not alone a solid and satisfactory good. It must therefore stand as a part and not as yet the last or highest expression of the final cause of Nature.

4. Similar to the point of being identical.
5. The many in one (a borrowing from Coleridge).
6. A distilling apparatus.

Chapter IV . Language

A third use which Nature subserves to man is that of Language. Nature is the vehicle of thought, and in a simple, double, and threefold degree.

1. Words are signs of natural facts.

2. Particular natural facts are symbols of particular spiritual facts.

3. Nature is the symbol of spirit.

1. Words are signs of natural facts. The use of natural history is to give us aid in supernatural history. The use of the outer creation is to give us language for the beings and changes of the inward creation. Every word which is used to express a moral or intellectual fact, if traced to its root, is found to be borrowed from some material appearance. *Right* originally means *straight; wrong* means *twisted. Spirit* primarily means *wind; transgression,* the crossing of a *line; supercilious,* the *raising of the eye-brow*. We say the *heart* to express emotion, the *head* to denote thought; and *thought* and *emotion* are, in their turn, words borrowed from sensible things, and now appropriated to spiritual nature. Most of the process by which this transformation is made, is hidden from us in the remote time when language was framed; but the same tendency may be daily observed in children. Children and savages use only nouns or names of things, which they continually convert into verbs, and apply to analogous mental acts.

2. But this origin of all words that convey a spiritual import,—so conspicuous a fact in the history of language,—is our least debt to nature. It is not words only that are emblematic; it is things which are emblematic. Every natural fact is a symbol of some spiritual fact.[7] Every appearance in nature corresponds to some state of the mind, and that state of the mind can only be described by presenting that natural appearance as its picture. An enraged man is a lion, a cunning man is a fox, a firm man is a rock, a learned man is a torch. A lamb is innocence; a snake is subtle spite; flowers express to us the delicate affections. Light and darkness are our familiar expression for knowledge and ignorance; and heat for love. Visible distance behind and before us, is respectively our image of memory and hope.

Who looks upon a river in a meditative hour, and is not reminded of the flux of all things? Throw a stone into the stream, and the circles that propagate themselves are the beautiful type of all influence. Man is conscious of a universal soul within or behind his individual life, wherein, as in a firmament, the natures of Justice,

---

7. This passage owes much to the Swedish theologian and mystic Emanuel Swedenborg (1688–1772), whose doctrine of correspondence between the inner and outer worlds underlies much of Emerson's thought.

Truth, Love, Freedom, arise and shine. This universal soul, he calls Reason: it is not mine or thine or his, but we are its; we are its property and men.[8] And the blue sky in which the private earth is buried, the sky with its eternal calm, and full of everlasting orbs, is the type of Reason. That which, intellectually considered, we call Reason, considered in relation to nature, we call Spirit. Spirit is the Creator. Spirit hath life in itself. And man in all ages and countries, embodies it in his language, as the FATHER.

It is easily seen that there is nothing lucky or capricious in these analogies, but that they are constant, and pervade nature. These are not the dreams of a few poets, here and there, but man is an analogist, and studies relations in all objects. He is placed in the centre of beings, and a ray of relation passes from every other being to him. And neither can man be understood without these objects, nor these objects without man. All the facts in natural history taken by themselves, have no value, but are barren like a single sex. But marry it to human history, and it is full of life. Whole Floras, all Linnæus' and Buffon's volume, are but dry catalogues of facts;[9] but the most trivial of these facts, the habit of a plant, the organs, or work, or noise of an insect, applied to the illustration of a fact in intellectual philosophy, or, in any way associated to human nature, affects us in the most lively and agreeable manner. The seed of a plant,—to what affecting analogies in the nature of man, is that little fruit made use of, in all discourse, up to the voice of Paul, who calls the human corpse a seed,—"It is sown a natural body; it is raised a spiritual body."[1] The motion of the earth round its axis, and round the sun, makes the day, and the year. These are certain amounts of brute light and heat. But is there no intent of an analogy between man's life and the seasons? And do the seasons gain no grandeur or pathos from that analogy? The instincts of the ant are very unimportant considered as the ant's; but the moment a ray of relation is seen to extend from it to man, and the little drudge is seen to be a monitor, a little body with a mighty heart, then all its habits, even that said to be recently observed, that it never sleeps, become sublime.

Because of this radical[2] correspondence between visible things and human thoughts, savages, who have only what is necessary, converse in figures. As we go back in history, language becomes more picturesque, until its infancy, when it is all poetry; or, all spiritual facts are represented by natural symbols.[3] The same sym-

---

8. As he regularly does, Emerson uses Reason to mean something like what we think of as the intuitive powers of the mind and Understanding to mean the rational powers.
9. Carl von Linné ("Linnaeus"), Swedish naturalist (1707–78); Comte de Buffon (1707–88), French naturalist.
1. I Corinthians 15.44.

2. Fundamental (literally from the "root").
3. The superseded theory of language was a Romantic commonplace, familiar to Emerson from Percy Bysshe Shelley's *A Defense of Poetry* (1821): "In the infancy of society every author is necessarily a poet."

bols are found to make the original elements of all languages. It has moreover been observed, that the idioms of all languages approach each other in passages of the greatest eloquence and power. And as this is the first language, so is it the last. This immediate dependence of language upon nature, this conversion of an outward phenomenon into a type of somewhat in human life, never loses its power to affect us. It is this which gives that piquancy to the conversation of a strong-natured farmer or back-woodsman, which all men relish.

Thus is nature an interpreter, by whose means man converses with his fellow men. A man's power to connect his thought with its proper symbol, and so utter it, depends on the simplicity of his character, that is, upon his love of truth and his desire to communicate it without loss. The corruption of man is followed by the corruption of language. When simplicity of character and the sovereignty of ideas is broken up by the prevalence of secondary desires, the desire of riches, the desire of pleasure, the desire of power, the desire of praise,—and duplicity and falsehood take place of simplicity and truth, the power over nature as an interpreter of the will, is in a degree lost; new imagery ceases to be created, and old words are perverted to stand for things which are not; a paper currency is employed when there is no bullion in the vaults. In due time, the fraud is manifest, and words lose all power to stimulate the understanding or the affections. Hundreds of writers may be found in every long-civilized nation, who for a short time believe, and make others believe, that they see and utter truths, who do not of themselves clothe one thought in its natural garment, but who feed unconsciously upon the language created by the primary writers of the country, those, namely, who hold primarily on nature.

But wise men pierce this rotten diction and fasten words again to visible things; so that picturesque language is at once a commanding certificate that he who employs it, is a man in alliance with truth and God. The moment our discourse rises above the ground line of familiar facts, and is inflamed with passion or exalted by thought, it clothes itself in images. A man conversing in earnest, if he watch his intellectual processes, will find that always a material image, more or less luminous, arises in his mind, cotemporaneous with every thought, which furnishes the vestment of the thought. Hence, good writing and brilliant discourse are perpetual allegories. This imagery is spontaneous. It is the blending of experience with the present action of the mind. It is proper creation. It is the working of the Original Cause through the instruments he has already made.

These facts may suggest the advantage which the country-life possesses for a powerful mind, over the artificial and curtailed life of cities. We know more from nature than we can at will communicate. Its light flows into the mind evermore, and we forget its presence. The poet, the orator, bred in the woods, whose scenes have been nourished by their fair and appeasing changes, year after year, without design and without heed,—shall not lose their lesson altogether, in the roar of cities or the broil of politics. Long hereafter, amidst agitation and terror in national councils,—in the hour of revolution,—these solemn images shall reappear in their morning lustre, as fit symbols and words of the thoughts which the passing events shall awaken. At the call of a noble sentiment, again the woods wave, the pines murmur, the river rolls and shines, and the cattle low upon the mountains, as he saw and heard them in his infancy. And with these forms, the spells of persuasion, the keys of power are put into his hands.

3. We are thus assisted by natural objects in the expression of particular meanings. But how great a language to convey such pepper-corn informations! Did it need such noble races of creatures, this profusion of forms, this host of orbs in heaven, to furnish man with the dictionary and grammar of his municipal speech? Whilst we use this grand cipher to expedite the affairs of our pot and kettle, we feel that we have not yet put it to its use, neither are able. We are like travellers using the cinders of a volcano to roast their eggs. Whilst we see that it always stands ready to clothe what we would say, we cannot avoid the question, whether the characters are not significant of themselves. Have mountains, and waves, and skies, no significance but what we consciously give them, when we employ them as emblems of our thoughts? The world is emblematic. Parts of speech are metaphors because the whole of nature is a metaphor of the human mind. The laws of moral nature answer to those of matter as face to face in a glass. "The visible world and the relation of its parts, is the dial plate of the invisible."[4] The axioms of physics translate the laws of ethics.[5] Thus, "the whole is greater than its part;" "reaction is equal to action;" "the smallest weight may be made to lift the greatest, the difference of weight being compensated by time;" and many the like propositions, which have an ethical as well as physical sense. These propositions have a much more extensive and universal sense when applied to human life, than when confined to technical use.

In like manner, the memorable words of history, and the proverbs of nations, consist usually of a natural fact, selected as a picture or parable of a moral truth.[6] Thus; A rolling stone gathers no moss; A bird in the hand is worth two in the bush; A cripple in the right way, will beat a racer in the wrong; Make hay whilst the

4. Emerson copied the Swedenborg quotation from the *New Jerusalem Magazine* (July 1832), p. 437 (*JMN* IV.33).
5. The quotation is adapted from Mme. De Staël's *Germany* (1813): "Not a mathematical axiom but is a moral rule" (*JMN* III.255).

6. A list of proverbs in *JMN* (VI.138–141) includes several of these, the one about the cripple in the race being attributed to Francis Bacon's *The Advancement of Learning*, II, and the one about the full cup being attributed to Robert Leighton's *Select Works*.

sun shines; 'T is hard to carry a full cup even; Vinegar is the son of wine; The last ounce broke the camel's back; Long-lived trees make roots first;—and the like. In their primary sense these are trivial facts, but we repeat them for the value of their analogical import. What is true of proverbs, is true of all fables, parables, and allegories.

This relation between the mind and matter is not fancied by some poet, but stands in the will of God, and so is free to be known by all men. It appears to men, or it does not appear. When in fortunate hours we ponder this miracle, the wise man doubts, if, at all other times, he is not blind and deaf;

> ——"Can these things be,
> And overcome us like a summer's cloud,
> Without our special wonder?"[7]

for the universe becomes transparent, and the light of higher laws than its own, shines through it. It is the standing problem which has exercised the wonder and the study of every fine genius since the world began; from the era of the Egyptians and the Brahmins, to that of Pythagoras, of Plato, of Bacon, of Leibnitz, of Swedenborg.[8] There sits the Sphinx at the road-side, and from age to age, as each prophet comes by, he tries his fortune at reading her riddle.[9] There seems to be a necessity in spirit to manifest itself in material forms; and day and night, river and storm, beast and bird, acid and alkali, preëxist in necessary Ideas in the mind of God, and are what they are by virtue of preceding affections,[1] in the world of spirit. A Fact is the end or last issue of spirit. The visible creation is the terminus or the circumference of the invisible world. "Material objects," said a French philosopher, "are necessarily kinds of *scoriæ* of the substantial thoughts of the Creator, which must always preserve an exact relation to their first origin; in other words, visible nature must have a spiritual and moral side."[2]

This doctrine is abstruse, and though the images of "garment," "scoriæ," "mirror," &c., may stimulate the fancy, we must summon the aid of subtler and more vital expositors to make it plain. "Every scripture is to be interpreted by the same spirit which gave it forth,"—is the fundamental law of criticism.[3] A life in harmony with nature, the love of truth and of virtue, will purge the eyes to understand her text. By degrees we may come to know the primi-

7. *Macbeth*, III.iv.110–112 (Emerson misquotes "these" for "such").
8. For Emerson, representatives of "every fine genius since the world began" (*Early Lectures*, I.224).
9. In Greek mythology, the winged monster with a lion's body and the head and breasts of a woman who perched on a rock near Thebes and challenged every passerby with a riddle; if they answered incorrectly, she killed them. When Oedi-

pus answered it correctly, she killed herself.
1. Modifying emotions.
2. Guillaume Oegger, *The True Messiah* (1829), which Emerson had seen in a manuscript translation, perhaps by Elizabeth Peabody. Scoria: slag or refuse left after metal has been smelted from ore.
3. From the English Quaker, George Fox (1624–91) (*JMN* IV.31).

tive sense of the permanent objects of nature, so that the world shall be to us an open book, and every form significant of its hidden life and final cause.

A new interest surprises us, whilst, under the view now suggested, we contemplate the fearful extent and multitude of objects; since "every object rightly seen, unlocks a new faculty of the soul."[4] That which was unconscious truth, becomes, when interpreted and defined in an object, a part of the domain of knowledge, —a new amount to the magazine[5] of power.

Chapter V. Discipline[6]

In view of this significance of nature, we arrive at once at a new fact, that nature is a discipline. This use of the world includes the preceding uses, as parts of itself.

Space, time, society, labor, climate, food, locomotion, the animals, the mechanical forces, give us sincerest lessons, day by day, whose meaning is unlimited. They educate both the Understanding and the Reason. Every property of matter is a school for the understanding,—its solidity or reistance, its inerita, its extension, its figure, its divisibility. The understanding adds, divides, combines, measures, and finds everlasting nutriment and room for its activity in this worthy scene. Meantime, Reason transfers all these lessons into its own world of thought, by perceiving the analogy that marries Matter and Mind.

1. Nature is a discipline of the understanding in intellectual truths. Our dealing with sensible objects is a constant exercise in the necessary lesson of difference, of likeness, of order, of being and seeming, of progressive arrangement; of ascent from particular to general; of combination to one end of manifold forces. Porportioned to the importance of the organ to be formed, is the extreme care with which its tuition[7] is provided,—a care pretermitted in no single case. What tedious training, day after day, year after year, never ending, to form the common sense; what continual reproduction of annoyances, inconveniences, dilemmas; what rejoicing over us of little men; what disputing of prices, what reckonings of interest,—and all to form the Hand of the mind;—to instruct us that "good thoughts are not better than good dreams, unless they be executed!"[8]

The same good office is performed by Property and its filial

4. From Coleridge's *Aids to Reflection* (1829), pp. 150–151 (*JMN* V.189).
5. Storehouse.
6. Whicher quotes the American literature anthologists Bradley, Beatty, and Long for their caution about the term "Discipline": "A trained ecclesiastic, Emerson utilizes the dualism of this word, signifying at once a controlled obedience to the absolute, and, secondly, the ecclesiastical discipline of practical rules affect-

ing conduct." The reference to "progressive arrangement" in paragraph 3 is a borrowing from Colridge's *The Friend* (1818). Emerson made a note on "what Coleridge defines Method, viz. progressive arrangement" (*JMN* III.299).
7. Guardianship; "pretermitted": neglected.
8. Adapted from Francis Bacon's essay *Of Great Place* (*JMN* V.136).

systems of debt and credit. Debt, grinding debt, whose iron face the widow, the orphan, and the sons of genius fear and hate;—debt, which consumes so much time, which so cripples and disheartens a great spirit with cares that seem so base, is a preceptor whose lessons cannot be foregone, and is needed most by those who suffer from it most. Moreover, property, which has been well compared to snow,—"if it fall level to-day, it will be blown into drifts to-morrow,"—is merely the surface action of internal machinery, like the index on the face of a clock. Whilst now it is the gymnastics of the understanding, it is hiving in the foresight of the spirit, experience in profounder laws.

The whole character and fortune of the individual is affected by the least inequalities in the culture of the understanding; for example, in the perception of differences. Therefore is Space, and therefore Time, that man may know that things are not huddled and lumped, but sundered and individual. A bell and a plough have each their use, and neither can do the office of the other. Water is good to drink, coal to burn, wool to wear; but wool cannot be drunk, nor water spun, nor coal eaten. The wise man shows his wisdom in separation, in gradation, and his scale of creatures and of merits, is as wide as nature. The foolish have no range in their scale, but suppose every man is as every other man. What is not good they call the worst, and what is not hateful, they call the best.

In like manner, what good heed, nature forms in us! She pardons no mistakes. Her yea is yea, and her nay, nay.

The first steps in Agriculture, Astronomy, Zoölogy, (those first steps which the farmer, the hunter, and the sailor take,) teach that nature's dice are always loaded; that in her heaps and rubbish are concealed sure and useful results.

How calmly and genially the mind apprehends one after another the laws of physics! What noble emotions dilate the mortal as he enters into the counsels of the creation, and feels by knowledge the privilege to Be! His insight refines him. The beauty of nature shines in his own breast. Man is greater that he can see this, and the universe less, because Time and Space relations vanish as laws are known.

Here again we are impressed and even daunted by the immense Universe to be explored. 'What we know, is a point to what we do not know.'[9] Open any recent journal of science, and weigh the problems suggested concerning Light, Heat, Electricity, Magnetism, Physiology, Geology, and judge whether the interest of natural science is likely to be soon exhausted.

Passing by many particulars of the discipline of nature we must not omit to specify two.

9. A saying ascribed both to Sir Isaac Newton (1642–1727), English mathematician and philosopher, and to Bishop Joseph Butler (1692–1752), the moralist.

The exercise of the Will or the lesson of power is taught in every event. From the child's successive possession of his several senses up to the hour when he saith, "thy will be done!"[1] he is learning the secret, that he can reduce under his will, not only particular events, but great classes, nay the whole series of events, and so conform all facts to his character. Nature is thoroughly mediate. It is made to serve. It receives the dominion of man as meekly as the ass on which the Saviour rode.[2] It offers all its kingdoms to man as the raw material which he may mould into what is useful. Man is never weary of working it up. He forges the subtile and delicate air into wise and melodious words, and gives them wing as angels of persuasion and command. More and more, with every thought, does his kingdom stretch over things, until the world becomes, at last, only a realized will,—the double of the man.

2. Sensible objects conform to the premonitions of Reason and reflect the conscience. All things are moral; and in their boundless changes have an unceasing reference to spiritual nature. Therefore is nature glorious with form, color, and motion, that every globe in the remotest heaven; every chemical change from the rudest crystal up to the laws of life; every change of vegetation from the first principle of growth in the eye of a leaf, to the tropical forest and antediluvian[3] coal-mine; every animal function from the sponge up to Hercules,[4] shall hint or thunder to man the laws of right and wrong, and echo the Ten Commandments. Therefore is nature always the ally of Religion: lends all her pomp and riches to the religious sentiment. Prophet and priest, David, Isaiah, Jesus, have drawn deeply from this source.

This ethical character so penetrates the bone and marrow of nature, as to seem the end for which it was made. Whatever private purpose is answered by any member or part, this is its public and universal function, and is never omitted. Nothing in nature is exhausted in its first use. When a thing has served an end to the uttermost, it is wholly new for an ulterior service. In God, every end is converted into a new means. Thus the use of Commodity, regarded by itself, is mean and squalid. But it is to the mind an education in the great doctrine of Use, namely, that a thing is good only so far as it serves; that a conspiring of parts and efforts to the production of an end, is essential to any being. The first and gross manifestation of this truth, is our inevitable and hated training in values and wants, in corn and meat.

It has already been illustrated, in treating of the significance of material things, that every natural process is but a version of a moral sentence. The moral law lies at the centre of nature and

1. Matthew 6.10 and 26.42.
2. Matthew 21.5.
3. Before the Flood which destroyed all living creatures not in Noah's ark (Genesis 6–9).
4. In Greek mythology the hero renowned for feats of strength.

radiates to the circumference. It is the pith and marrow of every substance, every relation, and every process. All things with which we deal, preach to us. What is a farm but a mute gospel? The chaff and the wheat, weeds and plants, blight, rain, insects, sun,—it is a sacred emblem from the first furrow of spring to the last stack which the snow of winter overtakes in the fields. But the sailor, the shepherd, the miner, the merchant, in their several resorts, have each an experience precisely parallel and leading to the same conclusions. Because all organizations are radically alike. Nor can it be doubted that this moral sentiment which thus scents the air, and grows in the grain, and impregnates the waters of the world, is caught by man and sinks into his soul. The moral influence of nature upon every individual is that amount of truth which it illustrates to him. Who can estimate this? Who can guess how much firmness the sea-beaten rock has taught the fisherman? how much tranquillity has been reflected to man from the azure sky, over whose unspotted deeps the winds forevermore drive flocks of stormy clouds, and leave no wrinkle or stain? how much industry and providence and affection we have caught from the pantomime of brutes? What a searching preacher of self-command is the varying phenomenon of Health!

Herein is especially apprehended the Unity of Nature,—the Unity in Variety,—which meets us everywhere. All the endless variety of things make a unique, an identical impression. Xenophanes complained in his old age, that, look where he would, all things hastened back to Unity.[5] He was weary of seeing the same entity in the tedious variety of forms. The fable of Proteus[6] has a cordial truth. Every particular in nature, a leaf, a drop, a crystal, a moment of time is related to the whole, and partakes of the perfection of the whole. Each particle is a microcosm, and faithfully renders the likeness of the world.

Not only resemblances exist in things whose analogy is obvious, as when we detect the type of the human hand in the flipper of the fossil saurus, but also in objects wherein there is great superficial unlikeness. Thus architecture is called 'frozen music,' by De Stael and Goethe.[7] 'A Gothic church,' said Coleridge, 'is a petrified religion.'[8] Michael Angelo maintained, that, to an architect, a knowledge of anatomy is essential.[9] In Haydn's oratorios, the notes present to the imagination not only motions, as, of the snake, the

5. Greek philosopher of 5th and 6th centuries B.C. who taught the unity of all existence (*JMN* III.369 and V.136).
6. Sea god who could change his shape so as to evade any captor; "cordial": vital, heartwarming.
7. Mme. De Stael (1766–1817), in *Corinne*, Book IV, Chap. 3 (*JMN* IV.40); Johann Wolfgang von Goethe (1749–1832), in his *Conversations with Eckermann* (*JMN* IV.337).
8. Coleridge, in his *Lecture on the General Character of the Gothic Mind in the Middle Ages* (1836) (*JMN* V.36).
9. From the sketch of Michelangelo in *Lives of Eminent Persons* (1833), p. 57 (*JMN* V.367–368).

stag, and the elephant, but colors also; as the green grass.[1] The granite is differenced in its laws only by the more or less of heat, from the river that wears it away. The river, as it flows, resembles the air that flows over it; the air resembles the light which traverses it with more subtile currents; the light resembles the heat which rides with it through Space. Each creature is only a modification of the other; the likeness in them is more than the difference, and their radical law is one and the same. Hence it is, that a rule of one art, or a law of one organization, holds true throughout nature. So intimate is this Unity, that, it is easily seen, it lies under the undermost garment of nature, and betrays its source in universal Spirit. For, it pervades Thought also. Every universal truth which we express in words, implies or supposes every other truth. *Omne verum vero consonat*.[2] It is like a great circle on a sphere, comprising all possible circles; which, however, may be drawn, and comprise it, in like manner. Every such truth is the absolute Ens[3] seen from one side. But it has innumerable sides.

The same central Unity is still more conspicuous in actions. Words are finite organs of the infinite mind. They cannot cover the dimensions of what is in truth. They break, chop, and impoverish it. An action is the perfection and publication of thought. A right action seems to fill the eye, and to be related to all nature. "The wise man, in doing one thing, does all; or, in the one thing he does rightly, he sees the likeness of all which is done rightly."[4]

Words and actions are not the attributes of mute and brute nature. They introduce us to that singular form which predominates over all other forms. This is the human. All other organizations appear to be degradations of the human form. When this organization appears among so many that surround it, the spirit prefers it to all others. It says, 'From such as this, have I drawn joy and knowledge. In such as this, have I found and beheld myself. I will speak to it. It can speak again. It can yield me thought already formed and alive.' In fact, the eye,—the mind,—is always accompanied by these forms, male and female; and these are incomparably the richest informations[5] of the power and order that lie at the heart of things. Unfortunately, every one of them bears the marks as of some injury; is marred and superficially defective. Nevertheless, far different from the deaf and dumb nature around them, these all rest like fountain-pipes on the unfathomed sea of thought and virtue whereto they alone, of all organizations, are the entrances.

1. Franz Joseph Haydn (1832–1809), Austrian composer (*JMN* V.137).
2. Every truth agrees with every other truth. "We say every truth supposes or implies every other truth" (*JMN* IV.376).
3. Abstract Being.

4. Paraphrase of Goethe's *Wilhelm Meister* from Carlyle's translation (*JMN* IV.75).
5. Products of the inward, form-giving capacity.

It were a pleasant inquiry to follow into detail their ministry to our education, but where would it stop? We are associated in adolescent and adult life with some friends, who, like skies and waters, are coextensive with our idea; who, answering each to a certain affection of the soul, satisfy our desire on that side; whom we lack power to put at such focal distance from us, that we can mend or even analyze them. We cannot chuse but love them. When much intercourse with a friend has supplied us with a standard of excellence, and has increased our respect for the resources of God who thus sends a real person to outgo our ideal; when he has, moreover, become an object of thought, and, whilst his character retains all its unconscious effect, is converted in the mind into solid and sweet wisdom,—it is a sign to us that his office is closing, and he is commonly withdrawn from our sight in a short time.

Chapter VI. Idealism

Thus is the unspeakable but intelligible and practicable meaning of the world conveyed to man, the immortal pupil, in every object of sense. To this one end of Discipline, all parts of nature conspire.

A noble doubt perpetually suggests itself, whether this end be not the Final Cause of the Universe; and whether nature outwardly exists. It is a sufficient account of that Appearance we call the World, that God will teach a human mind, and so makes it the receiver of a certain number of congruent sensations, which we call sun and moon, man and woman, house and trade. In my utter impotence to test the authenticity of the report of my senses, to know whether the impressions they make on me correspond with outlying objects, what difference does it make, whether Orion is up there in heaven, or some god paints the image in the firmament of the soul? The relations of parts and the end of the whole remaining the same, what is the difference, whether land and sea interact, and worlds revolve and intermingle without number or end,—deep yawning under deep,[6] and galaxy balancing galaxy, throughout absolute space, or, whether, without relations of time and space, the same appearances are inscribed in the constant faith of man. Whether nature enjoy a substantial existence without, or is only in the apocalypse[7] of the mind, it is alike useful and alike venerable to me. Be it what it may, it is ideal to me, so long as I cannot try the accuracy of my senses.

The frivolous make themselves merry with the Ideal theory,[8] as if its consequences were burlesque; as if it affected the stability of

---

6. From Psalms 42.7: "Deep calleth unto deep at the noise of thy waterspouts: all thy waves and thy billows are gone over me."
7. Revelation.

8. Emerson uses Bishop George Berkeley (1685–1753) as representative of the notion that we can only know ideas in the mind and cannot know material things in themselves.

nature. It surely does not. God never jests with us, and will not compromise the end of nature, by permitting any inconsequence in its procession. Any distrust of the permanence of laws, would paralyze the faculties of man. Their permanence is sacredly respected, and his faith therein is perfect. The wheels and springs of man are all set to the hypothesis of the permanence of nature. We are not built like a ship to be tossed, but like a house to stand. It is a natural consequence of this structure, that, so long as the active powers predominate over the reflective, we resist with indignation any hint that nature is more short-lived or mutable than spirit. The broker, the wheelwright, the carpenter, the tollman, are much displeased at the intimation.

But whilst we acquiesce entirely in the permanence of natural laws, the question of the absolute existence of nature, still remains open. It is the uniform effect of culture on the human mind, not to shake our faith in the stability of particular phenomena, as of heat, water, azote;[9] but to lead us to regard nature as a phenomenon, not a substance; to attribute necessary existence to spirit; to esteem nature as an accident and an effect.

To the senses and the unrenewed understanding, belongs a sort of instinctive belief in the absolute existence of nature. In their view, man and nature are indissolubly joined. Things are ultimates, and they never look beyond their sphere. The presence of Reason mars this faith. The first effort of thought tends to relax this despotism of the senses, which binds us to nature as if we were a part of it, and shows us nature aloof, and, as it were, afloat. Until this higher agency intervened, the animal eye sees, with wonderful accuracy, sharp outlines and colored surfaces. When the eye of Reason opens, to outline and surface are at once added, grace and expression. These proceed from imagination and affection, and abate somewhat of the angular distinctness of objects. If the Reason be stimulated to more earnest vision, outlines and surfaces become transparent, and are no longer seen; causes and spirits are seen through them. The best, the happiest moments of life, are these delicious awakenings of the higher powers, and the reverential withdrawing of nature before its God.

Let us proceed to indicate the effects of culture.[1] 1. Our first institution in the Ideal philosophy is a hint from nature herself.

Nature is made to conspire with spirit to emancipate us. Certain mechanical changes, a small alteration in our local position apprizes us of a dualism. We are strangely affected by seeing the shore from a moving ship, from a balloon, or through the tints of an unusual sky. The least change in our point of view, gives the whole world a pictorial air. A man who seldom rides, needs only to get

9. Nitrogen.
1. In the sense of the effects of awaken- ing thought; in the next sentence, "Institution" means instruction.

into a coach and traverse his own town, to turn the street into a puppet-show. The men, the women,—talking, running, bartering, fighting,—the earnest mechanic,[2] the lounger, the beggar, the boys, the dogs, are unrealized[3] at once, or, at least, wholly detached from all relation to the observer, and seen as apparent, not substantial beings. What new thoughts are suggested by seeing a face of country quite familiar, in the rapid movement of the rail-road car! Nay, the most wonted objects, (make a very slight change in the point of vision,) please us most. In a camera obscura,[4] the butcher's cart, and the figure of one of our own family amuse us. So a portrait of a well-known face gratifies us. Turn the eyes upside down, by looking at the landscape through your legs, and how agreeable is the picture, though you have seen it any time these twenty years!

In these cases, by mechanical means, is suggested the difference between the observer and the spectacle,—between man and nature. Hence arises a pleasure mixed with awe; I may say, a low degree of the sublime is felt from the fact, probably, that man is hereby apprized, that, whilst the world is a spectacle, something in himself is stable.

2. In a higher manner, the poet communicates the same pleasure. By a few strokes he delineates, as on air, the sun, the mountain, the camp, the city, the hero, the maiden, not different from what we know them, but only lifted from the ground and float before the eye. He unfixes the land and the sea, makes them revolve around the axis of his primary thought, and disposes them anew. Possessed himself by a heroic passion, he uses matter as symbols of it. The sensual man conforms thoughts to things; the poet conforms things to his thoughts.[5] The one esteems nature as rooted and fast; the other, as fluid, and impresses his being thereon. To him, the refractory world is ductile and flexible; he invests dusts and stones with humanity, and makes them the words of the Reason. The imagination may be defined to be, the use which the Reason makes of the material world. Shakspeare possesses the power of subordinating nature for the purposes of expression, beyond all poets. His imperial muse tosses the creation like a bauble from hand to hand, to embody any capricious shade of thought that is uppermost in his mind. The remotest spaces of nature are visited, and the farthest sundered things are brought together, by a subtle spiritual connexion. We are made aware that magnitude of material things is merely relative, and all objects shrink and expand to serve the passion of the poet. Thus, in his sonnets, the lays of birds, the scents and dyes of flowers, he finds to be the *shadow* of his beloved;

2. Manual laborer.
3. Made unsubstantial.
4. Dark chamber or box with a lens or opening through which an image is projected in natural colors onto an opposite surface.
5. From Bacon's *The Advancement of Learning* (II.iv.2), but more directly from William Hazlitt's adaptation (*JMN* VI.227).

time, which keeps her from him, is his *chest*; the suspicion she has awakened, is her *ornament*;[6]

> The ornament of beauty is Suspect,
> A crow which flies in heaven's sweetest air.[7]

His passion is not the fruit of chance; it swells, as he speaks, to a city, or a state.

> No, it was builded far from accident;
> It suffers not in smiling pomp, nor falls
> Under the brow of thralling discontent;
> It fears not policy, that heretic,
> That works on leases of short numbered hours,
> But all alone stands hugely politic.[8]

In the strength of his constancy, the Pyramids[9] seem to him recent and transitory. And the freshness of youth and love dazzles him with its resemblance to morning.

> Take those lips away
> Which so sweetly were forsworn;
> And those eyes,—the break of day,
> Lights that do mislead the morn.

The wild beauty of this hyperbole, I may say, in passing, it would not be easy to match in literature.

This transfiguration which all material obejcts undergo through the passion of the poet,—this power which he exerts, at any moment, to magnify the small, to micrify the great,—might be illustrated by a thousand examples from his Plays. I have before me the Tempest, and will cite only these few lines.[1]

---

6. Emerson summarizes Shakespeare's Sonnet 98:

From you have I been absent in the spring,
When proud-pied April, dress'd in all his trim,
Hath put a spirit of youth in every thing,
That heavy Saturn laugh'd and leap'd with him.
Yet nor the lays of birds, nor the sweet smell
Of different flowers in ordour and in hue,
Could make me any summer's story tell,
Or from their proud lap pluck them where they grew;
Nor did I wonder at the lily's white,
Nor praise the deep vermilion in the rose;
They were but sweet, but figures of delight,
Drawn after you, you pattern of all

those.
Yet seemed it winter still, and, you away,
As with your shadow I with these did play.

Then Emerson refers to Sonnet 65 ("Shall Time's best jewel from Time's chest lie hid?").
7. Shakespeare's Sonnet 70.
8. Shakespeare's Sonnet 124.
9. Shakespeare's Sonnet 123 ("No, Time, thou shalt not boast that I do change: / Thy pyramids built up with newer might / To me are nothing novel, nothing strange; / They are but dressings of a former sight."); the following quotation is from *Measure for Measure* (V.i.1–4).
1. *The Tempest*, V.i. 46–48 (the 1836 text says "Ariel" instead of Prospero, a careless slip not preserved here); later quotations are from V.i.58–60, 64–68, and 79–82.

PROSPERO. The strong based promontory
Have I made shake, and by the spurs plucked up
The pine and cedar.

Prospero calls for music to sooth the frantic Alonzo, and his companions;

A solemn air, and the best comforter
To an unsettled fancy, cure thy brains
Now useless, boiled within thy skull.

Again;

The charm dissolves space
And, as the morning steals upon the night,
Melting the darkness, so their rising senses
Begin to chase the ignorant fumes that mantle
Their clearer reason.

Their understanding
Begins to swell: and the approaching tide
Will shortly fill the reasonable shores
That now lie foul and muddy.

The perception of real affinities between events, (that is to say, of *ideal* affinities, for those only are real,) enables the poet thus to make free with the most imposing forms and phenomena of the world, and to assert the predominance of the soul.

3. Whilst thus the poet delights us by animating[2] nature like a creator, with his own thoughts, he differs from the philosopher only herein, that the one proposes Beauty as his main end; the other Truth. But, the philosopher, not less than the poet, postpones the apparent order and relations of things to the empire of thought. "The problem of philosophy," according to Plato, "is, for all that exists conditionally, to find a ground unconditioned and absolute."[3] It proceeds on the faith that a law determines all phenomena, which being known, the phenomena can be predicted. That law, when in the mind, is an idea. Its beauty is infinite. The true philosopher and the true poet are one, and a beauty, which is truth, and a truth, which is beauty, is the aim of both. Is not the charm of one of Pltao's or Aristotle's definitions, strictly like that of the Antigone of Sophocles?[4] It is, in both cases, that a spiritual life has been imparted to nature; that the solid seeming block of matter has been pervaded and dissolved by a thought; that this feeble human being has penetrated the vast masses of nature with an informing soul, and recognised itself in their harmony, that is, seized their

2. Giving life to.
3. Emerson draws this quotation from Coleridge's *The Friend* (1818) (*JMN* VI.202).
4. Sophocles, Greek dramatist of the

fifth century B.C., wrote the tragedy *Antigone* in which the title character chooses death rather than violate her sacred duty to perform funeral rites for her slain brother.

law. In physics, when this is attained, the memory disburthens itself of its cumbrous catalogues of particulars, and carries centuries of observation in a single formula.

Thus even in physics, the material is ever degraded before the spiritual. The astronomer, the geometer, rely on their irrefragable analysis, and disdain the results of observation. The sublime remark of Euler on his law of arches, "This will be found contrary to all experience, yet is true;" had already transferred nature into the mind, and left matter like an outcast corpse.[5]

4. Intellectual science has been observed to beget invariably a doubt of the existence of matter. Turgot said, "He that has never doubted the existence of matter, may be assured he has no aptitude for metaphysical inquiries."[6] It fastens the attention upon immortal necessary uncreated natures, that is, upon Ideas; and in their beautiful and majestic presence, we feel that our outward being is a dream and a shade. Whilst we wait in this Olympus of gods, we think of nature as an appendix to the soul. We ascend into their region, and know that these are the thoughts of the Supreme Being. "These are they who were set up from everlasting, from the beginning, or ever the earth was. When he prepared the heavens, they were there; when he established the clouds above, when he strengthened the fountains of the deep. Then they were by him, as one brought up with him. Of them took he counsel."[7]

Their influence is proportionate. As objects of science, they are accessible to few men. Yet all men are capable of being raised by piety or by passion, into their region. And no man touches these divine natures, without becoming, in some degree, himself divine. Like a new soul, they renew the body. We become physically nimble and lightsome; we tread on air; life is no longer irksome, and we think it will never be so. No man fears age or misfortune or death, in their serene company, for he is transported out of the district of change. Whilst we behold unveiled the nature of Justice and Truth, we learn the difference between the absolute and the conditional or relative. We apprehend the absolute. As it were, for the first time, *we exist*. We become immortal, for we learn that time and space are relations of matter; that, with a perception of truth, or a virtuous will, they have no affinity.[8]

5. Finally, religion and ethics, which may be fitly called,—the practice of ideas, or the introduction of ideas into life,—have an analogous effect with all lower culture, in degrading nature and suggesting its dependence on spirit. Ethics and religion differ herein; that the one is the system of human duties commencing

5. Leonhard Euler (1707–83) was a Swiss mathematician and physicist; Emerson took the quotation from Coleridge's *Aids to Reflection* (1829) (*JMN* IV. 327, 332).
6. Anne Robert Jacques Turgot was an 18th-century French economist, author of a book on proofs of the existence of God (*JMN* II.212–213).
7. Proverbs 8.23–30.
8. An echo of Socrates' speech in the *Symposium*.

from man; the other, from God. Religion includes the personality
of God; Ethics does not. They are one to our present design. They
both put nature under foot. The first and last lesson of religion is,
"The things that are seen, are temporal; the things that are unseen
are eternal."[9] It puts an affront upon nature. It does that for the
unschooled, which philosophy does for Berkeley and Viasa.[1] The
uniform language that may be heard in the churches of the most
ignorant sects, is,—'Contemn the unsubstantial shows of the world;
they are vanities, dreams, shadows, unrealities; seek the realities of
religion.' The devotee flouts nature. Some theosophists[2] have arrived at a certain hostility and indignation towards matter, as the
Manichean[3] and Plotinus. They distrusted in themselves any looking back to these flesh-pots of Egypt. Plotinus was ashamed of his
body.[4] In short, they might all better say of matter, what Michael
Angelo said of external beauty, "it is the frail and weary weed, in
which God dresses the soul, which he has called into time."[5]

It appears that motion, poetry, physical and intellectual science,
and religion, all tend to affect our convictions of the reality of the
external world. But I own there is something ungrateful in expanding too curiously the particulars of the general proposition, that all
culture tends to imbue us with idealism. I have no hostility to
nature, but a child's love to it. I expand and live in the warm day
like corn and melons. Let us speak her fair. I do not wish to fling
stones at my beautiful mother, nor soil my gentle nest. I only wish
to indicate the true position of nature in regard to man, wherein to
establish man, all right education tends; as the ground which to
attain is the object of human life, that is, of man's connexion with
nature. Culture inverts the vulgar views of nature, and brings the
mind to call that apparent, which it uses to call real, and that real,
which it uses to call visionary. Children, it is true, believe in the
external world. The belief that it appears only, is an afterthought,
but with culture, this faith will as surely arise on the mind as did
the first.

The advantage of the ideal theory over the popular faith, is this,
that it presents the world in precisely that view which is most
desirable to the mind. It is, in fact, the view which Reason, both
speculative and practical, that is, philosophy and virtue, take. For,
seen in the light of thought, the world always is phenomenal;[6] and
virtue subordinates it to the mind. Idealism sees the world in God.

9. II Corinthians 4.18.
1. Berkeley, British idealist philosopher;
Viasa, reputed author of the Vedas,
the ancient sacred literature of Hindu-
ism (*JMN* V.123).
2. In the broad sense of those who attempt to establish direct contact with
divine principle through contemplation
and revelation.
3. Mani or Manes, 3rd-century Persian,
founded a religion based on the dualism
of good and evil.
4. Plotinus, Greek neo-platonical philosopher of 3rd century was not so much
"ashamed of his body" as of the fact that
his soul had to be contained in a body
(*JMN* III.251). The Israelites yearned
for the fleshpots of Egypt while in the
wilderness (Exodus 16.3).
5. Michelangelo's Sonnet 51 (F
Early Lectures, I.229).
6. Only an appearance.

It beholds the whole circle of persons and things, of actions and events, of country and religion, not as painfully accumulated, atom after atom, act after act, in an aged creeping Past, but as one vast picture, which God paints on the instant eternity, for the contemplation of the soul. Therefore the soul holds itself off from a too trivial and microscopic study of the universal tablet. It respects the end too much, to immerse itself in the means. It sees something more important in Christianity, than the scandals of ecclesiastical history or the niceties of criticsm; and, very incurious concerning persons or miracles, and not at all disturbed by chasms of historical evidence, it accepts from God the phenomenon, as it finds it, as the pure and awful form of religion in the world. It is not hot and passionate at the appearance of what it calls its own good or bad fortune, at the union or opposition of other persons. No man is its enemy. It accepts whatsoever befals, as part of its lesson. It is a watcher more than a doer, and it is a doer, only that it may the better watch.

Chapter VII. Spirit

It is essential to a true theory of nature and of man, that it should contain somewhat progressive. Uses that are exhausted or that may be, and facts that end in the statement, cannot be all that is true of this brave lodging wherein man is harbored, and wherein all his faculties find appropriate and endless exercise. And all the uses of nature admit of being summed in one, which yields the activity of man an infinite scope. Through all its kingdoms, to the suburbs and outskirts of things, it is faithful to the cause whence it had its origin. It always speaks of Spirit. It suggests the absolute. It is a perpetual effect. It is a great shadow pointing always to the sun behind us.

The aspect of nature is devout. Like the figure of Jesus, she stands with bended head, and hands folded upon the breast. The happiest man is he who learns from nature the lesson of worship.

Of that ineffable essence which we call Spirit, he that thinks most, will say least. We can foresee God in the coarse and, as it were, distant phenomena of matter; but when we try to define and describe himself, both language and thought desert us, and we are as helpless as fools and savages. That essence refuses to be recorded in propositions, but when man has worshipped him intellectually, the noblest ministry of nature is to stand as the apparition[7] of God. It is the great organ through which the universal spirit speaks to the individual, and strives to lead back the individual to it.

When we consider Spirit, we see that the views already presented do not include the whole circumference of man. We must add some related thoughts.

Three problems are put by nature to the mind; What is matter? Whence is it? and Whereto? The first of these questions only, the

7. Visible state.

ideal theory answers. Idealism saith: matter is a phenomenon, not a substance. Idealism acquaints us with the total disparity between the evidence of our own being, and the evidence of the world's being. The one is perfect; the other, incapable of any assurance; the mind is a part of the nature of things; the world is a divine dream, from which we may presently awake to the glories and certainties of day. Idealism is a hypothesis to account for nature by other principles than those of carpentry and chemistry. Yet, if it only deny the existence of matter, it does not satisfy the demands of the spirit. It leaves God out of me. It leaves me in the splendid labyrinth of my perceptions, to wander without end. Then the heart resists it, because it baulks the affections in denying substantive being to men and women. Nature is so pervaded with human life, that there is something of humanity in all, and in every particular. But this theory makes nature foreign to me, and does not account for that consanguinity which we acknowledge to it.

Let it stand then, in the present state of our knowledge, merely as a useful introductory hypothesis, serving to apprize us of the eternal distinction between the soul and the world.

But when, following the invisible steps of thought, we come to inquire, Whence is matter? and Whereto? many truths arise to us out of the recesses of consciousness. We learn that the highest is present to the soul of man, that the dread universal essence, which is not wisdom, or love, or beauty, or power, but all in one, and each entirely, is that for which all things exist, and that by which they are; that spirit creates; that behind nature, throughout nature, spirit is present; that spirit is one and not compound; that spirit does not act upon us from without, that is, in space and time, but spiritually, or through ourselves. Therefore, that spirit, that is, the Supreme Being, does not build up nature around us, but puts it forth through us, as the life of the tree puts forth new branches and leaves through the pores of the old. As a plant upon the earth, so a man rests upon the bosom of God; he is nourished by unfailing fountains, and draws, at his need, inexhaustible power. Who can set bounds to the possibilities of man? Once inspire the infinite, by being admitted to behold the absolute natures of justice and truth, and we learn that man has access to the entire mind of the Creator, is himself the creator in the finite. This view, which admonishes me where the sources of wisdom and power lie, and points to virtue as to

> "The golden key
> When opes the palace of eternity,"[8]

carries upon its face the highest certificate of truth, because it animates me to create my own world through the purification of my soul.

8. John Milton's *Comus*, 13–14.

The world proceeds from the same spirit as the body of man. It is a remoter and inferior incarnation of God, a projection of God in the unconscious. But it differs from the body in one important respect. It is not, like that, now subjected to the human will. Its serene order is inviolable by us. It is therefore, to us, the present expositor of the divine mind. It is a fixed point whereby we may measure our departure. As we degenerate, the contrast between us and our house is more evident. We are as much strangers in nature, as we are aliens from God. We do not understand the notes of birds. The fox and the deer run away from us; the bear and tiger rend us. We do not know the uses of more than a few plants, as corn and the apple, the potato and the vine. Is not the landscape, every glimpse of which hath a grandeur, a face of him? Yet this may show us what discord is between man and nature, for you cannot freely admire a noble landscape, if laborers are digging in the field hard by. The poet finds something ridiculous in his delight, until he is out of the sight of men.

Chapter VIII. Prospects

In inquiries respecting the laws of the world and the frame of things, the highest reason is always the truest. That which seems faintly possible—it is so refined, is often faint and dim because it is deepest seated in the mind among the eternal verities. Empirical science is apt to cloud the sight, and, by the very knowledge of functions and processes, to bereave the student of the manly contemplation of the whole. The savant[9] becomes unpoetic. But the best read naturalist who lends an entire and devout attention to truth, will see that there remains much to learn of his relation to the world, and that it is not to be learned by any addition or subtraction or other comparison of known quantities, but is arrived at by untaught sallies of the spirit, by a continual self-recovery, and by entire humility. He will perceive that there are far more excellent qualities in the student than preciseness and infallibility; that a guess is often more fruitful than an indisputable affirmation, and that a dream may let us deeper into the secret of nature than a hundred concerted experiments.

For, the problems to be solved are precisely those which the physiologist and the naturalist omit to state. It is not so pertinent to man to know all the individuals of the animal kingdom, as it is to know whence and whereto is this tyrannizing unity in his constitution, which evermore separates and classifies things, endeavouring to reduce the most diverse to one form. When I behold a rich landscape, it is less to my purpose to recite correctly the order and super-position of the strata, than to know why all thought of multitude is lost in a tranquil sense of unity. I cannot greatly honor

9. Learned person.

minuteness in details, so long as there is no hint to explain the relation between things and thoughts; no ray upon the *metaphysics* of conchology, of botany, of the arts, to show the relation of the forms of flowers, shells, animals, architecture, to the mind, and build science upon ideas. In a cabinet[1] of natural history, we become sensible of a certain occult recognition and sympathy in regard to the most bizarre forms of beast, fish, and insect. The American who has been confined, in his own country, to the sight of buildings designed after foreign models, is surprised on entering York Minster or St. Peter's at Rome, by the feeling that these structures are imitations also,—faint copies of an invisible archetype. Nor has science sufficient humanity, so long as the naturalist overlooks that wonderful congruity which subsists between man and the world; of which he is lord, not because he is the most subtile inhabitant, but because he is its head and heart, and finds something of himself in every great and small thing, in every mountain stratum, in every new law of color, fact of astronomy, or atmospheric influence which observation or analysis lay open. A perception of his mystery inspires the muse of George Herbert, the beautiful psalmist of the seventh century. The following lines are part of his little poem on Man[2]

> "Man is all symmetry,
> Full of proportions, one limb to another,
>   And to all the world besides.
>   Each part may call the farthest, brother;
> For head with foot hath private amity,
>   And both with moons and tides.
>
> "Nothing hath got so far
> But man hath caught and kept it as his prey;
>   His eyes dismount the highest star;
>   He is in little all the sphere.
> Herbs gladly cure our flesh, because that they
>   Find their acquaintance there.
>
> "For us, the winds do blow,
> The earth doth rest, heaven move, and fountains flow;
>   Nothing we see, but means our good,
>   As our delight, or as our treasure;
> The whole is either our cupboard of food,
>   Or cabinet of pleasure.
>
> "The stars have us to bed:
> Night draws the curtain; which the sun withdraws.
>   Music and light attend our head.
>   All things unto our flesh are kind,

---

1. Display case, or room containing many display cases. 2. Stanzas 1–4 and 6 of Herbert's *Man.*

In their descent and being; to our mind,
In their ascent and cause.

"More servants wait on man
Than he'll take notice of. In every path,
He treads down that which doth befriend him
When sickness makes him pale and wan.
Oh mighty love! Man is one world, and hath
Another to attend him."

The perception of this class of truths makes the eternal attraction which draws men to science, but the end is lost sight of in attention to the means. In view of this half-sight of science, we accept the sentence of Plato, that, "poetry comes nearer to vital truth than history."[3] Every surmise and vaticination[4] of the mind is entitled to a certain respect, and we learn to prefer imperfect theories, and sentences, which contain glimpses of truth, to digested systems which have no one valuable suggestion. A wise writer will feel that the ends of study and composition are best answered by announcing undiscovered regions of thought, and so communicating, through hope, new activity to the torpid spirit.

I shall therefore conclude this essay with some traditions of man and nature, which a certain poet sang to me;[5] and which, as they have always been in the world, and perhaps reappear to every bard, may be both history and prophecy.

The foundations of man are not in matter, but in spirit. But the element of spirit is eternity. To it, therefore, the longest series of events, the oldest chronologies are young and recent. In the cycle of the universal man, from whom the known individuals proceed, centuries are points, and all history is but the epoch of one degradation.

'We distrust and deny inwardly our sympathy with nature. We own and disown our relation to it, by turns. We are, like Nebuchadnezzar, dethroned, bereft of reason, and eating grass like an ox.[6] But who can set limits to the remedial force of spirit?

'A man is a god in ruins. When men are innocent, life shall be longer, and shall pass into the immortal, as gently as we awake from dreams. Now, the world would be insane and rabid, if these disorganizations should last for hundreds of years. It is kept in check by death and infancy. Infancy is the perpetual Messiah, which comes into the arms of fallen men, and pleads with them to return to paradise.

3. In copying two quotations from the *Edinburgh Review* Emerson blurred the attributions; here he quotes not from Plato but from section 9 of Aristotle's *Poetics* (*JMN* IV.261 and 173).
4. Foretelling, prophesying.
5. The poet is Emerson himself, in the same sort of private joke which he later uses in *The Poet*, but before writing this passage he had been seeing his neighbor, the arch-Transcendentalist and idealist Bronson Alcott, who was full of his own "Orphic Sayings," so the device is a little joke with Alcott, one of the first readers and admirers of *Nature*.
6. See Daniel 4.31–33.

'Man is the dwarf of himself. Once he was permeated and dissolved by spirit. He filled nature with his overflowing currents. Out from him sprang the sun and moon; from man, the sun; from woman, the moon. The laws of his mind, the periods of his actions externized themselves into day and night, into the year and the seasons. But, having made for himself this huge shell, his waters retired; he no longer fills the veins and veinlets; he is shrunk to a drop. He sees, that the structure still fits him, but fits him colossally. Say, rather, once it fitted him, now it corresponds to him from far and on high. He adores timidly his own work. Now is man the follower of the sun, and woman the follower of the moon. Yet sometimes he starts in his slumber, and wonders at himself and his house, and muses strangely at the resemblance betwixt him and it. He perceives that if his law is still paramount, if still he have elemental power, "if his word is sterling yet in nature," it is not conscious power, it is not inferior but superior to his will. It is Instinct." Thus my Orphic poet sang.

At present, man applies to nature but half his force. He works on the world with his understanding alone. He lives in it, and masters it by a penny-wisdom; and he that works most in it, is but a half-man, and whilst his arms are strong and his digestion good, his mind is imbruted and he is a selfish savage. His relation to nature, his power over it, is through the understanding; as by manure; the economic use of fire, wind, water, and the mariner's needle; steam, coal, chemical agriculture; the repairs of the human body by the dentist and the surgeon. This is such a resumption of power, as if a banished king should buy his territories inch by inch, instead of vaulting at once into his throne. Meantime, in the thick darkness, there are not wanting gleams of a better light,—occasional examples of the action of man upon nature with his entire force,—with reason as well as understanding. Such examples are; the traditions of miracles in the earliest antiquity of all nations; the history of Jesus Christ; the achievements of a principle, as in religious and political revolutions, and in the abolition of the Slave-trade; the miracles of enthusiasm,[7] as those reported of Swedenborg, Hohenlohe, and the Shakers;[8] many obscure and yet contested facts, now arranged under the name of Animal Magnetism;[9] prayer; eloquence; self-healing; and the wisdom of children. These are examples of Reason's momentary grasp of the sceptre; the exertions of a power which exists not in time or space, but an instantaneous instreaming causing power. The difference between the actual and the ideal force of man is happily figured by the schoolmen,[1] in saying, that the knowledge of man is an evening knowledge, *vespertina*

---

7. Those in a supernatural ecstasy or possession.
8. Leopold Franz Emmerich, Prince of Hohnlohe (1794–1849), reputed miracle healer; the Shakers, an offshoot of the Quakers, also believed in miraculous cures.
9. Hypnotism.

cognitio, but that of God is a morning knowledge, *matutina cognitio*.

The problem of restoring to the world original and eternal beauty, is solved by the redemption of the soul. The ruin or the blank, that we see when we look at nature, is in our own eye. The axis of vision is not coincident with the axis of things, and so they appear not transparent but opake. The reason why the world lacks unity, and lies broken and in heaps, is, because man is disunited with himself. He cannot be a naturalist, until he satisfies all the demands of the spirit. Love is as much its demand, as perception. Indeed, neither can be perfect without the other. In the uttermost meaning of the words, thought is devout, and devotion is thought. Deep calls unto deep.[2] But in actual life, the marriage is not celebrated. There are innocent men who worship God after the tradition of their fathers, but their sense of duty has not yet extended to the use of all their faculties. And there are patient naturalists, but they freeze their subject under the wintry light of the understanding. Is not prayer also a study of truth,—a sally of the soul into the unfound infinite? No man ever prayed heartily, without learning something. But when a faithful thinker, resolute to detach every object from personal relations, and see it in the light of thought, shall, at the same time, kindle science with the fire of the holiest affections, then will God go forth anew into the creation.

It will not need, when the mind is prepared for study, to search for objects. The invariable mark of wisdom is to see the miraculous in the common. What is a day? What is a year? What is summer? What is woman? What is a child? What is sleep? To our blindness, these things seem unaffecting. We make fables to hide the baldness of the fact and conform it, as we say, to the higher law of the mind. But when the fact is seen under the light of an idea, the gaudy fable fades and shrivels. We behold the real higher law. To the wise, therefore, a fact is true poetry, and the most beautiful of fables. These wonders are brought to our own door. You also are a man. Man and woman, and their social life, poverty, labor, sleep, fear, fortune, are known to you. Learn that none of these things is superficial, but that each phenomenon hath its roots in the faculties and affections of the mind. Whilst the abstract question occupies your intellect, nature brings it in the concrete to be solved by your hands. It were a wise inquiry for the closet,[3] to compare, point by point, especially at remarkable crises in life, our daily history, with the rise and progress of ideas in the mind.

So shall we come to look at the world with new eyes. It shall answer the endless inquiry of the intellect,—What is truth? and of the affections,—What is good? by yielding itself passive to the

1. Medieval scholastic philosophers (see *JMN* VI.179).

2. Psalms 42.7.
3. The scholar's private workroom.

educated Will. Then shall come to pass what my poet said; 'Nature is not fixed but fluid. Spirit alters, moulds, makes it. The immobility or bruteness of nature, is the absence of spirit; to pure spirit, it is fluid, it is volatile, it is obedient. Every spirit builds itself a house; and beyond its house, a world; and beyond its world, a heaven. Know then, that the world exists for you. For you is the phenomenon perfect. What we are, that only can we see. All that Adam had, all that Cæsar could, you have and can do. Adam called his house, heaven and earth; Cæsar called his house, Rome; you perhaps call yours, a cobler's trade; a hundred acres of ploughed land; or a scholar's garret. Yet line for line and point for point, your dominion is as great as theirs, though without fine names. Build, therefore, your own world. As fast as you conform your life to the pure idea in your mind, that will unfold its great proportions. A correspondent revolution in things will attend the influx of the spirit. So fast will disagreeable appearances, swine, spiders, snakes, pests, mad-houses, prisons, enemies vanish; they are temporary and shall be no more seen. The sordor and filths of nature the sun shall dry up, and the wind exhale. As when the summer comes from the south, the snow-banks melt, and the face of the earth becomes green before it, so shall the advancing spirit create its ornaments along its path, and carry with it the beauty it visits, and the song which enchants it; it shall draw beautiful faces, and warm hearts, and wise discourse, and heroic acts, around its way, until evil is no more seen. The kingdom of man over nature, which cometh not with observation,[4]—a dominion such as now is beyond his dream of God,—he shall enter without more wonder than the blind man feels who is gradually restored to perfect sight.'

1836

The American Scholar[1]

Mr. President, and Gentlemen,

I greet you on the re-commencement of our literary year. Our anniversary is one of hope, and, perhaps, not enough of labor. We do not meet for games of strength or skill, for the recitation of histories, tragedies and odes, like the ancient Greeks; for parliaments of love and poesy, like the Troubadours;[2] nor for the advancement of science, like our cotemporaries in the British and European capitals. Thus far, our holiday has been simply a friendly sign of the survival of the love of letters amongst a people too busy

4. Luke 17.20.
1. The text printed here is that of the first publication (Boston, 1837) as a pamphlet entitled *An Oration, Delivered before the Phi Beta Kappa Society, at Cambridge, August 31, 1837.* By altering the title to *The American Scholar* when he republished it in *Essays* (1841), Emerson expanded the application to all American college students and all others who dedicate themselves to thought.
2. Courtly poets of southern France, especially Provence, in the 12th and 13th centuries.

to give to letters any more. As such, it is precious as the sign of an indestructible instinct. Perhaps the time is already come, when it ought to be, and will be something else; when the sluggard intellect of this continent will look from under its iron lids and fill the post-poned expectation of the world with something better than the exertions of mechanical skill. Our day of dependence, our long apprenticeship to the learning of other lands, draws to a close. The millions that around us are rushing into life, cannot always be fed on the sere remains of foreign harvests. Events, actions arise, that must be sung, that will sing themselves. Who can doubt that poetry will revive and lead in a new age, as the star in the constellation Harp which now flames in our zenith, astronomers announce, shall one day be the pole-star for a thousand years.

In the light of this hope, I accept the topic which not only usage, but the nature of our association, seem to prescribe to this day,— the AMERICAN SCHOLAR. Year by year, we come up hither to read one more chapter of his biography. Let us inquire what new lights, new events and more days have thrown on his character, his duties and his hopes.

It is one of those fables, which out of an unknown antiquity, convey an unlooked for wisdom, that the gods, in the beginning, divided Man into men, that he might be more helpful to himself;[3] just as the hand was divided into fingers, the better to answer its end.

The old fable covers a doctrine ever new and sublime; that there is One Man,—present to all particular men only partially, or through one faculty; and that you must take the whole society to find the whole man. Man is not a farmer, or a professor, or an engineer, but he is all. Man is priest, and scholar, and statesman, and producer, and soldier. In the *divided* or social state, these functions are parcelled out to individuals, each of whom aims to do his stint of the joint work, whilst each other performs his. The fable implies that the individual to possess himself, must sometimes re-turn from his own labor to embrace all the other laborers. But unfortunately, this original unit, this fountain of power, has been so distributed to multitudes, has been so minutely subdivided and peddled out, that it is spilled into drops, and cannot be gathered. The state of society is one in which the members have suffered amputation from the trunk, and strut about so many walking monsters,—a good finger, a neck, a stomach, an elbow, but never a man.

Man is thus metamorphosed into a thing, into many things. The planter, who is Man sent out into the field to gather food, is seldom cheered by any idea of the true dignity of his ministry. He sees his bushel and his cart, and nothing beyond, and sinks into the farmer,

3. One such fable Emerson knew from Plato's *Symposium*.

instead of Man on the farm. The tradesman scarcely ever gives an ideal worth to his work, but is ridden by the routine of his craft, and the soul is subject to dollars. The priest becomes a form; the attorney, a statute-book; the mechanic, a machine; the sailor, a rope of a ship.

In this distribution of functions, the scholar is the delegated intellect. In the right state, he is, *Man Thinking*. In the degenerate state, when the victim of society, he tends to become a mere thinker, or, still worse, the parrot of other men's thinking.

In this view of him, as Man Thinking, the whole theory of his office[4] is contained. Him nature solicits, with all her placid, all her monitory pictures. Him the past instructs. Him the future invites. Is not, indeed, every man a student, and do not all things exist for the student's behoof? And, finally, is not the true scholar the only true master? But, as the old oracle said, "All things have two handles. Beware of the wrong one." In life, too often, the scholar errs with mankind and forfeits his privilege. Let us see him in his school, and consider him in reference to the main influences he receives.

I. The first in time and the first in importance of the influences upon the mind is that of nature. Every day, the sun; and, after sunset, night and her stars. Ever the winds blow; ever the grass grows. Every day, men and women, conversing, beholding and beholden. The scholar must needs stand wistful and admiring before this great spectacle. He must settle its value in his mind. What is nature to him? There is never a beginning, there is never an end to the inexplicable continuity of this web of God, but always circular power returning into itself. Therein it resembles his own spirit, whose beginning, whose ending he never can find—so entire, so boundless. Far, too, as her splendors shine, system on system shooting like rays, upward, downward, without centre, without circumference,—in the mass and in the particle nature hastens to render account of herself to the mind. Classification begins. To the young mind, every thing is individual, stands by itself. By and by, it finds how to join two things, and see in them one nature; then three, then three thousand; and so, tyrannized over by its own unifying instinct, it goes on tying things together, diminishing anomalies, discovering roots running under ground, whereby contrary and remote things cohere, and flower out from one stem. It presently learns, that, since the dawn of history, there has been a constant accumulation and classifying of facts. But what is classification but the perceiving that these objects are not chaotic, and are not foreign, but have a law which is also a law of the human mind? The astronomer discovers that geometry, a pure abstraction of the human mind, is the measure of planetary motion. The chemist finds proportions and intelligible method throughout matter: and science is nothing but the finding of analogy, identity in the most remote

4. Function.

parts. The ambitious soul sits down before each refractory fact; one after another, reduces all strange constitutions, all new powers, to their class and their law, and goes on forever to animate the last fibre of organization, the outskirts of nature, by insight.

Thus to him, to this school-boy under the bending dome of day, is suggested, that he and it proceed from one root; one is leaf and one is flower; relation, sympathy, stirring in every vein. And what is that Root? Is not that the soul of his soul?—A thought too bold—a dream too wild. Yet when this spiritual light shall have revealed the law of more earthly natures,—when he has learned to worship the soul, and to see that the natural philosophy that now is, is only the first gropings of its gigantic hand, he shall look forward to an ever expanding knowledge as to a becoming creator. He shall see that nature is the opposite of the soul, answering to it part for part. One is seal, and one is print. Its beauty is the beauty of his own mind. Its laws are the laws of his own mind. Nature then becomes to him the measure of his attainments. So much of nature as he is ignorant of, so much of his own mind does he not yet possess. And, in fine, the ancient precept, "Know thyself," and the modern precept, "Study nature," become at last one maxim.

II. The next great influence[5] into the spirit of the scholar, is, the mind of the Past,—in whatever form, whether of literature, of art, of institutions, that mind is inscribed. Books are the best type of the influence of the past, and perhaps we shall get at the truth—learn the amount of this influence more conveniently—by considering their value alone.

The theory of books is noble. The scholar of the first age received into him the world around; brooded thereon; gave it the new arrangement of his own mind, and uttered it again. It came into him—life; it went out from him—truth. It came to him—short-lived actions; it went out from him—immortal thoughts. It came to him —business; it went from him—poetry. It was—dead fact; now, it is quick[6] thought. It can stand, and it can go. It now endures, it now flies, it now inspires.[7] Precisely in proportion to the depth of mind from which it issued, so high does it soar, so long does it sing.

Or, I might say, it depends on how far the process had gone, of transmuting life into truth. In proportion to the completeness of the distillation, so will the purity and imperishableness of the product be. But none is quite perfect. As no air-pump can by any means make a perfect vacuum, so neither can any artist entirely exclude the conventional, the local, the perishable from his book, or write a book of pure thought that shall be as efficient, in all respects, to a remote posterity, as to cotemporaries, or rather to the second age. Each age, it is found, must write its own books; or rather, each

5. Inflowing.
6. "Business": busyness, activity; "quick": living.
7. Breathes in; "go": walk.

generation for the next succeeding. The books of an older period will not fit this.

Yet hence arises a grave mischief. The sacredness which attaches to the act of creation,—the act of thought,—is instantly transferred to the record. The poet chanting, was felt to be a divine man. Henceforth the chant is divine also. The writer was a just and wise spirit. Henceforward it is settled, the book is perfect; as love of the hero corrupts into worship of his statue. Instantly, the book becomes noxious. The guide is a tyrant. We sought a brother, and lo, a governor. The sluggish and perverted mind of the multitude, always slow to open to the incursions of Reason, having once so opened, having once received this book, stands upon it, and makes an outcry, if it is disparaged. Colleges are built on it. Books are written on it by thinkers, not by Man Thinking; by men of talent, that is, who start wrong, who set out from accepted dogmas, not from their own sight of principles. Meek young men grow up in libraries, believing it their duty to accept the views which Cicero, which Locke, which Bacon[8] have given, forgetful that Cicero, Locke and Bacon were only young men in libraries when they wrote these books.

Hence, instead of Man Thinking, we have the bookworm. Hence, the book-learned class, who value books, as such; not as related to nature and the human constitution, but as making a sort of Third Estate[9] with the world and the soul. Hence, the restorers of readings, the emendators, the bibliomaniacs of all degrees.

This is bad; this is worse than it seems. Books are the best of things, well used; abused, among the worst. What is the right use? What is the one end which all means go to effect? They are for nothing but to inspire. I had better never see a book than to be warped by its attraction clean out of my own orbit, and made a satellite instead of a system. The one thing in the world of value, is, the active soul,—the soul, free, sovereign, active. This every man is entitled to; this every man contains within him, although in almost all men, obstructed, and as yet unborn. The soul active sees absolute truth; and utters truth, or creates. In this action, it is genius; not the privilege of here and there a favorite, but the sound estate of every man. In its essence, it is progressive. The book, the college, the school of art, the institution of any kind, stop with some past utterance of genius. This is good, say they,—let us hold by this. They pin me down. They look backward and not forward. But

8. These examples are not especially apt, since none of the three wrote books at an unusually precocious age. As a young man Marcus Tullius Cicero (106–43 B.C.), Roman statesman, was best known for his oratory; John Locke (1632–1704), English philosopher and political thinker, wrote *Essay Concerning Human Understanding* (1690); before he was 40. Sir Francis Bacon (1561–1626), English statesman and philosopher, wrote his *Essays*.

9. On the analogy of the three-part division of estates of the realm, in which the third estate is the common people while the first estate is the nobility and the second the clergy.

genius always looks forward. The eyes of man are set in his fore-head, not in his hindhead. Man hopes. Genius creates. To create,—to create,—is the proof of a divine presence. Whatever talents may be, if the man create not, the pure efflux[1] of the Deity is not his:—cinders and smoke, there may be, but not yet flame. There are creative manners, there are creative actions, and creative words; manners, actions, words, that is, indicative of no custom or authority, but springing spontaneous from the mind's own sense of good and fair.

On the other part, instead of being its own seer, let it receive always from another mind its truth, though it were in torrents of light, without periods of solitude, inquest and self-recovery, and a fatal disservice is done. Genius is always sufficiently the enemy of genius by over-influence. The literature of every nation bear me witness. The English dramatic poets have Shakspearized now for two hundred years.

Undoubtedly there is a right way of reading,—so it be sternly subordinated. Man Thinking must not be subdued by his instruments. Books are for the scholar's idle times. When he can read God directly, the hour is too precious to be wasted in other mens' transcripts of their readings. But when the intervals of darkness come, as come they must,—when the soul seeth not, when the sun is hid, and the stars withdraw their shining,—we repair to the lamps which were kindled by their ray to guide our steps to the East again, where the dawn is. We hear that we may speak. The Arabian proverb says, "A fig tree looking on a fig tree, becometh fruitful."

It is remarkable, the character of the pleasure we derive from the best books. They impress us ever with the conviction that one nature wrote and the same reads. We read the verses of one of the great English poets, of Chaucer, of Marvell, of Dryden, with the most modern joy,—with a pleasure, I mean, which is in great part caused by the abstraction of all *time* from their verses. There is some awe mixed with the joy of our surprise, when this poet, who lived in some past world, two or three hundred years ago, says that which lies close to my own soul, that which I also had well nigh thought and said. But for the evidence thence afforded to the philosophical doctrine of the identity of all minds, we should suppose some pre-established harmony, some foresight of souls that were to be, and some preparation of stores for their future wants, like the fact observed in insects, who lay up food before death for the young grub they shall never see.

I would not be hurried by any love of system, by any exaggeration of instincts, to underrate the Book. We all know, that as the human body can be nourished on any food, though it were boiled grass and the broth of shoes, so the human mind can be fed by any

---

1. Flowing forth.

knowledge. And great and heroic men have existed, who had almost
no other information than by the printed page. I only would say,
that it needs a strong head to bear that diet. One must be an
inventor to read well. As the proverb says, "He that would bring
home the wealth of the Indies, must carry out the wealth of the
Indies." There is then creative reading, as well as creative writing.
When the mind is braced by labor and invention, the page of
whatever book we read becomes luminous with manifold allusion.
Every sentence is doubly significant, and the sense of our author is
as broad as the world. We then see, what is always true, that as the
seer's hour of vision is short and rare among heavy days and
months, so is its record, perchance, the least part of his volume. The
discerning will read in his Plato or Shakspeare, only that least
part,—only the authentic utterances of the oracle,—and all the rest
he rejects, were it never so many times Plato's and Shakspeare's.

Of course, there is a portion of reading quite indispensable to a
wise man. History and exact science he must learn by laborious
reading. Colleges, in like manner, have their indispensable office,—
to teach elements. But they can only highly serve us, when they aim
not to drill, but to create; when they gather from far every ray of
various genius to their hospitable halls, and, by the concentrated
fires, set the hearts of their youth on flame. Thought and knowledge
are natures in which apparatus and pretension avail nothing.
Gowns, and pecuniary foundations, though of towns of gold, can
never countervail the least sentence or syllable of wit. Forget this,
and our American colleges will recede in their public importance
whilst they grow richer every year.

III. There goes in the world a notion that the scholar should be a
recluse, a valetudinarian,—as unfit for any handiwork or public
labor, as a penknife for an axe. The so called "practical men" sneer
at speculative men, as if, because they speculate or *see*, they could
do nothing. I have heard it said that the clergy,—who are always
more universally than any other class, the scholars of their day,—
are addressed as women: that the rough, spontaneous conversation
of men they do not hear, but only a mincing and diluted speech.
They are often virtually disfranchised; and, indeed, there are advocates for their celibacy. As far as this is true of the studious classes,
it is not just and wise. Action is with the scholar subordinate, but it
is essential. Without it, he is not yet man. Without it, thought can
never ripen into truth. Whilst the world hangs before the eye as a
cloud of beauty, we can not even see its beauty. Inaction is cowardice, but there can be no scholar without the heroic mind. The
preamble of thought, the transition through which it passes from
the unconscious to the conscious, is action. Only so much do I
know, as I have lived. Instantly we know whose words are loaded
with life, and whose not.

The world,—this shadow of the soul, or *other me*, lies wide around. Its attractions are the keys which unlock my thoughts and make me acquainted with myself. I launch eagerly into this resounding tumult. I grasp the hands of those next me, and take my place in the ring to suffer and to work, taught by an instinct that so shall the dumb abyss be vocal with speech. I pierce its order; I dissipate its fear; I dispose of it within the circuit of my expanding life. So much only of life as I know by experience, so much of the wilderness have I vanquished and planted, or so far have I extended my being, my dominion. I do not see how any man can afford, for the sake of his nerves and his nap, to spare any action in which he can partake. It is pearls and rubies to his discourse. Drudgery, calamity, exasperation, want, are instructers in eloquence and wisdom. The true scholar grudges every opportunity of action past by, as a loss of power.

It is the raw material out of which the intellect moulds her splendid products. A strange process too, this, by which experience is converted into thought, as a mulberry leaf is converted into satin. The manufacture goes forward at all hours.

The actions and events of our childhood and youth are now matters of calmest observation. They lie like fair pictures in the air. Not so with our recent actions,—with the business which we now have in hand. On this we are quite unable to speculate. Our affections as yet circulate through it. We no more feel or know it, than we feel the feet, or the hand, or the brain of our body. The new deed is yet a part of life,—remains for a time immersed in our unconscious life. In some contemplative hour, it detaches itself from the life like a ripe fruit, to become a thought of the mind. Instantly, it is raised, transfigured; the corruptible has put on incorruption.[2] Always now it is an object of beauty, however base its origin and neighborhood. Observe, too, the impossibility of antedating this act. In its grub state, it cannot fly, it cannot shine,—it is a dull grub. But suddenly, without observation, the selfsame thing unfurls beautiful wings, and is an angel of wisdom. So is there no fact, no event, in our private history, which shall not, sooner or later, lose its adhesive inert form, and astonish us by soaring from our body into the empyrean.[3] Cradle and infancy, school and playground, the fear of boys, and dogs, and ferules,[4] the love of little maids and berries, and many another fact that once filled the whole sky, are gone already; friend and relative, profession and party, town and country, nation and world, must also soar and sing.

Of course, he who has put forth his total strength in fit actions, has the richest return of wisdom. I will not shut myself out of this globe of action and transplant an oak into a flower pot, there to hunger and pine; nor trust the revenue of some single faculty, and

2. "For this corruptible must put on in corruption, and this mortal must put on immortality" (1 Corinthians 15.53).

3. The highest reaches of heaven.
4. Rods used for punishing children.

exhaust one vein of thought, much like those Savoyards,[5] who, getting their livelihood by carving shepherds, shepherdesses, and smoking Dutchmen, for all Europe, went out one day to the mountain to find stock, and discovered that they had whittled up the last of their pine trees. Authors we have in numbers,[6] who have written out their vein, and who, moved by a commendable prudence, sail for Greece or Palestine, follow the trapper into the prairie, or ramble round Algiers to replenish their merchantable stock.

If it were only for a vocabulary the scholar would be covetous of action. Life is our dictionary. Years are well spent in country labors; in town—in the insight into trades and manufactures; in frank intercourse with many men and women; in science; in art; to the one end of mastering in all their facts a language, by which to illustrate and embody our perceptions. I learn immediately from any speaker how much he has already lived, through the poverty or the splendor of his speech. Life lies behind us as the quarry from whence we get tiles and copestones for the masonry of to-day. This is the way to learn grammar. Colleges and books only copy the language which the field and the workyard made.

But the final value of action, like that of books, and better than books, is, that it is a resource. That great principle of Undulation in nature, that shows itself in the inspiring and expiring of the breath; in desire and satiety; in the ebb and flow of the sea, in day and night, in heat and cold, and as yet more deeply ingrained in every atom and every fluid, is known to us under the name of Polarity,— these "fits of easy transmission and reflection," as Newton called them,[7] are the law of nature because they are the law of spirit.

The mind now thinks; now acts; and each fit reproduces the other. When the artist has exhausted his materials, when the fancy no longer paints, when thoughts are no longer apprehended, and books are a weariness,—he has always the resource *to live*. Character is higher than intellect. Thinking is the function. Living is the functionary. The stream retreats to its source. A great soul will be strong to live, as well as strong to think. Does he lack organ or medium to impart his truths? He can still fall back on this elemental force of living them. This is a total act. Thinking is a partial act. Let the grandeur of justice shine in his affairs. Let the beauty of affection cheer his lowly roof. Those "far from fame" who dwell and act with him, will feel the force of his constitution in the doings and passages of the day better than it can be measured by any public and designed display. Time shall teach him that the scholar loses no hour which the man lives. Herein he unfolds the sacred germ of his

---

5. Savoy is in the western Alps, where France, Italy, and Switzerland converge.
6. Emerson's contemporaries would have understood a reference to writers now unread, such as Nathaniel Parker Willis, as well as to two still-famous writers, James Fenimore Cooper, author of *The Prairie* (1827), and Washington Irving, author of *A Tour on the Prairies* (1835).
7. From the *Optics* (1704) of Sir Isaac Newton (1642–1727), English scientist and mathematician.

instinct screened from influence. What is lost in seemliness is gained in strength. Not out of those on whom systems of education have exhausted their culture, comes the helpful giant to destroy the old or to build the new, but out of unhandselled[8] savage nature, out of terrible Druids and Berserkirs, come at last Alfred and Shakspear.[9]

I hear therefore with joy whatever is beginning to be said of the dignity and necessity of labor to every citizen. There is virtue yet in the hoe and the spade, for learned as well as for unlearned hands. And labor is every where welcome; always we are invited to work; only be this limitation observed, that a man shall not for the sake of wider activity sacrifice any opinion to the popular judgments and modes of action.

I have now spoken of the education of the scholar by nature, by books, and by action. It remains to say somewhat of his duties.

They are such as become Man Thinking. They may all be comprised in self-trust. The office of the scholar is to cheer, to raise, and to guide men by showing them facts amidst appearances. He plies the slow, unhonored, and unpaid task of observation. Flamsteed and Herschel,[1] in their glazed observatory, may catalogue the stars with the praise of all men, and, the results being splendid and useful, honor is sure. But he, in his private observatory, cataloguing obscure and nebulous stars of the human mind, which as yet no man has thought of as such,—watching days and months, sometimes, for a few facts; correcting still his old records;—must relinquish display and immediate fame. In the long period of his preparation, he must betray often an ignorance and shiftlessness in popular arts, incurring the disdain of the able who shoulder him aside. Long he must stammer in his speech; often forego the living for the dead. Worse yet, he must accept—how often! poverty and solitude. For the ease and pleasure of treading the old road, accepting the fashions, the education, the religion of society, he takes the cross of making his own, and, of course, the self accusation, the faint heart, the frequent uncertainty and loss of time which are the nettles and tangling vines in the way of the self-relying and self-directed; and the state of virtual hostility in which he seems to stand to society, and especially to educated society. For all this loss and scorn, what offset? He is to find consolation in exercising the highest functions of human nature. He is one who raises himself from private considerations, and breathes and lives on public and illustrious thoughts. He is the world's eye. He is the world's heart. He is to resist the vulgar prosperity that retrogrades ever to barbarism, by

---

8. A handsel is a gift to express good wishes at the outset of some enterprise; apparently Emerson uses the word to mean something like unauspicious.
9. Uncivilized Celts and Anglo-Saxons; Alfred was the enlightened ninth-century King of the West Saxons.

1. John Flamsteed (1646–1719), English astronomer, first royal astronomer at Greenwich observatory; Sir William Herschel (1738–1822), German-born English astronomer, founder of sidereal astronomy. "Glazed": glass-roofed.

preserving and communicating heroic sentiments, noble biographies, melodious verse, and the conclusions of history. Whatsoever oracles the human heart in all emergencies, in all solemn hours has uttered as its commentary on the world of actions,—these he shall receive and impart. And whatsoever new verdict Reason from her inviolable seat pronounces on the passing men and events of to-day,—this he shall hear and promulgate.

These being his functions, it becomes him to feel all confidence in himself, and to defer never to the popular cry. He and he only knows the world. The world of any moment is the merest appearance. Some great decorum, some fetish of a government, some ephemeral trade, or war, or man, is cried up by half mankind and cried down by the other half, as if all depended on this particular up or down. The odds are that the whole question is not worth the poorest thought which the scholar has lost in listening to the controversy. Let him not quit his belief that a popgun is a popgun, though the ancient and honorable of the earth affirm it to be the crack of doom. In silence, in steadiness, in severe abstraction, let him hold by himself; add observation to observation; patient of neglect, patient of reproach, and bide his own time,—happy enough if he can satisfy himself alone that this day he has seen something truly. Success treads on every right step. For the instinct is sure that prompts him to tell his brother what he thinks. He then learns that in going down into the secrets of his own mind, he has descended into the secrets of all minds. He learns that he who has mastered any law in his private thoughts, is master to that extent of all men whose language he speaks, and of all into whose language his own can be translated. The poet in utter solitude remembering his spontaneous thoughts and recording them, is found to have recorded that which men in "cities vast" find true for them also. The orator distrusts at first the fitness of his frank confessions,—his want of knowledge of the persons he addresses,—until he finds that he is the complement of his hearers;—that they drink his words because he fulfils for them their own nature; the deeper he dives into his privatest secretest presentiment,—to his wonder he finds, this is the most acceptable, most public, and universally true. The people delight in it; the better part of every man feels, This is my music: this is myself.

In self-trust, all the virtues are comprehended. Free should the scholar be,—free and brave. Free even to the definition of freedom, "without any hindrance that does not arise out of his own constitution." Brave; for fear is a thing which a scholar by his very function puts behind him. Fear always springs from ignorance. It is a shame to him if his tranquillity, amid dangerous times, arise from the presumption that like children and women, his is a protected class; or if he seek a temporary peace by the diversion of his thoughts from politics or vexed questions, hiding his head like an ostrich in the flowering bushes, peeping into microscopes, and turning rhymes, as a boy whistles to keep his courage up. So is the danger a danger still: so is the fear worse. Manlike let him turn and face it. Let him look into its eye and search its nature, inspect its origin—see the whelping of this lion,—which lies no great way back; he will then find in himself a perfect comprehension of its nature and extent; he will have made his hands meet on the other side, and can henceforth defy it, and pass on superior. The world is his who can see through its pretension. What deafness, what stone-blind custom, what overgrown error you behold, is there only by sufferance,—by your sufferance. See it to be a lie, and you have already dealt it its mortal blow.

Yes, we are the cowed,—we the trustless. It is a mischievous notion that we are come late into nature; that the world was finished a long time ago. As the world was plastic and fluid in the hands of God, so it is ever to so much of his attributes as we bring to it. To ignorance and sin, it is flint. They adapt themselves to it as they may; but in proportion as a man has anything in him divine, the firmament flows before him, and takes his signet[2] and form. Not he is great who can alter matter, but he who can alter my state of mind. They are the kings of the world who give the color of their present thought to all nature and all art, and persuade men by the cheerful serenity of their carrying the matter, that this thing which they do, is the apple which the ages have desired to pluck, now at last ripe, and inviting nations to the harvest. The great man makes the great thing. Wherever Macdonald sits, there is the head of the table.[3] Linnæus makes botany the most alluring of studies and wins it from the farmer and the herb-woman. Davy, chemistry: and Cuvier, fossils.[4] The day is always his, who works in it with serenity and great aims. The unstable estimates of men crowd to him whose mind is filled with a truth, as the heaped waves of the Atlantic follow the moon.

For this self-trust, the reason is deeper than can be fathomed,—darker than can be enlightened. I might not carry with me the feeling of my audience in stating my own belief. But I have already shown the ground of my hope, in adverting to the doctrine that man is one. I believe man has been wronged: he has wronged himself. He has almost lost the light that can lead him back to his prerogatives. Men are become of no account. Men in history, men in the world of to-day are bugs, are spawn, and are called "the mass" and "the herd." In a century, in a millenium, one or two men; that is to say —one or two approximations to the right state of every man. All the rest behold in the hero or the poet their own green and crude being

2. Seal.
3. An old proverb says, "Where Macgregor sits, there is the head of the table"; Emerson substitutes another type name for a Scottish chief.

4. Carolus Linnaeus (1707–78), Swedish botanist; Sir Humphry Davy (1778–1829), English chemist; Georges Cuvier (1769–1832), French pioneer in comparative anatomy and paleontology.

—ripened; yes, and are content to be less, so *that* may attain to its full stature. What a testimony—full of grandeur, full of pity, is borne to the demands of his own nature, by the poor clansman, the poor partisan, who rejoices in the glory of his chief. The poor and the low find some amends to their immense moral capacity, for their acquiescence in a political and social inferiority. They are content to be brushed like flies from the path of a great person, so that justice shall be done by him to that common nature which it is the dearest desire of all to see enlarged and glorified. They sun themselves in the great man's light, and feel it to be their own element. They cast the dignity of man from their downtrod selves upon the shoulders of a hero, and will perish to add one drop of blood to make that great heart beat, those giant sinews combat and conquer. He lives for us, and we live in him.

Men such as they are, very naturally seek money or power; and power because it is as good as money,—the "spoils," so called, "of office." And why not? for they aspire to the highest, and this, in their sleep-walking, they dream is highest. Wake them, and they shall quit the false good and leap to the true, and leave government to clerks and desks. This revolution is to be wrought by the gradual domestication of the idea of Culture. The main enterprise of the world for splendor, for extent, is the upbuilding of a man. Here are the materials strown along the ground. The private life of one man shall be a more illustrious monarchy,—more formidable to its enemy, more sweet and serene in its influence to its friend, than any kingdom in history. For a man, rightly viewed, comprehendeth the particular natures of all men. Each philosopher, each bard, each actor, has only done for me, as by a delegate, what one day I can do for myself. The books which once we valued more than the apple of the eye, we have quite exhausted. What is that but saying that we have come up with the point of view which the universal mind took through the eyes of that one scribe; we have been that man, and have passed on. First, one; then, another; we drain all cisterns, and waxing greater by all these supplies, we crave a better and more abundant food. The man has never lived that can feed us ever. The human mind cannot be enshrined in a person who shall set a barrier on any one side to this unbounded, unboundable empire. It is one central fire which flaming now out of the lips of Etna, lightens the capes of Sicily; and now out of the throat of Vesuvius, illuminates the towers and vineyards of Naples.[5] It is one light which beams out of a thousand stars. It is one soul which animates all men.

But I have dwelt perhaps tediously upon this abstraction of the Scholar. I ought not to delay longer to add what I have to say, of nearer reference to the time and to this country.

Historically, there is thought to be a difference in the ideas which predominate over successive epochs, and there are data for marking

5. **Active volcanoes in eastern Sicily and western Italy.**

the genius of the Classic, of the Romantic, and now of the Reflective or Philosophical age.[6] With the views I have intimated of the oneness or the identity of the mind through all individuals, I do not much dwell on these differences. In fact, I believe each individual passes through all three. The boy is a Greek; the youth, romantic; the adult, reflective. I deny not, however, that a revolution in the leading idea may be distinctly enough traced.

Our age is bewailed as the age of Introversion. Must that needs be evil? We, it seems, are critical. We are embarrassed with second thoughts. We cannot enjoy any thing for hankering to know whereof the pleasure consists. We are lined with eyes. We see with our feet. The time is infected with Hamlet's unhappiness,—

"Sicklied o'er with the pale cast of thought."[7]

Is it so bad then? Sight is the last thing to be pitied. Would we be blind? Do we fear lest we should outsee nature and God, and drink truth dry? I look upon the discontent of the literary class as a mere announcement of the fact that they find themselves not in the state of mind of their fathers, and regret the coming state as untried; as a boy dreads the water before he has learned that he can swim. If there is any period one would desire to be born in,—is it not the age of Revolution; when the old and the new stand side by side, and admit of being compared; when the energies of all men are searched by fear and by hope; when the historic glories of the old, can be compensated by the rich possibilities of the new era? This time, like all times, is a very good one, if we but know what to do with it.

I read with joy some of the auspicious signs of the coming days as they glimmer already through poetry and art, through philosophy and science, through church and state.

One of these signs is the fact that the same movement which effected the elevation of what was called the lowest class in the state, assumed in literature a very marked and as benign an aspect. Instead of the sublime and beautiful, the near, the low, the common, was explored and poetised. That which had been negligently trodden under foot by those who were harnessing and provisioning themselves for long journeys into far countries, is suddenly found to be richer than all foreign parts. The literature of the poor, the feelings of the child, the philosophy of the street, the meaning of household life, are the topics of the time. It is a great stride. It is a sign—is it not? of new vigor, when the extremities are made active, when currents of warm life run into the hands and the feet. I ask not for the great, the remote, the romantic; what is doing in Italy or Arabia; what is Greek art, or Provencal Minstrelsy; I embrace the

6. Emerson proceeds to refute the self-excusing notion that his age was merely a time for criticism, not for genuinely creative achievements.
7. *Hamlet*, 3.1.85–87.

common, I explore and sit at the feet of the familiar, the low. Give me insight into to-day, and you may have the antique and future worlds. What would we really know the meaning of? The meal in the firkin; the milk in the pan; the ballad in the street; the news of the boat; the glance of the eye; the form and the gait of the body;—show me the ultimate reason of these matters;—show me the sublime presence of the highest spiritual cause lurking, as always it does lurk, in these suburbs and extremities of nature; let me see every trifle bristling with the polarity that ranges it instantly on an eternal law; and the shop, the plough, and the ledger, referred to the like cause by which light undulates and poets sing;—and the world lies no longer a dull miscellany and lumber room,[8] but has form and order; there is no trifle; there is no puzzle; but one design unites and animates the farthest pinnacle and the lowest trench.

This idea has inspired the genius of Goldsmith, Burns, Cowper, and, in a newer time, of Goethe, Wordsworth, and Carlyle. This idea they have differently followed and with various success. In contrast with their writing, the style of Pope, of Johnson, of Gibbon, looks cold and pedantic.[9] This writing is blood-warm. Man is surprised to find that things near are not less beautiful and wondrous than things remote. The near explains the far. The drop is a small ocean. A man is related to all nature. This perception of the worth of the vulgar, is fruitful in discoveries. Goethe, in this very thing the most modern of the moderns, has shown us, as none ever did, the genius of the ancients.

There is one man of genius who has done much for this philosophy of life, whose literary value has never yet been rightly estimated; —I mean Emanuel Swedenborg.[1] The most imaginative of men, yet writing with the precision of a mathematician, he endeavored to engraft a purely philosophical Ethics on the popular Christianity of his time. Such an attempt, of course, must have difficulty which no genius could surmount. But he saw and showed the connexion between nature and the affections of the soul. He pierced the emblematic or spiritual character of the visible, audible, tangible world. Especially did his shade-loving muse hover over and interpret the lower parts of nature; he showed the mysterious bond that allies moral evil to the foul material forms, and has given in epical parables a theory of insanity, of beasts, of unclean and fearful things.

Another sign of our times, also marked by an analogous political

8. Junk room.

9. Himself nurtured on such "cold and pedantic" writers as Alexander Pope, Samuel Johnson, and Edward Gibbon, in this passage Emerson conventionally contrasts them with the so-called pre-Romantics like Oliver Goldsmith, Robert Burns, and William Cowper and Romantics like Goethe, Wordsworth, and Carlyle, supposedly marked by greater attention to aspects of ordinary life.

1. No important critic after Emerson has taken up this advocacy of literary greatness in Emanuel Swedenborg (1688–1772), Swedish scientist and theologian. He was a passion of Emerson's because of intellectual and spiritual affinities, not intrinsic literary merit.

movement is, the new importance given to the single person. Every thing that tends to insulate the individual,—to surround him with barriers of natural respect, so that each man shall feel the world is his, and man shall treat with man as a sovereign state with a sovereign state;—tends to true union as well as greatness. "I learned," said the melancholy Pestalozzi,[2] "that no man in God's wide earth is either willing or able to help any other man." Help must come from the bosom alone. The scholar is that man who must take up into himself all the ability of the time, all the contributions of the past, all the hopes of the future. He must be an university of knowledges. If there be one lesson more than another which should pierce his ear, it is, The world is nothing, the man is all; in yourself is the law of all nature, and you know not yet how a globule of sap ascends; in yourself slumbers the whole of Reason; it is for you to know all, it is for you to dare all. Mr. President and Gentlemen, this confidence in the unsearched might of man, belongs by all motives, by all prophecy, by all preparation, to the American Scholar. We have listened too long to the courtly muses of Europe. The spirit of the American freeman is already suspected to be timid, imitative, tame. Public and private avarice make the air we breathe thick and fat. The scholar is decent, indolent, complaisant.[3] See already the tragic consequence. The mind of this country taught to aim at low objects, eats upon itself. There is no work for any but the decorous and the complaisant. Young men of the fairest promise, who begin life upon our shores, inflated by the mountain winds, shined upon by all the stars of God, find the earth below not in unison with these,—but are hindered from action by the disgust which the principles on which business is managed inspire, and turn drudges, or die of disgust,—some of them suicides. What is the remedy? They did not yet see, and thousands of young men as hopeful now crowding to the barriers for the career, do not yet see, that if the single man plant himself indomitably on his instincts, and there abide, the huge world will come round to him. Patience—patience;—with the shades of all the good and great for company; and for solace, the perspective of your own infinite life; and for work, the study and the communication of principles, the making those instincts prevalent, the conversion of the world. Is it not the chief disgrace in the world, not to be an unit;—not to be reckoned one character;—not to yield that peculiar fruit which each man was created to bear, but to be reckoned in the gross, in the hundred, or the thousand, of the party, the section, to which we belong; and our opinion predicted geographically, as the north, or the south. Not so, brothers and friends,—please God, ours shall not be so. We will

2. Johann Heinrich Pestalozzi (1746–1827), Swiss educator and benefactor of poor children, whose ideas on education influenced Emerson's friends Bronson Alcott and Elizabeth Peabody.
3. Too ready to please others.

walk on our own feet; we will work with our own hands; we will speak our own minds. Then shall man be no longer a name for pity, for doubt, and for sensual indulgence. The dread of man and the love of man shall be a wall of defence and a wreath of love around all. A nation of men will for the first time exist, because each believes himself inspired by the Divine Soul which also inspires all men.

1837

The Divinity School Address[1]

In this refulgent summer it has been a luxury to draw the breath of life. The grass grows, the buds burst, the meadow is spotted with fire and gold in the tint of flowers. The air is full of birds, and sweet with the breath of the pine, the balm-of-Gilead,[2] and the new hay. Night brings no gloom to the heart with its welcome shade. Through the transparent darkness pour the stars their almost spiritual rays. Man under them seems a young child, and his huge globe a toy. The cool night bathes the world as with a river, and prepares his eyes again for the crimson dawn. The mystery of nature was never displayed more happily. The corn and the wine have been freely dealt to all creatures, and the never-broken silence with which the old bounty goes forward, has not yielded yet one word of explanation. One is constrained to respect the perfection of this world, in which our senses converse. How wide; how rich; what invitation from every property it gives to every faculty of man! In its fruitful soils; in its navigable sea; in its mountains of metal and stone; in its forests of all woods; in its animals; in its chemical ingredients; in the powers and path of light, heat, attraction, and life, is it well worth the pith and heart of great men to subdue and enjoy it. The planters, the mechanics, the inventors, the astronomers, the builders of cities, and the captains, history delights to honor.

But the moment the mind opens, and reveals the laws which traverse the universe, and make things what they are, then shrinks the great world at once into a mere illustration and fable of this mind. What am I? and What is? asks the human spirit with a

---

1. *An Address Delivered before the Senior Class in Divinity College, Cambridge, Sunday Evening 15 July, 1838* was published as a pamphlet in Boston soon after it was given. That original text is followed here, though with the title used in *Essays* (1841). Outraged attacks appeared in newspapers and pamphlets, and Emerson cautioned himself in his journal to remain "steady." (Perry Miller, in *The Transcendentalists* [1950], reprints some of the documents in this brief furor, including the most notorious attack on Emerson, Andrews Norton's *The Latest Form of Infidelity*.) Emerson retracted nothing privately or publicly and was not invited back to Harvard for three decades, after the university had become more secular and Emerson's own international reputation had muted the charges against him.

2. An aromatic evergreen tree, named for the curative resin associated with Gilead in Jeremiah 8.22: "Is there no balm in Gilead; is there no physician there?"

curiosity new-kindled, but never to be quenched. Behold these out-running laws, which our imperfect apprehension can see tend this way and that, but not come full circle. Behold these infinite relations, so like, so unlike; many, yet one. I would study, I would know, I would admire forever. These works of thought have been the entertainments of the human spirit in all ages.

A more secret, sweet, and overpowering beauty appears to man when his heart and mind open to the sentiment of virtue. Then instantly he is instructed in what is above him. He learns that his being is without bound; that, to the good, to the perfect, he is born, low as he now lies in evil and weakness. That which he venerates is still his own, though he has not realized it yet. *He ought.* He knows the sense of that grand word, though his analysis fails entirely to render account of it. When in innocency, or when by intellectual perception, he attains to say,—'I love the Right; Truth is beautiful within and without, forevermore. Virtue, I am thine: save me: use me: thee will I serve, day and night, in great, in small, that I may be not virtuous, but virtue;'—then is the end of the creation answered, and God is well pleased.

The sentiment of virtue is a reverence and delight in the presence of certain divine laws. It perceives that this homely game of life we play, covers, under what seem foolish details, principles that astonish. The child amidst his baubles, is learning the action of light, motion, gravity, muscular force; and in the game of human life, love, fear, justice, appetite, man, and God, interact. These laws refuse to be adequately stated. They will not by us or for us be written out on paper, or spoken by the tongue. They elude, evade our persevering thought, and yet we read them hourly in each other's faces, in each other's actions, in our own remorse. The moral traits which are all globed into every virtuous act and thought,—in speech, we must sever, and describe or suggest by painful enumeration of many particulars. Yet, as this sentiment is the essence of all religion, let me guide your eyes to the precise objects of the sentiment, by an enumeration of some of those classes of facts in which this element is conspicuous.

The intuition of the moral sentiment is an insight of the perfection of the laws of the soul. These laws execute themselves. They are out of time, out of space, and not subject to circumstance. Thus; in the soul of man there is a justice whose retributions are instant and entire. He who does a good deed, is instantly ennobled himself. He who does a mean deed, is by the action itself contracted. He who puts off impurity, thereby puts on purity. If a man is at heart just, then in so far is he God; the safety of God, the immortality of God, the majesty of God do enter into that man with justice. If a man dissemble, deceive, he deceives himself, and goes out of acquaintance with his own being. A man in the view of absolute goodness, adores, with total humility. Every step so downward, is a step upward. The man who renounces himself, comes to himself by so doing.

See how this rapid intrinsic energy worketh everywhere, righting wrongs, correcting appearances, and bringing up facts to a harmony with thoughts. Its operation in life, though slow to the senses, is, at last, as sure as in the soul. By it, a man is made the Providence to himself, dispensing good to his goodness, and evil to his sin. Character is always known. Thefts never enrich; alms never impoverish; murder will speak out of stone walls. The least admixture of a lie,—for example, the smallest mixture of vanity, the least attempt to make a good impression, a favorable appearance,—will instantly vitiate the effect. But speak the truth, and all nature and all spirits help you with unexpected furtherance. Speak the truth, and all things alive or brute are vouchers, and the very roots of the grass underground there, do seem to stir and move to bear you witness. See again the perfection of the Law as it applies itself to the affections, and becomes the law of society. As we are, so we associate. The good, by affinity, seek the good; the vile, by affinity, the vile. Thus of their own volition, souls proceed into heaven, into hell.

These facts have always suggested to man the sublime creed, that the world is not the product of manifold power, but of one will, of one mind; and that one mind is everywhere, in each ray of the star, in each wavelet of the pool, active; and whatever opposes that will, is everywhere baulked and baffled, because things are made so, and not otherwise. Good is positive. Evil is merely privative,[3] not absolute. It is like cold, which is the privation of heat. All evil is so much death or nonentity. Benevolence is absolute and real. So much benevolence as a man hath, so much life hath he. For all things proceed out of this same spirit, which is differently named love, justice, temperance, in its different applications, just as the ocean receives different names on the several shores which it washes. All things proceed out of the same spirit, and all things conspire with it. Whilst a man seeks good ends, he is strong by the whole strength of nature. In so far as he roves from these ends, he bereaves himself of power, of auxiliaries; his being shrinks out of all remote channels, he becomes less and less, a mote, a point, until absolute badness is absolute death.

The perception of this law of laws always awakens in the mind a sentiment which we call the religious sentiment, and which makes our highest happiness. Wonderful is its power to charm and to command. It is a mountain air. It is the embalmer of the world. It is myrrh and storax, and chlorine and rosemary.[4] It makes the sky

3. I.e., not an active power, but the absence of a power.
4. One of the gifts the wise men brought to Jesus was myrrh, a perfume made from aromatic resins. Storax is also an aromatic resin. Chlorine, in this sense, is a greenish-yellow gas used for purification. Rosemary is an aromatic evergreen shrub of southern Europe and Asia Minor, used in cookery and perfumery.

and the hills sublime, and the silent song of the stars is it. By it, is the universe made safe and habitable, not by science or power. Thought may work cold and intransitive in things, and find no end or unity. But the dawn of the sentiment of virtue on the heart, gives and is the assurance that Law is sovereign over all natures; and the worlds, time, space, eternity, do seem to break out into joy.

This sentiment is divine and deifying. It is the beatitude of man. It makes him illimitable. Through it, the soul first knows itself. It corrects the capital mistake of the infant man, who seeks to be great by following the great, and hopes to derive advantages *from another,*—by showing the fountain of all good to be in himself, and that he, equally with every man, is a door into the deeps of Reason. When he says, "I ought;" when love warms him; when he chooses, warned from on high, the good and great deed; then, deep melodies wander through his soul from Supreme Wisdom. Then he can worship, and be enlarged by his worship; for he can never go behind this sentiment. In the sublimest flights of the soul, rectitude is never surmounted, love is never outgrown.

This sentiment lies at the foundation of society, and successively creates all forms of worship. The principle of veneration never dies out. Man fallen into superstition, into sensuality, is never wholly without the visions of the moral sentiment. In like manner, all the expressions of this sentiment are sacred and permanent in proportion to their purity. The expressions of this sentiment affect us deeper, greatlier, than all other compositions. The sentences of the oldest time, which ejaculate this piety, are still fresh and fragrant. This thought dwelled always deepest in the minds of men in the devout and contemplative East; not alone in Palestine, where it reached its purest expression, but in Egypt, in Persia, in India, in China. Europe has always owed to oriental genius, its divine impulses. What these holy bards said, all sane men found agreeable and true. And the unique impression of Jesus upon mankind, whose name is not so much written as ploughed into the history of this world, is proof of the subtle virtue of this infusion.

Meantime, whilst the doors of the temple stand open, night and day, before every man, and the oracles of this truth cease never, it is guarded by one stern condition; this, namely; It is an intuition. It cannot be received at second hand. Truly speaking, it is not instruction, but provocation, that I can receive from another soul. What he announces, I must find true in me, or wholly reject; and on his word, or as his second, be he who he may, I can accept nothing. On the contrary, the absence of this primary faith is the presence of degradation. As is the flood so is the ebb. Let this faith depart, and the very words it spake, and the things it made, become false and hurtful. Then falls the church, the state, art, letters, life. The doctrine of the divine nature being forgotten, a sickness infects and dwarfs the constitution. Once man was all; now he is an appendage, a nuisance. And because the indwelling Supreme Spirit cannot wholly be got rid of, the doctrine of it suffers this perversion, that the divine nature is attributed to one or two persons, and denied to all the rest, and denied with fury. The doctrine of inspiration is lost; the base doctrine of the majority of voices, usurps the place of the doctrine of the soul. Miracles, prophecy, poetry, the ideal life, the holy life, exist as ancient history merely; they are not in the belief, nor in the aspiration of society; but, when suggested, seem ridiculous. Life is comic or pitiful, as soon as the high ends of being fade out of sight, and man becomes near-sighted, and can only attend to what addresses the senses.

These general views, which, whilst they are general, none will contest, find abundant illustration in the history of religion, and especially in the history of the Christian church. In that, all of us have had our birth and nurture. The truth contained in that, you, my young friends, are now setting forth to teach. As the Cultus, or established worship of the civilized world, it has great historical interest for us. Of its blessed words, which have been the consolation of humanity, you need not that I should speak. I shall endeavor to discharge my duty to you, on this occasion, by pointing out two errors in its administration, which daily appear more gross from the point of view we have just now taken.

Jesus Christ belonged to the true race of prophets. He saw with open eye the mystery of the soul. Drawn by its severe harmony, ravished with its beauty, he lived in it, and had his being there. Alone in all history, he estimated the greatness of man. One man was true to what is in you and me. He saw that God incarnates himself in man, and evermore goes forth anew to take possession of his world. He said, in this jubilee of sublime emotion, 'I am divine. Through me, God acts; through me, speaks. Would you see God, see me; or, see thee, when thou also thinkest as I now think.' But what a distortion did his doctrine and memory suffer in the same, in the next, and the following ages! There is no doctrine of the Reason which will bear to be taught by the Understanding.[5] The understanding caught this high chant from the poet's lips, and said, in the next age, 'This was Jehovah come down out of heaven. I will kill you, if you say he was a man.' The idioms of his language, and the figures of his rhetoric, have usurped the place of his truth; and churches are not built on his principles, but on his tropes. Christianity became a Mythus,[6] as the poetic teaching of Greece and of Egypt, before. He spoke of miracles; for he felt that man's life was

---

5. Emerson reverses the common meaning of Reason, using it in the sense of intuitive, suprarational knowledge, while by Understanding he means knowledge arrived at through a logical reasoning process.

6. A cult deliberately fostered.

a miracle, and all that man doth, and he knew that this daily miracle shines, as the man is diviner. But the very word Miracle, as pronounced by Christian churches, gives a false impression; it is Monster. It is not one with the blowing clover and the falling rain.

He felt respect for Moses and the prophets; but no unfit tenderness at postponing their initial revelations, to the hour and the man that now is; to the eternal revelation in the heart. Thus was he a true man. Having seen that the law in us is commanding, he would not suffer it to be commanded. Boldly, with hand, and heart, and life, he declared it was God. Thus was he a true man. Thus is he, as I think, the only soul in history who has appreciated the worth of a man.

1. In thus contemplating Jesus, we become very sensible of the first defect of historical Christianity. Historical Christianity has fallen into the error that corrupts all attempts to communicate religion. As it appears to us, and as it has appeared for ages, it is not the doctrine of the soul, but an exaggeration of the personal, the positive, the ritual. It has dwelt, it dwells, with noxious exaggeration about the *person* of Jesus. The soul knows no persons. It invites every man to expand to the full circle of the universe, and will have no preferences but those of spontaneous love. But by this eastern monarchy of a Christianity, which indolence and fear have built, the friend of man is made the injurer of man. The manner in which his name is surrounded with expressions, which were once sallies of admiration and love, but are now petrified into official titles, kills all generous sympathy and liking. All who hear me, feel, that the language that describes Christ to Europe and America, is not the style of friendship and enthusiasm to a good and noble heart, but is appropriated and formal,—paints a demigod, as the Orientals or the Greeks would describe Osiris or Apollo.[7] Accept the injurious impositions of our early catachetical instruction, and even honesty and self-denial were but splendid sins, if they did not wear the Christian name. One would rather be

'A pagan suckled in a creed outworn,'[8]

than to be defrauded of his manly right in coming into nature, and finding not names and places, not land and professions, but even virtue and truth foreclosed and monopolized. You shall not be a man even. You shall not own the world; you shall not dare, and live after the infinite Law that is in you, and in company with the infinite Beauty which heaven and earth reflect to you in all lovely

---

7. Emerson associates Egypt (where Osiris was a fertility god) with the Orient and associates Greece (where Apollo was the god of the sun) with European culture.

8. From Wordsworth's sonnet *The World Is Too Much with Us.*

forms; but you must subordinate your nature to Christ's nature; you must accept our interpretations; and take his portrait as the vulgar draw it.

That is always best which gives me to myself. The sublime is excited in me by the great stoical doctrine, Obey thyself. That which shows God in me, fortifies me. That which shows God out of me, makes me a wart and a wen. There is no longer a necessary reason for my being. Already the long shadows of untimely oblivion creep over me, and I shall decease forever.

The divine bards are the friends of my virtue, of my intellect, of my strength. They admonish me, that the gleams which flash across my mind, are not mine, but God's; that they had the like, and were not disobedient to the heavenly vision.[9] So I love them. Noble provocations go out from them, inviting me also to emancipate myself; to resist evil; to subdue the world; and to Be. And thus by his holy thoughts, Jesus serves us, and thus only. To aim to convert a man by miracles, is a profanation of the soul. A true conversion, a true Christ, is now, as always, to be made, by the reception of beautiful sentiments. It is true that a great and rich soul, like his, falling among the simple, does so preponderate, that, as his did, it names the world. The world seems to them to exist for him, and they have not yet drunk so deeply of his sense, as to see that only by coming again to themselves, or to God in themselves, can they grow forevermore. It is a low benefit to give me something; it is a high benefit to enable me to do somewhat of myself. The time is coming when all men will see, that the gift of God to the soul is not a vaunting, overpowering, excluding sanctity, but a sweet, natural goodness, a goodness like thine and mine, and that so invites thine and mine to be and to grow.

The injustice of the vulgar tone of preaching is not less flagrant to Jesus, than it is to the souls which it profanes. The preachers do not see that they make his gospel not glad, and shear him of the locks of beauty and the attributes of heaven. When I see a majestic Epaminondas,[1] or Washington; when I see among my contemporaries, a true orator, an upright judge, a dear friend; when I vibrate to the melody and fancy of a poem; I see beauty that is to be desired. And so lovely, and with yet more entire consent of my human being, sounds in my ear the severe music of the bards that have sung of the true God in all ages. Now do not degrade the life and dialogues of Christ out of the circle of this charm, by insulation and peculiarity. Let them lie as they befel, alive and warm, part of human life, and of the landscape, and of the cheerful day.

2. The second defect of the traditionary and limited way of using

9. "I was not disobedient unto the heavenly vision" (Acts 26.19).
1. Theban general (418?–362 B.C.) whose military innovations helped end Sparta's dominance in Greece.

the mind of Christ is a consequence of the first; this, namely; that the Moral Nature, that Law of laws, whose revelations introduce greatness,—yea, God himself, into the open soul, is not explored as the fountain of the established teaching in society. Men have come to speak of the revelation as somewhat long ago given and done, as if God were dead. The injury to faith throttles the preacher; and the goodliest of institutions becomes an uncertain and inarticulate voice.

It is very certain that it is the effect of conversation with the beauty of the soul, to beget a desire and need to impart to others the same knowledge and love. If utterance is denied, the thought lies like a burden on the man. Always the seer is a sayer. Somehow his dream is told. Somehow he publishes it with solemn joy. Sometimes with pencil on canvas; sometimes with chisel on stone; sometimes in towers and aisles of granite, his soul's worship is builded; sometimes in anthems of indefinite music; but clearest and most permanent, in words.

The man enamored of this excellency, becomes its priest or poet. The office is coeval with the world. But observe the condition, the spiritual limitation of the office. The spirit only can teach. Not any profane man, not any sensual, not any liar, not any slave can teach, but only he can give, who has; he only can create, who is. The man on whom the soul descends, through whom the soul speaks, alone can teach. Courage, piety, love, wisdom, can teach; and every man can open his door to these angels, and they shall bring him the gift of tongues. But the man who aims to speak as books enable, as synods use, as the fashion guides, and as interest commands, babbles. Let him hush.

To this holy office, you propose to devote yourselves. I wish you may feel your call in throbs of desire and hope. The office is the first in the world. It is of that reality, that it cannot suffer the deduction of any falsehood. And it is my duty to say to you, that the need was never greater of new revelation than now. From the views I have already expressed, you will infer the sad conviction, which I share, I believe, with numbers, of the universal decay and now almost death of faith in society. The soul is not preached. The Church seems to totter to its fall, almost all life extinct. On this occasion, any complaisance, would be criminal, which told you, whose hope and commission it is to preach the faith of Christ, that the faith of Christ is preached.

It is time that this ill-suppressed murmur of all thoughtful men against the famine of our churches; this moaning of the heart because it is bereaved of the consolation, the hope, the grandeur, that come alone out of the culture of the moral nature; should be heard through the sleep of indolence, and over the din of routine. This great and perpetual office of the preacher is not discharged. Preaching is the expression of the moral sentiment in application to the duties of life. In how many churches, by how many prophets, tell me, is man made sensible that he is an infinite Soul; that the earth and heavens are passing into his mind; that he is drinking forever the soul of God? Where now sounds the persuasion, that by its very melody imparadises my heart, and so affirms its own origin in heaven? Where shall I hear words such as in elder ages drew men to leave all and follow,—father and mother, house and land, wife and child?[2] Where shall I hear these august laws of moral being so pronounced, as to fill my ear, and I feel ennobled by the offer of my uttermost action and passion? The test of the true faith, certainly, should be its power to charm and command the soul, as the laws of nature control the activity of the hands,—so commanding that we find pleasure and honor in obeying. The faith should blend with the light of rising and of setting suns, with the flying cloud, the singing bird, and the breath of flowers. But now the priest's Sabbath has lost the splendor of nature; it is unlovely; we are glad when it is done; we can make, we do make, even sitting in our pews, a far better, holier, sweeter, for ourselves.

Whenever the pulpit is usurped by a formalist, then is the worshipper defrauded and disconsolate. We shrink as soon as the prayers begin, which do not uplift, but smite and offend us. We are fain to wrap our cloaks about us, and secure, as best we can, a solitude that hears not. I once heard a preacher who sorely tempted me to say, I would go to church no more. Men go, thought I, where they are wont to go, else had no soul entered the temple in the afternoon. A snowstorm was falling around us. The snowstorm was real; the preacher merely spectral; and the eye felt the sad contrast in looking at him, and then out of the window behind him, into the beautiful meteor of the snow. He had lived in vain. He had no one word intimating that he had laughed or wept, was married or in love, had been commended, or cheated, or chagrined. If he had ever lived and acted, we were none the wiser for it. The capital secret of his profession, namely, to convert life into truth, he had not learned. Not one fact in all his experience, had he yet imported into his doctrine. This man had ploughed, and planted, and talked, and bought, and sold; he had read books; he had eaten and drunken; his head aches; his heart throbs; he smiles and suffers; yet was there not a surmise, a hint, in all the discourse, that he had ever lived at all. Not a line did he draw out of real history. The true preacher can always be known by this, that he deals out to the people his life,—

2. See Matthew 19.28–29: "And Jesus said unto them, Verily I say unto you, That ye which have followed me, in the regeneration when the Son of man shall sit in the throne of his glory, ye also shall sit upon twelve thrones, judging the twelve tribes of Israel. And every one that hath forsaken houses, or brethren, or sisters, or father, or mother, or wife, or children, or lands, for my name's sake, shall receive an hundredfold, and shall inherit everlasting life."

life passed through the fire of thought. But of the bad preacher, it could not be told from his sermon, what age of the world he fell in; whether he had a father or a child; whether he was a freeholder or a pauper; whether he was a citizen or a countryman; or any other fact of his biography.

It seemed strange that the people should come to church. It seemed as if their houses were very unentertaining, that they should prefer this thoughtless clamor. It shows that there is a commanding attraction in the moral sentiment, that can lend a faint tint of light to dulness and ignorance, coming in its name and place. The good hearer is sure he has been touched sometimes; is sure there is somewhat to be reached, and some word that can reach it. When he listens to these vain words, he comforts himself by their relation to his remembrance of better hours, and so they clatter and echo unchallenged.

I am not ignorant that when we preach unworthily, it is not always quite in vain. There is a good ear, in some men, that draws supplies to virtue out of very indifferent nutriment. There is poetic truth concealed in all the common-places of prayer and of sermons, and though foolishly spoken, they may be wisely heard; for, each is some select expression that broke out in a moment of piety from some stricken or jubilant soul, and its excellency made it remembered. The prayers and even the dogmas of our church, are like the zodiac of Denderah,[3] and the astronomical monuments of the Hindoos, wholly insulated from anything now extant in the life and business of the people. They mark the height to which the waters once rose. But this docility is a check upon the mischief from the good and devout. In a large portion of the community, the religious service gives rise to quite other thoughts and emotions. We need not chide the negligent servant. We are struck with pity, rather, at the swift retribution of his sloth. Alas for the unhappy man that is called to stand in the pulpit, and *not* give bread of life. Everything that befals, accuses him. Would he ask contributions for the missions, foreign or domestic? Instantly his face is suffused with shame, to propose to his parish, that they should send money a hundred or a thousand miles, to furnish such poor fare as they have at home, and would do well to go the hundred or the thousand miles, to escape. Would he urge people to a godly way of living;—and can he ask a fellow creature to come to Sabbath meetings, when he and they all know what is the poor uttermost they can hope for therein? Will he invite them privately to the Lord's Supper? He dares not. If no heart warm this rite, the hollow, dry, creaking formality is too plain, than that he can face a man of wit and energy, and put the invitation without terror. In the street, what has he to say to the

---

3. At Dandarah, a village in Upper Egypt, the ceiling of a ruined ancient temple is sculpted with astronomical scenes.

bold village blasphemer? The village blasphemer sees fear in the face, form, and gait of the minister.

Let me not taint the sincerity of this plea by any oversight of the claims of good men. I know and honor the purity and strict conscience of numbers of the clergy. What life the public worship retains, it owes to the scattered company of pious men, who minister here and there in the churches, and who, sometimes accepting with too great tenderness the tenet of the elders, have not accepted from others, but from their own heart, the genuine impulses of virtue, and so still command our love and awe, to the sanctity of character. Moreover, the exceptions are not so much to be found in a few eminent preachers, as in the better hours, the truer inspirations of all,—nay, in the sincere moments of every man. But with whatever exception, it is still true, that tradition characterizes the preaching of this country; that it comes out of the memory, and not out of the soul; that it aims at what is usual, and not at what is necessary and eternal; that thus, historical Christianity destroys the power of preaching, by withdrawing it from the exploration of the moral nature of man, where the sublime is, where are the resources of astonishment and power. What a cruel injustice it is to that Law, the joy of the whole earth, which alone can make thought dear and rich; that Law whose fatal sureness the astronomical orbits poorly emulate, that it is travestied and depreciated, that it is behooted and behowled, and not a trait, not a word of it articulated. The pulpit in losing sight of this Law, loses all its inspiration, and gropes after it knows not what. And for want of this culture, the soul of the community is sick and faithless. It wants nothing so much as a stern, high, stoical, Christian discipline, to make it know itself and the divinity that speaks through it. Now man is ashamed of himself; he skulks and sneaks through the world, to be tolerated, to be pitied, and scarcely in a thousand years does any man dare to be wise and good, and so draw after him the tears and blessings of his kind.

Certainly there have been periods when, from the inactivity of the intellect on certain truths, a greater faith was possible in names and persons. The Puritans in England and America, found in the Christ of the Catholic Church, and in the dogmas inherited from Rome, scope for their austere piety, and their longings for civil freedom. But their creed is passing away, and none arises in its room. I think no man can go with his thoughts about him, into one of our churches, without feeling that what hold the public worship had on men, is gone or going. It has lost its grasp on the affection of the good, and the fear of the bad. In the country,—neighborhoods, half parishes are *signing off*,—to use the local term. It is already beginning to indicate character and religion to withdraw from the religious meetings. I have heard a devout person, who prized the Sabbath, say in bitterness of heart, "On Sundays, it seems wicked to go to church." And the motive, that holds the best there, is now only a hope and a waiting. What was once a mere circumstance, that the best and the worst men in the parish, the poor and the rich, the learned and the ignorant, young and old, should meet one day as fellows in one house, in sign of an equal right in the soul,—has come to be a paramount motive for going thither.

My friends, in these two errors, I think, I find the causes of that calamity of a decaying church and a wasting unbelief, which are casting malignant influences around us, and making the hearts of good men sad. And what greater calamity can fall upon a nation, than the loss of worship? Then all things go to decay. Genius leaves the temple, to haunt the senate, or the market. Literature becomes frivolous. Science is cold. The eye of youth is not lighted by the hope of other worlds, and age is without honor. Society lives to trifles, and when men die, we do not mention them.

And now, my brothers, you will ask, What in these desponding days can be done by us? The remedy is already declared in the ground of our complaint of the Church. We have contrasted the Church with the Soul. In the soul, then, let the redemption be sought. In one soul, in your soul, there are resources for the world. Wherever a man comes, there comes revolution. The old is for slaves. When a man comes, all books are legible, all things transparent, all religions are forms. He is religious. Man is the wonderworker. He is seen amid miracles. All men bless and curse. He saith yea and nay, only. The stationariness of religion; the assumption that the age of inspiration is past, that the Bible is closed; the fear of degrading the character of Jesus by representing him as a man; indicate with sufficient clearness the falsehood of our theology. It is the office of a true teacher to show us that God is, not was; that He speaketh, not spake. The true Christianity,—a faith like Christ's in the infinitude of man,—is lost. None believeth in the soul of man, but only in some man or person old and departed. Ah me! no man goeth alone. All men go in flocks to this saint or that poet, avoiding the God who seeth in secret. They cannot see in secret; they love to be blind in public. They think society wiser than their soul, and know not that one soul, and their soul, is wiser than the whole world. See how nations and races flit by on the sea of time, and leave no ripple to tell where they floated or sunk, and one good soul shall make the name of Moses, or of Zeno, or of Zoroaster,[4] reverend forever. None assayeth the stern ambition to be the Self of the nation, and of nature, but each would be an easy secondary to some Christian scheme, or sectarian connexion, or some eminent man. Once leave your own knowledge of God, your own sentiment, and

---

4. "Moses": Hebrew lawgiver who led the exodus from Egypt; "Zeno": Greek philosopher (342?–270? B.C.), founder of Stoicism; "Zoroaster": Iranian religious reformer (sixth century B.C.), founder of religion still practiced by the Parsees.

take secondary knowledge, as St. Paul's, or George Fox's, or Swedenborg's,[5] and you get wide from God with every year this secondary form lasts, and if, as now, for centuries,—the chasm yawns to that breadth, that men can scarcely be convinced there is in them anything divine.

Let me admonish you, first of all, to go alone; to refuse the good models, even those most sacred in the imagination of men, and dare to love God without mediator or veil. Friends enough you shall find who will hold up to your emulation Wesleys and Oberlins,[6] Saints and Prophets. Thank God for these good men, but say, 'I also am a man.' Imitation cannot go above its model. The imitator dooms himself to hopeless mediocrity. The inventor did it, because it was natural to him, and so in him it has a charm. In the imitator, something else is natural, and he bereaves himself of his own beauty, to come short of another man's.

Yourself a newborn bard of the Holy Ghost,—cast behind you all conformity, and acquaint men at first hand with Deity. Be to them a man. Look to it first and only, that you are such; that fashion, custom, authority, pleasure, and money are nothing to you,—are not bandages over your eyes, that you cannot see,—but live with the privilege of the immeasurable mind. Not too anxious to visit periodically all families and each family in your parish connexion, —when you meet one of these men or women, be to them a divine man; be to them thought and virtue; let their timid aspirations find in you a friend; let their trampled instincts be genially tempted out in your atmosphere; let their doubts know that you have doubted, and their wonder feel that you have wondered. By trusting your own soul, you shall gain a greater confidence in other men. For all our penny-wisdom, for all our soul-destroying slavery to habit, it is not to be doubted, that all men have sublime thoughts; that all men do value the few real hours of life; they love to be heard; they love to be caught up into the vision of principles. We mark with light in the memory the few interviews, we have had in the dreary years of routine and of sin, with souls that made our souls wiser; that spoke what we thought; that told us what we knew; that gave us leave to be what we inly were. Discharge to men the priestly office, and, present or absent, you shall be followed with their love as by an angel.

And, to this end, let us not aim at common degrees of merit. Can we not leave, to such as love it, the virtue that glitters for the

5. St. Paul, the apostle to the Gentiles, hero of the book of Acts, and author of other books of the New Testament; George Fox (1624–91), English founder of the Society of Friends (Quakers); Emanuel Swedenborg (1688–1772), Swedish scientist and theologian.
6. John Wesley (1703–91) and his brother Charles (1707–88) founded the Methodist movement in the Church of England; Jean Frédéric Oberlin (1740–1826), Alsatian Lutheran clergyman and philanthropist, innnovator in children's education, honored by the naming of the town and college in Ohio.

commendation of society, and ourselves pierce the deep solitudes of absolute ability and worth? We easily come up to the standard of goodness in society. Society's praise can be cheaply secured, and almost all men are content with those easy merits; but the instant effect of conversing with God, will be, to put them away. There are sublime merits; persons who are not actors, not speakers, but influences; persons too great for fame, for display; who disdain eloquence; to whom all we call art and artist, seems too nearly allied to show and by-ends, to the exaggeration of the finite and selfish, and loss of the universal. The orators, the poets, the commanders encroach on us only as fair women do, by our allowance and homage. Slight them by preoccupation of mind, slight them, as you can well afford to do, by high and universal aims, and they instantly feel that you have right, and that it is in lower places that they must shine. They also feel your right; for they with you are open to the influx of the all-knowing Spirit, which annihilates before its broad noon the little shades and gradations of intelligence in the compositions we call wiser and wisest.

In such high communion, let us study the grand strokes of rectitude: a bold benevolence, an independence of friends, so that not the unjust wishes of those who love us, shall impair our freedom, but we shall resist for truth's sake the freest flow of kindness, and appeal to sympathies far in advance; and,—what is the highest form in which we know this beautiful element,—a certain solidity of merit, that has nothing to do with opinion, and which is so essentially and manifestly virtue, that it is taken for granted, that the right, the brave, the generous step will be taken by it, and nobody thinks of commending it. You would compliment a coxcomb doing a good act, but you would not praise an angel. The silence that accepts merit as the most natural thing in the world, is the highest applause. Such souls, when they appear, are the Imperial Guard of Virtue, the perpetual reserve, the dictators of fortune. One needs not praise their courage,—they are the heart and soul of nature. O my friends, there are resources in us on which we have not drawn. There are men who rise refreshed on hearing a threat; men to whom a crisis which intimidates and paralyzes the majority—demanding not the faculties of prudence and thrift, but comprehension, immovableness, the readiness of sacrifice,—comes graceful and beloved as a bride. Napoleon said of Massena,[7] that he was not himself until the battle began to go against him; then, when the dead began to fall in ranks around him, awoke his powers of combination, and he put on terror and victory as a robe. So it is in rugged crises, in unweariable endurance, and in aims which put sympathy

7. André Masséna (1758–1817), marshal of the Empire under Napoleon; the anecdote is taken from Barry Edward O'Meara's *Napoleon in Exile* (Boston, 1823).

out of question, that the angel is shown. But these are heights that we can scarce remember and look up to, without contrition and shame. Let us thank God that such things exist.

And now let us do what we can to rekindle the smouldering, nigh quenched fire on the altar. The evils of that church that now is, are manifest. The question returns, What shall we do? I confess, all attempts to project and establish a Cultus with new rites and forms, seem to me vain. Faith makes us, and not we it, and faith makes its own forms. All attempts to contrive a system, are as cold as the new worship introduced by the French to the goddess of Reason,[8]—to-day, pasteboard and fillagree, and ending to-morrow in madness and murder. Rather let the breath of new life be breathed by you through the forms already existing. For, if once you are alive, you shall find they shall become plastic[9] and new. The remedy to their deformity is, first, soul, and second, soul, and evermore, soul. A whole popedom[1] of forms, one pulsation of virtue can uplift and vivify. Two inestimable advantages Christianity has given us; first; the Sabbath, the jubilee of the whole world; whose light dawns welcome alike into the closet of the philosopher, into the garret of toil, and into prison cells, and everywhere suggests, even to the vile, a thought of the dignity of spiritual being. Let it stand forevermore, a temple, which new love, new faith, new sight shall restore to more than its first splendor to mankind. And secondly, the institution of preaching;—the speech of man to men,—essentially the most flexible of all organs, of all forms. What hinders that now, everywhere, in pulpits, in lecture-rooms, in houses, in fields, wherever the invitation of men or your own occasions lead you, you speak the very truth, as your life and conscience teach it, and cheer the waiting, fainting hearts of men with new hope and new revelation.

I look for the hour when that supreme Beauty, which ravished the souls of those Eastern men, and chiefly of those Hebrews, and through their lips spoke oracles to all time, shall speak in the West also. The Hebrew and Greek Scriptures contain immortal sentences, that have been bread of life to millions. But they have no epical integrity; are fragmentary; are not shown in their order to the intellect. I look for the new Teacher, that shall follow so far those shining laws, that he shall see them come full circle; shall see their rounding complete grace; shall see the world to be the mirror of the soul; shall see the identity of the law of gravitation with purity of heart; and shall show that the Ought, that Duty, is one thing with Science, with Beauty, and with Joy.

1838, 1841

---

8. A reference to the French "worship of Reason" promulgated in 1793 during the Reign of Terror.

9. Receptive to influences, capable of receiving new shapes.
1. I.e., rigid hierarchy.

The Poet[1]

A moody child and wildly wise
Pursued the game with joyful eyes,
Which chose, like meteors, their way,
And rived the dark with private ray:
They overleapt the horizon's edge,
Searched with Apollo's privilege;
Through man, and woman, and sea, and star,
Saw the dance of nature forward far;
Through worlds, and races, and terms, and times,
Saw musical order, and pairing rhymes.

Olympian bards who sung
Divine ideas below,
Which always find us young,
And always keep us so.

Those who are esteemed umpires of taste, are often persons who have acquired some knowledge of admired pictures or sculptures, and have an inclination for whatever is elegant; but if you inquire whether they are beautiful souls, and whether their own acts are like fair pictures, you learn that they are selfish and sensual. Their cultivation is local, as if you should rub a log of dry wood in one spot to produce fire, all the rest remaining cold. Their knowledge of the fine arts is some study of rules and particulars, or some limited judgment of color or form, which is exercised for amusement or for show. It is a proof of the shallowness of the doctrine of beauty, as it lies in the minds of our amateurs, that men seem to have lost the perception of the instant dependence of form upon soul. There is no doctrine of forms in our philosophy. We were put into our bodies, as fire is put into a pan, to be carried about; but there is no accurate adjustment between the spirit and the organ, much less is the latter the germination of the former. So in regard to other forms, the intellectual men do not believe in any essential dependence of the material world on thought and volition. Theologians think it a pretty air-castle to talk of the spiritual meaning of a ship or a cloud, of a city or a contract, but they prefer to come again to the solid ground of historical evidence; and even the poets are contented with a civil and conformed manner of living, and to write poems from the fancy, at a safe distance from their own experience. But the highest minds of the world have never ceased to explore the double meaning, or, shall I say, the quadruple, or the centuple, or much more manifold meaning, of every sensuous fact: Orpheus, Empedocles, Heraclitus, Plato, Plutarch, Dante, Swedenborg,[2] and the masters of sculpture, picture, and poetry. For we are not pans and

1. First published in *Essays, Second Series* (1844), the source of the present text, *The Poet* contains the fullest elaboration of Emerson's aesthetic ideas and his most incisive comments on contemporary poetry and criticism. The first prefatory poem is from one of Emerson's own uncompleted poems, and the second is from his *Ode to Beauty*.
2. Emerson mentions a legendary Greek poet, three Greek philosophers (of the fifth, sixth, and fourth centuries B.C.), a first-century-A.D. Greek biographer, a medieval Italian poet, and an 18th century Swedish scientist and mystic.

barrows, nor even porters of the fire and torchbearers, but children of the fire, made of it, and only the same divinity transmuted, and at two or three removes, when we know least about it. And this hidden truth, that the fountains whence all this river of Time, and its creatures, floweth, are intrinsically ideal and beautiful, draws us to the consideration of the nature and functions of the Poet, or the man of Beauty, to the means and materials he uses, and to the general aspect of the art in the present time.

The breadth of the problem is great, for the poet is representative. He stands among partial men for the complete man, and apprises us not of his wealth, but of the commonwealth. The young man reveres men of genius, because, to speak truly, they are more himself than he is. They receive of the soul as he also receives, but they more. Nature enhances her beauty, to the eye of loving men, from their belief that the poet is beholding her shows at the same time. He is isolated among his contemporaries, by truth and by his art, but with this consolation in his pursuits, that they will draw all men sooner or later. For all men live by truth, and stand in need of expression. In love, in art, in avarice, in politics, in labor, in games, we study to utter our painful secret. The man is only half himself, the other half is his expression.

Notwithstanding this necessity to be published, adequate expression is rare. I know not how it is that we need an interpreter; but the great majority of men seem to be minors, who have not yet come into possession of their own, or mutes, who cannot report the conversation they have had with nature. There is no man who does not anticipate a supersensual utility in the sun, and stars, earth, and water. These stand and wait to render him a peculiar service. But there is some obstruction, or some excess of phlegm in our constitution, which does not suffer them to yield the due effect. Too feeble fall the impressions of nature on us to make us artists. Every touch should thrill. Every man should be so much an artist, that he could report in conversation what had befallen him. Yet, in our experience, the rays or appulses have sufficient force to arrive at the senses, but not enough to reach the quick, and compel the reproduction of themselves in speech. The poet is the person in whom these powers are in balance, the man without impediment, who sees and handles that which others dream of, traverses the whole scale of experience, and its representative of man, in virtue of being the largest power to receive and to impart.

For the Universe has three children, born at one time, which reappear, under different names, in every system of thought, whether they be called cause, operation, and effect; or, more poetically, Jove, Pluto, Neptune; or, theologically, the Father, the Spirit, and the Son; but which we will call here, the Knower, the Doer, and the Sayer. These stand respectively for the love of truth, for the love of good, and for the love of beauty. These three are equal. Each is that which he is essentially, so that he cannot be surmounted or analyzed, and each of these three has the power of the others latent in him, and his own patent.

The poet is the sayer, the namer, and represents beauty. He is a sovereign, and stands on the centre. For the world is not painted, or adorned, but is from the beginning beautiful; and God has not made some beautiful things, but Beauty is the creator of the universe. Therefore the poet is not any permissive potentate, but is emperor in his own right. Criticism is infested with a cant of materialism, which assumes that manual skill and activity is the first merit of all men, and disparages such as say and do not, overlooking the fact, that some men, namely, poets, are natural sayers, sent into the world to the end of expression, and confounds them with those whose province is action, but who quit it to imitate the sayers. But Homer's words are as costly and admirable to Homer, as Agamemnon's victories are to Agamemnon.[3] The poet does not wait for the hero or the sage, but, as they act and think primarily, so he writes primarily what will and must be spoken, reckoning the others, though primaries also, yet, in respect to him, secondaries and servants; as sitters or models in the studio of a painter, or as assistants who bring building materials to an architect.

For poetry was all written before time was, and whenever we are so finely organized that we can penetrate into that region where the air is music, we hear those primal warblings, and attempt to write them down, but we lose ever and anon a word, or a verse, and substitute something of our own, and thus miswrite the poem. The men of more delicate ear write down these cadences more faithfully, and these transcripts, though imperfect, become the songs of the nations. For nature is as truly beautiful as it is good, or as it is reasonable, and must as much appear, as it must be done, or be known. Words and deeds are quite indifferent modes of the divine energy. Words are also actions, and actions are a kind of words.

The sign and credentials of the poet are, that he announces that which no man foretold. He is the true and only doctor;[4] he knows and tells; he is the only teller of news, for he was present and privy to the appearance which he describes. He is a beholder of ideas, and an utterer of the necessary and causal. For we do not speak now of men of poetical talents, or of industry and skill in metre, but of the true poet. I took part in a conversation the other day, concerning a recent writer of lyrics, a man of subtle mind, whose head appeared to be a music-box of delicate tunes and rhythms, and whose skill, and command of language, we could not sufficiently praise. But when the question arose, whether he was not only a lyrist, but a poet, we were obliged to confess that he is plainly a contemporary,

---

3. Emerson is comparing the author (Homer) with his character (Agamemnon, in the *Iliad*).
4. Teacher.

not an eternal man. He does not stand out of our low limitations, like a Chimborazo under the line,[5] running up from the torrid base through all the climates of the globe, with belts of the herbage of every latitude on its high and mottled sides; but this genius is the landscape-garden of a modern house, adorned with fountains and statues, with well-bred men and women standing and sitting in the walks and terraces. We hear, through all the varied music, the ground-tone of conventional life. Our poets are men of talents who sing, and not the children of music. The argument is secondary, the finish of the verses is primary.

For it is not metres, but a metre-making argument, that makes a poem,—a thought so passionate and alive, that, like the spirit of a plant or an animal, it has an architecture of its own, and adorns nature with a new thing. The thought and the form are equal in the order of time, but in the order of genesis the thought is prior to the form. The poet has a new thought: he has a whole new experience to unfold; he will tell us how it was with him, and all men will be the richer in his fortune. For, the experience of each new age requires a new confession, and the world seems always waiting for its poet. I remember, when I was young, how much I was moved one morning by tidings that genius had appeared in a youth who sat near me at table. He had left his work, and gone rambling none knew whither, and had written hundreds of lines, but could not tell whether that which was in him was therein told: he could tell nothing but that all was changed,—man, beast, heaven, earth, and sea. How gladly we listened! how credulous! Society seemed to be compromised. We sat in the aurora of a sunrise which was to put out all the stars. Boston seemed to be at twice the distance it had the night before, or was much farther than that. Rome,—what was Rome? Plutarch and Shakspeare were in the yellow leaf, and Homer no more should be heard of. It is much to know that poetry has been written this very day, under this very roof, by your side. What! that wonderful spirit has not expired! these stony moments are still sparkling and animated! I had fancied that the oracles were all silent, and nature had spent her fires, and behold! all night, from every pore, these fine auroras have been streaming. Every one has some interest in the advent of the poet, and no one knows how much it may concern him. We know that the secret of the world is profound, but who or what shall be our interpreter, we know not. A mountain ramble, a new style of face, a new person, may put the key into our hands. Of course, the value of genius to us is in the veracity of its report. Talent may frolic and juggle; genius realizes and adds. Mankind, in good earnest, have availed so far in understanding themselves and their work, that the foremost watchman on the peak announces his news. It is the truest word ever spoken, and

5. "Chimborazo": a mountain in Ecuador; "line": equator.

the phrase will be the fittest, most musical, and the unerring voice of the world for that time.

All that we call sacred history attests that the birth of a poet is the principal event in chronology. Man, never so often deceived, still watches for the arrival of a brother who can hold him steady to a truth, until he has made it his own. With what joy I begin to read a poem, which I confide in as an inspiration! And now my chains are to be broken; I shall mount above these clouds and opaque airs in which I live,—opaque, though they seem transparent,—and from the heaven of truth I shall see and comprehend my relations. That will reconcile me to life, and renovate nature, to see trifles animated by a tendency, and to know what I am doing. Life will no more be a noise; now I shall see men and women, and know the signs by which they may be discerned from fools and satans. This day shall be better than my birth-day: then I became an animal: now I am invited into the science of the real. Such is the hope, but the fruition is postponed. Oftener it falls, that this winged man, who will carry me into the heaven, whirls me into the clouds, then leaps and frisks about with me from cloud to cloud, still affirming that he is bound heavenward; and I, being myself a novice, am slow in perceiving that he does not know the way into the heavens, and is merely bent that I should admire his skill to rise, like a fowl or a flying fish, a little way from the ground or the water; but the all-piercing, all-feeding, and ocular[6] air of heaven, that man shall never inhabit. I tumble down again soon into my old nooks, and lead the life of exaggerations as before, and have lost my faith in the possibility of any guide who can lead me thither where I would be.

But leaving these victims of vanity, let us, with new hope, observe how nature, by worthier impulses, has ensured the poet's fidelity to his office of announcement and affirming, namely, by the beauty of things, which becomes a new, and higher beauty, when expressed. Nature offers all her creatures to him as a picture-language. Being used as a type, a second wonderful value appears in the object, far better than its old value, as the carpenter's stretched cord, if you hold your ear close enough, is musical in the breeze. "Things more excellent than every image," says Jamblichus,[7] "are expressed through images." Things admit of being used as symbols, because nature is a symbol, in the whole, and in every part. Every line we can draw in the sand, has expression; and there is no body without its spirit or genius. All form is an effect of character; all condition, of the quality of the life; all harmony, of health; (and, for this reason, a perception of beauty should be sympathetic, or proper only to the good.) The beautiful rests on the foundations of the necessary. The soul makes the body, as the wise Spenser teaches:—

6. Visible.
7. Neoplatonic philosopher of the fourth century A.D. (Neoplatonism: a mystical religious system combining features of Platonic and other Greek philosophies with features of Eastern religions, primarily Judaism and Christianity.)

"So every spirit, as it is most pure,
  And hath in it the more of heavenly light,
So it the fairer body doth procure
  To habit in, and it more fairly dight,
  With cheerful grace and amiable sight.
For, of the soul, the body form doth take,
For soul is form, and doth the body make."[8]

Here we find ourselves, suddenly, not in a critical speculation, but in a holy place, and should go very warily and reverently. We stand before the secret of the world, there where Being passes into Appearance, and Unity into Variety.

The Universe is the externisation of the soul. Wherever the life is, that bursts into appearance around it. Our science is sensual, and therefore superficial. The earth, and the heavenly bodies, physics, and chemistry, we sensually treat, as if they were self-existent; but these are the retinue of that Being we have. "The mighty heaven," said Proclus,[9] "exhibits, in its transfigurations, clear images of the splendor of intellectual perceptions; being moved in conjunction with the unapparent periods of intellectual natures." Therefore, science always goes abreast with the just elevation of the man, keeping step with religion and metaphysics; or, the state of science is an index of our self-knowledge. Since everything in nature answers to a moral power, if any phenomenon remains brute and dark, it is that the corresponding faculty in the observer is not yet active.

No wonder, then, if these waters be so deep, that we hover over them with a religious regard. The beauty of the fable proves the importance of the sense; to the poet, and to all others; or, if you please, every man is so far a poet as to be susceptible of these enchantments of nature: for all men have the thoughts whereof the universe is the celebration. I find that the fascination resides in the symbol. Who loves nature? Who does not? Is it only poets, and men of leisure and cultivation, who live with her? No; but also hunters, farmers, grooms, and butchers, though they express their affection in their choice of life, and not in their choice of words. The writer wonders what the coachman or the hunter values in riding, in horses, and dogs. It is not superficial qualities. When you talk with him, he holds these at as slight a rate as you. His worship is sympathetic; he has no definitions, but he is commanded in nature, by the living power which he feels to be there present. No imitation, or playing of these things, would content him; he loves the earnest of the northwind, of rain, of stone, and wood, and iron. A beauty not explicable, is dearer than a beauty which we can see to the end

8. *An Hymn in Honour of Beauty* (1596), by the English poet Edmund Spenser (1552–99).

9. Greek Neoplatonic philosopher (411–485).

of. It is nature the symbol, nature certifying the supernatural, body overflowed by life, which he worships, with coarse, but sincere rites.

The inwardness, and mystery, of this attachment, drives men of every class to the use of emblems. The schools of poets, and philosophers, are not more intoxicated with their symbols, than the populace with theirs. In our political parties, compute the power of badges and emblems. See the great ball which they roll from Baltimore to Bunker hill![1] In the political processions, Lowell goes in a loom, and Lynn in a shoe, and Salem in a ship. Witness the cider-barrel, the log-cabin, the hickory-stick, the palmetto, and all the cognizances of party. See the power of national emblems. Some stars, lilies, leopards, a crescent, a lion, an eagle, or other figure, which came into credit God knows how, on an old rag of bunting, blowing in the wind, on a fort, at the ends of the earth, shall make the blood tingle under the rudest, or the most conventional exterior. The people fancy they hate poetry, and they are all poets and mystics!

Beyond this universality of the symbolic language, we are apprised of the divineness of this superior use of things, whereby the world is a temple, whose walls are covered with emblems, pictures, and commandments of the Deity, in this, that there is no fact in nature which does not carry the whole sense of nature; and the distinctions which we make in events, and in affairs, of low and high, honest and base, disappear when nature is used as a symbol. Thought makes every thing fit for use. The vocabulary of an omniscient man would embrace words and images excluded from polite conversation. What would be base, or even obscene, to the obscene, becomes illustrious, spoken in a new connexion of thought. The piety of the Hebrew prophets purges their grossness. The circumcision is an example of the power of poetry to raise the low and offensive. Small and mean things serve as well as great symbols. The meaner the type by which a law is expressed, the more pungent it is, and the more lasting in the memories of men: just as we choose the smallest box, or case, in which any needful utensil can be carried. Bare lists of words are found suggestive, to an imaginative and excited mind; as it is related of Lord Chatham, that he was accustomed to read in Bailey's Dictionary,[2] when he was preparing to speak in Parliament. The poorest experience is rich enough for all the purposes of expressing thought. Why covet a knowledge of new facts? Day and night, house and garden, a few books, a few actions, serve us as well as would all trades and all spectacles. We are far from having exhausted the significance of the few symbols we use.

1. This passage mentions a recent political stunt; in the next sentence towns are symbolized by major products.
2. William Pitt (1708–78), English statesman, famous for his oratory; Nathan (or Nathaniel) Bailey (d. 1742) published *An University Etymological English Dictionary* (1721), which ran through many editions.

We can come to use them yet with a terrible simplicity. It does not need that a poem should be long. Every word was once a poem. Every new relation is a new word. Also, we use defects and deformities to a sacred purpose, so expressing our sense that the evils of the world are such only to the evil eye. In the old mythology, mythologists observe, defects are ascribed to divine natures, as lameness to Vulcan, blindness to Cupid, and the like, to signify exuberances.

For, as it is dislocation and detachment from the life of God, that makes things ugly, the poet, who re-attaches things to nature and the Whole,—re-attaching even artificial things, and violations of nature, to nature, by a deeper insight,—disposes very easily of the most disagreeable facts. Readers of poetry see the factory-village, and the railway, and fancy that the poetry of the landscape is broken up by these; for these works of art are not yet consecrated in their reading; but the poet sees them fall within the great Order not less than the bee-hive, or the spider's geometrical web. Nature adopts them very fast into her vital circles, and the gliding train of cars she loves like her own. Besides, in a centred mind, it signifies nothing how many mechanical inventions you exhibit. Though you add millions, and never so surprising, the fact of mechanics has not gained a grain's weight. The spiritual fact remains unaltered, by many or by few particulars; as no mountain is of any appreciable height to break the curve of the sphere. A shrewd country-boy goes to the city for the first time, and the complacent citizen is not satisfied with his little wonder. It is not that he does not see all the fine houses, and know that he never saw such before, but he disposes of them as easily as the poet finds place for the railway. The chief value of the new fact, is to enhance the great and constant fact of Life, which can dwarf any and every circumstance, and to which the belt of wampum, and the commerce of America, are alike.

The world being thus put under the mind for verb and noun, the poet is he who can articulate it. For, though life is great, and fascinates, and absorbs,—and though all men are intelligent of the symbols through which it is named,—yet they cannot originally use them. We are symbols, and inhabit symbols; workmen, work, and tools, words and things, birth and death, all are emblems; but we sympathize with the symbols, and, being infatuated with the economical uses of things, we do not know that they are thoughts. The poet, by an ulterior intellectual perception, gives them a power which makes their old use forgotten, and puts eyes, and a tongue, into every dumb and inanimate object. He perceives the independence of the thought on the symbol, the stability of the thought, the accidency and fugacity of the symbol. As the eyes of Lyncæus[3] were said to see through the earth, so the poet turns the world to

_____

3. In Greek mythology, the keenest-sighted crewman on the *Argo*, in which Jason sailed in search of the Golden Fleece.

glass, and shows us all things in their right series and procession. For, through that better perception, he stands one step nearer to things, and sees the flowing or metamorphosis; perceives that thought is multiform; that within the form of every creature is a force impelling it to ascend into a higher form; and, following with his eyes the life, uses the forms which express that life, and so his speech flows with the flowing of nature. All the facts of the animal economy, sex, nutriment, gestation, birth, growth, are symbols of the passage of the world into the soul of man, to suffer there a change, and reappear a new and higher fact. He uses forms according to the life, and not according to the form. This is true science. The poet alone knows astronomy, chemistry, vegetation, and animation, for he does not stop at these facts, but employs them as signs. He knows why the plain, or meadow of space, was strown with these flowers we call suns, and moons, and stars; why the great deep is adorned with animals, with men, and gods; for, in every word he speaks he rides on them as the horses of thought.

By virtue of this science the poet is the Namer, or Language-maker, naming things sometimes after their appearance, sometimes after their essence, and giving to every one its own name and not another's, thereby rejoicing the intellect, which delights in detachment or boundary. The poets made all the words, and therefore language is the archives of history, and, if we must say it, a sort of tomb of the muses. For, though the origin of most of our words is forgotten, each word was at first a stroke of genius, and obtained currency, because for the moment it symbolized the world to the first speaker and to the hearer. The etymologist finds the deadest word to have been once a brilliant picture. Language is fossil poetry. As the limestone of the continent consists of infinite masses of the shells of animalcules, so language is made up of images, or tropes, which now, in their secondary use, have long ceased to remind us of their poetic origin. But the poet names the thing because he sees it, or comes one step nearer to it than any other. This expression, or naming, is not art, but a second nature, grown out of the first, as a leaf out of a tree. What we call nature, is a certain self-regulated motion, or change; and nature does all things by her own hands, and does not leave another to baptise her, but baptises herself; and this through the metamorphosis again. I remember that a certain poet[4] described it to me thus:

> Genius is the activity which repairs the decays of things, whether wholly or partly of a material and finite kind. Nature, through all her kingdoms, insures herself. Nobody cares for planting the poor fungus: so she shakes down from the gills of one agaric countless spores, any one of which, being preserved, transmits new billions of spores to-morrow or next day. The

4. A private joke: the poet is Emerson himself.

new agaric of this hour has a chance which the old one had not. This atom of seed is thrown into a new place, not subject to the accidents which destroyed its parent two rods off. She makes a man; and having brought him to ripe age, she will no longer run the risk of losing this wonder at a blow, but she detaches from him a new self, that the kind may be safe from accidents to which the individual is exposed. So when the soul of the poet has come to ripeness of thought, she detaches and sends away from it its poems or songs,—a fearless, sleepless, deathless progeny, which is not exposed to the accidents of the weary kingdom of time: a fearless, vivacious offspring, clad with wings (such was the virtue of the soul out of which they came), which carry them fast and far, and infix them irrecoverably into the hearts of men. These wings are the beauty of the poet's soul. The songs, thus flying immortal from their mortal parent, are pursued by clamorous flights of censures, which swarm in far greater numbers, and threaten to devour them; but these last are not winged. At the end of a very short leap they fall plump down, and rot, having received from the souls out of which they came no beautiful wings. But the melodies of the poet ascend, and leap, and pierce into the deeps of infinite time.

So far the bard taught me, using his freer speech. But nature has a higher end, in the production of new individuals, than security, namely, *ascension*, or, the passage of the soul into higher forms. I knew, in my younger days, the sculptor who made the statue of the youth which stands in the public garden. He was, as I remember, unable to tell directly, what made him happy, or unhappy, but by wonderful indirections he could tell. He rose one day, according to his habit, before the dawn, and saw the morning break, grand as the eternity out of which it came, and, for many days after, he strove to express this tranquillity, and, lo! his chisel had fashioned out of marble the form of a beautiful youth, Phosphorus,[5] whose aspect is such, that, it is said, all persons who look on it become silent. The poet also resigns himself to his mood, and that thought which agitated him is expressed, but *alter idem*,[6] in a manner totally new. The expression is organic, or, the new type which things themselves take when liberated. As, in the sun, objects paint their images on the retina of the eye, so they, sharing the aspiration of the whole universe, tend to paint a far more delicate copy of their essence in his mind. Like the metamorphosis of things into higher organic forms, is their change into melodies. Over everything stands its dæmon, or soul, and, as the form of the thing is reflected by the eye, so the soul of the thing is reflected by a melody. The sea, the mountain-ridge, Niagara, and every flower-bed, pre-exist, or super-exist, in pre-cantations, which sail like odors in the air, and when

5. The Greek god associated with the morning star.
6. The same, yet different.

any man goes by with an ear sufficiently fine, he overhears them, and endeavors to write down the notes, without diluting or depraving them. And herein is the legitimation of criticism, in the mind's faith, that the poems are a corrupt version of some text in nature, with which they ought to be made to tally. A rhyme in one of our sonnets should not be less pleasing than the iterated nodes of a sea-shell, or the resembling difference of a group of flowers. The pairing of the birds is an idyl, not tedious as our idyls are; a tempest is a rough ode, without falsehood or rant: a summer, with its harvest sown, reaped, and stored, is an epic song, subordinating how many admirably executed parts. Why should not the symmetry and truth that modulate these, glide into our spirits, and we participate the invention of nature?

This insight, which expresses itself by what is called Imagination, is a very high sort of seeing, which does not come by study, but by the intellect being where and what it sees, by sharing the path, or circuit of things through forms, and so making them translucid to others. The path of things is silent. Will they suffer a speaker to go with them? A spy they will not suffer; a lover, a poet, is the transcendency of their own nature,—him they will suffer. The condition of true naming, on the poet's part, is his resigning himself to the divine *aura*[7] which breathes through forms, and accompanying that.

It is a secret which every intellectual man quickly learns, that, beyond the energy of his possessed and conscious intellect, he is capable of a new energy (as of an intellect doubled on itself), by abandonment to the nature of things; that, beside his privacy of power as an individual man, there is a great public power, on which he can draw, by unlocking, at all risks, his human doors, and suffering the ethereal tides to roll and circulate through him: then he is caught up into the life of the Universe, his speech is thunder, his thought is law, and his words are universally intelligible as the plants and animals. The poet knows that he speaks adequately, then, only when he speaks somewhat wildly, or, "with the flower of the mind;" not with the intellect, used as an organ, but with the intellect released from all service, and suffered to take its direction from its celestial life; or, as the ancients were wont to express themselves, not with intellect alone, but with the intellect inebriated by nectar. As the traveller who has lost his way, throws his reins on his horse's neck, and trusts to the instinct of the animal to find his road, so must we do with the divine animal who carries us through this world. For if in any manner we can stimulate this instinct, new passages are opened for us into nature, the mind flows into and through things hardest and highest, and the metamorphosis is possible.

7. **Distinctive quality.**

This is the reason why bards love wine, mead, narcotics, coffee, tea, opium, the fumes of sandal-wood and tobacco, or whatever other species of animal exhilaration. All men avail themselves of such means as they can, to add this extraordinary power to their normal powers; and to this end they prize conversation, music, pictures, sculpture, dancing, theatres, travelling, war, mobs, fires, gaming, politics, or love, or science, or animal intoxication, which are several coarser or finer *quasi*-mechanical substitutes for the true nectar, which is the ravishment of the intellect by coming nearer to the fact. These are auxiliaries to the centrifugal tendency of a man, to his passage out into free space, and they help him to escape the custody of that body in which he is pent up, and of that jail-yard of individual relations in which he is enclosed. Hence a great number of such as were professionally expressors of Beauty, as painters, poets, musicians, and actors, have been more than others wont to lead a life of pleasure and indulgence; all but the few who received the true nectar; and, as it was a spurious mode of attaining freedom, as it was an emancipation not into the heavens, but into the freedom of baser places, they were punished for that advantage they won, by a dissipation and deterioration. But never can any advantage be taken of nature by a trick. The spirit of the world, the great calm presence of the creator, comes not forth to the sorceries of opium or of wine. The sublime vision comes to the pure and simple soul in a clean and chaste body. That is not an inspiration which we owe to narcotics, but some counterfeit excitement and fury. Milton says, that the lyric poet may drink wine and live generously, but the epic poet, he who shall sing of the gods, and their descent unto men, must drink water out of a wooden bowl.[8] For poetry is not 'Devil's wine,' but God's wine. It is with this as it is with toys. We fill the hands and nurseries of our children with all manner of dolls, drums, and horses, withdrawing their eyes from the plain face and sufficing objects of nature, the sun, and moon, the animals, the water, and stones, which should be their toys. So the poet's habit of living should be set on a key so low and plain, that the common influences should delight him. His cheerfulness should be the gift of the sunlight; the air should suffice for his inspiration, and he should be tipsy with water. That spirit which suffices quiet hearts, which seems to come forth to such from every dry knoll of sere grass, from every pine-stump, and half-imbedded stone, on which the dull March sun shines, comes forth to the poor and hungry, and such as are of simple taste. If thou fill thy brain with Boston and New York, with fashion and covetousness, and wilt stimulate thy jaded senses with wine and French coffee, thou shalt find no radiance of wisdom in the lonely waste of the pinewoods.

If the imagination intoxicates the poet, it is not inactive in other

8. In Milton's *Sixth Latin Elegy*.

men. The metamorphosis excites in the beholder an emotion of joy. The use of symbols has a certain power of emancipation and exhilaration for all men. We seem to be touched by a wand, which makes us dance and run about happily, like children. We are like persons who come out of a cave or cellar into the open air. This is the effect on us of tropes,[9] fables, oracles, and all poetic forms. Poets are thus liberating gods. Men have really got a new sense, and found within their world, another world, or nest of worlds; for, the metamorphosis once seen, we divine that it does not stop. I will not now consider how much this makes the charm of algebra and the mathematics, which also have their tropes, but it is felt in every definition; as, when Aristotle defines *space* to be an immovable vessel, in which things are contained;—or, when Plato defines a *line* to be a flowing point; or, *figure* to be a bound of solid; and many the like. What a joyful sense of freedom we have, when Vitruvius announces the old opinion of artists, that no architect can build any house well, who does not know something of anatomy. When Socrates, in Charmides, tells us that the soul is cured of its maladies by certain incantations, and that these incantations are beautiful reasons, from which temperance is generated in souls; when Plato calls the world an animal; and Timæus affirms that the plants also are animals; or affirms a man to be a heavenly tree, growing with his root, which is his head, upward; and, as George Chapman, following him, writes,—

"So in our tree of man, whose nervie root
        Springs in his top;"

when Orpheus speaks of hoariness as "that white flower which marks extreme old age;" when Proclus calls the universe the statue of the intellect; when Chaucer, in his praise of 'Gentilesse,' compares good blood in mean condition to fire, which, though carried to the darkest house betwixt this and the mount of Caucasus, will yet hold its natural office, and burn as bright as if twenty thousand men did it behold; when John saw, in the apocalypse, the ruin of the world through evil, and the stars fall from heaven, as the figtree casteth her untimely fruit; when Æsop reports the whole catalogue of common daily relations through the masquerade of birds and beasts;—we take the cheerful hint of the immortality of our essence, and its versatile habit and escapes, as when the gypsies say, "it is in vain to hang them, they cannot die."[1]

The poets are thus liberating gods. The ancient British bards had for the title of their order, "Those who are free throughout the world." They are free, and they make free. An imaginative book renders us much more service at first, by stimulating us through its tropes, than afterward, when we arrive at the precise sense of the author. I think nothing is of any value in books, excepting the transcendental and extraordinary. If a man is inflamed and carried away by his thought, to that degree that he forgets the authors and the public, and heeds only this one dream, which holds him like an insanity, let me read his paper, and you may have all the arguments and histories and criticism. All the value which attaches to Pythagoras, Paracelsus, Cornelius Agrippa, Cardan, Kepler, Swedenborg, Schelling, Oken,[2] or any other who introduces questionable facts into his cosmogony, as angels, devils, magic, astrology, palmistry, mesmerism,[3] and so on, is the certificate we have of departure from routine, and that here is a new witness. That also is the best success in conversation, the magic of liberty, which puts the world, like a ball, in our hands. How cheap even the liberty then seems; how mean to study, when an emotion communicates to the intellect the power to sap and upheave nature: how great the perspective! nations, times, systems, enter and disappear, like threads in tapestry of large figure and many colors; dream delivers us to dream, and, while the drunkenness lasts, we will sell our bed, our philosophy, our religion, in our opulence.

There is good reason why we should prize this liberation. The fate of the poor shepherd, who, blinded and lost in the snowstorm, perishes in a drift within a few feet of his cottage door, is an emblem of the state of man. On the brink of the waters of life and truth, we are miserably dying. The inaccessibleness of every thought but that we are in, is wonderful. What if you come near to it,—you are as remote, when you are nearest, as when you are farthest. Every thought is also a prison; every heaven is also a prison. Therefore we love the poet, the inventor, who in any form, whether in an ode, or in an action, or in looks and behavior, has yielded us a new thought. He unlocks our chains, and admits us to a new scene.

This emancipation is dear to all men, and the power to impart it, as it must come from greater depth and scope of thought, is a measure of intellect. Therefore all books of the imagination endure, all which ascend to that truth, that the writer sees nature beneath him, and uses it as his exponent.[4] Every verse or sentence, possessing this virtue, will take care of its own immortality. The religions

2. Emerson combines a Greek mathematician and mystic philosopher of the sixth century B.C., a 16th-century Swiss alchemist, a 16th-century German physician; a 16th-century Italian mathematician, a 17th-century German astronomer, an 18th-century Swedish statesman and mystic, a 19th-century German philosopher, and a 19th-century German naturalist.
3. Hypnotism.
4. Means of expounding his beliefs.

of the world are the ejaculations[5] of a few imaginative men.

But the quality of the imagination is to flow, and not to freeze. The poet did not stop at the color, or the form, but read their meaning; neither may he rest in this meaning, but he makes the same objects exponents of his new thought. Here is the difference betwixt the poet and the mystic, that the last nails a symbol to one sense, which was a true sense for a moment, but soon becomes old and false. For all symbols are fluxional; all language is vehicular and transitive, and is good, as ferries and horses are, for conveyance, not as farms and houses are, for homestead. Mysticism consists in the mistake of an accidental and individual symbol for an universal one. The morning-redness happens to be the favorite meteor to the eyes of Jacob Behmen,[6] and comes to stand to him for truth and faith; and he believes should stand for the same realities to every reader. But the first reader prefers as naturally the symbol of a mother and child, or a gardener and his bulb, or a jeweller polishing a gem. Either of these, or of a myriad more, are equally good to the person to whom they are significant. Only they must be held lightly, and be very willingly translated into the equivalent terms which others use. And the mystic must be steadily told,—All that you say is just as true without the tedious use of that symbol as with it. Let us have a little algebra, instead of this trite rhetoric,—universal signs, instead of these village symbols,—and we shall both be gainers. The history of hierarchies seems to show, that all religious error consisted in making the symbol too stark and solid, and, at last, nothing but an excess of the organ of language.

Swedenborg, of all men in the recent ages, stands eminently for the translator of nature into thought. I do not know the man in history to whom things stood so uniformly for words. Before him the metamorphosis continually plays. Everything on which his eye rests, obeys the impulses of moral nature. The figs become grapes whilst he eats them. When some of his angels affirmed a truth, the laurel twig which they held blossomed in their hands. The noise which, at a distance, appeared like gnashing and thumping, on coming nearer was found to be the voice of disputants. The men, in one of his visions, seen in heavenly light, appeared like dragons, and seemed in darkness: but, to each other, they appeared as men, and, when the light from heaven shone into their cabin, they complained of the darkness, and were compelled to shut the window that they might see.

There was this perception in him, which makes the poet or seer, an object of awe and terror, namely, that the same man, or society of men, may wear one aspect to themselves and their companions, and a different aspect to higher intelligences. Certain priests, whom

---

5. Throwings forth.   6. German mystic (1575–1624).

he describes as conversing very learnedly together, appeared to the children, who were at some distance, like dead horses: and many the like misappearances. And instantly the mind inquires, whether these fishes under the bridge, yonder oxen in the pasture, those dogs in the yard, are immutably fishes, oxen, and dogs, or only so appear to me, and perchance to themselves appear upright men; and whether I appear as a man to all eyes. The Bramins and Pythagoras propounded the same question, and if any poet has witnessed the transformation, he doubtless found it in harmony with various experiences. We have all seen changes as considerable in wheat and caterpillars. He is the poet, and shall draw us with love and terror, who sees, through the flowing vest, the firm nature, and can declare it.

I look in vain for the poet whom I describe. We do not, with sufficient plainness, or sufficient profoundness, address ourselves to life, nor dare we chaunt our own times and social circumstance. If we filled the day with bravery, we should not shrink from celebrating it. Time and nature yield us many gifts, but not yet the timely man, the new religion, the reconciler, whom all things await. Dante's praise is, that he dared to write his autobiography in colossal cipher, or into universality. We have yet had no genius in America, with tyrannous eye, which knew the value of our incomparable materials, and saw, in the barbarism and materialism of the times, another carnival of the same gods whose picture he so much admires in Homer; then in the middle age; then in Calvinism. Banks and tariffs, the newspaper and caucus, methodism and unitarianism, are flat and dull to dull people, but rest on the same foundations of wonder as the town of Troy, and the temple of Delphos,[7] and are as swiftly passing away. Our logrolling, our stumps and their politics,[8] our fisheries, our Negroes, and Indians, our boasts, and our repudiations, the wrath of rogues, and the pusillanimity of honest men, the northern trade, the southern planting, the western clearing, Oregon, and Texas, are yet unsung. Yet America is a poem in our eyes; its ample geography dazzles the imagination, and it will not wait long for metres. If I have not found that excellent combination of gifts in my countrymen which I seek, neither could I aid myself to fix the idea of the poet by reading now and then in Chalmers's collection of five centuries of English poets.[9] These are wits, more than poets,

7. "Troy": the site of the Trojan War in Asia Minor; "Delphos": the home of the Delphic oracle, or prophetess, in Greece.
8. "Logrolling" seems to be used in the metaphorical sense of exchanging political favors; "stumps" refers to the practice political orators had of addressing audiences from any makeshift platform, even a tree stump. Just below,

"boasts" is the common correction for the first edition's "boats"; Emerson is contrasting the optimism of the states as they sold bonds here and abroad with their seemingly blithe repudiation of states' debts when grandiose projects fell through.
9. A commonly used set compiled by Alexander Chalmers (1759–1834), Scottish journalist and biographer.

though there have been poets among them. But when we adhere to the ideal of the poet, we have our difficulties even with Milton and Homer. Milton is too literary, and Homer too literal and historical.

But I am not wise enough for a national criticism, and must use the old largeness a little longer, to discharge my errand from the muse to the poet concerning his art.

Art is the path of the creator to his work. The paths, or methods, are ideal and eternal, though few men ever see them, not the artist himself for years, or for a lifetime, unless he come into the conditions. The painter, the sculptor, the composer, the epic rhapsodist, the orator, all partake one desire, namely, to express themselves symmetrically and abundantly, not dwarfishly and fragmentarily. They found or put themselves in certain conditions, as, the painter and sculptor before some impressive human figures; the orator, into the assembly of the people; and the others, in such scenes as each has found exciting to his intellect; and each presently feels the new desire. He hears a voice, he sees a beckoning. Then he is apprised, with wonder, what herds of dæmons hem him in. He can no more rest; he says, with the old painter, "By God, it is in me, and must go forth of me." He pursues a beauty, half seen, which flies before him. The poet pours out verses in every solitude. Most of the things he says are conventional, no doubt; but by and by he says something which is original and beautiful. That charms him. He would say nothing else but such things. In our way of talking, we say, 'That is yours, this is mine;' but the poet knows well that it is not his; that it is as strange and beautiful to him as to you; he would fain hear the like eloquence at length. Once having tasted this immortal ichor,[1] he cannot have enough of it, and, as an admirable creative power exists in these intellections, it is of the last importance that these things get spoken. What a little of all we know is said! What drops of all the sea of our science are baled up! and by what accident it is that these are exposed, when so many secrets sleep in nature! Hence the necessity of speech and song; hence these throbs and heart-beatings in the orator, at the door of the assembly, to the end, namely, that thought may be ejaculated as Logos, or Word.

Doubt not, O poet, but persist. Say, 'It is in me, and shall out.' Stand there, baulked and dumb, stuttering and stammering, hissed and hooted, stand and strive, until, at last, rage draw out of thee that *dream*-power which every night shows thee is thine own; a power transcending all limit and privacy, and by virtue of which a man is the conductor of the whole river of electricity. Nothing walks, or creeps, or grows, or exists, which must not in turn arise and walk before him as exponent of his meaning. Comes he to that

1. In Greek myth, blood of the gods; but Emerson may mean nectar, the drink of the gods.

power, his genius is no longer exhaustible. All the creatures, by pairs and by tribes, pour into his mind as into a Noah's ark, to come forth again to people a new world. This is like the stock of air for our respiration, or for the combustion of our fireplace, not a measure of gallons, but the entire atmosphere if wanted. And therefore the rich poets, as Homer, Chaucer, Shakspeare, and Raphael, have obviously no limits to their works, except the limits of their lifetime, and resemble a mirror carried through the street, ready to render an image of every created thing.

O poet! a new nobility is conferred in groves and pastures, and not in castles, or by the sword-blade, any longer. The conditions are hard, but equal. Thou shalt leave the world, and know the muse only. Thou shalt not know any longer the times, customs, graces, politics, or opinions of men, but shalt take all from the muse. For the time of towns is tolled from the world by funereal chimes, but in nature the universal hours are counted by succeeding tribes of animals and plants, and by growth of joy on joy. God wills also that thou abdicate a manifold and duplex life, and that thou be content that others speak for thee. Others shall be thy gentlemen, and shall represent all courtesy and worldly life for thee; others shall do the great and resounding actions also. Thou shalt lie close hid with nature, and canst not be afforded to the Capitol or the Exchange.[2] The world is full of renunciations and apprenticeships, and this is thine: thou must pass for a fool and a churl for a long season. This is the screen and sheath in which Pan[3] has protected his well-beloved flower, and thou shalt be known only to thine own, and they shall console thee with tenderest love. And thou shalt not be able to rehearse the names of thy friends in thy verse, for an old shame before the holy ideal. And this is the reward: that the ideal shall be real to thee, and the impressions of the actual world shall fall like summer rain, copious, but not troublesome, to thy invulnerable essence. Thou shalt have the whole land for thy park and manor, the sea for thy bath and navigation, without tax and without envy; the woods and the rivers thou shalt own; and thou shalt possess that wherein others are only tenants and boarders. Thou true land-lord! sea-lord! air-lord! Wherever snow falls, or water flows, or birds fly, wherever day and night meet in twilight, wherever the blue heaven is hung by clouds, or sown with stars, wherever are forms with transparent boundaries, wherever are outlets into celestial space, wherever is danger, and awe, and love, there is Beauty, plenteous as rain, shed for thee, and though thou shouldest walk the world over, thou shalt not be able to find a condition inopportune or ignoble.

1844

---

2. Stock exchange.
3. In Greek myth, the god of woods and fields, represented with goat's legs, horns, and ears.

Experience

The lords of life, the lords of life,—
I saw them pass,
In their own guise,
Like and unlike,
Portly and grim,
Use and Surprise,
Surface and Dream,
Succession swift, and spectral Wrong,
Temperament without a tongue,
And the inventor of the game
Omnipresent without name;—
Some to see, some to be guessed,
They marched from east to west:
Little man, least of all,
Among the legs of his guardians tall,
Walked about with puzzled look:—
Him by the hand dear nature took;
Dearest nature, strong and kind,
Whispered, 'Darling, never mind!
Tomorrow they will wear another face,
The founder thou! these are thy race!'[1]

Where do we find ourselves? In a series of which we do not know the extremes, and believe that it has none. We wake and find ourselves on a stair; there are stairs below us, which we seem to have ascended; there are stairs above us, many a one, which go upward and out of sight. But the Genius[2] which, according to the old belief, stands at the door by which we enter, and gives us the lethe[3] to drink, that we may tell no tales, mixed the cup too strongly, and we cannot shake off the lethargy now at noonday. Sleep lingers all our lifetime about our eyes, as night hovers all day in the boughs of the fir-tree. All things swim and glitter. Our life is not so much threatened as our perception. Ghostlike we glide through nature, and should not know our place again. Did our birth fall in some fit of indigence and frugality in nature, that she was so sparing of her fire and so liberal of her earth, that it appears to us that we lack the affirmative principle, and though we have health and reason, yet we have no superfluity of spirit for new creation? We have enough to live and bring the year about, but not an ounce to impart or to invest. Ah that our Genius were a little more of a genius! We are like millers on the lower levels of a stream, when the factories above them have exhausted the water. We too fancy that the upper people must have raised their dams.

1. First published in *Essays, Second Series* (Boston, 1844), *Experience* emerged in 1843 and 1844 during Emerson's broodings following the death of his young son Waldo in January, 1842, rather than being derived from a lecture, as most of his essays were. David W. Hill has shown that some of the more optimistic passages derive from journal entries made after Waldo's death, while some of the darker passages were first drafted before 1842, so no simple autobiographical reading is tenable. Still, it is the intensity of concentration following Waldo's death and the new and ruthless determination to tell the truth as he saw it that give the essay a strong claim to being Emerson's masterpiece. The epigraph is by Emerson.
2. Governing or guardian spirit.
3. Water from the river of forgetfulness in the underworld of Greek myth.

If any of us knew what we were doing, or where we are going, then when we think we best know! We do not know today whether we are busy or idle. In times when we thought ourselves indolent, we have afterwards discovered, that much was accomplished, and much was begun in us. All our days are so unprofitable while they pass, that 'tis wonderful where or when we ever got anything of this which we call wisdom, poetry, virtue. We never got it on any date calendar day. Some heavenly days must have been intercalated somewhere, like those that Hermes won with dice of the Moon, that Osiris[4] might be born. It is said, all martyrdoms looked mean when they were suffered. Every ship is a romantic object, except that we sail in. Embark, and the romance quits our vessel, and hangs on every other sail in the horizon. Our life looks trivial, and we shun to record it. Men seem to have learned of the horizon the art of perpetual retreating and reference. 'Yonder uplands are rich pasturage, and my neighbor has fertile meadow, but my field,' says the querulous farmer, 'only holds the world together.' I quote another man's saying; unluckily, that other withdraws himself in the same way, and quotes me. 'Tis the trick of nature thus to degrade today; a good deal of buzz, and somewhere a result slipped magically in. Every roof is agreeable to the eye, until it is lifted; then we find tragedy and moaning women, and hard-eyed husbands, and deluges of lethe, and the men ask, 'What's the news?' as if the old were so bad. How many individuals can we count in society? how many actions? how many opinions? So much of our time is preparation, so much is routine, and so much retrospect, that the pith of each man's genius contracts itself to a very few hours. The history of literature—take the net result of Tiraboschi, Warton, or Schlegel,[5] —is a sum of very few ideas, and of very few original tales,—all the rest being variation of these. So in this great society wide lying around us, a critical analysis would find very few spontaneous actions. It is almost all custom and gross sense. There are even few opinions, and these seem organic in the speakers, and do not disturb the universal necessity.

What opium is instilled into all disaster! It shows formidable as we approach it, but there is at last no rough rasping friction, but the most slippery sliding surfaces. We fall soft on a thought. *Ate Dea*[6] is gentle,

> "Over men's heads walking aloft,
> With tender feet treading so soft."[7]

4. Chief Egyptian god. The following story is told in Plutarch's *Morals*: the sun god forbade his wife Rhea to give birth on any day of the year, but Hermes won five new days from the moon, during which Osiris could be born.
5. Girolamo Tiraboschi (1731–94); Thomas Warton (1728–90), and either Friedrich von Schlegel (1772–1829) or his brother August Wilhelm von Schlegel (1767–1845), historians, respectively, of Italian, British, and European literature.
6. The goddess of mischief or fatal recklessness.
7. The *Iliad*, Book 19.

People grieve and bemoan themselves, but it is not half so bad with them as they say. There are moods in which we court suffering, in the hope that here, at least, we shall find reality, sharp peaks and edges of truth. But it turns out to be scene-painting and counterfeit. The only thing grief has taught me, is to know how shallow it is. That, like all the rest, plays about the surface, and never introduces me into the reality, for contact with which, we would even pay the costly price of sons and lovers. Was it Boscovich[8] who found out that bodies never come in contact? Well, souls never touch their objects. An innavigable sea washes with silent waves between us and the things we aim at and converse with. Grief too will make us idealists. In the death of my son, now more than two years ago, I seem to have lost a beautiful estate,—no more. I cannot get it nearer to me. If tomorrow I should be informed of the bankruptcy of my principal debtors, the loss of my property would be a great inconvenience to me, perhaps, for many years; but it would leave me as it found me,—neither better nor worse. So is it with this calamity: it does not touch me: some thing which I fancied was a part of me, which could not be torn away without tearing me, nor enlarged without enriching me, falls off from me, and leaves no scar. It was caducous.[9] I grieve that grief can teach me nothing, nor carry me one step into real nature. The Indian who was laid under a curse, that the wind should not blow on him, nor water flow to him, nor fire burn him, is a type of us all. The dearest events are summer-rain, and we the Para coats[1] that shed every drop. Nothing is left us now but death. We look to that with a grim satisfaction, saying, there at least is reality that will not dodge us.

I take this evanescence and lubricity of all objects, which lets them slip through our fingers then when we clutch hardest, to be the most unhandsome part of our condition. Nature does not like to be observed, and likes that we should be her fools and playmates. We may have the sphere for our cricket-ball, but not a berry for our philosophy. Direct strokes she never gave us power to make; all our blows glance, all our hits are accidents. Our relations to each other are oblique and casual.

Dream delivers us to dream, and there is no end to illusion. Life is a train of moods like a string of beads, and, as we pass through them, they prove to be many-colored lenses which paint the world their own hue, and each shows only what lies in its focus. From the mountain you see the mountain. We animate what we can, and we see only what we animate. Nature and books belong to the eyes that see them. It depends on the mood of the man, whether he shall see the sunset or the fine poem. There are always sunsets, and there is always genius; but only a few hours so serene that we can relish

8. Ruggiero Giuseppe Boscovich (1711–87), Italian physicist who advanced a molecular theory of matter.

9. Not long-lasting.
1. Rubber overcoats.

nature or criticism. The more or less depends on structure or temperament. Temperament is the iron wire on which the beads are strung. Of what use is fortune or talent to a cold and defective nature? Who cares what sensibility or discrimination a man has at some time shown, if he falls asleep in his chair? or if he laugh and giggle? or if he apologize? or is affected with egotism? or thinks of his dollar? or cannot go by food? or has gotten a child in his boyhood? Of what use is genius, if the organ is too convex or too concave, and cannot find a focal distance within the actual horizon of human life? Of what use, if the brain is too cold or too hot, and the man does not care enough for results, to stimulate him to experiment, and hold him up in it? or if the web is too finely woven, too irritable by pleasure and pain, so that life stagnates from too much reception, without due outlet? Of what use to make heroic vows of amendment, if the same old law-breaker is to keep them? What cheer can the religious sentiment yield, when that is suspected to be secretly dependent on the seasons of the year, and the state of the blood? I knew a witty physician who found theology in the biliary duct, and used to affirm that if there was disease in the liver, the man became a Calvinist, and if that organ was sound, he became a Unitarian.[2] Very mortifying is the reluctant experience that some unfriendly excess or imbecility neutralizes the promise of genius. We see young men who owe us a new world, so readily and lavishly they promise, but they never acquit the debt; they die young and dodge the account: or if they live, they lose themselves in the crowd.

Temperament also enters fully into the system of illusions, and shuts us in a prison of glass which we cannot see. There is an optical illusion about every person we meet. In truth, they are all creatures of given temperament, which will appear in a given character, whose boundaries they will never pass: but we look at them, they seem alive, and we presume there is impulse in them. In the moment it seems impulse; in the year, in the lifetime, it turns out to be a certain uniform tune which the revolving barrel of the music-box must play. Men resist the conclusion in the morning, but adopt it as the evening wears on, that temper prevails over everything of time, place, and condition, and is inconsumable in the flames of religion. Some modifications the moral sentiment avails to impose, but the individual texture holds its dominion, if not to bias the moral judgments, yet to fix the measure of activity and of enjoyment.

I thus express the law as it is read from the platform of ordinary life, but must not leave it without noticing the capital exception. For temperament is a power which no man willingly hears any one

2. I.e., the Calvinistic sense of Original Sin is seen as an intellectual manifestation of a bodily disease; the Unitarian view of man has none of the Calvinistic preoccupation with eternal damnation for all but the select few, the elect.

praise but himself. On the platform of physics, we cannot resist the contracting influences of so-called science. Temperament puts all divinity to rout. I know the mental proclivity of physicians. I hear the chuckle of the phrenologists.[3] Theoretic kidnappers and slave-drivers, they esteem each man the victim of another, who winds him round his finger by knowing the law of his being, and by such cheap signboards as the color of his beard, or the slope of his occiput, reads the inventory of his fortunes and character. The grossest ignorance does not disgust like this impudent knowingness. The physicians say, they are not materialists; but they are:—Spirit is matter reduced to an extreme thinness: O *so* thin!—But the definition of *spiritual* should be, *that which is its own evidence*. What notions do they attach to love! what to religion! One would not willingly pronounce these words in their hearing, and give them the occasion to profane them. I saw a gracious gentleman who adapts his conversation to the form of the head of the man he talks with! I had fancied that the value of life lay in its inscrutable possibilities; in the fact that I never know, in addressing myself to a new individual, what may befall me. I carry the keys of my castle in my hand, ready to throw them at the feet of my lord, whenever and in what disguise so ever he shall appear. I know he is in the neighborhood hidden among vagabonds. Shall I preclude my future, by taking a high seat, and kindly adapting my conversation to the shape of heads? When I come to that, the doctors shall buy me for a cent.——'But, sir, medical history; the report to the Institute; the proven facts!'—I distrust the facts and the inferences. Temperament is the veto or limitation-power in the constitution, very justly applied to restrain an opposite excess in the constitution, but absurdly offered as a bar to original equity. When virtue is in presence, all subordinate powers sleep. On its own level, or in view of nature, temperament is final. I see not, if one be once caught in this trap of so-called sciences, any escape for the man from the links of the chain of physical necessity. Given such an embryo, such a history must follow. On this platform, one lives in a sty of sensualism, and would soon come to suicide. But it is impossible that the creative power should exclude itself. Into every intelligence there is a door which is never closed, through which the creator passes. The intellect, seeker of absolute truth, or the heart, lover of absolute good, intervenes for our succor, and at one whisper of these high powers, we awake from ineffectual struggles with this nightmare. We hurl it into its own hell, and cannot again contract ourselves to so base a state.

The secret of the illusoriness is in the necessity of a succession of moods or objects. Gladly we would anchor, but the anchorage is quicksand. This onward trick of nature is too strong for us: *Pero si*

3. Pseudoscientists who claimed to read character by the formation of the skull.

muove.[4] When, at night, I look at the moon and stars, I seem stationary, and they to hurry. Our love of the real draws us to permanence, but health of body consists in circulation, and sanity of mind in variety or facility of association. We need change of objects. Dedication to one thought is quickly odious. We house with the insane, and must humor them; then conversation dies out. Once I took such delight in Montaigne, that I thought I should not need any other book; before that, in Shakspeare; then in Plutarch; then in Plotinus; at one time in Bacon; afterwards in Goethe; even in Bettine;[5] but now I turn the pages of either of them languidly, whilst I still cherish their genius. So with pictures; each will bear an emphasis of attention once, which it cannot retain, though we fain would continue to be pleased in that manner. How strongly I have felt of pictures, that when you have seen one well, you must take your leave of it; you shall never see it again. I have had good lessons from pictures, which I have since seen without emotion or remark. A deduction must be made from the opinion, which even the wise express of a new book or occurrence. Their opinion gives me tidings of their mood, and some vague guess at the new fact, but is nowise to be trusted as the lasting relation between that intellect and that thing. The child asks, 'Mamma, why don't I like the story as well as when you told it me yesterday?' Alas, child, it is even so with the oldest cherubim of knowledge. But will it answer thy question to say, Because thou wert born to a whole, and this story is a particular? The reason of the pain this discovery causes us (and we make it late in respect to works of art and intellect), is the plaint of tragedy which murmurs from it in regard to persons, to friendship and love.

That immobility and absence of elasticity which we find in the arts, we find with more pain in the artist. There is no power of expansion in men. Our friends early appear to us as representatives of certain ideas, which they never pass or exceed. They stand on the brink of the ocean of thought and power, but they never take the single step that would bring them there. A man is like a bit of Labrador spar,[6] which has no lustre as you turn it in your hand, until you come to a particular angle; then it shows deep and beautiful colors. There is no adaptation or universal applicability in men, but each has his special talent, and the mastery of successful men consists in adroitly keeping themselves where and when that turn shall be oftenest to be practised. We do what we must, and call it by

4. "It moves, all the same"—Galileo's muttered protest after the Inquisition (tribunal of the Roman Catholic church charged with suppressing heresy) had forced him to retract the idea that the earth revolves around the sun.
5. Michel de Montaigne (1533–92), French essayist; Plutarch (46?–120?), Greek biographer of famous Greeks and Romans; Plotinus (205?–270?), Egyp-tian-born Roman Neoplatonist philosopher; Sir Francis Bacon (1561–1626), English essayist, philosopher, and statesman; Johann Wolfgang von Goethe (1749–1832), German poet and dramatist; Elizabeth ("Bettine") von Arnim (1785–1859), whose purported correspondence with Goethe was published in 1835.
6. Labradorite, crystalline rock.

the best names we can, and would fain have the praise of having intended the result which ensues. I cannot recall any form of man who is not superfluous sometimes. But is not this pitiful? Life is not worth the taking, to do tricks in.

Of course, it needs the whole society, to give the symmetry we seek. The parti-colored wheel must revolve very fast to appear white. Something is learned too by conversing with so much folly and defect. In fine, whoever loses, we are always of the gaining party. Divinity is behind our failures and follies also. The plays of children are nonsense, but very educative nonsense. So it is with the largest and solemnest things, with commerce, government, church, marriage, and so with the history of every man's bread, and the ways by which he is to come by it. Like a bird which alights nowhere, but hops perpetually from bough to bough, is the Power which abides in no man and in no woman, but for a moment speaks from this one, and for another moment from that one.

But what help from these fineries or pedantries? What help from thought? Life is not dialectics. We, I think, in these times, have had lessons enough of the futility of criticism. Our young people have thought and written much on labor and reform, and for all that they have written, neither the world nor themselves have got on a step. Intellectual tasting of life will not supersede muscular activity. If a man should consider the nicety of the passage of a piece of bread down his throat, he would starve. At Education-Farm,[7] the noblest theory of life sat on the noblest figures of young men and maidens, quite powerless and melancholy. It would not rake or pitch a ton of hay; it would not rub down a horse; and the men and maidens it left pale and hungry. A political orator wittily compared our party promises to western roads, which opened stately enough, with planted trees on either side, to tempt the traveller, but soon became narrow and narrower, and ended in a squirrel-track, and ran up a tree. So does culture with us; it ends in head-ache. Unspeakably sad and barren does life look to those, who a few months ago were dazzled with the splendor of the promise of the times. "There is now no longer any right course of action, nor any self-devotion left among the Iranis."[8] Objections and criticism we have had our fill of. There are objections to every course of life and action, and the practical wisdom infers an indifferency, from the omnipresence of objection. The whole frame of things preaches indifference. Do not craze yourself with thinking, but go about your business anywhere. Life is not intellectual or critical, but sturdy. Its chief good is for well-mixed people who can enjoy what they find, without question. Nature hates peeping and our mothers speak her very sense

7. Brook Farm, the Transcendentalist commune at West Roxbury, Mass.
8. From the Persian *Desatir*, ancient scriptures credited to Zoroaster, sixth-century B.C. founder of the Parsee religion.

when they say, "Children, eat your victuals, and say no more of it." To fill the hour,—that is happiness; to fill the hour, and leave no crevice for a repentance or an approval. We live amid surfaces, and the true art of life is to skate well on them. Under the oldest mouldiest conventions, a man of native force prospers just as well as in the newest world, and that by skill of handling and treatment. He can take hold anywhere. Life itself is a mixture of power and form, and will not bear the least excess of either. To finish the moment, to find the journey's end in every step of the road, to live the greatest number of good hours, is wisdom. It is not the part of men, but of fanatics, or of mathematicians, if you will, to say, that, the shortness of life considered, it is not worth caring whether for so short a duration we were sprawling in want, or sitting high. Since our office is with moments, let us husband them. Five minutes of today are worth as much to me, as five minutes in the next millennium. Let us be poised, and wise, and our own, today. Let us treat the men and women well: treat them as if they were real: perhaps they are. Men live in their fancy, like drunkards whose hands are too soft and tremulous for successful labor. It is a tempest of fancies, and the only ballast I know, is a respect to the present hour. Without any shadow of doubt, amidst this vertigo of shows and politics, I settle myself ever the firmer in the creed, that we should not postpone and refer and wish, but do broad justice where we are, by whomsoever we deal with, accepting our actual companions and circumstances, however humble or odious, as the mystic officials to whom the universe has delegated its whole pleasure for us. If these are mean and malignant, their contentment, which is the last victory of justice, is a more satisfying echo to the heart, than the voice of poets and the casual sympathy of admirable persons. I think that however a thoughtful man may suffer from the defects and absurdities of his company, he cannot with affection deny to any set of men and women, a sensibility to extraordinary merit. The coarse and frivolous have an instinct of superiority, if they have not a sympathy, and honor it in their blind capricious way with sincere homage.

The fine young people despise life, but in me, and in such as with me are free from dyspepsia, and to whom a day is a sound and solid good, it is a great excess of politeness to look scornful and to cry for company. I am grown by sympathy a little eager and sentimental, but leave me alone, and I should relish every hour and what it brought me, the potluck of the day, as heartily as the oldest gossip in the bar-room. I am thankful for small mercies. I compared notes with one of my friends who expects everything of the universe, and is disappointed when anything is less than the best, and I found that I begin at the other extreme, expecting nothing, and am always full of thanks for moderate goods. I accept the clangor and jangle of contrary tendencies. I find my account in sots and bores also. They give a reality to the circumjacent picture, which such a vanishing meteorous appearance can ill spare. In the morning I awake, and find the old world, wife, babes, and mother, Concord and Boston, the dear old spiritual world, and even the dear old devil not far off. If we will take the good we find, asking no questions, we shall have heaping measures. The great gifts are not got by analysis. Everything good is on the highway. The middle region of our being is the temperate zone. We may climb into the thin and cold realm of pure geometry and lifeless science, or sink into that of sensation. Between these extremes is the equator of life, of thought, of spirit, of poetry,—a narrow belt. Moreover, in popular experience, everything good is on the highway. A collector peeps into all the picture-shops of Europe, for a landscape of Poussin, a crayon-sketch of Salvator; but the Transfiguration, the Last Judgment, the Communion of St. Jerome, and what are as transcendent as these, are on the walls of the Vatican, the Uffizii, or the Louvre, where every footman may see them;[9] to say nothing of nature's pictures in every street, of sunsets and sunrises every day, and the sculpture of the human body never absent. A collector recently bought at public auction, in London, for one hundred and fifty-seven guineas,[1] an autograph of Shakspeare: but for nothing a school-boy can read Hamlet, and can detect secrets of highest concernment yet unpublished therein. I think I will never read any but the commonest books,—the Bible, Homer, Dante, Shakspeare, and Milton. Then we are impatient of so public a life and planet, and run hither and thither for nooks and secrets. The imagination delights in the woodcraft of Indians, trappers, and bee-hunters. We fancy that we are strangers, and not so intimately domesticated in the planet as the wild man, and the wild beast and bird. But the exclusion reaches them also; reaches the climbing, flying, gliding, feathered and four-footed man. Fox and woodchuck, hawk and snipe, and bittern, when nearly seen, have no more root in the deep world than many, and are just such superficial tenants of the globe. Then the new molecular philosophy shows astronomical interspaces betwixt atom and atom, shows that the world is all outside: it has no inside.

The mid-world is best. Nature, as we know her, is no saint. The lights of the church, the ascetics, Gentoos and Grahamites,[2] she does not distinguish by any favor. She comes eating and drinking and sinning. Her darlings, the great, the strong, the beautiful, are not children of our law, do not come out of the Sunday School, nor weigh their food, nor punctually keep the commandments. If we will be strong with her strength, we must not harbor such disconso-

---

9. Nicolas Poussin (1594–1665), French painter; Salvator Rosa (1615–73), Italian painter of wild landscapes. The *Transfiguration* is that by Raphael, in Rome; the *Last Judgment* is Michelangelo's, in Florence; and the *Communion of St. Jerome* is that by Il Domenichino, in Paris. The collector hunts for minor paintings in out-of-the-way shops while the great paintings are in museums where anyone may see them.

1. British gold coin worth one shilling more than a pound.

2. Hindu sectarians or contemporary food-faddists (from Sylvester Graham [1794–1851], vegetarian whose efforts at food reform are memorialized in the graham cracker).

late consciences, borrowed too from the consciences of other nations. We must set up the strong present tense against all the rumors of wrath, past or to come. So many things are unsettled which it is of the first importance to settle,—and, pending their settlement, we will do as we do. Whilst the debate goes forward on the equity of commerce, and will not be closed for a century or two, New and Old England may keep shop. Law of copyright and international copyright[3] is to be discussed, and, in the interim, we will sell our books for the most we can. Expediency of literature, reason of literature, lawfulness of writing down a thought, is questioned; much is to say on both sides, and, while the fight waxes hot, thou, dearest scholar, stick to thy foolish task, add a line every hour, and between whiles add a line. Right to hold land, right of property, is disputed, and the conventions convene, and before the vote is taken, dig away in your garden, and spend your earnings as a waif or godsend to all serene and beautiful purposes. Life itself is a bubble and a skepticism, and a sleep within a sleep. Grant it, and as much more as they will,—but thou, God's darling! heed thy private dream: thou wilt not be missed in the scorning and skepticism: there are enough of them: stay there in thy closet, and toil, until the rest are agreed what to do about it. Thy sickness, they say, and thy puny habit, require that thou do this or avoid that, but know that thy life is a flitting state, a tent for a night, and do thou, sick or well, finish that stint. Thou art sick, but shalt not be worse, and the universe, which holds thee dear, shall be the better.

Human life is made up of the two elements, power and form, and the proportion must be invariably kept, if we would have it sweet and sound. Each of these elements in excess makes a mischief as hurtful as its defect. Everything runs to excess: every good quality is noxious, if unmixed, and, to carry the danger to the edge of ruin, nature causes each man's peculiarity to superabound. Here, among the farms, we adduce the scholars as examples of this treachery. They are nature's victims of expression. You who see the artist, the orator, the poet, too near, and find their life no more excellent than that of mechanics or farmers, and themselves victims of partiality, very hollow and haggard, and pronounce them failures,—not heroes, but quacks,—conclude very reasonably, that these arts are not for man, but are disease. Yet nature will not bear you out. Irresistible nature made men such, and makes legions more of such, every day. You love the boy reading in a book, gazing at a drawing, or a cast: yet what are these millions who read and behold, but incipient writers and sculptors? Add a little more of that quality which now reads and sees, and they will seize the pen and chisel. And if one remembers how innocently he began to be an artist, he perceives that nature joined with his enemy. A man is a golden impossibility.

3. Not passed by the American Congress until 1891.

The line he must walk is a hair's breadth. The wise through excess of wisdom is made a fool.

How easily, if fate would suffer it, we might keep forever these beautiful limits, and adjust ourselves, once for all, to the perfect calculation of the kingdom of known cause and effect. In the street and in the newspapers, life appears so plain a business, that manly resolution and adherence to the multiplication-table through all weathers, will insure success. But ah! presently comes a day, or is it only a half-hour, with its angel-whispering,—which discomfits the conclusions of nations and of years! Tomorrow again, everything looks real and angular, the habitual standards are reinstated, common sense is as rare as genius,—is the basis of genius, and experience is hands and feet to every enterprise;—and yet, he who should do his business on this understanding, would be quickly bankrupt. Power keeps quite another road than the turnpikes of choice and will, namely, the subterranean and invisible tunnels and channels of life. It is ridiculous that we are diplomatists, and doctors, and considerate people: there are no dupes like these. Life is a series of surprises, and would not be worth taking or keeping, if it were not. God delights to isolate us every day, and hide from us the past and the future. We would look about us, but with grand politeness he draws down before us an impenetrable screen of purest sky, and another behind us of purest sky. 'You will not remember,' he seems to say, 'and you will not expect.' All good conversation, manners, and action, come from a spontaneity which forgets usages, and makes the moment great. Nature hates calculators; her methods are saltatory and impulsive. Man lives by pulses; our organic movements are such; and the chemical and ethereal agents are undulatory and alternate; and the mind goes antagonizing on, and never prospers but by fits. We thrive by casualties. Our chief experiences have been casual. The most attractive class of people are those who are powerful obliquely, and not by the direct stroke: men of genius, but not yet accredited: one gets the cheer of their light, without paying too great a tax. Theirs is the beauty of the bird, or the morning light, and not of art. In the thought of genius there is always a surprise; and the moral sentiment is well called "the newness," for it is never other; as new to the oldest intelligence as to the young child,—"the kingdom that cometh without observation."[4] In like manner, for practical success, there must not be too much design. A man will not be observed in doing that which he can do best. There is a certain magic about his properest action, which stupefies your powers of observation, so that though it is done before you, you wist not of it. The art of life has a pudency, and will not be exposed. Every man is an impossibility, until he is born; every thing impossible, until we see a success. The ardors of piety agree at last with the coldest skepticism,—that nothing is of us or

4. Luke 17.20.

our works,—that all is of God. Nature will not spare us the smallest leaf of laurel. All writing comes by the grace of God, and all doing and having. I would gladly be moral, and keep due metes and bounds, which I dearly love, and allow the most to the will of man, but I have set my heart on honesty in this chapter, and I can see nothing at last, in success or failure, than more or less of vital force supplied from the Eternal. The results of life are uncalculated and uncalculable. The years teach much which the days never know. The persons who compose our company, converse, and come and go, and design and execute many things, and somewhat comes of it all, but an unlooked for result. The individual is always mistaken. He designed many things, and drew in other persons as coadjutors, quarrelled with some or all, blundered much, and something is done; all are a little advanced, but the individual is always mistaken. It turns out somewhat new, and very unlike what he promised himself.

The ancients, struck with this irreducibleness of the elements of human life to calculation, exalted Chance into a divinity, but that is to stay too long at the spark,—which glitters truly at one point,— but the universe is warm with the latency of the same fire. The miracle of life which will not be expounded, but will remain a miracle, introduces a new element. In the growth of the embryo, Sir Everard Home,[5] I think, noticed that the evolution was not from one central point, but co-active from three or more points. Life has no memory. That which proceeds in succession might be remembered, but that which is co-existent, or ejaculated from a deeper cause, as yet far from being conscious, knows not its own tendency. So is it with us, now skeptical, or without unity, because immersed in forms and effects all seeming to be of equal yet hostile value, and now religious, whilst in the reception of spiritual law. Bear with these distractions, with this coetaneous growth of the parts: they will one day be *members*, and obey one will. On that one will, on that secret cause, they nail our attention and hope. Life is hereby melted into an expectation or a religion. Underneath the inharmonious and trivial particulars, is a musical perfection, the Ideal journeying always with us, the heaven without rent or seam. Do but observe the mode of our illumination. When I converse with a profound mind, or if at any time being alone I have good thoughts, I do not at once arrive at satisfactions, as when, being thirsty, I drink water, or go to the fire, being cold: no! but I am at first apprised of my vicinity to a new and excellent region of life. By persisting to read or to think, this region gives further sign of itself, as it were in flashes of light, in sudden discoveries of its profound beauty and repose, as if the clouds that covered it parted at intervals, and showed the approaching traveller the inland mountains,

5. Scottish surgeon (1756–1832).

with the tranquil eternal meadows spread at their base, whereon flocks graze, and shepherds pipe and dance. But every insight from this realm of thought is felt as initial, and promises a sequel. I do not make it; I arrive there, and behold what was there already. I make! O no! I clap my hands in infantine joy and amazement, before the first opening to me of this august magnificence, old with the love and homage of innumerable ages, young with the life of life, the sunbright Mecca of the desert. And what a future it opens! I feel a new heart beating with the love of the new beauty. I am ready to die out of nature, and be born again into this new yet unapproachable America I have found in the West.

> "Since neither now nor yesterday began
> These thoughts, which have been ever, nor yet can
> A man be found who their first entrance knew."[6]

If I have described life as a flux of moods, I must now add, that there is that in us which changes not, and which ranks all sensations and states of mind. The consciousness in each man is a sliding scale, which identifies him now with the First Cause, and now with the flesh of his body; life above life, in infinite degrees. The sentiment from which it sprung determines the dignity of any deed, and the question ever is, not, what you have done or forborne, but, at whose command you have done or forborne it.

Fortune, Minerva,[7] Muse, Holy Ghost,—these are quaint names, too narrow to cover this unbounded substance. The baffled intellect must still kneel before this cause, which refuses to be named,—ineffable cause, which every fine genius has essayed to represent by some emphatic symbol, as, Thales by water, Anaximenes by air, Anaxagoras by ($Nov\varsigma$) thought, Zoroaster by fire, Jesus and the moderns by love:[8] and the metaphor of each has become a national religion. The Chinese Mencius[9] has not been the least successful in his generalization. "I fully understand language," he said, "and nourish well my vast-flowing vigor."—"I beg to ask what you call vast-flowing vigor?"—said his companion. "The explanation," replied Mencius, "is difficult. This vigor is supremely great, and in the highest degree unbending. Nourish it correctly, and do it no injury, and it will fill up the vacancy between heaven and earth. This vigor accords with and assists justice and reason, and leaves no hunger."—In our more correct writing, we give to this generalization the name of Being, and thereby confess that we have arrived as far as we can go. Suffice it for the joy of the universe, that we have not arrived at a wall, but at interminable oceans. Our life seems not

---

6. A free translation of the conclusion of one of the heroine's speeches in Sophocles' *Antigone* (lines 456–57).
7. Roman goddess of wisdom.
8. The first three are Greek philosophers of, respectively, the seventh, sixth, and

fifth centuries B.C.; Zoroaster is the sixth-century-B.C. Persian founder of the fire worship of the Parsees.
9. Meng-tsu, third-century-B.C. compiler of doctrines of Confucianism.

present, so much as prospective; not for the affairs on which it is wasted, but as a hint of this vast-flowing vigor. Most of life seems to be mere advertisement of faculty: information is given us not to sell ourselves cheap; that we are very great. So, in particulars, our greatness is always in a tendency or direction, not in an action. It is for us to believe in the rule, not in the exception. The noble are thus known from the ignoble. So in accepting the leading of the sentiments, it is not what we believe concerning the immortality of the soul, or the like, but *the universal impulse to believe*, that is the material circumstance, and is the principal fact in the history of the globe. Shall we describe this cause as that which works directly? The spirit is not helpless or needful of mediate organs. It has plentiful powers and direct effects. I am explained without explaining, I am felt without acting, and where I am not. Therefore all just persons are satisfied with their own praise. They refuse to explain themselves, and are content that new actions should do them that office. They believe that we communicate without speech, and above speech, and that no right action of ours is quite unaffecting to our friends, at whatever distance; for the influence of action is not to be measured by miles. Why should I fret myself, because a circumstance has occurred, which hinders my presence where I was expected? If I am not at the meeting, my presence where I am, should be as useful to the commonwealth of friendship and wisdom, as would be my presence in that place. I exert the same quality of power in all places. Thus journeys the mighty Ideal before us; it never was known to fall into the rear. No man ever came to an experience which was satiating, but his good is tidings of a better. Onward and onward! In liberated moments, we know that a new picture of life and duty is already possible; the elements already exist in many minds around you, of a doctrine of life which shall transcend any written record we have. The new statement will comprise the skepticisms, as well as the faiths of society, and out of unbeliefs a creed shall be formed. For, skepticisms are not gratuitous or lawless, but are limitations of the affirmative statement, and the new philosophy must take them in, and make affirmations outside of them, just as much as it must include the oldest beliefs.

It is very unhappy, but too late to be helped, the discovery we have made, that we exist. That discovery is called the Fall of Man. Ever afterwards, we suspect our instruments. We have learned that we do not see directly, but mediately, and that we have no means of correcting these colored and distorting lenses which we are, or of computing the amount of their errors. Perhaps these subject-lenses have a creative power; perhaps there are no objects. Once we lived in what we saw; now, the rapaciousness of this new power, which threatens to absorb all things, engages us. Nature, art, persons, letters, religions,—objects, successively tumble in, and God is but one of its ideas. Nature and literature are subjective phenomena; every evil and every good thing is a shadow which we cast. The street is full of humiliations to the proud. As the fop contrived to dress his bailiffs in his livery, and make them wait on his guests at table, so the chagrins[1] which the bad heart gives off as bubbles, at once take form as ladies and gentlemen in the street, shopmen or barkeepers in hotels, and threaten or insult whatever is threatenable and insultable in us. 'Tis the same with our idolatries. People forget that it is the eye which makes the horizon, and the rounding mind's eye which makes this or that man a type of representative of humanity with the name of hero or saint. Jesus the "providential man," is a good man on whom many people are agreed that these optical laws shall take effect. By love on one part, and by forbearance to press objection on the other part, it is for a time settled, that we will look at him in the centre of the horizon, and ascribe to him the properties that will attach to any man so seen. But the longest love or aversion has a speedy term. The great and crescive[2] self, rooted in absolute nature, supplants all relative existence, and ruins the kingdom of mortal friendship and love. Marriage (in what is called the spiritual world) is impossible, because of the inequality between every subject and every object. The subject is the receiver of Godhead, and at every comparison must feel his being enhanced by that cryptic might. Though not in energy, yet by presence, this magazine[3] of substance cannot be otherwise than felt: nor can any force of intellect attribute to the object the proper deity which sleeps or wakes forever in every subject. Never can love make consciousness and ascription equal in force. There will be the same gulf between every me and thee, as between the original and the picture. The universe is the bride of the soul. All private sympathy is partial. Two human beings are like globes, which can touch only in a point, and, whilst they remain in contact, all other points of each of the spheres are inert; their turn must also come, and the longer a particular union lasts, the more energy of appetency[4] the parts not in union acquire.

Life will be imaged, but cannot be divided nor doubled. Any invasion of its unity would be chaos. The soul is not twin-born, but the only begotten, and though revealing itself as child in time, child in appearance, is of a fatal and universal power, admitting no co-life. Every day, every act betrays the ill-concealed deity. We believe in ourselves, as we do not believe in others. We permit all things to ourselves, and that which we call sin in others, is experiment for us. It is an instance of our faith in ourselves, that men never speak of crime as lightly as they think: or, every man thinks a latitude safe for himself, which is nowise to be indulged to another. The act

1. Ill-humored feelings.
2. Increasing.
3. Stored supply.
4. Strong impulse toward union.

looks very differently on the inside, and on the outside; in its quality, and in its consequences. Murder in the murderer is no such ruinous thought as poets and romancers will have it; it does not unsettle him, or fright him from his ordinary notice of trifles: it is an act quite easy to be contemplated, but in its sequel, it turns out to be a horrible jangle and confounding of all relations. Especially the crimes that spring from love, seem right and fair from the actor's point of view, but, when acted, are found destructive of society. No man at last believes that he can be lost, nor that the crime in him is as black as in the felon. Because the intellect qualifies in our own case the moral judgments. For there is no crime to the intellect. That is antinomian or hypernomian,[5] and judges law as well as fact. "It is worse than a crime, it is a blunder," said Napoleon, speaking the language of the intellect. To it, the world is a problem in mathematics or the science of quantity, and it leaves out praise and blame, and all weak emotions. All stealing is comparative. If you come to absolutes, pray who does not steal? Saints are sad, because they behold sin, (even when they speculate,) from the point of view of the conscience, and not of the intellect; a confusion of thought. Sin seen from the thought, is a diminution or *less*: seen from the conscience or will, it is pravity or *bad*. The intellect names it shade, absence of light, and no essence. The conscience must feel it as essence, essential evil. This it is not: it has an objective existence, but no subjective.

Thus inevitably does the universe wear our color, and every object fall successively into the subject itself. The subject exists, the subject enlarges; all things sooner or later fall into place. As I am, so I see; use what language we will, we can never say anything but what we are; Hermes, Cadmus, Columbus, Newton, Buonaparte, are the mind's ministers.[6] Instead of feeling a poverty when we encounter a great man, let us treat the new comer like a travelling geologist, who passes through our estate, and shows us good slate, or limestone, or anthracite, in our brush pasture. The partial action of each strong mind in one direction, is a telescope for the objects on which it is pointed. But every other part of knowledge is to be pushed to the same extravagance, ere the soul attains her due sphericity. Do you see that kitten chasing so prettily her own tail? If you could look with her eyes, you might see her surrounded with hundreds of figures performing complex dramas, with tragic and comic issues, long conversations, many characters, many ups and downs of fate,—and meantime it is only puss and her tail. How

5. Against or beyond the control of law.
6. I.e., great gods or men of legend and history are servants of the human mind because our subjectivity uses them to light up areas of our own being. (Hermes is the Greek god of invention; Cadmus the mythical inventor of the alphabet and creator of the Thebans by sowing dragon's teeth; Columbus discovered America; Newton discovered the law of gravity; and Napoleon Bonaparte in Emerson's childhood was the conqueror of much of Europe.)

long before our masquerade will end its noise of tamborines, laughter, and shouting, and we shall find it was a solitary performance?—A subject and an object,—it takes so much to make the galvanic circuit complete, but magnitude adds nothing. What imports it whether it is Kepler[7] and the sphere; Columbus and America; a reader and his book; or puss with her tail?

It is true that all the muses and love and religion hate these developments, and will find a way to punish the chemist, who publishes in the parlor the secrets of the laboratory. And we cannot say too little of our constitutional necessity of seeing things under private aspects, or saturated with our humors. And yet is the God the native of these bleak rocks. That need makes in morals the capital virtue of self-trust. We must hold hard to this poverty, however scandalous, and by more vigorous self-recoveries, after the sallies of action, possess our axis more firmly. The life of truth is cold, and so far mournful; but it is not the slave of tears, contritions, and perturbations. It does not attempt another's work, nor adopt another's facts. It is a main lesson of wisdom to know your own from another's. I have learned that I cannot dispose of other people's facts; but I possess such a key to my own, as persuades me against all their denials, that they also have a key to theirs. A sympathetic person is placed in the dilemma of a swimmer among drowning men, who all catch at him, and if he gives so much as a leg or a finger, they will drown him. They wish to be saved from the mischiefs of their vices, but not from their vices. Charity would be wasted on this poor waiting on the symptoms. A wise and hardy physician will say, *Come out of that*, as the first condition of advice.

In this our talking America, we are ruined by our good nature and listening on all sides. This compliance takes away the power of being greatly useful. A man should not be able to look other than directly and forthright. A preoccupied attention is the only answer to the importunate frivolity of other people: an attention, and to an aim which makes their wants frivolous. This is a divine answer, and leaves no appeal, and no hard thoughts. In Flaxman's drawing of the Eumenides of Æschylus, Orestes supplicates Apollo, whilst the Furies sleep on the threshold.[8] The face of the god expresses a shade of regret and compassion, but calm with the conviction of the irreconcilableness of the two spheres. He is born into other politics, into the eternal and beautiful. The man at his feet asks for his interest in turmoils of the earth, into which his nature cannot enter.

---

7. Johannes Kepler, 16th-century German physicist and pioneer in laws of planetary motion.
8. John Flaxman (1755–1826), English illustrator. In the clearer modern usage, the title of Aeschylus's play *The Eume-* *nides* would be italicized; in the scene depicted by Flaxman, the Furies, or Eumenides, who have pursued Orestes since his murder of his adulterous mother, are temporarily lulled by the power of Apollo, who sanctioned the murder.

And the Eumenides there lying express pictorially this disparity. The god is surcharged with his divine destiny.

Illusion, Temperament, Succession, Surface, Surprise, Reality, Subjectiveness,—these are threads on the loom of time, these are the lords of life. I dare not assume to give their order, but I name them as I find them in my way. I know better than to claim any completeness for my picture. I am a fragment, and this is a fragment of me. I can very confidently announce one or another law, which throws itself into relief and form, but I am too young yet by some ages to compile a code. I gossip for my hour concerning the eternal politics. I have seen many fair pictures not in vain. A wonderful time I have lived in. I am not the novice I was fourteen, nor yet seven years ago. Let who will ask, where is the fruit? I find a private fruit sufficient. This is a fruit,—that I should not ask for a rash effect from meditations, counsels, and the hiving of truths. I should feel it pitiful to demand a result on this town and county, an overt effect on the instant month and year. The effect is deep and secular[9] as the cause. It works on periods in which mortal lifetime is lost. All I know is reception; I am and I have: but I do not get, and when I have fancied I had gotten anything, I found I did not. I worship with wonder the great Fortune. My reception has been so large, that I am not annoyed by receiving this or that superabundantly. I say to the Genius, if he will pardon the proverb, *In for a mill, in for a million*. When I receive a new gift, I do not macerate my body to make the account square, for, if I should die, I could not make the account square. The benefit overran the merit the first day, and has overran the merit ever since. The merit itself, so-called, I reckon part of the receiving.

Also, that hankering after an overt or practical effect seems to me an apostasy. In good earnest, I am willing to spare this most unnecessary deal of doing. Life wears to me a visionary face. Hardest, roughest action is visionary also. It is but a choice between soft and turbulent dreams. People disparage knowing and the intellectual life, and urge doing. I am very content with knowing, if only I could know. That is an august entertainment, and would suffice me a great while. To know a little, would be worth the expense of this world. I hear always the law of Adrastia,[1] "that every soul which had acquired any truth, should be safe from harm until another period."

I know that the world I converse with in the city and in the farms, is not the world I *think*. I observe that difference, and shall observe it. One day, I shall know the value and law of this discrepance. But I have not found that much was gained by manipular

---

9. Lasting from century to century.
1. Another name for Nemesis or Des-

tiny. The quotation is from the *Phaedrus* by Plato.

attempts to realize the world of thought. Many eager persons successively make an experiment in this way, and make themselves ridiculous. They acquire democratic manners, they foam at the mouth, they hate and deny. Worse, I observe, that, in the history of mankind, there is never a solitary example of success,—taking their own tests of success. I say this polemically, or in reply to the inquiry, why not realize your world? But far be from me the despair which prejudges the law by a paltry empiricism,—since there never was a right endeavor, but it succeeded. Patience and patience, we shall win at the last. We must be very suspicious of the deceptions of the element of time. It takes a good deal of time to eat or to sleep, or to earn a hundred dollars, and a very little time to entertain a hope and an insight which becomes the light of our life. We dress our garden, eat our dinners, discuss the household with our wives, and these things make no impression, are forgotten next week; but in the solitude to which every man is always returning, he has a sanity and revelations, which in his passage into new worlds he will carry with him. Never mind the ridicule, never mind the defeat: up again, old heart!—it seems to say,—there is victory yet for all justice; and the true romance which the world exists to realize, will be the transformation of genius into practical power.

1844

Hymn Sung at the Completion of the Concord Monument, April 19, 1836

By the rude bridge that arched the flood,
  Their flag to April's breeze unfurled,
Here once the embattled farmers stood,
  And fired the shot heard round the world.

The foe long since in silence slept;   5
  Alike the conqueror silent sleeps;
And Time the ruined bridge has swept
  Down the dark stream which seaward creeps.

On this green bank, by this soft stream,
  We set to-day a votive stone;   10
That memory may their deed redeem,
  When, like our sires, our sons are gone.

Spirit, that made those heroes dare
  To die, or leave their children free,
Bid Time and Nature gently spare   15
  The shaft we raise to them and thee.

1836

Each and All

Little thinks, in the field, yon red-cloaked clown,[1]
Of thee from the hill-top looking down;
The heifer that lows in the upland farm,
Far-heard, lows not thine ear to charm;
The sexton, tolling his bell at noon,   5
Deems not that great Napoleon
Stops his horse, and lists with delight,
Whilst his files sweep round yon Alpine height;
Nor knowest thou what argument
Thy life to thy neighbor's creed has lent.   10
All are needed by each one;
Nothing is fair or good alone.
I thought the sparrow's note from heaven,
Singing at dawn on the alder bough;
I brought him home, in his nest, at even;   15
He sings the song, but it cheers not now,
For I did not bring home the river and sky;—
He sang to my ear,—they sang to my eye.
The delicate shells lay on the shore;
The bubbles of the latest wave   20
Fresh pearls to their enamel gave;
And the bellowing of the savage sea
Greeted their safe escape to me.
I wiped away the weeds and foam,
I fetched my sea-born treasures home;   25
But the poor, unsightly, noisome things
Had left their beauty on the shore,
With the sun, and the sand, and the wild uproar.
The lover watched his graceful maid,
As 'mid the virgin train she strayed,   30
Nor knew her beauty's best attire
Was woven still by the snow-white choir.
At last she came to his hermitage,
Like the bird from the woodlands to the cage;—
The gay enchantment was undone,   35
A gentle wife, but fairy none.
Then I said, 'I covet truth;
Beauty is unripe childhood's cheat;
I leave it behind with the games of youth.'—
As I spoke, beneath my feet   40
The ground-pine curled its pretty wreath,
Running over the club-moss burrs;
I inhaled the violet's breath;
Around me stood the oaks and firs;
Pine-cones and acorns lay on the ground,   45
Over me soared the eternal sky,

1. Peasant.

Full of light and of deity;
Again I saw, again I heard,
The rolling river, the morning bird;—
Beauty through my senses stole;   50
I yielded myself to the perfect whole.

1846

The Rhodora
On Being Asked, Whence Is the Flower?

In May, when sea-winds pierced our solitudes,
I found the fresh Rhodora in the woods,
Spreading its leafless blooms in a damp nook,
To please the desert and the sluggish brook.
The purple petals, fallen in the pool,   5
Made the black water with their beauty gay;
Here might the red-bird come his plumes to cool,
And court the flower that cheapens his array.
Rhodora! if the sages ask thee why
This charm is wasted on the earth and sky,   10
Tell them, dear, that if eyes were made for seeing,
Then Beauty is its own excuse for being:
Why thou wert there, O rival of the rose!
I never thought to ask, I never knew;
But, in my simple ignorance, suppose   15
The self-same Power that brought me there brought you.

1846

The Snow-Storm

Announced by all the trumpets of the sky,
Arrives the snow, and, driving o'er the fields,
Seems nowhere to alight: the whited air
Hides hills and woods, the river, and the heaven,
And veils the farm-house at the garden's end.   5
The sled and traveller stopped, the courier's feet
Delayed, all friends shut out, the housemates sit
Around the radiant fireplace, enclosed
In a tumultuous privacy of storm.

Come see the north wind's masonry.   10
Out of an unseen quarry evermore
Furnished with tile, the fierce artificer
Curves his white bastions with projected roof
Round every windward stake, or tree, or door.
Speeding, the myriad-handed, his wild work   15
So fanciful, so savage, nought cares he
For number or proportion. Mockingly,
On coop or kennel he hangs Parian wreaths;[1]

1. I.e., sculpted in white, from the mar-   the Aegean sea, for sculptors of classical
ble quarried in the island of Paros, in   Greece.

A swan-like form invests the hidden thorn;
Fills up the farmer's lane from wall to wall,   20
Maugre[2] the farmer's sighs; and, at the gate,
A tapering turret overtops the work.
And when his hours are numbered, and the world
Is all his own, retiring, as he were not,
Leaves, when the sun appears, astonished Art   25
To mimic in slow structures, stone by stone,
Built in an age, the mad wind's night-work,
The frolic architecture of the snow.

                                              1846

Merlin[1]

I

Thy trivial harp will never please
Or fill my craving ear;
Its chords should ring as blows the breeze,
Free, peremptory, clear.
No jingling serenader's art,   5
Nor tinkle of piano strings,
Can make the wild blood start
In its mystic springs.
The kingly bard
Must smite the chords rudely and hard,   10
As with hammer or with mace;
That they may render back
Artful thunder, which conveys
Secrets of the solar track,
Sparks of the supersolar blaze.   15
Merlin's blows are strokes of fate,
Chiming with the forest tone,
When boughs buffet boughs in the wood;
Chiming with the gasp and moan
Of the ice-imprisoned flood;   20
With the pulse of manly hearts;
With the voice of orators;
With the din of city arts;
With the cannonade of wars;
With the marches of the brave;   25
And prayers of might from martyrs' cave.

Great is the art,
Great be the manners, of the bard.
He shall not his brain encumber
With the coil of rhythm and number;   30
But, leaving rule and pale forethought,
He shall aye[2] climb

2. Despite.
1. Here, the type of a great poet (not
the magician-prophet of Arthurian legend).
2. Always.

For his rhyme.
'Pass in, pass in,' the angels say,
'In to the upper doors,   35
Nor count compartments of the floors,
But mount to paradise
By the stairway of surprise.'

Blameless master of the games,
King of sport that never shames,   40
He shall daily joy dispense
Hid in song's sweet influence.
Things[3] more cheerly live and go,
What time the subtle mind
Sings aloud the tune whereto   45
Their pulses beat,
And march their feet,
And their members are combined.

By Sybarites[4] beguiled,
He shall no task decline;   50
Merlin's mighty line
Extremes of nature reconciled,—
Bereaved a tyrant of his will,
And made the lion mild.
Songs can the tempest still,   55
Scattered on the stormy air,
Mould the year to fair increase,
And bring in poetic peace.

He shall not seek to weave,
In weak, unhappy times,   60
Efficacious rhymes;
Wait his returning strength.
Bird, that from the nadir's floor
To the zenith's top can soar,
The soaring orbit of the muse exceeds that
          journey's length.   65
Nor profane affect to hit
Or compass that, by meddling wit,
Which only the propitious mind
Publishes when 'tis inclined.
There are open hours   70
When the God's will sallies free,
And the dull idiot might see
The flowing fortunes of a thousand years;—
Sudden, at unawares,
Self-moved, fly-to the doors   75
Nor sword of angels could reveal
What they conceal.

3. Later texts read "Forms."
4. Like people from Sybaris, the Greek
city in Italy notorious for wealth and
hedonistic indulgence.

II

The rhyme of the poet
Modulates the king's affairs;
Balance-loving Nature   80
Made all things in pairs.
To every foot its antipode;
Each color with its counter glowed;
To every tone beat answering tones,
Higher or graver;   85
Flavor gladly blends with flavor;
Leaf answers leaf upon the bough;
And match the paired cotyledons.
Hands to hands, and feet to feet,
Coeval grooms and brides;[5]   90
Eldest rite, two married sides
In every mortal meet.
Light's far furnace shines,
Smelting balls and bars,
Forging double stars,   95
Glittering twins and trines.
The animals are sick with love,
Lovesick with rhyme;
Each with all propitious time
Into chorus wove.   100

Like the dancers' ordered band,
Thoughts come also hand in hand;
In equal couples mated,
Or else alternated;
Adding by their mutual gage,   105
One to other, health and age.
Solitary fancies go
Short-lived wandering to and fro,
Most like to bachelors,
Or an ungiven maid,   110
Not ancestors,
With no posterity to make the lie afraid,
Or keep truth undecayed.
Perfect-paired as eagle's wings,
Justice is the rhyme of things;   115
Trade and counting use
The self-same tuneful muse;
And Nemesis,[6]
Who with even matches odd,
Who athwart space redresses   120
The partial wrong,

5. Later texts read "In one body grooms and brides."
6. Here, the imposer of order, not the personification of divine disapproval and punishment.

Fills the just period,
And finishes the song.

Subtle rhymes, with ruin rife,
Murmur in the house of life,   125
Sung by the Sisters[7] as they spin;
In perfect time and measure they
Build and unbuild our echoing clay,
As the two twilights of the day
Fold us music-drunken in.   130

1846

FROM JOURNALS AND LETTERS[1]

From Journals

[Sadness after Thirty]

[*August 1, 1835, Concord*] After thirty a man wakes up sad every morning excepting perhaps five or six until the day of his death.

[Aftermath of the Divinity School Address]

[*August 31, 1838, Concord*] Yesterday at φ B.K. anniversary.[2] Steady, steady. I am convinced that if a man will be a true scholar, he shall have perfect freedom. The young people & the mature hint at odium, & aversion of faces to be presently encountered in society. I say no: I fear it not. No scholar need fear it. For if it be true that he is merely an observer, a dispassionate reporter, no partisan, a singer merely for the love of music, his is a position of perfect immunity: to him no disgusts can attach; he is invulnerable. The vulgar[3] think he would found a sect & would be installed & made much of. He knows better & much prefers his melons & his woods. Society has no bribe for me, neither in politics, nor church, nor

---

7. The Fates, in Greek mythology.

1. Emerson's journals and notebooks have been newly edited by several scholars, led by the late William H. Gilman and published meticulously by Harvard University Press as *The Journals and Miscellaneous Notebooks of Ralph Waldo Emerson.* Since the Havard edition does not print "clear text" but shows Emerson's revisions, some of the quotations here have been simplified to show only the final readings. The six-volume edition of *The Letters of Ralph Waldo Emerson* excludes most letters previously published in one collection or another, so the letters printed here are drawn from various sources indicated in the footnotes. Passages from the journals and letters are printed chronologically, but because Emerson sometimes failed to date journal entries the date given may be merely the first one which occurs prior to the entry.

Annotations are light, since the selections are meant to be suggestive of the diverse contents of the journals and letters, not comprehensive, even on a topic of such enduring interest as Emerson's ambivalence toward Thoreau. Together the journal entries and the letters afford the best view of Emerson the man, in both his private and public aspects.

2. Phi Beta Kappa. Emerson had delivered his oration on the "American Scholar" at the previous celebration, but on the 1838 anniversary he was merely in the audience. The warnings of ostracism which he heard on August 30, 1838, had to do with the growing hostility toward the address he had made on July 15, 1838, to the senior class of the Divinity School.

3. The masses; ordinary, insensitive people.

college, nor city. My resources are far from exhausted. If they will
not hear me lecture, I shall have leisure for my book which wants
me. Beside[,] it is an universal maxim worthy of all acceptation
that a man may have that allowance which he takes. Take the place
& attitude to which you see your unquestionable right, & all men
acquiesce. Who are these murmurers, these haters, these revilers?
Men of no knowledge, & therefore no stability. The scholar on the
contrary is sure of his point, is fast-rooted, & can securely predict
the hour when all this roaring multitude shall roar *for* him.

Analyze the chiding opposition & it is made up of such timidities,
uncertainties, & no opinions, that it is not worth dispersing.

From To Thomas Carlyle (Concord, October 17, 1838)

[*Delayed Reactions to the Divinity School Address*]

In a letter within a twelvemonth I have urged you to pay us a
visit in America, & in Concord. I have believed that you would
come, one day, & do believe it. But if, on your part, you have been
generous & affectionate enough to your friends here—or curious
enough concerning our society to wish to come, I think you must
postpone, for the present, the satisfaction of your friendship & your
curiosity. At this moment, I would not have you here, on any
account. The publication of my "Address to the Dvinity College,"
(copies of which I sent you) has been the occasion of an outcry in
all our leading local newspapers against my "infidelity," "pantheism," & "atheism." The writers warn all & sundry against me, &
against whatever is supposed to be related to my connexion of
opinion, &c; against Transcendentalism, Goethe & *Carlyle*. I am
heartily sorry to see this last aspect of the storm in our washbowl.[4]
For, as Carlyle is nowise guilty, & has unpopularities of his own, I
do not wish to embroil him in my parish-differences. You were
getting to be a great favorite with us all here, and are daily a
greater, with the American public, but just now, *in Boston*, where I
am known as your editor, I fear you lose by the association. Now it
is indispensable to your right influence here, that you should never
come before our people as one of a clique, but as a detached, that
is, universally associated man; so I am happy, as I could not have
thought, that you have not yet yielded yourself to my entreaties. Let
us wait a little until this foolish clam[or] be overblown. My position is fortunately such as to put me quite out of the reach of any
real inconvenience from the panic strikers or the panic struck; &,
indeed, so far as this uneasiness is a necessary result of mere inaction of mind, it seems very clear to me that, if I live, my neighbors
must look for a great many more shocks, & perhaps harder to
bear.

4. The intense, though sporadic and
local, hostility resulting from his address to the Harvard Divinity School,
described in footnote 2, above.

From Journals

[*Challenging Thoreau to Write His Opinions into Good Poetry*]

[*November 10, 1838, Concord*] My brave Henry Thoreau walked with me to Walden this P.M. and complained of the proprietors who compelled him to whom as much as to any the whole world belonged, to walk in a strip of road & crowded him out of all the rest of God's earth. He must not get over the fence: but to the building of that fence he was no party. Suppose, he said, some great proprietor, before he was born, had bought up the whole globe. So had he been hustled out of nature. Not having been privy to any of these arrangements he does not feel called on to consent to them & so cuts fishpoles in the woods without asking who has a better title to the wood than he. I defended of course the good Institution as a scheme not good but the best that could be hit on for making the woods & waters & fields available to Wit & Worth, & for restraining the bold bad man. At all events, I begged him, having this maggot of Freedom & Humanity in his brain, to write it out into good poetry & so clear himself of it. He replied, that he feared that that was not the best way; that in doing justice to the thought, the man did not always do justice to himself: the poem ought to sing itself: if the man took too much pains with the expression he was not any longer the Idea himself. I acceded & confessed that this was the tragedy of Art that the Artist was at the expense of the Man; & hence, in the first age, as they tell, the Sons of God printed no epics, carved no stone, painted no picture, built no railroad; for the sculpture, the poetry, the music, & architecture, were in the Man. And truly Bolts & Bars do not seem to me the most exalted or exalting of our institutions. And what other spirit reigns in our intellectual works? We have literary property. The very recording of a thought betrays a distrust that there is any more or much more as good for us. If we felt that the Universe was ours[,] that we dwelled in eternity & advance into all wisdom we should be less covetous of these sparks & cinders. Why should we covetously build a St Peter's, if we had the seeing Eye which beheld all the radiance of beauty & majesty in the matted grass & the overarching boughs? Why should a man spend years upon the carving an Apollo who looked Apollos into the landscape with every glance he threw?

[*Young Waldo's Physical World*]

[*January 30, 1842, Concord*] What he[5] looked upon is better, what he looked not upon is insignificant. The morning of Friday I woke at 3 oclock, & every cock in every barnyard was shrilling with

5. Waldo Emerson (1836–42), Emerson's son.

the most unnecessary noise. The sun went up the morning sky with all his light, but the landscape was dishonored by this loss. For this boy in whose remembrance I have both slept & awaked so oft, decorated for me the morning star, & the evening cloud, how much more all the particulars of daily economy; for he had touched with his lively curiosity every trivial fact & circumstance in the household the hard coal & the soft coal which I put into my stove; the wood of which he brought his little quota for grandmothers fire, the hammer, the pincers, & file, he was so eager to use; the microscope, the magnet, the little gobe, & every trinket & instrument in the study; the loads of gravel on the meadow the nests in the henhouse and many & many a little visit to the doghouse and to the barn,— For every thing he had his own name & way of thinking his own pronunciation & manner. And every word came mended from that tongue. A boy of early wisdom, of a grave & even majestic deportment, of a perfect gentleness

[*Young Waldo's Human World*]

[*January* 30(?), 1842, *Concord*] The boy had his full swing in this world Never I think did a child enjoy more he had been thoroughly respected by his parents & those around him & not interfered with; and he had been the most fortunate in respect to the influences near him for his Aunt Elizabeth[6] had adopted him from his infancy & treated him ever with that plain & wise love which belongs to her and, as she boasted, had never given him sugar plums. So he was won to her & always signalized her arrival as a visit to him & left playmates playthings & all to go to her. Then Mary Russell[7] had been his friend & teacher for two summers with true love & wisdom. Then Henry Thoreau had been one of the family for the last year, & charmed Waldo by the variety of toys whistles boats popguns & all kinds of instruments which he could make & mend; & possessed his love & respect by the gentle firmness with which he always treated him. Margaret Fuller & Caroline Sturgis[8] had also marked the boy & caressed & conversed with him whenever they were here. Meantime every day his Grandmother gave him his reading lesson & had by patience taught him to read & spell; by patience & by love for she loved him dearly.

[*Thoreau's Fault of Unlimited Contradiction*]

[*August* 25, 1843, *Concord*] H. D. T. sends me a paper[9] with the old fault of unlimited contradiction. The trick of his rhetoric is soon learned. It consists in substituting for the obvious word &

---

6. Elizabeth Hoar, who had been engaged to Emerson's dead brother Charles.
7. The private teacher of Emerson's children.

8. A young Bostonian Transcendentalist, frequent guest of the Emersons.
9. *A Winter Walk*, published in *The Dial*, October, 1843.

thought its diametrical antagonist. He praises wild mountains & winter forests for their domestic air; snow & ice for their warmth; villagers & wood choppers for their urbanity[;] and the wilderness for resembling Rome & Paris. With the constant inclination to dispraise cities & civilization, he yet can find no way to honour woods & woodmen except by paralleling them with towns & townsmen. W[illiam] E[llery] C[hanning] declares the piece is excellent: but it makes me nervous & wretched to read it, with all its merits.

To Walter Whitman (July 21, 1855, Concord)

[*The Wonderful Gift of* Leaves of Grass]

I am not blind to the worth of the wonderful gift of "Leaves of Grass." I find it the most extraordinary piece of wit and wisdom that America has yet contributed. I am very happy in reading it, as great power makes us happy. It meets the demand I am always making of what seemed the sterile & stingy nature, as if too much handiwork or too much lymph[1] in the termperament, were making our western wits fat & mean. I give you joy of your free & brave thought. I have great joy in it. I find incomparable things said incomparably well, as they must be. I find the courage of treatment, which so delights me, and which large perception only can inspire. I greet you at the beginning of a great career, which yet must have had a long foreground somewhere, for such a start. I rubbed my eyes a little to see if this sunbeam were no illusion; but the solid sense of the book is a sober certainty. It has the best of merits, namely, of fortifying & encouraging.

I did not know until I, last night, saw the book advertised in a newspaper, that I could trust the name as real & available for a post-office. I wish to see my benefactor, & have felt much like striking my tasks, & visiting New York to pay you my respects.

From Journals

[The Frustration of Trying to Talk to Thoreau]

[*February 29, 1856, Concord*] If I knew only Thoreau, I should think cooperation of good men impossible. Must we always talk for victory, & never once for truth, for comfort, & joy? Centrality he has, & penetration, strong understanding, & the higher gifts,—the insight of the real or from the real, & the moral rectitude that belongs to it; but all this & all his resources of wit & invention are lost to me in every experiment, year after year, that I make, to hold intercourse with his mind. Always some weary captious paradox to fight you with, & the time & temper wasted.

1. Here, a sluggish or phlegmatic substance.

NATHANIEL HAWTHORNE
1804–1864

Hawthorne was born on Independence Day, 1804, in Salem, Massachusetts, a descendant of Puritan immigrants; one ancestor had been a judge in the Salem witchcraft trials. The family, like the seaport town, was on the decline. When his sea-captain father died in Dutch Guiana in 1808, his mother's brothers took responsibility for his education. In his early teens he lived three years as free as "a bird of the air" at Sebago Lake, in Maine (then still a part of Massachusetts), acquiring a love of tramping which he always kept. By his midteens he was reading eighteenth-century novelists like Henry Fielding, Tobias Smollett, and Horace Walpole as well as contemporary writers like William Godwin and Sir Walter Scott, and forming an ambition to be a writer himself. At Bowdoin College shyness caused him to try to evade the obligatory public declamations, but in social clubs he formed smoking, card-playing, and drinking friendships; two fellow members of the Democratic literary society, Horatio Bridge and Franklin Pierce, later President, became lifelong friends; Longfellow, another classmate, belonged to the rival Federalist society. Hawthorne kept outdoors a good deal at the bucolic college but managed, as he later said, to read "desultorily right and left." At the graduation ceremonies in 1825, Longfellow spoke optimistically on the possibility that "Our Native Writers" could achieve lasting fame. Hawthorne went home to Salem and became a writer, but he was agonizingly slow in winning acclaim.

Hawthorne's years between 1825 and 1837 have fascinated his biographers and critics. Hawthorne himself took pains to propagate the notion that he had lived as a hermit who left his upstairs room only for nighttime walks and hardly communicated even with his mother and sisters. Twentieth-century scholars have shown that although in fact Hawthorne was intensely committed to his writing and was steeping himself in colonial history more than the political issues of his time, he socialized in Salem, had several more or less serious flirtations, kept in touch with Pierce and Bridge, among others, and spent most of the summers knocking about all over New England (an uncle owned stage-lines). He even got as far as Detroit one year. Often called his apprenticeship, these dozen years in fact encompassed as well his period of finest creativity. The first surviving piece of his true apprenticework is the historical novel *Fanshawe*, which Hawthorne paid to have published in 1828 and then quickly suppressed.

Over the next several years Hawthorne tried unsuccessfully to find a publisher for collections of the tales he was writing. In chagrin he burned *Seven Tales of My Native Land* (including one or two stories of witchcraft) though at least one of the seven, *Alice Doane's Appeal*, survives in an altered form. By 1829 he was negotiating—again fruitlessly—for the publication of a volume called *Provincial Tales*, which included *The Gentle Boy*, as well, apparently, as *Roger Malvin's Burial* and *My Kinsman, Major Molineux*. In tales like these he had found his special—though highly unsatisfactory—outlets for publication: magazines and the literary annuals that were issued each fall as genteel Christmas gifts. For his tales Hawthorne got a few dollars each and no fame at all, since publication in the annuals was anonymous. He continued to strive to interest a bookseller in his tales, offering what could have been a remarkable volume called "The Story Teller," in which the title character wandered about New England telling his stories in dramatic settings and circumstances. One story, *Mr. Higginbotham's Catastrophe,* reached print in its narrative frame, but the editor of the *New-England Magazine* scrapped the frame for *Young Goodman Brown* and others which are now known as isolated items instead of interrelated elements in a larger whole. The biographer Randall Stewart plausibly suggests that "*The Story Teller*" "would have united in one work Hawthorne's imaginative and reportorial faculties as none of his published writings quite do." In 1836 Hawthorne turned to literary hackwork, making an encyclopedia for the Boston publisher Samuel G. Goodrich, whose annual, *The Token,* had become the regular market for his tales. In the same year Bridge secretly persuaded Goodrich to publish a collection of Hawthorne's tales by promising to repay any losses. *Twice-Told Tales* appeared in March, 1837, with Hawthorne's name on the title page; the title was a self-deprecating allusion to Shakespeare's *King John* 3.4: "Life is as tedious as a twice-told tale / Vexing the dull eare of a drowsie man." The book was reviewed in England as well as the United States, and opened up what Hawthorne called "an intercourse with the world." A notebook entry written sometime in 1836 was only a little premature: "In this dismal and sordid chamber FAME was won."

Throughout the early stories, both those collected in *Twice-Told Tales* and those he left for later gleaning, Hawthorne mused obsessively over a small range of psychological themes: the consequences of pride, selfishness, and secret guilt; the conflict between lighthearted and somber attitudes toward life; the difficulty of preventing isolation from leading to coldness of heart; the impingement of the past (especially the Puritan past) upon the present; the futility of comprehensive social reforms; the impossibility of eradicating sin from the human heart. Above all, his theme was curiosity about the recesses of other men's and women's beings. About this theme he was always ambivalent, for he knew that his success as a writer depended upon his keen psychological analysis of people he met, while he could never forget that invasion of the sanctity of another's personality may harden the heart even as it enriches the mind. He knew that there was "something of the hawk-eye" about him, and that the line was vague between prurient curiosity and legitimate artistic study of character. At his best, he was a master of psychological insight, and some of his power of psychological burrowing remained with him throughout his career, even in the romances which were left unfinished at his death.

The year 1837 was the start of Hawthorne's public literary career; it also marked the end of his single-minded dedication to his work. In the fall of 1838 Elizabeth Peabody, a Salemite who was to become a major force in American educational reform, sought out the new local celebrity. When Hawthorne met her sister Sophia, twenty-nine and an invalid, his life abruptly changed course. Within a few months he and Sophia were engaged. To save money for marriage, Hawthorne worked as salt and coal measurer in the Boston Custom House during 1839 and 1840, then the next year invested in the utopian community Brook Farm, more as a business venture than as a philosophical gesture; the only return, however, was the locale he later used for *The Blithedale Romance* (1852). During his engagement, Hawthorne's main literary productions were letters to Sophia —full of ironical self-deprecation, satirical reportage, and romantic effusions. In December, 1841, he wrote Evert A. Duyckinck and Cornelius Mathews, New York magazine editors, that his early stories had grown out of quietude and seclusion, the lack of which would probably prevent him from writing any more. Marriage, not literature, became Hawthorne's new career long before the actual ceremony in July, 1842. As he rather severely put it, "when a man has taken upon himself to beget children, he has no longer any right to a life of his own."

The first three years of marriage, spent at the Old Manse in Concord, the home of Emerson's ancestors, seemed idyllic to the Hawthornes, but a hoped-for novel never materialized. By now comfortably familiar with accounts of the Puritan and Revolutionary past, he wrote a child's history of colonial and revolutionary New England, *Grandfather's Chair* (1841) and four years later a rewriting of Bridge's *Journal of an African Cruiser*. *Mosses from an Old Manse* (1846) consisted mainly of new tales, but among the early ones first collected in it were *Roger Malvin's Burial* and *Young Goodman Brown*. His literary earnings were not rising, but his reputation was, partly through his own shrewd creation of a public persona. Knowing that certain readers who delight in realism would be disturbed by the shadowiness of some of his stories, he anticipated the worst that could be said, declaring in the whimsical survey of his career in the headnote to *Rappaccini's Daughter* that "M. de l'Aubépine" (French for "Hawthorne") had "an inveterate love of allegory, which is apt to invest his plots and characters with the aspect of scenery and people in the clouds, and to steal away the human warmth out of his conceptions." Any hostility, of course, was disarmed by such self-criticism, and in the introductory essay for *Mosses from an Old Manse* Hawthorne pursued his strategy of evoking for himself an equivalent of the Miltonic fit audience though few, yet enlarging that audience without letting his readers feel they were part of a mob. Hawthorne insisted winningly both on his ultimate reserve—his refusal to "serve up" his own heart delicately fried—and on his eagerness to communicate with his chosen audience. Even after he attained a large readership, he knew the value of trading on his own early obscurity so as to make a reader feel like a special discoverer of a rarity yet unshared by the many. In the 1851 edition of *Twice-Told Tales*, Hawthorne observed that the author, "on the internal evidence of his sketches, came to be regarded as a mild, shy, gentle, melancholic, exceedingly sensitive, and not very forcible man, hiding his blushes under an assumed name, the quaintness of which was supposed, somehow or other, to symbolize his personal and literary traits." While summarizing the image critics had conceived of him, he helped fix that image for a century and more as *the* Hawthorne.

Through long service to the local Democrats, Hawthorne was named Surveyor of the Port of Salem in 1846. The office was something of a sinecure, but his forenoons—always his most productive hours—had to be spent at the Custom House, and he wrote little. Hawthorne was thrown out of office by the new Whig administration in June, 1849, amid a furious controversy in the newspapers. He then spent a summer of "great diversity and severity" of emotion climaxed by his mother's death. In September he was at work upon *The Scarlet Letter*, which he planned as a long tale to make up half a volume called "*Old Time Legends; together with Sketches, Experimental and Ideal.*" Besides the long introduction, *The Custom House*, which was Hawthorne's means of revenging himself on the Salem Whigs who had ousted him, he planned to include some still uncollected tales. James Fields, the young associate of the publisher William D. Ticknor, persuaded him that a longer fiction would sell better than another collection of stories, and Hawthorne obligingly expanded his manuscript. Although it was frequently denounced as licentious or morbid, *The Scarlet Letter* (1850) was nevertheless a literary sensation in the United States and Great Britain, and Hawthorne was proclaimed as the finest American romancer. There had already been many novels set in Puritan New England, and many more followed, but *The Scarlet Letter* remains the single classic of the group, appealing to tastes of changing generations in different ways; perhaps the most powerful appeal has not changed at all: the remarkable way Hawthorne manages to evoke emotional sympathy for the heroine even when he is condemning her actions.

During a year and a half in the Berkshires of western Massachusetts, where Melville became his "not-too-distant neighbor," Hawthorne wrote *The House of the Seven Gables* (1851), assembled *The Snow Image*, mainly from very early pieces, and wrote for children *A Wonder-Book* (1852). Escaping from the rigors of the Berkshire winters, he wrote *The Blithedale Romance* (1852) in West Newton; then in the first home he had owned, the Wayside at Concord, he put together a political biography of his friend Franklin Pierce for the campaign of 1852 and worked up *The Tanglewood Tales* (1853), prettified stories from mythology. This productivity was broken when President Pierce appointed him American consul at Liverpool. The consulship came as a blessing despite the disruption of his new life at Concord, for his literary income was not enough to support his family, which now included a son and two daughters.

At Liverpool (1853–57) Hawthorne was an uncommonly industrious consul; he had always been more comfortable among businessmen and politicians than among literary people. Tireless in sightseeing among ancient inns, castles, and other public buildings, he also set himself a rigorous course of gallery-going and elaborately recorded his observations in his notebooks. Exposed to great museums for the first time, Hawthorne surprised himself with his affinity for the seventeenth-century Dutch masters of genre painting, deciding that those painters "accomplish all they aim at, —a praise, methinks, which can be given to no other men since the world began." He forced himself—fortified with liquor—to make the required public speeches, and late in his consulship let himself be lionized during an extended trip to London. A stay in Italy—starting in the miserably cold first months of 1858—ate deeply into the more than $30,000 he had earned at Liverpool, and malaria nearly killed his daughter Una. Except during her illness, he kept up his minutely detailed tourist's account, as well as a record of the family's contacts with the English and American colony of painters, sculptors, and writers. Many pages of the notebooks went nearly verbatim into a book which he began in Florence in 1858 and finished late in 1859, after his return to England. This romance, suggested by the statue of a faun attributed to the classical Greek sculptor Praxiteles, was published in London (1860) as *Transformation* and in the United States under Hawthorne's preferred title, *The Marble Faun*.

The Hawthornes came home in June, 1860, during the general acclaim of the new romance, and set about fitting up the Wayside; this project was a considerable drain on Hawthorne's savings, which were already depleted by prolonged residence abroad after resigning his consulship and by generous, though unwise, loans to friends. His literary stature made even his abolitionist neighbors respectful toward him, but Hawthorne was keenly aware that his sympathy for the South ran counter to the mood of neighbors such as Emerson and Thoreau. For the *Atlantic Monthly* Fields solicited a series of sketches which Hawthorne adapted from his English notebooks. Fields paid well, but he was pressing Hawthorne into overwork. Despite short excursions designed to restore his vigor, Hawthorne's physical and psychic energies waned steadily. Humiliated by his weakness, he intermittently forced himself to work on his literary projects, especially the English sketches which he published as *Our Old Home* (1863), loyally dedicating it to Pierce, who because of his southern sympathies was now anathema to many northerners. Hawthorne began four romances, overlapping attempts to grapple with two major themes, an American claimant to an ancestral English estate and the search for an elixir of life. He finished none of them before his death in May, 1864, while traveling in New Hampshire with Pierce. He was buried in the Sleepy Hollow Cemetery at Concord. Alcott, Emerson, Fields, Holmes, Longfellow, and Lowell were among his pallbearers.

My Kinsman, Major Molineux[1]

After the kings of Great Britain had assumed the right of appointing the colonial governors,[2] the measures of the latter seldom met with the ready and general approbation, which had been paid to those of their predecessors, under the original charters. The people looked with most jealous scrutiny to the exercise of power, which did not emanate from themselves, and they usually rewarded the rulers with slender gratitude, for the compliances, by which, in softening their instructions from beyond the sea, they had incurred the reprehension of those who gave them. The annals of Massachusetts Bay will inform us, that of six governors, in the space of about forty years from the surrender of the old charter, under James II., two were imprisoned by a popular insurrection; a third, as Hutchinson[3] inclines to believe, was driven from the province by the whizzing of a musket ball; a fourth, in the opinion of the same historian, was hastened to his grave by continual bickerings with the house of representatives; and the remaining two, as well as their successors, till the Revolution, were favored with few and brief

---

1. The text here is that of the first printing in *The Token* for 1832, where the story is identified as being "By the Author of 'Sights from a Steeple.'"
2. I.e., after 1684, when the British government annulled the Massachusetts charter.
3. The particular annals, or year-by-year

histories, that Hawthorne has in mind are *The History of the Colony and Province of Massachusetts-Bay* (1764, 1767) by the last Royal governor, Thomas Hutchinson (1711–80). James II (1633–1701) reigned briefly (1685–88) before being exiled to France in the Glorious Revolution.

intervals of peaceful sway. The inferior members of the court party,[4] in times of high political excitement, led scarcely a more desirable life. These remarks may serve as preface to the following adventures, which chanced upon a summer night, not far from a hundred years ago. The reader, in order to avoid a long and dry detail of colonial affairs, is requested to dispense with an account of the train of circumstances, that had caused much temporary inflammation of the popular mind.

It was near nine o'clock of a moonlight evening, when a boat crossed the ferry with a single passenger, who had obtained his conveyance, at that unusual hour, by the promise of an extra fare. While he stood on the landing-place, searching in either pocket for the means of fulfilling his agreement, the ferryman lifted a lantern, by the aid of which, and the newly risen moon, he took a very accurate survey of the stranger's figure. He was a youth of barely eighteen years, evidently country-bred, and now, as it should seem, upon his first visit to town. He was clad in a coarse grey coat, well worn, but in excellent repair; his under garments were durably constructed of leather, and sat tight to a pair of serviceable and well-shaped limbs; his stockings of blue yarn, were the incontrovertible handiwork of a mother or a sister; and on his head was a three-cornered hat, which in its better days had perhaps sheltered the graver brow of the lad's father. Under his left arm was a heavy cudgel, formed of an oak sapling, and retaining a part of the hardened root; and his equipment was completed by a wallet,[5] not so abundantly stocked as to incommode the vigorous shoulders on which it hung. Brown, curly hair, well-shaped features, and bright, cheerful eyes, were nature's gifts, and worth all that art could have done for his adornment.

The youth, one of whose names was Robin, finally drew from his pocket the half of a little province-bill[6] of five shillings, which, in the depreciation of that sort of currency, did but satisfy the ferryman's demand, with the surplus of a sexangular piece of parchment valued at three pence. He then walked forward into the town, with as light a step, as if his day's journey had not already exceeded thirty miles, and with as eager an eye, as if he were entering London city, instead of the little metropolis of a New England colony. Before Robin had proceeded far, however, it occurred to him, that he knew not whither to direct his steps; so he paused, and looked up and down the narrow street, scrutinizing the small and mean wooden buildings, that were scattered on either side.

'This low hovel cannot be my kinsman's dwelling,' thought he, 'nor yonder old house, where the moonlight enters at the broken casement; and truly I see none hereabouts that might be worthy of him. It would have been wise to inquire my way of the ferryman,

4. The pro-Crown party. 6. Local paper money.
5. Knapsack.

and doubtless he would have gone with me, and earned a shilling from the Major for his pains. But the next man I meet will do as well.'

He resumed his walk, and was glad to perceive that the street now became wider, and the houses more respectable in their appearance. He soon discerned a figure moving on moderately in advance, and hastened his steps to overtake it. As Robin drew nigh, he saw that the passenger was a man in years, with a full periwig of grey hair, a wide-skirted coat of dark cloth, and silk stockings rolled about his knees. He carried a long and polished cane, which he struck down perpendicularly before him, at every step; and at regular intervals he uttered two successive hems, of a peculiarly solemn and sepulchral intonation. Having made these observations, Robin laid hold of the skirt of the old man's coat, just when the light from the open door and windows of a barber's shop, fell upon both their figures.

'Good evening to you, honored Sir,' said he, making a low bow, and still retaining his hold of the skirt. 'I pray you to tell me whereabouts is the dwelling of my kinsman, Major Molineux?'

The youth's question was uttered very loudly; and one of the barbers, whose razor was descending on a well-soaped chin, and another who was dressing a Ramillies wig,[7] left their occupations, and came to the door. The citizen, in the meantime, turned a long favored countenance upon Robin, and answered him in a tone of excessive anger and annoyance. His two sepulchral hems, however, broke into the very centre of his rebuke, with most singular effect, like a thought of the cold grave obtruding among wrathful passions.

'Let go my garment, fellow! I tell you. I know not the man you speak of. What! I have authority, I have—hem, hem—authority; and if this be the respect you show your betters, your feet shall be brought acquainted with the stocks,[8] by daylight, tomorrow morning!'

Robin released the old man's skirt, and hastened away, pursued by an ill-mannered roar of laughter from the barber's shop. He was at first considerably surprised by the result of his question, but, being a shrewd youth, soon thought himself able to account for the mystery.

'This is some country representative,' was his conclusion, 'who has never seen the inside of my kinsman's door, and lacks the breeding to answer a stranger civilly. The man is old, or verily— I might be tempted to turn back and smite him on the nose. Ah, Robin, Robin! even the barber's boys laugh at you, for choosing such a guide! You will be wiser in time, friend Robin.'

He now became entangled in a succession of crooked and narrow

7. Elaborately plaited wig named for Ramillies, Belgium.
8. Instrument of punishment having a heavy wooden frame with holes for confining the ankles and sometimes the wrists as well.

streets, which crossed each other, and meandered at no great distance
from the water-side. The smell of tar was obvious to his nostrils, the
masts of vessels pierced the moonlight above the tops of the buildings, and the numerous signs, which Robin paused to read, informed him that he was near the centre of business. But the streets
were empty, the shops were closed, and lights were visible only in
the second stories of a few dwelling-houses. At length, on the corner
of a narrow lane, through which he was passing, he beheld the
broad countenance of a British hero swinging before the door of an
inn, whence proceeded the voices of many guests. The casement of
one of the lower windows was thrown back, and a very thin curtain
permitted Robin to distinguish a party at supper, round a well-
furnished table. The fragrance of the good cheer steamed forth into
the outer air, and the youth could not fail to recollect, that the last
remnant of his travelling stock of provision had yielded to his
morning appetite, and that noon had found, and left him, dinner-
less.

'Oh, that a parchment three-penny might give me a right to sit
down at yonder table,' said Robin, with a sigh. 'But the Major will
make me welcome to the best of his victuals; so I will even step
boldly in, and inquire my way to his dwelling.'

He entered the tavern, and was guided by the murmur of voices,
and fumes of tobacco, to the public room. It was a long and low
apartment, with oaken walls, grown dark in the continual smoke,
and a floor, which was thickly sanded, but of no immaculate purity.
A number of persons, the larger part of whom appeared to be
mariners, or in some way connected with the sea, occupied the
wooden benches, or leather-bottomed chairs, conversing on various
matters, and occasionally lending their attention to some topic of
general interest. Three or four little groups were draining as many
bowls of punch, which the great West India trade had long since
made a familiar drink in the colony. Others, who had the aspect of
men who lived by regular and laborious handicraft, preferred the
insulated bliss of an unshared potation, and became more taciturn
under its influence. Nearly all, in short, evinced a predilection for
the Good Creature[9] in some of its various shapes, for this is a vice,
to which, as the Fast-day[1] sermons of a hundred years ago will
testify, we have a long hereditary claim. The only guests to whom
Robin's sympathies inclined him, were two or three sheepish
countrymen, who were using the inn somewhat after the fashion of
a Turkish Caravansary;[2] they had gotten themselves into the darkest corner of the room, and, heedless of the Nicotian[3] atmosphere,

9. Hawthorne is playing upon the warning against food fanatics in 1 Timothy
4.4: "For every creature of God is good,
and nothing to be refused, if it be received with thanksgiving."
1. Days set apart for public penitence.

2. An inn built around a court for ac-
commodating caravans.
3. Heavy with tobacco fumes (from
Jean Nicot, who introduced tobacco into
France when he was French ambassador
at Lisbon).

were supping on the bread of their own ovens, and the bacon cured in their own chimney-smoke. But though Robin felt a sort of brotherhood with these strangers, his eyes were attracted from them, to a person who stood near the door, holding whispered conversation with a group of ill-dressed associates. His features were separately striking almost to grotesqueness, and the whole face left a deep impression in the memory. The forehead bulged out into a double prominence, with a vale between; the nose came boldly forth in an irregular curve, and its bridge was of more than a finger's breadth; the eyebrows were deep and shaggy, and the eyes glowed beneath them like fire in a cave.

While Robin deliberated of whom to inquire respecting his kinsman's dwelling, he was accosted by the innkeeper, a little man in a stained white apron, who had come to pay his professional welcome to the stranger. Being in the second generation from a French protestant, he seemed to have inherited the courtesy of his parent nation; but no variety of circumstance was ever known to change his voice from the one shrill note in which he now addressed Robin.

'From the country, I presume, Sir?' said he, with a profound bow. 'Beg to congratulate you on your arrival, and trust you intend a long stay with us. Fine town here, Sir, beautiful buildings, and much that may interest a stranger. May I hope for the honor of your commands in respect to supper?'

'The man sees a family likeness! the rogue has guessed that I am related to the Major!' thought Robin, who had hitherto experienced little superfluous civility.

All eyes were now turned on the country lad, standing at the door, in his worn three-cornered hat, grey coat, leather breeches, and blue yarn stockings, leaning on an oaken cudgel, and bearing a wallet on his back. Robin replied to the courteous innkeeper, with such an assumption of consequence, as befitted the Major's relative.

'My honest friend,' he said, 'I shall make it a point to patronise your house on some occasion, when—' here he could not help lowering his voice—'I may have more than a parchment three-pence in my pocket. My present business,' continued he, speaking with lofty confidence, 'is merely to inquire the way to the dwelling of my kinsman, Major Molineux.'

There was a sudden and general movement in the room, which Robin interpreted as expressing the eagerness of each individual to become his guide. But the innkeeper turned his eyes to a written paper on the wall, which he read, or seemed to read, with occasional recurrences to the young man's figure.

'What have we here?' said he, breaking his speech into little dry fragments. "Left the house of the subscriber, bounden servant,[4]

---

4. A person bound by contract to servitude for seven years (or another set period), usually in repayment for transportation to the colonies.

Hezekiah Mudge—had on when he went away, grey coat, leather breeches, master's third best hat. One pound currency reward to whoever shall lodge him in any jail in the province." 'Better trudge, boy, better trudge.'

Robin had began to draw his hand towards the lighter end of the oak cudgel, but a strange hostility in every countenance, induced him to relinquish his purpose of breaking the courteous innkeeper's head. As he turned to leave the room, he encountered a sneering glance from the bold-featured personage whom he had before noticed; and no sooner was he beyond the door, than he heard a general laugh, in which the innkeeper's voice might be distinguished, like the dropping of small stones into a kettle.

'Now is it not strange,' thought Robin, with his usual shrewdness, 'is it not strange, that the confession of an empty pocket, should outweigh the name of my kinsman, Major Molineux? Oh, if I had one of these grinning rascals in the woods, where I and my oak sapling grew up together, I would teach him that my arm is heavy, though my purse be light!'

On turning the corner of the narrow lane, Robin found himself in a spacious street, with an unbroken line of lofty houses on each side, and a steepled building at the upper end, whence the ringing of a bell announced the hour of nine. The light of the moon, and the lamps from numerous shop windows, discovered people promenading on the pavement, and amongst them, Robin hoped to recognise his hitherto inscrutable relative. The result of his former inquiries made him unwilling to hazard another, in a scene of such publicity, and he determined to walk slowly and silently up the street, thrusting his face close to that of every elderly gentleman, in search of the Major's lineaments. In his progress, Robin encountered many gay and gallant figures. Embroidered garments, of showy colors, enormous periwigs, gold-laced hats, and silver hilted swords, glided past him and dazzled his optics. Travelled youths, imitators of the European fine gentlemen of the period, trod jauntily along, half-dancing to the fashionable tunes which they hummed, and making poor Robin ashamed of his quiet and natural gait. At length, after many pauses to examine the gorgeous display of goods in the shop windows, and after suffering some rebukes for the impertinence of his scrutiny into people's faces, the Major's kinsman found himself near the steepled building, still unsuccessful in his search. As yet, however, he had seen only one side of the thronged street; so Robin crossed, and continued the same sort of inquisition down the opposite pavement, with stronger hopes than the philosopher seeking an honest man,[5] but with no better fortune. He had arrived about midway towards the lower end, from which his course began, when he overheard the approach of some one, who struck down a cane on

5. Diogenes, the Greek philosopher (412?–323 B.C.), carried a lantern about in daytime in his search for an honest man.

the flag-stones at every step, uttering, at regular intervals, two sepulchral hems.

'Mercy on us!' quoth Robin, recognising the sound.

Turning a corner, which chanced to be close at his right hand, he hastened to pursue his researches, in some other part of the town. His patience was now wearing low, and he seemed to feel more fatigue from his rambles since he crossed the ferry, than from his journey of several days on the other side. Hunger also pleaded loudly within him, and Robin began to balance the propriety of demanding, violently and with lifted cudgel, the necessary guidance from the first solitary passenger, whom he should meet. While a resolution to this effect was gaining stength, he entered a street of mean appearance, on either side of which, a row of ill-built houses was straggling towards the harbor. The moonlight fell upon no passenger along the whole extent, but in the third domicile which Robin passed, there was a half-opened door, and his keen glance detected a woman's garment within.

'My luck may be better here,' said he to himself.

Accordingly, he approached the door, and beheld it shut closer as he did so; yet an open space remained, sufficing for the fair occupant to observe the stranger, without a corresponding display on her part. All that Robin could discern was a strip of scarlet petticoat, and the occasional sparkle of an eye, as if the moonbeams were trembling on some bright thing.

'Pretty mistress,'—for I may call her so with a good conscience, thought the shrewd youth, since I know nothing to the contrary— 'my sweet pretty mistress, will you be kind enough to tell me whereabouts I must seek the dwelling of my kinsman, Major Molineux?'

Robin's voice was plaintive and winning, and the female, seeing nothing to be shunned in the handsome country youth, thrust open the door, and came forth into the moonlight. She was a dainty little figure, with a white neck, round arms, and a slender waist, at the extremity of which her scarlet petticoat jutted out over a hoop, as if she were standing in a balloon. Moreover, her face was oval and pretty, her hair dark beneath the little cap, and her bright eyes possessed a sly freedom, which triumphed over those of Robin.

'Major Molineux dwells here,' said this fair woman.

Now her voice was the sweetest Robin had heard that night, the airy counterpart of a stream of melted silver; yet he could not help doubting whether that sweet voice spoke gospel truth. He looked up and down the mean street, and then surveyed the house before which they stood. It was a small, dark edifice of two stories, the second of which projected over the lower floor; and the front apartment had the aspect of a shop for petty commodities.

'Now truly I am in luck,' replied Robin, cunningly, 'and so indeed is my kinsman, the Major, in having so pretty a housekeeper. But I prithee trouble him to step to the door; I will deliver him a message from his friends in the country, and then go back to my lodgings at the inn.'

'Nay, the Major has been a-bed this hour or more, said the lady of the scarlet petticoat; 'and it would be to little purpose to disturb him to night, seeing his evening draught was of the strongest. But he is a kind-hearted man, and it would be as much as my life's worth, to let a kinsman of his turn away from the door. You are the good old gentleman's very picture, and I could swear that was his rainy-weather hat. Also, he has garments very much resembling those leather—But come in, I pray, for I bid you hearty welcome in his name.'

So saying, the fair and hospitable dame took our hero by the hand; and though the touch was light, and the force was gentleness, and though Robin read in her eyes what he did not hear in her words, yet the slender waisted woman, in the scarlet petticoat, proved stronger than the athletic country youth. She had drawn his half-willing footsteps nearly to the threshold, when the opening of a door in the neighborhood, startled the Major's housekeeper, and, leaving the Major's kinsman, she vanished speedily into her own domicile. A heavy yawn preceded the appearance of a man, who, like the Moonshine of Pyramus and Thisbe, carried a lantern,[6] needlessly aiding his sister luminary in the heavens. As he walked sleepily up the street, he turned his broad, dull face on Robin, and displayed a long staff, spiked at the end.

'Home, vagabond, home!' said the watchman, in accents that seemed to fall asleep as soon as they were uttered. 'Home, or we'll set you in the stocks by peep of day!'

'This is the second hint of the kind,' thought Robin. 'I wish they would end my difficulties, by setting me there to-night.'

Nevertheless, the youth felt an instinctive antipathy towards the guardian of midnight order, which at first prevented him from asking his usual question. But just when the man was about to vanish behind the corner, Robin resolved not to lose the opportunity, and shouted lustily after him—

'I say, friend! will you guide me to the house of my kinsman, Major Molineux?'

The watchman made no reply, but turned the corner and was gone; yet Robin seemed to hear the sound of drowsy laughter stealing along the solitary street. At that moment, also, a pleasant titter saluted him from the open window above his head; he looked up, and caught the sparkle of a saucy eye; a round arm beckoned to him, and next he heard light footsteps descending the staircase within. But Robin, being of the household of a New England clergyman, was a good youth, as well as a shrewd one; so he resisted temptation, and fled away.

6. In Shakespeare's *Midsummer Night's Dream*, 5.1, the craftsmen's play within a play.

He now roamed desperately, and at random, through the town, almost ready to believe that a spell was on him, like that, by which a wizard of his country, had once kept three pursuers wandering, a whole winter night, within twenty paces of the cottage which they sought. The streets lay before him, strange and desolate, and the lights were extinguished in almost every house. Twice, however, little parties of men, among whom Robin distinguished individuals in outlandish attire, came hurrying along, but though on both occasions they paused to address him, such intercourse did not at all enlighten his perplexity. They did but utter a few words in some language of which Robin knew nothing, and perceiving his inability to answer, bestowed a curse upon him in plain English, and hastened away. Finally, the lad determined to knock at the door of every mansion that might appear worthy to be occupied by his kinsman, trusting that perseverance would overcome the fatality which had hitherto thwarted him. Firm in this resolve, he was passing beneath the walls of a church, which formed the corner of two streets, when, as he turned into the shade of its steeple, he encountered a bulky stranger, muffled in a cloak. The man was proceeding with the speed of earnest business, but Robin planted himself full before him, holding the oak cudgel with both hands across his body, as a bar to further passage.

'Halt, honest man, and answer me a question,' said he, very resolutely. 'Tell me, this instant, whereabouts is the dwelling of my kinsman, Major Molineux?'

'Keep your tongue between your teeth, fool, and let me pass,' said a deep, gruff voice, which Robin partly remembered. 'Let me pass, I say, or I'll strike you to the earth!'

'No, no, neighbor!' cried Robin, flourishing his cudgel, and then thrusting its larger end close to the man's muffled face. 'No, no, I'm not the fool you take me for, nor do you pass, till I have an answer to my question. Whereabouts is the dwelling of my kinsman, Major Molineux?'

The stranger, instead of attempting to force his passage, stept back into the moonlight, unmuffled his own face and stared full into that of Robin.

'Watch here an hour, and Major Molineux will pass by,' said he.

Robin gazed with dismay and astonishment, on the unprecedented physiognomy of the speaker. The forehead with its double prominence, the broad-hooked nose, the shaggy eyebrows, and fiery eyes, were those which he had noticed at the inn, but the man's complexion had undergone a singular, or more properly, a two-fold change. One side of the face blazed of an intense red, while the other was black as midnight, the division line being in the broad bridge of the nose; and a mouth, which seemed to extend from ear to ear, was black or red, in contrast to the color of the cheek. The effect was as if two individual devils, a fiend of fire and a fiend of darkness, had united themselves to form this infernal visage. The stranger grinned in Robin's face, muffled his party-colored features, and was out of sight in a moment.

'Strange things we travellers see!' ejaculated Robin.

He seated himself, however, upon the steps of the church-door, resolving to wait the appointed time for his kinsman's appearance. A few moments were consumed in philosophical speculations, upon the species of the *genus homo*, who had just left him, but having settled this point shrewdly, rationally, and satisfactorily, he was compelled to look elsewhere for amusement. And first he threw his eyes along the street; it was of more respectable appearance than most of those into which he had wandered, and the moon, 'creating, like the imaginative power, a beautiful strangeness in familiar objects,' gave something of romance to a scene, that might not have possessed it in the light of day. The irregular, and often quaint architecture of the houses, some of whose roofs were broken into numerous little peaks; while others ascended, steep and narrow, into a single point; and others again were square; the pure milk-white of some of their complexions, the aged darkness of others, and the thousand sparklings, reflected from bright substances in the plastered walls of many; these matters engaged Robin's attention for awhile, and then began to grow wearisome. Next he endeavored to define the forms of distant objects, starting away with almost ghostly indistinctness, just as his eye appeared to grasp them; and finally he took a minute survey of an edifice, which stood on the opposite side of the street, directly in front of the church-door, where he was stationed. It was a large square mansion, distinguished from its neighbors by a balcony, which rested on tall pillars, and by an elaborate gothic window, communicating therewith.

'Perhaps this is the very house I have been seeking,' thought Robin.

Then he strove to speed away the time, by listening to a murmur, which swept continually along the street, yet was scarcely audible, except to an unaccustomed ear like his; it was a low, dull, dreamy sound, compounded of many noises, each of which was at too great a distance to be separately heard. Robin marvelled at this snore of a sleeping town, and marvelled more, whenever its continuity was broken, by now and then a distant shout, apparently loud where it originated. But altogether it was a sleep-inspiring sound, and to shake off its drowsy influence, Robin arose, and climbed a window-frame, that he might view the interior of the church. There the moonbeams came trembling in, and fell down upon the deserted pews, and extended along the quiet aisles. A fainter, yet more awful radiance, was hovering round the pulpit, and one solitary ray had dared to rest upon the opened page of the great bible. Had Nature, in that deep hour, become a worshipper in the house, which man had builded? Or was that heavenly light the visible sanctity of the place, visible because no earthly and impure feet were within the walls? The scene made Robin's heart shiver with a sensation of loneliness, stronger than he had ever felt in the remotest depths of his native woods; so he turned away, and sat down again before the door. There were graves around the church, and now an uneasy thought obtruded into Robin's breast. What if the object of his search, which had been so often and so strangely thwarted, were all the time mouldering in his shroud? What if his kinsman should glide through yonder gate, and nod and smile to him in passing dimly by?

'Oh, that any breathing thing were here with me!' said Robin.

Recalling his thoughts from this uncomfortable track, he sent them over forest, hill, and stream, and attempted to imagine how that evening of ambiguity and weariness, had been spent by his father's household. He pictured them assembled at the door, beneath the tree, the great old tree, which had been spared for its huge twisted trunk, and venerable shade, when a thousand leafy brethren fell. There, at the going down of the summer sun, it was his father's custom to perform domestic worship, that the neighbors might come and join with him like brothers of the family, and that the wayfaring man might pause to drink at that fountain, and keep his heart pure by freshening the memory of home. Robin distinguished the seat of every individual of the little audience; he saw the good man in the midst, holding the scriptures in the golden light that shone from the western clouds; he beheld him close the book, and all rise up to pray. He heard the old thanksgivings for daily mercies, the old supplications for their continuance, to which he had so often listened in weariness, but which were now among his dear remembrances. He perceived the slight inequality of his father's voice when he came to speak of the Absent One; he noted how his mother turned her face to the broad and knotted trunk, how his elder brother scorned, because the beard was rough upon his upper lip, to permit his features to be moved; how his younger sister drew down a low hanging branch before her eyes; and how the little one of all, whose sports had hitherto broken the decorum of the scene, understood the prayer for her playmate, and burst into clamorous grief. Then he saw them go in at the door; and when Robin would have entered also, the latch tinkled into its place, and he was excluded from his home.

'Am I here, or there?' cried Robin, starting; for all at once, when his thoughts had become visible and audible in a dream, the long, wide, solitary street shone out before him.

He aroused himself, and endeavored to fix his attention steadily upon the large edifice which he had surveyed before. But still his mind kept vibrating between fancy and reality; by turns, the pillars of the balcony lengthened into the tall, bare stems of pines, dwindled down to human figures, settled again in their true shape and size, and then commenced a new succession of changes. For a single moment, when he deemed himself awake, he could have sworn that a visage, one which he seemed to remember, yet could not absolutely name as his kinsman's, was looking towards him from the Gothic window. A deeper sleep wrestled with, and nearly overcame him, but fled at the sound of footsteps along the opposite pavement. Robin rubbed his eyes, discerned a man passing at the foot of the balcony, and addressed him in a loud, peevish, and lamentable cry.

'Halloo, friend! must I wait here all night for my kinsman, Major Molineux?'

The sleeping echoes awoke, and answered the voice; and the passenger, barely able to discern a figure sitting in the oblique shade of the steeple, traversed the street to obtain a nearer view. He was himself a gentleman in his prime, of open, intelligent, cheerful, and altogether prepossessing countenance. Perceiving a country youth, apparently homeless and without friends, he accosted him in a tone of real kindness, which had become strange to Robin's ears.

'Well, my good lad, why are you sitting here?' inquired he. 'Can I be of service to you in any way?'

'I am afraid not, Sir,' replied Robin, despondingly; 'yet I shall take it kindly, if you'll answer me a single question. I've been searching half the night for one Major Molineux; now, Sir, is there really such a person in these parts, or am I dreaming?'

'Major Molineux! The name is not altogether strange to me,' said the gentleman, smiling. 'Have you any objection to telling me the nature of your business with him?'

Then Robin briefly related that his father was a clergyman, settled on a small salary, at a long distance back in the country, and that he and Major Molineux were brothers' children. The Major, having inherited riches, and acquired civil and military rank, had visited his cousin in great pomp a year or two before; had manifested much interest in Robin and an elder brother, and, being childless himself, had thrown out hints respecting the future establishment of one of them in life. The elder brother was destined to succeed to the farm, which his father cultivated, in the interval of sacred duties; it was therefore determined that Robin should profit by his kinsman's generous intentions, especially as he had seemed to be rather the favorite, and was thought to possess other necessary endowments.

'For I have the name of being a shrewd youth,' observed Robin, in this part of his story.

'I doubt not you deserve it,' replied his new friend, good naturedly; 'but pray proceed.'

'Well, Sir, being nearly eighteen years old, and well grown, as you see,' continued Robin, raising himself to his full height, 'I thought it high time to begin the world. So my mother and sister put me in handsome trim, and my father gave me half the remnant of his last year's salary, and five days ago I started for this place, to pay the Major a visit. But would you believe it, Sir? I crossed the ferry a little after dusk, and have yet found nobody that would show me the way to his dwelling; only an hour or two since, I was told to wait here, and Major Molineux would pass by.'

'Can you describe the man who told you this?' inquired the gentleman.

'Oh, he was a very ill-favored fellow, Sir,' replied Robin, 'with two great bumps on his forehead, a hook nose, fiery eyes, and, what struck me as the strangest, his face was of two different colors. Do you happen to know such a man, Sir?'

'Not intimately,' answered the stranger, 'but I chanced to meet him a little time previous to your stopping me. I believe you may trust his word, and that the Major will very shortly pass through this street. In the mean time, as I have a singular curiosity to witness your meeting, I will sit down here upon the steps, and bear you company.'

He seated himself accordingly, and soon engaged his companion in animated discourse. It was but of brief continuance, however, for a noise of shouting, which had long been remotely audible, drew so much nearer, that Robin inquired its cause.

'What may be the meaning of this uproar?' asked he. 'Truly, if your town be always as noisy, I shall find little sleep, while I am an inhabitant.'

'Why, indeed, friend Robin, there do appear to be three or four riotous fellows abroad to-night,' replied the gentleman. 'You must not expect all the stillness of your native woods, here in our streets. But the watch will shortly be at the heels of these lads, and—'

'Aye, and set them in the stocks by peep of day,' interrupted Robin, recollecting his own encounter with the drowsy lantern-bearer. 'But, dear Sir, if I may trust my ears, an army of watchmen would never make head against such a multitude of rioters. There were at least a thousand voices went to make up that one shout.'

'May not one man have several voices, Robin, as well as two complexions?' said his friend.

'Perhaps a man may; but heaven forbid that a woman should!' responded the shrewd youth, thinking of the seductive tones of the Major's housekeeper.

The sounds of a trumpet in some neighboring street, now became so evident and continual, that Robin's curiosity was strongly excited. In addition to the shouts, he heard frequent bursts from many instruments of discord, and a wild and confused laughter filled up the intervals. Robin rose from the steps, and looked wistfully towards a point, whither several people seemed to be hastening.

'Surely some prodigious merrymaking is going on,' exclaimed he.

'I have laughed very little since I left home, Sir, and should be sorry to lose an opportunity. Shall we just step round the corner by that darkish house, and take our share of the fun?'

'Sit down again, sit down, good Robin,' replied the gentleman, laying his hand on the skirt of the grey coat. 'You forget that we must wait here for your kinsman; and there is reason to believe that he will pass by, in the course of a very few moments.'

The near approach of the uproar had now disturbed the neighborhood; windows flew open on all sides; and many heads, in the attire of the pillow, and confused by sleep suddenly broken, were protruded to the gaze of whoever had leisure to observe them. Eager voices hailed each other from house to house, all demanding the explanation, which not a soul could give. Half-dressed men hurried towards the unknown commotion, stumbling as they went over the stone steps, that thrust themselves into the narrow foot-walk. The shouts, the laughter, and the tuneless bray, the antipodes of music, came onward with increasing din, till scattered individuals, and then denser bodies, began to appear round a corner, at the distance of a hundred yards.

'Will you recognise your kinsman, Robin, if he passes in this crowd?' inquired the gentleman.

'Indeed, I can't warrant it, Sir; but I'll take my stand here, and keep a bright look out,' answered Robin, descending to the outer edge of the pavement.

A mighty stream of people now emptied into the street, and came rolling slowly towards the church. A single horseman wheeled the corner in the midst of them, and close behind him came a band of fearful wind-instruments, sending forth a fresher discord, now that no intervening buildings kept it from the ear. Then a redder light disturbed the moonbeams, and a dense multitude of torches shone along the street, concealing by their glare whatever object they illuminated. The single horseman, clad in a military dress, and bearing a drawn sword, rode onward as the leader, and, by his fierce and variegated countenance, appeared like war personified; the red of one cheek was an emblem of fire and sword; the blackness of the other betokened the mourning which attends them. In his train, were wild figures in the Indian dress, and many fantastic shapes without a model, giving the whole march a visionary air, as if a dream had broken forth from some feverish brain, and were sweeping visibly through the midnight streets. A mass of people, inactive, except as applauding spectators, hemmed the procession in, and several women ran along the sidewalks, piercing the confusion of heavier sounds, with their shrill voices of mirth of terror.

'The double-faced fellow has his eye upon me,' muttered Robin, with an indefinite but uncomfortable idea, that he was himself to bear a part in the pageantry.

The leader turned himself in the saddle, and fixed his glance full upon the country youth, as the steed went slowly by. When Robin had freed his eyes from those fiery ones, the musicians were passing before him, and the torches were close at hand; but the unsteady brightness of the latter formed a veil which he could not penetrate. The rattling of wheels over the stones sometimes found its way to his ear, and confused traces of a human form appeared at intervals, and then melted into the vivid light. A moment more, and the leader thundered a command to halt; the trumpets vomited a horrid breath, and held their peace; the shouts and laughter of the people died away, and there remained only an universal hum, nearly allied to silence. Right before Robin's eyes was an uncovered cart. There the torches blazed the brightest, there the moon shone out like day, and there, in tar-and-feathery dignity, sate his kinsman, Major Molineux!

He was an elderly man, of large and majestic person, and strong, square features, betokening a steady soul; but steady as it was, his enemies had found the means to shake it. His face was pale as death, and far more ghastly; the broad forehead was contracted in his agony, so that the eyebrows formed one dark grey line; his eyes were red and wild, and the foam hung white upon his quivering lip. His whole frame was agitated by a quick, and continual tremor, which his pride strove to quell, even in those circumstances of overwhelming humiliation. But perhaps the bitterest pang of all was when his eyes met those of Robin; for he evidently knew him on the instant, as the youth stood witnessing the foul disgrace of a head that had grown grey in honor. They stared at each other in silence, and Robin's knees shook, and his hair bristled, with a mixture of pity and terror. Soon, however, a bewildering excitment began to seize upon his mind; the preceding adventures of the night, the unexpected appearance of the crowd, the torches, the confused din, and the hush that followed, the spectre of his kinsman reviled by that great multitude, all this, and more than all, a perception of tremendous ridicule in the whole scene, affected him with a sort of mental inebriety. At that moment a voice of sluggish merriment saluted Robin's ears; he turned instinctively, and just behind the corner of the church stood the lantern-bearer, rubbing his eyes, and drowsily enjoying the lad's amazement. Then he heard a peal of laughter like the ringing of silvery bells; a woman twitched his arm, a saucy eye met his, and he saw the lady of the scarlet petticoat. A sharp, dry cachinnation appealed to his memory, and, standing on tiptoe in the crowd, with his white apron over his head, he beheld the courteous little innkeeper. And lastly, there sailed over the heads of the multitude a great, broad laugh, broken in the midst by two deep sepulchral hems; thus—

'Haw, haw, haw—hem, hem—haw, haw, haw, haw!'

The sound proceeded from the balcony of the opposite edifice, and thither Robin turned his eyes. In front of the Gothic window stood the old citizen, wrapped in a wide gown, his grey periwig exchanged for a nightcap, which was thrust back from his forehead, and his silk stockings hanging down about his legs. He supported himself on his polished cane in a fit of convulsive merriment, which manifested itself on his solemn old features, like a funny inscription on a tomb-stone. Then Robin seemed to hear the voices of the barbers; of the guests of the inn; and of all who had made sport of him that night. The contagion was spreading among the multitude, when, all at once, it seized upon Robin, and he sent forth a shout of laughter that echoed through the street; every man shook his sides, every man emptied his lungs, but Robin's shout was the loudest there. The cloud-spirits peeped from their silvery islands, as the congregated mirth went roaring up the sky! The Man in the Moon heard the far bellow; 'Oho,' quoth he, 'the old Earth is frolicsome to-night!'

When there was a momentary calm in that tempestuous sea of sound, the leader gave the sign, and the procession resumed its march. On they went, like fiends that throng in mockery round some dead potentate, mighty no more, but majestic still in his agony. On they went, in counterfeited pomp, in senseless uproar, in frenzied merriment, trampling all on an old man's heart. On swept the tumult, and left a silent street behind.

.   .   .   .

'Well, Robin, are you dreaming?' inquired the gentleman, laying his hand on the youth's shoulder.

Robin started, and withdrew his arm from the stone post, to which he had instinctively clung, while the living stream rolled by him. His cheek was somewhat pale, and his eye not quite so lively as in the earlier part of the evening.

'Will you be kind enough to show me the way to the Ferry?' said he, after a moment's pause.

'You have then adopted a new subject of inquiry?' observed his companion, with a smile.

'Why, yes, Sir,' replied Robin, rather dryly. 'Thanks to you, and to my other friends, I have at last met my kinsman, and he will scarce desire to see my face again. I begin to grow weary of a town life, Sir. Will you show me the way to the Ferry?'

'No, my good friend Robin, not to-night, at least,' said the gentleman. 'Some few days hence, if you continue to wish it, I will speed you on your journey. Or, if you prefer to remain with us, perhaps, as you are a shrewd youth, you may rise in the world, without the help of your kinsman, Major Molineux.'

1832, 1837

Young Goodman Brown[1]

Young goodman[2] Brown came forth, at sunset, into the street of Salem village, but put his head back, after crossing the threshold, to exchange a parting kiss with his young wife. And Faith, as the wife was aptly named, thrust her own pretty head into the street, letting the wind play with the pink ribbons of her cap, while she called to goodman Brown.

'Dearest heart,' whispered she, softly and rather sadly, when her lips were close to his ear, 'pr'y thee, put off your journey until sunrise, and sleep in your own bed to-night. A lone woman is troubled with such dreams and such thoughts, that she's afeard of herself, sometimes. Pray, tarry with me this night, dear husband, of all nights in the year!'

'My love and my Faith,' replied young goodman Brown, 'of all nights in the year, this one night must I tarry away from thee. My journey, as thou callest it, forth and back again, must needs be done 'twixt now and sunrise. What, my sweet, pretty wife, dost thou doubt me already, and we but three months married!'

'Then, God bless you!' said Faith, with the pink ribbons, 'and may you find all well, when you come back.'

'Amen!' cried goodman Brown. 'Say thy prayers, dear Faith, and go to bed at dusk, and no harm will come to thee.'

So they parted; and the young man pursued his way, until, being about to turn the corner by the meeting-house, he looked back, and saw the head of Faith still peeping after him, with a melancholy air, in spite of her pink ribbons.

'Poor little Faith!' thought he, for his heart smote him. 'What a wretch am I, to leave her on such an errand! She talks of dreams, too. Methought, as she spoke, there was trouble in her face, as if a dream had warned her what work is to be done to-night. But, no, no! 't would kill her to think it. Well; she's a blessed angel on earth; and after this one night, I'll cling to her skirts and follow her to Heaven.'

With this excellent resolve for the future, goodman Brown felt himself justified in making more haste on his present evil purpose. He had taken a dreary road, darkened by all the gloomiest trees of the forest, which barely stood aside to let the narrow path creep through, and closed immediately behind. It was all as lonely as could be; and there is this peculiarity in such a solitude, that the traveler knows not who may be concealed by the innumerable

---

1. The text followed here is that of the first publication, in the *New-England Magazine* (April, 1835); the story was ascribed to "the author of 'The Gray Champion,'" which had appeared in the same magazine three months earlier.

2. Hawthorne puns on the title used to address a man of humble birth and the moral implications of "good man"; what with "Brown" as a surname, the hero is equivalent to Young Mister Anybody.

trunks and the thick boughs overhead; so that, with lonely foot-steps, he may yet be passing through an unseen multitude.

'There may be a devilish Indian behind every tree,' said goodman Brown, to himself; and he glanced fearfully behind him, as he added, 'What if the devil himself should be at my very elbow!'

His head being turned back, he passed a crook of the road, and looking forward again, beheld the figure of a man, in grave and decent attire, seated at the foot of an old tree. He arose, at goodman Brown's approach, and walked onward, side by side with him.

'You are late, goodman Brown,' said he. 'The clock of the Old South was striking as I came through Boston; and that is full fifteen minutes agone.'[3]

'Faith kept me back awhile,' replied the young man, with a tremor in his voice, caused by the sudden appearance of his com-panion, though not wholly unexpected.

It was now deep dusk in the forest, and deepest in that part of it where these two were journeying. As nearly as could be discerned, the second traveler was about fifty years old, apparently in the same rank of life as goodman Brown, and bearing a considerable resem-blance to him, though perhaps more in expression than features. Still, they might have been taken for father and son. And yet, though the elder person was as simply clad as the younger, and as simple in manner too, he had an indescribable air of one who knew the world, and would not have felt abashed at the governor's dinner-table, or in king William's[4] court, were it possible that his affairs should call him thither. But the only thing about him, that could be fixed upon as remarkable, was his staff, which bore the likeness of a great black snake, so curiously wrought, that it might almost be seen to twist and wriggle itself, like a living serpent. This, of course, must have been an ocular deception, assisted by the uncertain light.

'Come, goodman Brown!' cried his fellow-traveler, 'this is a dull pace for the beginning of a journey. Take my staff, if you are so soon weary.'

'Friend,' said the other, exchanging his slow pace for a full stop, 'having kept covenant by meeting thee here, it is my purpose now to return whence I came. I have scruples, touching the matter thou wot'st of.'

'Sayest thou so?' replied he of the serpent, smiling apart. 'Let us walk on, nevertheless, reasoning as we go, and if I convince thee not, thou shalt turn back. We are but a little way in the forest, yet.'

'Too far, too far!' exclaimed the goodman, unconsciously resum-ing his walk. 'My father never went into the woods on such an errand, nor his father before him. We have been a race of honest

---

3. This speed could only be supernatural.
4. William of Orange, first cousin and husband of Queen Mary II, with whom he jointly ruled England, 1689–1702.

men and good Christians, since the days of the martyrs.[5] And shall
I be the first of the name of Brown, that ever took this path, and
kept'—

'Such company, thou wouldst say,' observed the elder person,
interpreting his pause. 'Good, goodman Brown! I have been as well
acquainted with your family as with ever a one among the Puritans;
and that's no trifle to say. I helped your grandfather, the constable,
when he lashed the Quaker woman so smartly through the streets of
Salem. And it was I that brought your father a pitch-pine knot,
kindled at my own hearth, to set fire to an Indian village, in king
Philip's[6] war. They were my good friends, both; and many a
pleasant walk have we had along this path, and returned merrily
after midnight. I would fain be friends with you, for their sake.'

'If it be as thou sayest,' replied goodman Brown, 'I marvel they
never spoke of these matters. Or, verily, I marvel not, seeing that
the least rumor of the sort would have driven them from New-
England. We are a people of prayer, and good works, to boot, and
abide no such wickedness.'

'Wickedness or not,' said the traveler with the twisted staff, 'I
have a very general acquaintance here in New-England. The deacons
of many a church have drunk the communion wine with me; the
selectmen, of divers towns, make me their chairman; and a majority
of the Great and General Court[7] are firm supporters of my interest.
The governor and I, too—but these are state-secrets.'

'Can this be so!' cried goodman Brown, with a stare of amazement at his undisturbed companion. 'Howbeit, I have nothing to do
with the governor and council; they have their own ways, and are
no rule for a simple husbandman,[8] like me. But, were I to go on
with thee, how should I meet the eye of that good old man, our
minister, at Salem village? Oh, his voice would make me tremble,
both Sabbath-day and lecture-day!'[9]

Thus far, the elder traveler had listened with due gravity, but now
burst into a fit of irrepressible mirth, shaking himself so violently,
that his snake-like staff actually seemed to wriggle in sympathy.

'Ha! ha! ha!' shouted he, again and again; then composing himself, 'Well, go on, goodman Brown, go on; but, pr'y thee, don't kill
me with laughing!'

'Well, then, to end the matter at once,' said goodman Brown,
considerably nettled, 'there is my wife, Faith. It would break her
dear little heart; and I'd rather break my own!'

5. I.e., during the reign of the Catholic
Mary Tudor of England (1553–58), called
"Bloody Mary" for her persecution of
Protestants. Common reading in New
England was John Foxe's *Acts and Mon-
uments* (1563), soon known as the *Book
of Martyrs*; it concluded with horrifically
detailed accounts of martyrdoms under
Mary.

6. Indian leader of the Wampanoags who
waged war (1675–76) against the New
England colonists.
7. The legislature.
8. Usually, farmer; here, man of ordinary
status.
9. Midweek sermon day, Wednesday or
Thursday.

'Nay, if that be the case,' answered the other, 'e'en go thy ways, goodman Brown. I would not, for twenty old women like the one hobbling before us, that Faith should come to any harm.'

As he spoke, he pointed his staff at a female figure on the path, in whom goodman Brown recognized a very pious and exemplary dame, who had taught him his catechism, in youth, and was still his moral and spiritual adviser, jointly with the minister and deacon Gookin.

'A marvel, truly, that goody Cloyse[1] should be so far in the wilderness, at night-fall!' said he. 'But, with your leave, friend, I shall take a cut through the woods, until we have left this Christian woman behind. Being a stranger to you, she might ask whom I was consorting with, and whither I was going.'

'Be it so,' said his fellow-traveler. 'Betake you to the woods, and let me keep the path.'

Accordingly, the young man turned aside, but took care to watch his companion, who advanced softly along the road, until he had come within a staff's length of the old dame. She, meanwhile, was making the best of her way, with singular speed for so aged a woman, and mumbling some indistinct words, a prayer, doubtless, as she went. The traveler put forth his staff, and touched her withered neck with what seemed the serpent's tail.

'The devil!' screamed the pious old lady.

'Then goody Cloyse knows her old friend?' observed the traveler, confronting her, and leaning on his writhing stick.

'Ah, forsooth, and is it your worship, indeed?' cried the good dame. 'Yea, truly is it, and in the very image of my old gossip, goodman Brown, the grandfather of the silly fellow that now is. But, would your worship believe it? my broomstick hath strangely disappeared, stolen, as I suspect, by that unhanged witch, goody Cory, and that, too, when I was all anointed with the juice of smallage and cinque-foil and wolf's-bane—[2]

'Mingled with fine wheat and the fat of a new-born babe,' said the shape of old goodman Brown.

'Ah, your worship knows the receipt,' cried the old lady, cackling aloud. 'So, as I was saying, being all ready for the meeting, and no horse to ride on, I made up my mind to foot it; for they tell me, there is a nice young man to be taken into communion to-night. But now your good worship will lend me your arm, and we shall be there in a twinkling.'

'That can hardly be,' answered her friend. 'I may not spare you my arm, goody Cloyse, but here is my staff, if you will.'

So saying, he threw it down at her feet, where, perhaps, it as-

---

1. Hawthorne uses historical names of people involved in the Salem witchcraft trials. "Goody" means "goodwife" and was a polite title for a married woman of humble rank.

2. Plants associated with witchcraft: wild celery or parsley; a five-lobed plant of the rose family (from the Latin for "five fingers"); hooded, poisonous plant known as monkshood ("bane" means "poison").

sumed life, being one of the rods which its owner had formerly lent
to the Egyptian Magi.[3] Of this fact, however, goodman Brown
could not take cognizance. He had cast up his eyes in astonishment,
and looking down again, beheld neither goody Cloyse nor the ser-
pentine staff, but his fellow-traveler alone, who waited for him as
calmly as if nothing had happened.

'That old woman taught me my catechism!' said the young man;
and there was a world of meaning in this simple comment.

They continued to walk onward, while the elder traveler exhorted
his companion to make good speed and persevere in the path, discoursing so aptly, that his arguments seemed rather to spring up in
the bosom of his auditor, than to be suggested by himself. As they
went, he plucked a branch of maple, to serve for a walking-stick,
and began to strip it of the twigs and little boughs, which were wet
with evening dew. The moment his fingers touched them, they became strangely withered and dried up, as with a week's sunshine.
Thus the pair proceeded, at a good free pace, until suddenly, in a
gloomy hollow of the road, goodman Brown sat himself down on
the stump of a tree, and refused to go any farther.

'Friend,' said he, stubbornly, 'my mind is made up. Not another
step will I budge on this errand. What if a wretched old woman do
choose to go to the devil, when I thought she was going to Heaven!
Is that any reason why I should quit my dear Faith, and go after
her?'

'You will think better of this, by-and-by,' said his acquaintance,
composedly. 'Sit here and rest yourself awhile; and when you feel
like moving again, there is my staff to help you along.'

Without more words, he threw his companion the maple stick,
and was as speedily out of sight, as if he had vanished into the
deepening gloom. The young man sat a few moments, by the road-
side, applauding himself greatly, and thinking with how clear a
conscience he should meet the minister, in his morning-walk, nor
shrink from the eye of good old deacon Gookin. And what calm
sleep would be his, that very night, which was to have been spent so
wickedly, but purely and sweetly now, in the arms of Faith! Amidst
these pleasant and praiseworthy meditations, goodman Brown heard
the tramp of horses along the road, and deemed it advisable to
conceal himself within the verge of the forest, conscious of the
guilty purpose that had brought him thither, though now so happily
turned from it.

On came the hoof-tramps and the voices of the riders, two grave
old voices, conversing soberly as they drew near. These mingled
sounds appeared to pass along the road, within a few yards of the
young man's hiding-place; but owing, doubtless, to the depth of the
gloom, at that particular spot, neither the travelers nor their steeds

---

3. See Exodus 7.11 for the magicians of
Egypt who duplicated Aaron's feat of
casting down his rod before Pharaoh and
making it turn into a serpent.

were visible. Though their figures brushed the small boughs by the way-side, it could not be seen that they intercepted, even for a moment, the faint gleam from the strip of bright sky, athwart which they must have passed. Goodman Brown alternately crouched and stood on tip-toe, pulling aside the branches, and thrusting forth his head as far as he durst, without discerning so much as a shadow. It vexed him the more, because he could have sworn, were such a thing possible, that he recognized the voices of the minister and deacon Gookin, jogging along quietly, as they were wont to do, when bound to some ordination or ecclesiastical council. While yet within hearing, one of the riders stopped to pluck a switch.

'Of the two, reverend Sir,' said the voice like the deacon's, 'I had rather miss an ordination-dinner than to-night's meeting. They tell me that some of our community are to be here from Falmouth[4] and beyond, and others from Connecticut and Rhode-Island; besides several of the Indian powows,[5] who, after their fashion, know almost as much deviltry as the best of us. Moreover, there is a goodly young woman to be taken into communion.'

'Mighty well, deacon Gookin!' replied the solemn old tones of the minister. 'Spur up, or we shall be late. Nothing can be done, you know, until I get on the ground.'

The hoofs clattered again, and the voices, talking so strangely in the empty air, passed on through the forest, where no church had ever been gathered, nor solitary Christian prayed. Whither, then, could these holy men be journeying, so deep into the heathen wilderness? Young goodman Brown caught hold of a tree, for support, being ready to sink down on the ground, faint and over-burthened with the heavy sickness of his heart. He looked up to the sky, doubting whether there really was a Heaven above him. Yet, there was the blue arch, and the stars brightening in it.

'With Heaven above, and Faith below, I will yet stand firm against the devil!' cried goodman Brown.

While he still gazed upward, into the deep arch of the firmament, and had lifted his hands to pray, a cloud, though no wind was stirring, hurried across the zenith, and hid the brightening stars. The blue sky was still visible, except directly overhead, where this black mass of cloud was sweeping swiftly northward. Aloft in the air, as if from the depths of the cloud, came a confused and doubtful sound of voices. Once, the listener fancied that he could distinguish the accents of town's-people of his own, men and women, both pious and ungodly, many of whom he had met at the communion-table, and had seen others rioting at the tavern. The next moment, so indistinct were the sounds, he doubted whether he had heard aught but the murmur of the old forest, whispering without a wind. Then

4. Town on Cape Cod, about 70 miles from Salem.
5. Medicine men. Usually spelled "pow-

wow" and later used to refer to any conference or gathering.

came a stronger swell of those familiar tones, heard daily in the sunshine, at Salem village, but never, until now, from a cloud of night. There was one voice, of a young woman, uttering lamentations, yet with an uncertain sorrow, and entreating for some favor, which, perhaps, it would grieve her to obtain. And all the unseen multitude, both saints and sinners, seemed to encourage her onward.

'Faith!' shouted goodman Brown, in a voice of agony and desperation; and the echoes of the forest mocked him, crying—'Faith! Faith!' as if bewildered wretches were seeking her, all through the wilderness.

The cry of grief, rage, and terror, was yet piercing the night, when the unhappy husband held his breath for a response. There was a scream, drowned immediately in a louder murmur of voices, fading into far-off laughter, as the dark cloud swept away, leaving the clear and silent sky above goodman Brown. But something fluttered lightly down through the air, and caught on the branch of a tree. The young man seized it, and beheld a pink ribbon.

'My Faith is gone!' cried he, after one stupefied moment. 'There is no good on earth; and sin is but a name. Come, devil! for to thee is this world given.'

And maddened with despair, so that he laughed loud and long, did goodman Brown grasp his staff and set forth again, at such a rate, that he seemed to fly along the forest-path, rather than to walk or run. The road grew wilder and drearier, and more faintly traced, and vanished at length, leaving him in the heart of the dark wilderness, still rushing onward, with the instinct that guides mortal man to evil. The whole forest was peopled with frightful sounds; the creaking of the trees, the howling of wild beasts, and the yell of Indians; while, sometimes, the wind tolled like a distant church-bell, and sometimes gave a broad roar around the traveler, as if all Nature were laughing him to scorn. But he was himself the chief horror of the scene, and shrank not from its other horrors.

'Ha! ha! ha!' roared goodman Brown, when the wind laughed at him. 'Let us hear which will laugh loudest! Think not to frighten me with your deviltry! Come witch, come wizard, come Indian powow, come devil himself! and here comes goodman Brown. You may as well fear him as he fear you!'

In truth, all through the haunted forest, there could be nothing more frightful than the figure of goodman Brown. On he flew, among the black pines, brandishing his staff with frenzied gestures, now giving vent to an inspiration of horrid blasphemy, and now shouting forth such laughter, as set all the echoes of the forest laughing like demons around him. The fiend in his own shape is less hideous, than when he rages in the breast of man. Thus sped the demoniac on his course, until, quivering among the trees, he saw a red light before him, as when the felled trunks and branches of a clearing have been set on fire, and throw up their lurid blaze against the sky, at the hour of midnight. He paused, in a lull of the tempest that had driven him onward, and heard the swell of what seemed a hymn, rolling solemnly from a distance, with the weight of many voices. He knew the tune; it was a familiar one in the choir of the village meeting-house. The verse died heavily away, and was length-ened by a chorus, not of human voices, but of all the sounds of the benighted wilderness, pealing in awful harmony together. Goodman Brown cried out; and his cry was lost to his own ear, by its unison with the cry of the desert.

In the interval of silence, he stole forward, until the light glared full upon his eyes. At one extremity of an open space, hemmed in by the dark wall of the forest, arose a rock, bearing some rude, natural resemblance either to an altar or a pulpit, and surrounded by four blazing pines, their tops a flame, their stems untouched, like candles at an evening meeting. The mass of foliage, that had over-grown the summit of the rock, was all on fire, blazing high into the night, and fitfully illuminating the whole field. Each pendent twig and leafy festoon was in a blaze. As the red light arose and fell, a numerous congregation alternately shone forth, then disappeared in shadow, and again grew, as it were, out of the darkness, peopling the heart of the solitary woods at once.

'A grave and dark-clad company!' quoth goodman Brown.

In truth, they were such. Among them, quivering to-and-fro, between gloom and splendor, appeared faces that would be seen, next day, at the council-board of the province, and others which, Sabbath after Sabbath, looked devoutly heavenward, and benig-nantly over the crowded pews, from the holiest pulpits in the land. Some affirm, that the lady of the governor was there. At least, there were high dames well known to her, and wives of honored hus-bands, and widows, a great multitude, and ancient maidens, all of excellent repute, and fair young girls, who trembled, lest their mothers should espy them. Either the sudden gleams of light, flash-ing over the obscure field, bedazzled goodman Brown, or he recog-nized a score of the church-members of Salem village, famous for their especial sanctity. Good old deacon Gookin had arrived, and waited at the skirts of that venerable saint, his revered pastor. But, irreverently consorting with these grave, reputable, and pious people, these elders of the church, these chaste dames and dewy virgins, there were men of dissolute lives and women of spotted fame, wretches given over to all mean and filthy vice, and suspected even of horrid crimes. It was strange to see, that the good shrank not from the wicked, nor were the sinners abashed by the saints. Scattered, also, among their pale-faced enemies, were the Indian priests, or powows, who had often scared their native forest with more hideous incantations than any known to English witchcraft.

'But, where is Faith?' thought goodman Brown; and, as hope came into his heart, he trembled.

Another verse of the hymn arose, a slow and solemn strain, such as the pious love, but joined to words which expressed all that our nature can conceive of sin, and darkly hinted at far more. Unfathomable to mere mortals is the lore of fiends. Verse after verse was sung, and still the chorus of the desert swelled between, like the deepest tone of a mighty organ. And, with the final peal of that dreadful anthem, there came a sound, as if the roaring wind, the rushing streams, the howling beasts, and every other voice of the unconverted wilderness, were mingling and according with the voice of guilty man, in homage to the prince of all. The four blazing pines threw up a loftier flame, and obscurely discovered shapes and visages of horror on the smoke-wreaths, above the impious assembly. At the same moment, the fire on the rock shot redly forth, and formed a glowing arch above its base, where now appeared a figure. With reverence be it spoken, the apparition bore no slight similitude, both in garb and manner, to some grave divine of the New-England churches.

'Bring forth the converts!' cried a voice, that echoed through the field and rolled into the forest.

At the word, goodman Brown stept forth from the shadow of the trees, and approached the congregation, with whom he felt a loathful brotherhood, by the sympathy of all that was wicked in his heart. He could have well nigh sworn, that the shape of his own dead father beckoned him to advance, looking downward from a smoke-wreath, while a woman, with dim features of despair, threw out her hand to warn him back. Was it his mother? But he had no power to retreat one step, nor to resist, even in thought, when the minister and good old deacon Gookin, seized his arms, and led him to the blazing rock. Thither came also the slender form of a veiled female, led between Goody Cloyse, that pious teacher of the catechism, and Martha Carrier, who had received the devil's promise to be queen of hell. A rampant hag was she! And there stood the proselytes, beneath the canopy of fire.

'Welcome, my children,' said the dark figure, 'to the communion of your race![6] Ye have found, thus young, your nature and your destiny. My children, look behind you!"

They turned; and flashing forth, as it were, in a sheet of flame, the fiend-worshippers were seen; the smile of welcome gleamed darkly on every visage.

'There,' resumed the sable form, 'are all whom ye have reverenced from youth. Ye deemed them holier than yourselves, and shrank from your own sin, contrasting it with their lives of right-

---

6. The *New-England Magazine* erroneously printed "grave," corrected to "race" in *Mosses from an Old Manse* (1846).

eousness, and prayerful aspirations heavenward. Yet, here are they all, in my worshipping assembly! This night it shall be granted you to know their secret deeds; how hoary-bearded elders of the church have whispered wanton words to the young maids of their households; how many a woman, eager for widow's weeds, has given her husband a drink at bed-time, and let him sleep his last sleep in her bosom; how beardless youths have made haste to inherit their fathers' wealth; and how fair damsels—blush not, sweet ones!— have dug little graves in the garden, and bidden me, the sole guest, to an infant's funeral. By the sympathy of your human hearts for sin, ye shall scent out all the places—whether in church, bedchamber, street, field, or forest—where crime has been committed, and shall exult to behold the whole earth one stain of guilt, one mighty blood-spot. Far more than this! It shall be your's to penetrate, in every bosom, the deep mystery of sin, the fountain of all wicked arts, and which, inexhaustibly supplies more evil impulses than human power—than my power, at its utmost!—can make manifest in deeds. And now, my children, look upon each other.'

They did so; and, by the blaze of the hell-kindled torches, the wretched man beheld his Faith, and the wife her husband, trembling before that unhallowed altar.

'Lo! there ye stand, my children,' said the figure, in a deep and solemn tone, almost sad, with its despairing awfulness, as if his once angelic nature could yet mourn for our miserable race. 'Depending upon one another's hearts, ye had still hoped, that virtue were not all a dream. Now are ye undeceived! Evil is the nature of mankind. Evil must be your only happiness. Welcome, again, my children, to the communion of your race!'

'Welcome!' repeated the fiend-worshippers, in one cry of despair and triumph.

And there they stood, the only pair, as it seemed, who were yet hesitating on the verge of wickedness, in this dark world. A basin was hollowed, naturally, in the rock. Did it contain water, reddened by the lurid light? or was it blood? or, perchance, a liquid flame? Herein did the Shape of Evil dip his hand, and prepare to lay the mark of baptism upon their foreheads, that they might be partakers of the mystery of sin, more conscious of the secret guilt of others, both in deed and thought, than they could now be of their own. The husband cast one look at his pale wife, and Faith at him. What polluted wretches would the next glance shew them to each other, shuddering alike at what they disclosed and what they saw!

'Faith! Faith!' cried the husband. 'Look up to Heaven, and resist the Wicked One!'

Whether Faith obeyed, he knew not. Hardly had he spoken, when he found himself amid calm night and solitude, listening to a roar of the wind, which died heavily away through the forest. He staggered against the rock and felt it chill and damp, while a hanging twig, that had been all on fire, besprinkled his cheek with the coldest dew.

The next morning, young goodman Brown came slowly into the street of Salem village, staring around him like a bewildered man. The good old minister was taking a walk along the graveyard, to get an appetite for breakfast and meditate his sermon, and bestowed a blessing, as he passed, on goodman Brown. He shrank from the venerable saint, as if to avoid an anathema. Old deacon Gookin was at domestic worship, and the holy words of his prayer were heard through the open window. 'What God doth the wizard pray to?' quoth goodman Brown. Goody Cloyse, that excellent old Christian, stood in the early sunshine, at her own lattice, catechising a little girl, who had brought her a pint of morning's milk. Goodman Brown snatched away the child, as from the grasp of the fiend himself. Turning the corner by the meeting-house, he spied the head of Faith, with the pink ribbons, gazing anxiously forth, and bursting into such joy at sight of him, that she skipt along the street, and almost kissed her husband before the whole village. But, goodman Brown looked sternly and sadly into her face, and passed on without a greeting.

Had goodman Brown fallen asleep in the forest, and only dreamed a wild dream of a witch-meeting?

Be it so, if you will. But, alas! it was a dream of evil omen for young goodman Brown. A stern, a sad, a darkly meditative, a distrustful, if not a desperate man, did he become, from the night of that fearful dream. On the Sabbath-day, when the congregation were singing a holy psalm, he could not listen, because an anthem of sin rushed loudly upon his ear, and drowned all the blessed strain. When the minister spoke from the pulpit, with power and fervid eloquence, and, with his hand on the open bible, of the sacred truths of our religion, and of saint-like lives and triumphant deaths, and of future bliss or misery unutterable, then did goodman Brown turn pale, dreading, lest the roof should thunder down upon the gray blasphemer and his hearers. Often, awakening suddenly at midnight, he shrank from the bosom of Faith, and at morning or eventide, when the family knelt down at prayer, he scowled, and muttered to himself, and gazed sternly at his wife, and turned away. And when he had lived long, and was borne to his grave, a hoary corpse, followed by Faith, an aged woman, and children and grand-children, a goodly procession, besides neighbors, not a few, they carved no hopeful verse upon his tomb-stone; for his dying hour was gloom.

1835

The May-Pole of Merry Mount[1]

There is an admirable foundation for a philosophic romance, in the curious history of the early settlement of Mount Wallaston, or Merry Mount. In the slight sketch here attempted, the facts, recorded on the grave pages of our New England annalists, have wrought themselves, almost spontaneously, into a sort of allegory. The masques, mummeries, and festive customs, described in the text, are in accordance with the manners of the age. Authority, on these points may be found in Strutt's Book of English Sports and Pastimes.[2]

Bright were the days at Merry Mount, when the May-Pole[3] was the banner-staff of that gay colony! They who reared it, should their banner be triumphant, were to pour sun-shine over New England's rugged hills, and scatter flower-seeds throughout the soil. Jollity and gloom were contending for an empire. Midsummer eve[4] had come, bringing deep verdure to the forest, and roses in her lap, of a more vivid hue than the tender buds of Spring. But May, or her mirthful spirit, dwelt all the year round at Merry Mount, sporting with the Summer months, and revelling with Autumn, and basking in the glow of Winter's fireside. Through a world of toil and care, she flitted with a dreamlike smile, and came hither to find a home among the lightsome hearts of Merry Mount.

Never had the May-Pole been so gaily decked as at sunset on midsummer eve. This venerated emblem was a pine tree, which had preserved the slender grace of youth, while it equalled the loftiest height of the old wood monarchs. From its top streamed a silken banner, colored like the rainbow. Down nearly to the ground, the pole was dressed with birchen boughs, and others of the liveliest green, and some with silvery leaves, fastened by ribbons that fluttered in fantastic knots of twenty different colors, but no sad ones. Garden flowers, and blossoms of the wilderness, laughed gladly forth amid the verdure, so fresh and dewy, that they must have grown by magic on that happy pine tree. Where this green and flowery splendor terminated, the shaft of the May-Pole was stained with the seven brilliant hues of the banner at its top. On the lowest green bough hung an abundant wreath of roses, some that had been gathered in the sunniest spots of the forest, and others, of still richer blush, which the colonists had reared from English seed. Oh, people of the Golden Age, the chief of your husbandry, was to raise flowers!

1. The text is that of the first printing in *The Token* (1836), where the story is ascribed to "the Author of 'The Gentle Boy.'"
2. Joseph Strutt, *The Sports and Pastimes of the People of England* (London, 1801). Hawthorne also knew Nathaniel Morton's *New England Memorial* (1669), which drew on William Bradford's manuscript history *Of Plymouth Plantation*.

3. In English tradition the tall pole placed in a prominent place in a village where on the first of May flower-bedecked young people could dance around it after a night of gathering new vegetation and blossoms in the woods. Puritans condemned the custom as a sexual orgy.
4. The 20th of June, the day before the longest day of the year.

But what was the wild throng that stood hand in hand about the May-Pole? It could not be, that the Fauns and Nymphs, when driven from their classic groves and homes of ancient fable, had sought refuge, as all the persecuted did, in the fresh woods of the West. These were Gothic monsters, though perhaps of Grecian ancestry. On the shoulders of a comely youth, uprose the head and branching antlers of a stag; a second, human in all other points, had the grim visage of a wolf; a third, still with the trunk and limbs of a mortal man, showed the beard and horns of a venerable he-goat. There was the likeness of a bear erect, brute in all but his hind legs, which were adorned with pink silk stockings. And here again, almost as wondrous, stood a real bear of the dark forest, lending each of his fore paws to the grasp of a human hand, and as ready for the dance as any in that circle. This inferior nature rose half-way, to meet his companions as they stooped. Other faces wore the similitude of man or woman, but distorted or extravagant, with red noses pendulous before their mouths, which seemed of awful depth, and stretched from ear to ear in an eternal fit of laughter. Here might be seen the Salvage Man,[5] well known in heraldry, hairy as a baboon, and girdled with green leaves. By his side, a nobler figure, but still a counterfeit, appeared an Indian hunter, with feathery crest and wampum belt. Many of this strange company wore fools-caps, and had little bells appended to their garments, tinkling with a silvery sound, responsive to the inaudible music of their gleesome spirits. Some youths and maidens were of soberer garb, yet well maintained their places in the irregular throng, by the expression of wild revelry upon their features. Such were the colonists of Merry Mount, as they stood in the broad smile of sunset, round their venerated May-Pole.

Had a wanderer, bewildered in the melancholy forest, heard their mirth, and stolen a half-affrighted glance, he might have fancied them the crew of Comus,[6] some already transformed to brutes, some midway between man and beast, and the others rioting in the flow of tipsey jollity that foreran the change. But a band of Puritans, who watched the scene, invisible themselves, compared the masques to those devils and ruined souls, with whom their superstition peopled the black wilderness.

Within the ring of monsters, appeared the two airiest forms, that had ever trodden on any more solid footing than a purple and golden cloud. One was a youth, in glistening apparel, with a scarf of the rainbow pattern crosswise on his breast. His right hand held a gilded staff, the ensign[7] of high dignity among the revellous, and his left grasped the slender fingers of a fair maiden, not less gaily decorated than himself. Bright roses glowed in contrast with the

---

5. Person clad in foliage to represent a savage, as in medieval and Renaissance pageantry.

6. The god of revelry, here associated with Milton's *Comus* (1634).
7. Sign, token.

dark and glossy curls of each, and were scattered round their feet, or had sprung up spontaneously there. Behind this lightsome couple, so close to the May-Pole that its boughs shaded his jovial face, stood the figure of an English priest, canonically dressed, yet decked with flowers, in Heathen fashion, and wearing a chaplet of the native vine leaves. By the riot of his rolling eye, and the pagan decorations of his holy garb, he seemed the wildest monster there, and the very Comus of the crew.

'Votaries of the May-Pole,' cried the flower-decked priest, 'merrily, all day long, have the woods echoed to your mirth. But be this your merriest hour, my hearts! Lo, here stand the Lord and Lady of the May, whom I, a clerk[8] of Oxford, and high priest of Merry Mount, am presently to join in holy matrimony. Up with your nimble spirits, ye morrice-dancers, green-men, and glee-maidens,[9] bears and wolves, and horned gentlemen! Come; a chorus now, rich with the old mirth of Merry England, and the wilder glee of this fresh forest; and then a dance, to show the youthful pair what life is made of, and how airily they should go through it! All ye that love the May-Pole, lend your voices to the nuptial song of the Lord and Lady of the May!'

This wedlock was more serious than most affairs of Merry Mount, where jest and delusion, trick and fantasy, kept up a continual carnival. The Lord and Lady of the May, though their titles must be laid down at sunset, were really and truly to be partners for the dance of life, beginning the measure that same bright eve. The wreath of roses, that hung from the lowest green bough of the May-Pole, had been twined for them, and would be thrown over both their heads, in symbol of their flowery union. When the priest had spoken, therefore, a riotous uproar burst from the rout of monstrous figures.

'Begin you the stave,[1] reverend Sir,' cried they all; 'and never did the woods ring to such a merry peal, as we of the May-Pole shall send up!'

Immediately a prelude of pipe, cittern,[2] and viol, touched with practised minstrelsy, began to play from a neighboring thicket, in such a mirthful cadence, that the boughs of the May-Pole quivered to the sound. But the May Lord, he of the gilded staff, chancing to look into his Lady's eyes, was wonderstruck at the almost pensive glance that met his own.

'Edith, sweet Lady of the May,' whispered he, reproachfully, 'is your wreath of roses a garland to hang above our graves, that you look so sad? Oh, Edith, this is our golden time! Tarnish it not by

8. In Anglican usage, lay minister who assists the parish clergyman.
9. Participants in an English folk dance (originally "Moorish dance"); men be-
decked in greenery; girl singers.
1. Stanza.
2. Guitar with pear-shaped body.

any pensive shadow of the mind; for it may be, that nothing of futurity will be brighter than the mere remembrance of what is now passing.'

'That was the very thought that saddened me! How came it in your mind too?' said Edith, in a still lower tone than he; for it was high treason to be sad at Merry Mount. 'Therefore do I sigh amid this festive music. And besides, dear Edgar, I struggle as with a dream, and fancy that these shapes of our jovial friends are visionary, and their mirth unreal, and that we are no true Lord and Lady of the May. What is the mystery in my heart?'

Just then, as if a spell had loosened them, down came a little shower of withering rose leaves from the May-Pole. Alas, for the young lovers! No sooner had their hearts glowed with real passion, than they were sensible of something vague and unsubstantial in their former pleasures, and felt a dreary presentiment of inevitable change. From the moment that they truly loved, they had subjected themselves to earth's doom of care, and sorrow, and troubled joy, and had no more a home at Merry Mount. That was Edith's mystery. Now leave we the priest to marry them, and the masquers to sport round the May-Pole, till the last sunbeam be withdrawn from its summit, and the shadows of the forest mingle gloomily in the dance. Meanwhile, we may discover who these gay people were.

Two hundred years ago, and more, the old world and its inhabitants became mutually weary of each other. Men voyaged by thousands to the West; some to barter glass beads, and such like jewels, for the furs of the Indian hunter; some to conquer virgin empires; and one stern band to pray. But none of these motives had much weight with the colonists of Merry Mount. Their leaders were men who had sported so long with life, that when Thought and Wisdom came, even these unwelcome guests were led astray, by the crowd of vanities which they should have put to flight. Erring Thought and perverted Wisdom were made to put on masques, and play the fool. The men of whom we speak, after losing the heart's fresh gaiety, imagined a wild philosophy of pleasure, and came hither to act out their latest day-dream. They gathered followers from all that giddy tribe, whose whole life is like the festal days of soberer men. In their train were minstrels, not unknown in London streets; wandering players, whose theatres had been the halls of noblemen; mummeries, rope-dancers, and mountebanks,[3] who would long be missed at wakes, church-ales, and fairs; in a word, mirth-makers of every sort, such as abounded in that age, but now began to be discountenanced by the rapid growth of Puritanism. Light had their footsteps been on land, and as lightly they came across the sea. Many had been maddened by their previous troubles into a gay

---

3. Masked actors; tightrope walkers; showmen who "climb on a bench" to hawk medicines or (as here) to tell stories or do tricks.

despair; others were as madly gay in the flush of youth, like the
May Lord and his Lady; but whatever might be the quality of their
mirth, old and young were gay at Merry Mount. The young deemed
themselves happy. The elder spirits, if they knew that mirth was but
the counterfeit of happiness, yet followed the false shadow wilfully,
because at least her garments glittered brightest. Sworn triflers of a
life-time, they would not venture among the sober truths of life, not
even to be truly blest.

All the hereditary pastimes of Old England were transplanted
hither. The King of Christmas was duly crowned, and the Lord of
Misrule⁴ bore potent sway. On the eve of Saint John,⁵ they felled
whole acres of the forest to make bonfires, and danced by the blaze
all night, crowned with garlands, and throwing flowers into the
flame. At harvest time, though their crop was of the smallest, they
made an image with the sheaves of Indian corn, and wreathed it
with autumnal garlands, and bore it home triumphantly. But what
chiefly characterized the colonists of Merry Mount, was their
veneration for the May-Pole. It has made their true history a poet's
tale. Spring decked the hallowed emblem with young blossoms and
fresh green boughs; Summer brought roses of the deepest blush, and
the perfected foliage of the forest; Autumn enriched it with that red
and yellow gorgeousness, which converts each wildwood leaf into a
painted flower; and Winter silvered it with sleet, and hung it round
with icicles, till it flashed in the cold sunshine, itself a frozen sun-
beam. Thus each alternate season did homage to the May-Pole, and
paid it a tribute of its own richest splendor. Its votaries danced
round it, once, at least, in every month; sometimes they called it
their religion, or their altar; but always, it was the banner-staff of
Merry Mount.

Unfortunately, there were men in the new world, of a sterner
faith than these May-Pole worshippers. Not far from Merry Mount
was a settlement of Puritans, most dismal wretches, who said their
prayers before daylight, and then wrought in the forest or the corn-
field, till evening made it prayer time again. Their weapons were
always at hand, to shoot down the straggling savage. When they met
in conclave, it was never to keep up the old English mirth, but to
hear sermons three hours long, or to proclaim bounties on the heads
of wolves and the scalps of Indians. Their festivals were fast-days,
and their chief pastime the singing of psalms. Woe to the youth or
maiden, who did but dream of a dance! The selectman nodded to
the constable; and there sat the light-heeled reprobate in the stocks;
or if he danced, it was round the whipping-post, which might be
termed the Puritan May-Pole.

A party of these grim Puritans, toiling through the difficult
woods, each with a horse-load of iron armor to burthen his foot-

steps, would sometimes draw near the sunny precincts of Merry Mount. There were the silken colonists, sporting round their May-Pole; perhaps teaching a bear to dance, or striving to communicate their mirth to the grave Indian; or masquerading in the skins of deer and wolves, which they had hunted for that especial purpose. Often, the whole colony were playing at blindman's bluff, magistrates and all with their eyes bandaged, except a single scape-goat, whom the blinded sinners pursued by the tinkling of the bells at his garments. Once, it is said, they were seen following a flower-decked corpse, with merriment and festive music, to his grave. But did the dead man laugh? In their quietest times, they sang ballads and told tales, for the edification of their pious visiters; or perplexed them with juggling tricks; or grinned at them through horse-collars; and when sport itself grew wearisome, they made game of their own stupidity, and began a yawning match. At the very least of these enormities, the men of iron shook their heads and frowned so darkly, that the revellers looked up, imagining that a momentary cloud had overcast the sunshine, which was to be perpetual there. On the other hand, the Puritans affirmed, that, when a psalm was pealing from their place of worship, the echo, which the forest sent them back, seemed often like the chorus of a jolly catch, closing with a roar of laughter. Who but the fiend, and his fond slaves, the crew of Merry Mount, had thus disturbed them! In due time, a feud arose, stern and bitter on one side, and as serious on the other as any thing could be, among such light spirits as had sworn allegiance to the May-Pole. The future complexion of New England was involved in this important quarrel. Should the grisly saints establish their jurisdiction over the gay sinners, then would their spirits darken all the clime, and make it a land of clouded visages, of hard toil, of sermon and psalm, forever. But should the banner-staff of Merry Mount be fortunate, sunshine would break upon the hills, and flowers would beautify the forest, and late posterity do homage to the May-Pole!

After these authentic passages from history, we return to the nuptials of the Lord and Lady of the May. Alas! we have delayed too long, and must darken our tale too suddenly. As we glanced again at the May-Pole, a solitary sun-beam is fading from the summit, and leaves only a faint golden tinge, blended with the hues of the rain bow banner. Even that dim light is now withdrawn, relinquishing the whole domain of Merry Mount to the evening gloom, which has rushed so instantaneously from the black surrounding woods. But some of these black shadows have rushed forth in human shape.

Yes: with the setting sun, the last day of mirth had passed from Merry Mount. The ring of gay masquers was disordered and broken; the stag lowered his antlers in dismay; the wolf grew weaker than a lamb; the bells of the morrice dancers tinkled with tremulous affright. The Puritans had played a characteristic part in the May-Pole mummeries. Their darksome figures were intermixed with the wild shapes of their foes, and made the scene a picture of the moment, when waking thoughts start up amid the scattered fantasies of a dream. The leader of the hostile party stood in the centre of the circle, while the rout of monsters cowered around him, like evil spirits in the presence of a dread magician. No fantastic foolery could look him in the face. So stern was the energy of his aspect, that the whole man, visage, frame, and soul, seemed wrought of iron, gifted with life and thought, yet all of one substance with his head-piece and breast-plate. It was the Puritan of Puritans; it was Endicott[6] himself!

'Stand off, priest of Baal!'[7] said he, with a grim frown, and laying no reverent hand upon the surplice. 'I know thee, Claxton![8] Thou art the man, who couldst not abide the rule even of thine own corrupted church,[9] and hast come hither to preach iniquity, and to give example of it in thy life. But now shall it be seen that the Lord hath sanctified this wilderness for his peculiar people. Woe unto them that would defile it! And first for this flower-decked abomination, the altar of thy worship!'

And with his keen sword, Endicott assaulted the hallowed May-Pole. Nor long did it resist his arm. It groaned with a dismal sound; it showered leaves and rose-buds upon the remorseless enthusiast; and finally, with all its green boughs, and ribbons, and flowers, symbolic of departed pleasures, down fell the banner-staff of Merry Mount. As it sank, tradition says, the evening sky grew darker, and the woods threw forth a more sombre shadow.

'There,' cried Endicott, looking triumphantly on his work, 'there lies the only May-Pole in New-England! The thought is strong within me, that, by its fall, is shadowed forth the fate of light and idle mirth-makers, amongst us and our posterity. Amen, saith John Endicott!'

'Amen!' echoed his followers.

But the votaries of the May-Pole gave one groan for their idol. At the sound, the Puritan leader glanced at the crew of Comus, each a figure of broad mirth, yet, at this moment, strangely expressive of sorrow and dismay.

'Valiant captain,' quoth Peter Palfrey, the Ancient[1] of the band, 'what order shall be taken with the prisoners?'

'I thought not to repent me of cutting down a May-Pole,' replied Endicott, 'yet now I could find in my heart to plant it again, and

6. John Endicott (1589?–1665), several times Governor of the Massachusetts colony.
7. For the slaying of the prophets of the fertility god Baal, see 1 Kings 18.
8. "Did Governor Endicott speak less positively, we should suspect a mistake here. The Reverend Mr. Claxton, though an eccentric, is not known to have been an immoral man. We rather doubt his identity with the priest of Merry Mount" [Hawthorne's note].
9. That is, the Anglican Church.
1. Lieutenant.

give each of these bestial pagans one other dance round their idol. It would have served rarely for a whipping-post!'

'But there are pine trees enow,' suggested the lieutenant.

'True, good Ancient,' said the leader. 'Wherefore, bind the heathen crew, and bestow on them a small matter of stripes apiece, as earnest of our future justice. Set some of the rogues in the stocks to rest themselves, so soon as Providence shall bring us to one of our own well-ordered settlements, where such accommodations may be found. Further penalties, such as branding and cropping of ears, shall be thought of hereafter.'

'How many stripes for the priest?' inquired Ancient Palfrey.

'None as yet,' answered Endicott, bending his iron frown upon the culprit. 'It must be for the Great and General Court[2] to determine, whether stripes and long imprisonment, and other grievous penalty, may atone for his transgressions. Let him look to himself! For such as violate our civil order, it may be permitted us to show mercy. But woe to the wretch that troubleth our religion!'

'And this dancing bear,' resumed the officer. 'Must he share the stripes of his fellows?'

'Shoot him through the head!' said the energetic Puritan. 'I suspect witchcraft in the beast.'

'Here be a couple of shining ones,' continued Peter Palfrey, pointing his weapon at the Lord and Lady of the May. 'They seem to be of high station among these mis-doers. Methinks their dignity will not be fitted with less than a double share of stripes.'

Endicott rested on his sword, and closely surveyed the dress and aspect of the hapless pair. There they stood, pale, downcast, and apprehensive. Yet there was an air of mutual support, and of pure affection, seeking aid and giving it, that showed them to be man and wife, with the sanction of a priest upon their love. The youth, in the peril of the moment, had dropped his gilded staff, and thrown his arm about the Lady of the May, who leaned against his breast, too lightly to burthen him, but with weight enough to express that their destinies were linked together, for good or evil. They looked first at each other, and then into the grim captain's face. There they stood, in the first hour of wedlock, while the idle pleasures, of which their companions were the emblems, had given place to the sternest cares of life, personified by the dark Puritans. But never had their youthful beauty seemed so pure and high, as when its glow was chastened by adversity.

'Youth,' said Endicott, 'ye stand in an evil case, thou and thy maiden wife. Make ready presently; for I am minded that ye shall both have a token to remember your wedding-day!'

'Stern man,' exclaimed the May Lord, 'How can I move thee? Were the means at hand, I would resist to the death. Being power-

2. Massachusetts legislature.

less, I entreat! Do with me as thou wilt; but let Edith go untouched!'

'Not so,' replied the immitigable zealot. 'We are not wont to show an idle courtesy to that sex, which requireth the stricter discipline. What sayest thou, maid? Shall thy silken bridegroom suffer thy share of the penalty, besides his own?'

'Be it death,' said Edith, 'and lay it all on me!'

Truly, as Endicott had said, the poor lovers stood in a woeful case. Their foes were triumphant, their friends captive and abased, their home desolate, the benighted wilderness around them, and a rigorous destiny, in the shape of the Puritan leader, their only guide. Yet the deepening twilight could not altogether conceal, that the iron man was softened; he smiled, at the fair spectacle of early love; he almost sighed, for the inevitable blight of early hopes.

'The troubles of life have come hastily on this young couple,' observed Endicott. 'We will see how they comport themselves under their present trials, ere we burthen them with greater. If, among the spoil, there be any garments of a more decent fashion, let them be put upon this May Lord and his Lady, instead of their glistening vanities. Look to it, some of you.'

'And shall not the youth's hair be cut?' asked Peter Palfrey, looking with abhorrence at the love-lock and long glossy curls of the young man.

'Crop if forthwith, and that in the true pumpkin shell fashion,'[3] answered the captain. 'Then bring them along with us, but more gently than their fellows. There be qualities in the youth, which may make him valiant to fight, and sober to toil, and pious to pray; and in the maiden, that may fit her to become a mother in our Israel,[4] bringing up babes in better nurture than her own hath been. Nor think ye, young ones, that they are the happiest, even in our lifetime of a moment, who misspend it in dancing round a May-Pole!'

And Endicott, the severest Puritan of all who laid the rock-foundation of New England, lifted the wreath of roses from the ruin of the May-Pole, and threw it, with his own gauntleted hand, over the heads of the Lord and Lady of the May. It was a deed of prophecy. As the moral gloom of the world overpowers all systematic gaiety, even so was their home of wild mirth made desolate amid the sad forest. They returned to it no more. But, as their flowery garland was wreathed of the brightest roses that had grown there, so, in the tie that united them, were intertwined all the purest and best of their early joys. They went heavenward, supporting each other along the difficult path which it was their lot to tread, and never wasted one regretful thought on the vanities of Merry Mount.

1835

3. Roundhead style, close-cropped in Puritan fashion.
4. Endicott makes the standard 17th- century Puritan identification of the New England settlers with the Jews, another persecuted, God-chosen minority.

Rappaccini's Daughter
Writings of Aubépine[1]

We do not remember to have seen any translated specimens of the productions of M. de l'Aubépine;[2] a fact the less to be wondered at, as his very name is unknown to many of his own countrymen, as well as to the student of foreign literature. As a writer, he seems to occupy an unfortunate position between the Transcendentalists (who, under one name or another, have their share in all the current literature of the world), and the great body of pen-and-ink men who address the intellect and sympathies of the multitude. If not too refined, at all events too remote, too shadowy and unsubstantial in his modes of development, to suit the taste of the latter class, and yet too popular to satisfy the spiritual or metaphysical requisitions of the former, he must necessarily find himself without an audience; except here and there an individual, or possibly an isolated clique. His writings, to do them justice, are not altogether destitute of fancy and originality; they might have won him greater reputation but for an inveterate love of allegory, which is apt to invest his plots and characters with the aspect of scenery and people in the clouds, and to steal away the human warmth out of his conceptions. His fictions are sometimes historical, sometimes of the present day, and sometimes, so far as can be discovered, have little or no reference either to time or space. In any case, he generally contents himself with a very slight embroidery of outward manners, —the faintest possible counterfeit of real life,—and endeavors to create an interest by some less obvious peculiarity of the subject. Occasionally, a breath of nature, a rain-drop of pathos and tenderness, or a gleam of humor, will find its way into the midst of his fantastic imagery, and make us feel as if, after all, we were yet within the limits of our native earth. We will only add to this very cursory notice, that M. de l'Aubépine's productions, if the reader chance to take them in precisely the proper point of view, may amuse a leisure hour as well as those of a brighter man; if otherwise, they can hardly fail to look excessively like nonsense.

Our author is voluminous; he continues to write and publish with as much praiseworthy and indefatigable prolixity, as if his efforts were crowned with the brilliant success that so justly attends those of Eugene Sue.[3] His first appearance was by a collection of stories, in a long series of volumes, entitled "*Contes deux fois racontées.*"[4] The titles of some of his more recent works (we quote from

---

1. The text is from the first publication in *The Democratic Review* (December, 1844).
2. French for "Hawthorne." What follows is a facetious account of Hawthorne's own career.

3. French novelist (1804–57), author of *The Wandering Jew* and other popular works.
4. *Twice-Told Tales* (1837), Hawthorne's first volume (except for the anonymous and suppressed *Fanshawe*).

memory) are as follows:—"*Le Voyage Céleste à Chemin de Fer,*" 3 tom. 1838. "*Le nouveau père Adam et la nouvelle mère Eve,*" 2 tom. 1839. "*Roderic; ou le Serpent à l'estomac,*" 2 tom. 1840. "*Le Culte du Feu,*" a folio volume of ponderous research into the religion and ritual of the old Persian Ghebers, published in 1841. "*La Soirée du Château en Espagne,*" 1 tom. 8vo. 1842; and "*L'Artiste du Beau; ou le Papillon Mécanique,*" 5 tom. 4to. 1843.[5] Our somewhat wearisome persual of this startling catalogue of volumes has left behind it a certain personal affection and sympathy, though by no means admiration, for M. de l'Aubépine; and we would fain do the little in our power towards introducing him favorably to the American public. The ensuing tale is a translation of his "*Béatrice; ou La Belle Empoisonneuse,*" recently published in "*La Revue Anti-Aristocratique.*"[6] This journal, edited by the Comte de Bearhaven,[7] has, for some years past, led the defence of liberal principles and popular rights, with a faithfulness and ability worthy of all praise.

Rappaccini's Daughter

A young man, named Giovanni Guasconti, came, very long ago, from the more southern region of Italy, to pursue his studies at the University of Padua. Giovanni, who had but a scanty supply of gold ducats in his pocket, took lodgings in a high and gloomy chamber of an old edifice, which looked not unworthy to have been the palace of a Paduan noble, and which, in fact, exhibited over its entrance the armorial bearings of a family long since extinct. The young stranger, who was not unstudied in the great poem of his country, recollected that one of the ancestors of this family, and perhaps an occupant of this very mansion, had been pictured by Dante as a partaker of the immortal agonies of his Inferno. These reminiscences and associations, together with the tendency to heartbreak natural to a young man for the first time out of his native sphere, caused Giovanni to sigh heavily, as he looked around the desolate and ill-furnished apartment.

"Holy Virgin, signor," cried old dame Lisabetta, who, won by the youth's remarkable beauty of person, was kindly endeavoring to give the chamber a habitable air, "what a sigh was that to come out of a young man's heart! Do you find this old mansion gloomy? For the love of heaven, then, put your head out of the window, and you will see as bright sunshine as you have left in Naples."

---

5. In these mock-bibliographical citations "tom." (the abbreviation for "tome," French for "volume") and "8vo" and "4vo" ("octavo" and quarto") are jokes: Hawthorne's tales took up only a few magazine pages each. Except for the imaginary *Evening in a Castle in Spain,* the titles refer to stories by Hawthorne: *The Celestial Railroad, The New Adam and Eve, Egotism; or, The Bosom-Serpent, Fire-Worship,* and *The Artist of the Beautiful.*
6. *The Democratic Review.*
7. Hawthorne's friend, John O'Sullivan, editor of *The Democratic Review.*

Guasconti mechanically did as the old woman advised, but could not quite agree with her that the Lombard sunshine was as cheerful as that of southern Italy. Such as it was, however, it fell upon a garden beneath the window, and expended its fostering influences on a variety of plants, which seemed to have been cultivated with exceeding care.

"Does this garden belong to the house?" asked Giovanni.

"Heaven forbid, signor!—unless it were fruitful of better pot-herbs than any that grow there now," answered old Lisabetta. "No: that garden is cultivated by the own hands of Signor Giacomo Rappaccini, the famous Doctor, who, I warrant him, has been heard of as far as Naples. It is said he distils these plants into medicines that are as potent as a charm. Oftentimes you may see the signor Doctor at work, and perchance the signora his daughter, too, gathering the strange flowers that grow in the garden."

The old woman had now done what she could for the aspect of the chamber, and, commending the young man to the protection of the saints, took her departure.

Giovanni still found no better occupation than to look down into the garden beneath his window. From its appearance, he judged it to be one of those botanic gardens, which were of earlier date in Padua than elsewhere in Italy, or in the world. Or, not improbably, it might once have been the pleasure-place of an opulent family; for there was the ruin of a marble fountain in the centre, sculptured with rare art, but so wofully shattered that it was impossible to trace the original design from the chaos of remaining fragments. The water, however, continued to gush and sparkle into the sunbeams as cheerfully as ever. A little gurgling sound ascended to the young man's window, and made him feel as if the fountain were an immortal spirit, that sung its song unceasingly, and without heeding the vicissitudes around it; while one century embodied it in marble, and another scattered the garniture on the soil. All about the pool into which the water subsided, grew various plants, that seemed to require a plentiful supply of moisture for the nourishment of gigantic leaves, and, in some instances, flowers gorgeously magnificent. There was one shrub in particular, set in a marble vase in the midst of the pool, that bore a profusion of purple blossoms, each of which had the lustre and richness of a gem; and the whole together made a show so resplendent that it seemed enough to illuminate the garden, even had there been no sunshine. Every portion of the soil was peopled with plants and herbs, which, if less beautiful, still bore tokens of assiduous care; as if all had their individual virtues, known to the scientific mind that fostered them. Some were placed in urns, rich with old carving, and others in common garden-pots; some crept serpent-like along the ground, or climbed on high, using whatever means of ascent was offered them. One plant had wreathed itself round a statue of Vertumnus,[8] which was thus quite veiled and shrouded in a drapery of hanging foliage, so happily arranged that it might have served a sculptor for a study.

While Giovanni stood at the window, he heard a rustling behind a screen of leaves, and became aware that a person was at work in the garden. His figure soon emerged into view, and showed itself to be that of no common laborer, but a tall, emaciated, sallow, and sickly-looking man, dressed in a scholar's garb of black. He was beyond the middle term of life, with grey hair, a thin grey beard, and a face singularly marked with intellect and cultivation, but which could never, even in his more youthful days, have expressed much warmth of heart.

Nothing could exceed the intentness with which this scientific gardener examined every shrub which grew in his path; it seemed as if he was looking into their inmost nature, making observations in regard to their creative essence, and discovering why one leaf grew in this shape, and another in that, and wherefore such and such flowers differed among themselves in hue and perfume. Nevertheless, in spite of the deep intelligence on his part, there was no approach to intimacy between himself and these vegetable existences. On the contrary, he avoided their actual touch, or the direct inhaling of their odors, with a caution that impressed Givoanni most disagreeably; for the man's demeanor was that of one walking among malignant influences, such as savage beasts, or deadly snakes, or evil spirits, which, should he allow them one moment of license, would wreak upon him some terrible fatality. It was strangely frightful to the young man's imagination, to see this air of insecurity in a person cultivating a garden, that most simple and innocent of human toils, and which had been alike the joy and labor of the unfallen parents of the race. Was this garden, then, the Eden of the present world?—and this man, with such a perception of harm in what his own hands caused to grow, was he the Adam?

The distrustful gardener, while plucking away the dead leaves or pruning the too luxuriant growth of the shrubs, defended his hands with a pair of thick gloves. Nor were these his only armor. When, in his walk through the garden, he came to the magnificent plant that hung its purple gems beside the marble fountain, he placed a kind of mask over his mouth and nostrils, as if all this beauty did but conceal a deadlier malice. But finding his task still too dangerous, he drew back, removed the mask, and called loudly, but in the infirm voice of a person affected with inward disease:

"Beatrice!—Beatrice!"

"Here am I, my father! What would you?" cried a rich and youthful voice from the window of the opposite house; a voice as

8. The god of the seasons (and vegetation produced by the changing seasons).

rich as a tropical sunset, and which made Giovanni, though he knew not why, think of deep hues of purple or crimson, and of perfumes heavily delectable.—"Are you in the garden?"

"Yes, Beatrice," answered the gardener, "and I need your help."

Soon there emerged from under a sculptured portal the figure of a young girl, arrayed with as much richness of taste as the most splendid of the flowers, beautiful as the day, and with a bloom so deep and vivid that one shade more would have been too much. She looked redundant with life, health, and energy; all of which attributes were bound down and compressed, as it were, and girdled tensely, in their luxuriance, by her virgin zone.[9] Yet Giovanni's fancy must have grown morbid, while he looked down into the garden; for the impression which the fair stranger made upon him was as if here were another flower, the human sister of those vegetable ones, as beautiful as they—more beautiful than the richest of them—but still to be touched only with a glove, nor to be approached without a mask. As Beatrice came down the garden-path, it was observable that she handled and inhaled the odor of several of the plants, which her father had most sedulously avoided.

"Here, Beatrice," said the latter,—"see how many needful offices require to be done to our chief treasure. Yet, shattered as I am, my life might pay the penalty of approaching it so closely as circumstances demand. Henceforth, I fear, this plant must be consigned to your sole charge."

"And gladly will I undertake it," cried again the rich tones of the young lady, as she bent towards the magnificent plant, and opened her arms as if to embrace it. "Yes, my sister, my splendor, it shall be Beatrice's task to nurse and serve thee; and thou shalt reward her with thy kisses and perfumed breath, which to her is as the breath of life!"

Then, with all the tenderness in her manner that was so strikingly expressed in her words, she busied herself with such attentions as the plant seemed to require; and Giovanni, at his lofty window, rubbed his eyes, and almost doubted whether it were a girl tending her favorite flower, or one sister performing the duties of affection to another. The scene soon terminated. Whether Doctor Rappaccini had finished his labors in the garden, or that his watchful eye had caught the stranger's face, he now took his daughter's arm and retired. Night was already closing in; oppressive exhalations seemed to proceed from the plants, and steal upward past the open window; and Giovanni, closing the lattice, went to his couch, and dreamed of a rich flower and beautiful girl. Flower and maiden were different and yet the same, and fraught with some strange peril in either shape.

9. Wide girdlelike belt customarily worn by unmarried girls.

But there is an influence in the light of morning that tends to rectify whatever errors of fancy, or even of judgment, we may have incurred during the sun's decline, or among the shadows of the night, or in the less wholesome glow of moonshine. Giovanni's first movement on starting from sleep, was to throw open the window, and gaze down into the garden which his dreams had made so fertile of mysteries. He was surprised, and a little ashamed, to find how real and matter-of-fact an affair it proved to be, in the first rays of the sun, which gilded the dew-drops that hung upon leaf and blossom, and, while giving a brighter beauty to each rare flower, brought everything within the limits of ordinary experience. The young man rejoiced, that, in the heart of the barren city, he had the privilege of overlooking this spot of lovely and luxuriant vegetation. It would serve, he said to himself, as a symbolic language, to keep him in communion with nature. Neither the sickly and thought-worn Doctor Giacomo Rappaccini, it is true, nor his brilliant daughter were now visible; so that Giovanni could not determine how much of the singularity which he attributed to both, was due to their own qualities, and how much to his wonder-working fancy. But he was inclined to take a most rational view of the whole matter.

In the course of the day, he paid his respects to Signor Pietro Baglioni, professor of medicine in the University, a physician of eminent repute, to whom Giovanni had brought a letter of introduction. The professor was an elderly personage, apparently of genial nature, and habits that might almost be called jovial; he kept the young man to dinner, and made himself very agreeable by the freedom and liveliness of his conversation, especially when warmed by a flask or two of Tuscan wine. Giovanni, conceiving that men of science, inhabitants of the same city, must needs be on familiar terms with one another, took an opportunity to mention the name of Dr. Rappaccini. But the professor did not respond with so much cordiality as he had anticipated.

"Ill would it become a teacher of the divine art of medicine," said Professor Pietro Baglioni, in answer to a question of Giovanni, "to withhold due and well-considered praise of a physician so eminently skilled as Rappaccini. But, on the other hand, I should answer it but scantily to my conscience, were I to permit a worthy youth like yourself, Signor Giovanni, the son of an ancient friend, to imbibe erroneous ideas respecting a man who might hereafter chance to hold your life and death in his hands. The truth is, our worshipful Doctor Rappaccini has as much science as any member of the faculty—with perhaps one single exception—in Padua, or all Italy. But there are certain grave objections to his professional character."

"And what are they?" asked the young man.

"Has my friend Giovanni any disease of body or heart, that he is so inquisitive about physicians?" said the Professor, with a smile.

"But as for Rappaccini, it is said of him—and I, who know the man well, can answer for its truth—that he cares infinitely more for science than for mankind. His patients are interesting to him only as subjects for some new experiment. He would sacrifice human life, his own among the rest, or whatever else was dearest to him, for the sake of adding so much as a grain of mustard-seed to the great heap of his accumulated knowledge."

"Methinks he is an awful[1] man, indeed," remarked Guasconti, mentally recalling the cold and purely intellectual aspect of Rappaccini. "And yet, worshipful Professor, is it not a noble spirit? Are there many men capable of so spiritual a love of science?"

"God forbid," answered the Professor, somewhat testily—"at least, unless they take sounder views of the healing art than those adopted by Rappaccini. It is his theory, that all medicinal virtues are comprised within those substances which we term vegetable poisons. These he cultivates with his own hands, and is said even to have produced new varieties of poison, more horribly deleterious than Nature, without the assistance of this learned person, would ever have plagued the world with. That the signor Doctor does less mischief than might be expected, with such dangerous substances, is undeniable. Now and then, it must be owned, he has effected—or seemed to effect—a marvellous cure. But, to tell you my private mind, Signor Giovanni, he should receive little credit for such instances of success—they being probably the work of chance—but should be held strictly accountable for his failures, which may justly be considered his own work."

The youth might have taken Baglioni's opinions with many grains of allowance, had he known that there was a professional warfare of long continuance between him and Doctor Rappaccini, in which the latter was generally thought to have gained the advantage. If the reader be inclined to judge for himself, we refer him to certain black-letter tracts on both sides, preserved in the medical department of the University of Padua.

"I know not, most learned Professor," returned Giovanni, after musing on what had been said of Rappaccini's exclusive zeal for science—"I know not how dearly this physician may love his art; but surely there is one object more dear to him. He has a daughter."

"Aha!" cries the Professor with a laugh. "So now our friend Giovanni's secret is out. You have heard of this daughter, whom all the young men in Padua are wild about, though not half a dozen have ever had the good hap to see her face. I know little of the Signora Beatrice, save that Rappaccini is said to have instructed her deeply in his science, and that, young and beautiful as fame reports her, she is already qualified to fill a professor's chair. Perchance her

1. The word carries some of the sense of "awe-striking."

father destines her for mine! Other absurd rumors there be, not worth talking about, or listening to. So now, Signor Giovanni, drink off your glass of Lacryma."[2]

Guasconti returned to his lodgings somewhat heated with the wine he had quaffed, and which caused his brain to swim with strange fantasies in reference to Doctor Rappaccini and the beautiful Beatrice. On his way, happening to pass by a florist's, he bought a fresh bouquet of flowers.

Ascending to his chamber, he seated himself near the window, but within the shadow thrown by the depth of the wall, so that he could look down into the garden with little risk of being discovered. All beneath his eye was a solitude. The strange plants were basking in the sunshine, and now and then nodding gently to one another, as if in acknowledgment of sympathy and kindred. In the midst, by the shattered fountain, grew the magnificent shrub, with its purple gems clustering all over it; they glowed in the air, and gleamed back again out of the depths of the pool, which thus seemed to overflow with colored radiance from the rich reflection that was steeped in it. At first, as we have said, the garden was a solitude. Soon, however, —as Giovanni had half-hoped, half-feared, would be the case,—a figure appeared beneath the antique sculptured portal, and came down between the rows of plants, inhaling their various perfumes, as if she were one of those beings of old classic fable, that lived upon sweet odors. On again beholding Beatrice, the young man was even startled to perceive how much her beauty exceeded his recollection of it; so brilliant, so vivid in its character, that she glowed amid the sunlight, and, as Giovanni whispered to himself, positively illuminated the more shadowy intervals of the garden path. Her face being now more revealed than on the former occasion, he was struck by its expression of simplicity and sweetness; qualities that had not entered into his idea of her character, and which made him ask anew, what manner of mortal she might be. Nor did he fail again to observe, or imagine, an analogy between the beautiful girl and the gorgeous shrub that hung its gem-like flowers over the fountain; a resemblance which Beatrice seemed to have indulged a fantastic humor in heightening, both by the arrangement of her dress and the selection of its hues.

Approaching the shrub, she threw open her arms, as with a passionate ardor, and drew its branches into an intimate embrace; so intimate, that her features were hidden in its leafy bosom, and her glistening ringlets all intermingled with the flowers.

"Give me thy breath, my sister," exclaimed Beatrice; "for I am faint with common air! And give me this flower of thine, which I separate with gentlest fingers from the stem, and place it close beside my heart."

With these words, the beautiful daughter of Rappaccini plucked

2. A still Italian wine grown near Vesuvius.

one of the richest blossoms of the shrub, and was about to fasten it in her bosom. But now, unless Giovanni's draughts of wine had bewildered his senses, a singular incident occurred. A small orange-colored reptile of the lizard or chameleon species, chanced to be creeping along the path, just at the feet of Beatrice. It appeared to Giovanni—but, at the distance from which he gazed, he could scarcely have seen anything so minute—it appeared to him, how-ever, that a drop or two of moisture from the broken stem of the flower descended upon the lizard's head. For an instant, the reptile contorted itself violently, and then lay motionless in the sunshine. Beatrice observed this remarkable phenomenon, and crossed herself, sadly, but without surprise; nor did she therefore hesitate to arrange the fatal flower in her bosom. There it blushed, and almost glim-mered with the dazzling effect of a precious stone, adding to her dress and aspect the one appropriate charm, which nothing else in the world could have supplied. But Giovanni, out of the shadow of his window bent forward and shrank back, and murmured and trembled.

"Am I awake? Have I my senses?" said he to himself. "What is this being?—beautiful, shall I call her?—or inexpressibly terrible?"

Beatrice now strayed carelessly through the garden, approaching closer beneath Giovanni's window, so that he was compelled to thrust his head quite out of its concealment in order to gratify the intense and painful curiosity which she excited. At this moment, there came a beautiful insect over the garden wall; it had perhaps wandered through the city and found no flowers nor verdure among those antique haunts of men, until the heavy perfumes of Doctor Rappaccini's shrubs had lured it from afar. Without alighting on the flowers, this winged brightness seemed to be attracted by Beatrice, and lingered in the air and fluttered about her head. Now here it could not be but that Giovanni Guasconti's eyes deceived him. Be that as it might, he fancied that while Beatrice was gazing at the insect with childish delight, it grew faint and fell at her feet!—its bright wings shivered! it was dead!—from no cause that he could discern, unless it were the atmosphere of her breath. Again Beatrice crossed herself and sighed heavily, as she bent over the dead insect.

An impulsive movement of Giovanni drew her eyes to the win-dow. There she beheld the beautiful head of the young man—rather a Grecian than an Italian head, with fair, regular features, and a glistening of gold among his ringlets—gazing down upon her like a being that hovered in mid-air. Scarcely knowing what he did, Gio-vanni threw down the bouquet which he had hitherto held in his hand.

"Signora," said he, "there are pure and healthful flowers. Wear them for the sake of Giovanni Guasconti!"

"Thanks, Signor," replied Beatrice, with her rich voice, that came forth as it were like a gush of music; and with a mirthful expression half childish and half woman-like. "I accept your gift, and would fain recompense it with this precious purple flower; but if I toss it into the air, it will not reach you. So Signor Guasconti must even content himself with my thanks."

She lifted the bouquet from the ground, and then as if inwardly ashamed at having stepped aside from her maidenly reserve to respond to a stranger's greeting, passed swiftly homeward through the garden. But, few as the moments were, it seemed to Giovanni when she was on the point of vanishing beneath the sculptured portal, that his beautiful bouquet was already beginning to wither in her grasp. It was an idle thought; there could be no possibility of distinguishing a faded flower from a fresh one at so great a distance.

For many days after the incident, the young man avoided the window that looked into Doctor Rappaccini's garden, as if something ugly and monstrous would have blasted his eye-sight, had he been betrayed into a glance. He felt conscious of having put himself, to a certain extent, within the influence of an unintelligible power, by the communication which he had opened with Beatrice. The wisest course would have been, if his heart were in any real danger, to quit his lodgings and Padua itself, at once; the next wiser, to have accustomed himself, as far as possible, to the familiar and day-light view of Beatrice; thus bringing her rigidly and systematically within the limits of ordinary experience. Least of all, while avoiding her sight, should Giovanni have remained so near this extraordinary being, that the proximity and possibility even of intercourse, should give a kind of substance and reality to the wild vagaries which his imagination ran riot continually in producing. Guasconti had not a deep heart—or at all events, its depths were not sounded now—but he had a quick fancy, and an ardent southern temperament, which rose every instant to a higher fever-pitch. Whether or no Beatrice possessed those terrible attributes—that fatal breath—the affinity with those so beautiful and deadly flowers—which were indicated by what Giovanni had witnessed, she had at least instilled a fierce and subtle poison into his system. It was not love, although her rich beauty was a madness to him; nor horror, even while he fancied her spirit to be imbued with the same baneful essence that seemed to pervade her physical frame; but a wild offspring of both love and horror that had each parent in it, and burned like one and shivered like the other. Giovanni knew not what to dread; still less did he know what to hope; *hope* and *dread* kept a continual warfare in his breast, alternately vanquishing one another and starting up afresh to renew the contest. Blessed are all simple emotions, be they dark or bright! It is the lurid intermixture of the two that produces the illuminating blaze of the infernal regions.

Sometimes he endeavored to assuage the fever of his spirit by a rapid walk through the streets of Padua, or beyond its gates; his footsteps kept time with the throbbings of his brain, so that the walk was apt to accelerate itself to a race. One day, he found himself arrested; his arm was seized by a portly personage who had turned back on recognizing the young man, and expended much breath in overtaking him.

"Signor Giovanni!—stay, my young friend!" cried he. "Have you forgotten me? That might well be the case, if I were as much altered as yourself."

It was Baglioni, whom Giovanni had avoided, ever since their first meeting, from a doubt that the professor's sagacity would look too deeply into his secrets. Endeavoring to recover himself, he stared forth wildly from his inner world into the outer one, and spoke like a man in a dream:

"Yes; I am Giovanni Guasconti. You are Professor Pietro Baglioni. Now let me pass!"

"Not yet—not yet, Signor Giovanni Guasconti," said the Professor, smiling, but at the same time scrutinizing the youth with an earnest glance.—"What; did I grow up side by side with your father, and shall his son pass me like a stranger, in these old streets of Padua? Stand still, Signor Giovanni; for we must have a word or two, before we part."

"Speedily, then, most worshipful Professor, speedily!" said Giovanni, with feverish impatience. "Does not your worship see that I am in haste?"

Now, while he was speaking, there came a man in black along the street, stooping and moving feebly, like a person in inferior health. His face was all overspread with a most sickly and sallow hue, but yet so pervaded with an expression of piercing and active intellect, that an observer might easily have overlooked the merely physical attributes, and have seen only this wonderful energy. As he passed, this person exchanged a cold and distant salutation with Baglioni, but fixed his eyes upon Giovanni with an intentness that seemed to bring out whatever was within him worthy of notice. Nevertheless, there was a peculiar quietness in the look, as if taking merely a speculative, not a human interest, in the young man.

"It is Doctor Rappaccini!" whispered the Professor, when the stranger had passed.—"Has he ever seen your face before?"

"Not that I know," answered Giovanni, starting at the name.

"He *has* seen you!—he must have seen you!" said Baglioni, hastily. "For some purpose or other, this man of science is making a study of you. I know that look of his! It is the same that coldly illuminates his face, as he bends over a bird, a mouse, or a butterfly, which, in pursuance of some experiment, he has killed by the perfume of a flower;—a look as deep as nature itself, but without nature's warmth of love. Signor Giovanni, I will stake my life upon it, you are the subject of one of Rappaccini's experiments!"

"Will you make a fool of me?" cried Giovanni, passionately. "*That*, Signor Professor, were an untoward experiment."

"Patience, patience!" replied the imperturbable Professor.—"I tell thee, my poor Giovanni, that Rappaccini has a scientific interest in thee. Thou hast fallen into fearful hands! And the Signora Beatrice? What part does she act in this mystery?"

But Guasconti, finding Baglioni's pertinacity intolerable, here broke away, and was gone before the Professor could again seize his arm. He looked after the young man intently, and shook his head.

"This must not be," said Baglioni to himself. "The youth is the son of my old friend, and should not come to any harm from which the arcana of medical science can preserve him. Besides, it is too insufferable an impertinence in Rappaccini, thus to snatch the bud out of my own hands, as I may say, and make use of him for his infernal experiments. This daughter of his! It shall be looked to. Perchance, most learned Rappaccini, I may foil you where you little dream of it!"

Meanwhile, Giovanni had pursued a circuitous route, and at length found himself at the door of his lodgings. As he crossed the threshold, he was met by old Lisabetta, who smirked and smiled, and was evidently desirous to attract his attention; vainly, however, as the ebullition of his feelings had momentarily subsided into a cold and dull vacuity. He turned his eyes full upon the withered face that was puckering itself into a smile, but seemed to behold it not. The old dame, therefore, laid her grasp upon his cloak.

"Signor!—Signor!" whispered she, still with a smile over the whole breadth of her visage, so that it looked not unlike a grotesque carving in wood, darkened by centuries—"Listen, Signor! There is a private entrance into the garden!"

"What do you say?" exclaimed Giovanni, turning quickly about, as if an inanimate thing should start into feverish life.—"A private entrance into Doctor Rappaccini's garden!"

"Hush! hush!—not so loud!" whispered Lisabetta, putting her hand over his mouth. "Yes; into the worshipful Doctor's garden, where you may see all his fine shrubbery. Many a young man in Padua would give gold to be admitted among those flowers."

Giovanni put a piece of gold into her hand.

"Show me the way," said he.

A surmise, probably excited by his conversation with Baglioni, crossed his mind, that this interposition of old Lisabetta might perchance be connected with the intrigue, whatever were its nature, in which the Professor seemed to suppose that Doctor Rappaccini was involving him. But such a suspicion, though it disturbed Giovanni, was inadequate to restrain him. The instant he was aware of the possibility of approaching Beatrice, it seemed an absolute necessity of his existence to do so. It mattered not whether she were angel or demon; he was irrevocably within her sphere, and must obey the law that whirled him onward, in ever lessening circles, towards a result which he did not attempt to foreshadow. And yet, strange to say, there came across him a sudden doubt, whether this intense interest on his part were not delusory—whether it were really of so deep and positive a nature as to justify him in now thrusting himself into an incalculable position—whether it were not merely the fantasy of a young man's brain, only slightly, or not at all, connected with his heart!

He paused—hesitated—turned half about—but again went on. His withered guide led him along several obscure passages, and finally undid a door, through which, as it was opened, there came the sight and sound of rustling leaves, with the broken sunshine glimmering among them. Giovanni stepped forth, and forcing himself through the entanglement of a shrub that wreathed its tendrils over the hidden entrance, he stood beneath his own window, in the open area of Doctor Rappaccini's garden.

How often is it the case, that, when impossibilities have come to pass, and dreams have condensed their misty substance into tangible realities, we find ourselves calm, and even coldly self-possessed, amid circumstances which it would have been a delirium of joy or agony to anticipate! Fate delights to thwart us thus. Passion will choose his own time to rush upon the scene, and lingers sluggishly behind, when an appropriate adjustment of events would seem to summon his appearance. So was it now with Giovanni. Day after day, his pulses had throbbed with feverish blood, at the improbable idea of an interview with Beatrice, and of standing with her, face to face, in this very garden, basking in the oriental sunshine of her beauty, and snatching from her full gaze the mystery which he deemed the riddle of his own existence. But now there was a singular and untimely equanimity within his breast. He threw a glance around the garden to discover if Beatrice or her father were present, and perceiving that he was alone, began a critical observation of the plants.

The aspect of one and all of them dissatisfied him; their gorgeousness seemed fierce, passionate, and even unnatural. There was hardly an individual shrub which a wanderer, straying by himself through a forest, would not have been startled to find growing wild, as if an unearthly face had glared at him out of the thicket. Several, also, would have shocked a delicate instinct by an appearance of artificialness, indicating that there had been such commixture, and, as it were, adultery of various vegetable species, that the production was no longer of God's making, but the monstrous offspring of man's depraved fancy, glowing with only an evil mockery of beauty. They were probably the result of experiment, which, in one or two cases, had succeeded in mingling plants individually lovely into a compound possessing the questionable and ominous character that distinguished the whole growth of the garden. In fine, Giovanni recognized but two or three plants in the collection, and those of a kind that he well knew to be poisonous. While busy with these contemplations, he heard the rustling of a silken garment, and turning, beheld Beatrice emerging from beneath the sculptured portal.

Giovanni had not considered with himself what should be his deportment; whether he should apologize for his intrusion into the garden, or assume that he was there with the privity, at least, if not the desire of Doctor Rappaccini or his daughter. But Beatrice's manner placed him at his ease, though leaving him still in doubt by what agency he had gained admittance. She came lightly along the path, and met him near the broken fountain. There was surprise in her face, but brightened by a simple and kind expression of pleasure.

"You are a connoisseur in flowers, Signor," said Beatrice with a smile, alluding to the bouquet which he had flung her from the window. "It is no marvel, therefore, if the sight of my father's rare collection has tempted you to take a nearer view. If he were here, he could tell you many strange and interesting facts as to the nature and habits of these shrubs, for he has spent a life-time in such studies, and this garden is his world."

"And yourself, lady"—observed Giovanni—"if fame says true— you, likewise, are deeply skilled in the virtues indicated by these rich blossoms, and these spicy perfumes. Would you deign to be my instructress, I should prove an apter scholar than under Signor Rappaccini himself."

"Are there such idle rumors?" asked Beatrice, with the music of a pleasant laugh. "Do people say that I am skilled in my father's science of plants? What a jest is there! No; though I have grown up among these flowers, I know no more of them than their hues and perfume; and sometimes, methinks I would fain rid myself of even that small knowledge. There are many flowers here, and those not the least brilliant, that shock and offend me, when they meet my eye. But, pray, Signor, do not believe these stories about my science. Believe nothing of me save what you see with your own eyes."

"And must I believe all that I have seen with my own eyes?" asked Giovanni pointedly, while the recollection of former scenes made him shrink. "No, Signora, you demand too little of me. Bid me believe nothing, save what comes from your own lips."

It would appear that Beatrice understood him. There came a deep flush to her cheek; but she looked full into Giovanni's eyes, and responded to his gaze of uneasy suspicion with a queen-like haughtiness.

"I do so bid you, Signor!" she replied. "Forget whatever you may have fancied in regard to me. If true to the outward senses, still it may be false in its essence. But the words of Beatrice Rappaccini's lips are true from the heart outward. Those you may believe!"

A fervor glowed in her whole aspect, and beamed upon Giovanni's consciousness like the light of truth itself. But while she spoke, there was a fragrance in the atmosphere around her, rich and delightful, though evanescent, yet which the young man, from an indefinable reluctance, scarcely dared to draw into his lungs. It might be the odor of the flowers. Could it be Beatrice's breath, which thus embalmed her words with a strange richness, as if by steeping them in her heart? A faintness passed like a shadow over Giovanni, and flitted away; he seemed to gaze through the beautiful girl's eyes into her transparent soul, and felt no more doubt or fear.

The tinge of passion that had colored Beatrice's manner vanished; she became gay, and appeared to derive a pure delight from her communion with the youth, not unlike what the maiden of a lonely island might have felt, conversing with a voyager from the civilized world. Evidently her experience of life had been confined within the limits of that garden. She talked now about matters as simple as the day-light or summer-clouds, and now asked questions in reference to the city, or Giovanni's distant home, his friends, his mother, and his sisters; questions indicating such seclusion, and such lack of familiarity with modes and forms, that Giovanni responded as if to an infant. Her spirit gushed out before him like a fresh rill, that was just catching its first glimpse of the sunlight, and wondering at the reflections of earth and sky which were flung into its bosom. There came thoughts, too, from a deep source, and fantasies of a gem-like brilliancy, as if diamonds and rubies sparkled upward among the bubbles of the fountain. Ever and anon, there gleamed across the young man's mind a sense of wonder, that he should be walking side by side with the being who had so wrought upon his imagination—whom he had idealized in such hues of terror—in whom he had positively witnessed such manifestations of dreadful attributes—that he should be conversing with Beatrice like a brother, and should find her so human and so maiden-like. But such reflections were only momentary; the effect of her character was too real, not to make itself familiar at once.

In this free intercourse, they had strayed through the garden, and now, after many turns among its avenues, were come to the shattered fountain, beside which grew the magnificent shrub with its treasury of glowing blossoms. A fragrance was diffused from it, which Giovanni recognized as identical with that which he had attributed to Beatrice's breath, but incomparably more powerful. As her eyes fell upon it, Giovanni beheld her press her hand to her bosom, as if her heart were throbbing suddenly and painfully.

"For the first time in my life," murmured she, addressing the shrub, "I had forgotten thee!"

"I remember, Signora," said Giovanni, "that you once promised to reward me with one of these living gems for the bouquet, which I had the happy boldness to fling to your feet. Permit me now to pluck it as a memorial of this interview."

He made a step towards the shrub, with extended hand. But Beatrice darted forward, uttering a shriek that went through his heart like a dagger. She caught his hand, and drew it back with the whole force of her slender figure. Giovanni felt her touch thrilling through his fibres.

"Touch it not!" exclaimed she, in a voice of agony. "Not for thy life! It is fatal!"

Then, hiding her face, she fled from him, and vanished beneath the sculptured portal. As Giovanni followed her with his eyes, he beheld the emaciated figure and pale intelligence of Doctor Rappaccini, who had been watching the scene, he knew not how long, within the shadow of the entrance.

No sooner was Guasconti alone in his chamber, than the image of Beatrice came back to his passionate musings, invested with all the witchery that had been gathering around it ever since his first glimpse of her, and now likewise imbued with a tender warmth of girlish womanhood. She was human: her nature was endowed with all gentle and feminine qualities; she was worthiest to be worshipped; she was capable, surely, on her part, of the height and heroism of love. Those tokens, which he had hitherto considered as proofs of a frightful peculiarity in her physical and moral system, were now either forgotten, or, by the subtle sophistry of passion, transmuted into a golden crown of enchantment, rendering Beatrice the more admirable, by so much as she was the more unique. Whatever had looked ugly, was now beautiful; or, if incapable of such a change, it stole away and hid itself among those shapeless half-ideas, which throng the dim region beyond the day-light of our perfect consciousness. Thus did Giovanni spend the night, nor fell asleep, until the dawn had begun to awake the slumbering flowers in Doctor Rappaccini's garden, whither his dreams doubtless led him. Up rose the sun in his due season, and flinging his beams upon the young man's eyelids, awoke him to a sense of pain. When thoroughly aroused, he became sensible of a burning and tingling agony in his hand—in his right hand—the very hand which Beatrice had grasped in her own, when he was on the point of plucking one of the gem-like flowers. On the back of that hand there was now a purple print, like that of four small fingers, and the likeness of a slender thumb upon his wrist.

Oh, how stubbornly does love—or even that cunning semblance of love which flourishes in the imagination, but strikes no depth of root into the heart—how stubbornly does it hold its faith, until the moment come, when it is doomed to vanish into thin mist! Giovanni wrapt a handkerchief about his head, and wondered what evil thing had stung him, and soon forgot his pain in a reverie of Beatrice.

After the first interview, a second was in the inevitable course of what we call fate. A third; a fourth; and a meeting with Beatrice in the garden was no longer an incident in Giovanni's daily life, but the whole space in which he might be said to live; for the anticipation and memory of that ecstatic hour made up the remainder. Nor was it otherwise with the daughter of Rappaccini. She watched for the youth's appearance, and flew to his side with confidence as unreserved as if they had been playmates from early infancy—as if they were such playmates still. If, by any unwonted chance, he failed to come at the appointed moment, she stood beneath the window, and sent up the rich sweetness of her tones to float around him in his chamber, and echo and reverberate throughout his heart —"Giovanni! Giovanni! Why tarriest thou? Come down!"—And down he hastened into that Eden of poisonous flowers.

But, with all this intimate familiarity, there was still a reserve in Beatrice's demeanor, so rigidly and invariably sustained, that the idea of infringing it scarcely occurred to his imagination. By all appreciable signs, they loved; they had looked love, with eyes that conveyed the holy secret from the depths of one soul into the depths of the other, as if it were too sacred to be whispered by the way; they had even spoken love, in those gushes of passion when their spirits darted forth in articulated breath, like tongues of long-hidden flame; and yet there had been no seal of lips, no clasp of hands, nor any slightest caress, such as love claims and hallows. He had never touched one of the gleaming ringlets of her hair; her garment—so marked was the physical barrier between them—had never been waved against him by a breeze. On the few occasions when Giovanni had seemed tempted to overstep the limit, Beatrice grew so sad, so stern, and withal wore such a look of desolate separation, shuddering at itself, that not a spoken word was requisite to repel him. At such times, he was startled at the horrible suspicions that rose, monster-like, out of the caverns of his heart, and stared him in the face; his love grew thin and faint as the morning-mist; his doubts alone had substance. But when Beatrice's face brightened again, after the momentary shadow, she was transformed at once from the mysterious, questionable being, whom he had watched with so much awe and horror; she was now the beautiful and unsophisticated girl, whom he felt that his spirit knew with a certainty beyond all other knowledge.

A considerable time had now passed since Giovanni's last meeting with Baglioni. One morning, however, he was disagreeably surprised by a visit from the Professor, whom he had scarcely thought of for whole weeks, and would willingly have forgotten still longer. Given up, as he had long been, to a pervading excitement, he could tolerate no companions, except upon condition of their perfect sympathy with his present state of feeling. Such sympathy was not to be expected from Professor Baglioni.

The visitor chatted carelessly, for a few moments, about the gossip of the city and the University, and then took up another topic.

"I have been reading an old classic author lately," said he, "and met with a story[3] that strangely interested me. Possibly you may remember it. It is of an Indian prince, who sent a beautiful woman as a present to Alexander the Great. She was as lovely as the dawn, and gorgeous as the sunset; but what especially distinguished her was a certain rich perfume in her breath—richer than a garden of Persian roses. Alexander, as was natural to a youthful conqueror, fell in love at first sight with this magnificent stranger. But a certain sage physician, happening to be present, discovered a terrible secret in regard to her."

"And what was that?" asked Giovanni, turning his eyes downward to avoid those of the Professor.

"That this lovely woman," continued Baglioni, with emphasis, "had been nourished with poisons from her birth upward, until her whole nature was so imbued with them, that she herself had become the deadliest poison in existence. Poison was her element of life. With that rich perfume of her breath, she blasted the very air. Her love would have been poison!—her embrace death! Is not this a marvellous tale?"

"A childish fable," answered Giovanni, nervously starting from his chair. "I marvel how your worship finds time to read such nonsense, among your graver studies."

"By the by," said the Professor, looking uneasily about him, "what singular fragrance is this in your apartment? Is it the perfume of your gloves? It is faint, but delicious, and yet, after all, by no means agreeable. Were I to breathe it long, methinks it would make me ill. It is like the breath of a flower—but I see no flowers in the chamber."

"Nor are there any," replied Giovanni, who had turned pale as the Professor spoke; "nor, I think, is there any fragrance, except in your worship's imagination. Odors, being a sort of element combined of the sensual and the spiritual, are apt to deceive us in this manner. The recollection of a perfume—the bare idea of it—may easily be mistaken for a present reality."

"Aye; but my sober imagination does not often play such tricks," said Baglioni; "and were I to fancy any kind of odor, it would be that of some vile apothecary drug, wherewith my fingers are likely enough to be imbued. Our worshipful friend Rappaccini, as I have heard, tinctures his medicaments with odors richer than those of Araby. Doubtless, likewise, the fair and learned Signora Beatrice would minister to her patients with draughts as sweet as a maiden's breath. But wo to him that sips them!"

Giovanni's face evinced many contending emotions. The tone in which the Professor alluded to the pure and lovely daughter of

3. In Sir Thomas Browne's *Vulgar Errors* (1646) or elsewhere.

Rappaccini was a torture to his soul; and yet, the intimation of a view of her character, opposite to his own, gave instantaneous distinctness to a thousand dim suspicions, which now grinned at him like so many demons. But he strove hard to quell them, and to respond to Baglioni with a true lover's perfect faith.

"Signor Professor," said he, "you were my father's friend—perchance, too, it is your purpose to act a friendly part towards his son. I would fain feel nothing towards you, save respect and deference. But I pray you to observe, Signor, that there is one subject on which we must not speak. You know not the Signora Beatrice. You cannot, therefore, estimate the wrong—the blasphemy, I may even say—that is offered to her character by a light or injurious word."

"Giovanni!—my poor Giovanni!" answered the Professor, with a calm expression of pity, "I know this wretched girl far better than yourself. You shall hear the truth in respect to the poisoner Rappaccini, and his poisonous daughter. Yes; poisonous as she is beautiful! Listen; for even should you do violence to my grey hairs, it shall not silence me. That old fable of the Indian woman has become a truth, by the deep and deadly science of Rappaccini, and in the person of the lovely Beatrice!"

Giovanni groaned and hid his face.

"Her father," continued Baglioni, "was not restrained by natural affection from offering up his child, in this horrible manner, as the victim of his insane zeal for science. For—let us do him justice—he is as true a man of science as ever distilled his own heart in an alembic. What, then, will be your fate? Beyond a doubt, you are selected as the material of some new experiment. Perhaps the result is to be death—perhaps a fate more awful still! Rappaccini, with what he calls the interest of science before his eyes, will hesitate at nothing."

"It is a dream!" muttered Giovanni to himself, "surely it is a dream!"

"But," resumed the professor, "be of good cheer, son of my friend! It is not yet too late for the rescue. Possibly, we may even succeed in bringing back this miserable child within the limits of ordinary nature, from which her father's madness has estranged her. Behold this little silver vase! It was wrought by the hands of the renowned Benvenuto Cellini,[4] and is well worthy to be a love-gift to the fairest dame in Italy. But its contents are invaluable. One little sip of this antidote would have rendered the most virulent poisons of the Borgias[5] innocuous. Doubt not that it will be as efficacious against those of Rappaccini. Bestow the vase, and the precious liquid within it, on your Beatrice, and hopefully await the result."

Baglioni laid a small, exquisitely wrought silver phial on the

4. Benvenuto Cellini (1500–71), Italian goldsmith and sculptor.
5. Renaissance Italian family influential in church and government and notorious for cruelty and licentiousness.

table, and withdrew, leaving what he had said to produce its effect upon the young man's mind.

"We will thwart Rappaccini yet!" thought he, chuckling to himself, as he descended the stairs. "But, let us confess the truth of him, he is a wonderful man!—a wonderful man indeed! A vile empiric, however, in his practice, and therefore not to be tolerated by those who respect the good old rules of the medical profession!"

Throughout Giovanni's whole acquaintance with Beatrice, he had occasionally, as we have said, been haunted by dark surmises as to her character. Yet, so thoroughly had she made herself felt by him as a simple, natural, most affectionate and guileless creature, that the image now held up by Professor Baglioni, looked as strange and incredible, as if it were not in accordance with his own original conception. True, there were ugly recollections connected with his first glimpses of the beautiful girl; he could not quite forget the bouquet that withered in her grasp, and the insect that perished amid the sunny air, by no ostensible agency, save the fragrance of her breath. These incidents, however, dissolving in the pure light of her character, had no longer the efficacy of facts, but were acknowledged as mistaken fantasies, by whatever testimony of the senses they might appear to be substantiated. There is something truer and more real, than what we can see with the eyes, and touch with the finger. On such better evidence, had Giovanni founded his confidence in Beatrice, though rather by the necessary force of her high attributes, than by any deep and generous faith, on his part. But, now, his spirit was incapable of sustaining itself at the height to which the early enthusiasm of passion had exalted it; he fell down, grovelling among earthly doubts, and defiled therewith the pure whiteness of Beatrice's image. Not that he gave her up; he did but distrust. He resolved to institute some decisive test that should satisfy him, once for all, whether there were those dreadful peculiarities in her physical nature, which could not be supposed to exist without some corresponding monstrosity of soul. His eyes, gazing down afar, might have deceived him as to the lizard, the insect, and the flowers. But if he could witness, at the distance of a few paces, the sudden blight of one fresh and healthful flower in Beatrice's hand, there would be room for no further question. With this idea, he hastened to the florist's, and purchased a bouquet that was still gemmed with the morning dew-drops.

It was now the customary hour of his daily interview with Beatrice. Before descending into the garden, Giovanni failed not to look at his figure in the mirror; a vanity to be expected in a beautiful young man, yet, as displaying itself at that troubled and feverish moment, the token of a certain shallowness of feeling and insincerity of character. He did gaze, however, and said to himself, that his features had never before possessed so rich a grace, nor his eyes such vivacity, nor his cheeks so warm a hue of superabundant life.

"At least," thought he, "her poison has not yet insinuated itself into my system. I am no flower to perish in her grasp!"

With that thought, he turned his eyes on the bouquet, which he had never once laid aside from his hand. A thrill of indefinable horror shot through his frame, on perceiving that those dewy flowers were already beginning to droop; they wore the aspect of things that had been fresh and lovely, yesterday. Giovanni grew white as marble, and stood motionless before the mirror, staring at his own reflection there, as at the likeness of something frightful. He remembered Baglioni's remark about the fragrance that seemed to pervade the chamber. It must have been the poison in his breath! Then he shuddered—shuddered at himself! Recovering from his stupor, he began to watch, with curious eye, a spider that was busily at work, hanging its web from the antique cornice of the apartment, crossing and re-crossing the artful system of interwoven lines, as vigorous and active a spider as ever dangled from an old ceiling. Giovanni bent towards the insect, and emitted a deep, long breath. The spider suddenly ceased its toil; the web vibrated with a tremor originating in the body of the small artizan. Again Giovanni sent forth a breath, deeper, longer, and imbued with a venomous feeling out of his heart; he knew not whether he were wicked or only desperate. The spider made a convulsive gripe with his limbs, and hung dead across the window.

"Accursed! Accursed!" muttered Giovanni, addressing himself. "Hast thou grown so poisonous, that this deadly insect perishes by the breath?"

At that moment, a rich, sweet voice came floating up from the garden:—

"Giovanni! Giovanni! It is past the hour! Why tarriest thou! Come down!"

"Yes," muttered Giovanni again. "She is the only being whom my breath may not slay! Would that it might!"

He rushed down, and in an instant, was standing before the bright and loving eyes of Beatrice. A moment ago, his wrath and despair had been so fierce that he could have desired nothing so much as to wither her by a glance. But, with her actual presence, there came influences which had too real an existence to be at once shaken off; recollections of the delicate and benign power of her feminine nature, which had so often enveloped him in a religious calm; recollections of many a holy and passionate outgush of her heart, when the pure fountain had been unsealed from its depths, and made visible in its transparency to his mental eye; recollections which, had Giovanni known how to estimate them, would have assured him that all this ugly mystery was but an earthly illusion, and that, whatever mist of evil might seem to have gathered over her, the real Beatrice was a heavenly angel. Incapable as he was of such high faith, still her presence had not utterly lost its magic. Giovanni's rage was quelled into an aspect of sullen insensibility. Beatrice, with a quick spiritual sense, immediately felt that there was a gulf of blackness between them, which neither he nor she could pass. They walked on together, sad and silent, and came thus to the marble fountain, and to its pool of water on the ground, in the midst of which grew the shrub that bore gem-like blossoms. Giovanni was affrighted at the eager enjoyment—the appetite, as it were—with which he found himself inhaling the fragrance of the flowers.

"Beatrice," asked he abruptly, "whence came this shrub?"

"My father created it," answered she, with simplicity.

"Created it! created it!" repeated Giovanni. "What mean you, Beatrice?"

"He is a man fearfully acquainted with the secrets of nature," replied Beatrice; "and, at the hour when I first drew breath, this plant sprang from the soil, the offspring of his science, of his intellect, while I was but his earthly child. "Approach it not!" continued she, observing with terror that Giovanni was drawing nearer to the shrub. "It has qualities that you little dream of. But I, dearest Giovanni,—I grew up and blossomed with the plant, and was nourished with its breath. It was my sister, and I loved it with a human affection: for—alas! hast thou not suspected it? there was an awful doom."

Here Giovanni frowned so darkly upon her that Beatrice paused and trembled. But her faith in his tenderness re-assured her, and made her blush that she had doubted for an instant.

"There was an awful doom," she continued,—"the effect of my father's fatal love of science—which estranged me from all society of any kind. Until Heaven sent thee, dearest Giovanni, Oh! how lonely was thy poor Beatrice!"

"Was it a hard doom?" asked Giovanni, fixing his eyes upon her.

"Only of late have I known how hard it was," answered she tenderly. "Oh, yes; but my heart was torpid, and therefore quiet."

Giovanni's rage broke forth from his sullen gloom like a lightning-flash out of a dark cloud.

"Accursed one!" cried he, with venomous scorn and anger. "And finding thy solitude wearisome, thou hast severed me, likewise, from all the warmth of life, and enticed me into thy region of unspeakable horror!"

"Giovanni!" exclaimed Beatrice, turning her large bright eyes upon his face. The force of his words had not found its way into her mind; she was merely wonder-struck.

"Yes, poisonous thing!" repeated Giovanni, beside himself with passion. "Thou has done it! Thou has blasted me! Thou hast filled my veins with poison! Thou hast made me as hateful, as ugly, as loathsome and deadly a creature as thyself,—a world's wonder of hideous monstrosity! Now—if our breath be happily as fatal to ourselves as to all others—let us join our lips in one kiss of unutterable hatred, and so die!"

"What has befallen me?" murmured Beatrice, with a low moan out of her heart. "Holy Virgin pity me, a poor heart-broken child!"

"Thou! Dost thou pray?" cried Giovanni, still with the same fiendish scorn. "Thy very prayers, as they come from thy lips, taint the atmosphere with death. Yes, yes; let us pray! Let us to church, and dip our fingers in the holy water at the portal! They that come after us will perish as by a pestilence. Let us sign crosses in the air! It will be scattering curses abroad in the likeness of holy symbols!"

"Giovanni," said Beatrice calmly, for her grief was beyond passion, "why dost thou join thyself with me thus in those terrible words? I, it is true, am the horrible thing thou namest me. But thou!—what hast thou to do, save with one other shudder at my hideous misery, to go forth out of the garden and mingle with thy race, and forget that there ever crawled on earth such a monster as poor Beatrice?"

"Dost thou pretend ignorance?" asked Giovanni, scowling upon her. "Behold! This power have I gained from the pure daughter of Rappaccini!"

There was a swarm of summer-insects flitting through the air, in search of the food promised by the flower-odors of the fatal garden. They circled round Giovanni's head, and were evidently attracted towards him by the same influence which had drawn them, for an instant, within the sphere of several of the shrubs. He sent forth a breath among them, and smiled bitterly at Beatrice, as at least a score of the insects fell dead upon the ground.

"I see it! I see it!" shrieked Beatrice. "It is my father's fatal science? No, no, Giovanni; it was not I! Never, never! I dreamed only to love thee, and be with thee a little time, and so to let thee pass away, leaving but thine image in mine heart. For, Giovanni—believe it—though my body be nourished with poison, my spirit is God's creature, and craves love as its daily food. But my father!—he has united us in this fearful sympathy. Yes; spurn me!—tread upon me!—kill me! Oh, what is death, after such words as thine? But it was not I! Not for a world of bliss would I have done it!"

Giovanni's passion had exhausted itself in its outburst from his lips. There now came across a sense, mournful, and not without tenderness, of the intimate and peculiar relationship between Beatrice and himself. They stood, as it were, in an utter solitude, which would be made none the less solitary by the densest throng of human life. Ought not, then, the desert of humanity around them to press this insulated pair close together? If they should be cruel to one another, who was there to be kind to them? Besides, thought Giovanni, might there not still be a hope of his returning within the limits of ordinary nature, and leading Beatrice—the redeemed Beatrice—by the hand? Oh, weak, and selfish, and unworthy spirit, that could dream of an earthly union and earthly happiness as possible, after such deep love had been so bitterly wronged as was Beatrice's love by Giovanni's blighting words! No, no; there could be no such hope. She must pass heavily, with that broken heart, across the borders—she must bathe her hurts in some fount of Paradise, and forget her grief in the light of immortality—and *there* be well!

But Giovanni did not know it.

"Dear Beatrice," said he, approaching her, while she shrank away, as always at his approach, but now with a different impulse— "dearest Beatrice, our fate is not yet so desperate. Behold! There is a medicine, potent, as a wise physician has assured me, and almost divine in its efficacy. It is composed of ingredients the most opposite to those by which thy awful father has brought this calamity upon thee and me. It is distilled of blessed herbs. Shall we not quaff it together, and thus be purified from evil?"

"Give it me!" said Beatrice, extending her hand to receive the little silver phial which Giovanni took from his bosom. She added, with a peculiar emphasis; "I will drink—but do thou await the result."

She put Baglioni's antidote to her lips; and, at the same moment, the figure of Rappaccini emerged from the portal, and came slowly towards the marble fountain. As he drew near, the pale man of science seemed to gaze with a triumphant expression at the beautiful youth and maiden, as might an artist who should spend his life in achieving a picture or a group of statuary, and finally be satisfied with his success. He paused—his bent form grew erect with conscious power, he spread out his hand over them, in the attitude of a father imploring a blessing upon his children. But those were the same hands that had thrown poison into the stream of their lives! Giovanni trembled. Beatrice shuddered nervously, and pressed her hand upon her heart.

"My daughter," said Rappaccini, "thou art no longer lonely in the world! Pluck one of those precious gems from thy sister shrub, and bid thy bridegroom wear it in his bosom. It will not harm him now! My science, and the sympathy between thee and him, have so wrought within his system, that he now stands apart from common men, as thou dost, daughter of my pride and triumph, from ordinary women. Pass on, then, through the world, most dear to one another, and dreadful to all besides!"

"My father," said Beatrice, feebly—and still, as she spoke, she kept her hand upon her heart—"wherefore didst thou inflict this miserable doom upon thy child?"

"Miserable!" exclaimed Rappaccini. "What mean you, foolish girl? Dost thou deem it misery to be endowed with marvellous gifts, against which no power nor strength could avail an enemy? Misery, to be able to quell the mightiest with a breath? Misery, to be as terrible as thou art beautiful? Wouldst thou, then, have preferred the condition of a weak woman, exposed to all evil, and capable of none?"

"I would fain have been loved, not feared," murmured Beatrice, sinking down upon the ground.—"But now it matters not; I am going, father, where the evil, which thou hast striven to mingle with my being, will pass away like a dream—like the fragrance of these poisonous flowers, which will no longer taint my breath among the flowers of Eden. Farewell, Giovanni! Thy words of hatred are like lead within my heart—but they, too, will fall away as I ascend. Oh, was there not, from the first, more poison in thy nature than in mine?"

To Beatrice—so radically had her earthly part been wrought upon by Rappaccini's skill—as poison had been life, so the powerful antidote was death. And thus the poor victim of man's ingenuity and of thwarted nature, and of the fatality that attends all such efforts of perverted wisdom, perished there, at the feet of her father and Giovanni. Just at that moment, Professor Pietro Baglioni looked forth from the window, and called loudly, in a tone of triumph mixed with horror, to the thunder-stricken man of science:

"Rappaccini! Rappaccini! And is *this* the upshot of your experiment?"

1844

HENRY WADSWORTH LONGFELLOW
1807–1882

Longfellow was born in Portland, Maine (then still a part of Massachusetts), on February 27, 1807, and died on March 24, 1882, in Cambridge, Massachusetts, the most beloved American poet of his time. His father sent him to Bowdoin, thinking that he would become a lawyer. Instead, Longfellow became so proficient a student of languages that Bowdoin created for him a professorship of modern languages, then one of only a handful in the country. With support from his father, Longfellow studied languages in Europe for three years before taking up his work at Bowdoin in 1829. In Spain, Washington Irving was hospitable, and Longfellow's prose romance *Outre-Mer* (1833–35) was in loving imitation of *The Sketch-Book*. Having concentrated on the Romance languages during his first European stay,

Longfellow returned to perfect himself in Germanic languages, a condition for his becoming a professor at Harvard late in 1836. He took teaching seriously, although in the early years he spent most of his time instilling the rudiments of foreign languages (for which he wrote and published his own textbooks) without being able to teach the literatures. Later, at Harvard, he taught an extraordinary range of European literatures of many periods and thereby became an incalculable force in American cultural life. It would be hard, also, to overestimate the importance of his anthology *The Poets and Poetry of Europe* (1845) in bringing home to the ordinary reader the rich variety of European literatures. His own poetry became a means of teaching readers of his day something of the possible range of poetic subject matter and techniques, ancient, medieval, and modern. Irving had been notably successful in domesticating European subject matter while employing a British prose style; now Longfellow domesticated European meters, as in his adaptation of classical Greek meters to tell the story of Evangeline Belle-fontaine, set in the recent North American past, or in using Finnish folk meter in his celebration of American Indian legends in *Hiawatha*. Longfellow became a great teacher of the masses. If his worst fault is that he made poetry seem so easy to write that anyone could do it, his greatest virtue is that he made poetry seem worth reading and worth writing.

Longfellow married in 1831, during his professorship at Bowdoin, but in 1835, during his second European trip, his wife died after miscarrying. Longfellow stayed on, fulfilling his commitment to Harvard, and before he returned home he had met Fanny Appleton, the Boston heiress who was to become his second wife. She was slow to return his affection, and he embarrassed her by the transparent account of their meeting in the prose romance *Hyperion* (1839), but after their marriage in 1843 their life was idyllic. Longfellow's father-in-law bought the couple, as a wedding gift, Craigie House in Cambridge, a mansion George Washington had used as headquarters and where Longfellow himself had been renting rooms. Their life was elegant. Emerson, who lived amply enough in Concord, was intimidated: "If Socrates were here, we could go and talk with him; but Longfellow we cannot go and talk with; there is a palace, and servants, and a row of bottles of different colored wines, and wine glasses, and fine coats." But the sumptuousness proved supportive and encouraging to Longfellow's poetry and to his work at Harvard until he resigned in 1854. Popular as he was, Longfellow could not make a living from his poetry. In 1855 and 1856, for instance, the phenomenal sales of *Hiawatha* brought his total earnings from poetry to around $3,700 and $7,400, but in the 1840s and 1850s his average annual income from poetry hardly exceeded his Harvard salary of $1,500 ($1,800 after 1845). In 1861 Mrs. Longfellow was fatally burned as she was sealing up locks of her daughters' hair. In his grief Longfellow turned to translating the entire *Divine Comedy* of Dante, making the labor the occasion for regular meetings with friends such as James Russell Lowell and the young William Dean Howells, who had lived in Venice. Longfellow's last decades were uneventful, except for one final visit to Europe in 1868–69, during which Queen Victoria gave him a private audience. His seventy-fifth birthday was celebrated nationally. Of his death his brother and official biographer wrote: "The long, busy, blameless life was ended. The loneliness of separation was over. He was dead. But the world was better and happier for his having lived."

A Psalm of Life[1]

'Life that shall send
A challenge to its end,
And when it comes, say, 'Welcome, friend.'[2]

WHAT THE HEART OF THE YOUNG MAN SAID
TO THE PSALMIST

I

Tell me not, in mournful numbers,[3]
　　Life is but an empty dream!
For the soul is dead that slumbers,
　　And things are not what they seem.

II

Life is real—life is earnest—　　　　　　　5
　　And the grave is not its goal:
Dust thou art, to dust returnest,
　　Was not spoken of the soul.

III

Not enjoyment, and not sorrow,
　　Is our destin'd end or way;　　　　　　10
But to *act*, that each to-morrow
　　Find us farther than to-day.

IV

Art is long, and time is fleeting,[4]
　　And our hearts, though stout and brave,
Still, like muffled drums, are beating　　　15
　　Funeral marches to the grave.

V

In the world's broad field of battle,
　　In the bivouac of Life,
Be not like dumb, driven cattle!
　　Be a hero in the strife!　　　　　　　20

VI

Trust no Future, howe'er pleasant!
　　Let the dead Past bury its dead!
Act—act in the glorious Present!
　　Heart within, and God o'er head!

VII

Lives of great men all remind us　　　　　25
　　We can make *our* lives sublime,
And, departing, leave behind us
　　Footsteps on the sands of time.

1. The text is that of the first publication, in the *Knickerbocker or New-York Monthly Magazine* (September, 1838). The poem was collected in *Voices of the Night* (Cambridge: John Owen, 1839).
2. Slightly misquoted from *Wishes to His Supposed Mistress* by the English poet Richard Crashaw (c. 1613–49). Longfellow included the Crashaw poem in a volume he edited, *The Waif: A Collec-* *tion of Poems* (Cambridge: John Owen, 1845).
3. Meters, rhythms.
4. A paraphrase of Seneca's complaint, "Vita brevis est, ars longa" (*De Brevitate vitae* 1, 1). The meaning of "ars" or "art" is clearer in Chaucer's *The Parliament of Fowls*, line 1: "The lyf so short, the craft so long to lerne."

VIII

Footsteps, that, perhaps another,
        Sailing o'er life's solemn main,
A forlorn and shipwreck'd brother,
        Seeing, shall take heart again.   30

IX

Let us then be up and doing,
        With a heart for any fate;
Still achieving, still pursuing,   35
        Learn to labor and to wait.

                                        1838, 1839

Mezzo Cammin[1]

Boppard on the Rhine. August 25, 1842

Half of my life is gone, and I have let
    The years slip from me and have not fulfilled
    The aspiration of my youth, to build
    Some tower of song with lofty parapet.
Not indolence, nor pleasure, nor the fret   5
    Of restless passions that would not be stilled,
    But sorrow, and a care that almost killed,
    Kept me from what I may accomplish yet;
Though, half-way up the hill, I see the Past
    Lying beneath me with its sounds and sights,—   10
    A city in the twilight dim and vast,
With smoking roofs, soft bells, and gleaming lights,—
    And hear above me on the autumnal blast
    The cataract of Death far thundering from the heights.

1842   1886

My Lost Youth[1]

Often I think of the beautiful town
    That is seated by the sea;
Often in thought go up and down
    The pleasant streets of that dear old town,

1. The text is that of the first printing in *Life of Henry Wadsworth Longfellow*, ed. Samuel Longfellow (Boston: Ticknor and Company, 1886), Vol. 1, p. 404. The sonnet was evidently too personal an assessment for Longfellow to publish it in his lifetime. The title comes from the opening line of Dante's *Inferno*, "Nel mezzo del cammin di nostra vita," "Midway in the journey of our life" (i.e., 35 years old, half the Biblical ideal of threescore years and 10, according to Psalm 90.10).

1. Longfellow wrote this poem about his hometown of Portland, Maine, in March, 1855, at Cambridge, deriving the refrain from lines in John Scheffer's *The History of Lapland* (1674): "A Youth's desire is the desire of the wind, / All his essaies / Are long delaies, / No issue can they find." ("Essaies" or "essays": attempts; "issue": outlet.) The text is that of the first printing in *Putnam's Monthly Magazine*, Vol. 6 (August, 1855). It was reprinted in *The Courtship of Miles Standish and Other Poems* (Boston: Ticknor and Fields, 1858).

And my youth comes back to me.
  And a verse of a Lapland song
  Is haunting my memory still:
"A boy's will is the wind's will,
And the thoughts of youth are long, long thoughts."   5

I can see the shadowy lines of its trees,   10
  And catch, in sudden gleams,
The sheen of the far-surrounding seas,
And islands that were the Hesperides[2]
  Of all my boyish dreams.
    And the burden of that old song,   15
    It murmurs and whispers still:
"A boy's will is the wind's will,
And the thoughts of youth are long, long thoughts."

I remember the black wharves and the slips,
  And the sea-tides tossing free;   20
And Spanish sailors with bearded lips,
And the beauty and mystery of the ships,
  And the magic of the sea.
    And the voice of that wayward song
    Is singing and saying still: 25
"A boy's will is the wind's will,
And the thoughts of youth are long, long thoughts."

I remember the bulwarks by the shore,
  And the fort upon the hill;
The sun-rise gun, with its hollow roar,   30
The drum-beat repeated o'er and o'er,
  And the bugle wild and shrill.
    And the music of that old song
    Throbs in my memory still:
"A boy's will is the wind's will,   35
And the thoughts of youth are long, long thoughts."

I remember the sea-fight far away,
  How it thundered o'er the tide![3]
And the dead captains, as they lay
In their graves, o'erlooking the tranquil bay,   40
  Where they in battle died.
    And the sound of that mournful song
    Goes through me with a thrill:
"A boy's will is the wind's will,
And the thoughts of youth are long, long thoughts."   45

---

2. In Greek mythology, fabled islands where the golden apples grew.
3. The American *Enterprise* and the British *Boxer* fought near Portland in 1813. Both captains were killed and carried ashore for burial.

I can see the breezy dome of groves,
   The shadows of Deering's Woods;
And the friendships old and the early loves
Come back with a Sabbath sound, as of doves
   In quiet neighborhoods.   50
      And the verse of that sweet old song,
        It flutters and murmurs still:
"A boy's will is the wind's will,
And the thoughts of youth are long, long thoughts."

I remember the gleams and glooms that dart   55
   Across the schoolboy's brain;
The song and the silence in the heart,
That in part are prophecies, and in part
   Are longings wild and vain.
      And the voice of that fitful song   60
        Sings on, and is never still:
"A boy's will is the wind's will,
And the thoughts of youth are long, long thoughts."

There are things of which I may not speak;
   There are dreams that cannot die;   65
There are thoughts that make the strong heart weak,
And bring a pallor into the cheek,
   And a mist before the eye.
      And the words of that fatal song
        Come over me like a chill: 70
"A boy's will is the wind's will,
And the thoughts of youth are long, long thoughts."

Strange to me now are the forms I meet
   When I visit the dear old town;
But the native air is pure and sweet,   75
And the trees that o'ershadow each well-known street,
   As they balance up and down,
      Are singing the beautiful song,
        Are sighing and whispering still:
"A boy's will is the wind's will,   80
And the thoughts of youth are long, long thoughts."

And Deering's Woods are fresh and fair,
   And with joy that is almost pain
My heart goes back to wander there,
And among the dreams of the days that were,   85
   I find my lost youth again.
      And the strange and beautiful song,
        The groves are repeating it still:
"A boy's will is the wind's will,
And the thoughts of youth are long, long thoughts."   90
1855   1855

JOHN GREENLEAF WHITTIER
1807–1892

John Greenleaf Whittier was born on December 17, 1807, on a farm near Haverhill, Massachusetts, of a Quaker family. No longer persecuted in New England, Quakers were still a people apart, and Whittier grew up with a sense of being different from most of his neighbors. Labor on the debt-ridden farm overstrained his health in adolescence, and thereafter throughout his long life he suffered from intermittent physical collapses. At fourteen, having had only meager education in a household suspicious of non-Quaker literature, he found in the Scottish poet Robert Burns a model for imitation, one using a regional dialect, dealing with homely subjects, and displaying a strong social conscience. His first poem was published in 1826 in a local newspaper run by another young man, William Lloyd Garrison, whose dedication to the antislavery movement was to affect Whittier's life profoundly. In 1827 Garrison helped persuade Whittier's father that the young poet deserved more education, and Whittier supported himself through two terms at Haverhill Academy. During this time and later Whittier was near serious courtships, but like many of his relatives, he never married; among the obstacles were his Quakerism, his poverty, and his commitment to abolitionism. In 1836, six years after his father's death, Whittier and his mother and sisters moved from the farm to the house in nearby Amesbury, Massachusetts, which he owned until his death.

In his twenties Whittier became editor of various newspapers, some of regional importance. He was elected for a term to the Massachusetts legislature (1835) and became a behind-the-scenes force in the Whig party, and later in the antislavery Liberty party, which he helped to found in 1839. The turning point in his career came in 1833 with the publication of his abolitionist manifesto *Justice and Expediency*, in which Whittier concluded that there was only one practicable and just scheme of emancipation: "Immediate abolition of slavery; an immediate acknowledgment of the great truth, that man cannot hold property in man; an immediate surrender of baneful prejudice to Christian love; an immediate practical obedience to the command of Jesus Christ: 'Whatsoever ye would that men should do unto you, do ye even so to them.'" Over the next three decades Whittier paid for his principles in many ways, some subtle, some as overt as being mobbed and stoned in 1835. The climactic danger came in 1838 when Whittier, in disguise, joined a mob to save some of his papers as his office was ransacked and burned.

From the 1830s through the 1850s Whittier was a working editor associated with abolitionist papers, becoming the sort of man he was to describe in *The Tent on the Beach* (1867): "a dreamer born, / Who, with a mission to fulfil, / Had left the Muses' haunts to turn / The crank of an opinion-mill, / Making his rustic reed of song / A weapon in the war with wrong." Yet he continued to write about his own region, one legacy from his family being a rich oral history. His first book, *Legends of New England* (1831), had included stories in both prose and poetry. His first book of poetry was *Lays of My Home* (1843), and the prose *Supernatural-*

ism of New England followed in 1847. *Leaves from Margaret Smith's Journal* (1849) is a fictional re-creation of colonial life in the form of the diary of a young woman. Through his fictional and historical prose and through his poetry Whittier was setting a very early example of faithful treatment of American village and rural life which later local colorists and regionalists were to follow: the elderly Whittier's paternal interest in the career of Sarah Orne Jewett epitomizes this influence. But from the beginning a crucial problem for Whittier had been how to be true to the occasional beauty of rural life without portraying it in the sentimental manner which prevailed at the time. Whittier succeeded best in some late poems, especially *Snow-Bound* (1866) and the "Prelude" to *Among the Hills* (1868). Whittier's reputation began undergoing a change in the late 1850s, when abolitionism had ceased to be almost as much abhorred in the North as in the South; partly the new favor he received was a result of the founding in 1857 of the *Atlantic Monthly*, which was always hospitable to his poems, humorous folk legends as well as militant odes. *Snow-Bound* brought Whittier extraordinary acclaim and immediate financial security; although one of the themes of the poem was his sense of his own approaching death, Whittier ironically lived another quarter century during which he was revered as a great American poet. He died on September 7, 1892.

Ichabod![1]

So fallen! so lost! the light withdrawn
    Which once he wore!
The glory from his gray hairs gone
    Forevermore!

Revile him not—the Tempter hath   5
    A snare for all;
And pitying tears, not scorn and wrath,
    Befit his fall!

Oh! dumb be passion's stormy rage,
    When he who might   10
Have lighted up and led his age,
    Falls back in night.

Scorn! would the angels laugh, to mark
    A bright soul driven,
Fiend-goaded, down the endless dark,   15
    From hope and heaven!

Let not the land, once proud of him,
    Insult him now,

1. *Ichabod!* is an attack on the statesman Daniel Webster, whose championing of the Fugitive Slave Bill (the part of the Compromise of 1850 which provided that northern states must return runaway slaves caught within their borders) made him anathema to the abolitionists. The title is from 1 Samuel 4.21: "And she named the child Ichabod, saying, The glory is departed from Israel." The text is that of the first printing in *Songs of Labor, and Other Poems* (1850).

Nor brand with deeper shame his dim,
    Dishonored brow.   20

But let its humbled sons, instead,
    From sea to lake,
A long lament, as for the dead,
    In sadness make.

Of all we loved and honored, nought   25
    Save power remains—
A fallen angel's pride of thought,
    Still strong in chains.

All else is gone; from those great eyes
    The soul has fled: 30
When faith is lost, when honor dies,
    The man is dead!

Then, pay the reverence of old days
    To his dead fame;
Walk backward, with averted gaze,   35
And hide the shame![2]

1850

Prelude to *Among the Hills*[1]

Along the roadside, like the flowers of gold
That tawny Incas[2] for their gardens wrought,
Heavy with sunshine droops the golden-rod,
And the red pennons of the cardinal-flowers
Hang motionless upon their upright staves.   5
The sky is hot and hazy, and the wind,
Wing-weary with its long flight from the south,
Unfelt; yet, closely scanned, yon maple leaf
With faintest motion, as one stirs in dreams,
Confesses it. The locust by the wall   10
Stabs the noon-silence with his sharp alarm.
A single hay-cart down the dusty road
Creaks slowly, with its driver fast asleep
On the load's top. Against the neighboring hill,
Huddled along the stone wall's shady side,   15
The sheep show white, as if a snow-drift still
Defied the dog-star.[3] Through the open door

2. By this allusion to Genesis 9.20–25 Whittier equates Webster's shame to that of Noah after the flood, who in drunkenness sprawled naked in his cave.
1. From the first printing, in *Among the Hills, and Other Poems* (Boston: Fields, Osgood, & Co., 1869).

2. An allusion to the belief that gold was so plentiful among the Inca Indians of Peru that they fashioned golden ornamental flowers for their gardens.
3. Sirius, star visible near the sun at dawn during the torrid "dog days" of August.

A drowsy smell of flowers—gray heliotrope,
And white sweet-clover, and shy mignonette—
Comes faintly in, and silent chorus lends   20
To the pervading symphony of peace.

No time is this for hands long overworn
To task their strength; and (unto Him be praise
Who giveth quietness!) the stress and strain
Of years that did the work of centuries   25
Have ceased, and we can draw our breath once more
Freely and full. So, as yon harvesters
Make glad their nooning underneath the elms
With tale and riddle and old snatch of song,
I lay aside grave themes, and idly turn   30
The leaves of Memory's sketch-book, dreaming o'er
Old summer pictures of the quiet hills,
And human life, as quiet, at their feet.

And yet not idly all. A farmer's son,
Proud of field-lore and harvest craft, and feeling 35
All their fine possibilities, how rich
And restful even poverty and toil
Become when beauty, harmony, and love
Sit at their humble hearth as angels sat
At evening in the patriarch's tent, when man   40
Makes labor noble, and his farmer's frock
The symbol of a Christian chivalry
Tender and just and generous to her
Who clothes with grace all duty; still, I know
Too well the picture has another side,—   45
How wearily the grind of toil goes on
Where love is wanting, how the eye and ear
And heart are starved amidst the plenitude
Of nature, and how hard and colorless
Is life without an atmosphere. I look   50
Across the lapse of half a century,
And call to mind old homesteads, where no flower
Told that the spring had come, but evil weeds,
Nightshade and rough-leaved burdock in the place
Of the sweet doorway greeting of the rose   55
And honeysuckle, where the house walls seemed
Blistering in sun, without a tree or vine
To cast the tremulous shadow of its leaves
Across the curtainless windows from whose panes
Fluttered the signal rags of shiftlessness;   60
Within, the cluttered kitchen-floor, unwashed
(Broom-clean I think they called it); the best room
Stifling with cellar damp, shut from the air
In hot midsummer, bookless, pictureless
Save the inevitable sampler hung   65

Over the fireplace, or a mourning-piece,[4]
A green-haired woman, peony-cheeked, beneath
Impossible willows; the wide-throated hearth
Bristling with faded pine-boughs half concealing
The piled-up rubbish at the chimney's back;   70
And, in sad keeping with all things about them,
Shrill, querulous women, sour and sullen men,
Untidy, loveless, old before their time,
With scarce a human interest save their own
Monotonous round of small economies,[5]   75
Or the poor scandal of the neighborhood;
Blind to the beauty everywhere revealed,
Treading the May-flowers with regardless feet;
For them the song-sparrow and the bobolink
Sang not, nor winds made music in the leaves;   80
For them in vain October's holocaust
Burned, gold and crimson, over the hills,
The sacramental mystery of the woods.
Church-goers, fearful of the unseen Powers,
But grumbling over pulpit-tax and pew-rent,[6]   85
Saving, as shrewd economists, their souls
And winter pork with the least possible outlay
Of salt and sanctity; in daily life
Showing as little actual comprehension
Of Christian charity and love and duty,   90
As if the Sermon on the Mount[7] had been
Outdated like a last year's almanac:
Rich in broad woodlands and in half-tilled fields,
And yet so pinched and bare and comfortless,
The veriest straggler limping on his rounds,   95
The sun and air his sole inheritance,
Laughed at a poverty that paid its taxes,
And hugged his rags in self-complacency!

Not such should be the homesteads of a land
Where whoso wisely wills and acts may dwell   100
As king and lawgiver, in broad-acred state,
With beauty, art, taste, culture, books, to make
His hour of leisure richer than a life
Of fourscore to the barons of old time,
Our yeoman[8] should be equal to his home   105
Set in the fair, green valleys, purple walled,
A man to match his mountains, not to creep
Dwarfed and abased below them. I would fain
In this light way (of which I needs must own

4. A piece of art in memory of a departed relative.
5. Management of domestic affairs, particularly those involving the budget.
6. Fees to support the minister and pay for the use of a pew.

7. Matthew 5–7, Jesus' fullest statement of the absolute behavior he expects of his followers in contrast to the conventional ways of this world.
8. Farmer.

With the knife-grinder of whom Canning[9] sings,　　110
"Story, God bless you! I have none to tell you!")
Invite the eye to see and heart to feel
The beauty and the joy within their reach,—
Home, and home loves, and the beatitudes
Of nature free to all. Haply in years　　115
That wait to take the places of our own,
Heard where some breezy balcony looks down
On happy homes, or where the lake in the moon
Sleeps dreaming of the mountains, fair as Ruth,
In the old Hebrew pastoral, at the feet　　120
Of Boaz,[1] even this simple lay of mine
May seem the burden of a prophecy,
Finding its late fulfilment in a change
Slow as the oak's growth, lifting manhood up
Through broader culture, finer manners, love,　　125
And reverence, to the level of the hills.

O Golden Age, whose light is of the dawn,
And not of sunset, forward, not behind,
Flood the new heavens and earth, and with thee bring
All the old virtues, whatsoever things　　130
Are pure and honest and of good repute,
But add thereto whatever bard has sung
Or seer has told of when in trance and dream
They saw the Happy Isles of prophecy!
Let Justice hold her scale, and Truth divide　　135
Between the right and wrong; but give the heart
The freedom of its fair inheritance;
Let the poor prisoner, cramped and starved so long,
At Nature's table feast his ear and eye
With joy and wonder; let all harmonies　　140
Of sound, form, color, motion, wait upon
The princely guest, whether in soft attire
Of leisure clad, or the coarse frock of toil.
And, lending life to the dead form of faith,
Give human nature reverence for the sake　　145
Of One who bore it, making it divine
With the ineffable tenderness of God;
Let common need, the brotherhood of prayer,
The heirship of an unknown destiny,
The unsolved mystery round about us, make　　150

---

9. During the 1790s, as a way of turning English public opinion against the French Revolution, the statesman George Canning (1770–1827) wrote for *The Anti-Jacobin*, a paper, as its title says, opposed to the most radical French faction. Canning's *The Friend of Humanity and the Knife-Grinder*, extremely popular in Whittier's time, is a satire of misplaced humanitarianism and bleeding-heart liberalism. The line Whittier quotes is the drink-loving knife-grinder's brusque retort to the torrential address of the would-be philanthropist.
1. See Ruth 3 for the story of how the young widow, an ancestress of David, reminded Boaz of his family obligation to marry her.

> A man more precious than the gold of Ophir.[2]
> Sacred, inviolate, unto whom all things
> Should minister, as outward types and signs
> Of the eternal beauty which fulfils
> The one great purpose of creation, Love,   155
> The sole necessity of Earth and Heaven!

1869

2. Source of treasures of gold brought to King Solomon (1 Kings 10.11).

EDGAR ALLAN POE
1809–1849

The life of Poe is the most melodramatic of any of the major American writers of his generation. Determining the facts has proved difficult, since lurid legend became entwined with fact even before he died. Some legends were spread by Poe himself. Given to claiming that he was born in 1811 or 1813 and had written certain poems far earlier than he had, Poe also exaggerated the length of his attendance at the University of Virginia and, in imitation of Lord Byron, fabricated a "quixotic expedition to join the Greeks, then struggling for liberty." Two days after Poe's death his supposed friend Rufus Griswold, a prominent anthologizer of American literature, began a campaign of character assassination in which he ultimately rewrote Poe's correspondence so as to alienate many of his friends who could only assume that Poe had treacherously maligned them behind their backs. Griswold's forgeries went unexposed for many years, poisoning every biographer's image of Poe, and legend still feeds upon half truth in much writing on him.

Yet biographers now possess a great deal of factual evidence about most periods of Poe's life. His mother, Elizabeth Arnold, had been an actress, prominent among the wandering seaport players in a profession which was then considered disreputable. She was a teenage widow when she married David Poe, Jr., in 1806. Poe, also an actor, worked up to choice supporting roles before liquor destroyed his career. Edgar, the Poes' second child, was born in Boston on January 19, 1809; a year later David Poe deserted the family. In December, 1811, Elizabeth Poe died at twenty-four while acting in Richmond, Virginia, and her husband disappeared, probably dying soon afterward at the age of twenty-seven.

The disruptions of Poe's first two years were followed by apparent security, for John Allan, a young Richmond merchant, took him in as the children were parceled out. As "Master Allan," Poe accompanied the family to England in 1815, where he attended good schools. On their return in 1820 the boy continued in school, but under his own last name. During Poe's adolescence uncertainty about his future and shameful certainty about his past affected his feelings—and those of his prosperous playmates. Around 1824, Allan's attitude toward the boy changed; one rumor suggests that Edgar took the side of his foster mother in a quarrel. Poe spent most of 1826 at the new University of Virginia, doing well in his studies, although he was already drinking. Under the pretext that Allan had not provided him an adequate allowance, he gambled, and lost some $2,000—"debts of honor" which a gentleman must repay. Allan had just inherited a fortune of several hundred thousand dollars (with purchasing power of several million today), but he refused to pay Poe's debts. After a quarrel with Allan in March, 1827, Poe looked up his father's relatives in Baltimore and then went on to his birthplace, where he paid for the printing of *Tamerlane and Other Poems*, "By a Bostonian." Before its publication, "Edgar A. Perry" had joined the army. Poe was partially reconciled with Allan in March, 1829, just after Mrs. Allan died. Released from the army with the rank of sergeant major, Poe sought Allan's influence to gain him an appointment to West Point, although he was past the age limit for admission.

While he was waiting for the appointment, Poe shortened *Tamerlane*, revised other poems, and added new ones to make up a second volume, *Al Aaraaf, Tamerlane, and Minor Poems*, published at Baltimore in December, 1829. He entered West Point in June, 1830, but felt he could not fit into life at the academy without supplemental income, and Allan was interested in his own life, not Poe's. Just after Poe went to West Point a woman in Richmond bore Allan twin sons. In October, 1830, Allan married again and within a month his new wife was pregnant. Losing any remaining hope that if he dutifully pursued a military career he might become Allan's heir, Poe got himself expelled by missing classes and roll calls. Supportive friends among the cadets made up a subscription for his *Poems*, published in May, 1831. In this third volume Poe revised some earlier poems and for the first time included versions of both *To Helen* (the famous "Helen, thy beauty is to me," not a later, inferior poem of the same title) and *Israfel*.

Poe's mature career—from his twenty-first year to his death in his fortieth year—was spent in four literary centers: Baltimore, Richmond, Philadelphia, and New York. The Baltimore years—mid-1831 to late 1835—were marked by great industry and comparative sobriety. Poe lived in sordid poverty among his once-prosperous relatives, including his poetaster brother who died in 1831; his Grandmother Poe, whose death in 1835 cut off a Revolutionary widow's pension of $240 per annum on which the household relied; his aunt Maria Poe Clemm; and her daughter Virginia, whom Poe secretly married in 1835, when she was thirteen. Poe's first story, *Metzengerstein* (later subtitled *In Imitation of the German*) was published in the Philadelphia *Saturday Courier*, anonymously, in January, 1832, and other stories appeared in the same paper through the year. By early 1833, Poe was projecting a volume of eleven stories, *Tales of the Folio Club*, never published under that title. In May, 1833, he sent the *New-England Magazine* one of a set of *Eleven Tales of the Arabesque*—apparently the same eleven; a postscript added to the manuscript said simply, "I am poor." With his *Tales of the Folio Club*, Poe impressed all three judges of a contest in the Baltimore *Saturday Visiter*. One judge, the novelist John P. Kennedy, became a loyal mentor, offering timely money and advice.

Poe returned to Richmond in 1835, twenty-six years old, as assistant editor of T. L. White's new *Southern Literary Messenger*, at a salary of $540 a year, subsistence wages even in the 1830s. Allan was dead, survived by three small legitimate sons, and Poe had no contact with the widow. From the start, White deplored what he called Poe's tendency to "sip the juice," and gave him editorial duties without commensurate recognition or authority, even though the circulation of the magazine rose swiftly under Poe's guidance. The *Messenger* published stories by Poe, but it was through his critical pieces that he gained a national reputation as a reviewer in the virulently sarcastic British manner—a literary hatchetman.

Fired from the *Messenger* early in 1837, Poe took his aunt and his wife (whom he had publicly remarried in May, 1836) to New York City, where for two years he lived hand to mouth on the fringes of the publishing world, selling a few stories and reviews. He had written a short novel, *The Narrative of Arthur Gordon Pym*, in Richmond, where White ran two installments in the *Messenger* early in 1837. *Harper's* finally brought it out in July, 1838, but it earned him neither money nor reputation, since it purported only to be edited by Poe. In 1838 Poe moved to Philadelphia, where for weeks the family survived on bread and molasses. But he continued writing, and *Ligeia* appeared in the Baltimore *American Museum* in September, 1838, where other stories and poems followed. Resorting to literary hackwork just as Hawthorne was doing, Poe put his name on *The Conchologist's First Book* (1839). In May, 1839, he got his first steady job in over two years, as co-editor of *Burton's Gentleman's Magazine.* There he published book reviews and stories, among them *The Fall of the House of Usher* and *William Wilson*. Late in 1839, a Philadelphia firm published *Tales of the Grotesque and Arabesque*, but it sold badly. Poe was now at the height of his powers as a writer of tales, though his personal life continued unstable, as did his career as an editor. William Burton fired him for drinking in May, 1840, but recommended him to George Graham, who carried on Burton's magazine as *Graham's*. Throughout 1841, Poe was with *Graham's* as co-editor, courting subscribers by articles on cryptography and on character as revealed in handwriting. In January, 1842, Virginia Poe, not yet twenty, burst a blood vessel in her throat (she lived only five more years). Leaving *Graham's* in some unhappiness, Poe revived a project for his own magazine, now to be called *The Stylus*. In 1843 he worked at times for the Philadelphia weekly *Saturday Museum*. On a trip to Washington seeking a patronage job (and subscriptions to *The Stylus*) he reportedly was so drunk when he called on President Tyler that he wore his cloak inside out.

In April, 1844, Poe moved his family to New York City, where he wrote for newspapers and worked as subeditor on the *Sunday Times*. Poe's most successful year was 1845. The February issue of *Graham's* contained James Russell Lowell's complimentary article on Poe, and *The Raven* appeared in the February *American Review* after advance publication in the New York *Evening Mirror*. Capitalizing on the sensation the poem created, Poe lectured on "Poets of America" and became a principal reviewer for the new weekly, the *Broadway Journal. The Raven* won him entrée into the literary life of New York. One new literary acquaintance, Evert A. Duyckinck, soon to be Melville's friend also, selected a dozen of Poe's stories for a collection brought out by Wiley & Putnam in June and arranged for the same firm to publish *The Raven and Other Poems* in November. Having acquired critical clout despite a growing number of enemies, Poe had great hopes for the *Broadway Journal*, of which he became sole owner; but it failed early in 1846. Meanwhile Poe was marring his new opportunities by drinking.

With fame the tempo of Poe's life spun into a blur of literary feuds, flirtations with literary ladies, and drinking bouts which ended in quarrels.

Virginia's death in January, 1847, slowed the tempo: during much of that year Poe was seriously ill himself—perhaps with a brain lesion—and drinking steadily. He worked away at *Eureka,* a prose statement of a theory of the universe, and soon after Virginia's death he wrote *Ulalume.* The year 1848 was frenetic, culminating in a brief engagement to Helen Power Whitman of Providence; his letters to her are effusively hysterical. He flirted with Mrs. Nancy Richmond of Lowell, Massachusetts, in equally desperate letters, and may—as he wrote her—have tried to commit suicide by taking laudanum. He managed to write a little still, the story *Hop-Frog* and the poem *Annabel Lee.* While headed South in June, 1849, he drank on the train and got off in Philadelphia to seek asylum, he said, from two men who were trying to kill him. In Richmond he spent two improbably happy months, being received into society by his childhood friends and becoming engaged to the sweetheart of his teens, the now-widowed Elmira Royster Shelton. He gave lectures and readings, and joined the Sons of Temperance. On the way to accept a hundred dollars for editing the poems of a Philadelphia woman, he stopped off in Baltimore, broke his temperance pledge, and was found senseless near a polling place on an Election Day (October 3). Taken to a hospital, he died on October 7, 1849, "of congestion of the brain."

If Poe had disappeared from the American literary scene after publishing his third volume of poems in 1831, a literary historian grubbing among privately printed nineteenth-century collections of poetry would have classified him (once his authorship of the anonymous *Tamerlane* had been established) as an odd American imitator of major British Romantics like Lord Byron and Percy Bysshe Shelley as well as then-popular ones like Thomas Moore. In both form and content Poe's early poetry is typically Romantic, although of an unusually limited range. Well before his twenty-first birthday he had earned the right to call himself a poet, but by British standards he was not an important one.

It was the handful of poems which Poe wrote a decade and a half later that made him famous as a poet. *The Raven* brought him international celebrity, and poems like *Ulalume* and *The Bells* soon enhanced that fame among Poe's constantly enlarging posthumous audience. These poems became standard declamation pieces in schools and remained so well into the present century. In subject matter they progress little beyond the Romantic gothicism of Poe's early years, but in technique they are remarkable. Innumerable young people have learned to love poetry from them and have continued to love poetry even after they stopped loving only Poe. There could be worse fates for a man who started out as a belated, second-rate imitator of first- and second-rate British Romantics.

But the bulk of Poe's collected writings consists of his criticism, and his most abiding ambition was to become a powerful critic. Just as he had modeled his poems and first tales upon British examples (or British imitations of the German), he took his critical concepts from treatises on aesthetics by late eighteenth-century Scottish Common-Sense philosophers (later modified by his borrowings from A. W. Schlegel and Coleridge) and took his stance as a reviewer from the slashing critics of the British quarterlies. Poe's employers were often uneasy about their reviewer, both because his virulence brought reproaches (though it was good for business) and because they suspected that for all his stress on aesthetic principles, Poe's reviews were apt to be unjust to writers he was jealous of and laudatory toward others he wished to curry favor with. But Poe's basic critical principles were consistent enough, however he deviated from them in his reviewing. He thought poetry should appeal only to the sense of beauty, not truth; informational poetry, poetry of ideas, or any sort of didactic poetry was illegitimate. Holding that the true poetic emotion was a vague sensory state, he set himself against realistic details in poetry, although the prose tale, with truth as one object, could profit from the discreet use of specifics. Both poems and tales should be short enough to be read in one sitting; otherwise the unity of effect would be dissipated. In Poe's view, good writers calculate their effects precisely. At a time when even famous poets such as Longfellow rarely wrote a poem of sustained coherence, Poe's reaction, with the stress on forethought, seems understandable. But his criticism is often dogmatic and self-serving, weakened partly because it was applied to some of the most wretched writing a reviewer ever had to discuss, for Poe never had the luxury of reviewing only worthwhile volumes.

Poe's first tales have proved hard to classify—are they burlesques of popular kinds of fiction or serious attempts at contributing to or somehow altering those genres? Poe's own comments tend to becloud his intentions rather than to clarify them. In 1836 his benefactor John P. Kennedy wrote him: "Some of your *bizarreries* have been mistaken for satire—and admired too in that character. *They* deserved it, but *you* did not, for you did not intend them so. I like your grotesque—it is of the very best stamp; and I am sure you will do wonders for yourself in the comic—I mean the seriotragicomic." Poe's reply is tantalizing: "You are nearly, but not altogether right in relation to the satire of some of my Tales. Most of them were *intended* for half banter, half satire—although I might not have fully acknowledged this to be their aim even to myself." The problem of determining the nature of a given work—imitation? satire? spoof? hoax?—is crucial in Poe criticism.

At the core of Poe's defenses of his stories is the hardheadedness of a professional writer who wanted to crack the popular market. Such stories, he claimed, were the products of superior minds disciplining themselves to the task at hand, not the indulgences of Romantic genius. Poe worked hard at structuring his tales of aristocratic madmen, self-tormented murderers, neurasthenic necrophiliacs, and other deviant types so as to produce the greatest possible horrific effects on the reader. In the detective story, which Poe created when he was thirty-two, with all its major conventions complete, the structuring was equally contrived, although the effect desired was one of awe at the brilliance of his preternatural logician-hero. Seriously as he took the writing of his tales, Poe never claimed that prose writing was for him, as he said poetry was, a "passion," not merely a "purpose."

Other American writers, from Poe's time to ours, have often been uneasy about him. The "jingle man," Ralph Waldo Emerson is supposed to have called him, and Henry James thought that enthusiasm for Poe was "the mark of a decidedly primitive stage of reflection," while T. S. Eliot said Poe's intellect was that of "a highly gifted young person before puberty." Yet no other American writer, except possibly Mark Twain, has been so thoroughly absorbed by later writers—writers as diverse as E. A. Robinson, Frank Norris, Theodore Dreiser, William Faulkner, as well as

…

the great Russian-American player of complex Poesque games, Vladimir Nabokov. Some American literary critics and historians have always been hard pressed to understand why foreign writers like Charles Baudelaire and Stéphane Mallarmé could idolize Poe and translate his works lovingly, why the French Symbolist poets could draw on him for their aesthetic ideas, how August Strindberg could fantasize that because he was born in 1849 Poe's spirit had passed to him, how the influence of someone so childish could seem profound when it came back to English indirectly, through foreigners Poe had influenced. Some American critics have often felt reproached when British writers such as Dante Gabriel Rossetti, Algernon Swinburne, Robert Louis Stevenson, Arthur Conan Doyle, and George Bernard Shaw expressed delight in Poe or indebtedness to him. More than a century and a quarter after his death, American critics are still taking sides about Poe, hailing him as a pioneering aesthetician, psychological investigator, and literary technician, or else reviling him as an absurd fraud, a subliterary vulgarian. But whatever his influence on artists of the past and present, and whatever his status with literary critics and historians, Poe's reputation with the reading public—through the whole range of literacy—is more assured than that of any other major American writer of his century, again with the possible exception of Mark Twain. For the professional writer that Poe struggled to be, that is probably a fate even better than being precisely understood and logically classified.

Sonnet—To Science[1]

SCIENCE! meet daughter of old Time thou art
  Who alterest all things with thy peering eyes!
Why prey'st thou thus upon the poet's heart,
  Vulture! whose wings are dull realities!
How should he love thee—or how deem thee wise   5
  Who wouldst not leave him, in his wandering,
To seek for treasure in the jewell'd skies
  Albeit, he soar with an undaunted wing?
Hast thou not dragg'd Diana[2] from her car,
  And driv'n the Hamadryad[3] from the wood   10
To seek a shelter in some happier star?
  The gentle Naiad[4] from her fountain-flood?
The elfin from the green grass? and from me
  The summer dream beneath the shrubbery?

1829, 1845

1. The text is from *The Raven and Other Poems* (1845). Both in 1829 and 1831 the sonnet, untitled, was printed as a proem to *Al Aaraaf*; in 1845 the poem retained its place but carried the title first used in an 1843 reprinting. *Sonnet—To Science* is built upon the Romantic commonplace that the scientific spirit destroys beauty, a notion well exemplified by Wordsworth's *The Tables Turned* ("Sweet is the lore which Nature brings;/Our med- dling intellect/Misshapes the beauteous forms of things:—/We murder to dissect") and by Keats's *Lamia* ("Philosophy will clip an angel's wings").
2. Roman goddess of the moon (imaged as a chariot or car which she drives through the sky).
3. Wood nymph in Greek and Roman mythology, often thought of as living within a tree and perishing with it.
4. Nymph living in brooks or fountains.